ENVIRONMENTAL
PLANNING
1939–1969

VOLUME III

The author has been given full access to official documents. He alone is responsible for the statements made and the views expressed.

ENVIRONMENTAL PLANNING 1939–1969

Volume III

NEW TOWNS POLICY

BY

J. B. CULLINGWORTH

LONDON
HER MAJESTY'S STATIONERY OFFICE

Printed in England for Her Majesty's Stationery Office by Ebenezer Baylis & Son Ltd.
The Trinity Press, Worcester, and London
Dd 595917 K8 4/79

CONTENTS

Page

INTRODUCTION   xiii

PART ONE

I THE BIRTH OF THE OFFICIAL NEW TOWNS POLICY   3

Planning for London   3
Machinery for New Town Development   6
Stevenage   9
A Private Enterprise New Town?   10
W. S. Morrison's Proposals on Machinery   11
The Change of Government   12
The Reith Committee   13
Discussion with Local Authorities   15
Ministerial Discussions   18
Drafting the Bill   23
The Bill in Parliament   25
Annex: Stevenage   27

II MINISTERIAL DECISIONS ON THE FIRST NEW TOWNS   32

Silkin's Paper on New Towns   33
Westwood's Paper on Scottish New Towns   38
Jay's Paper   40
Consideration by the Dalton Committee May 1946   43
The Capital Cost of New Towns   45
    Silkin's Paper   45
    Westwood's Paper   47
    Barnes' Paper   48
Discussion at the Dalton Committee Meeting 1946   50
The Cost of Transport Facilities for New Towns   52
The Cost of East Kilbride   55
New Towns in Scotland   56
Review of New Towns for England and Wales   57
New Town at Mobberley   59
Aycliffe New Town   60
New Towns in Scottish Mining Areas   61
Welwyn Garden City and Hatfield   62
Silkin Faces Mounting Opposition   66
The 1947 Review of New Town Proposals   67
Provincial New Towns   73

Contents

Easington (Peterlee)   73
South Wales   75
Other Proposals   76
The Economic Crisis   78
The New Towns in April 1948   80
Pitsea-Laindon (Basildon)   82
Scottish New Towns   86
A New Town at Bracknell   89
New Towns in South Wales   92
     Church Village-Tonteg   92
     Cwmbran-Pontnewydd   93
New Towns in Cheshire   95
Loss of Agricultural Land   101
Peterlee New Town   102
Corby New Town   108
The Abandonment of Church Village New Town   110
The End of the First Round of New Towns   112
     Holiday New Town   113
Fourteen New Towns   114

III NEW TOWN POLICY IN THE FIFTIES   116

The Town Development Bill   116
Rent Restriction in the New Towns   117
Butler Presses for Economies   117
The MHLG/Treasury Report   120
Butler Asks 'Can We Afford the New Towns?'   122
Macmillan's Policy Review   125
Thorneycroft's Reply to Macmillan's Review   129
The Scottish Statement   130
Consideration by the Economic Policy Committee   133
Macmillan's Co-ordinated Study   134
     Relative Costs of Housing in Old and New Towns   136
     Reducing the Ultimate Size of New Towns   137
     Effectiveness of Decentralisation   137
     Future Organisation of the New Towns   138
Thorneycroft's Case: Industrial Implications   139
The Scottish Situation   140
Discussion at the Economic Policy Committee   141
Operation Round-Up   142
Sandys Takes Over   148
Cumbernauld   149
After Glasgow . . . Manchester?   151
Hook New Town   155
Annex: A Private Enterprise New Town   162

IV NEW TOWN POLICY UNDER REVIEW 1960–64   164

The Beginnings of a Change in Policy   164
New Towns for Liverpool and Birmingham   166
The Ministerial Committee on Birmingham Housing   168
Dawley New Town   173
A Second New Town for the West Midlands?   174
The Fourth Scottish New Town: Livingston   175

Contents

Population Growth and Regional Development	178
The Population and Employment Report	176
The North East and Scotland	186
Washington	188
Irvine	190
Joseph Asks for More New Towns	192
A New Town for Manchester	193
The South East Study	196
Problems of Implementation	201

V New Towns Policy 1964–69 — **207**

Review of the South East Study	207
Jay's Letter to Crossman	215
Review of Policy for the South East	216
Regional Policies	218
A New Town for Manchester	219
Planning for the Year 2000	223
North Buckinghamshire New Town (Milton Keynes)	228
The New Towns Working Group	233
The New Towns Programme	234
The Need for New Towns	237
Cost of the New Town Programme	239
Housing	240
Industrial Employment	241
Regional Implications	242
Rephasing of the New Towns Programme	243
Recommendations of the Working Group	244
Consideration by Ministers	245
Jay's Paper on London Overspill	246
Ashford	249
South Hampshire	252
Central Lancashire New Town	253
Dawley–Wellington–Oakengates	258
Wellington–Oakengates: Ministerial Discussion	260
Industrial Development Crisis at Dawley	264
The Humberside Report	267
Ipswich	269
Post Inquiry Developments	271
The Treasury Case Against Ipswich	273
Review of London's Population Trends	275
Ipswich Abandoned	278
The Welsh New Towns	279
A New Town for Mid-Wales	279
Llantrisant	283
Overview	286

PART TWO — **289**

VI Organisational Issues — **291**

Appointment of Corporation Members	291
The Standing Ministerial Conference	297

Contents

Ministerial Doubts on Machinery, 1948   300
The Working Party on Payment of Members   306
Public Statements by Development Corporations   309
The Treasury Report on Development Corporations   312
The Future Ownership Issue   316
  The Views of the New Town Chairmen   322
  Political Pressure for Action   327
  Policy Issues   329
  Cabinet Discussion   334
The Commission for the New Towns   341
  The Bill in Parliament   341
  The Organisation of the Commission   342
  The Role of the Commission   344
  The Future of the Commission   347
Research Organisation 1947–50   348
The Welwyn Research Saga   362
The Resumption of Research on New Towns   366
New Towns Information Bureau   370
The Working Party on New Towns Structure 1968–69   372
The New Towns Association   384

VII HOUSING ISSUES   385

Housing Rents and Subsidies   385
Selection of Tenants   399
The Town Development Act 1952   404
The Revised Selection Procedure   406
The Housing Subsidies Act 1956   412
The Special Housing Allocation   415
The London Dispersal Liaison Group   417
Better Class Housing in the New Towns   419
Owner Occupation in New Towns   427
  The Sale of Council Houses   427
  Sale of New Town Housing   429
  The Report on Ownership and Management of
    Housing in the New Towns   438
  Policies to Increase Owner Occupation   442
  Concessions to Sitting Tenants   445

VIII FINANCIAL ISSUES   448

The Financial Framework   448
Policy and Finance   450
The Cost of a New Town   451
Comparative Costs of New and Expanded Towns   454
The New Towns Research Group 1963   457
Objections to 'Piecemeal' Decisions   460
The Study Group on Economic Criteria 1964–65   462
  Social Criteria   465
  First Draft Report   467
  Progress of the Study Group   470
The NIESR Report on Town Structure, Size and Cost   473

Contents

The New Towns Working Group 1967 — 474
Treasury Apprehensions and Management Accounts — 477
The Philosopher's Stone — 484

IX EXPANDED TOWNS POLICY — 486

Early Thinking on Expanded Towns — 486
The Town Development Bill — 497
The Early Operation of the Town Development Act — 500
The Housing Subsidies Act 1956 — 501
Disappointing Progress — 502
Review of Machinery for Town Expansion — 504
New Town Machinery for Town Expansion? — 509
A Regional Development Agency? — 512
'Partnership' New Towns — 517
The 1965 Review of Town Development — 518
Scottish Expanded Towns — 520

EPILOGUE — 525

X NEW TOWNS AND GOVERNMENT — 527

New Towns and Urban Problems — 532
Agricultural Land — 535
Housing Policies — 536
Central Control — 538

APPENDICES

A Distribution of Industry Policy — 543
B Agricultural Land — 564
C Land Acquisition — 581
D Parliamentary Control — 587
E Report of the Interdepartmental Group on Administrative and Legislative Arrangements Needed for the Development of Satellite or New Towns (Pepler Report) 1944 — 592
F New Town Statistics — 603
G List of Ministers — 608
H List of Abbreviations — 616

INDEX — 619

DESIGNATED NEW TOWNS AND THE ABERCROMBIE PROPOSALS

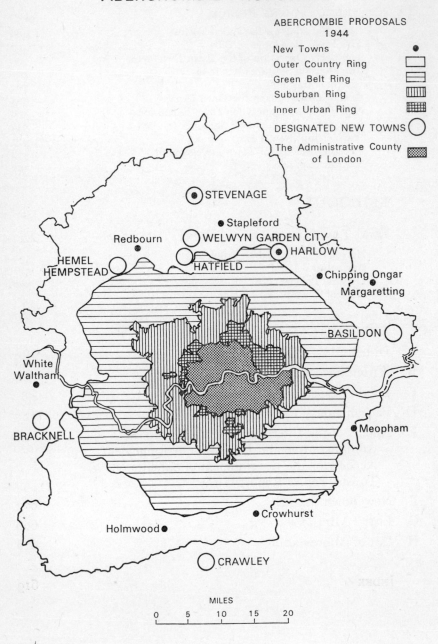

ABERCROMBIE PROPOSALS
1944

New Towns   ●
Outer Country Ring
Green Belt Ring
Suburban Ring
Inner Urban Ring
DESIGNATED NEW TOWNS   ○
The Administrative County
of London

● STEVENAGE

● Stapleford
● WELWYN GARDEN CITY
● HARLOW
HEMEL
HEMPSTEAD   HATFIELD
Redbourn
● Chipping Ongar
● Margaretting
BASILDON ○
White
Waltham
BRACKNELL
● Meopham
● Crowhurst
Holmwood ●
○ CRAWLEY

MILES

0   5   10   15   20

Cartographic Services PCH
Department of the Environment

© Crown copyright 1976

NEW TOWNS 1969

INTRODUCTION

THIS is the third volume of the history of environmental planning which spans the thirty years from 1939 to 1969. The first volume discussed the early 'reconstruction' period up to the passing of the 1947 Town and Country Planning Act.* There the main focus was on the establishment of the new physical planning machinery and the nationalisation of development rights. A later volume will continue that story from 1947 to the end of the 'sixties. Two major areas of policy, however, were reserved for separate treatment—national parks and access to the countryside, and new towns. The former was dealt with in volume II,† while the latter is the subject matter of this volume.

It was the original intention to confine this history of new towns to an account of Cabinet and Cabinet committee deliberations, with only minor reference to departmental files where this was thought necessary to illuminate particular points. This was the approach adopted in the first volume; but it rapidly proved quite inadequate for the present subject. In the words of a retired permanent secretary who kindly commented on early drafts, the Cabinet papers reveal only 'the tip of the iceberg'. Indeed, they reveal only the tips of a large number of icebergs, and an account largely based on Cabinet papers would be episodic, tantalising and frequently incomprehensible. On the other hand, once one moves from Cabinet papers to departmental files, the basic criterion for selection of material is lost. The interconnections, ramifications and complexities of policies are truly seen as the real problems of government, and the historian is faced with similar dilemmas to those facing politicians. It is impossible to master all the facts or to be sure that all the relevant facts have been collated. It is difficult to sift fact from opinion. And, above all, one is overwhelmed by the volume of material.

For example, chapter II provides an account of the arguments which Silkin, Westwood and Woodburn deployed over a period of four and a half years to secure the acquiescence in principle of their colleagues to each of the first generation new towns. This, however, reflects only the middle stage of a long and complex story which, if told in full, would include the Barlow report, the Abercrombie reports, the powerful stimulation of the Town and Country Planning Association, early government commitments to an urban decentralisation policy (particularly in relation to London and Glasgow), and

---

* J. B. Cullingworth, *Reconstruction and Land Use Planning 1939–1947*, HMSO, 1975.
† G. E. Cherry, *National Parks and Recreation in the Countryside*, HMSO, 1975.

negotiations with local authorities and a multitude of government departments. And, after Silkin had secured the approval of his Cabinet colleagues and run the gauntlet of outstanding objections on agricultural, industrial, economic and financial grounds (to which the account in chapter II refers), there was the subsequent story of the formal designation procedures, the appointment of development corporations and the actual development of the towns.

Again, many 'new town issues' were inextricably inter-related with broader issues, for example of national housing policy. Policies in relation to housing in the new towns cannot be understood except by reference to this wider framework. Similarly, since government has to allocate resources between alternative—and often conflicting —objectives, no account of new towns would be adequate if it did not refer to these wider areas of debate and the clashes of policy which inevitably arose. Perhaps the clearest example of this is in the clash between interregional and intraregional objectives: given a limited amount of mobile industry, what priorities should be accorded to the London new towns as compared with the development areas? What proportion of resources should go to new towns in the south-east and the north-west?

Even wider questions are relevant: how many new towns were needed? How could they be costed and compared with alternative forms of new development such as expanding towns or peripheral development? Was the machinery for review, for research and for control adequate? How important was it to safeguard agricultural land—and how could this be assessed?

All these—and many more—issues came before the Cabinet or its committees. Some were the subject of lengthy discussion but many received only fleeting attention. Sometimes a matter was resolved by 'inviting' ministers to consult further with each other, but more frequently committees of officials were established to examine a problem in greater depth or to thrash out an interdepartmental compromise.

Clearly, to have restricted the history to those issues which came before the Cabinet and its committees would have resulted in a gross distortion of the real sequence of events. Yet, once one moves from this arena, it is quite impossible to devise criteria for deciding what should be included and what should be omitted. Moreover, since new towns inevitably straddle the responsibilities of several departments the historian is faced not only with the problem of selecting files from the main ministry concerned, but also of deciding which other ministries should be examined.

There is no satisfactory solution to this problem and, in the event, the selection was restricted, in the main, to the files of the Ministry of Town and Country Planning, the Department of Health for

Scotland (and their successors) and the Treasury. This inevitably does less than justice to other departments such as those responsible for agriculture or industrial location policy, but there are even more intractable problems. The files of the 'selected' departments are gargantuan in number. Though helpfully some are labelled 'policy' files (or, more enigmatically, 'general questions' files), this is inevitably an inadequate guide. The line between 'policy' and 'administration' is an unclear one and, even if it is clear at one point in time, it can be transformed by an unpredictable turn of events. The historian thus faces an insoluble problem. It is impossible to consult all the files: it is even impossible to judge which will be relevant to the issues which appear to be important. The final result is difficult to defend, though it is neither capricious nor idiosyncratic.

This is not intended as an extended apologia for the shortcomings of this volume. It is intended simply to explain why it was felt necessary to go beyond Cabinet papers to departmental files, and to stress that, having so decided, no firm basis remained for determining where to stop. The approach adopted was to identify major issues which warranted extensive use of departmental papers. Initially this was done by reference to Cabinet discussions, followed by an examination of departmental records. Drafts were prepared and advice then sought from the departments concerned. The final judgement rested with the author, and it is for the reader to assess the adequacy of this.

In the outcome, the first part of the volume presents a chronological account based mainly on Cabinet discussions. In the second part, selected policy issues are discussed at some length together with an account of the expanded towns policy: here the main sources are typically the files of departments. Some important matters will be dealt with, in a broader context, in a following volume: this applies particularly to land policies—the purchase and sale of land, and the basis for compensation and sale prices. A short note on this is, however, provided in one of the appendices.

It was not easy to decide how much analysis should be given of distribution of industry policy. This was frequently before ministers both generally and specifically in relation to new towns. It was also, of course, closely related to regional policies and became more so as new towns came to be regarded as instruments of regional policy in the 'sixties. There was therefore justification for an extensive treatment of the subject. But it became clear that, since this would necessarily lead into major issues of economic planning, it would inordinately extend the scope of the history. Instead, some account is given in the chronological chapters, and an appendix presents both a summary of general policies and a discussion of their application in the new towns.

A more difficult problem arose on the administrative and financial relationship between the departments, the Treasury, the new town development corporations and the local authorities. The crux of the problem lies in the complex detail with which these relationships had to deal. Much of this has to be shed if a reasonably comprehensible account is to be provided, yet it is in the fine points of detail that the essence of the relationships is to be seen. There is no satisfactory solution to this in the context of a wide-ranging history, though an attempt has been made in the second part of the volume to deal as clearly as possible with specific issues. Given the sources used the account essentially relates to the stance of Whitehall. Matters undoubtedly appeared differently to the development corporations and the local authorities (as the issues arising on the industrial selection scheme illustrated*). It was these bodies who had the task of translating government policies and decisions into practice. But that is another story.

Some explanation of the nature of an 'official' history is necessary in the light of the misunderstandings revealed by the critical comments made by reviewers of earlier volumes in this series. Significantly, attempts have been made by other 'official' historians to avoid the use of the term because of the confusion to which it can give rise.† But the term is too well established to be rejected now; and, in any case, it does indicate a particular type of history. It certainly does not imply any seal of official approval—as the standard disclaimer at the front of the volume underlines. (Neither, of course, does any critical comment imply official censure of the person or event to which it applies.) In truth the adjective merely indicates that the history has been commissioned by the Government, that official records have been made freely available, and that assistance has been rendered by serving civil servants. An author who has unrestricted access to Cabinet and departmental records within the closed period and, in my case, up to the recent past, has a rare privilege. He has to use this, however, within certain official constraints and to avoid, so far as the story allows him, the personalisation of issues with which the Government of the day were collectively concerned.

The account is based on official records in London and Edinburgh and, while advice and comment has been given by past and present officials in the relevant departments, there has been no systematic interviewing of ministers or officials or staffs of the development corporations. The reason for this is a purely practical one: it would have been quite impossible, in the time available, to undertake the

---

* See chapter VII.
† See, for example, S. W. Roskill, 'Some Reasons for Official History', *Library Association Record*, Vol 65, 1963, p. 93.

systematic interviewing of even the main *dramatis personae* in a history which extends over a period of thirty years.

Furthermore, little attempt could be made to relate the events recorded here to the wider context of social and economic change of which they formed a part. This again was a necessary price which had to be paid for the opportunity of detailing the history of new towns policy over such a lengthy period.

The result is, in significant ways, tantalising and inadequate; but the objective of the history was to bring together in a coherent form that part of the fuller story which could be gleaned from the official records without transgressing the conventions which apply to the 'closed period'. It is intended as a contribution to the understanding of what was involved, predominantly in Whitehall, in deciding upon and implementing the new towns policy.

The impression is inevitably and falsely created of what a reviewer of a previous volume termed an 'hermetically sealed world'. It is for others to correct this, but hopefully they will find this partial history a useful source for supplementing material which is easier of access. In the words of an official Public Record Office publication:

> The published histories cannot tell the whole story; they should be regarded as guides and works of reference which can provide the framework for further research, and to be read along with the memoirs, diaries and letters of . . . officials and politicians, and with the original material unfolding in the Public Record Office under the 30-year rule.*

For my part I have found the task a fascinating one, and the opportunity to delve into the inner workings of British government has been most rewarding.

I have been greatly helped, first and foremost by my colleague, Mr S. S. Wilson, whose experience and knowledge have been invaluable, and by Mr F. Schaffer, whose guidance has been unstinting. In accordance with convention, many others who have assisted me must remain anonymous—particularly officials in the Departments of Agriculture, Environment, and Industry, the Treasury and the Scottish Office. And without the good offices of the record keepers and librarians of the various departments, my work would have been impossible. Special thanks go to those in the Cabinet Office, the Treasury, the Department of the Environment and the Scottish Office who met my constant requests with efficiency and an almost embarrassing enthusiasm. They provided me with an *embarras de richesse*.

Acknowledgement must also be gratefully made to the staff of DOE who prepared the maps and the material for the statistical appendix.

J. B. Cullingworth

Cabinet Office   May 1977

---

* S. S. Wilson, *The Cabinet Office to 1945*, HMSO, 1975, p. 123.

PART ONE

CHAPTER I

The Birth of the Official New Towns Policy

MUCH has been written on the development of thinking about new towns—from Ebenezer Howard and earlier, to the Barlow report on the Distribution of the Industrial Population.* This official history starts with the acceptance, in the early nineteen-forties, of the relevance of new towns to the postwar problems of reconstruction.

Popular discussion centred on the idea of new towns: a tangible manifestation of the 'Better Britain' which was to be built after the war. Government, on the other hand, had to translate the idea into workable legislative, administrative and financial terms. As this chapter demonstrates, this was by no means an easy matter.

Despite the strong lobby of the Garden City Association (later to become the Town and Country Planning Association) and the increasing popularity of the idea of new towns, government pronouncements tended not to be explicit. Though the policy was early accepted that 'the decentralisation, decongestion and redevelopment of our big towns do constitute a primary objective of policy of His Majesty's Government',† it was far less clear how this was to be achieved and what role would be played by new towns.

Planning for London‡

The major focus of attention within the Ministry of Town and Country Planning was on the London problem (a fact which did not go unnoticed by other departments). A simple explanation for this was not merely that London clearly had enormous problems, but also that more preparatory planning had been undertaken for this region than for anywhere else in Britain. The reasons for this lie in the bomb damage suffered by London and the early moves of the City of London and the London County Council in preparing for postwar redevelopment. As early as March 1941 Lord Reith asked these two authorities to make a start on provisional redevelopment plans which would be quickly followed by 'the extension of planning over the outer areas'. The City of London instructed their surveyor, and the LCC their architect and planning officer, to prepare these

---

* See Department of the Environment Bibliography No. 65.
† HL Debates, Vol 133, Col 182, 27 September 1944.
‡ MHLG Files P1/20001, P1/20001/1/2 and 114542/A/3.

provisional plans. The LCC also appointed Professor Abercrombie as consultant.

Abercrombie stipulated that 'he would have to take within his purview a wider area than the county'. It was not long before the home counties authorities heard of this, and they expressed anxiety lest 'they might have a plan sprung on them which affected their interests but had been prepared without any consultation with them'. G. L. Pepler (chief technical adviser to the Ministry of Town and Country Planning) stepped into the breach ('very privately') and suggested to the local authorities that an outline plan should be prepared for the whole region 'by an independent expert such as Professor Abercrombie'. 'Very fortunately, this suggestion commended itself to them' and, in October 1941, they wrote to Reith urging that the local authorities 'should take a constructive part in the planning of their areas and suggesting that they should form a committee to confer with Professor Abercrombie and the city corporation in the preparation of redevelopment plans affecting areas outside London'.

An informal conference, chaired by Reith, was held in January 1942. Reith steered the conference so that the request to appoint Abercrombie to produce an outline plan for Greater London (with boundaries to be determined by Abercrombie) should appear to come from the local authorities. Informal discussions then took place with LCC officials who (somewhat reluctantly) agreed that it was necessary to make use of the Standing Conference on London Regional Planning. Eventually the minister (now Portal) wrote to the chairman of the standing conference:

'My predecessor, Lord Reith, took the view, with which I agree, that in planning the reconstruction of the London region a beginning should be made with the central areas, particularly in view of the fact that enemy bombing had been largely concentrated on the centre. Accordingly the London County Council and the Corporation of the City of London were invited by him to prepare provisional plans of redevelopment for the county and city respectively. I understand that these plans are now in an advanced stage of preparation and the time is arriving when consideration should be given to the question of planning the area surrounding the County of London. In this connection my predecessor was recently approached by representatives of some of the county councils of the home counties.

I hope that the conception of a regional plan for the area surrounding London, which, in many ways, forms a composite whole with the city and county, will generally commend itself. The plan would, I need hardly say, be based on present facts but could and should be sufficiently flexible to enable any necessary adjustments to be made as the war proceeds and as the post-war prospects emerge with greater clarity. The plan for the area surrounding London, and those for the county and the city, although separate and distinct, would need to be closely co-ordinated, so as to form together a comprehensive plan for the whole of the region.'

After a great deal of informal consultation and formal sparring, the standing conference agreed (in May 1942) to the preparation of a Greater London Plan by Abercrombie.

In February of the following year, a MTCP minute commented that the preparation of plans for London was 'not very satisfactory'. Three separate plans were being prepared: for the City, the LCC, and the Greater London area. But the latter two were being prepared by the same man (Abercrombie) and were well advanced:

'The plan is prepared. It has been conceived and brought forth in secret and is understood now to be under consideration by the appropriate leaders of the county council. Fear of speculation in land has (possibly rightly) dictated this policy of secrecy.'

At some time, the other interested parties would be brought into consultation and, finally, the scheme would be presented to the Ministry of Town and Country Planning—'probably rather suddenly':

'The planning of London is as much a matter for the authorities controlling it as for the department and whilst for the time being there would be advantage in the Government providing the full cost, I envisage a permanent technical planning body supported mainly if not entirely by contributions from all the authorities concerned.

In the early stages the all-important thing would be the technical preparation of a plan or scheme untramelled except in the very widest sense by consideration of boundaries or other irrelevant (from the planning point of view) local government considerations.

Later I would contemplate the establishment of a permanent regional council for planning in the Greater London area. This might be a local government body but to its actual status and functions I have not given detailed consideration. It should however have executive functions, though clearly it would be necessary for other authorities to carry out statutory planning at a lower level. Alternatively the Government might retain full control through a commission.'

A draft of Abercrombie's Greater London Plan was submitted to the ministry in the spring of 1944. The immediate reaction of the technical staff of the ministry was that the drafting was so poor as to require substantial rewriting. The report 'bears the imprint of many hands, hands of so divergent a character and ability, and occasionally of accuracy, as to make publication of the report in its present form impossible'.

A large number of such side-issues occupied the time of departmental officials, but the report was eventually published in December 1944. It proposed a redistribution of London's population on a massive scale. A million people were to move: 383,000 to eight or ten 'new satellite towns outside the green belt area', 100,000 to areas 'wholly outside the metropolitan area', 164,000 to existing towns 'outside the Greater London area and 40–50 miles distant', and the remainder to towns and estates within Greater London.

The new satellite towns proposed were:

		Maximum ultimate population
Berkshire	White Waltham	60,000
Essex	Chipping Ongar	60,000
	Harlow	60,000
	Margaretting	30,000
Herts	Stevenage	60,000
	Redbourn	60,000
	Stapleford	25,000
Kent	Meopham	40,000
Surrey	Crowhurst	60,000
	Holmwood	60,000

*Machinery for New Town Development**

Meanwhile, the ministry had begun to give serious attention to the legislative, administrative and financial problems that would be involved in the planning and building of new towns. At that time, official thinking in the department was on the lines of responsibility resting with local authorities. In a minute of 27 October 1943 it was argued that 'there are difficulties of principle in the way of action by the State in fostering a young community'. On the one hand, 'the individual who is dissatisfied by the way he is governed locally would lose his right of throwing his council out'; on the other, 'the State might give preferential treatment to its own child by a higher standard of provision than it is prepared to pay for elsewhere'. The conclusion was that 'it would therefore be far better to use the machinery of local government and to make powers available to the county council to do all that is necessary under a government guarantee'. It was known that several county councils were 'nibbling at this sort of idea'.†

To pursue the matter further, a group was set up in January 1944 under the chairmanship of Pepler, with representatives from the Ministry of Health, 'to make proposals as to the administrative and legislative arrangements needed for the development of satellite or new towns'. In their report, which was finalised in August 1944, the group considered that 'movement of population will generally take the form of additions to established small towns or large villages

---

* MHLG Files 91650/12 and 91650/1; and Secretary's Bill Papers 234B.

† Several county councils (including Somerset and Lancashire) had approached the ministry on the need for adequate legislative provision for satellite towns to accommodate overspill from congested towns. This led to a number of meetings between county clerks and Pepler. Counties were encouraged to proceed with forward planning, while the ministry were urged to settle the outlines of the necessary legislation and the issue of compensation for compulsory land acquisition.

rather than that of the creation of entirely new towns on virgin soil'.*
This meant that the receiving area would be a moderate-sized
borough, or an urban or a rural district, whereas the exporting
authority would usually be a county borough. In view of the strength
of the latter, the former might be apprehensive of 'a raid upon their
territory in the form of extensive land purchase by the exporting
town, or an invitation by the exporting town to collaborate on its
own terms'. Accordingly, the group considered that the county
council for the receiving area should either support the receiving
authority in agreement with the exporting authority, or that the
county council should itself undertake the development with the
assistance of both the exporting and the receiving authorities.

It was thought, however, that there would probably be difficulty in
cases where there was no local authority with adequate experience or
resources, or where the county council would not accept responsibility, or where the exporting authority would not be prepared to
co-operate. They therefore considered that it would be advisable to
create a joint developing body, representing the exporting and
receiving authorities and the county council of the receiving area,
with the co-option of private individuals. Where a joint developing
body was established, 'it should have complete control from the
commencement of the scheme with the object of producing a
balanced township, whether its immediate object is to absorb the
overspill of the exporting town or towns, or to create a new town
open to all comers. Its aim should be to secure the town's complete
physical development within a reasonable time'. To this end, there
should be an executive joint planning committee to undertake
planning. Land acquired compulsorily should be transferred to the
joint developing body, which would be responsible for the preparation of roads and services and for 'the erection and estate management of buildings, houses (not all working class), shops, community
centres, schools etc, and some industrial buildings, sufficiently to
establish a nucleus and bring the town up to the stage at which
private enterprise would be attracted and would progressively
undertake independent development'. The joint developing body as
sole landlord would receive the estate revenue, rents etc, in addition
to the existing state subsidies for housing, but for all other purposes
should be financed by loans from the Public Works Loan Board.
Ultimately 'all works and buildings of a public character should be
handed over by the joint developing body to the appropriate local
authority at cost'.

Although the group gave a broad outline of their ideas for a joint
developing body, they were careful not to dismiss the possibility of
direct participation by individual local authorities. They therefore

---

* The report is reproduced in appendix E.

recommended that 'the Minister of Town and Country Planning should determine in consultation with the Minister of Health which authority should be given charge of satellite development and, failing agreement, on what terms or whether the responsibility should be placed in the hands of a joint developing body'. At the time of the Pepler report and subsequently, the problem was viewed primarily in terms of planning and therefore appropriate to the Ministry of Town and Country Planning. The housing aspect appears to have been secondary, and the Ministry of Health (the department then responsible for housing) had a lesser role.

Before the report of the Pepler group was finalised, officials of the ministry had asked parliamentary counsel to draft provisions which could be submitted to the minister for his approval enabling some form of authority to be established to develop new towns, and it was suggested that this might be included in the Town and Country Planning Bill which was then in active preparation. The reaction of parliamentary counsel was that, in the time available, it was quite impossible 'to work up ideas which are still at the egg-stage' and which had not been the subject of interdepartmental discussion or Cabinet agreement. Although the proposal was dropped at the time, amendments were introduced (forming S9 and 12 of the Town and Country Planning Act 1944) enabling a promoting local authority to acquire land in the area of another authority and by agreement with the latter, for the relocation of population or industry.*

Meanwhile the report of the Pepler group was circulating within the ministry and, in a minute of 26 September 1944, W. G. Holford (technical adviser to the ministry) commented that with 'existing authorities already burdened with other responsibilities, there would be a risk of inadequate finance, unconcentrated effort, and local jealousy . . . Would not an independent board financed by the exchequer be a simpler solution? This does not mean of course that local authority interests would be ignored, but that the board would not be simply the local authorities in another guise'.

At a meeting of officials in December 1944 it was felt the organisation for developing a new town might take one of four forms:

1. The receiving authority backed by the county council in agreement with the exporting authority.
2. The county council with the assistance of both the exporting and receiving authorities.
3. An *ad hoc* joint developing body representative of the appropriate authorities, with the addition of co-opted individuals.

---

* See Volume I of this History (*Reconstruction and Land Use Planning 1939–1947*), pp. 135–137 (hereafter referred to as *History Vol. I*).

4. A development association set up at the instance of the central government and specially constituted to carry through or direct all operations for the building of new towns or large extensions of existing towns.

As the problem was likely to vary in different areas, the solution should provide variety in method of approach and operation. So far as finance was concerned, officials recognised that there would be a tendency for both the exporting and the importing authorities to think they would suffer substantial loss—the former by reason of reduction of population and of rateable value, and the latter in shouldering the burden of development costs for an unprofitable influx of population. It was agreed that the question of organisation, and the legislation required, should be put to ministers, and that the Ministry of Health would further examine the financial implications for local authorities.

Stevenage*

The Abercrombie Plan for Greater London had been circulated to the local authorities concerned at the end of December 1944, and its many implications came under review by those authorities and by an interdepartmental committee (GLP) comprising representatives of the Ministries of Town and Country Planning, Agriculture, Health, Labour, War Transport and the Board of Trade. By March 1945, the GLP Committee felt that preparatory decisions were required about the new towns, and recommended Stevenage as the first experiment. Accordingly, W. S. Morrison (Minister of Town and Country Planning) wrote to Woolton (Minister of Reconstruction) on 12 May 1945 enclosing the draft of a paper to the Reconstruction Committee saying that 'an excellent opportunity presents itself at Stevenage' which was 'well suited to serve as a first experiment'. Its situation was generally attractive, it was well served by road and rail, it was 'relatively acceptable' to the Ministry of Agriculture, and it had already proved attractive to a number of small industries. A site on the northern side of London was preferable to one on the southern side since the connections with the industrial north and midlands were better and the need for 'thinning out' was greater. Indeed, it was understood that the Borough of Tottenham was considering Stevenage in its examination of 'the possibilities of thinning out on a large-scale'. It was similarly thought that the London County Council would be interested, since their 'quasi-satellites' (mainly housing estates) nearer to the built-up area of London would only satisfy their immediate postwar needs.

W. S. Morrison therefore proposed that the Ministry of Town and

---

* R(45)45, MHLG File 91650/16 and Ministry of Reconstruction File 1293.

Country Planning should undertake a survey of the Stevenage site and prepare a town plan in outline. The creation of 'an instrument to carry out the purpose' was, he said, a difficult problem, which had already been studied in general terms and 'its further pursuit can be more precisely focused as soon as an urgent proposition of this kind is available for examination in definite and concrete form . . . It will be important that no agency—whether exporting authority, statutory undertaking, private developers or *ad hoc* body —able and prepared to take a part should be debarred from doing so through lack of legislative ways and means or through financial impediments that could properly be removed'. This draft paper, raised to ministerial level (in the context of Stevenage) the issue which had been dealt with in the Pepler report. (A copy of the draft had been supplied to the Ministry of Health, who commented that 'surely the question whether the proposed town is to be built by a public utility body or a local government body does not depend on any physical survey of the *locus in quo*'.)

Woolton's reply to W. S. Morrison of 17 May 1945 was that before the Reconstruction Committee discussed Stevenage, he wished to have more definite information about the plans for bringing the new town into existence, since any public announcement 'would invite questions about organisation'. To frame the reply to Woolton, the ministry set up a Satellite and New Town Committee, with representatives from the Ministry of Health and the Treasury. They reached the conclusion that 'a government corporation was likely to be the appropriate form for Stevenage', and that in advance of legislation, the land for Stevenage should be acquired under S35 of the 1932 Planning Act. The Treasury made it clear, however, that they were doubtful of the attitude of a Conservative Government to satellite policy; and the abortive paper to the Reconstruction Committee was redrafted with a view to obtaining ministerial agreement to the principle of satellite development, but with muted reference to Stevenage.

A Private Enterprise New Town?*

Meanwhile, between February and April 1945, informal approaches were made to the department by an architect (Alistair MacDonald) on behalf of a building society (Co-operative Permanent, with financial backing) who were considering the creation of a new town on alternative sites near London (at Brickendon Bury in Hertfordshire or at Ongar in Essex). It was proposed that Silkin—then an opposition MP—should be chairman of a company to buy the land, but 'it must have an assurance from you (Pepler) that you would enforce the transfer to us at a proper valuation'. On the

* MHLG File 91650/8.

strength of this approach, W. S. Morrison was encouraged to think that the initiative for some new towns might come from 'non-official sources'. Thus was born the idea of a private enterprise new town—an idea which stayed in the arena of discussion even after the return of the Labour Government.*

W. S. Morrison's Proposals on Machinery†

W. S. Morrison redrafted his paper and circulated it on 25 July 1945. It referred to the Barlow report and its 'demonstration' of the need for a policy of planned decentralisation, as well as the Government's acceptance of this. It also referred to the Abercrombie plans which indicated how this policy could be implemented, ie by measures which included the creation of satellite towns. It proposed the early 'establishment of one or two satellite towns which would make a major contribution to the housing problem in the London area; they would, if wisely planned, act as an example, guide and spur to local authorities; and perhaps no less important, would show that the Government means business'.

The urgency of a decision was stressed. Firm conclusions on the means by which the Abercrombie plans could be implemented . . .

'. . . are fast becoming urgent, particularly in view of the necessity of carrying out a very extensive housing programme as soon as conditions permit. The Ministry of Town and Country Planning and the Ministry of Health, in collaboration with other departments, have already gone a long way in agreeing sites for development in the first and second years after the war. In some cases this has had to be done irrespective of wider planning considerations and in the light only of the paramount necessity for providing houses with the least possible delay. Acceptance of some of the sites proposed by the LCC for their immediate programme, for instance, has been conceded as a safety-valve measure, even although the sites do not wholly accord with desirable planning principles.

In view of the time which it takes to select sites, prepare plans and carry out other preliminaries to development, the same situation will arise again, unless we prepare now for the second stage (ie for the third year after the war and onwards). Accordingly there would, in my opinion, be great advantage in beginning now, under government auspices, to promote the establishment of one or two satellite towns.'

As there were 'obvious weaknesses' in the structure of local government to undertake such development (and since these could

---

* After he became Minister of Town and Country Planning Silkin received a deputation on 18 October 1945 consisting of two MPs, the ex-chairman of the TUC (George Gibson) and the architect (MacDonald) who wished to find out 'whether he would react favourably to the idea that a public utility society should be formed to develop a satellite town in conjunction with local authorities'. Silkin replied that there was no statutory power under which he could authorise a public utility society to undertake all aspects of a satellite town, and that before going much further he wished to have the views of the Reith Committee. The approach was not pursued though it was not until 20 March 1946 that the possibility of participation by private enterprise was finally eliminated.
† LP(45)128 (originally HA(45)24).

not immediately be radically changed), other means had to be found, and it was therefore proposed that new legislation should provide for two types of organisation. Where two or more local authorities desired to take an active part in the establishment of a satellite town (or where exceptionally the Government had to act without the active help of local authorities or non-official bodies) the organisation would take the form of a government-sponsored corporation. Where the initiative came from non-official sources, a company with limited profits would be set up under the Companies Acts.

In the first case the corporation would be managed by a board nominated by the interested local authorities and appointed by the minister. The land required would be compulsorily purchased and the corporation would be financed by government loans. Services would be provided either by the corporation or by the local authorities in the area. In due course a new local authority could be created to take over all assets and liabilities, and the corporation would then be dissolved.

In the second case, the company would be financed from non-official sources, its memorandum and articles being drawn up in agreement with the minister. Land would be compulsorily acquired by the minister and leased to the company, whose relationship to local authorities and others would be that of an ordinary estate developer. It would continue in existence independently of any new local authority which might in due course be created.

The paper emphasised the need for a large scale effort from the Government as a whole—the Board of Trade for assisting the synchronisation of movement of industry and population; the Ministry of Health for the programming and allocation of housing, and for the problems of water supply and sewerage; the Ministry of Agriculture and Fisheries for the orderly withdrawal of land in farming use and for drainage problems; the Ministry of Fuel and Power to facilitate arrangements for gas and electricity; the Ministry of Education for schools; the Ministry of Works for allocation of building permits; the Ministry of Labour and National Service for assistance in the supply of building and civil engineering labour; the Ministry of War Transport for improvements in communication; and so forth. The total public loan capital required to establish a new town of 50,000 persons would be of the order of £10m spread over the period of development and made up as to 60 per cent for housing, 15 per cent for other building, 15 per cent for site development and services, and 10 per cent for land. The paper proposed that Stevenage should be selected as the site of the first satellite.

The Change of Government

No action was taken on W. S. Morrison's paper owing to the fall of the Caretaker Government. Morrison was succeeded as Minister of Town and Country Planning by L. Silkin (whose appointment dated from 4 August 1945). On 14 August 1945, Silkin circulated three papers* to the Lord President's Committee (which under Herbert Morrison and subject to the Cabinet, dealt with matters on the home front). These dealt with the control of land use,† satellite towns and national parks.‡

Each of these papers referred to the proposals of the previous Government, gave general endorsement to them, and sought approval to the introduction of legislation for their implementation. They were submitted at a time when the new Government had been in office for barely two weeks and when the war with Japan had ended unexpectedly a few days previously. The country was suddenly faced with a vast range of problems in the turnover to a peace economy; in addition, the Government were committed to an extensive programme of nationalisation. The ministers in the new Government thus had a surfeit of problems in their own spheres and, not surprisingly, were reluctant to be hustled into hasty action on satellite towns which would involve heavy and unknown continuing commitments and which, in any event, would be unlikely to afford much relief to the housing position for some time.

Among the points in the Labour Party manifesto before the election had been an undertaking 'to bring forward proposals for improving the law with regard to compensation and betterment so as to secure for the future the best use of land in the public interest, including proper reservation of open spaces and the best location of industry and housing'; nothing had been said about new towns. Nevertheless, within nine months of taking office, the Government introduced a New Towns Bill, which took precedence over the promised measure on compensation and betterment.

The route whereby this reversal was achieved involves discussion of the reports of the Reith Committee, the views of local authorities, and the inability of ministers to settle the terms of the measure on compensation and betterment. As it would be confusing to deal with these steps in their strict chronological sequence, each will be dealt with separately, but their interplay over the period should be borne in mind.

The Reith Committee§

Silkin, who himself was under pressure from the Town and Country Planning Association, had realised that there would be

---

* LP(45)134, 135 and 136.
† See *History Vol. I*, p. 183 *et seq.*
‡ See *History Vol. II*, p. 49 *et seq.*
§ MHLG File 91650/20.

reluctance on the part of his colleagues to giving any priority to new towns, and it was with this in mind that (jointly with the Secretary of State for Scotland) he appointed a departmental committee (publicly announced on 19 October 1945). The terms of reference were:

> 'to consider the general questions of the establishment, development, organisation and administration that will arise in the promotion of new towns in furtherance of a policy of planned decentralisation from congested urban areas; and in accordance therewith to suggest guiding principles on which such towns should be established and developed as self-contained and balanced communities for work and living'.

Lord Reith was appointed as chairman. As Minister of Works and Buildings in 1941, he had instigated the London County Council to call for the Forshaw and Abercrombie reports, and was known to be an advocate of planning. Several of the other members (including F. J. Osborn) had been active in the garden city movement, and Silkin could therefore reasonably expect a favourable report to add to the pressure he was beginning to exert on his colleagues.

The committee had to work quickly, but it was considerably helped (and influenced) by the extensive amount of work which had already been undertaken within the ministry. A first interim report (Cmd 6759) was hurried through because Silkin wanted to make progress with Stevenage and therefore urgently needed advice on the form of the agency which was to develop the new town. The second interim report (Cmd 6794), which dealt with other legislative matters was even more hurried since the Bill was brought forward by several months, following the postponement of the Development Rights Bill. The final report (Cmd 6876), though produced only nine months after the establishment of the committee, appeared several weeks after the publication of the Bill.

The first interim report (dated 21 January 1946) related mainly to the type of agency which should be responsible for development and estate management. It rejected 'ordinary commercial enterprise' or a housing association and, though it considered that an 'authorised association' under S35 of the Act of 1932, or a local authority sponsored corporation might be suitable in some cases, it felt that a government-sponsored corporation financed by the exchequer would be most suitable. The committee's second interim report (dated 9 April 1946) was largely concerned with the powers the agency should have for the acquisition of land; but the committee also discussed the position of the agency when the town had been developed and concluded 'by a large majority' that it should continue in being as a land-owner, rather than that ownership should pass to the local authority. Apart from this recommendation about future ownership —which Silkin rejected—most of the substance of the two interim

reports was embodied in the Bill which was published on 17 April
1946.

The final report of the Reith Committee (dated 25 July 1946) was
a comprehensive examination of the problems which would be
encountered in creating a new town. Although the committee had
completed their task within nine months, it was unfortunate that
their final report was not available while the Bill was passing through
Parliament, when politicians would have had a clearer idea of what
it was for which they were giving legislative authority. But the
generality of the review made by the committee was accepted by the
minister and was welcomed by local authorities. In certain important
aspects, however, the recommendations were not accepted by the
Government. In their final report there was a strong recommendation for the creation of a central advisory commission as a body to
which the corporations would have recourse for detached and well-
founded advice and guidance, able to resist 'the pressure towards
centralisation and uniformity . . . to fortify the position of ministers
when under sectional pressure', and to leave the corporations, while
subject to ministerial direction in major policy, with 'the fullest
freedom in ideas and execution'. Implicit in their thinking was a
claim for ready access to public funds—a claim which was hardly
consistent with the principles of peace-time finance and that of
ministerial responsibility. Inevitably therefore there was a greater
degree of central control than the Reith Committee had wanted.

Discussion with Local Authorities*

Silkin invited the local authority associations to a meeting in
October 1945 at which he explained that, though he had not yet
received Cabinet authority to proceed with legislation for the
development of new towns, he was anxious to obtain the views of
local authorities as early as possible. There was a need to create
new towns for the relief of congestion of large cities, but the Act of
1932 was inadequate for the purposes of a properly balanced
development. Subject to the views of the Reith Committee, he had
tentatively decided that there should be set up a corporation for each
new town. The members of the corporations would be appointed by
him after consultation with the local authorities concerned. He would
acquire the land and lease or transfer it to the corporation; the
outline plan would be prepared by the corporation after consultation
with local authorities; and the corporation would be empowered to
provide necessary services where the existing agencies were unable
to do so. The existing functions of local authorities would not be
disturbed and, after a period of years, the corporation would hand

---

* Secretary's Bill Papers, Vol 249B, and Lord President's File 1352.

over to an existing or new local authority. Normally the corporation would build working class houses, the exporting local authorities having a right of nomination, on conditions (including a rate contribution) for the tenancies. The corporation might dispose of some of its land to local authorities who would themselves build; private enterprise would have its place; and the legislation might provide for development by companies formed under the Companies Acts.

In answer to questions, Silkin said he hoped shortly to make known which areas were suitable for new towns. He hoped that no special inducements would be necessary to persuade industry to move and did not anticipate any great difficulty in attracting people to a new town even if it were a long distance from the parent town. As to the initiation of any particular project, he contemplated discussion between exporting and importing local authorities, the county council and himself, and expected that the decision would be arrived at in agreement with the local authorities concerned. Lord Latham on behalf of the London County Council agreed that the lines on which the minister was approaching the problem were 'sensible and practical'. The representative of the Rural District Councils Association said that in view of the conflicting interests of the various local authorities, a corporation was desirable. The others present said that, though they had been unable to consult their constituents, they could see no serious objections to the minister's proposals.

Shortly after this meeting with the local authority associations, Silkin met the joint planning committees and the county councils in the London area who set up an advisory committee under an independent chairman (Clement Davies) to examine and arrive at an agreed outline plan which could, with the minister's approval, serve as a broad directive to the planning and other authorities in the Greater London region. Members of the advisory committee and officials of the GLP committee were meeting continuously at the end of 1945 and early in 1946 and making a full examination of the Abercrombie proposals for satellite towns. Several of these were rejected: White Waltham because of its proximity to an airfield, and the loss of land of high agricultural value; Margaretting because it lay too close to Chelmsford; Redbourn and Stapleford because they were too close to other towns in Hertfordshire; Meopham and Crowhurst in view of their doubtful industrial potential; and Holmwood in the light of its amenity value and its proximity to Dorking. There was general agreement on the other three Abercrombie sites (ie Chipping Ongar, Harlow and Stevenage); Crawley was added as an attractive site to the south of London and in partial substitution for the proposal for Holmwood; and Hemel Hempstead was substituted for Redbourn. Stevenage was agreed by ministers in

November 1945, and in view of the concensus between the advisory and GLP committees, Silkin was able to press his colleagues for approval to the other four towns (ie Chipping Ongar, Harlow, Crawley and Hemel Hempstead) in April 1946.*

In March 1946 Silkin met the associations of local authorities again and informed them that he hoped to present the New Towns Bill before Easter. Two major points were now settled: there would be a government-sponsored corporation only; and secondly, when the job of the corporation was substantially done, the assets and liabilities would be handed over to a local authority.

Silkin's statement on these two issues is worth reproducing *in extenso*:

'In October last my mind had not been made up, and since that date I and Lord Reith's Committee have been considering the matters at issue. The interim report has now been received from the Reith Committee, and I propose to deal with the major points on which I intend to depart from the committee's recommendations. I now favour one type of corporation only—a government-sponsored corporation—and am rejecting all other kinds.

Dealing with those now rejected, the Reith Committee does not favour private enterprise, since such an undertaking as a new town is not a fit subject for private enterprise; such a responsibility should be a matter for a public corporation. There should be ample scope for private enterprise to play its part, under the umbrella of the government-sponsored corporation, for leases of blocks of land within the area of a new town could be granted for the purpose of development in accordance with approved overall planning and detailed plans. Charitable corporations to permit a charitable or non-profit-making institution to promote a new town would import the difficulty of definition and the impossibility in practice of differentiating between these and organisations set up by builders.

I reject also the local government sponsored corporation, which is the Reith Committee's second best choice. No proposal has been received from any local authority to create a new town since 1932. The rights of existing local authorities must be respected and they cannot be expected to favour the descent of a large authority from outside coming into their area to create a new town. The rights of a would-be exporting authority to export population from an overcrowded area to an importing authority were and would be protected. From a financial point of view, the Government would, in any case, have to take the responsibility, and the task must therefore be sponsored by the Government. Co-operation between the exporting and importing area authority is essential and can be satisfactorily obtained by representations made to and through the government-sponsored corporation. It is nevertheless most necessary that members of these authorities who are also members of the corporation should not regard themselves as delegates to the corporation.

I differ from the Reith Committee in the ultimate fate of the corporation. It is the Committee's view that the corporation should continue indefinitely, living side-by-side with the local authority, as, for example, at Welwyn, but I think that, when its job is substantially done, the corporation must go, and the assets and liabilities handed over to a local authority.'

---

* See below, p. 21.

The reaction of the local authority spokesmen was generally favourable. Lord Latham, on behalf of the London County Council, endorsed the decision for a government-sponsored agency, but felt that the LCC, as an exporting authority, could not subsidise an estate where it did not own the freehold. Sir Miles Mitchell, on behalf of the Association of Municipal Corporations, had no serious objection to a statutory corporation, but felt there should be room for a municipal corporation. He also objected strongly to a rate contribution when the houses were not owned by an exporting authority. The County Councils Association supported the government-sponsored corporation, but did not look with favour on a municipal corporation. In reply, Silkin said that it was not intended to compel local authorities to make rate contribution payments. These would be payable by agreement between the corporation and the exporting authority which would benefit from the development of the new town.*

Ministerial Discussions†

Having launched the Reith Committee, Silkin sought the agreement of the Lord President's Committee to make an early public statement of his intention to proceed with legislation for new towns as a means of checking city sprawl, which would be on the general lines of the proposals of his predecessor. This was objected to on the grounds that it was difficult to agree to such a statement while the whole question was being considered by the Reith Committee. Moreover, it would have an adverse effect on the efforts being made to induce industrialists to establish themselves in the development area. At a later meeting, Silkin argued that in the absence of an early public statement of intention, local authorities would start housing developments in the green belt areas. A counter view was that it was dangerous to proceed until the Government were 'able to see how the new towns would fit into the general industrial picture'. Otherwise they might deprive existing industrial areas of those industries

---

* This proposal was dropped (for a time) partly because of local authority opposition. A minute of 11 April 1946 from the Economic Section to the Lord President noted that 'since the object is to secure dispersal from congested areas, some means should be found for ensuring that the new towns are mainly populated by the "decanting" process and neither by migration from uncongested areas nor by attracting industries that would otherwise have gone to development areas. The suggestion that local authorities in the congested areas should contribute to the cost of rehousing in the new towns needs critical examination from this point of view. What is wanted is *encouragement* of migration from the congested area, and *discouragement* of migration from elsewhere'. For further discussion, see Chapter III p. 128 and Chapter VII p. 406, *et seq.*

† MHLG Files 91650/16 and 91650/17 and Ministry of Reconstruction File 1352; LP(45)214, LP(45)128, LP(45)40th Meeting, 1 November 1945, LP(45)43rd Meeting, 16 November 1945, LP(45)251, LP(45)45th Meeting, 30 November 1945, LP(46)50, LP(46)8th Meeting, 1 March 1946, LP(46)79, LP(46)12th Meeting, 5 April 1946, LP(46)88, CP(46)142, LP(46)13th Meeting, 12 April 1946, LP(DI)(46)3rd and later Meetings and CM(46)35th Conclusions, 15 April 1946.

without which they could not provide full employment. Nevertheless, in November 1945 the LP Committee expressed general approval of the proposal to establish satellite towns in suitable cases, but asked that the implications should be further considered before the Government were finally committed to acceptance.

In response to this invitation, Silkin submitted a paper on 23 November 1945 and to it attached a report by the official interdepartmental committee on the Greater London Plan (GLP). This noted that Greater London constituted 'the leading area for decentralisation'. The ten 'Abercrombie sites' were being examined, but not all were likely to be chosen. Special attention was being given to expanding existing towns. It was thought that it would be possible to get development started on two satellites within two or three years. These would be completed in five to seven years; meanwhile three or four others might be started. It was not anticipated that water and sewerage would lag behind housing development and, accordingly, planned decentralisation would not increase the claims on labour and materials. It was of first importance that industry should move concurrently with population, and with a strong government drive and a carefully controlled programme this should be attained. The Board of Trade had a list of firms anxious to rebuild, whose decentralisation was desirable, but who satisfied the Board that they should continue to be located in Greater London —'there will therefore be no clash with development area policy . . . and no danger of depriving existing industrial areas of industries needed for the maintenance of full employment'.

Many London boroughs were anxious to participate in satellite projects by exporting both population and industry, and some were well advanced with proposals, particularly for Stevenage, where 'the initial experiment' should be made. The GLP Committee were continuing their examination of sites and associated matters, and when that had been completed it would be desirable to issue a public statement for the information and guidance of planning authorities, farmers, industrialists, developers and other interested parties.

Two points are worthy of emphasis at this stage: the urgency of the issue as seen by Silkin, and the concept of a satellite town (a term which, rather misleadingly, was still used interchangeably with 'new town'). As to urgency, Silkin's paper noted:

'We are already having to look beyond the selection of sites for the first two years of our housing programme. Hitherto we have had to accept considerable encroachment onto the precious reserves of green space in the nearer neighbourhood of London. The pressure both for housing and industrial sites continues unabated. We cannot delay, therefore, in our preparations *now* for the next stage, ie the third year and after. For this we must either select and press on with the development of sites further afield, or turn our back on the London plans and permit a return to the wasteful development of the inter-war years.'

The concept of satellite towns was the antithesis of this interwar suburban development:

'By satellite towns I mean self-contained, balanced communities for both work and living. Steps are being taken to ensure that by careful organisation and concerted action, and with the powerful assistance of governmental influences, this object is secured; and that, although they will remain within the sphere of influence of the metropolis for certain specialised and major purposes, eg university life or theatreland, these towns will not repeat the mistake of the dormitory suburbs. They will be built beyond the green belt (which will be preserved under planning control reinforced by forthcoming legislation) in pleasant surroundings and on inexpensive land; and be of a size to provide homes, industry, shopping and recreation ready to hand and under attractively planned conditions. They will recreate the type of town that has form and develops a character of its own.'

Silkin asked for the approval of his colleagues to an immediate announcement that legislation would be introduced in the next session of Parliament; and to the purchase of the Stevenage land. In the discussion on Silkin's paper, it was proposed that public reference to satellite towns, other than Stevenage, should be deferred till there was agreement on the precise plans. A general statement that a few towns were to be set up near London would not help in detailed planning, and would discourage industry from transferring from London to the development areas. Moreover, proposals should not be formulated entirely in terms of London's needs: one or more of the early schemes should be in some other part of the country.

The LP Committee agreed that the purchase of land at Stevenage should proceed, but asked Silkin to bring later projects for approval in each case and to bear in mind the requirements of large urban areas outside London. Until the Reith Committee had completed their work (which Silkin was asked to expedite) and comprehensive proposals on the 'local government problems' involved had been put before the committee, 'no announcement should be made about the introduction of general legislation on satellite towns during the currency of the present Parliament'.

The reference to no announcement of general legislation 'during the currency of the present Parliament' was intended to put an end to further discussion on new towns pending full consideration of the report of the Reith Committee at some unknown date in future. From the point of view of Silkin and his department this implied concentration on the general problems of planning and more particularly on the increasing complexities of the Development Rights Bill to deal with compensation and betterment. Nevertheless, the position at the end of November 1945 was that ministers had accepted in principle the concept of new towns and had authorised the purchase of land at Stevenage.

The complexities of the Development Rights Bill, however, were so difficult of solution that, by the early part of 1946, it became apparent that there was little hope of introducing and passing the Bill in the 1945–46 session. In February of 1946, Silkin proposed to the LP Committee that it should be deferred and that, instead, he should introduce the Satellite Towns Bill. The main difficulty was that the question of land purchase by a central land commission had not been settled* and, if the Development Rights Bill were to proceed, it would have to exclude provision for such acquisition. As the drafting of the Bill proceeded, it became increasingly evident that, if a decision was eventually taken in favour of 'central purchase', the resulting (separate) Bill would so significantly affect a large number of the provisions of the Development Rights Bill that the latter Bill would have to be virtually 'rewritten'—only a year after it had been passed. But, while this Bill could be deferred for a year, it was imperative for the Satellite Towns Bill to be passed in the current session. The argument here was twofold. Silkin felt that he could hardly expect to have two Bills in the 1946–47 session. Secondly, while he could 'carry on without legislation' on satellite towns for a time, he could not do so for long. Silkin was confident that the Bill would not be 'seriously controversial' and it might perhaps run to only twenty clauses.

The argument was not entirely convincing, and doubts were expressed on the possibility of drafting the Satellite Towns Bill so quickly. Nevertheless, the LP Committee agreed (with evident relief) to the postponement of the Development Rights Bill and gave Silkin authority to 'press on' with the Satellite Towns Bill. Undaunted by these legislative difficulties, Silkin returned to the committee one month later with proposals for new towns at Harlow, Chipping Ongar, Hemel Hempstead and Crawley—in addition to Stevenage. (He commented that the 'urgent legislation' which was being drafted 'should greatly facilitate the task in view'.) These towns had been unanimously recommended by the GLP Committee, and he was anxious to make speedy progress because of the difficult London housing situation. When this proposal was discussed, it was suggested that the claims of other parts of the country should be considered before decisions were reached on the London projects. Dalton (Chancellor of the Exchequer) pointed out that there was no reference to cost and that he had not been consulted: he asked that the matter should be deferred. It was agreed that Silkin should submit a memorandum on costs, and that it would be convenient to consider this when the draft of the New Towns Bill was ready.

* See *History Vol. I*, p. 220 *et seq.*

A few days later, Silkin circulated two papers—one on the finance of new town development, and the other (submitted jointly by Silkin and Westwood, Secretary of State for Scotland) covering the seventh draft of the New Towns Bill.

For a new town of 50,000 people, to be developed over ten years, it was broadly estimated that capital expenditure chargeable to public funds would be of the order of £19m. (This excluded certain public sector items such as hospitals, premises for government departments and additional railway facilities.) This figure of £19m is perhaps of less intrinsic interest (particularly in view of the inflation which later took place) than the assumptions on which it was based. It was assumed that the development would be spread fairly evenly over the ten-year period and that, at the end of this time, it would have reached a stage at which the undertaking of the development corporation could be transferred to the local authority for the new town. It was also assumed that private developers would build half of the middle-class houses and a large part of the shops, offices and factories, and all the cinemas, banks and hotels. All working-class houses would be provided by the development corporation. These would have to be built at public cost in any case, whether in the new town or elsewhere. Extending this line of thought to services such as roads and sewerage and water schemes, 'something on factories and possibly also on shops', estimates were made of the *additional* public expenditure due to the establishment of a new town as compared with the expansion of existing towns. If it were assumed that the latter would involve a higher proportion of private enterprise building, the estimate gave an additional cost to public funds of about twenty per cent but, if the same proportion of local authority development were assumed, the additional cost estimate fell to less than ten per cent. Much was heard of this point in the discussions about new towns, both at this time and later.

Exchequer grants on annual deficiencies were also envisaged. These were considered to be necessary in view of the inevitable time-lag between the date on which expenditure was incurred on development and the return on such expenditure in the form of rents and ground rents. It was thought that, during the first five years, the annual grant required to meet this deficit might be between £30,000 and £40,000. 'Thereafter, the financial position will depend among other things upon the appreciation of central values which the development of the town will produce.'

The 'full' new town programme contemplated at this time (at least by Silkin and Westwood) was for a total of at least twenty-six new towns. There would be thirteen for London (in the main, major extensions of existing small towns) and seven in the rest of England and Wales 'for centres such as Manchester, Leeds, Liverpool, possibly

Plymouth, and in Durham'. In Scotland, there would be six to eight new towns, of which three or four would have populations of 10,000 to 15,000. The whole programme would provide for the movement of just over one million people, of whom about half would come from the Greater London area. Eventually some £380m of public loan capital might be involved, but this would be spread over 'ten years or more' and the draft Bill asked for '£100m only . . . to ensure the successful launching of the scheme'. The figure was, however, provisional and had not yet been agreed with the Chancellor of the Exchequer.

When the two papers were discussed at the LP Committee, there was concern about the geographical balance of the new towns programme: it was thought that, though the Bill was an essential contribution towards the solution of the London housing problem, insufficient attention had been given to other regions of Britain. This issue was referred for further consideration—in the event to the Subcommittee on the Distribution of Industry [*sic*] who decided that only industry 'moving completely' from congested areas should be allowed in new towns. This was to prevent firms from expanding by opening factories in the new towns while retaining their original premises in a congested area.

The Bill itself had an easy passage through the LP Committee, though Dalton demurred at the proposed borrowing powers of £100m. He suggested discussions on this between the Treasury and the ministry. (A figure of £50m was later agreed.) The Bill was submitted to the Cabinet, who gave approval on 15 April 1946. It was introduced in the House of Commons on 17 April 1946 by Silkin and Westwood, and was accompanied by a white paper (Cmd 6801) explaining the application and modification of the provisions of the Town and Country Planning Act 1944 relating to land acquisition.

Drafting the Bill*

In anticipation of ministerial approval, the department had prepared during August 1945 (ie before the Reith Committee were appointed) a draft of instructions outlining the features which might be embodied in the Bill, and this draft was discussed informally with parliamentary counsel on 28 August 1945, who not unnaturally took the view that he could take no action until he knew the place the Bill would occupy in the Government's legislative programme. The draft was kept under review during the following months and, immediately after the decision of the LP Committee on 1 March 1946, the detailed instructions were sent. A cardinal point was the nature of the agency to be responsible for the development of the

---

* Secretary's Bill Papers, Volume 249B, MHLG File 91650/16 and Ministry of Reconstruction File 1352.

new town, and it was contemplated that in most cases this would be a government-sponsored corporation, but 'provision should be made for other agencies, ie by corporations sponsored by local authorities, by limited liability companies or bodies analogous to authorised associations under S35 of the Act of 1932'.

At a meeting between Silkin and his officials of 5 March 1946 it is recorded that in view of 'the incidence of the financial risk, the nomination of the members, and the degree of government control' [*sic*], provision for a local authority-sponsored corporation should not be included. While the corporation would normally be government-sponsored, 'the Bill to be drawn up in terms of an authorised association, and if possible drafted so as to exclude ordinary commercial enterprise; . . . It was agreed that the Bill should provide for as wide a control by the minister as possible; it would be within the minister's discretion as to what extent he would exercise the control'. The differing types of agency had given rise to complexities in drafting and in a letter of 18 March 1946 parliamentary counsel warned 'there may be many problems relating to local government generally, the very nature of which we have not yet fully apprehended. The Bill introduces into the existing local government system a new type of authority which is not a local government authority, but is to be responsible for the building up of what amounts to a major local government unit'.

In revised instructions from the department on 20 March 1946 all references to agencies other than a government-sponsored corporation disappeared. (At his meeting with the associations of local authorities on 26 March 1946, Silkin said he had rejected all other forms:* this ended the argument for the time being about the nature of the organisation which had occupied much attention since the Pepler Report, but, as emerged towards the end of 1948, ministers had doubts whether some of the larger local authorities should not participate in the development of new towns.)†

Apart from this major point of organisation, the drafting of the Bill gave rise to many difficulties, including the arrangements for winding up the corporations and transfer to local authorities, land acquisition (which incorporated by reference much previous legislation), and the relationship of the corporations to local authorities and statutory undertakers, which were matters in which several government departments were concerned. A suggestion by a Treasury official that there should be some parliamentary approval to a new town was not pressed.‡

---

* See p. 17 above.
† See Chapter II, p. 85.
‡ The Treasury view was that 'there is serious objection to leaving the final decision in the hands of the minister without any parliamentary control'. The issue arose again in 1952 and 1963: see appendix D.

The Bill in Parliament

The Bill received an unopposed second reading in the House of Commons on 8 May 1946. W. S. Morrison (who had been Minister of Town and Country Planning in the previous Government) gave it general support. The only sour note came from Hinchingbrooke who referred to the Stevenage controversy which was then active, and denounced the Bill as 'frankly totalitarian in form'.*

In standing committee, only one amendment (to give protection to 'the requirements of food production') was pressed to a division, but was rejected. An amendment to enable local authorities to promote new towns was withdrawn after Silkin had explained that he had found no enthusiasm on their part to accept responsibility; the money would have to be found by the exchequer in any case, and if the members of the corporation were drawn from a wider field than would be possible from any individual local authority, they would probably form a better corporation. A further amendment to enable 'authorised associations' to sponsor new towns was withdrawn after a full discussion, in the course of which Silkin argued that they could not possibly have or command the resources required. An amendment to establish a central advisory commission (as recommended in the Reith Report) was withdrawn after Silkin had explained that while he naturally wanted co-ordination and exchange of ideas, he was not satisfied that a statutory body was the best method, and that if an advisory commission were wanted it could be set up without legislation.

The report stage was taken on 4 July 1946, and a new clause moved by Silkin was agreed to clarify the arrangements for winding up the corporations when their work was done. Several opposition amendments which would have had the effect of limiting the powers of corporations were negatived. The Bill had an unopposed third reading in the Commons on 5 July 1946, though it was again condemned by Hinchingbrooke as 'a State experiment in the life and happiness of our people and in my opinion like all State experiments, it will work havoc, bitterness and grave social damage'.†

In the Lords, the Bill was commended by Reith as generally embodying the recommendations in the two interim reports of his committee, but he was concerned by the number of references to Treasury approval. He could understand Treasury intervention and control where the body was to be permanently subsidised but although the corporations would have to run on borrowed money for a while, in due course they should be self-supporting, and should have freedom of action from the minister and the Treasury comparable with that of an ordinary commercial concern. Several

---

* HC Debates, Vol 422, Col 1154, 8 May 1946.
† HC Debates, Vol 424, Col 2536, 5 July 1946.

comments were made about the difficulties of the Scottish adaptation clause, with the suggestion that there should have been a separate Bill for Scotland. The Bill was unopposed, and after some minor amendments in committee received Royal Assent on 1 August 1946.

The New Towns Bill was very much simpler than the Planning Bill which it replaced in the legislative programme. This was not, however, the only difference. The concept of new towns was widely accepted and had an easy parliamentary passage. The 'development rights' scheme on the other hand raised intense opposition. Curiously, the main 'opposition' to the New Towns Bill came from within the Government from ministers who were concerned about the apparent preoccupation with the problems of London and the effect which the proposed London new towns would have on policies for the distribution of industry and the depressed areas. There was a fear —which proved justified—that London planning (whatever its inadequacies in relation to the size of the London problem) was running ahead of provincial planning. It took all Silkin's skill and determination to steer his proposals through Whitehall and the Cabinet.

The story does not stop here of course. This first chapter is intended to cover the period up to the passing of legislation, not its operation thereafter. But while the boundary line between the formulation of policy by way of legislative provision and its implementation was clear in relation to the development rights scheme, with the new towns it was blurred in the extreme. Indeed, one cannot help wondering if part of Silkin's success was a result of his almost brazen start to the new towns programme—and also if this was not part of the reason for some of the opposition of his ministerial colleagues.

As we shall see, he eventually had to pay dearly for his enthusiasm. The 'Stevenage Case' not only delayed the new towns programme: more subtly it dampened some of the broadly based support which the programme initially had—in Westminster, in Whitehall and in the country at large. Other problems—of shortages of labour and materials, of the fuel crisis and the dollar crisis—delayed the programme. The time needed to prepare new town plans and sites proved much greater than had been anticipated, and increasing doubts about the viability of the large programme for new towns became evident. By the time Silkin left office, in 1950, there was little to show for the efforts he had put into making the new towns possible. But he had laid the foundation, and by the time he died in 1972 the new towns had grown in number to twenty-eight and in population by nearly a million.

The following chapter documents the history of new towns policy during the remainder of Silkin's reign. The Stevenage story, however, is more easily dealt with separately and is presented as an annex to this chapter.

ANNEX

*Stevenage**

As Stevenage was the first of the new towns to be designated, and the one which encountered more local opposition than most, a brief account of its earlier history is appropriate.

Before the war the Stevenage Urban District Council had prepared a preliminary plan for an expansion of population from 7,000 to 30,000. No action was taken on this plan during the war but, in anticipation of the Abercrombie Plan for Greater London, officials of the Ministry of Town and Country Planning investigated the locality as a possible site for a new town and, on a confidential basis, were in touch with county and district officials on a range of matters including the drainage and sewerage problems involved, and the identification and referencing of the properties whose acquisition was likely.

The Abercrombie Plan was published in December 1944 and contained proposals for a number of new towns (including Stevenage). Following consideration by the GLP Committee, Silkin announced in Parliament on 5 March 1946† his general endorsement of the Abercrombie proposals, including decentralisation into new towns twenty to fifty miles from London. This was followed by a Written Answer on 12 March 1946‡ in which it was stated that a start would be made on the development of a satellite town at Stevenage, but that for its full development 'further powers are needed and the necessary legislation will be introduced as soon as possible'.

This was the first official intimation to the inhabitants of Stevenage that their small country town had been selected for the new experiment, and a local agitation immediately began. It is difficult now to judge how far the complaints of lack of consultation were justified. Officials of the local authorities were certainly aware confidentially of what was afoot. Members of the county council and of joint planning committees (but possibly not members of Stevenage UDC) had been consulted on the generality of the Abercrombie proposals. An official of the ministry met members of the UDC for the first time in October 1945, when he explained the proposals fully and, although he asked that they should be kept confidential for the time being, a garbled account was given to the press. The probability is that there was a failure in communication and that inadequate attention in the early stages was given to local susceptibilities,

---

* MHLG Files 91650/260/5, 91650/260/1, 91650/260/29/1 : and CM(47)25th Conclusions, 27 February 1947. See also Franklin and others v Minister of Town and Country Planning—2 All Eng 289.
† HC Debates, Vol 420, Cols 189–192, 5 March 1946.
‡ HC Debates, Vol 420, Col 198, 12 March 1946.

particularly those of the UDC who had some pride in their pre-war plan.

After several meetings between officials of the ministry and members of the UDC in April 1946, it was arranged that Silkin should meet members of the UDC on 6 May and address a public meeting in the evening of that day. In his speech Silkin referred to the Barlow report and the need for decentralisation from London, the Reith reports, the New Towns Bill, the possibilities for Stevenage 'where, as elsewhere, change was inevitable', and the deficiencies of the pre-war plan. He made a plea for 'this new town to be built in order to provide for the happiness and welfare of some 60,000 men, women and children . . . The project will go forward, because it must go forward'. The public meeting was disorderly.

On 18 May 1946 the UDC conducted a poll of the local government electors, with the following result:

In favour	913
Qualified approval	282
Entirely opposed	1,316

In sending the result of the poll to the ministry, the council asked for a public inquiry, and they were informed that in the event of the Bill which was then before Parliament becoming law, the minister would be prepared to consider sympathetically any application for a public inquiry to be held into a draft order to designate the Stevenage area as the site of a new town.

During the summer of 1946, the Bill was proceeding through Parliament, and the ministry were actively engaged in discussion with the Ministry of Agriculture and other interests about the precise boundaries of the area to be designated. At the same time, 1,100 local inhabitants of Stevenage were joining a residents' protection society which conducted a vigorous campaign in opposition to the proposal. Meanwhile, Silkin was making soundings about possible members of the new corporation, and on 2 July letters were sent to Hertfordshire County Council, Stevenage UDC, Hertford RDC, Hitchin RDC and to the London County Council and six metropolitan borough councils who might be interested in the new town for their overspill. The letter explained that a designation order was likely but that, in advance of this, the minister wished to set up a small informal advisory committee (most if not all of whom would later be formally appointed as members of the development corporation), and invited the local authorities to make nominations. The local authorities between them made forty nominations, and on 2 August 1946 the minister announced the names of the eight he had appointed to the advisory committee; four had been nominated by the local authorities and four were independent persons:

Clough Williams-Ellis	Architect (chairman)
Mrs. Monica Felton	Member of the Hertfordshire County Council (deputy chairman)
Campbell Allen	Director John Lewis Partnership (building and financial operations)
Hilary Atkinson	Staff of Labour Party HQ
Frank Corbett	Mayor of Wood Green Borough Council; Head of Legal Department of National Union of Railwaymen
W. J. Grimshaw	Member of Hornsey Borough Council; (accountant)
P. J. Ireton	Member of Stevenage UDC and of Hertfordshire County Council; (railway clerk)
Mrs. Elizabeth McAllister	Editor of 'Town and Country Planning'

Royal Assent was given to the Bill on 1 August 1946, the draft designation order was promulgated and, in view of the objections received, a local inquiry was held at Stevenage on 7 and 8 October by Arnold Morris (an inspector of the ministry) who made a brief opening statement that the purpose was to hear representations in connection with the minister's proposals. He said that the details of the plan, which would be determined by the corporation to be appointed, would not be considered, but representations could be made as to the appropriateness of the application of the New Towns Act to Stevenage, to the projected size and general character of the town, and, in general terms, to the inclusion of particular land within the designation area.

Objections were voiced either in person or by counsel on behalf of a number of local farmers, the residents' protection society, the Stevenage UDC, the Hertford RDC, two parish councils, the Lee Conservancy and Catchment Boards, and the Metropolitan Water Board (the Hertfordshire County Council held a watching brief, but did not appear as an objector). There was no cross examination of the objectors to test the force of their objections, or to place them in perspective with public policy. In his report of 31 October 1946 the inspector concluded:

'Most of the objections coincided on three main points—

   (i) That the place would be merely a dormitory town.

  (ii) That a 60,000 population town at Stevenage would coalesce with Welwyn, Hitchin and Letchworth into one urban community.

(iii) That transport facilities, particularly rail, were unequal to any increased demands.

I feel that these objections are inescapable and that cross-examination could not have removed the impression that they are genuine reasons against the choice of locality . . . In any case I suggest that the Stevenage project might well be held up until a safer example of the new town principle can be advanced as the first under the Act.'

A departmental comment was 'either Stevenage is a proper place for a new town or it is not: my own view is that insufficient evidence has been adduced to make the minister change his mind'. The secretary minuted the minister endorsing this view and adding:

'Perusal of the report reinforces the view that it is unnecessary and indeed unreasonable to expect the inspector to make any general recommendations as to merits. He cannot have the necessary background and what we want is a report of the objections and in particular recommendations about any adjustment of the boundary line in the light of the objections. I entirely agree . . . that the inquiry has not brought forward any major factor to override your original decision that there should be a new town at Stevenage with boundaries as proposed in the draft order.'

Silkin decided to proceed. A formal letter was sent to the objectors on 8 November 1946, and the designation order was made on 11 November 1946. There is no indication that before doing so he consulted his colleagues, although he may have mentioned it at the meeting of the DI Committee on 7 November 1946 (when approval was given for two new towns in Scotland, in spite of Silkin's reluctance).* After the order was made, hurried (and formal) consultation took place with local authorities (as required by the Act) about the appointment of members of the development corporation, which was formally constituted on 5 December; the membership was identical with that of the advisory committee formed four months previously. (Most of the local authorities who had earlier been invited to submit names for the advisory committee made vigorous protest that their nominees had not been selected.)

The validity of the Stevenage designation order was promptly challenged on behalf of the residents' protection society and, on 20 February 1947, the high court held in favour of the objectors on the ground that the minister had made up his mind before the public inquiry into the objections which he had not therefore considered fairly. As this would have defeated government policy, the Cabinet on 27 February 1947, on the submission of the attorney general, agreed that the case should go to appeal and that, in the meantime, legislation should be drafted to preclude the courts from reviewing ministerial decisions under the New Towns Act and similar measures. (In the event legislation proved unnecessary.) A month later, the

* See below, pp. 61–62.

court of appeal reversed the earlier judgement, and this reversal was upheld by the House of Lords on 24 July 1947 on the ground that the process of designation was an administrative act and that no heavier duty lay on the minister than that of carrying out in good faith the procedure prescribed in the Act. While this litigation was proceeding, the minister felt unable to authorise the corporation to proceed with land acquisition. Shortly after the litigation was settled, the Government clamped down on capital expenditure generally, and so far as Stevenage was concerned the number of men who could be employed on construction work was limited to seventy-five.

Early changes in the chairmanship of the corporation added some unsettlement. Clough Williams-Ellis resigned in August 1947 and was succeeded by Sir Thomas Gardiner (previously director-general of the Post Office) in October 1947; Sir Thomas resigned in October 1948 and was succeeded by the Rev. Charles Jenkinson (leader of the Leeds City Council) who died in August 1949; he was succeeded by Mrs. Monica Felton, then the chairman of the Peterlee corporation, but previously (December 1946–April 1948) the deputy chairman of Stevenage; Mrs Felton was dismissed in June 1951 for failure to attend a meeting of the Public Accounts Committee and for unexplained absence from the country, and was succeeded by Sir Thomas Bennett (the chairman of Crawley), who held the appointment till May 1953.

Restriction on capital expenditure was tight until 1950 and by the end of that year twenty new houses had been completed although 600 were in course of construction. But much preliminary work had been undertaken. The master plan was approved in February 1950 and, during that year, agreement was reached on the sewerage and water problems, and large scale civil engineering works were in hand. In their first report for the year ending 31 March 1948 the corporation noted that 'relations with existing Stevenage residents have steadily improved'; in 1949, 'our public relations have been greatly improved'; in 1950 periodic informal meetings with the UDC 'have served a most useful purpose in promoting mutual understanding'; and, in 1951 'this year under review has seen the beginning of large-scale development of the new town and encouraging progress has been made in both civil engineering and building projects'. The report for 1951 noted that 'a considerable number of enquiries have been made by industrialists for sites in the industrial area, but none of them has so far been able to satisfy all the requirements of the Board of Trade, and so obtain an industrial development certificate and building licence'. Nevertheless, in spite of the difficulties at the start, the new town was well under way within five years of its designation.

CHAPTER II

Ministerial Decisions on the First New Towns

MINISTERIAL discussions on new towns during the preparation and passage of the Bill were—with the exception of Stevenage—inconclusive. This was not because it was felt that decisions would have to await the passing of the Bill (which was a foregone conclusion) ; nor was it because of any basic disagreement in principle on the desirability of new towns. A major doubt was on the relationship between the geographical distribution of the proposed new towns and the Government's distribution of industry policy. Although investigations were under way on the need for, and the possible location of, provincial new towns, it was the London new town proposals which were furthest advanced. Silkin stressed the urgency of the London problem but, although this was not disputed, other ministers argued that since resources were limited, the claims of other parts of the country (in particular south Wales, the Clyde Valley and the north of England) should be considered before decisions were reached on the London proposals. There were fears that the development of a number of new towns in the London area would not only commit a disproportionate share of exchequer funds, but would also conflict with the policy of stimulating growth in development areas. These fears were further increased by uncertainties on the cost of new towns.

Matters came to a head in April 1946 when the Lord President's Committee (of which Herbert Morrison was chairman) discussed a paper by Silkin which sought authority to promote four new towns at Harlow, Chipping Ongar, Hemel Hempstead and Crawley.* At the instigation of Dalton (Chancellor of the Exchequer) it was agreed that a small committee of ministers should be appointed 'to examine the plans for the establishment of new towns both in the Greater London area and elsewhere in the United Kingdom, and to determine the priority in this matter to be afforded to different parts of the country'.

In the event, all issues relating to the location of new towns were referred to the newly established Distribution of Industry Subcommittee of the Lord President's Committee under the chairmanship of Dalton. It was at the early meetings of this Dalton Committee

---

* LP(46)79, LP(46)12th Meeting, 5 April 1946 and LP(46)13th Meeting, 12 April 1946.

that the initial policy issues in relation to new towns were thrashed out. It is therefore appropriate to deal at some length with the papers which were prepared for and discussed by the committee.

At the first meeting, on 1 May 1946, Dalton proposed that a new town should be established in each of the three main development areas (the north-east, south Wales and Scotland). In the north-east, Dalton suggested Ferryhill, and in south Wales, a site between Swansea and Cardiff, possibly at Bridgend, 'designed to draw labour from the townships of the Rhondda Valley'. The then current proposals for Scottish new towns (East Kilbride, Cumbernauld, Bishopton and Houston) were all in a development area. Silkin accepted in principle the development of new towns in development areas but stressed the amount of detailed investigation and regional consultation which would be required before exact sites could be determined.

Silkin and Westwood were asked to submit reports on the establishment of new towns in the three main development areas for consideration. These were produced quickly and were discussed on 23 May 1946 together with a paper written by Douglas Jay (then in the Prime Minister's Office) on 'New Towns and the Distribution of Industry'.

*Silkin's Paper on New Towns**

Though asked to deal with development areas, Silkin's paper dealt with the whole of England and Wales. Examination of the problem was proceeding 'in every region where there was a prima facie case', but London had been given first priority because there the problem was both the most complicated and the most urgent. Sufficient progress had nevertheless been made elsewhere to enable him to make specific proposals for the first instalment of the programme for the country as a whole.

The proposals for decentralisation from London as formulated in the Greater London Plan and amended in submissions made by an interdepartmental committee of officials envisaged some 300,000 people in 'satellites'. The overall proposals were as follows:

Quasi-satellites	125,000
Expanded towns in the region	341,390
Expanded towns outside the region	267,000
Satellites	300,850
	1,034,240

The 'satellites' were Chipping Ongar (an additional population of

---

* LP(DI)(46)12.

44,300), Harlow (54,300), Stevenage (50,500), Hemel Hempstead (41,750), and Crawley (40,000). Still under consideration were a 'western' new town in the White Waltham area (40,000), and a southern or south-eastern satellite, possibly at Meopham (30,000).

There were a further five other towns 'the degree of whose contemplated expansion [might] point to the creation of a government corporation': Hatfield (an additional population of 19,000), Newbury (20,000), Aylesbury (30,000), Bletchley (32,500), and Basingstoke (20,000). At this stage, Letchworth and Welwyn were omitted on the assumption that 'they could and would prefer to look after themselves'.

If these proposals were accepted, out of a total decentralisation from London of 1,034,240, the new towns to be developed by the government-sponsored corporations would account for about two-fifths, whilst over half of the decentralisation would go to existing centres of population.

The nature and extent of the need for new towns throughout the rest of England and Wales had not yet been examined in the same detail as had been done for the London area, but Silkin outlined the factors 'which had come to the notice of his department on the planning problems of certain areas'.

For Manchester 'the need for extension and decentralisation was urgent, and plans were far advanced', although Silkin had not been able to approve the method proposed by the city for putting them into effect. Manchester had been hoping themselves to build a new town within extended boundaries, either on an island site in the middle of Cheshire or on a site connected with the existing city area. Cheshire County Council had been pressing, on the other hand, that Manchester's overspill should be housed by means of the expansion of a large number of existing towns. They were strongly opposed to 'an enclave of Manchester in Cheshire', but it was believed that their opposition to a single new town would disappear with the passage of the New Towns Bill under which such a town would be built and managed by a government corporation—not by Manchester City Council. Silkin added that he understood that Lancashire County Council took a similar view. He proposed to pursue matters with the local authorities concerned in the immediate future.

In the Liverpool area, the Merseyside Plan had recommended peripheral development in spurs with wedges of open space as an alternative to a new town, which in this area would almost certainly involve development on some of the most valuable agricultural land in the country. Planning opinion was divided on this point, and the Merseyside Plan itself involved building on first class agricultural land. Silkin was advised that there might well be a case for a new town in the Wigan area and also for an expansion of Ellesmere Port.

No general outline plan had been made for Birmingham. A long-term programme of blight redevelopment was proposed by the city council, but the scale of the displacement of population involved was not known. It was thus impossible to form any view whether a new town might be desirable for accommodating the displaced population or whether it could more conveniently be accommodated in extensions of existing large towns, or even on 'the large amount of open land' within the city boundaries.

Sheffield City Council wanted to provide for their overspill in peripheral expansion on the basis that most of the industries of Sheffield were very closely tied to the city area. It was, however, open to question whether such a means would, by itself, be adequate to cope with the whole problem, and Silkin was having the matter examined more closely.

Leeds were thinking in terms of one or two new townships, within the city boundaries, while the West Riding County Council preferred that some of the existing towns in the county should be further built up. The need for and best form of such decentralisation was being examined.

Abercrombie's proposal for a satellite town for Hull at Burton Constable was opposed by the city council because it would be outside the city boundary. Moreover, there was no general agreement on planning grounds that Hull needed a 'satellite'.

Bradford had been mentioned as possibly needing a new town, but the matter was in a very early stage, and it was doubtful whether there was really a need.

There was a need to build some 30,000 houses for Bristol and there might be a prima facie case for erecting these in a separate town. The city council, however, were contemplating building within their present boundaries, thereby increasing density and 'damaging some of the city's natural amenities'. There was a promising site for a possible new town at Chipping Sodbury, and Silkin proposed to draw the attention of the city council to this and to have discussions with them.

Both Leicester and Nottingham were contemplating the building of considerable numbers of houses on large tracts outside their own boundaries, but it was not yet clear whether the best course would be to segregate these in new towns or to build up existing townships and villages.

Portsmouth would require to build some 30–60,000 houses (the figures varied) and had a site, which had been purchased some time ago, at Leigh Park, but a new town might also prove to be desirable.

There was a considerable overspill to be re-accommodated from Plymouth, but whether this was to be done in the form of a new town was bound up with the city's application to the Boundary Commission for a large extension of their area.

All these were cases of decentralisation to relieve congestion, but new towns were also seen as possible solutions to the problems of other areas. In the south Derbyshire and Leicestershire coalfield area, for example, problems of large-scale subsidence were anticipated, and the needs of future development might require the creation of one or two new towns. In Durham there was a major problem 'of bringing people together into a new centre where new and more varied employment could be found for them'. The Durham coalfield contained some 'derelict communities' where the coal seams were worked out, and it was proposed in one case to regroup population currently housed in an area of this type in a new town at Aycliffe, adjacent to a new industrial area based on the royal ordnance factory.

At the first meeting of the Dalton Committee, it had been suggested that new towns might be established at Bridgend and Ferryhill as part of the reconstruction programmes respectively of south Wales and north-east England. Silkin had then stated that a good deal of detailed work, including discussions at the regional level, would be needed before any conclusion could be reached. He now suggested that there might be other places in south Wales which should also be considered but, though he had 'great sympathy with the needs of these areas and thought that new towns might well be necessary', he was not yet ready to make any proposals since 'the necessary research had not been completed'.

Silkin continued that in development areas the major problem was that of attracting new industry, and it was not envisaged that this would ordinarily need a new town. But development areas, like other areas, had problems of congestion which might need to be met in this way and had, moreover, the special problem, of which the Durham case was an instance, 'of collecting people into new communities in order to provide appropriate employment for them'. Many industries which would settle in new towns would not be potential candidates for any of the development areas. They might be unable to move without taking their workpeople with them, and if they did this the advantage to the development area was lost. There might also be difficulties about markets, linking of processes, and so forth. Moreover, the control which would be exercised by the corporations through the leasing of industrial sites in new towns would be 'very much more complete than anything hitherto experienced in the history of planning', and would enable the corporations with the encouragement of the Government, to refrain from making industrial sites available to industries which could properly be induced to settle in a development area. Finally, on the short-term view, a great many industries which were at that time urgently seeking a site would not be able to wait for the construction of a new town, and would, therefore, go elsewhere. A proportion of these would find their way into the development areas.

Silkin stressed that it was vital that the new towns programme should be soundly based and conceived. Before a complete and final programme for the whole country could be formulated, much further detailed research was required. This was proceeding; good progress was being made; and proposals would be submitted as soon as it was complete. But enough was already known to enable certain interim decisions to be made, and he recommended that the preparatory work needed for the establishment of six further new towns, of which four would be in the London area, one in a development area and one elsewhere in the provinces, should begin at once.

He thought that there would be general agreement that the case of London was by far the most urgent. Indeed, if the immediate programme had regard only to pressure of need, it would probably be initially confined to new towns for the London area (with the possible addition of one for Manchester). Nearly a quarter of the population of the whole country was in the Greater London area; the congestion was very grave; and the degree of the housing shortage far exceeded that of any provincial city, owing largely to the fact that war damage had been far more severe. The scale, therefore, on which housing sites had to be found within the following few years was such that they could not all be provided by normal extensions of existing towns outside the green belt ring. Some sites, to meet immediate needs, had already been allocated in the green belt area, but any further encroachment on the green belt would be contrary to the Government's declared policy. Nevertheless, the pressure for the allocation of further sites in the green belt ring would almost certainly prove irresistible unless adequate alternatives were available for development without delay. When all allowance was made for the practicable expansions of the larger towns, there was a residual need which could be met only by the development of new towns. Moreover, it had to be remembered that the problem was not that of the London County Council area alone but also of the many large and congested contiguous areas, such as East and West Ham, Tottenham, Edmonton, Walthamstow, Willesden and Croydon.

In order to secure the right location for large new centres of population it was essential to lose no opportunity of inducing industry to go to the selected centres. There was opportunity within the following two or three years if sites were available, 'but if they are not, there is grave danger that the opportunity will be lost'. The period from the time at which the first steps for the creation of a new town were undertaken to the time when the building sites actually became available was unavoidably lengthy, and for this further reason it was essential to the implementation of the Government's declared policy that the preparatory steps for a sufficient number of new towns should be put in hand at once.

Silkin therefore sought authority of the Dalton Committee to proceed at once with the preliminary steps for the construction of six new towns (in addition to Stevenage which had already received approval) so that formal action could be taken as soon as the New Towns Bill had become law.

The six towns were Chipping Ongar, Harlow, Crawley and Hemel Hempstead; Aycliffe; and a new town for Manchester. A proposal for a new town in south Wales would be submitted as soon as the necessary research had been undertaken.

*Westwood's Paper on Scottish New Towns**

Westwood's paper indentified two areas of central Scotland where new towns were required—the Clyde Valley (which, at that time, embraced the greater part of the Scottish development area) where there was a need to provide for housing for 'overspill' from the highly congested urban areas and, at the same time, to promote industrial growth 'as an integral part of the development area policy'; and secondly in Fife and in the Lothians to meet the needs of the new coalfields in those areas.

The proposals for the establishment of new towns in the Clyde Valley area arose out of the recommendations recently made in Abercrombie's report for the Clyde Valley Regional Planning Advisory Committee. Glasgow, with a population of about 1,100,000, was one of the most congested areas in Great Britain, 700,000 people being huddled together in and around the city centre within a space of three square miles, at densities ranging up to 127 houses to the acre. The dwellings were mainly of the one and two-room type, and in some of the central wards the percentage of such dwellings was as high as 93 per cent.

Industrial congestion in the central areas of Glasgow was equally acute. Housing and industry were inextricably mixed up, and industrial concerns had no room to expand. There was an urgent need for relocating industry in better surroundings and for introducing new industries on a substantial scale to secure a properly balanced industrial structure. The Board of Trade estimated that, to remedy unemployment in Glasgow, about six million square feet of new factory accommodation were required—a figure which took no account of the need for relocating industries currently accommodated in unsatisfactory premises.

Glasgow could not continue expanding outwards as this would lead to the city and the surrounding towns becoming one large urban

* LP(DI)(46)13.

sprawl. A planned policy of decongestion and decentralisation was urgently needed. Similar problems of housing and industrial congestion existed on a smaller scale in other towns in the region such as Greenock and Clydebank.

Against this background, the Clyde Valley Committee had recommended the establishment of four new towns in the area—at East Kilbride in north Lanarkshire (about seven miles from the centre of Glasgow), at Bishopton in Renfrewshire (about ten miles from the centre of Glasgow), at Houston in Renfrewshire (about twelve miles) and at Cumbernauld in Dunbartonshire (about twelve miles). In addition, the committee proposed the extension of a number of existing towns elsewhere in the region. Each of these four new towns would ultimately have a population of between 50,000 and 60,000 and would provide for an overspill from Glasgow and other areas (such as Greenock) of 200,000 to 250,000 people.

Westwood accepted in principle the committee's basic recommendation that the provision of new towns in the Clyde Valley area was essential for securing the decongestion of Glasgow and the properly balanced provision of the new housing and industrial facilities that were so urgently needed in this part of the Scottish development area.

He was in broad agreement with the Clyde Valley Committee as to the areas in which the new towns should be developed and was satisfied that the establishment of a new town at East Kilbride should be regarded as the first priority. Lanarkshire County Council were anxious to make an immediate start with the building of a substantial number of houses at East Kilbride and it was clear that these houses had to be planned as part of the new town. He therefore sought the authority of his colleagues to initiate early discussions with all the local authorities concerned on the basis that the Clyde Valley Committee's proposals were accepted in principle by the Government and that the establishment of a new town at East Kilbride would be put in hand as a matter of priority.

In Fife and the Lothians substantial development of new coalfields were under way, and in the next decade or so these areas would become the principal coalmining areas in Scotland. In the next few years new sinkings would take place in three main areas in the Lothians. The working of these new pits would involve the rapid build-up of an additional labour force of 10,000 to 15,000 mineworkers, the majority of whom would be drawn from other parts of the country, and new housing accommodation would have to be provided for them. He was anxious to ensure that these houses were built in the right places as part of 'properly planned communities constituting a complete break from the outmoded conception of the mining town'. In some cases it would be appropriate to provide the necessary housing and other facilities by expanding some of the existing towns; in other cases it would be necessary to develop new towns with populations ranging from 10,000 to 15,000. He proposed to consider with the Minister of Fuel and Power and the local authorities concerned the precise areas in which new communities should be established and hoped to submit specific proposals at an early date.

Jay's Paper*

Both Silkin and Westwood presented their cases for new towns with confidence and with an implied assumption that new towns were self-evidently essential elements of policy. Not so Douglas Jay. His paper (presented by Dalton with a covering note indicating his broad agreement with Jay's argument) was dispassionate, thoughtful and questioning. To Silkin and Westwood it must have seemed academic.

He argued that the proposal to establish a new town was substantially a proposal to influence the distribution of industry and population; and unless it was seen clearly as such in all its bearings, the eventual effects might be different from what was intended. Currently, attempts were being made (rightly in his view) to carry out two policies simultaneously. First, there was the policy of redistributing industry from areas where the demand for labour exceeded the supply (mainly London and the Midlands) to areas where the supply exceeded the demand (mainly development areas). The objective here was 'to correct the dominating urge of industry towards London'. This had been shown conclusively by the Barlow report (and still more by wartime labour supply experience) 'to be causing great economic inefficiency and waste at both ends'. It meant failure to use resources in the distressed areas, and unnecessary duplication of them in London.

Secondly, there was the policy of the 'decongestion' of population from 'huge scale overgrown areas' such as London. This policy sprang from a social rather than an economic motive, and it sought to mitigate overcrowding rather than unemployment. There was now general agreement that, when the problem reached the London scale, the satellite town was the only long-term solution. It was also agreed that if population moved out, industry had to move out also.

The crucial issue was that of planning the outward movement of industry from the congested areas to the new towns, and the strict reservation of industrial facilities in those towns for firms from the congested areas. If this were tackled properly, the new towns would achieve decongestion successfully without causing undesirable effects elsewhere; but if it were not tackled successfully, the new

* LP(DI)(46)17.

towns would tend to draw both population and industry from other parts of the country. The result would be the creation of worse or new distressed areas in, for example, the north and west. Experience had shown that this was a very real danger. Welwyn and Letchworth were quoted as 'undoubted examples of the causes of extreme unemployment on the north-east coast before the war'. Similarly the growth of Slough had created unemployment in south Wales. The wartime labour supply and manpower experience, in which towns to the north and west of London were sucking population from the development areas, left no doubt of this.

It followed, Jay continued, that the creation of new towns, particularly in the London area, had to be most carefully planned if new unemployment in the development areas was not to be created as a result. It would be difficult to restrain the rush of businessmen to some of the new towns suggested. A new factory in Stevenage, Hatfield, or Newbury was 'every tired businessman's dream, and no half-hearted or slipshod administrative methods will hold him back'. In each new town therefore, the objectives had to be, first, to ensure that the population actually came from the congested area and not from elsewhere; and, secondly (and more important still), to ensure that the industrial facilities in the new towns were strictly reserved for firms from the congested areas.

The first point meant, of course, not that someone from Sheffield could not live in Stevenage, but that there was a countervailing decrease in the housing accommodation and population of central London corresponding to the increase in Stevenage. In Jay's view, it was not clear from Silkin's paper how this was to be secured. The second point required that the industrial facilities in the new towns should be strictly reserved for firms from the congested areas. If a new factory in Stevenage were taken by a firm from Newcastle, the inevitable effect would be unemployment in Newcastle, increased labour shortage in London, and eventually a further net growth of population, industry and overcrowding in London. If this process were not stopped at the source by the refusal of new factories in the satellite towns to any but firms from congested areas, the forces at work would be too strong to resist it later. It was also essential to realise that satellite factories could not be allocated to firms expanding from the congested areas. If London firms were to take new factories in Stevenage in addition to their existing London factories, the result would be a net growth in the industry, housing and population of the London area. It was therefore necessary to ensure that the firms moving from central London to Stevenage and the other towns vacated an amount of space roughly equivalent to that which they took in the new town. It was this, rather than the actual building of new towns in development areas, that was the real safeguard against the creation of unemployment in development areas as a result of the new towns policy. Indeed, it was possible that a case could be made against the building of any new towns in development areas on the two grounds that there was an excess of social capital there already, and more should not be created; and that the new towns policy was one of 'decongestion' which did not arise in the development areas. On the whole these two arguments were not conclusive since there was another strong ground for the placing of new towns in development areas, namely that the creation of new towns (which meant the creation of a great many physical services) took a material place in the country's investment programme. In current conditions of general manpower shortage, there was thus a case for beginning the new town policy in development areas rather than in London, the area of most intense labour shortage.

On balance, however, Jay thought that the social and economic arguments together probably justified starting one or two new town projects in London and in the development areas together. The Scottish proposal for a new town at East Kilbride should be supported on all grounds, since both the decongestion and the development areas arguments applied. There was also a strong special case for the Fife proposals, which might indirectly (by transfer of population) help to relieve unemployment in Lanarkshire. Moreover, there was a strong special case for a moderate-sized new town on the north side of the Aycliffe royal ordnance factory, since the industrial facilities were already present and communications were good. This town, however, would not need to be on the scale of the proposed London satellites. There was a similar, though perhaps less strong case for enlarging Bridgend, on the assumption that there was no need to adhere rigidly to figures as large as 50,000 or 60,000 for new towns.

The proposals for London (and also for cities such as Manchester, Liverpool and Birmingham, which were set out in Silkin's paper) were examples of 'decongestion proper'; and the principles suggested for decongestion should apply strictly. Jay suggested that since these were not stated explicitly in Silkin's paper, the committee might think it worth laying it down as a strict condition of 'decongestion new towns' that the industrial facilities should be reserved for firms moving (and not expanding) from the congested area; and that the increase in housing accommodation in the satellite should be demonstrably balanced by decrease in the congested area.

Jay added as a final comment that, if mistakes were to be avoided, and the difficulties encountered at Stevenage circumvented, it might be worth proceeding fairly cautiously with the 'decongestion' satellites, and not laying down a target population too rigidly.

Consideration by the Dalton Committee May 1946*

In presenting his paper, Silkin stressed that, though his department was actively considering the need for new towns in other parts of the country, there was no doubt that the decongestion of London was the most urgent problem to be faced, and it was for this reason that he proposed to give the London area five of the first seven new towns to be built. The extreme urgency of the London problem was due to the much greater degree of damage which London had suffered from enemy action. No fewer than 100,000 houses in the area had been totally destroyed during the war, and unless new towns were got under way at the earliest possible moment, it would prove impossible to resist the demand of the London County Council to develop housing estates in the green belt.

He had already decided that he would reject the proposal of the LCC to develop a cottage estate of 800 acres at Chessington for about 20,000 people.† But insistence on the abandonment of the Chessington site was not enough :‡ above all, alternative provision had to be made, and the only alternative was a series of new towns.

Silkin had an ally here in Bevan, who, as Minister of Health, was responsible for the housing programme and for the determination of the compulsory purchase order which the LCC had submitted for Chessington. He agreed that, without a new town at Crawley, it would be impossible to resist the demand for a new housing estate at Chessington. The Dalton Committee were convinced, and the Crawley proposal was agreed.

Another issue discussed at this meeting was the 'nearness' of the new towns to London. Silkin discounted this criticism. He argued that thirty to forty miles was the maximum distance over which it would be possible to persuade firms to move. This, of course, was an issue of major importance, particularly in view of Jay's analysis. The Dalton Committee accepted the argument and agreed that in 'decongestion new towns' industrial facilities would be provided only for firms moving from the congested area whose problem they were designed to solve.

Nevertheless, the other London new town proposals ran into

---

* LP(DI)(46)3rd Meeting, 23 May 1946, LP(46)88 and Treasury File SS 385/02.

† This decision was submitted by Silkin to the Lord President's Committee (LP(46) 119). Though he had agreed to 'quasi-satellites' at Aveley, Loughton, Chigwell, Dagnam Park and Oxhey, he could not agree to the Chessington proposal which would have the result of closing up an important wedge of open country extending into the built-up area of London at Surbiton. Quite apart from its intrinsic undesirability, to give approval to development in this area would be a severe discouragement to the local authorities who had been 'endeavouring to conform to the canons of good planning often at some detriment to their own short-term interests'.

‡ Silkin also attacked the LCC on two other grounds : their insistence on the need to develop very large estates (primarily for one class of resident, and inevitably located in the green belt) ; and their rooted objection to accepting, as a contribution to their housing problem, any development (whether by themselves or any other body) on land of which they did not own the freehold.

43

heavy weather. This stemmed from Treasury alarm at the financial implications of the programme. As one Treasury minute put it:

'I feel some alarm at the way Town and Country Planning multiply their projects without so much as mentioning finance. They have an enormous programme of land acquisition in blitzed cities, estimated to cost over £500m, apart altogether from the costs of redevelopment. They have an unknown but very large sum in prospect under the compensation proposals. They are pressing hard for a scheme for central purchase of all publicly owned land . . . And now they are multiplying new towns at a cost of about £15m a time.'

At the meeting, Dalton expressed his concern about the 'lack of clarity' on the financial implications of the programme. The financial clauses of the New Towns Bill were based on the assumption that the new towns programme would require some £50m over the first five years, but if the new towns at Hemel Hempstead, Chipping Ongar, and Harlow were approved (in addition to Crawley and Stevenage) little money would be available for the creation of new towns elsewhere in the country. He thought, therefore, that the committee should have before them more detailed estimates of the costs involved in creating each of the new towns proposed in Silkin's paper, before final approval was given to the creation of the three additional towns which were proposed for the London area.

Silkin undertook to submit a memorandum on the cost of the new towns proposed, but pointed out that the figure of £50m to which Dalton had referred should be ample to provide for the early development of a considerable number of new towns, as the bulk of the expenditure would not be incurred until the house construction had got well under way.

Barnes (Minister of Transport) welcomed the Chancellor's suggestions and offered to submit a note showing the cost involved in providing adequate transport facilities for the new towns in prospect.

So far as the provincial new towns were concerned, Silkin stressed that 'active consideration' was not being slowed down by his department's concentration on the London problem. Though proposals were less advanced, progress was being made and agreement was requested in principle to a new town at Aycliffe. (This was approved.) South Wales was more difficult—as Bevan underlined when he expressed his 'grave doubts' on whether this was a satisfactory solution to the problem: he had no objection to providing sufficient houses at Bridgend to enable full use to be made of the local royal ordnance factory, but he did not like the idea of creating new centres of population which would draw off population from the existing towns and villages and destroy the very rich communal life which they had developed. In his opinion, the solution to the south Wales problem was 'to pump industry into the existing centres of population'.

There was apparently little discussion on the other provincial new towns, though it was minuted that consideration of the Manchester problem should be deferred to a later date.

Westwood did not need to argue his case for the Scottish towns so fully since his proposals nicely met the requirements of both physical planning policy and the distribution of industry policy. Approval was given to a rapid start of East Kilbride and to the elaboration of specific proposals for new towns in Fife and the Lothians. Concern was, however, expressed on the danger of creating 'new single-industry towns which might themselves become distressed areas when the new coalfields began to be worked out'.

The Capital Cost of New Towns

Dalton's concern over the cost of the new towns programme stimulated a great deal of work in the various departments concerned, and three papers were prepared for the Dalton Committee. These were presented in May 1946 by Silkin, Westwood and Barnes.*

SILKIN'S PAPER

Silkin's paper consisted of a memorandum by his departmental officials and a covering note by himself. The memorandum provided additional detail on the previously given estimate† of £19m—the cost to public funds of building a new town of 50,000 persons over a period of ten years. Of the £19m, £15·5m would be borne by the development corporation (paid out of advances from the consolidated fund) and £3·5m by local authorities, made up as follows:

		£
Land, roads, sewerage and water		2,860,000
Educational premises, community centres, swimming baths, etc.		2,250,000
Housing		
Working-class	£10,000,000	
Middle-class	1,910,000	
		11,910,000
Public and commercial buildings, factories, shops, etc.		1,980,000
TOTAL		£19,000,000

---

* LP(DI(46)22, 23 and 24.
† In LP(46)88; see also CP(46)142 and the Financial and Explanatory Memorandum to the New Towns Bill.

Provision was made in the estimate for the construction of all working class houses (viz 10,530) and half the middle-class houses (viz 1,315). The estimate would be reduced to the extent that private enterprise undertook the building of houses for which provision had been made in the estimate. For the purpose of the estimate it was assumed that there would be some fall in the current level of building costs; the assumed average cost of building a working-class house was £950 (exclusive of site and development costs).

The estimate did not include the cost of hospitals or premises required for government departments, nor any contribution by the development corporation towards the capital cost of the provision of electricity and gas services or towards the cost of additional railway facilities that might be needed in consequence of the provision of a new town; nor did it include the cost of purchasing any built-up nucleus in the new town area. It was assumed that private developers would undertake the construction of at least half of the middle-class houses and a large part of the shops, offices and factories, and all cinemas, banks, churches and hotels.

An issue of particular concern was the comparative costs of building a new town and expanding existing towns. In his covering note, Silkin made much of this point: if instead of creating new towns, the necessary housing and other development took place elsewhere, the cost to public funds would not be lessened by more than 10 to 20 per cent. He was satisfied that every new town would save public money. The land for new towns would be bought at a figure which would be often little more than one-twentieth of the cost of fringe land, resulting in a saving of perhaps £3m. When the only alternative was expensive central land, at perhaps £10,000 an acre, the saving was many times greater. Moreover, the saving in housing subsidies in such a case would be formidable; for 125,000 houses there could be a total saving, on the current rate of subsidy, of £181,600 a year for sixty years. Moreover, in a carefully planned long-term development, taking place mainly on previously undeveloped land, there was a substantial saving in the provision of public utilities, since 'the patchwork adaptations and extemporisations' needed in an area which was being laid out afresh and redeveloped were avoided.

The estimate related to a 'typical' town of 50,000 additional population. Actual estimates for individual towns were not feasible but Silkin, somewhat blandly, expressed the view that there was no reason to expect wide individual variations.

The New Towns Bill provided for advances to development corporations up to £50m. It was envisaged that some £37m would be needed over the first five years of the programme in England and Wales; by 1948 six new towns would be under way and additional new towns would be started as indicated in the table below. (The six new towns were Stevenage, Crawley, Chipping Ongar, Harlow, Hemel Hempstead and Aycliffe.)

Estimated capital expenditure to be met from public funds in the development of new towns on the basis of the assumed programme, during a period of five years following the passing of the New Towns Bill, from (say) the end of July 1946 to 31 July 1951 England and Wales

		Expenditure by :					
		Development Corporations		Local Authorities		Total	
Year	Number of New Towns	In the Year £m	Cumulative £m	In the Year £m	Cumulative £m	In the Year £m	Cumulative £m
1946–47	1	0·25	0·25	—	—	0·25	0·25
1947–48	6	3·0	3·25	1·0	1·0	4·0	4·25
1948–49	7	4·6	7·85	2·2	3·2	6·8	11·05
1949–50	9	9·0	16·85	2·8	6·0	11·8	22·85
1950–51	12	14·05	30·9	3·8	9·8	17·85	40·70
1951–52	15	6·01	36·91	1·6	11·4	7·61	48·31

WESTWOOD'S PAPER

While Silkin's estimate related to a 'typical' new town, Westwood was concerned with the specific case of East Kilbride which had been approved by the Dalton Committee as a priority project. Nevertheless, it was too early to produce anything more than 'a very broad general estimate', and a number of assumptions had to be made. These were: first, that the development of the new town would be spread over a period of ten years and that the average cost of building and civil engineering work during that period would be 12·5 per cent below existing prices; secondly, that the development corporation would construct all the working-class houses in the new town (approximately 10,500) and half (approximately 1,300) of the other houses; thirdly, that the development corporation would provide most of the shops in housing areas and only a few of the shops in the main shopping centre; fourthly, that the Board of Trade would develop an industrial estate providing employment for about 5,000 workers and that the development corporation would provide factory buildings for 2,500 additional workers; and finally, that private enterprise would undertake the construction of the remainder of the houses, shops and factories and all cinemas, banks, offices, hotels, etc.

The total expenditure likely to be borne by public funds was £23·7m shared between the development corporation (£17m), the local authority (£5·7m), and the Board of Trade (£1m).

The estimates made no provision for expenditure on the building of hospitals or premises for government departments or for any contributions by the development corporation to statutory undertakers in respect of electricity or gas services or additional railway facilities, nor did they include the cost of acquiring any properties in the existing village of East Kilbride.

On the assumption that the New Towns Bill would come into operation by the end of July 1946, and that a development corporation was set up shortly afterwards for the development of East Kilbride, it was estimated that the total amount of advances from the consolidated fund to the development corporation during the five years August 1946 to August 1951 would be £7·8m.

BARNES' PAPER

Barnes had offered to prepare a memorandum on the cost of providing adequate transport facilities for the proposed new towns but, in the event, his paper dealt with the much wider issue of the capital investment required (but, in his view, unlikely to be achieved) on transport facilities in the London area. The cost of servicing the new towns (and the 'decentralised population') was relegated to an appendix. In essence, his argument was that the problem of providing adequate transport facilities for London was a huge one even if there were no new towns: the new towns would make it even more difficult.

He began by stressing the wider issue of the existing commitments to transport improvements and of the probable requirements which had to be envisaged as part of the planning programme of the London area over the following decade. He dealt, in the main, with railway works but he reminded the committee that, in addition, 'vast expenditure' would have to be undertaken on the replanning and rebuilding of highways for facilitating movement to or within the central area or for enabling through traffic to by-pass the centre.

If they were to be able to serve adequately the existing and prospective traffic needs of London and the surrounding areas, the railway companies and the London Passenger Transport Board had to incur very large sums in extending and improving their services, properties and equipment. They were already committed to the £40m programme embodied in the London Passenger Transport (Agreement) Act 1935, of which over £26m had already been spent and a further £20m remained to complete the programme, including the extension of the Central London Railway eastwards to Loughton and round the Fairlop Loop and westwards to Ruislip, and the electrification of the LNER from Liverpool Street to Shenfield. These were of the first priority and were already in hand.

Many of the older main line terminal stations needed complete modernisation. A plan for the rebuilding of Euston Station had already been approved at an estimated cost of £2·5m. King's Cross and probably other stations would have to be rebuilt as soon as conditions allowed.

The development of London Airport and the importance of providing the quickest possible access between it and the centre of London were likely to necessitate (apart from local services) the provision of a special high-speed railway track which might cost anything from £5·5m to £12·5m according to the scheme adopted. The urgency of this work would be all the greater if the improvement of the road route were delayed owing to the difficulty over rehousing.

The railway improvements needed in central London had been the subject of a full and expert examination by a committee under the chairmanship of Professor Inglis whose report had recently been issued. They had recommended schemes estimated to cost approximately £240m, about half of which should, they considered, be completed within ten to fifteen years. The most urgent involved the construction of 58 route miles of railway in tunnel through central London, which they regarded as necessary to provide proper facilities across London and to avoid increasing congestion on the roads.

Apart from all these works of improvement, the transport authorities had of course to do a vast amount of work by way of repair of war damage and overtaking arrears of maintenance accumulated during the six years of war.

The relative priority of most of the work had yet to be determined, but much of it was needed to serve existing populations and to avoid conditions of stagnation in the heart of the metropolis. The development of new towns at Stevenage and elsewhere combined with other outward movements of population was broadly estimated to involve railway works over and above these, at a cost which might be in the region of £60m.

In summary, Barnes foresaw the need for expenditure on railway works alone in the London area of something like £150m over a ten-year period. This was irrespective of the cost of providing the transport facilities necessary to serve the proposed policy of decentralisation and distribution of population:

'Even if the country can afford all this expenditure during the next decade, I doubt if it will be physically possible to carry it out and I feel bound, therefore, to warn my colleagues that having regard to the urgent importance of facilitating movement and avoidance of congestion in the central areas, I cannot promise that all the railway works required in connection with the Greater London development can be executed within the next ten years.'

Discussion at the Dalton Committee Meeting 1946

These three papers were discussed by the Dalton Committee in June 1946. Silkin, though admitting that his figures 'could not be more than a rough guess', felt that they over-estimated rather than under-estimated the costs of new town development. He also repeated his warning about the urgency of the situation, and asked for approval to the Chipping Ongar, Harlow and Hemel Hempstead proposals. (In this he was again supported by Bevan who argued that the establishment of a new town should, in the long run, represent a profitable investment to the State.) In addition to securing cheap land, the State would have the advantage of being able to plan sewerage and other common services rationally and economically, and he saw no reason why the State should not, like private builders, derive a reasonable profit from the houses it erected.

It was essential, however, that the new towns programme should be phased so as to fit in with the Government's general employment policy and with the ten-year programme of housebuilding and slum clearance which he was in the course of preparing. Finally, Silkin thought that, in planning new towns, particular care should be taken to avoid the segregation of classes. Such a segregation would mean that the districts in which the cheaper houses were concentrated would come to be regarded as socially undesirable, and their inhabitants would wish to leave them whenever they could afford to do so.

Barnes was in favour of the creation of new towns 'wherever such development could be justified', but thought that the committee should be aware of the very considerable capital cost involved in providing transport facilities for the new towns proposed in the London area, and that this aspect of the problem should be considered carefully in relation to the other urgent transport schemes that ought to be undertaken within the next ten years. On current estimates railway works alone in the London area would call for an expenditure of something like £150m during this period irrespective of the cost of providing the transport facilities required by new towns and other measures of decentralisation which he put at £60m. Even if the country could afford this expenditure, he doubted whether it would be physically possible to carry it out.

Moreover, he felt that there was some danger of duplicating housing development in rebuilding on blitzed sites in the centre of London at the same time as the new towns were being developed, beyond the green belt, to serve the same populations. It was not easy to move Londoners outside the central metropolitan area if they did not wish to go, and it might turn out that the great majority of the population for whom the new towns were intended would remain in London, leaving the new towns themselves to be settled by people from other parts of the country. He would, therefore, like to see the approved new town programme for the London area confined for the moment to Stevenage and Crawley, so that the transport implications of the programme as a whole could be subject to thorough examination.

Bevan, on the other hand, said that rebuilding on blitzed sites concurrently with the building of new towns involved no duplication of effort. Building in the blitzed areas was proceeding according to an approved plan and would not by itself solve the London housing programme. Additional development had to take place outside the built-up areas and **if it** did not take place in new towns it would do so by further uncontrolled sprawl into the green belt. In his view, the Government should prohibit all further encroachment upon the green belt. This could be done only if the necessary accommodation could be provided in new towns.

To Silkin there were no grounds for believing that transport facilities for the new towns would involve any substantial capital expenditure that would not have to be incurred in any case. The new towns would not be London dormitories and, if they were not built, transport facilities would have to be provided for the further scattered development around London which was the only alternative.

Dalton, summing up the discussion, said that the general opinion of the committee seemed to be in favour of proceeding with the proposed new towns at Chipping Ongar, Harlow, and Hemel Hempstead provided that the development programme was properly co-ordinated with the Government's general employment policy and the national housing programme. Nevertheless, it was clear that, in the first place, the committee would have to be able to form some idea of the cost involved in providing transport facilities for these towns and for Crawley and Stevenage. The point at issue, he thought, was by how much the provision of transport facilities for the five new towns proposed would increase the cost that would have in any event to be incurred on communications in the London region during the next ten years, having regard to the fact that an outward movement of population from London whether into new towns or into the green belt was inevitable. The value of such a report would be increased if it could include some comparison of the cost of providing transport to a carefully planned new town like those proposed by Silkin, compared with the cost of providing the same facilities for a town which 'grew up haphazard'. He accordingly suggested that officials of the appropriate departments should be instructed to examine this problem as a matter of urgency.

East Kilbride raised a very specific question: why was it estimated to cost some £4·7m more than a new town for a comparable population in the London region? A further report was called for.

The Cost of Transport Facilities for New Towns*

The report by officials of the Ministries of Transport and Town and Country Planning was duly prepared and circulated, with a covering memorandum by Barnes, to the Dalton Committee on 10 July 1946.

Officials, not surprisingly, found it impracticable to make any straight comparison between the cost likely to be incurred over the following ten years on railway facilities for a planned dispersal, as proposed, and a hypothetical unplanned movement. The latter inevitably depended on a number of suppositions, the nature and effect of which was open to wide variation. Improvements in the Outer London Area would ultimately become necessary in any event, but possibly not so soon in the case of unplanned growth as under a programme of planned dispersal. They did not feel able to suggest any closer guide than that, against the estimate of £60m for works in the Outer London Area to meet a planned dispersal, an expenditure that might range between £20m and £40m, according to circumstances, might be expected if matters were allowed to take their own course.

Any difference in cost between railway works required in the Outer London Area for planned and unplanned dispersal respectively, though possibly substantial, would be relatively small in comparison with the cost of work in the inner area, which was needed in either case. Of greater importance was the question as to whether the necessary facilities could be provided in phase with the building programme. They suggested that the essential question was to settle the priority of the schemes in the light of the capital expenditure to be incurred and the resources in labour, materials and finance which could be made available within the period.

Much of the basis of Barnes' main argument was swept away by a footnote to the estimates of the costs of works required for the new towns which pointed out that a great deal of the investment would probably be needed whether or not the new towns were built. Barnes shifted his tack somewhat: the main problem was more one of timing and priorities than of comparative costs. He also advanced a number of further points which had to be taken into consideration.

First, as a transport problem, the service to the new towns could not be divorced from that of increased populations resulting from 'infilling' of existing communities along the same lines of route. This process of infilling would be likely to be essentially of a dormitory nature.

* LP(DI)(46)37 and LP(DI)(46)7th Meeting, 10 July 1946.

Secondly, while the amount of travel per head of population in the case of new towns such as were proposed was estimated as being about half that resulting from dispersal by general infilling, the fact that the new towns were to be planned to provide industrial occupation for their populations meant that provision had to be made for freight services, fuel, raw materials and finished products considerably greater than would be needed for settlements largely of a dormitory character.

Thirdly, the effective capacity of lines in the outer parts of the area would largely depend on the provision of additional facilities for the accommodation of increased passenger traffic at the central terminals and for its distribution from those terminals to the ultimate destinations. The cost of these would be relatively much greater than the cost of works in the outer area.

The incidence and timing of London Transport improvements had to be considered as a whole in relation to the labour and finance which might reasonably be expected to be available. On neither of these decisive factors could any clear lead be given. Barnes had already given a figure of £150m as the expenditure that was likely to be required on the railways in the London area during the following decade, irrespective of planned dispersal. He now provided a more detailed statement and also produced a list of highway works which should be undertaken. These works were estimated to cost £125m, of which at least £50m should actually be expended in ten years. All these works had to compete for the limited supply of civil engineering labour in the area as well as for the available resources of technical staffs. They would also make large drafts on the exchequer since it had to be assumed that the greater part of the expenditure would, of necessity, be financed by the Government in one way or another. These considerations underlined the importance of well-planned priority in the allocation of all resources.

The detailed list of railway works given in the report are not reproduced here, but it is appropriate to refer to one item, namely the railway works needed for Chipping Ongar new town. Though no explanation is recorded, it was noted that 'no practical proposal' had yet been devised, but the minimum cost might be £5·5m and could 'well be very much greater'. The proposed new town at Chipping Ongar was abandoned shortly afterwards.

At the Dalton Committee meeting on 10 July, there was general acceptance of the view that the main issue relevant to the new towns was the timing of railway investment rather than its costs. Silkin said that he did not regard the ambitious proposals for improving the transport facilities to Harlow and Hemel Hempstead at a total cost of £34·5m as really essential to their development. If his proposals were approved, he would not press that these transport projects should be given high priority. Indeed, they implied that new towns would have much more of the character of dormitory suburbs than was the intention. In his view, the really essential transport needs of the towns were quite modest (consisting of such things as sidings and improved stations).

He pressed for immediate authorisation for proceeding with his plans for Hemel Hempstead and Harlow. This was agreed, with the rider that it did not commit the Minister of Transport to give special priority to the major transport schemes to serve these two towns which were contemplated in the report of the officials.*

Silkin was also asked at the meeting (by Dalton) about the progress being made on proposals for further provincial new towns. He replied that discussion had reached an advanced stage with local authorities in the West Riding on the establishment of a new town to relieve overcrowding in Leeds and Bradford; that discussions were also proceeding with the Manchester authorities; and that active consideration was being given to the siting of a new town in south Wales, possibly at Bridgend.

The outcome of the meeting was an approval in principle to new towns in the West Riding ('to house the overflow of population from Leeds and Bradford') and in south Wales 'possibly at Bridgend'. Silkin was also 'invited' to consult the Minister of Agriculture and Fisheries before finally selecting the site for any proposed new town.

---

* These works included the widening and electrification of the line to Harlow, and the widening of two main line routes and a branch line for Hemel Hempstead and N W Hertfordshire, together with the provision of a connecting line from Hemel Hempstead to a point between Boxmoor and Apsley. The total cost of these and unspecified 'other' works was estimated at £34·5m.

Barnes was not happy with the Dalton Committee's decision and, on 9 September 1946, wrote to Dalton saying that he found it difficult to believe that it was 'one which could be adhered to in practice':

'What will happen if, in accordance with it, we proceed to plant new industrial towns at points where there are no transport facilities adequate to deal with the traffic to which they give rise? Even if we accept in large measure that these new towns will provide employment for practically all their inhabitants (and I confess that I am very doubtful whether this ideal is in fact attainable) they are bound to place additional peak-hour traffic on the railways to and from London, and when this occurs on a line on which there is no spare capacity, trains will be unable to meet the additional demands upon them. In many cases it will not be the inhabitants of the new towns who will be crowded out, but persons who seek to join the trains at stations between them and London. The Minister of Transport, rather than the Minister of Town and Country Planning, will then have to bear the brunt of public criticism of the travelling conditions which result, and ultimately of course complaint of lack of foresight and provision will fall upon and discredit the Government as a whole. To proceed with the establishment of these new towns, plus any additional "infilling" at other places en route, without providing for their transport services would not merely be bad planning, but the negation of any planning at all.'

Barnes pressed for a reconsideration of the decision but this was rejected. (Treasury File 2SS 385/02 and Cab 124/885.)

The Cost of East Kilbride*

While Silkin had estimated that the cost to public funds of a typical new town in England and Wales would be £19m, Westwood's estimate for East Kilbride, at £23·7m, was very much higher. In a paper to the Dalton Committee he set out the reasons for this major difference. One major factor, of course, was that while the figures for East Kilbride related to a specific site, Silkin's related to the cost of the works which would 'normally be required for the purposes of any new town'. Less ambiguously, he noted that the development of a particular site in England might cost 'somewhat more or somewhat less . . . depending on the nature and configuration of the site and the extent to which water, sewerage and other services were available'. It followed that any comparison between the two estimates would be 'apt to be misleading'.

Such statements would not have been likely to commend themselves to the committee without some harder evidence of the reasons for the higher estimates for the particular development at East Kilbride: this Westwood provided by detailing the main items where his figures were greatly in excess of Silkin's. This is set out in the following table.

The Cost of a 'Typical' New Town Compared With East Kilbride

		Silkin's Estimate for a 'typical' new town in England and Wales £	Westwood's Estimate for East Kilbride £	Excess of Scottish over English Estimate £
1.	Roads	1,360,000	1,750,000	390,000
2.	Sewerage	550,000	1,000,000	450,000
3.	Water	450,000	850,000	400,000
4.	Educational buildings	2,000,000	2,600,000	600,000
5.	Housing			
	(i) Working class	10,003,500	10,500,000	496,500
	(ii) Middle class	1,906,750	2,000,000	93,250
6.	Public and commercial buildings	500,000	1,300,000	800,000
7.	Factories	750,000	1,500,000	750,000
8.	Miscellaneous	329,750	1,000,000	670,250

A series of notes explained the reasons for specific differences. For example, the Scottish estimates took account of the need for replanning the approach roads to the proposed new town at East Kilbride and of the fact that the road construction would be carried out on a

---

* LP(DI)(46)30

somewhat undulating site. They also took into account the fact that there would be more than one drainage area at East Kilbride (ie more than one drainage system and purification works) because of the nature of the site.

The reason for the higher Scottish estimate for water was that a new reservoir providing a gravitation supply was required for East Kilbride whereas the English estimates made no provision for a reservoir but merely for bores and pumping stations. On 'educational buildings', the English and Scottish figures represented an attempt to estimate the cost of the provision of schools at modern standards. Both were rough estimates, and 'it is possible that the Scottish figure is too high or that the English figure is too low'. It was added that it was necessary to 'keep in mind that building costs are higher in Scotland than in England'.

House-building costs were also higher in Scotland than in England. The Scottish figures assumed that a working-class house would cost £1,000 and a non-working-class house £1,500. The comparable English figures were £950 and £1,450.

The Scottish estimates for public and commercial buildings assumed that a wider range of provision would be made in the first ten years of the development of the new town. The Scottish figures also took account of the need for providing a fire station, police station, administrative offices, libraries, halls, etc.

East Kilbride was in the Scottish development area and the Scottish estimate for factories included a figure of £1m representing the cost of an industrial estate developed by the Board of Trade. The English estimate made no provision for any industrial building by the Board of Trade and assumed that the bulk of the factory provision would be carried out by private enterprise.

Finally, the Scottish estimates allowed a round sum for miscellaneous items. This figure represented 'less than five per cent of the total cost of the development of the new town'.

The minutes of the Dalton Committee meeting merely record that this report was noted and that Westwood was invited to circulate 'in due course' a report on progress at East Kilbride.

New Towns in Scotland*

East Kilbride was one of the four new towns proposed in the Abercrombie Clyde Valley Plan. The case for these had been put to the committee but, though specific authority had been given to East Kilbride, the question of further new towns in the Clyde Valley had not yet been considered. In July 1946 Westwood presented the case for a further new town at Bishopton. Essentially this was two-fold:

---

* LP(DI)(46)45 and LP(DI)(46)8th Meeting, 31 July 1946.

to provide new industrial facilities to the west of Glasgow to relieve unemployment in the city itself, and to meet the problem of the residential and industrial congestion of Greenock—an area hemmed in by the Clyde on one side and steep hills on the other.

Westwood also returned to the possibility of a new town in Fife, on which he had previously been authorised to work out detailed proposals with the local authorities concerned. He had now concluded (and both the Minister of Fuel and Power and the President of the Board of Trade agreed) that, in addition to the considerable housing developments which would be carried out by local authorities in the Kirkcaldy and Buckhaven-Leven districts, two new townships should be developed in central Fife as soon as possible. One of these towns would be in the Lochgelly-Cowdenbeath area, and the other in the Leslie-Markinch area. Each of the towns would cater for an additional population of the order of 20,000 people, and would be planned so as to provide ample facilities for new industrial development in order to ensure a properly balanced industrial structure. The new townships would be centrally situated near the main railway lines and the proposed new trunk road running through Fife from the north to the south via the Forth road bridge.

Westwood was thus asking for approval to proceed with these three additional new towns in Scotland. The prospect of four Scottish new towns inevitably raised the question as to whether (in Dalton's words) this 'would give that country a disproportionate share of the initial programmes as compared with England and Wales'. The Cabinet papers record only that while the Secretary of State for Scotland thought that the case for all the three additional new towns was justified, that most urgently needed was the one in the Lochgelly-Cowdenbeath area of Fife. This was, in the event, the only one approved at this stage. (The site was later found to be unsuitable and the proposal was abandoned.*)

Review of New Towns for England and Wales†

In a paper prepared by Silkin for the same meeting (in July 1946), he provided a general survey of the current situation on proposals for further new towns.

A possible alternative to Chipping Ongar was under consideration following the report of the advisory committee on London regional planning. In the meantime, to meet the urgent housing needs in the short term period, Silkin had asked the Joint Planning Committee in south and west Essex to carry out a thorough survey of land available for housing in their areas.

---

* See p. 87 below.
† LP(DI)(46)44 and LP(DI)(46)8th Meeting, 31 July 1946.

At Aycliffe, progress had been made with site surveys. The planned population would be 15,000–20,000 (the level at which the Reith Committee felt that a new town could be self-sufficient in public services and amenities). However, it was intended to plan the town in such a way that it would be capable of expansion to at least 30,000 if this proved desirable in the light of employment growth at the royal ordnance factory.

Further consideration of the Leeds situation had led Silkin to conclude that the question of provision for the overspill of Leeds and Bradford ought to be further examined as part of a wider problem of overspill from towns in the West Riding generally, including the Dewsbury-Morley-Batley group of towns. This further investigation would necessarily take some time, and meanwhile Silkin felt that it would be undesirable to put forward any definite proposal. The need in this case was not, in his judgement, of the same order of urgency as elsewhere since the authorities concerned were in a position to meet their housing needs for some time to come without recourse to a new town.

The position in Manchester was still under discussion, but for south Wales doubts about the relevance of new towns were emerging. Discussions were leading to the 'tentative' conclusion that there was:

> 'no reason to suspect that the population and employment problems of the rural areas, coast towns or mining valleys would lead to new towns. Any needs for rehousing could be met by developing housing sites within the area of the authorities affected which in some cases may involve the development of new neighbourhood units.'

The position in respect of the fringe areas of the coalfield to the east and south, where the big wartime factories were situated— (Bridgend, Glascoed, the Treforest Trading Estate, etc)—and where further industrial development was taking place, was not so clear. These factories drew their workers from large distances. Following local discussions, Silkin had now reached the conclusion that Bridgend could probably cope with its problem by normal (though rapid) development of the town. As regards the others the position might be met by building up existing townships, but a case could possibly be established for 'a couple of small new townships' of 20,000 or more. One might be in the Pontypool area (near Glascoed and a big new nylon factory, and the Lucas factory at Cwmbran) and the other in the Pontypridd-Llantrisant area near the Treforest Trading Estate.

> 'The whole problem is a complex one and I do not think it will be possible to propound a definite solution till the investigations at present proceeding have been carried a stage further.'

New Town at Mobberley*

A more detailed discussion of a proposed new town for Manchester at Mobberley (Cheshire) took place in October 1946. Silkin explained that Manchester had 'some of the worst overcrowding in the country'. Unless a substantial part of the city's population could be 'exported', it would be impossible for the city to make a start of the implementation of the *City of Manchester Plan*. Since the surrounding areas to the east and west had overspill problems of their own, the only alternative to a considerable growth of Manchester to the north and south was the creation of one or more new towns. The principal objections to further growth of the city itself were that it was already 'inconveniently elongated' from north to south, and any further 'creep' into Cheshire in particular would mean continuous urban development southward from Manchester, thus removing the countryside 'even further from the doors of city-dwellers'.

Manchester had agreed that the proper solution was an independent new town in Cheshire, and had suggested a site at Mobberley some twelve miles to the south of the city. Though a more distant site would have been preferable, interdepartmental discussions had shown that there were strong objections to the alternatives. Areas further west were ruled out by subsidence difficulties due to brine pumping, while any site further south 'would deprive farmers of valuable agricultural land in an area hitherto unaffected by urban penetration'. Railway consideration also favoured Mobberley as against a more southerly site.

In view of the urgency of Manchester's housing needs the choice, in Silkin's view, was between a new town at Mobberley and a gradual sprawl of the city over the area separating it from Mobberley. In addition to making it possible to preserve an appreciable break of open land between built-up areas, the new town was thought to have the advantage that industry as well as population would be attracted to it from Manchester, 'thus enabling it to achieve a measure of economic independence and develop a life and character of its own, so avoiding the danger of development merely as a dormitory area for the city'.

It was estimated that of the 76,000 new houses required for Manchester's overspill population only 33,000 would be built inside the city boundary. Probably not more than half of the remaining 42,000 could be accommodated in Mobberley, since the total population contemplated for the new town would not exceed 60,000, and Salford and Stretford also might be obliged to look beyond existing communities in an attempt to relieve serious overcrowding. Nevertheless, the Mobberley proposal was seen to represent a large part of the answer to Manchester's most pressing difficulties,

---

* LP(DI)(46)75 and LP(DI)(46)10th Meeting, 23 October 1946.

particularly as the building force then employed on the city's Wythenshawe estate might complete the major part of its work in 1948 and be available for switching to other building within reasonable distance of the city early in 1949. Silkin asked for agreement in principle to the new town proposal: this would give time for the designation of the area, hearing of objections, preparation of plan and preliminary work on the site to be completed by the time building operations came to an end at Wythenshawe.

Silkin's proposal was agreed on condition that industries would be drawn only from the Manchester-Salford area and that consultations took place with the Ministers of Agriculture and Transport, both of whom had 'views' on siting.

*Aycliffe New Town**

Aycliffe had been earlier proposed as a new town for a population of between 15,000 and 20,000 but 'capable of further expansion to 30,000'. Even these low figures, however, gave rise to anxiety in the area that the new town would have undesirable effects. In particular it was feared that it would draw miners away from the coalfields 'which would obviously be highly undesirable in view of the great need for coal'; and that it would adversely affect the redevelopment of nearby towns such as Bishop Auckland. This was Dalton's constituency, and the local authorities of the area pressed on him their 'vehement' opposition to the Aycliffe proposal. Dalton, however, was in favour of the new town as a means of 'killing unemployment in this most difficult area', but in a letter to Silkin he warned that 'it will need very careful handling if we are to avoid a general line-up of Labour controlled local authorities' against it.

The outcome was a limitation of Aycliffe to a population of 10,000—'at least in the first instance'. Agreement was reached on this figure with the local authorities, and Silkin maintained that 'in the particular circumstances of this area', a town of this size 'could be constituted as a satisfactory urban unit'.

Among the particular circumstances of the area was the fact that it was probable that as many as 3,500 of the 6,000 employees at the royal ordnance factory would be women, most of whom would be likely to wish to remain in their existing towns.

The Board of Trade felt that it might be more prudent to plan for a larger population in order to provide for employment 'if and when' the local coal seams were exhausted, but the general feeling of the Dalton Committee (as minuted) was that 'it would be sufficient to provide only for 10,000 people'. It was this population size which was initially approved.

---

* LP(DI)(46)75, LP(DI)(46)10th Meeting, 23 October 1946 and Treasury File SS 385/02.

New Towns in Scottish Mining Areas*

The position in the Scottish mining areas was very different. The Lanarkshire coalfields were progressively declining, and major new sinkings were planned in Fife, Clackmannan, Stirling and the Lothians, and in central Ayrshire. There was thus a need to provide housing on a very substantial scale in new and expanding mining areas.

In a paper to the Dalton Committee, Westwood stressed that, while some new housing could be provided by additions to existing villages, it was necessary in the case of the larger proposals to establish entirely new communities. These were required not only to provide housing for miners but also to enable development of a balanced character to take place 'providing employment for members of the miners' families, and with social amenities and facilities up to modern standards'. New towns were proposed for two areas where large scale development was urgently required—in East Fife at Leslie-Markinch, and in central Ayrshire at Sinclairston.

Two new pits were to be sunk near the Leslie-Markinch area (in 1951 and 1957) ultimately providing employment for some 4,300 miners. Additionally, housing was required for several hundred miners who were living in unfit or overcrowded houses in the vicinity. To accommodate a mining population of the order of 4,500 in a properly balanced community, a total population of around 30,000 was necessary. A new town of this size was therefore proposed on a site adjoining the small towns of Leslie and Markinch. The site had been agreed by government departments and the local authorities concerned, and was capable of rapid development.

In the Sinclairston area, two new sinkings were planned, the first providing employment for upwards of 2,000 miners and the other employment for about 500 miners. These new pits would not come into production until 1953–57, but there was an immediate need in the area for about 500 houses to replace unfit and overcrowded houses in the surrounding villages. In addition, nearly 500 new houses were required for additional miners who could be employed to increase production at existing pits. Ayrshire County Council were pressing for a first development of 500 houses in the area, and Westwood thought that it was essential that this development should be planned as part of the new township. Taking into account the labour requirements of the proposed new sinkings, of expanded production at existing collieries, and of the needs of general industry to secure a properly balanced industrial structure in this expanding mining area, the new town should ultimately have a population of about 30,000 people. The site at Sinclairston, which was 6·5 miles

---

* LP(DI)(46)94 and LP(DI)(46)11th Meeting, 7 November 1946.

due east of the town of Ayr, had been selected after consultation with the Ministry of Fuel and Power, the Board of Trade, the Ministry of Labour and the County Council. Rail facilities were available direct to the site and the road communications were excellent.

Westwood therefore sought approval to his proposals for these two new townships and to the immediate commencement of the necessary planning work.

At the Dalton Committee meeting in November 1946 Silkin, though seeing 'no objection on the merits of the proposals', suggested that the new towns would not be required for several years. They would involve a drain on the limited financial programme, and he felt it would suffice to authorise 'preparatory measures'.

Westwood argued that it was essential to mining developments that he should be able to proceed immediately with the proposals. Housing accommodation was needed in any case, and though local authorities had the necessary powers to make the provision, they allocated their houses in accordance with their lists and not necessarily to miners. Some houses would be required immediately for the two new mines.

In discussion 'the need to watch the proportion between Scotland and England and Wales' in the new town programme was recognised. Dalton pointed out that £50m had been allotted to the programme initially, but that for his part he would give favourable consideration to further allocation when this was used up. It was decided to authorise Westwood to proceed as proposed 'as soon as conditions permitted', and in consultation with the interested departments.

Welwyn Garden City and Hatfield*

Silkin had explicitly omitted Welwyn (and Letchworth) from his new town plans 'on the assumption that they can and will prefer to look after themselves'.† Hatfield, however, was identified as a town where the envisaged expansion 'may point to the erection of a government corporation'. (Others were Newbury, Aylesbury, Bletchley and Basingstoke.)

In November 1946 Silkin brought before the Dalton Committee a proposal that Welwyn and Hatfield should be expanded as two new towns under one development corporation. This proposal gave rise to considerable debate. Silkin noted that there was general agreement between departments both on the desirability of expansion in these two areas and on its scale. The issue was simply

---

* LP(DI)(46)97, LP(DI)(46)101, LP(DI)(46)93 and LP(DI)(46)12th Meeting, 27 November 1946; LP(DI)(46)102 and LP(DI)(46)13th Meeting, 11 December 1946; and Treasury File SS 385/02.

† See p. 34 above.

that of the instrument to be used for the expansion. Welwyn and Hatfield were both on the main railway line some five miles south of Stevenage. Hatfield was twenty miles from King's Cross, and Welwyn a little more than two miles to the north. Although the two towns would probably remain separate, they presented a single inter-related planning problem. For this reason alone a single development corporation was appropriate; but there were other reasons. In the case of Hatfield there was little doubt that the rural district council could not carry out satisfactorily a rapid expansion of their village to three times its existing size. In the case of Welwyn, the garden city company, which was responsible for almost all of the existing development, could probably carry out the expansion but, in Silkin's opinion, ownership of a town by a private company operating for profit was not satisfactory, and when moving the second reading of the New Towns Bill he had made it quite clear that he did not intend new towns to be developed by 'authorised undertakings'. This view had been generally accepted. Since a development corporation was in any event necessary for Hatfield, there was everything to be said for entrusting to it simultaneously the expansion of Welwyn, though he hoped that the company would co-operate, that members of the company would serve on the development corporation and that the corporation would be able to use their building resources and organisation.

Anticipating objections to the proposal for new town development so close to Stevenage and before Stevenage itself was well launched, Silkin stressed the attractiveness of both Welwyn and Hatfield to industry moving from inner London. Early expansion was inevitable and decisions were urgent. Already there had been applications for industrial development in the area. A major expansion of the De Havilland Works (from 5,700 employees to 8,000 or possibly even 10,000) and a move of British Drug Houses to Hatfield were expected.

The Dalton Committee, however, did not see the issue in the straightforward terms suggested by Silkin. The expansion of the De Havilland works had not been agreed, and protracted discussions on the British Drug Houses move had not yet reached a conclusion which was acceptable to them. Belcher (parliamentary secretary, Board of Trade) recommended a deferment of any decision on these grounds, adding that the past expansion of Welwyn had been efficiently carried out by the garden city company. The company had paid due attention to the need to create a balanced community and had been very co-operative in carrying out government policy. Finally he doubted whether the expansion of Hatfield could be carried out with the speed which Silkin implied: the demands for building labour in the Welwyn, St Albans and Stevenage area were too great. In any case, the plans of neither the De Havilland Company nor the British Drug Houses justified speedy action. He accepted the incapability of the Hatfield RDC to carry out major expansion, but suggested that the task might be given to either the Stevenage or the Hemel Hempstead development corporation.

Belcher was supported by Tomlinson (Minister of Works) and Jay. Important issues of principle were involved. The committee had previously decided that the industrial facilities in new and expanding towns required for 'decongestion' of London should be used for firms transferring from central London and not by expansions of London firms. If the latter were allowed, there would be an acceleration of the over-growth of London which had done so much harm before the war, both to the Metropolis and to the old depressed areas. The acceptance of Silkin's arguments about De Havilland and British Drug Houses would also make it impossible to refuse a similar request from other firms in the London region; and it was all too clear 'where this process would end'.

Furthermore, it had to be borne in mind that the total projected load on London's building labour and resources for several years ahead was much greater than it could bear and clearly the greatest restraint in starting new schemes had to be exercised.

The Treasury supported this line of argument. Indeed they felt that 'it is time to call a halt to these projects until the existing ones have made some headway'. An internal minute noted:

> 'The purpose of the "new towns" technique is to secure ordered and compact development instead of "sprawl". It is applied where the job of development —zoning, timing and provision of public utility services in advance of the creation of rateable value etc—is administratively and financially beyond local resources; and where, moreover, a deliberate and concerted government effort is needed so as to direct development to the chosen spot instead of elsewhere . . . The case for applying it here is weak. There is no question of having to direct development to Hatfield and Welwyn. Developers are already straining at the leash.'

The minute continued by arguing that the existing agencies should be allowed to get on with the job, adding that the Hatfield councillors would have the benefit of the ministry's guidance, 'and on sunny afternoons they can cross the fields to Stevenage and pick up hints'.

More seriously the Treasury complained that the ministry were 'too eager to centralise not merely the control but the execution of planning'. What they now needed was experience, 'not further opportunities for it'.

With this weight of opposition, no approval was to be expected at the November meeting, and the issue was deferred. Silkin lost no time, however, in bringing his proposals back to the committee at their next meeting when he reiterated the attractiveness of both Welwyn and Hatfield and the inevitability of growth.

The expansion of Welwyn to accommodate a population of at least 35,000 and of Hatfield to accommodate a population of 30,000 had been agreed by all the departments concerned and by the Clement Davies Advisory Committee, whose report had now been published (though the committee put the figure for Hatfield at 25,000). Expansions on this scale were inevitable. The Welwyn UDC and the garden city company were both pressing for a decision on the ultimate size of Welwyn (which they wished to be 50,000 instead of 35,000) in order that they could get ahead with plans to carry out the expansion. The pressure from Hatfield was currently less acute, but it was very probable that British Drug Houses would move out to this area, ministers having already agreed in principle that the firm should be found accommodation in the Greater London area, and Hatfield providing the likeliest location. In any event Hatfield would certainly expand.

The only question to be resolved was whether these expansions should be carried out under the control of a development corporation or should be left to the local authorities and, in the case of Welwyn, the garden city company. The committee had accepted the arguments in relation to Hatfield and, since there was a very strong case for both towns to be developed by a single development corporation, it followed that the company should be superseded.

Skirting round the objection to the De Havilland expansion, Silkin argued that the Welwyn proposal was in no way dependent upon it. Even if De Havilland were not allowed to expand he would still wish to increase Welwyn to a population of at least 35,000.

The grounds for argument thus began to shift. Wilmot (Minister of Supply) expressed his apprehension at the projected creation of so many new towns around the periphery of London. The proximity of these towns to each other and to the congested area of London would result in continuation of the London suburban sprawl and they would inevitably become dormitory towns. Was it worth while facing the upheaval involved in uprooting industry unless it was to be re-established well beyond the reach of London suburbia, for example in the development areas? If dislocation had to be faced, firms would be willing to move the greater distance.

Key (parliamentary secretary, Minister of Health) supported the view that the new towns should be placed further away from London. Already the development agreed to at Stevenage and Harlow was causing difficulty in regard to water and sewerage, and if similar developments were now to go ahead at Welwyn and Hatfield, the authorities concerned would be faced with an impossible position. However, both Isaacs (Minister of Labour) and

Belcher held that Londoners would not be prepared to move more than twenty-five miles out. Tomlinson (Minister of Works) and Strauss (parliamentary secretary, Minister of Transport) expressed concern at the size of the total programme in relation to the resources available. Dalton supported this and again raised the question of the lack of balance between proposals for London and the rest of the country.

Silkin argued eloquently, as he had done on previous occasions, about the urgency of the London problem and the urgent need for decisions irrespective of the currently available resources. There was much planning to be done before development could start and, in any case, the new towns would take their proper place in the national housing programme.

The outcome of the discussion was twofold. Silkin's proposals for Welwyn and Hatfield were approved in principle on condition that 'no commitment should be entered into in regard to labour and materials' and that no announcement should be made for the time being. Secondly, Silkin was asked to prepare a full statement of the new town proposals for London and the rest of the country, showing what claims on labour and materials would be involved.

Silkin Faces Mounting Opposition
Up to the end of 1946, Silkin had found it unnecessary to argue the precise merits and justification of the particular sites he proposed for London new towns, as the sites had been accepted by the advisory (Clement Davies) committee and by the official GLP Committee, where any objections by other departments on agricultural and other grounds had been overcome. The arguments he had had to face at the ministerial level had been in general terms relating to the overall cost, or to the distribution of industry, or to the undue prominence given to the London problem.

But from now on he faced increasing opposition to his proposals. In addition to the claims being made on resources, the Treasury were worried about the finance of the new towns programme and the ability of the ministry to handle it. They were becoming convinced that Silkin's department was 'attempting too much too soon' and was in danger of producing 'nothing but frustration and apologies'. In their view, the ministry 'ought to acquire practical experience and produce some concrete results before they add to the volume of their projects on hand'. Moreover, as soon as the draft designation orders were published, considerable local opposition arose, and Stevenage, Hemel Hempstead and Harlow were all challenged in the courts. It was against this increasingly hostile background that Silkin produced his review paper. He was also compelled from now on to give much greater explanation and justification for proposals for further new towns.

The 1947 Review of New Town Proposals*

Silkin produced his 'comprehensive review' in February 1947. The document was a meaty one which it is appropriate to discuss in some detail.

Five new towns (Stevenage, Crawley, Hemel Hempstead, Harlow and Welwyn-Hatfield) had been approved in the London area, but the future programme urgently required two additional new towns, one to the east and one to the west. In the east, the Great London Plan had proposed Meopham in Kent and Chipping Ongar in Essex. Both were 'uncomfortably close' to London (around twenty miles). Chipping Ongar also presented acute transport difficulties. Sites at a greater distance from London were under investigation. To the west, White Waltham had been proposed in the Greater London Plan. The Ministry of Agriculture opposed the site, as did the Air Departments (who were anxious to retain the use of the airfield). Silkin, therefore, had decided to abandon the proposal, and alternative sites were being investigated up to fifty miles distant. One possibility was Bracknell (thirty-two miles from London). If sites could be found in these two directions, there would be a total of seven new towns for London, 'fairly well distributed to the north, south, east and west'. He reminded the committee that the Greater London Plan had proposed eight new towns, to be selected from ten recommended sites. However, one of Silkin's (Welwyn-Hatfield) did not originate in the plan: though expansion of these two communities was proposed, it had not been envisaged that this would be undertaken by a development corporation. On this rather curious arithmetic basis, Silkin argued that 'the true comparison between my new towns and those in the plan is six to eight'.

Those which were not being pursued were Stapleford ('too close to Hertford'); Margaretting ('too close to Chelmsford'); Crowhurst ('too close to Crawley'); and Holmwood in Surrey ('country too good'). Silkin pointed out that new towns were only part of the proposals in the Greater London Plan for carrying through the 'decentralisation' of $1\frac{1}{4}$ million Londoners. Well over half of these were to be accommodated by the expansion of existing towns; and the distinction between the expansion of an existing town and the creation of a new town could 'sometimes be very fine'. He might have to propose that some of the planned expansion should, in the event, be dealt with as new towns; but his current review dealt only with the new towns so far envisaged.

In the provinces, Silkin had hoped that a designation order for a new town for Manchester-Salford overspill could have been made,

---

* LP(DI)(47)12, LP(DI)(47)2nd Meeting, 5 February 1947, and Lord President's File 191/34.

but the site at Mobberley which Manchester had selected (and which had been approved by the Dalton Committee in October 1946) might be unsuitable because of threatened subsidence due to salt winning. A further survey was being made.

For Leeds, the city council and the West Riding county council had proposed Sherburn-in-Elmet, but Silkin had rejected this on the grounds that it was too close (eleven miles) to Leeds. He had requested that a search should be made some twenty-five miles distant, probably to the north.

Investigations were continuing in south Wales (Pontypool and Pontypridd), Durham (Easington), west Cumberland and south Derbyshire (to 'replace' Swadlincote which was subject to increasing subsidence).

Other provincial towns in which there was an overspill problem which might create a need for a new town were Liverpool, Bristol, Hull and Sunderland. Surveys were in progress to establish the best way of dealing with the overspill problem from these and other towns.

In short, it was still too early to draw up a firm programme. Nevertheless, for the purpose of estimating the demand for labour and materials, a provisional programme had been assumed on the basis of six new towns drawing on the London labour market and six drawing on provincial markets (including one new town at some distance from London). This programme envisaged five new towns starting by mid-1947, five between mid-1947 and mid-1948, and two between mid-1948 and mid-1949.

5 new towns to start by mid-1947	Stevenage, Crawley, Hemel Hempstead, Harlow and Aycliffe
5 new towns to start between mid-1947 and mid-1948	Welwyn-Hatfield; alternatives to Meopham, White Waltham and Mobberley; and one other in the provinces
2 new towns to start between mid-1948 and mid-1949	Both in the provinces

It was the intention that, if possible, each new town providing for 50–60,000 people should be completed within ten years from commencement. All the towns were assumed to provide for a population of 50–60,000 (except Aycliffe which would provide only for 10,000 and was to be completed over a period of three to four years). The figure of 50–60,000 was chosen, not because the towns would necessarily be of that size but because this was the maximum likely size, and therefore gave the maximum demand likely to be made on labour and materials. It also gave some margin on the number of towns—two small ones might be substituted for one large one. On these assumptions it was calculated that the labour requirements would rise from 2,500 in 1947–48 to 36,000 in 1950–51. On a ten-year programme the peak would be reached in the sixth year (ie 1954–55). No further details were given as to how these figures were derived.

It had been agreed between Silkin's department and the Ministry of Health (the department responsible for housing) that the new towns' labour force should come out of the overall allocation to housing, since the creation of the new towns was a part of the housing programme. However, it was being suggested to the Headquarters Building Committee that in so far as the new towns' force would be occupied on non-housing operations (eg the building of shops, factories, schools, public buildings), the overall allocation to housing should be increased. It was estimated that sixty per cent of the new towns' force would be engaged on housing including site development, and forty per cent on non-housing operations.

No separate computation was prepared of the demand for materials since that was made by the Ministry of Works in relation to the whole building demand; and it was their responsibility to keep the total building programme in step with availability of materials.

The New Towns Act 1946 provided that £50m might be advanced to development corporations in the United Kingdom without further parliamentary authority. The assumption was that this would be sufficient for the first five years. The provisional programme (which took no account of Scottish proposals) would, it was estimated, entail a capital expenditure, including expenditure on the acquisition of land, of approximately the following amounts:

$$£ \text{ million}$$

1947–48	5·4
1948–49	10·9
1949–50	17·15
1950–51	22·68
	56·13

If the programme were adhered to, therefore, it would be necessary, taking account of Scottish proposals, to seek further parliamentary authority for expenditure four years after the passing of the Act. Somewhat disarmingly Silkin suggested that it was unlikely that the programme would in fact be adhered to, since not all the new towns would be capable of being built at this rate. He was sure, however, that it was desirable to plan for the new towns *starting* in the years suggested, if not sooner; and it was not until more detailed surveys had been made in relation to each town, of the actual building and civil engineering problems involved that he could estimate the precise rate of build-up for each town. His department were suggesting to the Headquarters Building Committee that the current estimate should be accepted, subject to review when the detailed plans for each town had been worked out. Under the arrangements by which the new towns' labour force would be shown as part of the total allocation to housing, the labour not taken up by the corporations would continue to be available for normal housing operations, 'so that no harm will be done'.

Silkin's paper continued with a resumé of the rationale for new towns. Three categories were mentioned: overspill, industry's need for new population in a particular place (as at Aycliffe), and the need to provide improved living conditions for scattered communities (as in Durham, south Wales and Cumberland). At this point the first reference in Cabinet papers was made to the possibility of a new town at Pitsea and Laindon in Essex (later known as Basildon). The passage is worth quoting in full:

> 'Not all proposals for rebuilding poverty-stricken communities as new towns, at initial exchequer cost, can be accepted in this category however. The proposal of the advisory committee on London regional planning (a committee of planning authorities under the chairmanship of Clement Davies, which was appointed to report on Professor Abercrombie's Greater London Plan) that Pitsea and Laindon in Essex, two shabby bungalow communities, should be developed as a new town of 50,000 is a case in point. I am not anxious to accept responsibility for the redevelopment of this area under the New Towns Act, as in view of the extensive development which has already taken place, I do not think that a satisfactory new town would result; but I may be very strongly pressed by the local authorities in the particular case, especially as development in the area is probably inevitable, and I may have to return to the subcommittee for specific consideration.'

Finally, Silkin commented on the distance a new town should be from its 'parent town'. The view had been expressed at previous meetings that a distance of twenty to twenty-five miles was not enough. Welwyn-Hatfield (Silkin insisted on referring to them as a single planned development) was, in his view, exceptional in that some expansion was irresistible, and he was anxious to secure that the expansion should be undertaken by a public, not a private, authority, and should be devoted to the decentralisation of London. His general aim, however, was to ensure that additional new towns were sited at least thirty and preferably forty miles from London; and at least twenty-five miles from a provincial town.

It had to be remembered, however, that a new town was completely dependent for success on the willingness both of industries and of people to move to it. The Board of Trade would not fix any particular distance as being the most that industry would move, since it depended so much on the direction and on the transport facilities. Thus, they expected London industry to be unwilling to move more than twenty to twenty-five miles into the eastern counties; but on the west, they regarded Reading (thirty-six miles) as attractive to London industrialists.

People were probably less willing to move a long distance than industry. One member of the family at least might want to continue working or attending school in the parent town for a time, and it might well be that some travelling between the two towns must at any rate be possible for the first year or two of the new town's existence if people were to be willing to move. However, if travelling time was at least an hour, and sufficient employment were provided locally, this would very soon dwindle to a negligible amount, as had, in fact, happened at Welwyn. It was almost impossible to test effectively what would be the reaction of workers in three, four or five years' time to a proposal that they should move with industry to a new town forty or fifty miles distant (or, say, thirty miles in the provinces), but the view of such local authorities as had discussed the problem with Silkin was that it would very seriously reduce the willingness to move. The Reith Committee had suggested that the new towns in the Greater London area need not be more than twenty-five miles from the centre; from other great towns a distance of ten to fifteen miles might be enough.

When Silkin's paper was discussed by the Dalton Committee in February 1947, doubt was expressed as to whether agreement had been given at the previous meeting for Welwyn-Hatfield to be developed by a development corporation. Silkin was asked to settle the point with Dalton.*

Considerable concern was expressed at the ambitious nature of Silkin's programme and the over-concentration on the London area. It was suggested that it would be advisable to start on one or more of the towns already approved and devote effort to their completion: this would give the public confidence in the new towns policy and would yield valuable experience. Silkin objected that such a policy would inevitably lead to housing developments in the green belt: the problem was so large that a major new town programme for London was essential. So far as the provinces were concerned, the situation was under investigation and discussion in Manchester-Salford, Leeds, south Wales, Durham, west Cumberland, Liverpool, Bristol, Hull, Sunderland and Swadlincote.

---

* A later paper reported that, following a discussion with Dalton, a development corporation was to be established (LP(DI)(47)91).

The committee agreed that Silkin should 'press on' with the new towns already approved and report back, at an early date, on progress for new towns in the provinces.

Later in February 1947, Dalton wrote to Silkin that the growth of London was not being checked, and that the new towns near London would make it an even stronger magnet for people from the older industrial areas. He suggested that it would be better to concentrate on making the older towns attractive in order to retain their population, and promote any new towns in the provinces. He added:

'Why should a family live in some dirty survival of the industrial revolution if they can easily find accommodation in a spruce new town or suburb in the home counties? Surely it would be better to concentrate on making attractive these older towns so that they would retain their populations, than to provide the means by which the scales would be tipped even more out of balance and in favour of an even greater mass of our population being concentrated in the home counties. That is why I have steadily urged upon you the need to press on with new towns in the provinces.

It is natural that enthusiasm should have centred on the new towns round London, since that is the only area for which a plan already existed. Looking at the national picture, however, is it not an elementary mistake to begin with the Abercrombie Plan, just because it is ready?

Before we embark on the very great expenditure of money that the new town proposals involve, and before we irrevocably allocate to them large shares of our very scarce resources in men and materials, I think there is need for a real national survey of the problem. The present lack of provincial projects in the new town programme is a very serious weakness. We do not want to make mistakes now, the full consequences of which we shall reap over many years.'

Though not explicit, this note by the Chancellor reflected the apprehensions of the Treasury early in 1947 that the new town policy was a very expensive way of solving the housing shortage, and their doubts about the capacity of the Ministry of Town and Country Planning to handle a large programme of development.*

Simultaneously with these hesitations on the part of his colleagues, the validity of the designation order for Stevenage had been challenged, and on 20 February 1947 the High Court had upset the order. The Cabinet agreed that the case should go to appeal (which was later successful), but the incident had a depressing effect as, until the case was disposed of, the minister was unable to authorise

---

* A Treasury minute of February 1947 is illustrative:

'At the official level we are very uneasy about the capacity of the ministry to handle a large new town programme. We feel they are far too inclined to bite off more than they can chew. They have as yet no practical experience—that is of course nobody's fault—and we feel they ought to acquire some and prove their capacity on a limited scheme rather than start up all over the place before they have acquired the know-how . . . With the great demands which the initial implementation of the Town and Country Planning Bill will make on the ministry's administrative resources, there is everything to be said on administrative grounds for limiting their new town commitment.' (Treasury File SS 385/02.)

the corporation to acquire land. Nevertheless, Silkin continued to investigate the possibilities for further new towns and, in August 1947, presented a further memorandum on proposals for new towns in the provinces. Three specific proposals were submitted for new towns in development areas—at Easington (County Durham), at Talbot Green-Church Village and Blackwood-Pontllanfraith in south Wales.

Provincial New Towns*

EASINGTON (PETERLEE)

The proposal for a new town at Easington had been put forward by the rural district council in 1946.† Easington was situated on the Durham coast between West Hartlepool and Seaham Harbour. It had been suggested at the Dalton Committee that this district was

---

* LP(DI)(47)80, LP(DI)(47)92, LP(DI)(47)13th Meeting, 6 August 1947 and Treasury File SS 385/02.

† The proposal came from C. W. Clarke, the engineer and surveyor to the council. A full account is given in *Farewell Squalor* which was written by Clarke and published in December 1946. The 'author's note' with which the report ends is of particular interest and is reproduced here in full:

'The original report was presented to the Council in December, 1946, and was agreed to unanimously. Draft plans were also prepared on 25 inch ordnance maps to give some idea of how the site could be planned and these, together with photographs and charts, have been added to the book which is now published under the title of "Farewell Squalor". This title does not bear any relation whatsoever to the actual homes of the people but to the design, outlook, position and amenities of the sub-standard structures which we have been pleased to call houses.

At the moment, the naming of the new town has not been considered. Many names have come to my mind; some having their derivation from local history, some coined from the names of our present villages and others from the names of members of the Government.

I have reviewed each one of them from all angles and have come to the conclusion that this new town should bear the name of some local man who, during his life time, went fearlessly and courageously forward for the good and uplift of the people of this district. A man who was a power both in bodily physique and mental ability and whose statue would grace the town square, a man who had the courage of his own convictions—and there are few of these, a man whose very presence commanded respect and attention, a man who, had he lived today, would have supported this project whole heartedly, knowing full well that it will be a town for social and individual living, containing healthy and pleasant living conditions, facilities for education, recreation, pleasure and social intercourse, provided near to the homes so that they may be enjoyed to the full, as a normal happening of every day life and without being regarded as a luxury to be sought for in other places.

Having all these virtues in one single frame seems well nigh impossible. I am convinced, however, that there was one person whose life was moulded on these virtues and whose memory could be appropriately perpetuated by the naming of the new town—PETER-LEE. The neighbourhood unit names, I suggest, should preserve local colour by taking existing farms or features as their base, becoming "Howletch", "Oakerside" and "Yoden".

No jerry builders will be permitted in Peterlee. This scum of the building trades will not be allowed to stake a claim in this new town of ours. Their nefarious operations have been permitted long enough. Peterlee must be designed in all its phases by a modern and proven team of impartial experts and only the best is good enough.

Let us, therefore, close our eyes on the nineteenth century degradation and squalor, and let us only look with unseeing eyes on the sordid excrescence of the first decade of this century, let us blind ourselves to the septic and ugly building wens and ribbons perpetrated and planted on us between the wars, but let us open our eyes and look brightly forward and onward to the new town, the new living . . . Peterlee.'

too near the seaboard where employment was already good, and that it would be better to choose a site further to the west. After careful consideration of this point Silkin said that he had reached the conclusion that there was a real need for a new town in this district. The pits on the coast seemed to be assured of a long life and, since the mining populations would be tied to this area for a long time to come (which might not necessarily be the case with the communities around the pits to the west which often had a much shorter life), it was desirable to ensure that they were provided so far as possible with a decent setting in which to live. As regards employment there were substantial numbers currently out of work and these numbers were, he was informed, likely to grow as pits other than those on the coast closed down.

The district was a traditional colliery one, 'with coal mining dominating everything else'. The existing development was in the main 'deplorable', consisting very largely of unsatisfactory settlements of sub-standard houses at excessive densities erected alongside the pits by colliery owners. Even the interwar housing was not well sited, and the area as a whole was lacking in communal facilities and in amenities. Badly controlled industrial development, spoil heaps, derelict colliery buildings, dilapidated brick kilns and so forth were scattered throughout the area.

The population of the rural district at the time was around 80,000. It was estimated that during the following twenty years there would be a requirement for perhaps 10,000 houses. Silkin did not think that this housing, apart from 1,000 houses already programmed, should be 'reprovided' in the existing communities. By their nature, and even allowing for the improvements which would clearly have to be made in the years to come, these communities could never provide a really satisfactory life for the present population. The Easington RDC had therefore proposed that the 9,000 or so houses required should be provided in the form of a new town on a completely fresh site where a community offering all the features of a properly balanced town could be developed, including additional industry to help meet the need for employment for women and for men for whom work could not be found in the pits. The plans envisaged a town with a population of some 32,000 people. This would mean that forty per cent of the population of the rural district would be rehoused under conditions that would make possible a much more satisfactory life in the course of the next twenty years.

The site chosen lay between the existing settlements of Easington, Horden and Shotton. It included the amenity area of Castle Eden Dene, the character of which would be preserved. Since the site would be removed from the immediate neighbourhood of the collieries, a certain amount of travelling to work would be entailed, but this was no new feature in mining areas, and special attention would be given to the problem. Silkin said that he understood that the project had the full support of the Ministry of Fuel and Power and the National Coal Board as a measure designed to improve the living conditions of this area. No undue difficulty was expected in providing the necessary public services. The project had been extensively examined in the region with the other government departments and authorities concerned, and there was general agreement (subject to the reservation on travel-to-work) both on the need for the development and on the suitability of the site proposed. Silkin understood that the Ministry of Agriculture would have preferred the rehousing of this population to be carried out by extension of the existing communities rather than in the form of a new town because of the loss of a sizeable tract (say, 1,800 acres) of agricultural land. He gathered, however, that they were now prepared to agree to the programme of development for the first ten years but felt that taking the land for the second decade at this stage would be likely to have a bad effect on farming. There seemed, however, to be no reason why agricultural production should not be co-ordinated with the programme of development for the new town. It was, of course, necessary to acquire the whole of the land initially 'as is usual in these projects' so that the full development of the new town could be assured. They had suggested two other sites on land of less value agriculturally but these were both open to various solid objections, and he therefore had to press for the adoption of the proposed site which had been shown by investigation to be the only really suitable one in the area.

SOUTH WALES

South Wales had 'unique problems'. Though considerable progress had been made with the diversification of industry, the available evidence suggested that over a period of years there was likely to be some shift of population from those parts of the coalfield which were approaching exhaustion. Satisfactory sites for industry in the valleys themselves were limited and it would therefore be difficult to bring into them enough industry to absorb the probable surplus of workers. At the same time, the need for houses in south Wales was acute and though this need could be satisfied to some extent in the places in which it arose, the lack of adequate sites in some parts of the valleys meant that a portion of the demand would have to be met in the open parts of the valleys and towards the northern edge of the coastal plain where there was already a heavy demand for housing to provide for the industrial expansion of the previous ten years.

The idea of concentrating provision of housing and industry was, of course, not new and the *Outline Plan for South Wales* had again recommended this method of meeting the problem, with proposals for development on this basis in certain areas. The examination of these proposals was now in hand, but Silkin considered that it was desirable to give specially urgent consideration to proposals for development on a scale justifying the use of the new towns' machinery in two areas, at Talbot Green-Church Village and at Blackwood-Pontllanfraith. Discussions of these two proposals were proceeding at the regional physical planning committee as part of their examination of the outline plan as a whole. Suggestions for development there had also been received from local bodies.

Development in the Talbot Green-Church Village area, which was situated near Llantrisant and Pontypridd and was about twelve miles from Cardiff, would serve a wide area including the Treforest Trading Estate, Pontypridd and the Rhondda. Subject to a detailed examination of the site, it was considered that land was available for about 35,000 people. Communications were good and it would be possible to provide for the necessary expansion of public services.

Blackwood-Pontllanfraith was situated at the foot of the Rhymney and Sirhowy valleys about thirteen miles from Newport and sixteen miles from Cardiff. With an existing population of about 17,000 there was land available for approximately 35,000 additional people. Communications were good and there were modern collieries in operation. The main purpose of development here would be to provide satisfactory living conditions for those who worked in the area but lived some way off, and to provide for others who would be attracted by the housing and employment prospects.

OTHER PROPOSALS

Apart from the designation of Aycliffe, Silkin had little else to report. No progress had been made on the selection of a location for a Leeds new town, and site investigations in Cheshire for a Manchester new town were proving 'most troublesome'. Extensive investigations into the question of subsidence, including borings, had been carried out and it had been necessary to reject several sites. Discussions were continuing with the Geological Survey and others concerned, and Silkin was still hoping that it might be possible to find a suitable site in this area. In the meantime, however, he had started investigations into sites further afield at Crowton in Cheshire (to the west of Northwich), at Eccleston (in the Chorley rural district of Lancashire) and in the Garstang-Inglewhite area (to the east of Fleetwood). Preliminary investigations had shown that all of these areas contained possibilities for new town development and these were being further explored. They would be considered not only from the point of view of taking overspill from the Manchester conurbation, but also in relation to other parts of Lancashire, including Merseyside.

In concrete terms, therefore, Silkin was seeking approval (in principle) only for the one new town at Easington. His memorandum had referred to the reluctant agreement of the Ministry of Agriculture to this proposal and this formed the major issue of debate at the Dalton Committee meeting in August 1947. The Minister of Agriculture (Williams) submitted a memorandum setting out his arguments (which clearly indicated that, far from reluctantly accepting Silkin's proposals, he still had strong objections to them). The proposed site comprised some of the best land in Durham, and the only substantial unspoiled rural area in Easington. Owing to the quality of the land, the proportion of arable was very high as compared with the average in County Durham. The eleven farms affected had a total area of over 1,900 acres of which not less than 1,400 were tillage land. The farms carried some 270 dairy cows and the average monthly milk sales were 11,500 gallons. At three pints per person per week this meant that close on 8,000 people were provided with their milk ration from this land, apart from all the other foods such as vegetables, oats, wheat, potatoes and livestock products.

It was Williams' view that a better alternative to the new town was the expansion of existing communities, and it was only because he appreciated the difficulties to which this would give rise and the advantages which might accrue from a new town that he had reluctantly agreed to a new town in principle. He had no wish to depart from this if the committee felt that a new town was desirable, but he still felt bound to oppose on agricultural grounds the suggested size and location of the town. He urged a reduction in size to a population of 10,000 (the balance being accommodated in neighbouring mining villages) and a relocation to a site which would be less damaging to agriculture. This site lay to the north of the one proposed by Silkin and included, as well as Easington Colliery, 'the not unpleasant village of Easington' itself. The main objection to this site was the inclusion in the area of Easington Colliery with the considerable scatter of interwar housing between it and Easington village, but this would presumably need to be tidied up in any case. Although he appreciated the advantages of beginning with a virgin site he suggested that, in this case, the agricultural objection to the use of the virgin site was such as to outweigh the difficulties presented by the alternative site.

Silkin's arguments, however, won the day and his proposals were approved (subject only to consultation with the Minister of

Transport which he had failed to undertake—and for which he was rebuked).*

With hindsight it is surprising that little reference was apparently made to difficulties which might arise over the effect of the new town on the sterilisation of coal. The minutes merely record that the National Coal Board wanted other building in the Easington area to be stopped in order to avoid the sterilisation of coal (which would also safeguard agricultural land); and that the support ascribed in Silkin's memorandum to the Ministry of Fuel and Power and the NCB was conditional on an agreement on siting in view of the need to avoid unnecessary sterilisation of coal. The difficulties to which this might give rise were not fully appreciated at the time, but they were shortly to become a major problem.†

The Economic Crisis‡

At this juncture, it is appropriate to refer to certain political events which had their implications for new town policy. On 18 August 1947 Dalton wrote to Silkin that 'in the present economic emergency we shall be bound to look again at the policy of new towns and until we have done so it would be most unfortunate if any action were taken to press on with something on which we may, before long, have to go into reverse'. He therefore asked that there should be no further commitments for expenditure, pending reviews of the capital investment programme.

As the 1947 economic crisis worsened, the new towns programme (as with other investment programmes) came under increasingly critical analysis. An Investment Programmes Committee was established with the two major objectives of reducing the overall level of activity and of concentrating investment programmes on a smaller number of projects in order that more rapid progress could be made within an approved total. A report from this committee, of October 1947, noted that existing supplies of material were inadequate to complete all the investments which had been started. More and more materials of all kinds were being put into an ever growing total of unfinished work 'while the amount actually completed lags deplorably'. In the building sector, a house was now taking thirteen months to complete, compared with eight months two years previously. The number of unfinished houses was 50,000 more than planned. New towns were the subject of particular concern:

---

* Silkin's proposals were (now untypically) supported by the Treasury. In their view there was 'much more to be said, in present circumstances, for the "Aycliffe" type of new town which "pulls together" and diversifies an industrial area in the light of foreseen economic trends, than for the "Stevenage" type which takes overspill from a big town'. (Minute of 21.7.47, Treasury File SS 385/02/A.)

† See below, p. 102 *et seq.*

‡ MHLG File 90/149 and IPC(47)9.

'The trouble with the "overspill" new towns is that they require not only housing, which would otherwise have been in, for example, London's green belt, but also additional roads, railways, factories etc, a large part of which would not have been required on the fringe of an existing conurbation. In present circumstances, it is obviously very difficult to contemplate additional works of this sort. On the other hand, the new towns are in such an embryonic stage, lacking even the simplest basic water and sewerage services (except for small numbers, possibly up to about 5,000) that they will always tend to lag behind London's housing programme if a complete stop is put to them. This lag is such that the Ministry of Town and Country Planning has been reluctantly constrained to agree to an additional 100,000 people being put in areas originally designated as London's green belt.'

The smaller 'non-overspill' new towns did not present the same problems: they were intended to cater for immediate industrial needs or for new mining areas. The Investment Programmes Committee recommended that these should be allowed to continue. But the London new towns had to be retarded. These were to be allowed to proceed only with basic water and sewerage services employing in total not more than 300 men. Large works such as those at Stevenage should be postponed until 1949. These proposals, which formed part of much wider restrictions on investment, were accepted by the Government. Thus the London new towns programme was delayed just as it was beginning.

Other changes took place at this time which are relevant to the new towns story. In September 1947 Cripps, who had been President of the Board of Trade, was appointed Minister of Economic Affairs and, as part of the reorganisation which then took place, the LP(DI) Committee was in October 1947 reconstituted at a lower level as the Distribution of Industry Committee, with the Paymaster General (Marquand) as chairman (succeeded at the end of 1947 by Douglas Jay, the Financial Secretary, Treasury). Supervision of the new towns reverted to the Lord President's Committee.

On 12 November 1947 Dalton resigned from the Government. As Chancellor of the Exchequer and as chairman of the LP(DI) Committee, he had at best been lukewarm about the new town policy, and, in so far as he had accepted it, had regarded the towns as plums which should be fairly distributed throughout the country, including the development areas. With Herbert Morrison as the new overlord, a different line of approach developed. As leader of the London County Council before the war, and as Minister of Home Security during the war, he was well acquainted with the strengths and loyalties of local authorities. On the other hand, as the author of the Act of 1933 establishing the London Passenger Transport Board, he was a known advocate of the principle of public boards, and as chairman of the Cabinet Committee on the Socialisation of Industries, he was active in the nationalisation measures then passing through Parliament and which were depriving local authorities of their gas, electricity, and transport undertakings. He may have had an intuitive feeling that the process was going too far, and that local authorities were being weakened through the loss of their trading activities, and accordingly took the opportunity when new town proposals came before the committee of pressing their claims.

In view of the economic crisis and the ministerial changes, no further proposals for new towns were put forward by Silkin until April 1948.

The New Towns in April 1948*

In April 1948, Silkin presented a review of the new towns programme to the Lord President's Committee and asked for approval for a new town at Pitsea-Laindon.

Five areas had so far been designated for new town development round London: Stevenage (population 60,000), Crawley (50,000), Hemel Hempstead (60,000), Harlow (60,000), Welwyn-Hatfield (61,000); the last was still in the draft stage. Two areas had been designated in the provinces: Aycliffe (10,000), and Easington (30,000), both in County Durham.

The white paper on *Capital Investment in 1948* (Cmd 7268) had clearly stated that new towns designed to serve immediate industrial needs or mining areas should go ahead within the limits of the housing programme; but that work on new towns designed to provide for industry and population decentralised from overcrowded cities should in general be limited, during 1948, to starting the provision of water, sewerage and roads. In accordance with this decision, Aycliffe and Easington were going ahead as far as practicable. Both were still in the planning stage, but work would begin shortly. Meanwhile, the corporations of the first four London new towns were working on their plans, and were making such progress on the provision of initial services as was possible with the limited labour force allowed to them (300 workers between the four). The aim with these 'overspill' new towns was that they should be got into a state of readiness for extensive operations as and when building became possible. Silkin argued that this was essential if he was to be able to prevent the continued outward sprawl of London when current restrictions on building were relaxed.

In the provinces Silkin hoped, shortly after the middle of 1948, to designate an area at Mobberley in Cheshire to take some of the Manchester overspill. Manchester had proposed themselves to develop this area as a satellite, but he was satisfied that if it were

---

* LP(48)32 and LP(48)7th Meeting, 30 April 1948.

not to be simply a further extension of Manchester it had to be developed under the New Towns Act. Delay had been caused by the possibility that there was salt under the site—with consequent risk of subsidence—and borings were being made. To date no salt had been found but the borings were not yet complete. A site was being sought for a second new town for the Manchester area, but it was not yet possible to say where this would be.

There was still a possibility of a new town in south Wales. A plan had been produced (to be published in about three months' time) which proposed substantial new development at Pontllanfraith and at Cwmbran (Monmouthshire) and at or near Llantrisant (Glamorganshire). Whilst he had no reason for doubting the soundness of these proposals Silkin was not sure which of the places, if any, would best be dealt with under the New Towns Act. The proposals were being examined against the background of the plan as a whole. There was also the problem of housing workers for the new strip mill at Margam. This was to be discussed shortly by the Distribution of Industry Committee. Silkin was doubtful whether a new town proposal would emerge.

Although there were one or two more new town projects under examination, no other proposal in the provinces was sufficiently far advanced to be mentioned individually. The overspill problem was much less acute than in London. Liverpool overspill might create a need but that had yet to be assessed (there were wide divergences of opinion) and the area was a very difficult one in which to find suitable new town sites.

As for the London area, Silkin still had to find further sites in addition to an immediate proposal for Pitsea-Laindon. The Abercrombie Plan provided for the decentralisation of 1·25 million people. The five new towns 'so far found' provided, after allowing for their existing populations, for something under 0·25 million. The greater part of the 'overspill' had to be provided for by expanding existing communities (such as Slough, St Albans, Farnham, Letchworth, Newbury, Aylesbury, Bletchley, Chelmsford, Basingstoke, Ashford), but Silkin still wished to find at least three more new town sites, one to the south-east, one to the south-west, and one to the north-west. He felt that some of the proposed expansions might have to be carried out under the New Towns Act since they could be beyond the capabilities of the local authorities. To the south-west he expected, in any event, to propose fairly shortly a small new town at Bracknell in Berkshire; in the other directions he had as yet no proposals sufficiently firm to mention.

In view of the current economic difficulties and the limitation, during 1948, to 300 building workers on the four 'overspill' new towns so far designated round London, it might have been thought that there was no point in designating any others at this time. In Silkin's opinion, however, it was necessary to settle as soon as possible the part ultimately to be played by new towns in the 'London decentralisation'. The local authorities around London needed to know not only where development was to take place ('that broadly had been settled, though additional proposals might have to be made'): they also needed to know what would be carried through as new towns, and what they would be expected to do themselves under the Town and Country Planning Act. Further, in so far as some of the development was to be carried through by corporations under the New Towns Act, these corporations ought to be set up as soon as was reasonably possible.

Pitsea-Laindon (Basildon)

At Pitsea-Laindon, the development consisted of two separate communities (which had prewar populations of 8,000 and 8,750 respectively). It was proposed to build up the two communities into one town with a total population of 50,000 or more. The proposal was made originally by the advisory committee for London regional planning and was strongly supported by the Essex CC and the Billericay UDC. It was also urged by the county borough councils of West and East Ham, from which a large proportion of the population to be housed in the new town would come. Silkin had refused permission for housing development on Wanstead Flats because of the importance to east London of this open space, and this made it all the more necessary that he should propose an alternative solution.

Bevan (Minister of Health) supported the proposal because of the housing needs in the east of London, while other interested departments represented on the Greater London Plan Interdepartmental Committee had agreed in principle to development of the Pitsea-Laindon area.

The existing communities of Pitsea and Laindon consisted of very poor development, some of which would ultimately have to be cleared if a satisfactory new town were to be built. The first stage, however, was to develop the land separating these two communities for an additional population of 20–25,000. Once restrictions on building were relaxed, it would be possible to provide fairly quickly an outlet for the overcrowded districts of east London. Services existed and no very heavy preliminary expenditure on water, sewerage, or drainage was expected. It was probable, Silkin argued, that there would be fairly substantial development in this area, even if he did not take action under the New Towns Act; but it had been very strongly represented to him by the local authorities that only if this development were carried out by a development corporation would it have any chance of being carried our success-fully. The alternative would be that the urban district council and some of the London local authorities should themselves undertake housing operations on the available land, but this would not and could not result in an integrated and properly balanced town. Billericay Urban District Council and the West and East Ham County Borough Councils had given an undertaking that, if he would carry through the development under the New Towns Act, they would contribute to the provision of the various services. Moreover, Essex County Council (who had already spent consider-able sums on preserving amenity features in the neighbourhood) might be expected to help further in tidying up the area as the new town proceeded. The question whether this development was to be carried out under the New Towns Act had to be settled urgently. Land for housing was almost non-existent in the east of London, and the local authorities were pressing for a decision on whether he was prepared to take action in regard to Pitsea-Laindon, or whether they were to be left to their own resources to proceed as best they could. The London County Council had asked him to agree to a proposal that they should develop a big housing estate at Thorndon Park, between Hornchurch and Laindon. He was most unwilling to do this, as the proposed site was not only in the green belt, it was also located in an area which, if Pitsea-Laindon were developed, he would particularly wish to preserve.

Silkin therefore asked for approval to his proposal that Pitsea-Laindon should be developed under the New Towns Act as a new town with a total population of about 50,000.

Silkin's paper raised a number of general issues which were taken up in the discussion at the Lord President's Committee. Herbert Morrison asked whether the London County Council and the other London local authorities were systematically working towards the thinning out of the population in the main built-up area of London and showing a genuine desire to make the new towns policy a success. How far, for example, were the London County Council still developing cottage estates on the periphery of London?

Bevan said that he had initiated discussions with the London County Council about their housing programme and had decided not to approve any further acquisition by them of housing sites outside the county area, though they would be allowed to develop such sites as had already been approved. He was concerned about the co-ordination of the London County Council's housing plans with the housing plans of the new towns near London. If the work of preparing housing sites was spread out among a number of new towns, he was not sure that it would be possible to switch over quickly enough to housebuilding in new towns the resources which would be released as the London County Council's programme of housing outside their own area fell off. There might therefore be some advantage in concentrating most of the work of site preparation in one new town.

Silkin said that he believed that, in the London area, the development of new towns was reasonably well integrated with the work of the London local authorities. The new town development corporations would let houses only to people moving from the congested areas which the new towns were designed to relieve. Thus, Harlow had arranged to provide houses for families on the housing waiting lists of the local authorities whose area they served. Enquiries at Tottenham had indicated that ninety per cent of the people on the waiting list were prepared to go to the new town. Similarly, the new towns were taking their industries from the dispersal areas, and the development corporations had already received more applications than they could meet from firms in these areas.

Nevertheless, the committee asked Silkin 'to examine further the organisation of the initial provision of housing by the new town corporations in the London area, with a view to its effective co-ordination with the London County Council's housing programme'.

The question of a new town development corporation for Welwyn was again raised—this time by Morrison. It also became apparent that Silkin was thinking of similar action in relation to Letchworth. Morrison stressed that both had started as public-spirited ventures and that it might be thought unfair to supplant the companies unless there proved to be no way of inducing them to carry out the general Government policy. The local authorities concerned were probably under some misapprehension in thinking that a new town development corporation would be more amenable than the companies.

Silkin said that the question whether there should be a development corporation for Welwyn had already been exhaustively discussed. The position was complicated by the fact that there had to be new development both at Hatfield and Welwyn, and there was great advantage in the same organisation being in charge of both ventures. The local authority had presented formidable objections to the present operations of the company, notably in its policy of segregation and its control over cinemas, public-houses and shops. So far as Letchworth was concerned, he was in no way committed to the view that the company should be superseded, though he was under great pressure from the local authority. The company was now 'rather moribund' but it did not present some of the objectionable features of the Welwyn company. He proposed, therefore, to explore with representatives of the company whether it would be possible to bring in some fresh blood, including some representation from neighbouring local authorities.

The minutes record that the committee 'took note' of Silkin's proposals.

A wider question was then raised by Morrison as to whether more should not be done to enlist the help of the larger local authorities in the construction of new towns. Manchester had wanted to provide a new town, and it would be of advantage to the large progressive authorities to be entrusted with undertakings of this kind. It would, of course, have to be clearly understood that there was to be no repetition of the construction of one-class housing estates of the character of Becontree.

Some members of the committee supported this suggestion, and it was pointed out that in certain areas, including possibly Manchester, the local authority had the organisation and experience necessary for the provision of new housing on a large scale.

Silkin said that the question whether some of the larger local authorities should be allowed to construct new towns had been thrashed out when the New Towns Act was being drafted and had been rejected. Local authorities were not really anxious to provide new towns of the self-contained character proposed in the New Towns Act, and their natural inclination was to develop estates close to their boundaries which might eventually be incorporated in their areas. Only Manchester and Leeds had asked for these powers, and there was reason to believe that Manchester would seek eventually to incorporate Mobberley in the city if they were allowed to construct a new town there. The local authorities had never suggested that they should finance the new towns which they provided, but had assumed that the cost would fall on the exchequer. It would be difficult to justify the financing of a new town by the exchequer if control was to be entirely in the hands of the local authority; and it was particularly difficult in the Manchester area where the new town was intended to relieve congestion not only in Manchester but also in Salford and Stretford. He agreed that the larger authorities had an organisation for housebuilding of which the Government should make use, and he had accordingly proposed to Manchester that they should build, on behalf of the new town development corporation, a neighbourhood unit (which would house about 10,000 people) in the new town.* The London County Council showed no inclination to assist in this way, but he proposed to have further discussions with them and he would arrange that the Minister of Health should accompany him.

Judging by the minutes of that meeting, these general issues formed the main subject of discussion. So far as the Pitsea-Laindon proposal was concerned, there was apparently general agreement

---

* At this date, the proposal for a new town at Mobberley (which had been approved by the LP Committee) was still a live one.

and authority was given to Silkin's proposal for a new town with a total population of about 50,000.*

Scottish New Towns†

The proposal for a new town in the Bishopton area of Renfrewshire had not been accepted by the Dalton Committee in July 1946.‡ The view was then taken that an additional Scottish new town 'would upset the balance as between England and Wales on the one hand and Scotland on the other'.

By April 1948, further new towns had been approved south of the Border and, moreover, decisions on the future planning of the area had become urgent. The Secretary of State for Scotland (now Woodburn) therefore resubmitted the proposal to the Lord President's Committee. At the same time, the Scottish new town programme as a whole was reviewed. Apart from Bishopton there were proposals for new towns at Coylton and Lochgelly, as well as East Kilbride and Glenrothes which had been approved by ministers.

In East Kilbride, a development corporation had been appointed in August 1947 under the chairmanship of Sir Patrick Dollan. The corporation had adopted a development plan, after consultation with Abercrombie, Mears and Holford; had completed the technical preparation for an initial programme of housing development comprising about 136 houses, work on which was expected to start within about six weeks; and had initiated preliminary work on the main drainage and water services required for the new town which would be executed on their behalf by the Lanarkshire County Council. In addition, they had provided facilities for Department of Scientific and Industrial Research establishments to be set up in the new town area.

Glenrothes was to be developed in the Leslie-Markinch area of Fife to serve the expanding coalfields, including in particular the large new sinking at Rothes which was now being developed by the National Coal Board. A public inquiry had been held and a formal designation order for the new town would be made shortly. Plans had been prepared for an initial development of 150 houses by Fife County Council, and work on this development was expected to begin in the late summer.

Coylton was proposed as a new town to serve the expanding coalfields in North Ayrshire. Final test plans were being adjusted in the light of the mineral position and formal action to designate the area of the new town would be taken within the next few months.

---

* The issue of new town development by local authorities is further discussed in chapter VI, p. 300 *et seq*; see also chapter IX on expanded towns policy.

† LP(48)35, LP(48)7th Meeting, 30 April 1948, LP(49)90, LP(49)21st Meeting, 9 December 1949; and SDD File P/NT/HOU/2.

‡ See pp. 56–57.

Lochgelly was intended to provide grouped housing facilities and new industrial opportunities in an important area in Fife which was wholly dependent at the time on mining. Prior to the establishment of the National Coal Board, the site selected for the new town was declared to be free from the risk of mineral subsidence. The National Coal Board, however, had now re-surveyed the mineral possibilities of this area and, as a result of their revised plans, including in particular the development of new surface mines, it had been impossible to secure a suitable site of sufficient size which would be capable of early development. It was therefore necessary to defer Lochgelly, at least for the present, and alternative planning proposals were being considered. (The proposal was later abandoned.)

There were several reasons for a new town in the Bishopton area. In the first place, the Burgh of Greenock, which had a population of about 80,000, had almost completely exhausted all the immediately available sites within the existing burgh boundary both for new housing and for industrial development. The town, which was grossly congested before the war, suffered more extensive war damage than any other town in Scotland except Clydebank and in fact about 1,000 houses were destroyed. The total number of houses required amounted to 13,500. Of these, 5,000 could be built within the existing burgh boundaries but only as a part of a long term programme for the redevelopment of the central town area. The balance of 8,000 houses, including houses immediately required, would have to be located outside the present burgh boundary. The town was very closely hemmed in topographically and a properly planned extension incorporating this number of houses was not feasible.

The shortage of industrial sites was equally acute, and the current employment situation in Greenock presented grave and urgent problems. The total number of unemployed at the end of March 1948 was 2,000 or about six per cent of the population—the highest total number of unemployed in any town in Scotland except Glasgow. Moreover Greenock, with the immediately adjoining burgh of Port Glasgow, had a very ill-balanced industrial structure, 45 per cent of the insured population being dependent upon ship-building and marine engineering.

It was therefore essential to find additional land for housing and industrial development, and the bulk of the requirements could be met only outside the limits of the existing burgh, after taking full account of the long term possibilities of redevelopment. One possible solution—proposed by Greenock—was to permit the town to straggle south-westwards in the only direction open to expansion along the line of a relatively narrow valley—the Kip Valley—in such a way that isolated housing schemes would be built up to a distance as far away as five miles from the present town centre. Such a solution would, however, create a continuous elongated ribbon of development stretching for twelve miles from Port Glasgow through Greenock to the head of the valley and would locate the bulk of the new houses required in a situation remote from the main centres of existing and future employment to the east of Port Glasgow. Even this solution, however, would produce little additional land suitable for industrial development for Greenock itself and was not a solution which, as planning minister, Woodburn could approve. The alternative scheme for securing a grouped development with an ultimate target population of about 40–45,000 in the Bishopton-Houston area (recommended in Abercrombie's report), was in fact the only acceptable one (and had been recommended by the Scottish Physical Planning Committee).

This solution had the advantage of providing a grouped centre to serve the equally pressing needs of Renfrew Burgh, and would also assist in dealing with the overspill problem from Glasgow. The precise site of the new town had not yet been delimited, but the area provisionally selected was one which, in the opinion of the Board of Trade, was likely to be more attractive to industrialists than any other area in this part of Scotland. Moreover, this area was particularly convenient to serve the general requirements of east Renfrewshire where it was anticipated that there would continue to be a need for additional labour in existing enterprises, including in particular the Linwood Factory recently taken over by the Pressed Steel Company. Any shipyard workers who moved to the new town and wished to continue in their employment in Greenock and Port Glasgow would, of course, have to travel back to those towns, but the journey to the shipyards from the new town would be little greater than from the alternative housing sites in the Kip Valley, while other workers in the new town area would have employment facilities at hand which could not possibly be made available in the Kip Valley.

The Bishopton-Houston area lay about nine miles east of Greenock, about twelve miles west of Glasgow, and about four miles west of Renfrew. In Woodburn's view, it was therefore ideally situated to provide a combined solution for both the housing and industrial needs of each of these three towns, but it was impossible for these local authorities, singly or in combination, to undertake a grouped development on the lines proposed. Indeed, it was just this type of development for which the machinery of the New Town Act was designed.

An early decision in principle was required if the physical planning requirements for Renfrewshire as a whole were to be properly met and if the immediate housing and industrial site requirements of the local authorities were to be satisfied.

Woodburn's proposal ran into difficulties at the LP Meeting when Morrison stated that he had had a message from the Minister of State, Hector McNeil (MP for Greenock) who was currently abroad, raising objection to the new town and stressing the advantages of enlarging Greenock by the development of the Kip Valley. In the discussion, particular point was made of the fact that the proposed new town was very close to the existing built-up areas of Glasgow, Renfrew and Greenock: 'this would not have been allowed in England'. Nevertheless, the committee 'approved the proposal that there should be a new town at Bishopton-Houston if the Secretary of State considered, on further examination, that effect could not be given to the Minister of State's proposal'.

In December 1949 Woodburn brought the proposal back to the committee and assured them that the enlargement of Greenock was not practicable. The designation of Houston was approved (though it was later abandoned, largely because of the strong opposition of Greenock).

A New Town at Bracknell*

Advance notice of a proposal for a new town at Bracknell had been given to the LP Committee in April 1948. In July Silkin sought authority to proceed with the proposal.

Of the areas already designated for new town development around London, Hemel Hempstead lay to the north-west, Stevenage, Welwyn Garden City and Hatfield to the north, Harlow to the north-east and Crawley to the south. Another new town (to be known as Basildon) had been authorised in the Pitsea-Laindon area of Essex and this would provide an outlet to the east.

In the existing distribution of new towns for London, the outstanding gap was to the west and south-west, ie the sector lying between Hemel Hempstead and Crawley; and it was this gap which Bracknell would help to fill. Means had to be found to provide an outlet for the surplus population and industry of west Middlesex which was one of the most overcrowded areas of Greater London. In this area, covering eleven local authorities, the existing population was some 112,000 above the ultimate population proposed under the Greater London Plan. Broadly, this meant that between 25,000 and 30,000 houses to accommodate this excess population would have to be provided outside the west Middlesex area. The problem had been seriously aggravated by the development of London Airport which had not only reduced the amount of land which might otherwise

---

* LP(48)65 and LP(48)13th Meeting, 23 July 1948.

have been available for housing purposes within the area, but had also given rise to an additional housing demand from airport workers, estimated at a minimum of 3,500 houses. For many of the local authorities suffering most from overcrowding, notably Ealing, Southall, Twickenham, Brentford, Heston and Isleworth, Hayes and Harlington, the housing problem was not only acute but urgent. All of them had little housing land remaining within their boundaries and, unless they could be helped under the New Towns Act, they would need land elsewhere within the following two or three years. The estimated surplus population from these authorities alone was of the order of 75,000.

No surplus housing land could be found in the areas of neighbouring authorities, while large scale development further out in Middlesex would be at the expense of the metropolitan green belt which Silkin was determined to preserve. Other important factors were the need to protect the sand and gravel areas in west Middlesex for mineral purposes, and the market gardening areas in the interest of food production. Relief for west Middlesex housing, therefore, had to be sought further to the west. Various expansions of existing towns were proposed in this direction, in particular Basingstoke, Newbury, and Wokingham, but these could make only a limited contribution to a solution. A careful investigation showed that Bracknell was the only place in this sector suitable for large scale urban expansion.

Bracknell was a village of some 5,000 inhabitants on the London–Ascot–Reading Road, about seven miles south-west of Windsor, nine miles east of Reading and thirty-two miles from Charing Cross by rail. It was the administrative centre of Easthampstead Rural District Council. Silkin's proposal was that the village should be expanded to a town of 25,000 people.

The idea that a new town should be developed in this part of the country was first put forward in the *Greater London Plan* when it was suggested that a new town of 60,000 should be built at White Waltham, five miles north of Bracknell. Silkin had rejected this proposal, as it would have prevented the use of White Waltham airfield and would have involved the loss of land of high agricultural value. Bracknell was, therefore, put forward as an alternative. It was thought that development at Bracknell should be able to proceed fairly quickly, as soon as conditions permitted. Services existed and no very heavy expenditure on water supplies, drainage and sewerage was likely to be entailed. The land was mainly of a heathy character and no loss to agriculture would result from its use for development.

The interested government departments had been consulted and had agreed in principle to the development of the Bracknell area. The scheme was strongly supported by the Minister of Health.

Berkshire County Council and Easthampstead RDC were in favour of the proposal and were willing to co-operate to the full, while the local authorities of west Middlesex, who looked to a new town at Bracknell for relief of their housing problem, were pressing strongly for a decision to proceed with the scheme. It seemed unlikely that there would be any serious objection to the designation of the area for new town development.

The proposed new town was considerably smaller than any already approved in the London area. This was partly because of the physical limitations of the area and partly because of the un-desirability of any large expansion within a few miles of the neigh-bouring town of Wokingham. For both of these reasons Silkin was satisfied that Bracknell should not expand beyond a population of 25,000.

He had considered whether it would be possible for the rural district council to undertake the development which they were, in fact, at one stage anxious to do. A careful examination of the financial and organisational problems involved had been made and the conclusion was that the task would be quite beyond their resources. Silkin was, therefore, satisfied that if Bracknell were to be developed on the scale proposed, it had to be done under the machinery of the New Towns Act. Accordingly, he asked his colleagues to agree that Bracknell should be developed as a new town for a total population of 25,000.

The proposal was approved by the LP Committee in July 1948 though concern was expressed at the proximity of the site to London and the consequent danger of the new town becoming a dormitory area. The question of the 'balance' of the new towns programme was also raised again. Bracknell was the eighth new town approved for London, yet only two provincial new towns had been agreed. Silkin pointed out that resources were in fact being devoted to the development of Aycliffe and Easington in preference to any of the Greater London projects. It had not yet been possible to find a suitable site for a Manchester new town or to reach agreement with Leeds, who had proposed a site much too close to the city. A clear case for the provision of a new town in any other part of England and Wales had not yet been made, but enquiries into the possibility of developing new towns in Wales were still proceeding, and the position in the midlands and Staffordshire would be considered as soon as the local authorities' plans were available. It also had to be borne in mind that the need for new towns connected with the Greater London area was more acute and that local authorities in most parts of the provinces had been less active in preparing their plans.

It was at this meeting that an issue arose which developed into one of considerable concern and lengthy discussion. This was the question of the number of paid appointments involved in the execution of the new towns policy. Morrison asked whether it would not be possible to get more of the work done voluntarily and whether it was necessary to pay members of the new towns corporations other than the chairman and vice-chairman. He still felt that the possibility of entrusting the development of a new town to one of the larger local authorities was worth considering. Silkin was asked to circulate a memorandum on the possibility of reducing the number of paid appointments to new town corporations.*

New Towns in South Wales†

Two months later (in September 1948) Silkin proposed two new towns for south Wales: at Church Village-Tonteg (three miles from Pontypridd and two miles from the Treforest Trading Estate) and at Cwmbran-Pontnewydd (four miles north of Newport). He had earlier suggested that two new towns would be needed in south Wales, and it had been agreed that he should pursue further the possibilities of development at Church Village and Pontllanfraith (situated at the foot of the Rhymney-Sirhowy Valley thirteen miles from Newport and sixteen miles from Cardiff). Following further investigation of the probable concentration of existing collieries and sinkings of new ones, of industrial projects carried out and envisaged by the Board of Trade, and of the projects approved for the nationalisation of steel and tin plate, Silkin had come to the conclusion that the idea of a new town at Pontllanfraith should be dropped, and that Cwmbran–Pontnewydd should be substituted.

CHURCH VILLAGE-TONTEG

Church Village-Tonteg had a population of about 5,000 but there was, or shortly would be, local employment for upwards of 17,000 people. About 10,000 were currently employed at the Treforest Trading Estate, and it was estimated by the Board of Trade that the number would increase to 14,000. Additionally, a new colliery at Nantgarw would employ about 2,500, and there might also be other coalmining development in the area. It was necessary to drastically reduce the burden of the journey to work. Of the 10,000 workers at Treforest, around 7,000 travelled more than three miles and nearly 5,000 over five miles.

Account also had to be taken of probable movements into the area of people living in neighbouring mining valleys who would in time be obliged to find new homes, either as a result of concentration of

---

* This issue is discussed in detail in chapter VI.
† LP(48)73, LP(48)14th Meeting, 24 September 1948; and Lord President's File 1352/4.

existing collieries, or because of the difficulties in finding suitable housing sites in the valleys. The Welsh Board of Health had recently stated that practically all the available sites in the valleys had now been used, but it was not possible, in the absence of detailed surveys by the local planning authorities, to determine exactly how many people were likely to move on this account.

The area was suitable for expansion up to a population of 25,000. About 2,000 acres of medium and poor quality land were available for development. Roads and public services already existed and could be supplemented without much difficulty. The risk of subsidence was not greater than was to be expected in this part of the coalfield though care would be necessary to limit sterilisation of coking coal reserves. Natural physical features made it possible to develop the site separately from Pontypridd, and, in the view of the Board of Trade, no additional industry would be required to maintain this population.

CWMBRAN-PONTNEWYDD

At Cwmbran-Pontnewydd the existing population was about 12,000 and Silkin proposed expansion up to about 32,000. Provision of houses and other facilities was badly needed for reasons similar to those for the Church Village-Tonteg area. An additional 8,000 jobs were being provided, mostly in the metal, engineering and allied trades. With the exception of Treforest the area had received a greater proportion of new industry than any other in south Wales. A large percentage of this additional labour force would be obliged to travel to work from other areas. Already over 2,000 workers were travelling into the area from distances of five miles or more. Account had to be taken of likely movement of population from the neighbouring east Monmouthshire valleys, where concentration of collieries was probable and where, in the view of the National Coal Board, mining was not likely to continue on its current scale.

Adequate land existed for large scale development, and communications and public services could be provided for additional population without much difficulty. Though Cwmbran and Pontnewydd were situated only four miles north of Newport and four miles south of Pontypool, development could take place independently of both places. Facilities for an additional population of 20,000 persons should be provided in this area, and no additional industry would be required to maintain this population.

The provision of additional facilities of this order would in both areas entail a heavy financial and administrative responsibility which the planning authorities and the local authorities could not be expected to carry, especially since the task would include provision for population coming from other parts of the coalfield.

Silkin said that, if the proposals were approved by the LP Committee, he intended to proceed immediately with detailed site investigations, discussions with the local authority concerned, and the making of the draft designation orders. The committee, however, had some reservations. In the first place it was questioned whether the proposals did not assume too readily that people ought not to be expected to travel some three or four miles to work. The view that workers' houses should be immediately beside the factory was a discredited one, and workers (particularly in the London area) now travelled long distances.

New towns in Wales would largely draw their population from existing blighted areas. Would not it be better to redevelop these areas, making use of the services which they already had rather than to create new towns? Church Village-Tonteg was only three miles from Pontypridd and eight to ten miles from Cardiff, while Cwmbran-Pontnewydd was only four miles from Newport and four miles from Pontypool. There was thus some danger that both would become mere satellites of the neighbouring towns, and not new towns in the accepted sense of the term. Would it not be wasteful to set up fresh local authorities and provide separate local services?

In answer to these points, Silkin argued that, outside the London area, travelling facilities were less good and that it was in any event desirable, as a general policy, to reduce the amount of travelling which workers had to do and to bring their living accommodation within walking distance of their employment wherever possible. Moreover, the case for the two new towns in south Wales did not rest solely or mainly on travelling considerations but on the industrial development which had recently taken place or was projected. Subsidence due to mine workings rendered some of the existing built-up areas unsuitable for redevelopment. The clearing of parts of these areas and the redevelopment of others should go on simultaneously with the development of the new towns. There was unlikely to be a surplus of accommodation since the existing built-up areas were very congested and the process of redevelopment would involve some thinning out of their population.

It was difficult to find suitable sites in south Wales further from built-up areas. Development would be prohibited between the new town and the adjacent built-up areas and to that extent a belt of open country would be retained. The planned development of mining and industry in south Wales should secure that the inhabitants of the new towns would find work near their homes.

These arguments were persuasive, but the committee felt that while both new towns would be well situated from many points of view, their location would probably make them 'rather drab in appearance and there was much to be said for securing at least one site in a more attractive setting', such as the Vale of Glamorgan or the Rhymney-Sirhowy Valley, though the idea of a new town at Pontllanfraith had been dropped. It was accordingly suggested that the Church Village-Tonteg project should proceed but that the possibility of an alternative site to Cwmbran-Pontnewydd should be further considered.

This was agreed though, as we shall see,* Church Village-Tonteg was later abandoned because of future coal mining plans and the danger of major subsidence. Cwmbran was not further discussed by the committee, but was agreed in correspondence between Silkin and Morrison in March 1949.

New Towns in Cheshire†

In October 1946 approval had been given to a proposal to proceed with a new town at Mobberley in north Cheshire to absorb up to 60,000 of the population overspill from Manchester and other overcrowded towns in SE Lancashire.‡ In March 1949, Silkin reported that he had had to abandon the proposal on account of the risk of subsidence which had since been established. Manchester had acquiesced in this decision, but were now asking that they should be allowed to develop in the Mobberley area an estate for about 25,000 people, if sufficient safe land could be found (which he thought was the case). In view of their urgent need for additional land for housing (which had been impressed on him by the Minister of Health) Silkin felt that he had to agree to this. There was no likelihood of finding an alternative to Mobberley new town which could be started quickly (though, in the longer term, Congleton could be developed). Silkin therefore thought it was necessary that 'Manchester must be given something at Mobberley'. He understood that the Minister of Agriculture was 'not happy' about this new Mobberley proposal because the land which Manchester would need was valuable to agriculture: while he (ie the Minister of Agriculture) was prepared to accept a new town at Mobberley as making a substantial contribution to the problem of Manchester and SE Lancashire, it was more difficult for him to agree to the smaller scheme while at the same time being asked to agree to a new town further out which Silkin was proposing at Congleton. Nevertheless, there was no practicable alternative for Manchester's short term development which was not at least as damaging to agriculture, and Silkin said that he would ensure that the actual site to be developed was settled in consultation with the Minister of Agriculture and took

---

* See p. 110 below.
† LP(49)19, LP(49)21 and LP(49)6th Meeting, 18 March 1949.
‡ See pp. 59–60 above.

as little good agricultural land as was compatible with an estate for about 25,000 people.

The abandonment of Mobberley as a possible site for a new town made it necessary to find another site in Cheshire, and Silkin had come to the conclusion that the right course was to try and find 'one really big one'. There was a very large potential overspill from Manchester and adjoining areas 'to say nothing of Merseyside which certainly exceeds 200,000 and may be a good deal bigger'. A new town for 60,000 at Mobberley had never been envisaged as being more than a 'contribution' to the problem, and even had that gone forward, he had always had it in mind that he must find a second new town site as a matter of urgency in addition to anything that could be done by way of building up existing towns. Ideally, he thought that he still ought to find two new town sites to the south of Manchester, but the area was so difficult because of its high agricultural value, underlying salt, ICI developments and other factors, that he was sure that the right course was to concentrate on one area. For that, Congleton seemed to him to be the best site, and he proposed to develop it, subject to more detailed investigation of the site, if possible up to 120,000 population.

Congleton was in SE Cheshire, approximately twenty-two miles from Manchester and twelve miles from Stoke-on-Trent. Silkin had inspected the site himself and was satisfied that a good new town could be built here. The existing town had a population of approximately 15,000, and the additional development could be so laid out that it would not be hampered by what was there already. It was known that several of the local authorities concerned, including Cheshire County Council, would not be averse to development on the scale proposed, and substantial building up of this area was probably unavoidable in any event, owing to its easy accessibility by road and rail from both Manchester and the Potteries. The departments primarily concerned had been consulted, and with the exception of the Ministry of Agriculture, did not object. Industrial development to provide a self-contained town would be essential, and it was understood that the Board of Trade regarded Congleton as a reasonably promising location for the purpose. Major works would be needed to provide sufficient water, but this was likely to be unavoidable wherever a large new town was developed.

A good deal of further investigation would be needed before any decision could be reached about the best method of providing the necessary water, but it did not appear, after consultation with the Ministry of Health, that insuperable difficulty should be anticipated. The need for major water works, however, would inevitably limit the extent of development in the first few years—hence partly the need for letting Manchester have something at Mobberley in the interim.

Some land in this neighbourhood might be underlain by salt, and geological tests would be necessary before he could be sure of the stability of all the land that might be involved.

The principal difficulty at Congleton was the value of the land to agriculture. This difficulty arose throughout Cheshire. The project had been fully discussed with the Ministry of Agriculture, and Silkin thought that it was agreed that no alternative area could be suggested which would be feasible for adequate new town development and would be less damaging to their interests. At Congleton itself, the amount of damage to agriculture depended to some extent on the way in which the new town was developed. The most likely site for building was undoubtedly to the south of the existing community, but a large part of the necessary area, which for an additional population of about 100,000 would entail something like 6,000 acres, was good agricultural land. To the north-east of the existing town there was some land which was less valuable agriculturally, but which it would be very difficult to develop as part of the new town because it was cut off from the existing community (which must be incorporated), by difficult contours. Roads, rail access and the development of a satisfactory industrial area would all entail difficulties in the northern site. Nor would development to the north and north-east avoid the taking of some good agricultural land and he was not yet clear what the real difference to agriculture was as between the two alternatives. Silkin's technical advisers did not consider that a satisfactory new town could be built by using the land to the north and it was clear that development in that direction would be considerably more expensive than development to the south because of the cost of bridging etc. If, however, the development of a new town at Congleton could be approved in principle, Silkin was prepared to investigate further with the Ministry of Agriculture the precise area to be developed, and he would undertake to incorporate in the town as little land of high agricultural value as possible, even at the cost of difficulty in securing a satisfactory layout and additional expense on road and engineering services.

Silkin's obvious concern about the agricultural opposition to his proposals were well founded. The Minister of Agriculture (Williams) prepared a long memorandum for the LP Committee stating the agricultural case.

Diplomatically he started by admitting the exceptional difficulties of selecting an open site for a new town outside the belt of towns surrounding Manchester. To the south there was the fertile Cheshire plain which was uniformly excellent dual-purpose farm land; to the west was the south-west Lancashire plain, one of the most important areas of first class arable land in the country; while the Pennines bordered the north and the east. Thus, any new town in open unspoilt country would almost inevitably take high quality land and would be 'a severe blow for agriculture'.

From the agricultural standpoint, the overspill could best be accommodated by expanding some of the existing towns where the land was inherently poor or where it was already ruined for agriculture. For instance, in the extreme north-eastern tongue of Cheshire (within six to twelve miles from Manchester in the triangle formed by Stockport, Mossley and New Mills) there was an extensive area, 'capable of taking new population as well as re-developing existing declining towns', where the land was of only intermediate quality and very largely spoilt for farming by sporadic development; at Westhoughton (fourteen miles from Manchester, between Bolton and Wigan) land was very much affected by urban and industrial development, and some 3,500 acres would be available for development without serious loss to agriculture; the cotton towns of Lancashire (Bolton, Bury, Rochdale, etc), which had lost over 100,000 population during the previous thirty years, could also be redeveloped and expanded without serious agricultural opposition.

Williams pointed out that no firm figures of the extent of the overspill problem were available. Estimates varied, but the minimum population to be exported from Manchester alone had been put at 100,000 people. The figure of 200,000 quoted by Silkin included also the Merseyside area for which other outlets might be possible. In the Cheshire Plan, prepared by Dobson Chapman in 1947, very considerable expansion of a number of towns in Cheshire was advocated to meet Manchester's overspill. To some of these proposals there was strong agricultural objection, but others would be acceptable. A statement was produced of these proposals and the way in which they could be adapted to the satisfaction of the Ministry of Agriculture. Williams accepted that planned decentralisation of some of Manchester's industry and population to a number of other towns would be more difficult than to one large new town, but he argued that since Manchester's industries were firmly anchored to Manchester there was some doubt whether much of the industry could be moved anywhere. Until these possibilities of dealing with the problem had been more fully considered he felt that he had to question the expedient of one large new town and had to oppose a new town for 120,000 people sited on land which was of high quality by national as well as local standards.

The site considered for the 1946 proposal for a new town at Mobberley for 60,000 people included a strip of good land sandwiched between areas of poor land in the north-east and north-west. There was some justification for the loss of the good land because it formed a necessary part of the whole area, including a certain amount of land of rather lower quality. But the Manchester proposal for a town of 25,000 people would take only the good strip, which, moreover, would extend further south on to even better land. It had been proved that the poorer land on the east overlaid a salt field, and Tatton Park to the north-west was liable to subsidence (though the existence of salt deposits had not been proved by borings). The strip of good land was not of the same quality as land to the south, but it was nevertheless good on national standards and good by immediate local farming standards. The earlier proposal had been strongly opposed by farmers and the National Farmers' Union. Violent farming opposition to the present proposal was certain even if the southern extension of the site were excluded and Tatton Park was used for recreational purposes. Williams was therefore in a difficult position but, if it could be clearly demonstrated that there was no other means of early relief for Manchester's congestion and if the justification would be so stated as to convince public opinion that there was no alternative, he was reluctantly prepared to agree to the Mobberley proposal in principle, subject to further consideration on the precise boundaries of the site.

The site proposed for a new town, twenty-two miles south of Manchester on the south-west of Congleton would, Williams continued, absorb the whole or parts of 115 farms and take at least 5,500 acres of excellent land producing cereals, potatoes, and over a million gallons of milk a year. (Williams' detailed statement is reproduced overleaf.) Even on the high standards set in Cheshire, the quality of land and the standards of farm management were excellent. The site lay wholly in the valuable Cheshire Plain and, because it could produce either excellent grass or heavy arable crops, according to national needs or agricultural policy, it was a valuable asset and should remain in farming use. Except for a relatively small fringe adjacent to the town of Congleton the site was a rural unspoilt area. Moreover its development would inevitably lead to further agricultural loss by trespass and damage in the surrounding valuable agricultural land.

To the north-east of Congleton and south of the river Dane there was an area of lesser agricultural value which was inferior to the land in the Cheshire Plain. Together with land for industry further south on the eastern side of the Macclesfield–Stafford railway, there was an area which would accommodate a new town for up to 40,000–50,000 people. Though this included some good land, it was generally considerably inferior to land in the Cheshire Plain. Admittedly, the area would be more difficult and probably more costly to develop because of the contours, but these themselves would form natural scenic attractions within the town, and the surrounding hills would provide access lands where trespass would not cause serious damage to farming.

A new town to accommodate 120,000 people to the north of Congleton would involve large inroads on to land of comparable quality to that on the south-west, and Williams strongly opposed it for the same reasons. In fact, a new town for 120,000 anywhere at Congleton would be an extremely serious blow for agriculture, not only because of the loss of the land directly concerned but also because of its psychological effect on farmers generally and the four-year plan for agricultural expansion. If, therefore, a smaller new town on the north-east of Congleton were not acceptable, he had to resist the proposal for any new town in this vicinity:

'Approval to taking over 5,500 acres of some of the finest food producing land in the country would be completely at variance with the declared policy of conserving good farm land and if it were given at this time it would be embarrassing to the Government in the forthcoming debate on Lord Radnor's motion about the policy of using land resources for maximum food production.'

The agricultural case was thus a strong one, and Silkin found himself very much on the defensive when the issue was discussed at the

Statement by the Ministry of Agriculture on the
Estimated Produce of the Proposed Site for
Congleton New Town

Total Acreage of Agricultural Land	5,529 acres
Acreage of Arable Land	2,887 acres
Acreage of Wheat and Rye	354 acres
Estimated yield at 23 cwts per acre	407 tons
(National average 19·3 cwts per acre)	
Acreage of Potatoes	308 acres
Estimated yield at 8 tons per acre	2,464 tons
(National average 7 tons per acre)	
Acreage of Oats and Mixed Corn	945 acres
Estimated yield at 25 cwts per acre	1,181 tons
(National average 16·2 cwts per acre)	
Acreage of Green Crops	155 acres
Total Acreage of Temporary Ley (Approximately)	1,125 acres
Estimated yield 60 cwts per acre	3,375 tons
(National average 26 cwts per acre)	
Total Number of Cows	1,983
Total Head of Young Stock	548
Annual Milk Yield	1,018,956 gallons
Attested Milk Producers	
Number of Herds	7
Number of Cows	223
Number of Young Stock	63
Annual Milk Production	113,839 gallons

LP Committee in March 1949. Though he was able to show that little contribution to the Manchester problem could be expected from the Lancashire towns (because of their own severe problems of congestion), he was not able to persuade his colleagues to support him. Indeed, as the discussion proceeded, an increasing number of doubts arose. The Board of Trade had not had sufficient opportunity to examine the industrial prospects at Congleton and it was doubted whether sufficient Manchester industries could be induced to move there. Without employment, Congleton could develop only as a dormitory town, yet it was too far from Manchester for this to be practicable. In any case, the transport implications had not so far been considered (and, indeed, could not be until the proposal was more precise). The cost of the project also needed examination. A figure of £40m was mentioned, but the Treasury had not yet 'formed a view' on the financial implications.

Not surprisingly, Silkin was asked (in consultation with Agriculture, Health, Labour, Transport and Trade) to examine alternatives. Moreover, the concern of ministers on the loss of agricultural land (not only to housing and new towns but also to industry, playing fields and other developments) led them to ask Williams and Silkin (in consultation with the Secretary of State for Scotland) to prepare 'an appreciation of the extent to which current developments were encroaching upon the available acreage of agricultural land in this country'. Good arable land was strictly limited, and the progressive inroads upon it for development purposes were 'alarming' in amount. The cost of more concentrated development, such as the construction of flats in towns, would have to be balanced against the need for a flourishing agricultural industry.

Loss of Agricultural Land*

The 'appreciation' was duly produced. It was, however, greatly hedged with qualifications on the inadequacy of the available statistics. Indeed, the statistics were so inadequate that no clear conclusions were really possible. Nevertheless, the conclusion was drawn that attempts should be made to reduce the loss of agricultural land. The estimates indicated a loss to agriculture in England and Wales over the previous twenty-one years of 1,100,000 acres; the loss for the next twenty years was estimated at 620,000 acres. Williams proposed that development should be at higher densities and that there should be a greater use of poorer land even if this involved increased cost.

Silkin, on the other hand, said that he did not take an alarmist view of the situation though he agreed that every endeavour should be made to be economic in the use of land for development.

* LP(49)57, LP(49)60 and LP(49)15th Meeting, 15 July 1949.

The discussion was necessarily inconclusive except for a general agreement that better statistics should be secured and that the position should be kept under review.*

Peterlee New Town†

Although Peterlee (Easington) new town had been approved in August 1947,‡ and the designation order had been made on 10 March 1948, serious differences arose between the development corporation and the National Coal Board about reservation of land for underground working, particularly in the town centre.

The full story is a complicated and confused one but, in essence, the difficulties arose from the fact that the development corporation was not fully aware of the negotiations which had taken place (before the corporation was set up) between MTCP and the NCB. These negotiations had resulted in mutual agreement on the location and phasing of development. As a result, the NCB made no objections at the inquiry on the designation order for the new town. The development corporation, however, argued that their position 'was now governed entirely by the application of the New Towns Act to the Peterlee designated area and not by the informal [*sic*] negotiations that [the NCB] had entered into with the Ministry of Town and Country Planning in the early stages, before the development corporation had come into being'.

They had their own ideas as to how the master plan for the town should be designed and programmed. Though they were willing to discuss the ways in which the development of the new town could be phased to minimise the effects on coal mining, they could not accept a situation in which coal mining considerations should dictate the planning of the town.

The dispute reached deadlock and Silkin was forced to take the matter to the LP Committee in 1949. He explained that, in an attempt to reach a solution, he had sought technical advice from the chief development engineer of the Ministry of Works. His report (the Webster report) showed that the type of town desired could be built, but that the cost of buildings might be up to one-tenth more than in a non-coal mining area, and that it would take about four to five years longer to build than was at first estimated. Although some of the area (the 'red' zones) could never be built upon, and other parts (the 'amber' zones) could be built upon only after a period varying between two to five years after coal extraction, much of the former would not have been used for building even had no

---

* For further discussion, see appendix B.
† LP(49)28, LP(49)63, LP(49)7th Meeting, 25 March 1949, LP(49)16th Meeting, 22 July 1949; MHLG Files NT 265/55 series, and Lord President's File 1352/4.
‡ See pp. 77–78 above.

coal underlain it, and much of the latter would not have been essential in the early stages and could be dealt with by programming. Most important, the distribution of the three types of area (the third consisted of the 'green' zones available for a wide range of building immediately) was not such that any master plan based upon it would be 'ludicrous' or at any rate distorted in its layout or in the location of certain important buildings. There was no risk, for example, that the communal buildings of the town would have to be sited on the perimeter. Moreover, the distribution of the three types of area was not such that the time involved in extraction of coal and consequent subsidence would result in the period required to build the town being hopelessly drawn out or different building programmes being thrown out of balance. The precautions required to counter the risks of subsidence—a natural risk in mining areas—were not such as to prevent the normal facilities of a modern town being provided.

Silkin concluded that it might fairly be said that the effect of the Webster report was to leave unaffected the general principles which were accepted and the assumptions which were made when the project was first put forward and approved. These were that sterilisation of coal as a means of diminishing subsidence risks should be kept to the minimum consistent with the development of a comprehensive modern town, and that this dual objective should be achieved, as indeed it could only be achieved, by close working relationships between the corporation and the National Coal Board.

Silkin stressed that the idea of a new town at Peterlee had caught the imagination of the Durham mining community, the housing accommodation which it would provide was urgently required, and the Webster report showed that there was no reason why the scheme should not proceed. In these circumstances, it was in his view 'unthinkable that the plans for a new town on this site should be countermanded', or even suspended for a considerable period. He therefore sought authority to proceed with the scheme, on the understanding that he would consult with the Treasury if exceptional difficulties involving serious financial commitment came to light.

The immediate reaction of ministers to the report was to ask why the problem had not been brought to the attention of the Dalton Committee when the Peterlee proposal was being discussed.* Though due reference might have been made to the danger of subsidence it was clear that the committee had not envisaged this to

---

* In a letter of 16 March 1949 Morrison wrote to Silkin commenting that, even if (as Silkin stated) 'the risk of subsidence and other factors related to coalmining were not overlooked when the project was approved by ministers . . . they were certainly not fully brought out'.

be a major problem and certainly not one-which might raise serious doubts as to the advisability of the project. Silkin explained that before the corporation was established, there had been discussions between officers of the Ministry of Town and Country Planning and the NCB about the effect of mining operations on the development of the area. Agreement had been reached on a small area in which building work might proceed forthwith, and there had been an understanding about the sequence in which further development should take place. This, however, had proved unacceptable to the development corporation but their proposals were equally unacceptable to the National Coal Board.

It is clear from the departmental files that the development corporation felt that they could not develop the town adequately and efficiently within the framework of a series of constraints agreed before they were established. The National Coal Board, on the other hand, were greatly disturbed to find that these agreements were being questioned: they argued that all the problems relating to the 'co-ordination of surface and underground planning' had been settled before the designation order was made.

Silkin underlined the importance to the Government of an early agreement on a development plan which did not involve heavy additional expenditure: otherwise, the choice of the site would be criticised. Yet it was undesirable that the development of the new town should involve an embargo on the mining of coal over a considerable area, since the livelihood of those living in the new town would depend upon a prosperous mining industry in the neighbourhood. Nevertheless, it might, in the long run, be cheaper to reach agreement with the NCB that mining operations would not be conducted in the whole or in part of the 'amber' area, rather than that expensive protective works should be required for houses and other buildings erected in that area.

There was, at this time, no definite estimate of the additional cost which would be involved if strengthened structures were built in the 'amber' area. One estimate was £20 additional expenditure per house; but, if concrete rafts had to be built under the houses, the cost might be considerably higher.

It was also alleged that the development corporation at Peterlee was 'weak in business ability'. It currently consisted of the chairman, a university teacher and some local authority members. There were three vacancies which the minister was anxious to fill by finding individuals with business experience. One of the difficulties was the reluctance of the local authorities in the neighbourhood to accept the presence on the corporation of persons belonging to other political parties. It was felt that this attitude should not be accepted if it impaired the efficiency of the corporation. It was suggested that it would be useful if a representative of the NCB could be added to the corporation, but the Board were unwilling to consider this until broad agreement had been reached between the corporation and the Board on the development plan for the new town.*

The general feeling of the committee was that it would be necessary to proceed with the proposed construction of a new town at Peterlee, but that the size and other details of the project could not be decided until the position had been further examined. The Ministry of Fuel and Power and the National Coal Board would have to examine the Webster report, and discuss the position further with the Corporation. It was agreed that Silkin should arrange for a detailed examination of the plans for Peterlee by his department, in consultation with the Treasury, Ministry of Health, Ministry of Fuel and Power and the National Coal Board, and to report further to the committee whether an agreed scheme of development could be secured. A Peterlee working party was established and reported to the LP Committee in July 1949. The main outcome was that it proved impossible for the development corporation and the National Coal Board to reach an agreed solution.

Silkin argued that there could be no question of abandoning the new town. In addition to the most serious political consequences which this course would have, the decision to have a new town in the area 'had been profoundly welcomed by local public opinion and by miners throughout the country'. To abandon it would cause disappointment and disillusionment. The issue, therefore, was the basis on which the new town should now proceed. The report of the working party showed that the corporation had asked for two things in particular. First, they had asked that the NCB should sterilise at once a part of the site proposed for the town centre so that a stable site could be provided on which the relatively heavy buildings needed could be built without risk. The National Coal Board had offered so to arrange their programme of working that the site would be stable by 1957. They maintained that if the site were to be made stable at once (by stopping coal-getting which was approaching the site), the effect would be that 100 face workers would be put out of employment immediately and there would be a loss of production of about 250 tons a day. Silkin said that he could not believe that there was no alternative employment for 100 face workers in the area.

---

* An internal MTCP minute of 26 July 1948 noted that there were doubts 'about whether a group of so highly imaginative and temperamental people would work successfully together as a team. Being wise after the event, it would have been better to let them try out their ideas where the difficulties were not aggravated by coal'. Nevertheless, Silkin felt that the current management should be continued, with some 'strengthening'. An official commented that 'they would undoubtedly produce a new town different from the ordinary type which might be evolved, and that was all to the good'.

The matter was a most serious one for the corporation since it would mean that the town centre buildings could not be started for another seven years, and that the development of the town would not proceed in an orderly and balanced manner. In the circumstances he felt bound to press that this request of the corporation should be met.

Secondly, the corporation asked that three sites should be made available to them as stable land within varying periods so that they could accelerate progress, and provide more accommodation by the erection of flats (and thus use the available land economically and to the best advantage).

Silkin thought that the corporation had made out their case for all these sites and he supported them, though he recognised that the difficulties in the way of the third site seemed more formidable than the other two, because in this instance not only was there a question of sterilisation but the NCB maintained that the reorganisation plans for the colliery working this area would be affected. Even so, he thought that if such reorganisation of the work were necessary in the public interest there should be no insuperable difficulty in carrying it out.

At the LP Meeting in July 1949 Silkin said that there was no dispute that the development corporation were free to build scattered houses and schools over the whole site of the new town. The difficulty arose in regard to the town centre, where the corporation wished a stable site for relatively heavy buildings and three other sites where the corporation wished to build blocks of houses, including flats, at an early date. The town centre would cover an area of 60 acres and might sterilise up to 1,200,000 tons of coal. The other sites amounted to 300 acres. The coal involved at all the sites was about 3,000,000 tons. This loss would be spread over many years, and he considered that it was more important to provide housing and civic amenities in an area where they were greatly needed. Surely the National Coal Board could take steps to prevent unemployment among local coal miners, by a redistribution of their men?

Gaitskell (Minister of Fuel and Power) said that estimates of possible loss of coal with which he had been provided were between 3,000,000 and 4,000,000 tons. While the other building sites presented difficulty, particularly the 100 acres in the western half of the designated area, the main trouble was in regard to the town centre. He gathered (contrary to the view expressed by Silkin) that there was no great enthusiasm in the Durham mining community for the Peterlee new town, and that there would be considerable resentment if an immediate result was that 100 face workers were put out of employment. The coal in the western parts of Durham was becoming worked-out and the mining developments contemplated at Peterlee were part of a general shift of coal-mining to the eastern parts of the county.

The committee considered, but rejected, a suggestion that Peterlee should be abandoned as a new town, and a fresh site found. A good deal of preliminary work had already been done at Peterlee, and the objections on agricultural grounds to any possible alternative site were likely to be serious. In view of the extent to which the provision of housing in neighbouring mining communities was being restricted because of the housing which was to be provided at Peterlee, there was general agreement that it would be necessary to make progress with the development of the new town, including the town centre. Within this general objective, however, every endeavour should be made to reduce the loss of coal which was involved, in view of the importance of securing as much coal as could be profitably worked.

Silkin referred to the disquiet which members of the committee had earlier expressed about the weakness of the development corporation in business ability, and reported that he was now filling three vacancies on the corporation by the appointment of individuals 'with sound commercial and financial experience'.

The committee agreed that the land required by the development corporation should be made available to them notwithstanding the loss of coal which was involved. Though the matter ended thus so far as the Cabinet were concerned, the issue remained one of major contention for many years.

In concluding this summary of the initial difficulties faced in Peterlee, it is appropriate to point out that the National Coal Board had been formed on 1 January 1947—only seven months before the decision to proceed with the new town. It took some considerable time for this new organisation to settle down and for clear lines of responsibility between headquarters and the regions to be established. Moreover, they could have had little idea at this stage of what was involved by a new town development.

Thus two new organisations—the NCB and the development corporation—were wrestling both with their organisational problems and with the problems of a development of unprecedented character. In these circumstances it would not have been surprising to find both organisations seeking to establish their authority. In the process each would have appeared to the other as being difficult, frustrating and unco-operative.*

---

* It may be relevant to note the fact that Shinwell was MP for Easington and had been Minister of Fuel and Power from August 1945 to October 1947 (when he became Minister of Defence). The Cabinet papers, however, give no clue as to whether Shinwell took any part in the discussions.

*Corby New Town**

In July 1949 Silkin presented a memorandum to the LP Committee proposing a new town at Corby.

The Government had decided that Stewart and Lloyds' steelworks in the area were to double their capacity within the space of a few years. Their existing production labour was about 5,750: this figure was to increase to 6,400 by 1950–51, and ultimately to 10,000. This raised acute questions on the provision of the necessary houses, of shops, service industry and all the other social and communal facilities which would be needed. After discussion between Silkin's department and the Ministries of Health and of Supply, and in agreement with them, he had come to the conclusion that the expansion could be carried through satisfactorily only by the establishment of a development corporation under the New Towns Act.

The population of the urban district was about 14,000. Fifteen years earlier it had been little more than a village, and up to the war its expansion was carried out by Stewart and Lloyds. The firm had built most of the existing houses in the district, but they were not prepared to continue building houses, and Silkin did not think it desirable that they should do so. The choice therefore lay between leaving the urban district council 'to carry on as best they could' under the Housing Acts, or establishing a development corporation. There was already an acute overcrowding problem in the district in addition to which many workers were travelling long distances to work. The urban district council had undertaken a large housing programme, with just over 500 houses completed, over 500 under construction, and land acquired for a further 200 to 300. Nevertheless, this programme was insufficient to meet the existing needs and made no provision for the necessary expansion. Even so, it was straining the council's resources, and they were already asking the ministry for special financial assistance (to cover the cost of imported labour) for any further expansion.

The main factor which influenced Silkin in proposing action under the New Towns Act was that the current expansion was taking place 'without proper planning of the town', and without any prospect of the provision of social and communal services or of some diversification of employment. Northamptonshire County Council (the local planning authority) were anxious that a development corporation should be established, though the district council naturally did not want to be superseded by a corporation.

The minimum population to which Corby had to expand, providing only for the additional steelworkers and their families, would be approximately 30,000—twice the existing population. It was most

* LP(49)56 and LP(49)15th Meeting, 15 July 1949.

desirable, however, that some diversification of industry should be provided, particularly for women and for men, who, because of age, could not continue on heavy work in the steelworks. To make a reasonably satisfactory town, the minimum figure to be aimed at was 50,000. The Board of Trade, however, were disposed to think that 40,000 might be sufficiently large as Corby was in an exceptionally prosperous region having a well diversified industrial economy with other important manufacturing centres nearby. Silkin, himself, preferred a town of about 100,000: this would prevent it from being almost wholly dependent on the steelworks, and would provide a balanced and varied community. He was advised, however, that this would involve many serious difficulties, not least that of attracting other industry to the area. His current proposal therefore was that there should be an initial expansion to at least 40,000, with the possibility of an increase in this figure if further investigation and discussion with the departments principally concerned suggested that that was practicable and desirable.

Silkin promised that the usual consultations with interested departments would take place. In particular, the Ministry of Agriculture would be consulted about the precise area to be designated though, perhaps somewhat rashly, he suggested that it might not be possible to reach agreement on this until after the public inquiry had been held 'since it is essential that no time should be lost in starting the designation procedure'.

Silkin had support for his proposal from Bevan who agreed that the expansion of Corby was beyond the resources of the urban district council. Both the Minister of Agriculture and the President of the Board of Trade apparently accepted the desirability of the project but considered that the population limit should be 40,000. The argument of the Board of Trade was that a larger town would compete seriously with the development areas in the attraction of industries. Moreover, Corby was situated in a prosperous part of the country with a number of neighbouring towns with diversified industries: this would ensure that Corby did not reproduce the worst features of a one-industry town. Agricultural objections to a larger town were reinforced by the serious losses in Northamptonshire due to ironstone workings.

The Treasury expressed concern not only at the likely cost of Corby in particular, but of the cost of the total new towns programme. Financial commitments were of particular importance in the case of Corby, since industrial development had already taken place and there might not be much leasing of land for better-class houses. There appeared to be little hope that the exchequer would recoup itself for the heavy capital cost of new towns within the first ten or fifteen years of their operation. More generally, the time had arrived when the Government should form a view on the financial liability which was being incurred in respect of existing and prospective new towns.

This was accepted by the committee and, in giving approval to a new town at Corby ('capable of accommodating in all 40,000 inhabitants'), Silkin and Cripps were asked to submit a memorandum on the capital cost of new towns and on the extent to which these were likely to give rise to a continuing financial burden on the exchequer.*

The Abandonment of Church Village New Town†

In September 1948 the committee had tentatively approved Silkin's proposal for the establishment of two new towns in south Wales, one at Church Village near Pontypridd and the other at Cwmbran near Newport.‡ The area for the new town at Cwmbran was designated on 4 November 1949 and a development corporation was set up on 24 November. Severe problems, however, arose with the Church Village proposal and these were reported to the LP Committee in January 1950. At the time when the proposal had initially come before the committee, Silkin had been aware that coal had been and would be worked under part of the site, but there was no reason for thinking that the risk of subsidence was greater than normal in the south Wales coalfield. It was not until after the committee's decision that he learnt that the National Coal Board proposed to work important deep seams of coal by the method of horizon mining under most of the site. It became clear that this would greatly increase the risk of subsidence and he accordingly asked the Ministry of Works to investigate the question for him. While this investigation was proceeding he had an informal consultation with the local authorities affected, and he found that they were all in favour of his proposal, with the exception of the Rhondda Urban District.

The report from the Ministry of Works was extremely disquieting. Their view was that the working of the deep seams of coal would be liable to cause severe movements on the surface and to produce fissures several feet wide, extending to a great depth. These conditions were liable to affect the greater portion of the site and Silkin was advised that the extent and location of the subsidence was quite unpredictable. He had investigated the possibility of an alternative site off the coalfield, but had been forced to the conclusion that any site to the south of the coalfield would not only be at too great distance from the Treforest Trading Estate (which the new town

---

* See chapter VIII p. 451 *et seq.*
† LP(50)4 and LP(50)1st Meeting, 20 January 1950.
‡ See p. 95.

was mainly intended to serve) but would also be so close to Cardiff that the new town would have little chance of a separate existence. He had therefore arranged for discussions with the Divisional Coal Board in south Wales on the possibility of obtaining a site to the west of Church Village which would avoid the more valuable coal seams. It appeared from the discussion that such an arrangement might be practicable, and he accordingly selected an alternative site to the west and south of Church Village which, though not so suitable as the original site, would have housed a population of about 16,000. When, however, this site was put to the NCB he was informed that the most valuable part of it (from the point of view of development) lay over the deep seams of coal, and that its development would involve the sterilisation of at least 22 million tons, which the NCB felt it impossible to sacrifice. Silkin had previously considered the question of going even further west of Church Village, but had found this impossible.

Consultations with the Minister of Fuel and Power and the National Coal Board led to the conclusion that the Church Village site ought to be abandoned.

In the course of these various discussions it was suggested that a suitable site might be found in the neighbourhood of Caerphilly. Although Silkin regarded this site as much less suitable for a new town than Church Village, he would nevertheless have been prepared to consider an extension of Caerphilly up to 40,000 if sufficient ground could have been found; but here again the same difficulty about the working of deep coal seams arose. For a new town, about 2,600 acres would be needed, but the NCB were unwilling to concede anything beyond an area of about 1,000 acres which included the existing town of Caerphilly: 'that would be useless for a new town'.

If the proposal for a new town to serve the Treforest Trading Estate and the mines in the vicinity were to be abandoned, the implication would be an acceptance of the situation in which the Trading Estate would continue to be 'without a community of its own'. Additionally, large numbers of workers would have to continue to travel to their work from considerable distances. Some, no doubt, would be catered for in new local authority housing estates (assuming that sites could be found which were reasonably free from the risk of subsidence). Such scattered estates, however, could provide only for a proportion of the workers at the Trading Estate and in the mines. Moreover, they would perpetuate the existing type of unsatisfactory development in the south Wales valleys and could not provide the social and community facilities which would be found in a new town. Silkin regarded this as 'deplorable': and 'we shall almost certainly not get another opportunity of making something of this area'. But, sadly, he concluded that if there were no prospect of sterilising the coal underlying the Church Village or Caerphilly areas, there appeared to be no practicable alternative.

The outcome was predictable: the new town proposal was abandoned.

The End of the First Round of New Towns

The decision on Church Village was taken in January 1950. One month later a general election was held and the Labour Government was returned with a narrow majority. A further general election was held in October 1951 when a Conservative Government was returned.

No further new towns were designated in England and Wales for twelve years (in Scotland for six years). The following table shows the dates at which the proposals for new towns were first put before ministers collectively, when ministers approved the proposals, and when designation orders were made (after public notice and consideration of objections).

First mention to Cabinet Committee	Approved by Cabinet Committee		Designation Order
25 November 1945	30 November 1945	Stevenage	11 November 1946
29 March 1946	10 July 1946	Harlow	25 March 1947
29 March 1946	10 July 1946	Hemel Hempstead	4 February 1947
29 March 1946	23 May 1946	Crawley	9 January 1947
13 May 1946	23 May 1946	East Kilbride	6 May 1947
13 May 1946	23 October 1946	Aycliffe	19 April 1947
2 November 1946	7 November 1946	Glenrothes	30 June 1948
1 February 1947	26 July 1947	Welwyn	20 May 1948
1 February 1947	26 July 1947	Hatfield	20 May 1948
19 July 1947	6 August 1947	Peterlee	10 March 1948
17 April 1948	30 April 1948	Basildon	4 January 1949
20 July 1948	23 July 1948	Bracknell	17 June 1949
20 September 1948	8 March 1949	Cwmbran	4 November 1949
11 July 1949	15 July 1949	Corby	1 April 1950

The following sites were seriously proposed to ministers collectively, but were withdrawn before the designation procedure was put in motion.

First Mention to Cabinet Committee	Considered by Cabinet Committee		Withdrawn
29 March 1946	31 July 1946	Chipping Ongar (Essex)	1946
23 Oct 1946	18 March 1949	Mobberley (Cheshire)	1949
20 April 1948	9 Dec 1949	Bishopton-Houston	1950
20 Sep 1948	24 Sep 1948	Church Village (Monmouthshire)	1950
15 March 1949	18 March 1949	Congleton (Cheshire)	1952

Many potential sites had been suggested by local authorities and private individuals which had little merit, but the following are some of those which were more or less seriously considered by the department, although not specifically referred to ministers.*

Berkshire	–	Basingstoke
		Newbury
		Reading
Brecon	–	Ystradgynlais
Bucks	–	Verney (later developed as Milton Keynes)
Cheshire	–	Crowton
		Ellesmere Port
Cumberland	–	Egremont
		Seascale
Derbyshire	–	Swadlincote
Durham	–	Brandon
Flint	–	Mold
Gloucestershire	–	Chipping Sodbury
Hants	–	Leigh Park
Kent	–	Ashford
Lancashire	–	Eccleston–Chorley (later developed as the Central Lancashire New Town)
Staffordshire	–	Potteries
Suffolk	–	Haverhill
Yorkshire	–	Ripon

Another proposal which came to nothing was for a 'holiday new town'. On several occasions between 1947 and 1950 Silkin pressed his officials to give consideration to the possibility of such a town. He felt it would provide an opportunity for 'a fine experiment' which might serve to meet overspill needs, and also provide a stimulus to the development of tourism. He had Littlehampton in mind.

HOLIDAY NEW TOWN†

There were two distinct lines of thought which led Silkin to make this proposal. First, there was the need to provide more holiday accommodation. Under the heading 'more family holidays', the Labour Party policy statement *Labour Believes in Britain*, had proposed the establishment of 'a Holidays Council, with government support, to start providing modern reasonably priced holiday centres with accommodation for families'. (To this Silkin later added that 'ultimately a new town we are developing should aim at national and international conferences as one of its main undertakings'.)

---

* MHLG File 91650/302/3.
† MHLG File 91650/66.

Secondly, Silkin felt that there was force in the criticism that some of the first new towns were too near to London and that:

'the creation of a new town designed as a holiday resort might serve to take people out of London not just temporarily for a week's holiday but as a permanent population who would be occupied in the provision of holiday facilities for the ordinary holiday maker'.

This met 'with little enthusiasm within his department—one official commenting that 'anything more squalid and demoralising for the young and old than the backstairs life of a holiday resort cannot be imagined'. Great difficulties were foreseen in obtaining a reasonable balance of employment; existing holiday towns were unlikely to welcome government-sponsored competition—and above all it seemed extremely unlikely that ministers would be agreeable to investment (and additional industrial development) in a new town of this character.

However, Silkin persisted and, in August 1949, pressed the President of the Board of Trade (Harold Wilson)—who had responsibility for the British Tourist and Holidays Board—to agree to an interdepartmental study of the possibilities.

Wilson was unimpressed by the arguments. He pointed to the difficulties of finding sufficient mobile industry to meet the requirements of the development and other needy areas as well as those of the new towns already approved. Many existing holiday towns already suffered from a lack of industrial balance which gave rise to much seasonal unemployment which it was very difficult to cure. For these and similar reasons, the proposal lay 'quite outside practical possibilities'. Any examination of the possibilities would be a waste of the resources of both Silkin's and his departments.

Silkin was forced to accept this, though he did impress on his officials that the idea should not be dropped: it should be borne in mind as a possibility when sites were being investigated for further new towns.

The proposal, however, was not revived.

Fourteen New Towns

By the time of the election in February 1950, Silkin (for England and Wales) and Westwood and Woodburn (for Scotland) had secured the approval of their colleagues for eight new towns for London, two in Durham, one in the Midlands (Corby), one in south Wales (Cwmbran), and two in Scotland, and had subsequently guided these through the machinery of the Act of 1946 against varying degrees of local opposition. The merits and demerits of each particular site had been thoroughly canvassed at the official level before they were referred to ministers collectively but, although

Silkin and the Scottish ministers withdrew a few of their proposals, none which they pressed were rejected by their colleagues. Nevertheless, Silkin's proposals in particular had been met with a lack of enthusiasm during the four and a half years while he was pursuing his policy. This appears to have arisen (apart from apprehensions about the development areas) from three main doubts in the minds of his ministerial colleagues: on whether the resources being devoted to new towns might not be better employed in rehabilitating and expanding existing communities; on whether the organisational arrangements were adequate; and on whether the claims on the exchequer could be justified.

Doubts on the first were partly allayed by the Town Development Act 1952 which, though passed by a Conservative Government, was largely initiated by Dalton (who succeeded Silkin as Minister of Town and Country Planning in February 1950). This is discussed further in chapters III and IX. Problems of organisation arose in an acute but guarded form during 1948, but a suggestion for a national corporation was rejected, and participation by local authorities was side stepped. As chapter VI shows, the issue was a live one throughout the period covered by this history (and later). Finance flared up in 1949 and was under scrutiny thereafter. Chapter VIII deals with this at some length.

CHAPTER III

New Town Policy in the Fifties

THE Conservative Government took office on 26 October 1951, and four days later Harold Macmillan became Minister of Housing and Local Government—the new name for the Ministry of Local Government and Planning, designed to emphasise the new administration's interest in housing and reflecting a disillusionment with 'planning'. Nothing had been said in the Conservative manifesto specifically about the new towns though, more generally, a determination was expressed to 'simplify the administrative machine and prune waste and extravagance in every department; . . . to stop all further nationalisation; . . . the whole system of town planning and development charges needs drastic overhaul; . . . we shall seek to restore to local government the confidence and responsibility it has lost under Socialism'. But there was a feeling that the new towns had some of the attributes of the ground nuts scheme: by the end of 1950 the number of dwellings completed in the twelve towns in England and Wales was only 592, and even by the end of 1951 had risen to only 3,126. It was therefore inevitable that the policy should come under scrutiny.

The Town Development Bill*

As we shall see, this policy review took some time to complete and involved considerable argument between ministers, but the basis for one new approach lay to hand: the outline of a Bill to facilitate 'town development' by local authorities. The Minister of Local Government and Planning in the previous Government, Dalton, had submitted a memorandum on this to the Lord President's Committee and the proposals had been agreed. Work on the Bill, and negotiations with local authority associations proceeded, but the Government fell before all this could be completed. In November 1951, just three weeks after becoming Minister of Housing and Local Government, Macmillan submitted virtually the same paper to the Home Affairs Committee and secured their approval to the introduction of a Bill. The matter then passed to the Legislation Committee together with an additional proposal relating to the freehold

---

* LP(51)44, LP(51)17th Meeting, 20 July 1951, HA(51)3, HA(52)7, HA(52)1st Meeting, 18 January 1952, LC(52)2nd Meeting, 22 January 1952 and LC(52)3rd Meeting, 29 January 1952.

disposal of land. The New Towns Act and the Town and Country Planning Act precluded the minister from authorising the disposal of the freehold (or of a lease of more than 99 years) unless there were 'exceptional circumstances'. This restriction on ministerial discretion was 'inconsistent' with the policy of the Government on on the sale of council houses, and there was some indication that industrialists were being deterred from setting up factories in new towns unless they could obtain the freehold of the land on which the factories were to be established. Macmillan therefore wished 'to get rid of it without delay'. Though it was expected that the proposal would 'not be accepted quietly by the Opposition', Macmillan thought that 'both Parliament and the local authorities will realise that this is a removal of an unnecessary restriction which is desirable in the interest of rapid town expansions, and thus completely germane to the Town Development Bill, and that it is reasonable and proper to take the opportunity, by a simple amendment, to remove it at the same time for other planning purposes'. This was agreed by the Home Affairs and Legislation Committees.

An account of the background to the Town Development Bill and of its provisions is given in chapter IX.

Rent Restriction in the New Towns*

A further piece of tidying-up was attempted by Macmillan when he proposed that in the forthcoming Housing Subsidy Bill, provision should be made to exempt from rent restriction houses belonging to new town development corporations (and housing associations and similar non-profit-making bodies). This would bring them into line with local authorities who could spread the higher costs of new houses by raising rents of existing houses. New town development corporations were in all material respects comparable with local authorities but they could not adjust the rents of existing houses.

This proposal was discussed by the Home Affairs Committee in March 1952. Difficulties were foreseen and it was argued that a concession to public bodies might make it more difficult to amend the Acts later to help private landlords: on the other hand, to give public authorities some concession would make the injustice and unwisdom of continuing the present restrictions on private landlords more manifest, and opposition to general amending legislation might diminish. The proposal was dropped for the time being (but enacted by S.33 of the Housing Repairs and Rents Act 1954).

Butler Presses for Economies†

On 20 December 1951, Butler (Chancellor of the Exchequer)

---

* HA(52)34 and HA(52)7th Meeting, 7 March 1952.
† MHLG Files NT 62/5, NT 62/6 and Treasury File SS 385/02.

wrote to Macmillan asking for economies in the new towns, and urging that Congleton, which had been actively pursued by the previous Government, should not proceed. Macmillan replied on 29 January 1952 that the new towns were an essential part of the housing programme and that he was anxious to press on with the eight London towns, which by 1954 should be producing 10,000 houses a year; 'if they don't, the LCC will be striving to fill the gap—which will save neither public money, nor investment: it will just make a nasty mess'.

Butler wrote more fully to Macmillan on 7 April 1952. He stressed that he had no quarrel with the new towns as such, and he accepted Macmillan's view that they were an essential part of the housing programme:

> 'Even if it were open to us, it would be foolish to throw away, or even to jeopardise, all the preparatory work which has been going forward over the last five years, not to mention the capital that has been sunk into them. Our job, as I see it, is to shape this legacy from the late Government into an efficient and economical instrument for achieving the Conservative housing programme.'

For this purpose a critical examination was required, particularly in relation to investment and finance. In terms of investment the fourteen new towns were 'an alarming commitment'. Though the houses had to be built somewhere, locating them in new towns involved increased expenditure on the provision of main services and, in due course, on shops, offices, hospitals, entertainment buildings, public houses and other facilities. These were investments which were rigidly limited elsewhere.

Butler continued that, since new towns were not to become dormitories, factories would have to be built to provide work for both the present and the future occupants of the houses. Were the factories needed in the national interest this would not be a problem, but in fact the production departments could not find enough firms who wished to build factories for 'desirable' purposes who were also willing to go to the new towns. Many of the 'desirable' projects had to be sited alongside existing industry; others were reluctant to go to new towns because of the uncertainty of the labour supply, or for other reasons. In 1951 the Ministry of Housing had had to be given an allocation of £1m for licensing projects in new towns which other departments could not license out of their ordinary programmes. They were now asking for an allocation of £3·5m in 1953. It was politically and administratively difficult to agree to such a scale of investment in non-essential industrial development at a time when increasing restrictions were being put on building for manufacturing industry.

As regards finance, the burden of the new towns on public funds was mounting steadily, and it had proved necessary to put a Bill before the House which raised to £100m the total of advances which could be made to the corporations.* Butler submitted that it could not be assumed that the financial burden which the new towns method imposed—and would continue to impose—on the exchequer was less important than the purely physical burdens on the economy as a whole: 'steel may be short, but so is money'. These were considerations of major importance with long term implications for the future. He continued:

> 'We must not shut our eyes to them in an excess of anxiety to build houses anywhere and at all costs. It seems to me clear that what we need is a thorough examination of new towns policy not only—and not mainly—to make sure that no possibility of economy is being overlooked and that expenditure is being properly controlled, but also to see how the new towns should develop under the present Government. The New Towns Act has been on the Statute Book for some six years and I think that the time has come for a specific examination of the actual achievements to date and the future prospects of one or two of the new towns which have made most progress. We could then see what the capital expenditure has been in the light of progress so far made, what further capital expenditure will be necessary to bring them to a reasonably balanced state in which we could expect to dispose of them to local authorities, and what the prospects of disposal really are.'

Butler said that he had given careful thought to the way in which such a review should be conducted, and he proposed the establishment of a small committee consisting of Macmillan's parliamentary secretary, the parliamentary under-secretary Department of Health for Scotland and the financial secretary, Treasury under the chairmanship of a senior member of the Cabinet. He asked for Macmillan's views on this, but in the meantime, 'we must take no decisions about increasing the number of new towns'. So far as Congleton was concerned he hoped that Macmillan would be able to persuade Manchester 'to do it themselves with such assistance as may be appropriate under the Town Development Bill when it is passed'.

To this Macmillan replied on 9 April 1952, that he was 'glad you feel that we must make [the new towns] succeed and serve our purposes. This I am determined to do'. He was not happy about many features of the new towns, and when his proposals were ready, he would put them before his colleagues. In all this he would be most glad to use any help which Butler or his department could give, but he maintained that it was 'quite wrong' to think that houses built elsewhere than in new towns did not require main services, shops, offices, schools and so forth. These were needed wherever houses

---

* The Bill was passed as the New Towns Act 1952.

were built 'in quantity'. The relative cost as between new towns and large housing estates was 'no doubt a matter for examination, and I have been trying to get some figures'.

In an internal minute of 10 April 1952, Macmillan spelled out his views:

> 'My general point is that the creation of new towns is an exceptional, indeed unique, process and needs to be acknowledged and treated as such within the complex of government policy of which it forms a part. In other words, rules of policy which are right and necessary for the rest of the country may well be in flat contradiction to what is right and necessary in new towns, and the fact that they are not intended to be applied to new towns requires to be promulgated and accepted all round Whitehall (and Millbank). Administration cannot be carried on on a basis of an endless series of interdepartmental battles on individual cases each alleged to be exceptional. I should like to see a proper and intelligible new towns policy substituted for the present 'system' which seems to be no more than a generally inefficient process of wangling and wrangling on the part of officials the more bitter on both sides because as things stand both sides are naturally convinced that they are right —and as things stand, both are.'

This minute reflected not only irritation with the Treasury, but also the difficulties with the Board of Trade ('Millbank') and the production departments on the provision of factories to keep pace with the building of houses, with the Ministry of Works on building licences, and with the Ministry of Labour on starting dates. The field of irritation was, in fact, a wide one and extended to the 'ban' on office building; the troubles of the development corporations with local authorities particularly in providing roads which for traffic reasons ought to be constructed to a standard in excess of the needs of the corporation itself as a developer; and the complexity and delays involved in compulsory purchase order procedures.

The upshot was the setting up of a working party of officials from the Treasury and the ministry. This met frequently during the second part of 1952. Meanwhile on 24 June 1952, Macmillan had stated in answer to a parliamentary question that 'I do not intend to designate any more new towns in the near future . . . I think it is much more important to get on with building the new towns that have been designated than to designate a lot more.'* This reply went some distance to meet the apprehensions of the Treasury in that they were relieved of the prospect of arguing with the ministry about any extension of the existing programme.

The MHLG/Treasury Report†

The report of the working party (which extended to 45 foolscap pages) dealt in some detail with a wide range of issues, from aggregate

---

* HC Debates, Vol 502, Col 2013, 24 June 1952.
† MHLG File NT 62/6.

financial liability to the level of rents, from standards for roads to the capitalisation of interest, and from central control to profitability. Their major conclusion was that

'the economic prospects of the new towns will be a very nice run thing, and that there is no ground whatever for some of the optimistic assumptions all too frequently made. We cannot accept the views of some of the corporations that present deficits can be made good out of future profits. The building of a new town is a large scale, prolonged and extremely hazardous undertaking; and from a strictly financial point of view there is much more probability of a loss than a profit. This probability is enhanced while the provision of shops, factories and offices continue to be closely throttled back in the general economic interest . . . It should be added at once that the prospects of economic loss do not condemn the new towns. They are indispensable. The old pre-war practice of allowing building on the fringes of London and the other great towns has been allowed to the tolerable limit in the immediate post-war emergency while an alternative was being worked out. In the light of the social, economic and strategic considerations brought out in the Barlow report, a halt has to be called to the old practice in these areas.'

No immediate action was taken on this report, but while the Treasury were considering what steps might be taken to get ministers to review the whole programme, Macmillan put up an enthusiastic case to the Home Affairs Committee for a further increase in the borrowing limits from £100m to £200m.* He was, he said, 'dizzy with success'. Over 12,000 houses had been completed in the new towns of Great Britain; a further 9,000 were under construction, and over 18,000 were under contract. Nearly 1½ million square feet of factory space had been completed and an equal amount was being built.

Not surprisingly, there was Treasury objection to this, and it was argued that the heavy prospective demands on the money market for other purposes made the time inopportune for an increase as large as £100m. Moreover, there was concern at the mounting cost of the new towns, not only in respect of advances to the corporations, but also by the departments responsible for providing such facilities as health services and education.

The committee agreed that Macmillan should discuss with the Chancellor the sum to be specified in the Bill, and recorded their view that there was a prima facie case for a review by the ministers concerned of the existing policy of new town development. Later the same day (1 May 1953) Thorneycroft (President of the Board of Trade) wrote to the Chancellor suggesting that ministers should consider where the new towns policy was leading and proposing that the matter be referred to the Economic Affairs Committee (of which Butler was chairman) before it was again considered by the Home

---

* HA(53)40 and HA(53)9th Meeting, 1 May 1953.

Affairs Committee. Butler agreed and wrote to Macmillan on 5 May 1953 that a less expensive way had to be found for achieving the housing objective than the new town method. As an immediate step he proposed the abandonment of Cwmbran, where development had hardly started, and the disposal of Welwyn and Hatfield to the local authorities. On 6 May 1953 Butler and Macmillan agreed that the borrowing powers be increased by £50m. The New Towns Bill, increasing the limit to £150m, had an unopposed passage through Parliament and received royal assent on 31 July 1953.

Butler asks 'Can we afford the New Towns?'*

In May 1953 Butler circulated a memorandum to the Economic Policy Committee (of which he was chairman) setting out his doubts on the new town policy. He welcomed the view expressed by the Home Affairs Committee that 'a prima facie case had been established for a review by the ministers concerned of the existing policy for new towns development'.

He was disturbed by the heavy and increasing burden of the new towns on the budget, particularly 'below the line'. They were financed in the main by repayable advances from the consolidated fund. These advances were estimated to rise to £127m in 1954–55. Thereafter they would continue at a steady rate of about £44m a year for three or four years, making an aggregate of around £277m, after which they would begin to drop. On the latest estimate the potential exchequer commitments (ie the total liability which might eventually have to be met from the consolidated fund resulting from the activities of corporations so far established under the Act), were within the range of £250m to £275m and, by the time this aggregate expenditure had been incurred, repayment of advances to corporations might have amounted to £20m. In the meantime repayment of advances was being financed by further advances from the consolidated fund and the new towns were thus getting further and further into debt.

These were 'large sums of money'. The situation would be quite different if the investment were likely to result in 'I will not say a profit, but at least the prospect of avoiding a loss'. This was not the case. The MHLG/Treasury report had concluded that 'the building of a new town is a large scale, prolonged and extremely hazardous undertaking; and from a strictly financial point of view there is much more probability of a loss than a profit'.

In these circumstances he thought that it was essential to consider the alternatives to the current policy which was simply 'to acquiesce without further examination in policies inherited from our pre-

---

* EA(53)64, HA(53)9th Meeting, 1 May 1953, EA(53)65 and EA(53)16th Meeting, 13 May 1953.

decessors which are already so costly and are only now gathering momentum'. The advances from the consolidated fund were by no means the whole story. Whereas housing subsidy on council houses was shared between the exchequer and the rate fund in the proportion of three to one, in the new towns the exchequer paid the whole amount. Even more important were the outgoings on schools and other services, eg health, which had to keep pace with the houses. In a recent paper, the Minister of Education had calculated that as much as £25m could be saved over five years if, from 1955 onwards, policy was concentrated on redeveloping existing areas of population instead of continuing the present policy of new towns, expanded towns and housing estates:

> 'The essence of the matter, it seems to me, is whether we can in present circumstances afford a vast outlay of money and resources on a redistribution of the population which, however desirable, cannot be regarded as essential to our national survival.'

He did not expect that any uniform, and still less any easy, solution to this problem could be found. The fourteen new towns were at different stages of development and different expedients had to be applied in each individual case. At one end of the scale was Cwmbran where development had only just begun: 'I think we must consider whether it should continue.' At the other end of the scale were Welwyn and Hatfield 'which may well be ripe for immediate transfer on suitable terms to the local authorities concerned'. Others, like Corby and Hemel Hempstead, were closely related to local industries: here the Government should take an interest in, and indeed responsibility for, their development.

> 'I recognise that in some cases it would be uneconomic to call a sudden halt because substantial outlay has already been incurred on the provision of roads, main services and other basic works. But that is not to say that we must accept the new towns policy of the last Government without the most critical examination. In particular we must try to find sources of capital finance other than the consolidated fund and here I have particularly in mind the private developer who may have a substantial role to play in the future as he has done in the past.'

He suggested that the first step was to call for a factual analysis by officials of the individual circumstances of each of the fourteen new towns—an analysis which should bring out the steps which might be taken in each case to lighten the burden on the exchequer and the implications of those steps for housing policy and population planning. 'Pending this review we should hold our hand and limit decisions involving further development to the severest minimum.'

Macmillan's answer was brief and to the point: Butler's ideas 'are not novel, and had, in part at least, occurred to me'. But nothing could be done without legislation—'and of the most controversial character'. He nicely pointed out that since there was already so much legislation which was falling to him to put through 'I have shrunk from asking authority for another major Bill'.* The MHLG/Treasury enquiry had just been completed and 'it would be wiser to give some policy guidance to officials before setting them to work'. The matter might be considered by the Cabinet Committee on Housing Policy. 'Meanwhile, I must warn my colleagues that great questions of policy are involved. They cannot be adequately dealt with by an exchange of notes over the week-end.'

The Economic Policy Committee considered the papers by Butler and Macmillan in May 1953. Macmillan said that any change of policy would involve legislation which would be controversial. He would have preferred a central board to run the new towns on business lines in place of the independent corporations of varying quality which the present legislation required. It would then have been easier to begin the experiment of transferring the new towns to the local authorities as they reached an appropriate stage of development. While it was now hoped to rehouse much of the population within existing cities, to make use of the facilities which existed there, this would not be a complete solution. London could not rehouse more than sixty per cent of the people displaced by redevelopment, and unless the inevitable overflow were directed to the new towns, it would be impossible to prevent it spilling over into new housing estates in the green belts. If it were decided to change the existing policy for new towns this would have to be clearly stated in Parliament.

In the course of a full discussion a wide range of issues was raised: the possible curtailment at Cwmbran where development had only just begun, and which had no impact on the London problem; the difficulty of attracting industry to the new towns; the continued growth of London, and the replacement of factories which had been transferred to the new towns by other factories instead of by houses or offices. Macleod said that if present policies continued he would have to invest an increasing part of the limited resources of the Ministry of Health in the new towns, which might be used to better purpose elsewhere if development in the new towns were curtailed. The Glasgow problem was similar to that in London: 250,000 people should be moved out of the city, and if new towns were not to contribute there must be a large expansion of housing estates. It was suggested that the cost of creating new communities from scratch was more than the nation could afford; but in view of the large amount of preliminary work which had been done in the new towns

---

* He listed the 'comprehensive' Repairs and Housing Bill; a large Bill to amend the Town and Country Planning Act; an Equalisation Grant Bill; and probably another Rating and Valuation Bill.

it might be preferable to slow down other projected new housing schemes rather than curtail the new towns. Butler said his main concern was with the rapid growth of public expenditure and he pressed the need for a review of existing policy for new towns. The committee reached no decision, and it was agreed to resume discussion after Macmillan had submitted a further paper giving his advice on future policy, including the possibility of curtailing Cwmbran.

Macmillan's Policy Review

In October three memoranda—from Macmillan, Thorneycroft and Stuart (Secretary of State for Scotland)—were considered by the Economic Policy Committee.*

Macmillan started his paper with two quotations. One of these was of a character which was to become familiar in later papers: it was a quotation from *The House at Pooh Corner*:

> 'There's no Space. I never saw a more spreading lot of animals in my life, and all in the wrong places.'

The other, impishly, was a quotation from a speech by Boyd-Carpenter (currently financial secretary, Treasury) which he made in support of the 1946 New Towns Bill:

> 'If . . . this problem is not handled at once and vigorously, it will be too late, in this small and overcrowded island, to prevent large tracts of country from being spoiled by the erection of vast, unsuitable, inappropriate, inconvenient and badly-designed dormitory communities.'

The paper was untypically lengthy, and it exhibited contrasting styles: staccato and pungent statements interspersed by longer and more deliberate passages reminiscent of ministerial briefs prepared by civil servants. The beginning of the first main section—on decentralisation policy—is illustrative:

> 'We, like our predecessors, are committed to the policy of decentralisation. It commands wide popular support, including support in all quarters of the House of Commons.
> Our problem now is how best to ensure making a success of the policy. Nevertheless, it will be useful to consider what decentralisation really means; and also what alternatives we have got.
> We presumably agree that a very large number of new houses and flats will continue to be built. Between the wars an average of 210,000 houses were built each year. In the last six years before 1939 over 300,000 houses were built each year, rising to nearly 340,000 in 1938, of which 250,000 were unsubsidised. These figures refer to England and Wales.

---

* The papers were: Macmillan—EA(53)106; Thorneycroft—EA(53)111; Stuart—EA(53)122; these were discussed at EA(53)25th Meeting, 28 October 1953.

We cannot, therefore, envisage less than 200,000 new houses and flats a year
for many years to come (England and Wales), though the precise level must
depend on government policy at the time and on what private enterprise will
do. It is quite possible that the figure of 200,000 is too low, and that the level
may be nearer 250,000; it might be even higher. The need for new houses is
still very great and the stock must be continually renewed. 2¼ million houses
are over 100 years old; a further 1¾ are over 75 years old; a further ¾ are over
65 years old; and there is a terrible slum problem. About 1,300,000 families
have still not got a separate home. But let us take 200,000 new houses a year
as the minimum for England and Wales.

The housing need is greatest in the largest towns. Over half the houses that
will be built, say 120,000 to 130,000 a year, will be built for the benefit of the
people now living in Greater London, Greater Birmingham, Merseyside, the
Manchester group, Tyneside, Leeds, Sheffield, etc. This will happen whether
the houses continue to be built mainly by public authorities, as at present, or
whether private enterprise once again undertakes the greater share. The
main demand comes from the urban population.'

The argument gradually unfolded but, in summary, it continued
with a demonstration of the undesirability (in financial, social and
political terms) of 'great blocks of flats [which] have not an encouraging history either in Glasgow or Vienna'. Some 60,000 to
65,000 homes a year would have to be built outside the existing
built-up areas. For these there were two alternatives: 'to allow
building to flood out into open land, or to continue the policy of
planned decentralisation to new towns and towns capable of being
expanded'. Some of the houses could properly be built close to
existing towns, but to allow all to be so would mean 'throwing over
the Barlow report', abandoning the green belt and adding to the
already intolerable traffic congestion: 'it is not practical politics'.
Planned decentralisation did involve the exchequer in some
expenditure which would normally be borne on the rates (in contribution to provision of basic services, and part of the statutory
housing subsidy normally borne by local authorities), 'but this is all
expenditure which must be borne out of public funds, and this
comparatively small shift from the rates to the exchequer does not
seem too high a price to pay for the policy of decentralisation'. He
continued that there was some truth, 'but not much', in the point
that expenditure on basic services could have been avoided if new
building had been allowed to make maximum use of existing
services rather than been directed to undeveloped areas. The
capacity of existing services would soon have been exhausted, and
in the long run planned concentrations of population were more
economical than an endless process of adding to existing towns. The
Minister of Education had agreed that since the new houses must be
built somewhere outside existing built up areas, it made little
difference to the need for new schools whether they were built on
the fringe or further out.

The most difficult problem was industry. Here there were two major problems. One was whether enough industry could be induced to move out to the new towns, expanded towns and existing local authority housing estates to provide for the scale of decentralisation already undertaken or envisaged. The other was whether even if this were possible it could be done without prejudicing the development areas.

Macmillan's judgement was that there was sufficient industry willing or capable of being persuaded to move out to new towns and similar areas 'to encourage us to go ahead with our plans'. The more difficult problem arose with the threatened competition with the development areas which 'naturally troubles the President of the Board of Trade'. Courting wrath from that quarter, Macmillan continued:

> 'I am prepared to agree that any industry which is willing to move to a development area should go to that area, and should not be offered the alternative of a new or expanded town. But now that licensing is easier there is a good deal of industry which could be persuaded to move out to a new or expanded town, but which could not be led to move to a development area. That is the industry we want to get.
>
> Naturally, if we let it be known that any employer, willing to decentralise his business, but unwilling to go to a development area, will be allowed and indeed encouraged to move to a new or expanded town or an outer housing estate, this freedom may make it more difficult for the Board of Trade to interest an industrialist, thinking of decentralisation, in a development area. But I think we must take the risk. We cannot turn our backs on decentralisation now. Nor can we continue too rigid a control forever.'

He added that decentralisation of office staffs also ought to be encouraged and that 'substantial sections' of government departments might move to the new towns.

At this point—psychologically very apt—he declared that he did not intend to designate any more new towns (or, if he could help it, any further London County Council dormitory estates 'out in the blue'). 'The important thing is to get on as quickly as possible with the new towns—and get them finished.' Thereafter the future lay with expanded towns.

To this point Macmillan's argument had been addressed to the general issue of decentralisation and to the proposal 'that we should agree that the policy must continue; and that that being so we should agree that all necessary services, including roads, schools, shops, community buildings, playing fields, and above all employment must keep in step with housing'.

He then turned to the new towns themselves, and said he felt that the minister should have a freer hand than he had under the 1946 Act to hand over the undertaking to a local authority so soon as there was a local authority capable of carrying it on; and also a greater freedom to merge corporations or reorganise the whole structure of management. But legislation would be required on both points, and as he had introduced so many Bills already and was faced with so many more, he hesitated to act as a 'Parliamentary Oliver Twist'. Nevertheless he examined three possibilities of reducing the cost.

The first possibility was to slow down the pace of development in the new towns. This would be politically unwise since public opinion was strongly behind the idea of new towns, and the criticism generally made was that not enough was being done. It would also be financially unsound, as in the initial stages most of the expenditure on land and services was unremunerative, and most of the profitable development was still to come. The right policy was to get the towns as quickly as possible to the point where there was some return on the investment. Although Cwmbran was the town with the least justification, it was an indication that there was an alternative to further overcrowding of the industrial valleys, and to migration to London. It had been a gesture to Wales, and it could not be abandoned now.

The second possibility was to transfer the new towns to a local authority before completion. For this, legislation would be required, but it was hardly practical politics. It was not sensible to sell at a time when the most profitable development was still to come; and it was doubtful whether the authorities would take on the work at the present stage, even if they were competent to do so.

The third possibility was the best line to take: to transfer some of the cost. He had already told the London housing authorities that when a house in a new town was let to a tenant they had put forward, they should pay the rate contribution for ten years. He was encouraging private enterprise house building, and corporations were authorised to sell houses to owner occupiers. Industrialists were encouraged to build factories, and private enterprise to develop shops and offices. There was a good chance that property companies would be interested in the development of new town centres.

Macmillan concluded that, when it was possible to legislate, provision could be made for handing over the undertaking to the local authority, and to increase the minister's power to make general reforms and alterations in the structure. Until then it would be desirable to shift as much responsibility as possible for building to private enterprise and meanwhile get ahead with building new houses, factories and offices. Finally:

'since we are committed to these new towns we must do our best to see that they are successful . . . they are in my judgement worth the money, both socially and industrially. Maybe we would not have proposed this particular way of building them; but do not let that obscure the fact that they are good developments . . . The best hope of making them pay their way is to see that they are places which will attract prosperity . . . but they will not do so if we starve them of the things which made a town a good place to live in.'

Thorneycroft's Reply to Macmillan's Review

Not to be outdone by Macmillan's literary preface, Thorneycroft started his memorandum with a quotation from the Gospel According to St Luke:

'For which of you, intending to build a tower, sitteth not down first and counteth the cost, whether he have sufficient to finish it?
Lest haply, after he hath laid the foundation, and is not able to finish it, all that behold it begin to mock him, saying, this man began to build, and was not able to finish.'

This may have been good-humoured, but he was deadly serious. 60,000–65,000 homes a year on new sites outside existing congested areas (which was the basic assumption in Macmillan's paper) meant the provision of some 55,000 factory jobs, involving an investment in new factory building of the order of £40m, equivalent to one third of the total annual investment in building for manufacturing industry. It was extremely unlikely that industry would be willing or able to move on this scale. The only hope of doing so would be the offer of substantial inducements to industrialists, and at least equal inducements would have to be offered to those prepared to move to development areas.

It was true that over the previous five years jobs at the average rate of no more than 5,000 a year had been provided, or promised, in the Greater London new towns. This result had been achieved under the most favourable conditions: there was a back-log of building, and the effect of capital investment controls and physical controls over materials made it possible for the planners to offer strong inducements in some areas and effectively to prevent development elsewhere. Now much of the back-log had been overtaken, the remaining controls were 'little effective' to compel removals, and there was noticeably less footloose industry than before. Most applications for industrial development certificates were for extensions to existing premises. More and more industrialists were seeking to expand on the spot and the IDC procedure 'virtually unsupported' was not a sufficiently effective instrument to ensure that industry would move. Industry once established on a site would not readily move unless it was forced or bribed.

The accepted all-party policy had been to give precedence to development areas and unemployment areas for new industry. Thorneycroft stressed that the suggested departure from the existing policy of preferences for the development areas would be such a marked change from existing policy that it would have to be made the subject of a formal public announcement which the Government would have to be prepared to defend. 'Our political opponents would undoubtedly be only too glad to seize on such an announcement as an indication of our desertion of the development and unemployment areas.'

Moreover, the effect of the suggested programme on distribution of industry policy went deeper than its effect on development and unemployment areas. An extension of the policy of building houses in the 'decantation areas' around London and Birmingham beyond the capacity of industry to move out of the congested parts of these areas, would lead to the creation of an industrial vacuum. It would become increasingly difficult, if not impossible, to prevent industry from being drawn in from outside. The tendency would be to encourage the flow of industry towards the naturally attractive areas of the south, south-east, and midlands, and the whole purpose of the Barlow recommendations would be subverted.

Thorneycroft drew three conclusions from his analysis. First, the suggested housing programme in the 'decantation areas' was of such a size that he could see no prospect of its being 'matched with equivalent industry'. It had to be very substantially slowed down if industry and housing were to keep in step.

Secondly, to achieve even partial success in finding the necessary industry for the suggested programme would involve considerable expense by way of compensation etc, and additional amounts would have to be spent in connection with moves to development areas and unemployment areas.

Thirdly, Macmillan's proposals would mean such a radical change in the existing distribution of industry policy towards the development areas that it would be necessary to make a public statement.

The Scottish Statement

Stuart's paper was altogether more sober. The Scottish situation needed no literary introduction. To date, only two new towns were being built in Scotland—East Kilbride (designed to cater for decentralisation from Glasgow), and Glenrothes (which was part of the programme for opening up the extensive new east Fife coalfield).

The general policy issues raised by Macmillan also arose in Scotland, but there were some important differences in detail. In the first place, the Scottish local authorities had from the beginning co-operated fully as partners in the development of the Scottish new towns and had agreed to provide at their own cost the basic services of water, drainage, and highways (other than 'pure development' roads) in the new town areas subject only to some limited and largely recoverable financial aid from the corporations during the early and 'lean' years before the rateable value had built up sufficiently to secure the local authorities an adequate return. The Scottish local authorities had spent or were committed to spend about £5m on these services in the two new towns. The assumption by the Scottish local authorities of these responsibilities had, of course, relieved the development corporations and the Exchequer *pro tanto* of substantial liabilities but had imposed a corresponding strain on local rate-borne resources. Stuart maintained that the local authorities could not do more, and that to ask them to assume total responsibility for the new towns at the present time would be out of the question.

Secondly, as in the case of the English new towns, the full development value of these projects had yet to mature and it was only now that the real sources of revenue to the corporations, namely, rents from commercial and other remunerative premises, were beginning to build up.

Thirdly, the Scottish rating system under which the development corporations as landlords were saddled with substantial rate burdens in the form of owners' rates significantly affected the picture. For instance, in East Kilbride, out of every £1 of rent received by the new town development corporation they paid to the local authority not less than 12s 5d in the form of owners' rates and, in the case of house property, to recover this liability from the tenant would mean driving the rents up to impracticable levels. This was a fundamental and serious problem affecting the whole field of rateable property throughout Scotland which was being considered by a committee under Lord Sorn.*

Finally, the attraction of new industrial enterprise to the Scottish new towns was, of course, essential to their success. East Kilbride enjoyed the advantage of being in the Scottish Development Area and, thanks to the efforts of the President of the Board of Trade and the Minister of Supply, excellent progress had been made. There

---

* Scottish Home Department, *Report of the Scottish Valuation and Rating Committee*, Cmd 9244, 1954. Some startling illustrations of the problem were given in this report: 'Whereas the corporation of an English new town, in order to secure a return of £1 from their property, would require to charge a rent of £1 plus the cost of repairs, insurance and management, in Scotland it was necessary, in order to secure the same net return, to charge a rent of £5, which included £3 for owners' rates. To give some concrete examples, a house which would give an economic return in England at a rent of £122 would require to be let at a rent of £240 in Scotland to produce the same net return.'
'. . . in order to increase the income of the housing account by sums between £4 and £5 the county council require to increase their rents by £11, and the tenants' outlays rise by amounts varying between £17 12s 6d and £18 11s according to the incidence of special district rates. These fantastic results are produced not simply by owners' rates but by the combination in the Scottish system of owners' rates with valuation on the basis of actual rents, so that, as the owner puts up his rent to compensate himself for his rates outlay, rates are payable on rates in an indefinite progression.'

had also been established there the Mechanical Engineering Research Laboratory and other research substations of the Department of Scientific and Industrial Research giving employment to scientific and laboratory staff and skilled craftsmen. As a result, the provision of jobs at East Kilbride was actually running ahead of the provision of houses. At Glenrothes less progress had been made, but there a slower build-up had been expected since the town would grow into full maturity only after the new pits and the large new colliery sinkings were in full production (which would not be for several years). There were some doubts as to whether sufficient industry would be attracted to Glenrothes to provide a balanced employment for the population as it built up, but the problem was not an immediate one.

There was no prospect of stopping the two Scottish new towns or of transferring the total liability to the local authorities. There was, moreover, less likelihood in Scotland of a substantial measure of the liability being assumed by private enterprise. Both schemes were designed to fulfil national purposes which could not, except to a limited extent, be achieved by any local or private interest. East Kilbride, for example, although designed to cater largely for overspill from Glasgow, was also a project which would help to fulfil development area policy on the industrial side, and Glenrothes would draw its new population from widely scattered communities. It was part of an overall plan to develop the national asset represented by the substantial resources of unworked coal in east Fife.

In the Glasgow area, further decentralisation would undoubtedly be necessary. Despite the substantial progress which had been made with new housebuilding, Glasgow was still the most congested city in the United Kingdom. It was unthinkable that an attempt should be made to reproduce the high densities on redevelopment. When the time came for extensive slum clearance and rebuilding it would be possible to re-settle only about thirty per cent of the original populations of the congested districts. It was clear that about 100,000 houses would have to be found outside the present city limits. The problem was one of considerable urgency since all the available housing sites within Glasgow were being developed and there was no more scope for peripheral expansion without encroaching on land which was of the highest agricultural value or minerally unstable or was at such altitudes that it was not suitable for building. The problem of how these houses were to be provided was being examined at present by the local authorities who were to furnish the secretary of state with a report towards the end of the year; 'and I must warn my colleagues that further new town developments may well prove to be the only practicable solution'.

Stuart concluded by saying that he was considering what financial contribution the local authorities themselves could make, and the possibility of contributions from Glasgow towards re-housing costs in East Kilbride and elsewhere was under examination.

Consideration by the Economic Policy Committee

Ministers had an inconclusive discussion on these papers in October 1953.* Few new issues arose, though it was suggested that there might be a possibility of reducing the ultimate size of certain of the new towns. This, it was felt, might yield economies: some of the new towns were substantial and were in danger of creating their own transport difficulties or of becoming dormitories. It was also suggested that Welwyn, Hemel Hempstead and Hatfield might be handed over to the local authorities, but *per contra* it was pointed out that it could be profitable to develop them further before attempting to dispose of them. Finally, Macmillan was challenged on his contention that there was little real difference in cost between building in new and in existing towns.

It was agreed that it would be difficult for Macmillan to contemplate introducing further legislation in the near future to deal with the problem of new towns, but departmental agreement should be reached about the number of jobs which would be required by the rate of expansion envisaged by Macmillan and about the relative costs of houses in the new towns and elsewhere. Consideration should also be given to the possibility of reducing the ultimate size of the new towns and of handing over certain of them in the near future to local authorities. In the light of these further investigations, which the Minister of Housing and Local Government could co-ordinate, a further paper containing more precise proposals might be prepared for submission to the Economic Policy Committee.

Discussions proceeded at the official level to produce the study called for by ministers. Simultaneously, the department were putting forward to the Treasury for their approval a stream of proposals from the development corporations for fresh expenditure, which the Treasury was delaying or holding up. On a complaint from the department about the delay in a particular case, a Treasury official replied on 7 January 1954,† enquiring about progress on the study and continuing:

'The problem is to strike a proper middle course between the lavishness to which all town planners are prone and the cheese-paring economy which might in future years show itself to have been short-sighted.

---

* EA(53)25th Meeting, 28 October 1953.
† MHLG File NT 62/6.

We do not feel that the latter danger is at all a serious one. Indeed, there is no "incentive" for the new towns' corporations to be economical, except, of course, the fear of their chairmen that their reputations may suffer if the corporations show big losses at the end of the day. Even this, however, is not a lucid incentive, for one imagines that the ultimate loss or profit will depend upon the valuation at which the assets are taken over by the successor local authorities—and this is hardly likely to be determined on a very scientific basis.

Moreover, although it is obviously clearly desirable that the new towns should be as good as they can be made with the resources available, it must never be overlooked that they are being paid for by people who live in "old towns", and it is really rather anomalous that the taxpayers generally should have to provide amenities for the residents of the new towns which they do not have in their own towns. There is in fact a real question here of the ultimate standards to be provided for now in the new towns and the extent to which any of this work should be begun before the dwellers in these new towns have a financial stake in the enterprise. With these considerations in mind, what criteria do you recommend should be adopted in deciding what amenities should be planned for in the new towns?'

*Macmillan's Co-ordinated Study**

Macmillan's study was circulated to the Economic Policy Committee in March 1954. It dealt with the number of jobs required to match the housing programmes of the new and expanded towns in England and Wales, the relative costs of 'making the necessary housing provision' in old towns and new towns, the possibility of reducing the ultimate size of the new towns, the effectiveness of decentralisation, and the future ownership and organisation of the new towns.

Macmillan's department and the Board of Trade had agreed that decentralisation on the scale envisaged would entail 9,000–10,000 jobs in the new and expanded towns in 1954, rising to a peak of 13,000–14,000 in 1957, and thereafter falling as the new town housing programme ran down. Macmillan argued that, on experience to date, there was every reason to believe that the new towns could attract industry on this scale. 'They need have no difficulty, unless we make it for them.'

In any event 'the new towns are going concerns which cannot be stopped just like that'. Nor could their development be suddenly or drastically cut back. They would build upwards of 8,000 houses in 1954, and 10,000 in 1955. This could not be halted except by a violent interruption of development already started. Thereafter 'they should do even better' (up to about 11,000 houses in 1957), 'but that would be the peak'.

As to the expanded towns, only one (Bletchley) involving 300 houses a year, had yet started in the south. One (Worsley) had

---

* EA(54)27.

started in Lancashire, but this was so close to the 'parent' Salford that it did not 'involve new industry'. Swindon was about to start, but as employment was already expanding there 'it should not give any difficulty to the Board of Trade'. It had been agreed that the starting dates and pace of development would be related to the industrial prospects at the time, and would be settled in consultation with the Board of Trade.

The Ministry of Housing and Local Government proposed that:

'(a) the present building programmes of the new towns should continue as planned in 1954 and 1955;

(b) thereafter, only if experience shows that the corporations are unable to attract sufficient industry should there be any restriction of their housing programmes below the levels now contemplated;

(c) the position in the new towns should be reviewed, in consultation with the Board of Trade, at the beginning of 1955;

(d) meanwhile industry able and willing to move to a development area should go there and any other industry which needs to move or to expand should be encouraged to go to a new or expanding town— especially industry at present in the London area;

(e) close control should be exercised over the starting dates and pace of the expanded towns programmes in consultation with the Board of Trade.'

Macmillan, in a covering memorandum, noted the fears of the President of the Board of Trade that there was not, and could not be, enough industrial activity 'to feed both the new towns and the development areas'. He himself believed that it was not possible to make any worthwhile forecast of industrial building activity: there were too many unpredictable factors. He continued:

'I should certainly be most unwilling to slow the new towns down on some guess at what industry may or may not be prepared to invest in the years ahead. I agree that the pace of the towns should be conditioned by the industry they can get; but I think that they should be allowed to get what they can—subject only to steering to the development areas projects able and willing to go there. We are already committed to expenditure of over £100m in new towns; and they provide thoroughly efficient conditions for industry. It would really be folly to strangle them now; just as they begin to make their contribution to our economic strength, and just as we begin to see a return on our outlay.'

Macmillan reminded his colleagues that they had always accepted the reasons for new towns. It was only by supporting the new town policy (and following it up with 'town development') that it had been possible to restrain the outward sprawl of Greater London. He understood and sympathised with the anxiety of the President of the Board of Trade over the development areas, but he could not believe that it would be right:

'to tackle that problem by creating another; nor can I believe that to strangle the new towns would in practice make much contribution to the development areas. If we tell industry that its rate of building in the new towns is to be halved, will the other half go to the development areas? It will not. Perhaps a very little of what would otherwise go to a new town might be induced to go to a development area. The rest will either give it up altogether, or will break out in some place of its own choice.'

The expanding towns would go ahead very slowly and only in consultation with the Board of Trade. So far as possible, housing development would be steered to places where industry was already expanding. Town development did not constitute any great problem for the Board of Trade. The estimate that it might, in a few years' time, demand as many as 3,000 to 4,000 jobs a year was very much 'a shot in the dark'.

The second outstanding question was whether, in building the new towns, the Government should be prepared to keep all the necessary development in step: 'roads, schools, shops, community buildings, playing fields, health centres and so forth'. To some extent this involved his colleagues, who might have to sanction any grant-aid expenditure in new towns, 'although they may feel that they have more urgent cases waiting'. It also meant that Macmillan had to authorise the corporations to spend money (eg on community buildings), but the amount of money involved was extremely small in relation to the total being invested and, in any case, the Government was under severe criticism for failing to keep things in step:

> 'I am perfectly sure that if we want the investment to succeed the only way is to make the towns reasonably attractive places to live in. Private capital is prepared to invest in the new towns; in factories, shops, offices and houses. We need this. But we shall not get it on the scale we need unless we make it clear that the Government means to make the new towns succeed.'

RELATIVE COSTS OF HOUSING IN OLD AND NEW TOWNS

Discussions between officials had led to the conclusion that it was not possible to draw up a balance sheet between the cost of developing in new towns and the cost of the suggested alternative solution—concentrated development in high density flats in the slum clearance areas. There were too many factors involved which could not be reduced to financial terms—the social factors, the cost of transport and sites, the loss of agricultural land and the complicated question of services. In strictly financial terms, there was 'probably not much in it', provided that the density of development in slum clearance areas was sufficient to ensure that existing services, transport facilities etc were fully used. But, Macmillan continued:

> 'apart from and in addition to considerations of cost, the solution of the housing problem in any great English city does not lie in the provision of High Barbicans or High Paddingtons. They may be physically and theo-

retically possible but they are completely alien to the habits and tastes of the people who would be expected to live in them. Further, their size would result in inordinate demands in any urban, especially in a metropolitan, area for further open space for school sites, roads, etc. The London local authorities are building to higher and higher densities. In the central areas the London County Council are providing on average for about 140 people to the acre (in some schemes for even more) and this is as high as is reasonable. Some authorities are reluctant to build as densely as this, but the pressures are steadily pushing them up. Even so a large number of Londoners must be housed in new towns; and this is both less costly in terms of house-building and more acceptable to the people concerned than metropolitan skyscrapers.'

REDUCING THE ULTIMATE SIZE OF NEW TOWNS

A policy of reducing the ultimate size of the new towns seemed to have little to commend it, least of all considerations of economy. Working class housing in new towns, by far the greatest single element of expense, 'paid its way' (allowing for the normal subsidies), and this was more than could be said for most municipal housing. Factories, shops and offices made a profit. Schools cost much the same whether they were built, as they otherwise would be, on the fringe of old or in new towns. The one heavy block of expenditure which, from its nature, had to be incurred at the very commencement of a new town, and thus in advance of full need, was on services, roads, water and sewerage. The latter was a particularly formidable item and 'its end conditions its beginning'. The Government were already committed to £26m under this head, which covered the bulk of the expenditure: any significant reduction in the size of the towns would result in a sheer waste of much of this money. Indeed, there were strong economic and policy arguments which supported an increase in the target figure of some of the towns already under development. This would increase the amount of productive expenditure without any corresponding increase in the amount of the unproductive, and in the long run might lead to some saving of expenditure on basic services elsewhere.

EFFECTIVENESS OF DECENTRALISATION

One of the criticisms most frequently made of the new town policy was, Macmillan continued, that as fast as industry and population moved out to the new or expanding towns, more industry and more people poured into London. If a firm vacated industrial premises, any other firm could occupy them: they did not need a certificate from the Board of Trade. The only remedy was for the local planning authority to extinguish the industrial use, paying compensation. This meant buying the building, demolishing it, and using the land for something else such as open space, housing or schools. The authority received a grant from the department for any loss incurred in doing this; and the Town and Country Planning Bill recently introduced provided that this should be 50 per cent.* Previously in the County of London it had been only 20 per cent.

Even with this grant, however, the London County Council would feel able to extinguish only comparatively small and peculiarly ill-sited industrial uses:

> 'The money involved is too big. They would like a grant of 70 per cent to 80 per cent; then they might make a bold attack on the problem. But that would simply transfer the cost to the exchequer; and the money is still too big.'

The new grant arrangements would do something to extinguish some minor and badly sited industrial uses. For the rest, the only practicable way to tackle the problem was the imperfect one of steadily refusing to allow London to expand by refusing permission for industrial expansion, by reducing the stock of effective housing accommodation (slum replacement typically involved a reduction in population); and by steadily increasing the attraction of other towns, including the new and expanding towns. 'In short, a policy of squeeze in London and counter-pull elsewhere.'

The decentralisation policy was not being fully effective, in the sense that 'a flow-in to London' was not forcibly prevented; 'but the flow-in is not as great as the flow-out'. And, as it became more and more evident that conditions in London were not propitious for new industry, 'whereas conditions elsewhere were', the decentralisation policy should become increasingly successful.

FUTURE ORGANISATION OF THE NEW TOWNS

The New Towns Act envisaged that the future of the new towns lay with the local authorities. They were in due course to inherit all or most of the development owned by the corporations: houses, shops, factories and offices. Starting from this point, consideration had been given to the possibility of handing over some of the towns to the local authorities before they were completed. It was felt that this might be practicable in the case of Welwyn, Hemel and Hatfield. It would need legislation; and the opportunity should be taken as soon as practicable of giving the minister wider statutory powers to facilitate the handing over of new town development (and of merging corporations). But even if the power existed, there would be 'a very nice question as to the place and the time', if the exchequer was to get the best or even a fair bargain. It was certainly too soon at present, except perhaps in the case of Welwyn. Moreover, in looking to future policy in relation to new town development, the first question

---

* Town and Country Planning Act 1954.

to consider was 'whether handing over to the local authorities is our policy at all'.

When legislation became possible, he would have to consider more fundamental and far reaching changes in the structure of management and in the machinery of finance. Instead of contemplating transfer to local authorities 'as the sole ultimate heirs', provision might be made, not only for grouping existing corporations, but also for the establishment of a central corporation which would direct the main policy and carry it out through area boards (created from the merger on a geographical basis of existing corporations, for example a Hertfordshire area and an Essex area). Under this scheme, the central board might be not only a central executive supervising development; it might also have vested in it all the property hitherto belonging to individual corporations. It would thus be 'a sort of investment trust' covering the present new towns (and possibly holding further properties outside new town areas which it might be convenient for such a body to manage or to develop). Moreover, it would be worth consideration 'whether or not the trust should not and could not rely on private capital investment' though with a Treasury guarantee in the first instance. In addition to its function as a central executive and as a holding trust, the body would act as 'a disposals board guided by an enlightened self interest (which would be the national interest) and exercising a shrewd discretion as to what it disposed of, when it disposed, and to whom it disposed—local authority, statutory undertaker, private developer, or investor, individual or institution'. Equally it should be free to decide, 'if it thought expedient on investment grounds', to continue to hold certain development and its profit and revenue to the benefit of the exchequer.

Thorneycroft's Case: Industrial Implications*

Macmillan's enthusiasm for the new towns was not shared by the Board of Trade. In their view, to continue the building of new towns at the increased rate forecast for the following three years and, at the same time, to start a programme for expanded towns would have serious repercussions on the development areas. The development areas could not hope to compete with 'attractive offers of modern factories to rent in pleasant surroundings in model towns' which, in addition, had 'the powerful pull of the south-east of England on their side'. Moreover, the new towns would very probably attract industry back from the development areas. (Since the war about a half of the industry moving to these areas had come from London.)

---

* EA(54)44 and EA(54)51.

Between 1945 and 1948 the development areas (with under one-fifth of the population) obtained half of all new factory building, while London obtained five per cent. In 1953, the development areas' share had fallen to less than a fifth, whereas London's share had increased to one-third. Indeed, the London new towns and the London County Council estates alone obtained no less than a quarter of the total for Great Britain—considerably more than the total for the development areas.

The implications of Macmillan's proposals were, therefore, very serious for the regional distribution of industry policy. It was misleading to think of the new towns as simply a restraint on the outward sprawl of Greater London. In regional terms they added to the size of Greater London. They provided for 'orderly development', but they were essentially a part of a growing Greater London. Thorneycroft concluded:

> 'The new towns policy is a large and bold conception and I agree with the minister that there are powerful arguments to support it. But there are also powerful economic, as well as distribution of industry, arguments for going more slowly at the present time than the minister proposes. You can have too much even of a good thing and I cannot accept the arguments that the new towns must spend every penny that they have authority to borrow as swiftly as they can build houses, no matter what the repercussions on our economy and on other parts of the United Kingdom. They are already making rapid progress and they must, of course, continue to grow. I should certainly not be in favour of strangling them. But I suggest that they should not be allowed to grow at the increased rate which the minister proposes, or even at the 1953 rate.'

He further proposed that the expanded towns programme should be held back until the peak of the (reduced) new town programme was past. Industry should continue to be steered to the new towns only where it was essential that it should remain in or near London.

Monckton (Minister of Labour and National Service) added his support to this argument, stressing that, despite efforts to restrain the growth of London and the transfer of large numbers of workers to new towns and out-county estates, the total number of insured workers in Greater London continued to grow—from 4,800,000 in 1948 to 4,950,000 in 1951 and to 5,064,000 in 1953.

The Scottish Situation*

In Scotland there was no conflict between new towns policy and development area policy. Of the two Scottish new towns one (East Kilbride) was in a development area, and the other (Glenrothes) was in an area of expanding coal production. But the Secretary of State, James Stuart, was 'greatly disturbed' by the facts set out in Thorneycroft's paper and strongly underlined the need to continue

---

* EA(54)45.

'to pursue vigorously the policy of counteracting the magnetic attraction of south-east England'. Unemployment in the Scottish development area was more than double the national average, and in some black spots was as high as 7·5 per cent.

Stuart agreed with Macmillan's views on the undesirability of reducing the ultimate size of the new towns and 'the impracticability of redevelopment being a practical alternative to new towns' : such a choice was not open to the over-congested city of Glasgow. Indeed, further new towns would probably be necessary.

Stuart also agreed that, 'in due course' amending legislation would be needed on the structure of management and the machinery of finance. Here he thought that the possibility should be examined of bringing local government more formally into partnership with the development corporations both on management and finance. Experience in Scotland suggested, for instance, that a joint administration partly centrally appointed and partly formally representative of local government would produce a more representative management structure, would strengthen the case for requiring local government to bear a larger share of the finance, and would facilitate the ultimate disposal of the new town undertakings. The question of a greater measure of financial responsibility being assumed by local government was one which he would keep prominently in mind in connection with future proposals for dealing with the Glasgow problem.

*Discussion at the Economic Policy Committee**

The Economic Policy Committee met on 1 April 1954 and discussed these various papers together with one from Butler, listing the questions on which decisions were necessary—such as the size of the future new town programme and the financial arrangements and future organisation of the new towns. Most of these questions were deferred, but the committee agreed that projects capable of going to development areas or coming from outside Greater London should not be considered for new towns, and that the expanded towns programme should be kept under close review by the Ministry of Housing and Local Government, the Board of Trade and the Ministry of Labour.

During the discussion a much wider issue arose. Butler argued that from the point of view of the exchequer, the worst feature of the existing arrangements for the development of new towns was that the organisations responsible for expenditure did not have to find the necessary revenue. But, as Macmillan had pointed out, this issue was closely related to other problems of local government. He had

---

* EA(54)52, EA(54)8th Meeting, 1 April 1954 and CC(54)28th Conclusions, 13 April 1954.

already circulated a memorandum to the Cabinet on a comprehensive scheme for local government reform and was proposing that the wide issues involved should be referred to a new Cabinet committee. If the Cabinet accepted this, the same committee could also review new town policy. This was agreed and, as a result, consideration of new towns moved from the Economic Policy Committee to the newly established committee on local government reform.

Operation Round-Up*

The Committee on Local Government Reform was set up to consider a long and detailed series of proposals put forward by Macmillan in a paper headed *Operation Round-Up* and sub-titled 'a comprehensive scheme for local government'.

The preface to this had Macmillan's typical lightness of touch (the quotation on this occasion was 'a poor thing, but mine own'). For some time, he said, he had been 'worried about the large number of skeletons remaining in my ministerial cupboard'. Some had already been decently disposed of, while others were on their way to the burial ground, 'but many remain'. Important among these were several inter-related problems of the structure and finance of local government, the relationship of these to central government, and overspill to new and expanded towns. The full list was a formidable one and included rating, requisitioned housing, the finance of owner occupation, and housing subsidies:

> 'It may be asked whether these proposals are to be regarded as a "prospectus" or as a "last will and testament". Events must decide.'

This huge field is largely outside the boundaries of the current history, and our focus is solely on the new and expanded towns policy. Macmillan lost no time in presenting to the committee a cogent case for a continuation of the new town programme.

He reiterated that the new towns programme was not a ground nuts scheme. The new towns were doing well and had a good chance of proving 'a real success'. In any case, development had gone too far to be stopped, and the only prudent course to take was 'to press on as fast as practicable'. This was the best way of making a financial success of the venture. The time had arrived when it was necessary to start the building of shops in the town centres: 'here is the most profitable part of the new towns and we must surely cash in on it'.

Financial considerations thus urged a continuation of the new towns programme, but this did not dispose of the contrary argument based on the needs of development areas. Macmillan agreed

---

* C(54)111, LG(54)3, LG(54)4, and LG(54)2nd Meeting, 26 May 1954.

that firms capable of going to the development areas—and which could be induced to do so—should go there. He also agreed that the London new towns should be expected to draw their industry wholly from London. But firms which could not go to the development areas should be encouraged to go to new towns.

'I see no point in cutting back the natural progress of the new towns in the hope that this will induce more firms to go to development areas; while from my point of view—and, I venture to suggest, the Exchequer's—there is great objection to doing so . . . If we cut back the new towns, the industry they might have had will not go, I suggest, to the development areas; most of it will go to the "rest of the Greater London area" and to the "rest of Great Britain". This is really the vital point. We can ruin the new towns, but should we do any good to the development areas in the process? I do not think we would.'

Nevertheless, Macmillan accepted that industrial development had to dictate the pace of development in the new towns, and that it would be right to review their programme at the beginning of 1955 with the other ministers concerned.

Macmillan repeated his previous argument that a reduction in the planned ultimate size of new towns was a false economy and he again rehearsed his arguments. The peak of the foreseeable expenditure on main services from public funds had now been passed. If the new towns were stopped short before reaching their target populations, a proportion of this expenditure would be wasted. But, he added, this was not the main reason for adhering to the original targets—'or indeed to higher ones if more people can be housed within the areas selected and without additions to main services'. More important were the functions which the new towns served. The eight London new towns were being built to house Londoners: if these new towns were cut back, housing would have to be provided elsewhere. Since it was not possible to meet all needs within London, the only other alternative was development in the green belt—which was contrary to the policy of successive governments.

The four provincial new towns were being built to meet special needs: Corby for workers in Stewart and Lloyds; Aycliffe for workers on the trading estate; Peterlee for miners in the eastern Durham coal fields; and Cwmbran for workers in the existing factories between Newport and Pontypool. Macmillan thought it unlikely that it should be suggested that the targets set for any of these should be reduced. They were all comparatively small. Cwmbran was the most doubtful; but he did not think that the only Welsh new town could be cut in size.

In Greater London, the expanded town policy was complementary to the new town policy; in the north-west and the midlands it was alternative. Once again, so Macmillan argued, the position was that housebuilding had to be allowed somewhere: 'if we do not plan for it in convenient places we shall get it in inconvenient ones'. The policy set out to confine development to places where employment could be provided, where it would not add to the difficulties of the transport services, and where it was economical to provide main services such as water and sewerage. However, 'very few' expanded towns would be started in the next two or three years and even then the rate of development would be discussed in advance with the Board of Trade and the Ministry of Labour. The only cost to the exchequer in expanded towns lay in the contribution that had to be made to the development of basic services in order to get the building started in the right place; and possibly in some contribution to the part of housing cost normally borne by the rates (though for the most part this would be met by the local authorities for whose people the houses were built). This was all expenditure which had in any event to be borne on public funds; and the exchequer contribution was a small price to pay 'for getting the development where we want it instead of where we don't'.

On amenities in the new towns Macmillan agreed with the Chancellor that 'a nice balance must be kept'. It was unreasonable to expect that the general taxpayer should provide better amenities for the new towns than were provided in the general run of old towns of similar size and importance. 'I do not think that he should provide as much—nor anything like as much.' Old towns had cinemas, theatres, halls, public houses, recreation grounds, swimming baths, libraries, galleries, museums etc. In planning the new towns the development corporations left room for most of these, but they had no intention of providing them; nor would he agree to their doing so. 'That is for private enterprise, for the local authorities, for voluntary effort.'

All he wanted to do was to provide, in the early days of the towns, 'a few places for meeting and for recreation'. It was essential to make some minimum social provision of this kind while the towns were building up: and he was being pressed to do it by the churches and voluntary organisations.

'If we don't there is nowhere for the young people to go except the streets. £1 million in the next five years for all the towns would be sufficient; and there would, of course, be some counter-balancing revenue as rent would be charged for the use of the halls etc.

What has troubled the Chancellor on this is, I understand, that the development corporations cannot guarantee that community centres, if built, will be self-supporting. This is because they want them to be used by the various voluntary organisations (Boy Scouts, Girl Guides, Mothers' Union etc etc) which cannot pay an economic rent. The corporations will get as much rent as they can; but there may be some small charge which they will themselves have to bear.'

In reply to the suggestion that the standards being adopted in new towns were unnecessarily high, Macmillan pointed out that critics in the architectural press were saying they were too low. In order to save land and money, he had increased the proportion of 'people's houses' and had insisted on high density. But there was danger in this: 'we shall never interest private enterprise in the towns if they look like Poor People's Towns.'

Macmillan argued that the encouragement of private house building in new towns was largely part of the more general problem of 'stimulating private housebuilding anywhere' (and this came within another part of his *Operation Round-Up*).

> 'In the new towns there is the further problem that owner-occupiers have no cause to build in them until they are firmly established. What will encourage them is the development of the towns, and particularly of the town centres with the big shops and so forth. If we can get some offices to the towns (which I am most anxious to do but have until recently been stopped from doing by the ban on office building); if we can push on with the commercial development in the towns; and if we can get private enterprise moving generally on housebuilding—then I do not think that there will be any difficulty in stimulating private housebuilding in the new towns. But there must be offices and shops as well as factories.'

On the possibility of transfer of new towns to local authorities or to a new successor authority, Macmillan said: 'this is a difficult question which needs a great deal of thought'. Either course needed legislation, and this necessarily had to follow the legislation proposed in *Operation Round-Up*: 'so there is no need to reach a decision immediately'. A convenient place would be in any Bill for the reorganisation of local government, since that might well affect the ability of the authorities to take over the new towns, but such a Bill could not be introduced before the autumn of 1955 at the earliest. The case for a successor authority was that in the long run some of the new town undertakings should show a handsome profit which would off-set some—perhaps ultimately all—of the expenditure incurred: 'the Government ought therefore to keep some hold on this'. Macmillan also strongly disliked the idea of towns in which all the land and almost all the houses were owned by the local authorities. But there were also difficulties in the proposal for one large corporation owning most of the new town assets: 'that could be a powerful monopoly'.

Macmillan's paper had been lengthy, discursive, statistical and argumentative. The Financial Secretary (Boyd-Carpenter) followed it with a paper which accepted the substance of the arguments, but translated them into a series of draft conclusions which the Treasury would recommend as a basis for policy in the long run and the short term. Both papers were before the LG Committee on 26 May 1954. The President of the Board of Trade referred to the danger of the accelerating pace of housing development; the Ministers of Health and Education suggested that their ability to finance essential public services such as hospitals and schools might be a determining factor in deciding the future rate of growth; the Minister of Agriculture expressed concern that the LCC were 'scouring the countryside' and considering as suitable sites areas of good agricultural land. But notwithstanding these asides, there was general agreement with the Treasury recommendations and the conclusions of the committee were:

(a) the Government's long term policy should be to continue steadily with a controlled programme for the growth of the new towns;

(b) there should be an annual review by the Treasury and the Ministry of Housing and Local Government in consultation with other departments concerned to fix the rate of house-building and other development of new towns for two clear years ahead; this review should include questions of general policy (eg industrial location) which might affect the growth of new and expanded towns;

(c) the housing programme in each new town should not be allowed to run ahead of the industrial development there;

(d) the programmes for 1954 and 1955 should be approved, provided that they were in conformity with (c);

(e) firms which were capable of going to the development areas and which could be induced to do so, should go there;

(f) London new towns should be expected to draw their industry wholly from Greater London;

(g) the ultimate planning size of the London new towns should not be reduced, but further commitments for the provision of basic main services should not be entered into until it was absolutely necessary to go ahead;

(h) there should be an investigation of the future ultimate size and organisation of the four provincial new towns—Aycliffe, Peterlee, Corby and Cwmbran;

(i) a limited number of community centres should be authorised provided that where the centre was not self-supporting (in the sense that it did not cover its running cost and the capital charges) the corporation was prepared to charge the deficit to the rent account so that no additional charge fell on the exchequer;

(j) the number and standards of public buildings to be provided in the new towns should not be more lavish than those existing in the general run of other towns of comparable size and importance;

(k) private house building should be stimulated;

(l) the 'expanded towns' programme should be limited to ten towns, and should then be reconsidered by ministers; applications for special assistance should be approved only where the industrial prospect was satisfactory and where it seemed that the 'expanded town' would be able to stand on its own feet after a period of special assistance; the selection of towns for 'expansion' and the rate of development should be kept under close review by the Ministry of Housing and Local Government, the Board of Trade and the Ministry of Labour;

(m) consideration of the future constitution of the new towns should be deferred.

And so ended a battle between ministers which had lasted for two and a half years. It had begun with the political distrust by the Conservative Government of the policy of their predecessors. The slackening of economic activity in 1952 resulted in the Treasury line that any restrictions which could be placed on new towns were worth striving for, and that it was better to have town development schemes where the local authority met some of the costs rather than new towns where the whole cost fell on the exchequer, and which created a demand for more than a fair share of total investment. This line was reinforced by the Board of Trade who were apprehensive that the new towns were undermining their distribution of industry policy. The other side of the argument was that of the Ministry of Housing and Local Government (and the Scottish Office) who were committed to a policy of decentralisation, for which the new towns provided a partial solution, and which enjoyed a wide measure of popular support. Although doubtfully obvious at the time, an economic boom was getting under way by the end of 1953, and throughout 1954 most of the new towns were flourishing; any ideas about abandoning them were dropped, and the generally dismal outlook which had previously pertained evaporated. (An enthusiastic article in *The Economist* of 20 November 1954 was entitled *Britain's Boom Towns,* and concluded that 'the new towns seem likely to be solvent and in some cases profitable ventures').

The conclusions of the Committee on Local Government Reform of 26 May 1954 formed the basis of policy for the next few years. They enabled the Treasury and the ministry to approve a number of major development proposals from the development corporations which, to the irritation of the latter, had been held up during the ministerial discussions which had proceeded during the previous two years. In August 1954, the Treasury agreed that there should be a presumption in favour of the provision of a library, fire and police stations, post office, and a range of municipal buildings for the local authority—an understanding which went far to assist the development corporations in their planning for the new town centres.

The annual reviews called for by conclusion (b) of the ministerial meeting on 26 May 1954 were conducted by the Treasury at assistant secretary level with representatives of MHLG, the Board of Trade, the Ministry of Labour and, on occasion, the Scottish Office. Examination was made of the future house building programmes of the new and expanded towns in relation to the expected industrial development and demand, and minor adjustments resulted. By the end of the 1950s, industry in most of the London new towns was no longer lagging behind houses and a reasonably balanced programme was being achieved. The reviews gave opportunity for the ventilation of more general issues, such as the effects of rising costs, profitability, the level of rents, the point at which natural growth could be expected, and the scale of amenities.*

Sandys Takes Over†

On 18 October 1954, Macmillan became Minister of Defence and was succeeded as Minister of Housing and Local Government by Duncan Sandys. During Macmillan's three years of office, the new town policy had been under heavy attack by the Treasury and was regarded with some suspicion by other ministers. Development had been slow and there was relatively little to show in the form of completed buildings and even less of any financial return. Macmillan had kept his critics at bay largely by a policy of delaying his replies to their suggestions for curtailment or retrenchment, but in the meanwhile pressing ahead at the departmental and local levels with work of construction, and bringing many of the new towns to a state where their financial prospects were showing signs of improvement under the influence of the developing economic resurgence.

Sandys was more positively inclined to an expansion of the new towns programme. Early in 1955 he decided to meet the chairmen of the London new towns to explore the possibility of expanding them to take more London overspill. The chairmen, however, pressed 'that the best long-term solution . . . is the establishment of further new towns'. An internal MHLG minute commented:

'What the chairmen overlook is the intense dislike of new towns felt by ministers not directly responsible for them, the acute difficulty of finding another site within range of London, and the impracticability of doing now (especially since the Town Development Act was passed) a number of bold things which were quite feasible in the climate of 1946–50.'

* The results of the reviews were not directly reported to ministers, and by 1961 'they had become a desultory annual discussion which settled nothing about anything'. It was agreed departmentally that they had outlived their purpose and that *ad hoc* discussion was the best way in future of settling any new points as they arose. (MHLG Files 91650/26/55/13–15 and NT 55/1–4.)

† MHLG Files 91650/27/5/3 and 91650/27/11, and Treasury File SS 385/02.

Departmental consideration of the technical problems involved in the expansion of the London new towns followed. It was agreed that Welwyn, Hatfield, Stevenage and Hemel Hempstead should not go above their current population targets 'in view of the scrum in this part of Hertfordshire'. An aggregate increase of 100,000 for the other London new towns was suggested but, allowing for natural increase this implied only an extra 25,000 overspill from London. Sandys minuted:

> 'I would like you to consider whether it might be possible to find a suitable site which could receive a really large number of people, say about 200,000–250,000. A new town of this size ought not to have difficulty in attracting industrialists. It might well contribute towards some decentralisation of office employment in London, and would be a clear demonstration of the Government's intention to grapple with the problem of congestion in London.'

No direct action appears to have followed on this, but correspondence continued with the new town chairmen on the proposed expansions. This frequently became bogged down in argument about natural growth, the point at which building should cease, and when planned immigration should stop. In some cases negotiation with planning and local authorities followed, but the Treasury (at the annual review) were not enthusiastic for further expansions because of the commitments that were involved. In a letter to MHLG they stressed also that 'we shall certainly want to avoid implicating the Treasury in the financing of the second wave (ie of natural growth)'.

In the meantime, a much less contentious proposal came from north of the Border.

Cumbernauld*

In April 1955, Stuart, Secretary of State for Scotland, submitted a proposal to the Economic Policy Committee for the establishment of a new town at Cumbernauld. This was required to meet the urgent housing needs of Glasgow. Despite progress since the war, Glasgow had a housing problem of horrendous proportions. At least 100,000 new houses were required to replace slums, to relieve overcrowding and to meet shortages. Over 40,000 families in the city were still living in rooms, and overcrowding was such that 48,000 families were living at more than two persons per room. (By comparison, the London County Council area—which had four times Glasgow's population—had 13,000 families living at this density.) About 37 per cent of all houses in the city had no separate water closets and 50 per cent had no baths: the corresponding London figures were 2·6 and 14·4 per cent respectively.

---

* EP(55)3 and EP(55)1st Meeting, 28 April 1955.

In slum areas such as Gorbals, congestion was 'almost un-believably high': densities ranged from 400 to 700 persons per acre. Redevelopment on any substantial scale was not possible without a considerable overspill. This was estimated at about 50 per cent of the existing populations even if the cleared sites were rebuilt with high flats.

The city were building at the rate of 5,000 homes a year but could not maintain this programme since all vacant sites would be fully built up by 1957/58. Boundary extensions were ruled out by topography, mineral subsidence and the need for preserving what was left of the very inadequate green belt, the greater part of which consisted of high quality agricultural land.

In short, it was a matter of great urgency to get new developments started outside the city if the housing programme for Glasgow were not to come to a halt.

A joint committee of all the local authorities in the Clyde Valley area had had the problem under review for the previous two years. Though they had not yet been able to work out 'a complete scheme for dealing with the whole of Glasgow's overspill' (which in any case would probably involve a Scottish equivalent to the Town Develop-ment Act), they had recommended as a first step, the development of a new town at Cumbernauld, some thirteen miles north-east of Glasgow. This was supported strongly by Glasgow, by the joint committee and in the House. Preliminary technical investigations carried out by the Department of Health for Scotland showed that the Cumbernauld area could accommodate about 14,000 houses giving an ultimate population of about 50,000 people with some scope for expansion beyond that figure. It would be eighteen months to two years before houses could come 'off the line' at Cumbernauld, and an immediate decision was therefore necessary.

Lengthy negotiations had been carried out with Glasgow in an attempt to persuade them to participate financially and admini-stratively, but 'this has not been easy'. Glasgow maintained that their problem was proportionately four times as great as that of the London County Council and that, as the previous Government agreed to the development of eight new towns to deal with London overspill but only one for Glasgow, there was no good reason why the present Government should not assume full responsibility for a new town at Cumbernauld to cater exclusively for Glasgow. In this Glasgow had considerable support in the House.

Glasgow had eventually agreed to pay the statutory rate fund contribution for houses let to their nominees at Cumbernauld (averaging £14 a house for ten years). A 'clear understanding' had also been reached with the city that the exchequer could not accept the full burden of the expected deficit on the housing account; that the city would be asked to pay a supplementary rate contribution if other local authorities catering for Glasgow's overspill demanded such a payment; and that the total amount of this payment would be settled by the Secretary of State but would not exceed one-third of the deficit on the Cumbernauld project as a whole.

Stuart said that he was clear that the local authorities receiving Glasgow's overspill would require the city to make a very substantial contribution, 'since they will be most reluctant to accept any burden which would impose any substantial charge on their ratepayers'. Moreover, he had explained to the county council (Dunbartonshire) that, insofar as the increase in their rate income from the Cumbernauld development exceeded the loan charges and other annual expenditure on services provided there by the county council they would be expected to contribute from this 'rate income surplus' towards the deficit on the new town undertaking.

Stuart expressed his satisfaction that, 'after many months of difficult negotiation', these arrangements represented 'the best possible bargain to the exchequer'. They would ensure a community of interest between the Government, Glasgow and Dunbartonshire to secure the best possible return from rents and rates on the project and so keep the deficit to the minimum. Furthermore, he was hopeful that by relating the ultimate Cumbernauld settlement to the arrangements for dealing with Glasgow overspill generally, 'we can hope to get the economics of costs and rents for Glasgow housing into better balance'.

Nevertheless, in the discussion Butler stressed the need for a periodic review of the financial situation 'to keep the exchequer's liability to a minimum'. Subject to this, and an 'invitation' to the Secretary of State for Scotland and the President of the Board of Trade to consider further the industrial development of Cumbernauld,* the proposal was approved.

After Glasgow . . . Manchester?†

Among the points raised in the discussion on the Cumbernauld proposal was its likely effect in increasing the pressure for other new towns to assist with the problems of Manchester and possibly Birmingham. Whether or not there was any direct connection, just over one year later, in May 1956, a Cabinet committee was faced with a proposal for a major overspill development by Manchester at Lymm in Cheshire.

In support of this Sandys argued that, despite the objections of the

---

* The point at issue was the rents to be charged for factories in Cumbernauld. Thorneycroft did not wish to provide factories for rehousing Glasgow firms at uneconomic rents, since this would jeopardise his department's efforts in other Scottish development areas.

† HP(56)79, HP(56)80, HP(56)14th Meeting, 2 July 1956; HP(O)56 series; CC(57) 33rd Conclusions, 11 April 1957 and CC(57)47th Conclusions, 26 July 1957.

Minister of Agriculture, the scheme should go ahead for the simple reason that there was no practicable alternative. Manchester had applied, in 1953, for permission to carry out two large scale building schemes at Mobberley and Lymm. After a public inquiry, the application relating to Mobberley was unconditionally rejected. So far as Lymm was concerned, the then minister 'declined to approve', but made it clear that this was not necessarily a final rejection, and that his main reason for refusing the application was that the possibility of finding other suitable building sites on land of lesser agricultural value had not been sufficiently explored.

Since then a number of other suggested sites had been exhaustively investigated. Sandys had himself made a tour of the area and had held a series of meetings with representatives of Manchester and the county councils concerned. As a result he was now satisfied on four points. First, certain of the alternative sites proposed were not practicable, and the potentialities of others as an outlet for Manchester had been over-stated by the county councils concerned. Secondly, the organisation and building resources existed to enable Manchester to undertake a large scheme of comprehensive development (such as was suggested at Lymm) in addition to making full use of all other suitable sites. Thirdly, if such a scheme were to be carried out, there was no practical alternative to the area around Lymm. Finally, unless Manchester's efforts to deal with their vast housing and slum clearance problem were to be seriously retarded, permission had to be given to the proposed development at Lymm.

In addition to these local considerations, there was a wider question of financial policy involved. It was most desirable that, where large scale developments of this kind were necessary, the Government should not be expected to finance them. Manchester were fully prepared to finance the project at Lymm themselves, with the normal grants available under the Town Development Act. On the other hand, Birmingham and the London County Council were strongly pressing for the creation of more new towns financed wholly by the exchequer under the New Towns Act. If the scheme at Lymm materialised, Manchester's example would greatly strengthen the minister's hand in resisting these demands.

Sandys accordingly asked for the agreement of his colleagues that, when Manchester renewed their application for planning permission to build at Lymm he should (subject to any new factors which might emerge at the inquiry) approve the proposal.

Heathcoat Amory (Minister of Agriculture) strongly disagreed—which was the main reason why the matter came before a Cabinet committee. He argued that the Government had repeatedly declared their policy to preserve good agricultural land from development where land of lesser agricultural value could be used. The proposed large scale development at Lymm would mean taking 3,100 acres of the finest agricultural land in the country, 'and our attitude to this will be regarded by agricultural opinion, both inside and outside the House, as the acid test of our sincerity'.

Manchester's housing needs were recognised as being very great in 1954. Nevertheless, the decision taken then, after a full public inquiry, was that development at Lymm could not be permitted unless Manchester could prove a stronger case than that argued on their behalf. Unless it could be clearly demonstrated that the position was now worse than it was then, there was no ground for reversing the decision taken in October 1954.

In fact, he argued, Manchester's housing prospects had improved. Whereas in 1953 Manchester estimated that they had sites available for less than 19,000 houses, there were now sites in prospect for over 40,000 houses. These, if accepted by Manchester and fully developed, would cater for the requirements until 1971. Though it could not be foreseen whether every one of these sites would be fully developed this could not be advanced as a justification for taking 3,100 acres of first class land, 'primarily as an insurance policy'. The county councils had co-operated fully in the search for land for Manchester, and Cheshire was strongly opposed to the development of Lymm. He considered that Manchester had not proved the case for a revision of the 1954 decision. He was therefore strongly opposed to the development.

In arguing against the agricultural case, Sandys pointed out that the sites proposed in nearby towns and areas for a total of 40,000 houses were nearly all unsuitable. But even if these sites were in fact all suitable, the execution of a programme of this scale would depend on a number of smaller local authorities being able (which had to be considered doubtful) and willing (which not all of them were) to build houses at the rate required. These local authorities did not have good records in regard to house building; they could not undertake responsibility for this programme in addition to their own needs and, as their own needs would come first, any deficit would fall on the Manchester programme.

Moreover, it was essential that, in reducing the size of Manchester, industry should be exported as well as people. The Manchester authorities had been brought unwillingly to agree to this, and it had been made clear to them that any government support for their operations would depend upon it. But it would not be possible to induce industries to leave Manchester if the building programme were to be fragmented over the various separate sites which had been mentioned.

The case turned on whether the view was accepted that a greater contribution towards Manchester's problem, in terms of houses built, would be made if permission to build at Lymm were given.

As the scheme would destroy first class agricultural land and Manchester had failed to establish their case when the matter was considered three years earlier, Sandys had approached the further examination of the proposal with some bias against it and had placed the burden of proof entirely on Manchester. Now, after exhaustive consideration, not merely with the Manchester but separately and jointly with the Cheshire, Lancashire and Derbyshire County Councils as well, he was satisfied that the proposed scheme was fully justified.

Heathcoat Amory laid very great emphasis on the high agricultural value of the Lymm site. It was an unusually fertile, high yielding and well equipped area, and the proposed building development would spread over the land of between thirty and forty farms. In his opinion, Manchester had still not proved their case and, in view of the alternative sites which were available, the housing problem of the area was not yet serious enough to justify a commitment at this stage to surrender the best agricultural land to meet it.

'To commandeer the site at Lymm' would be regarded as a test case by the farming industry and by government supporters and, if a decision were taken now in favour of Manchester, the Government would have no prospect of being able to convince public opinion and the interests concerned that they were capable of holding a balance between the needs of housing and of agriculture in regard to the use of land.

The consensus of opinion among ministers was that a decision 'to alienate the site at Lymm to urban building development' would in fact be regarded as a test case by the agricultural industry and interested sections of public opinion, and would arouse great controversy. Nevertheless, there was support for the view that the problem which Manchester faced would not be solved simply by aggregating the possibilities of the development of outlets for the surplus population at a number of separate and unrelated sites. Industries would not in fact follow the population out of Manchester if this course were to be adopted. Proposals to disperse some part of Manchester's surplus population to developments at Crewe, Leyland and Chorley seemed at first sight unrealistic. Moreover, although the proposal regarding the site at Lymm was clearly something of a test case, it was also a relevant point that problems of excess population on the scale on which this problem occurred in Manchester could, in the nature of things, arise only in regard to very few cities.*

---

* It was also submitted that the case illustrated the need for re-examining the density standards of local planning authorities:

'With limited good agricultural land we had adopted a lower density ratio than most countries in the world, and we should not be able to avoid encroaching excessively on land needed for food production unless we adopted the policy of using less ground space and building higher.'

The Lymm proposal raised difficult issues of considerable political importance. This was underlined by Butler who said that the chairmen of both the 1922 Committee and the Agricultural Committee of the Conservative Party had approached him about it. At the same time, however, ministers clearly saw that there were political objections to rejecting Manchester's case. The matter proved difficult to resolve, and it was agreed that further study was required before a decision could be taken.

The first step was the preparation by officials of a factual report on Manchester's housing needs. This was considered by an *ad hoc* ministerial committee where the political difficulties of both solutions were well ventilated but not resolved. The matter then passed to the Cabinet where the now familiar arguments were again repeated. It was finally decided that the case had not been made out for taking a decision in favour of Manchester at the present time. Such a decision would cause great disquiet among government supporters and among the agricultural community. A further public inquiry would weaken the incentive to Manchester to seek any alternative solution, since they would concentrate their efforts on justifying their case before the inquiry. It was in any case premature to re-open an issue which had already been exhaustively examined within the last few years; and a decision to disallow Manchester's application for the time being could be justified on this ground.

Pressure for Lymm continued and although, in April 1957, the Cabinet again rejected the proposal, nonetheless on 26 July 1957 they agreed that there should be an independent inquiry. The inquiry was held by J. R. Willis QC in January 1958, and attracted strong opposition from the local authorities in Cheshire and from agricultural interests. Willis concluded that, while Lymm presented the easiest solution to Manchester's problem, there were other suitable sites available which were open to much less agricultural objection and which were more than sufficient to meet the need. The minister rejected Manchester's application for the Lymm scheme as well as a later request from the city for a government-sponsored new town to meet the city's overspill needs.

Hook New Town*

A rather different story attaches to the proposal by the London County Council to build a new town at Hook in Hampshire—though the outcome was similar.

The story commences early in 1957 when the LCC asked the ministry whether the Government would approve in principle the building of a new town by the council, and whether if a suitable site

---

* MHLG File 20001/25, HA(57)80, HA(57)16th Meeting, 8 July 1957, HA(57)101 and HA(57)20th Meeting, 1 August 1957.

were found the council could expect the appropriate subsidies and grants (then £24 per house per annum for sixty years and a 50 per cent grant towards the cost of main sewerage and water). In support of this, the LCC submitted detailed calculations of their housing problems. These were scrutinised by the technical officers of the ministry and discussed with LCC officials. The ministry agreed that there was certainly a short term need and that, 'unless the pace and scale of TDA action can be dramatically revolutionised, it is difficult to deny that direct action by LCC on a major scheme would provide the quickest and more certain relief'. However, if a large scale scheme were to be developed, 'there is a risk attached in that the justification for it falls within the probable margin of error of the statistical estimate of overspill'.

The ministry were also concerned about longer term implications. There was a danger of a 'hollow core' in London and a very large fall in the population of the county. Some fall below the development plan 1971 target of 3,150,000 seemed inevitable, but the LCC figures implied a fall to between 2·5 and 2·7 millions.

'So great a fall cannot be viewed with equanimity, particularly if it is not accompanied by a commensurate reduction in employment. Sites to house the overspill are only available beyond the green belt, and journeys to work involving even a substantial part of the additional 500,000 moving daily to Inner London would create intolerable congestion, expense and wastage of time.'

Discussions continued on these and related matters (for example, the possibility of minimising overspill by more rapid redevelopment and the likelihood—or otherwise—of the 1957 Rent Bill resulting in a substantial number of additional dwellings being provided by conversions). The LCC became increasingly impatient and, in May 1957, the Leader of the Council wrote to the minister (Brooke) appealing for 'a quick conclusion' to be brought to the statistical arguments:

'I would not for one moment dispute that the case for undertaking a project of this magnitude must be thoroughly well founded. In view of the time which has already been spent on these calculations, however, I am in the most serious anxiety lest theoretical conclusions, which can in the nature of the matter be based only on a vast complexity of hypotheses, each subject to a wide margin of error, should be allowed to obscure the plain facts of existing housing need. The painful evidence of this is brought home every day to all in any way connected with the problem, and, I venture to say, came within your own personal knowledge and experience in the service you have devotedly given to housing work on this council and elsewhere over a long period.

Can I appeal to you to bring to a quick conclusion any necessary consideration of the figures which have been called for and, if there can arise from them any doubt as to the need for our new town, to meet us at an early date to resolve it?

Even the certainty that this need would disappear through the operation of a variety of causes in the next generation, would not relieve us of responsibility to this one. A new town now might, in theory, produce a decline in the future population beyond what has been planned. It could not do so in fact; the magnetic attraction of the metropolis would soon redress the balance. We should have bought a breathing space, an opportunity to undertake planned redevelopments, and the price would not be thrown away, but invested in houses and a decent family life for hundreds of thousands who have no other hope of it.'

The secretary warned Brooke that the long term overspill requirement might well be less than the current housing shortage suggested. Already the population of London County had fallen to 3·25 million (only 100,000 above the 20-year target proposed in the development plan) and it was decreasing by 20,000 a year:

'It is impossible to say with exactitude what the population of the county *ought* ultimately to be. The Abercrombie and development plan targets were, of course, very broad, and assume redevelopment at certain densities which cannot (and should not) be achieved everywhere. On the other hand, nobody knows what effect the Rent Bill may have in increasing the density of population.

We all however agree that there is so much room for opening up London (more traffic space, more open space) that we need not really be afraid of another new town; and that bearing in mind the immediate housing need it would be impossible to tell the LCC that there is no case for their building themselves a new town.

What most bothers us is site. The LCC have said nothing about this officially; they have merely asked for approval "in principle" and assuming that a satisfactory site can be found. The trouble is that there can, in the nature of things, be no wholly satisfactory site. Nowhere in Great Britain (and certainly nowhere within 50 miles of London) can you find three or four thousand acres of land suitable for building, where water and sewerage will present no great difficulty, so situated as to be attractive to industry, with no significant value to agriculture, and unlikely to create strong local opposition.

I think it is true that to proceed by way of expansions would be the better course if it were administratively practicable. It has the advantages that you make full use of existing investment; that you can slow down—or stop—more easily than if you start a new town; and that you don't spoil unspoilt country. But nothing, so far as I can see, can make this method administratively practicable, except in a very small way.

The snag of approving a new town "in principle" is that we shall then have to go on and approve it, somewhere, in practice. But I think we must do it. We should, of course, make it clear that this is subject to a suitable site being found, adding perhaps that that is going to be no easy matter.'

Brooke agreed to send an 'interim reply' but asked 'ought I not to give Home Affairs Committee the opportunity to discuss the question of principle, in view of what is happening about Manchester?' This he did in July. The HA Committee decided to refer the matter to an interdepartmental group of officials who reported in August 1957. They concluded that there was no good reason why the LCC proposal should not be agreed in principle, though it should be made clear that this was subject to a site being found which was satisfactory from agricultural and other points of view. They should be asked to notify MHLG 'as soon as any sites emerged which were prima facie suitable, so that time was not wasted on detailed examination of sites which might be open to objection'. Any proposal would then be considered by the various departments concerned, and the county council 'warned off' if there were likely to be serious and well-founded objections.

In presenting the officials' report to the HA Committee, Brooke said that he was fully satisfied that there was in London no considerable amount of vacant land, or land ripe for development, which the LCC had neglected in putting forward their overspill proposals. The density of development on the land within the county allocated for housing would, overall, exceed 100 persons per acre. This was a relatively high figure, and it was impossible to increase it significantly without jettisoning the standards of schools and open spaces etc. These standards were, even as proposed, likely to be lower in the County of London than in the rest of Greater London. Moreover, the type of accommodation which would be inevitable at higher densities 'would not be what most ordinary families want'.

The examination by officials had not revealed any departmental reason why the LCC should not now be informed that their proposal to build a new town was approved in principle subject to warnings about agricultural land. Brooke noted that such a decision would commit the Government only to the payment of subsidies and grants 'appropriate to such development if a suitable site can be found'. He therefore invited his colleagues to agree 'because, apart from a new town built with government money which I rule out, there is no alternative method of enabling London to proceed with the solving of its unquestionably serious housing problem'. The proposal was agreed in principle but on condition that there would be no special exchequer assistance, that the chosen site was satisfactory from the agricultural and other points of view, and that progress on a scheme would be dependent upon the economic situation at the time.

The LCC proceeded to make an exhaustive search of possible sites including Ringwood, Newtown (near Newbury), Wooton Underwood (near Aylesbury) and Tadley (near Aldermaston). All of these were rejected for one reason or another, the main one being agricultural objection. By early 1958 attention was focused on Hook, and with the knowledge of the ministry but with no commitment on their part, the LCC opened negotiations with the Hampshire County Council. On 13 October 1958 Brooke minuted 'I have no doubt the LCC understand that if they approach Hampshire they must do it on their own and cannot quote us as backing them.' The approach to Hampshire met with a violent reaction from the county council and from local residents, and early in 1959 the clerk of the LCC sought the advice of the permanent secretary as to what steps should be taken next. On the one hand, the ministry had agreed in principle that there was need for a new town but, on the other, the LCC were most unwilling to proceed with a planning application for Hook, 'involving a public inquiry, with the possibility of its being turned down, and having to start all over again'.

However, within the ministry, officials had already 'gone over the ground again and [have] had second thoughts'. The secretary minuted the minister that this was partly because Hampshire had, in effect, told the LCC that there was no point in further discussion: quite apart from the argument that they had 'special difficulties resulting from the spread from the coastal towns which made the county unsuitable for a new town anywhere', they were 'unalterably opposed' to the Hook site.

> 'But our second thoughts are partly also due to the fact that we have never in our hearts been convinced that the LCC have a fool-proof case for a new town. Nor have we ever really liked the Hook site, though hard put to it to find a better. We believe that Hampshire might well make a damning case against it at inquiry.'

On the other hand, if the LCC were willing to finance a new town it was 'very difficult' to oppose them. Yet the long term overspill statistics were 'less and less convincing, as the population of the county falls (which it is doing steadily) and the average age of those that remain rises'. Moreover, town development (in spite of all its difficulties) was beginning to make a significant contribution.

Certainly a new town would enable the LCC to increase the pace and to get, perhaps, 10,000 additional families rehoused in the next five or six years, 'but we have always known that in accepting the case for a new town we have let the immediate needs stifle our doubts about the ultimate wisdom. No great harm would perhaps be done if there were a good site: but there isn't.' The plain fact was that there was no good site for a new town left within range of London, 'accepting that we must keep off good agricultural land'.

> 'All this makes us very uneasy about letting the LCC ride for what may well be a fall at Hook. Should we not warn them that we think they may fail and try to persuade them to soldier on with town expansions, including a major expansion of Newbury (though they may well reject this as being too far)? Of course if they decide to apply for Hook we can't stop them—and I think they may do so, if only because they have resolved to build a new town and no-one can suggest a better site for a genuine new town. But I think we ought to warn them.'

In February 1959, ministers discussed the situation. Brooke said that he was 'sorry for the LCC', but his private feelings were that it was unlikely that an LCC new town would in the end be built, and they ought to be made fully aware of the difficulties that lay in their path. He was doubtful whether, in view of the current rate of migration from the county, a new town would in the long term be justified. It might well be that the relief provided by existing new towns, by town development and by out-county estates would, together with migration, eventually solve the problem.

Discussing the possible locations, Brooke said that the Hook site was unpromising, and Hampshire were apparently irreconcilably opposed to it. Ringwood had at one time been favoured by Hampshire, but it seemed that it was too far away for the LCC, and the Board of Trade were doubtful whether industry would go there. The Tadley site was not altogether promising, because of its distance from the nearest railway, but as the Atomic Energy Authority, the Board of Trade and the Ministry of Agriculture were all prepared to support a new town there, it was worth further consideration. The possible expansion of Thatcham 'might also be looked at again', despite the fact that the LCC did not favour the Newbury area for a new town. This site had the advantage that the LCC would not be committed to a figure—'they would start with (say) 20,000 people, and then take stock before more were sent'.

Brooke said he thought that the secretary should see the LCC, explain the pros and cons of the various possibilities, and tell them that the Government's conclusion was that there was no site which was wholly satisfactory for a new town; and that, therefore, they would be up against difficulties created not by the Government but by the facts of the situation. It was important to make clear that it was not the Government that was putting difficulties in their way. He added, apropos the development of existing new towns, that he favoured the expansion of Bracknell and would be prepared to make this known in the near future if it involved no head-on clash with the National Farmers Union.

Brooke added that he was also concerned with 'the sort of mess' that existed in the Fleet–Aldershot area, and he thought that some agency should be found to clear up such messes and contribute to the rehousing of overspill population in the process. It might well be feasible 'to give a heart' to these areas which they lacked at present. In the particular case of Aldershot, he was unconvinced that the Army could not give up some of the heath-land in the area.

On 13 March 1959 ministry officials met members and officers of the LCC informally and said that while Hook might be as good a site as any, it was opposed by the Hampshire County Council on grounds which might on examination prove to be well founded. The most formidable objection was that it would be bad planning to site a town between Basingstoke and the Farnborough–Aldershot built-up area, 'which would mean an urban sprawl across the whole stretch'. A further objection was that to supply water to Hook would be difficult and costly. While the ministry could not forecast the result of any inquiry, it was possible that the objections to Hook might be so cogent that no government would be able to agree to a new town there. An alternative might be some expansion at Newbury (Berkshire), and the possibility of further development at the new town of Basildon. The representatives of the LCC said a town expansion for London overspill at a place like Newbury would involve the LCC in heavy expenses without the 'credits' which should come from commercial development in a town centre for a new town, but they agreed to give further consideration to the proposals.

The LCC continued with detailed investigation of the Hook site, but made no formal application for planning permission. Private negotiations took place during 1959 between the London and Hampshire County Councils, and, in March 1960, the secretary minuted the minister that a chance was developing 'that we can get this Hook project withdrawn'. The clerk of Hampshire County Council had been to see her. If the LCC would withdraw it, Hampshire was now prepared, with the agreement of the borough and district councils concerned, to propose a major expansion of Basingstoke (50,000 people to be added) and lesser expansions of Andover, Tadley (Aldermaston) and, if the War Office could be made to co-operate, Aldershot. These expansions would be carried out under the Town Development Act by Hampshire and the local council jointly (the LCC being invited to join in if they wished), 'Hampshire putting up most of the money'.

> 'It would be infinitely better planning—and it would be agreed. We should have trouble with Agriculture over Basingstoke and Andover—but they don't like Hook either. This would be a wonderful break for town development and a real chance of doing something for London without a violent row. I think we must make Agriculture accept it.
>
> I wait now to hear the LCC line. Personally I think the Hampshire offer one they ought to jump at; I also think that they have no real choice. If Hampshire came out with this at an inquiry into Hook that scheme would be doomed. The only question is I believe whether the LCC will accept graciously or ungraciously. I hope they would do the former—perhaps with a mutter that they'd have built a lovely town, but we can all bear that.'

The LCC accepted the position. The upshot was thus (in political terms) a satisfactory solution to what had threatened to be a difficult problem for the ministry who, having agreed in principle to a new town, might have found themselves directly responsible for rejecting a carefully considered proposal of the LCC.*

The Hook story illustrates some of the difficulties facing local authorities in attempting to solve the housing problems of the

---

* The extensive studies which were undertaken in connection with the Hook project were published by the LCC in 1961 under the title *The Planning of a New Town*.

conurbations (of which fuller discussion is given in chapter IX). Despite these difficulties, it remained government policy throughout the 'fifties not to embark on further new towns. It was held that town development formed a cheaper and more satisfactory method of securing dispersal. However it became increasingly clear that it was not an effective method. Few agreements were made between exporting and receiving authorities, and fewer still led to significant results. By the end of the 'fifties London, Manchester, Birmingham and Liverpool were reaching the limits of available land for housing. The pressures from these areas for overspill, coupled with concern at revised forecasts of population increase led, at the turn of the decade, to a review of policy and to the second generation of new towns. This is the subject of the following chapter. To complete this account of the 'fifties a short note is given on the proposal for a private enterprise new town.*

ANNEX: A Private Enterprise New Town†

Though there is no evidence in the Cabinet papers that the proposal for a private enterprise new town at Allhallows, Kent, ever came before the Cabinet, a short account of the proposal is appropriate here.

In May 1956 the Dolphin Development and Management Company Ltd (a wholly owned subsidiary of Richard Costain Ltd) submitted a proposal to Kent County Council for planning approval for the development of a balanced community of some 25,000 people in 7,600 dwellings with complete public and social services. The site proposed was at Allhallows on the Isle of Grain, in close proximity to the Kent refinery of British Petroleum which was then being expanded. The primary purpose was to provide accommodation for the workmen at the oil refinery, which then had 1,800 employees, most of whom lived in the Medway towns (1,400 of them travelling more than eleven miles to work daily). The scheme assumed further development of the refinery to a total of 2,900 workers but, to diversify employment and to avoid the social and economic problems inherent in a 'one industry' or 'company' town, forty acres of land were earmarked for an industrial estate, which might cater for a further 3,350 workers. Ancillary employment (shop assistants, school teachers, dustmen etc) was estimated at 6,250, giving a total of 12,500 jobs and a total population of 25,000.

The promoters had extensive experience of new town development: the managing director was W. E. Adams, lately general

---

* This period also saw the decision on the issue of the future ownership of the new towns and the establishment of the Commission for the New Towns. This is dealt with in chapter VI.

† MHLG File 2/2398/40621/20 deals with the early stages; the file dealing with the appeal (2398/40621/103) was destroyed in 1970.

manager of Harlow; another director was Sir Howard Roberts, lately clerk to the LCC; and among the consultants was Sir Frederick Gibberd, the consultant to Harlow. The physical characteristics of the scheme followed the usual pattern, with three separate residential neighbourhoods, each with its primary school, community facilities and local shopping. The central area would cater not only for the local population, but for 7,000 people living in the neighbouring villages, and for a summer weekend influx of 25,000. The town centre would contain sixty shops, offices, a cinema, library, health centre and municipal buildings. The promoters stated that they had already acquired the freehold of the 872 acres required for the scheme, but 'it is acknowledged immediately that the fullest consideration must be given to agricultural interests'.

As the promoters were expecting no grants from the central government or from local authorities, nothing was said about the financial arrangements in the planning application, but it later emerged that the cost was estimated at some £20m, towards which British Petroleum would participate to the extent of £2m.

In July 1956, the county council rejected the application for planning permission, mainly on the ground that it would seriously injure agricultural interests. The promoters appealed to the minister who, after a public inquiry, dismissed the appeal, saying that the site was of the highest agricultural value and ought to be kept in agricultural use unless there were the most compelling reasons for its development. The case presented by the promoters rested essentially on the need to provide accommodation near their work for the refinery workers, and while this was a desirable objective:

'some doubts remain in the minister's mind whether oil workers in the numbers suggested would prefer living in a town of the size and character proposed, rather than in the large urban centre of the Medway towns, where many are already living with their families, and where there are considerable compensating advantages in the form of established urban facilities on a considerable scale to set against the disadvantages of a long daily journey to work. The minister's conclusion is that strong as is the case made for the new town, it does not provide sufficient ground for sacrificing land which is of such outstanding value to agriculture.'*

* As the appeal file has been destroyed, the quotation above from the letter of rejection is taken from the article by Eric Adams in *The Town Planning Review* for October 1957. Letters on MHLG File 2/2398/40621/20 from the Ministry of Labour, Ministry of Fuel and Power and the Board of Trade reveal a lack of enthusiasm for the proposal. The Ministry of Agriculture were wholly opposed to the project.

CHAPTER IV

The New Town Policy Under Review 1960–64

*The Beginnings of a Change in Policy**

MINISTERS frequently find themselves in the position of defending a policy in public which they are seriously questioning in private. So it was with Brooke in early 1960. While publicly rejecting the prospect of further new towns, he was coming to the view, not only that more were necessary, but also that there would be widespread support for them. In March 1960 a MHLG official wrote: 'my minister says that, since the election, Conservative back-benchers have become much more sympathetically disposed to government new towns; what they cannot stand is great developments on this scale carried out by the big municipalities'. Simultaneously, the attitude at the official level in the Treasury was shifting:

> 'From the Treasury's point of view, it may initially seem better to have town development schemes where we only pay a grant to the local authority on some of the costs, rather than to have new town schemes where the whole of the cost falls on the exchequer. I think this is short sighted. It is clear that town development is not working, and it would probably never work. Meantime, its lack of success will be used to argue in favour of a much higher rate of grant than the present 50 per cent. (The amount is discretionary under the terms of the 1952 Act.) We should then be liable to pay out large sums of money without the control which we have in the case of the new towns, and, above all, without any return which the new towns will ultimately bring, and which the present London new towns are already beginning to bring. Town development is only a cheap alternative to new towns if, as now, it doesn't work. My own conclusion is that the Treasury should prefer new towns to town development if there has got to be an intensive effort to deal with overspill, but that our acceptance of new towns might well be in combination with another attempt to get somewhere on the one big outstanding difficulty of sewerage.'

This change in attitude was reflected in discussions and correspondence between the ministry and the Treasury. A ministry minute noted, in relation to the suggestion that 'we would be coming to the Treasury with a proposal to develop Skelmersdale as a new town', that there would be a 'sympathetic' response.

Thus, officials in the ministry, with the approval of Brooke, were sounding their official colleagues in the Treasury (and in the Board

---

* Treasury Files SS 48/186/09 and SS 355/02; and MHLG File 91650/15/2.

of Trade on the industrial implications) on the possibility of extending the new towns programme, and finding them generally receptive.
But before a change of policy could be adopted, the approval of
ministers collectively was needed, and Brooke took the opportunity
of raising the matter with the Cabinet in the course of a comprehensive paper on housing policy. He started by stressing that no new
towns had been started by the present Government for the relief of
overcrowded and congested towns. Further overspill building had
relied on local authority action, largely in the form of town development schemes based on agreement between the exporting and
receiving authorities. For a number of reasons (planning, financial,
administrative and political) progress had been slow. The London
County Council had made efforts to promote schemes and had had
some success, but elsewhere little had been achieved. However, a
number of provincial counties had received 'one or two sharp shocks
recently in the shape of threats by the exporting authorities to break
out for themselves' (Birmingham's demand for 2,500 acres in
Wythall, for example) and Brooke believed that there would now be
better progress in some of the difficult areas. Manchester seemed
likely to reach agreement on building 'what will virtually be a new
town' at Westhoughton. He was trying to achieve agreement between
Birmingham and the surrounding counties on two or three substantial schemes of town development. He was also intending to try
to persuade Liverpool to accept the policy of decentralisation, in
which Lancashire had always been prepared to co-operate. If he
could 'slightly improve the rate of government assistance for overspill, and be prepared when there is a strong case to start another
government new town, it would provide a fresh stimulus at a critical
moment'. Indeed there was prospect, within the next year, of
reaching agreement on solutions for all the main overspill problems
'which have caused so much trouble and heartburning since the
war'.

'We should be prepared, if the need is proved, to initiate the building of one
or two more new towns. I have mentioned the efforts I am making to improve
the at present almost non-existent rate of decentralisation from Birmingham
and Liverpool. If it proves, as it may, that for either or both action on a new
town scale is part of the solution, I am certain that we ought to be willing to
build those towns ourselves. In recent years we have taken the line that
if Birmingham or Liverpool or any other powerful authority need a new
town to relieve their congestion they should build it themselves; but it would
be very difficult now for themselves to raise the necessary capital quite apart
from which there is no doubt that building by a government agency is very
much more acceptable to the people in the county concerned than building
by one of these great municipalities. I should of course seek to agree any
specific proposal for the siting of a new town, or of any town expansion with
those of my colleagues principally concerned.'

New Towns for Liverpool and Birmingham*

Though it seems that there was no discussion on this at the full Cabinet meeting in June 1960, the issue was taken up by the Home Affairs Committee. Following further discussion with the local authorities concerned, Brooke had concluded that the solution to the overspill problem was to be found in a combination of town expansion and new town schemes. Attempts had been made to persuade Liverpool and Birmingham that, if they needed overspill schemes on a new town scale, they should provide them themselves, but neither Liverpool nor Birmingham had been willing to do so, 'and it has never been possible to explain convincingly why they should in view of what the Government is doing elsewhere; and in any event, if the job has to be done, I have not the slightest doubt it is better done by a new town corporation than by any local council'.

Liverpool had very little building land left inside the city, and 84,000 slums remained to be cleared. Despite rebuilding to high densities, only 50 per cent of the original population could be rehoused on the site. Three or four years' supply of housing land remained just outside the city boundary, but further expansion should be halted by a green belt to protect high quality agricultural land and prevent coalescence of urban areas. The three town expansion schemes at Ellesmere Port, Runcorn and Widnes were limited in size. Liverpool's need could be met only by an additional 'really large scheme'. There was only one suitable site—at Skelmersdale. This site was mainly in the Skelmersdale Urban District, though it overlapped the areas of three other district councils. All were 'small and weak', and it was clear that, even with help from Liverpool and Lancashire, a scheme under the Town Development Act was not viable. If development were to proceed on a scale and at a rate commensurate with Liverpool's housing needs, 'the only possible agency is a new town corporation'.

Skelmersdale would, of course, need industrial development. The expansion of the motor car industry on Merseyside would be likely to bring further industry in its wake, while Liverpool itself was bound to displace some industry in the course of redevelopment. Brooke hoped that the President of the Board of Trade would allow industry to move to Skelmersdale, though he accepted the principle that for industry moving from other parts of the country 'he must first be satisfied that it could not reasonably go to areas of high unemployment'. Brooke envisaged that Skelmersdale would eventually grow to a population of up to 80,000, taking overspill from Bootle as well as from Liverpool.

Birmingham was in a similar position with regard to housing land,

---

* HA(60)121 and HA(60)18th Meeting, 29 July 1960.

green belt policy and slum clearance. Brooke had recently rejected the city's proposals for building at Wythall in potential green belt land, and was committed to ensure that some other way was found of meeting 'the universally admitted need'. Small scale town expansion schemes were under way, but he hoped the surrounding county councils would take the lead in seeking agreement on two or three substantial schemes, with Birmingham making a more generous contribution than in the past. However, these developments alone would be inadequate and, if the Government were to embark on a new town (the case for which could not be disputed, as eight were being built for London), it would inspire the local authorities to do their part.

After much study, Swynnerton (Staffordshire) had been selected as the most suitable site for a large scheme. It had good communications and services, and the disused royal ordnance factory site would be very suitable for an industrial estate of some five to six hundred acres. However, it would be impossible to avoid taking for housing up to 5,000 acres of farmland, much of which was of high quality. The Minister of Agriculture had expressed a wish for Brooke to consider an alternative site at Dawley in Shropshire. Here much of the land was badly spoiled by old mineral workings and other scattered development, and the farmland was of relatively low quality. But the reclaiming of the derelict land and the removal of spoil heaps might prove 'altogether too expensive'. A detailed survey would be necessary before it could be determined whether a new town on the site was practicable. All this would delay an effective start at Dawley for two or three years longer than at Swynnerton— even if Dawley proved feasible.

In any case, the scale of the overspill problem in Birmingham and the Black Country was such (well over 150,000 people) that if Dawley proved to be suitable it would be needed in addition to Swynnerton and to such town expansion schemes as were likely to go ahead. Brooke therefore suggested that a scheme of 'moderate' size (say 50,000–60,000 ultimate population) should be started at Swynnerton and, at the same time, a detailed survey should be carried out at Dawley.

Brooke noted that the new town would be dependent for employment on such industry as was 'tied to the midlands' and which could not be expected to go to areas of high unemployment. Recent experience suggested that there would be sufficient, 'though progress may be slower than from the overspill point of view I would wish'.

Finally, Brooke urged that a decision should be taken quickly on both the Liverpool and the Birmingham proposals—partly to relieve uncertainty about the future and partly in order that slum clearance would not be seriously held up in the two cities in a few years' time.

Ministers accepted in principle the need for building further new towns in England and Wales 'and possibly also in Scotland'. It was agreed that this would be preferable to the development of schemes of similar magnitude by local authorities themselves, partly on general political grounds, and partly because it would be possible to ensure that the new town corporations set aside land for development by private enterprise. But they felt that the implications, and therefore the method of presentation, of this decision were important: 'there might be some advantage in presenting the operation as the end of a phase in housing policy, marking the final stage of the Government's campaign of slum clearance'.

On the specific proposals, the new town at Skelmersdale was acceptable if areas of good agricultural land were avoided as far as possible, if the local authorities undertook greater financial responsibilities, and if it were realised that the new town could not rank as high as areas of high unemployment for the purpose of industrial development certificates. Swynnerton presented very much more difficulty. The industrial development intended for the royal ordnance factory site would require some houses in any case, but to take 5,000 acres of good farmland would arouse strong criticism locally and from the Government's supporters. Development would be slowed by labour shortages in the Birmingham area, and its distance from Birmingham 'made it unattractive from the point of view of the distribution of industry'.

Reclamation of the Dawley site, on the other hand, could be presented as an 'imaginative project' which would do minimal damage to agriculture. This would go far to justify the additional building costs there. However, the elaborate survey required would further delay commencement, which could mean a slowing down of the Birmingham slum clearance programme at a politically sensitive time. If the survey were undertaken, it would be necessary to satisfy local pressures by saying that development at Swynnerton or elsewhere was not ruled out. But the Government should not be committed at that stage to more than one new town for overspill from Birmingham and the Black Country.

The new town at Skelmersdale was approved in principle, and Dawley was favoured in preference to Swynnerton. The Dawley area was to be surveyed, Swynnerton was to be considered further and political soundings taken, and the local authorities concerned were to be informed that the possibility of providing a new town elsewhere was not ruled out.

The Ministerial Committee on Birmingham Housing*
Pressure from Birmingham and difficulties over both Dawley and

* BH(61) series; C(61)121 and CC(61)46th Conclusions, 1 August 1961.

Swynnerton, however, led to the establishment of a ministerial committee in February 1961 'to consider the principles on which sites should be selected for new building to meet the future housing needs of Birmingham and other congested towns in the west midlands; and in the light of those principles, what particular areas for development should be suggested to the local authorities concerned'.

The committee met over a period of five months and finally agreed that Birmingham should be given permission to build on 600 acres of land at Wythall, that the local authorities concerned should be urged 'to proceed as rapidly as possible' at Redditch, Worcester and Daventry, and that a new town should be built at Dawley.

There was little dispute on the severity of the Birmingham housing problem. In the following twenty years, at least 500,000 houses would be required in the west midlands. Even with 'various space-saving expedients', 350,000 houses would have to be provided outside the remaining built-up area, using 60,000 acres of virgin land. 50,000 of these houses would have to be provided by public authorities. Birmingham presented an immediate problem. The city had at least 43,000 slum houses which would take forty years to clear. Meanwhile, obsolescence would add to the total. In three or four years' time, all the undeveloped sites of more than two acres in the city would have been used, and building activity would come to a halt.

There were three alternatives: to increase the density of development within Birmingham; to build in the green belt; or to build beyond the green belt.

The first alternative was quickly rejected. Redevelopment was already taking place at high densities and, though these 'had to be tolerated' in the inner areas of the city, it would be publicly unacceptable to attempt intensive development on suburban sites. It would be 'unrealistic' to expect local authorities to raise densities to house 'strangers' from Birmingham and, at the same time, increase the pressure on existing facilities in low density residential areas.

The second alternative (building in the green belt) appeared to offer the easiest solution, but it would precipitate 'a tremendous political storm'. The built-up area of Birmingham and adjoining towns was 'already too large', and Brooke could see no scope for adjusting the green belt boundaries, except perhaps at Wythall where he had previously refused Birmingham permission to build. Due to the urgency of the situation, it might be necessary to concede some 1,000 acres there although even this would be strongly opposed. This, however, would be totally at variance with numerous government pledges, with the policy announced on the Wythall decision, with the inspector's recommendations on the green belt boundary enquiries and with a host of other planning decisions.

Brooke therefore concluded that building beyond the green belt was the only practicable solution. It would be necessary to have an initial programme of two new towns (each with a population of 50,000–60,000) and two town expansions (each of 15,000–20,000). He had already announced Dawley as a possible new town site, and had Swynnerton in mind for the other. They would be the key to the solution, and could have houses ready more quickly than was possible under town expansion procedure.

Brooke gave the assurance that avoidance of good agricultural land was a main consideration in choosing a new town site, but some loss had to be faced to house an increasing population and improve living conditions. However, due to the large investment of exchequer funds, the site had, above all, to be one where a new town would prosper. In town expansion, the attitude of the receiving authority was the decisive factor, although the minister could use various powers of persuasion.

New and expanded towns 'must provide work as well as homes for the people who move there', and Brooke expected firms to move from the conurbation due to lack of room for expansion and displacement by redevelopment. This could be encouraged by the planning authorities and the Board of Trade. Only about one-fifth of the extra manufacturing jobs which would develop in the west midlands in the following twenty years would be needed for new towns and town expansions. The proposals would not damage the development districts which had to have priority, and he did not believe industry and labour from outside would be attracted to the proposed new areas of development.

The Board of Trade were less optimistic: they agreed that it was important that existing industry should move out, 'in theory matching the employment needs of the overspill schemes', but many firms in the Birmingham area were small, and 'agglomeration economies' were such that they could not afford to move far. Some firms would be able to expand on their playing fields, for example, and denial of an industrial development certificate for an extension would not cause them to move their existing factory. It was likely that industry would not move on a sufficient scale. As a result, new towns would have surplus workers, and the Board of Trade would be expected to steer the expansion schemes of existing firms to them. The development districts relied on the expansion projects of firms in the midlands and the south for their supply of new industry, and new towns near Birmingham would provide a strong alternative attraction. Overall they thought that the midlands would gain industry: 'a bad situation in an area of labour shortage'. They therefore proposed dormitory towns just beyond the green belt as the solution to Birmingham's problem, since workers could remain in their jobs, and no question of finding industry would arise.

Brooke raised strong objection to attempting to solve the problem by building dormitory settlements beyond the green belt. Since the war, successive governments had adopted the principle that publicly sponsored schemes for transferring overspill population should provide employment as well as houses in the reception area. Reversal of this policy in the west midlands would be regarded as 'putting the clock back a generation'. In addition to their effect on journey to work and the transport system, such estates had serious social disadvantages, confirmed by social surveys on the London 'out-county' estates. Building on the scale required *in* the green belt (the only practicable place for dormitory settlements) would mean effective abandonment of the green belt policy, and would set a precedent for private development.

There was much debate on this issue, and there was particular concern about the competition between new towns, existing overspill reception areas and unemployment areas for branch factories. Although existing overspill reception areas were small, each claimed new industry which had to be secured before the population moved. More were proposed for Manchester and London. Skelmersdale would require industry from the midlands or the south, and additional industry was needed for the London new towns to meet the youth employment problem. Glasgow was to have another new town whose industrial progress might be adversely affected by a contemporaneous new town in the midlands. It was recognised that town planners wished to get balanced communities of residential and industrial development, but 'however desirable, we can only afford social policies which industrial activity can support'.

From this discussion emerged the compromise proposal to build one new town 'as near Birmingham as possible . . . meaning that only a small number of additional jobs would need to be provided'. Accordingly a search was conducted for new town sites 'sufficiently close to Birmingham to allow movement of population and industry without social or economic disruption, but sufficiently far from development districts to avoid competing with them'. The tests applied were: good communications; distance from other large urban areas; cost of water and sewerage provision; freedom from flood risk; suitable topography; avoidance of good agricultural land, land used for or affected by mineral workings, green belt land, land of outstanding natural beauty and Forestry Commission or National Trust land. The prime essential was a site where a new town could thrive. It might have to include a small existing town, but this should not have more than 20,000 people, 'to avoid the situation

171

where a development corporation and an existing sizeable local authority would be at loggerheads'.

A field reconnaissance identified twenty-four potential sites, but after more detailed study these were narrowed down to five: Dawley, Swynnerton, Alcester, Ombersley and Penkridge. All but Dawley were on good agricultural land, and the last two had other disadvantages.

Development at Dawley would be more expensive than at Swynnerton since the land would cost more to acquire (being more developed) and there was the question of treating the spoil heaps whose low load-bearing capacity and subsidence risks would make structural precautions necessary, and raise sewerage costs above the average. In addition, transport facilities were inferior to Swynnerton. Large scale quarrying of fireclay would have to continue along one side of the site for thirty to forty years. However, an unsightly area would be rehabilitated, and the extra cost was not great in relation to the total cost of a town. Birmingham's city architect was to make a special study of the site with specialist assistance, but this would take a year and a decision was urgently required.

Swynnerton could be started and developed quickly. The planning authority could be relied on to prevent it coalescing with Stoke and Stafford which were 'rather close'. Brooke promised that there would be consultation with the Ministry of Agriculture on the problem of agricultural land, and that housing densities would be one-third greater than in the London new towns. He requested permission to proceed with the preliminary stages of a new town there, 'unless anyone could suggest anything better', making it clear that the Government were not irrevocably committed to the proposal. He hinted that the royal ordnance factory site would be used for industry anyway, attracting new population which would be housed more haphazardly in the absence of a new town.

A similar search for town expansion sites had identified several possible towns. In Daventry and Droitwich the county and borough councils both welcomed expansion, but the motives of Burton-on-Trent and Worcester were questioned since they only offered to take overspill when threatened with loss of their county borough status by the Local Government Commission. At Droitwich the local authorities were being encouraged to proceed with a scheme and there were good prospects for the expansion of Daventry.

Brooke's proposal for a new town at Swynnerton was hotly debated, and it was argued that it would compete both with the development districts and with Skelmersdale. It was too far from the conurbation for small firms and too close to Stoke and Newcastle-under-Lyme. It would attract industries with higher wage rates than those currently paid by the National Coal Board and other employers in the Potteries, at whose expense the new industries would be manned. Objections to Dawley were not as comprehensive, but it, too, would compete with the development districts and would not attract small firms.

As discussion proceeded, increasing attention was given to the possibility of a major expansion of Redditch. The Board of Trade favoured the site (since it was within commuting distance of Birmingham); there were no agricultural objections; and the council were in favour of development. Brooke thought that the area was suitable for 'a certain amount' of expansion but objected to a new town on the grounds that it would be a satellite to Birmingham: 'a discredited type of development which it would be quite wrong for the Government deliberately to create'. It would have no life of its own. It was too close to Birmingham for shops of the central area type and would thus lose the high rents vital to a new town's economic success. Although Swynnerton was the same distance from Stoke (population 270,000) the pull would be much weaker than that exercised by Birmingham (population 1,100,000) on Redditch. The resultant new town at Redditch would amount to an extension of the conurbation, 'contrary to national policy'. The existing nucleus was so large that the proper agency for expansion was the local authority who were now willing to expand.

However, it was clear that whatever provision could be made by way of town expansion schemes, there was still a requirement for a new town. In view of the objections to Swynnerton, it was agreed 'on balance' to proceed with Dawley.

The final outcome was approval to dormitory development by Birmingham on 600 acres at Wythall,* the encouragement of town expansion schemes at Redditch, Worcester and Daventry, and—'in principle'—a new town at Dawley.

Dawley New Town†

The promised survey of the Dawley site was carried out by Sheppard Fidler (the city architect of Birmingham) with the assistance of mining and other experts. The conclusions of this survey, together with a general review of the overspill problem in the west midlands, were presented to ministers in May 1962 by Hill (the new housing minister).

The survey showed that it would be possible to build 'a very satisfactory town' at Dawley with an ultimate population of between 80,000 and 90,000 (of which 50,000 would come from Birmingham). The area, which was only thirty miles west of Birmingham, would be

---

* Due to 'strenuous local opposition and the terms of the inspector's report of the public inquiry' the Wythall proposal was later rejected (C(62)44).

† HA(62)52 and HA(62)9th Meeting, 25 May 1962.

very attractive to industry if road communications were improved. The Minister of Transport was prepared to arrange this if the proposal for a new town were approved.

The cost of development at Dawley, however, would be high because so much of the land was covered by old pit heaps and shafts. An extra £2m (above normal costs) would be incurred on water, sewerage and levelling. This was probably a conservative figure; and there would be other costs which were difficult to estimate such as protection against subsidence. In all, a total additional cost of about £4m might have to be envisaged. In relation to the total cost of the new town (of the order of £70m to £80m) these additional costs were 'not large'; and, Hill added, 'since building here would mean clearing up a wide tract of dereliction, and making use of some otherwise useless land in a region where pressure on land is acute, I think it can be regarded as a worthwhile investment'. An additional factor of importance was that Shropshire County Council were in favour of the new town.

As with all new towns, heavy expenditure would have to be incurred on land acquisition and expansion of main services before revenue-earning development could make much progress, and thus deficits were inevitable in the early years. In Dawley the deficits would be bigger and would take longer to wipe off than in towns built on easier sites. However, the existing new towns in England and Wales were now beginning to make a revenue surplus overall, and this would steadily increase:

> 'So looking at the whole new town account we can expect profits to set against the early deficits on new ventures. In the long run Dawley too should be a profitable development, though the run will be longer than if we could use more level, unspoiled land.'

Hill's conclusion was that 'we should certainly go ahead with a new town at Dawley'. Such a decision would be warmly welcomed both in Birmingham and in the midlands generally. Ministers agreed.

A Second New Town for the West Midlands?

Dawley could not, by itself, meet all the needs of the west midlands. Hill had rejected Birmingham's application to build in the green belt at Wythall because of 'the bitterness of the local opposition', the fact that 'the inspector clearly thought that the land should be kept open if possible', and the immediate alternative provided for Birmingham at Castle Bromwich (where a substantial area of land had become available). Even so, the refusal of the Wythall application would place Birmingham in great difficulty in the near future. This difficulty now appeared greater than had been thought earlier following the completion of a detailed survey of housing needs and land capacity in the region. It was 'now more than ever clear that we are heading for real trouble in the west midlands'.

Hill's department had been having discussions with the city and the adjoining counties in an effort to obtain agreement on a programme which would be adequate for Birmingham's needs. Birmingham had been pressed to accept responsibility for one or two major town development schemes. Some progress had been made:

> 'For the first time Birmingham showed willingness to put some of its own resources into the development of small towns beyond the green belt to which industry and people could move from the city; and the counties, having won on Wythall, were anxious to co-operate. But all were firm that the Government ought to do more to help, and it is plain that their willingness to work together on redistribution is dependent on their being satisfied that the Government is doing its share.'

It was argued that the Government ought to be prepared to build at least two new towns in the midlands. Hill thought that, in relation to the size of the problem, this was reasonable:

> 'and I believe that if I can show willingness it may transform relations with the city and mean that they will, at least, take an active part in pushing decentralisation. Then we could, at last, show that we meant business and perhaps produce a programme over several years ahead which would demonstrate that we were tackling this most difficult housing problem with real determination.'

The only site which the authorities had so far been able to suggest for a new town other than Dawley was Swynnerton, which the Government had rejected earlier. But, with the existence there of the old royal ordnance factory, Staffordshire County Council believed that development was ultimately inevitable, and that it would be best carried out as a new town 'provided that it is not allowed to become very large'.

Hill did not ask for an immediate decision on Swynnerton: rather was he giving a warning that it might become a live issue again. In the meantime he urged that Dawley should be approved. A further new town, whether at Swynnerton or elsewhere, would need careful consideration 'when we have seen the strength of Birmingham's case'.*

The Fourth Scottish New Town: Livingston†

While the Birmingham situation was under review, the Secretary

---

* Swynnerton was again considered in July 1962 when the Secretary of State for War expressed a wish to dispose of the site for industrial development, while the President of the Board of Trade objected on the grounds that it conflicted with the distribution of industry policy. The matter was deferred pending a decision on a second new town for the midlands. In January 1963 it was agreed that the second new town should be Redditch: see p. 192 *et seq* below.

† HA(61)64, HA(61)10th Meeting, 16 June 1961, SEPD File NT 4/DES/5, and Treasury File 2AT 335/01.

of State for Scotland, Maclay, put forward proposals for an additional new town for Glasgow. Though progress was being made, both with the redevelopment of the city and with overspill (particularly to East Kilbride and Cumbernauld), it was clear that a gap would develop from about 1965 between overspill needs and overspill provision. The gap would amount to over 1,000 houses a year, rising to a higher level as the existing new towns reached their full capacity. In total, the excess demand would 'certainly suffice to populate a further new town of at least 50,000 inhabitants'.

Since a project of new town proportions took four to five years to achieve 'peak performance', Maclay had reached the conclusion that the stage had been reached when it was necessary to implement the qualified pledge contained in the Scottish election manifesto:

> 'We will press on with providing new homes and employment opportunities for Glasgow families moving out from the City's congested districts, and if another new town proves necessary it will be built.'

The industrial prospects of a further new town seemed promising in the light of experience of both the movement of firms from the city and of the attraction of new industry. Twenty-two firms had moved from Glasgow in the previous two years, and larger projects attracted to Scotland were tending to go to areas where they could be assured of an immediate local labour supply and of the additional advantages of drawing special skills from Glasgow. Instances quoted were the British Motor Corporation at Bathgate, Rootes at Linwood, and Skefco at Irvine, each of which had taken Glasgow overspill into account in planning their developments.

Maclay stressed that it would be a 'prerequisite' that Glasgow would make financial contributions in respect of each family rehoused in the new town from the city—'and this will be clearly established in formal discussions with Glasgow as and when I am authorised to undertake them'. Moreover, in line with Scottish practice, the cost of main services would be borne by the responsible local authorities. Though the new town development corporation would provide financial assistance in the early years, this would be on a temporary basis (until rate income became sufficient) and would be largely recoverable.

It was unlikely that housing accounts could 'initially' be made to balance, though industrial and commercial developments were 'likely to show a good margin of profit to the exchequer'. Nevertheless, there were good prospects of a 'more realistic attitude to rents on the part of local authorities', and it was anticipated that the existing new towns would soon be able to raise their rents very substantially.

This issue of housing finance was considered to be 'fundamental'.

Maclay's department had discussed the economic profitability of an additional new town with the Treasury in some detail, and it was the intention ('now that the Scottish valuation system has been brought on to a realistic basis')* to set targets of rent income in new towns which would not only be more closely linked with earning power and capacity to pay, but which would, 'so far as practicable', keep in reasonable step with rising costs and economic growth generally. Details had still to be agreed with the Treasury, and the policy would be extremely difficult to achieve if council house rents in Scotland remained 'at their present depressed level', but there were signs that the new rating valuations would influence local authority rent policies 'and I shall do what I can to bring about a "break through" on this front'. Action had been taken against 'the worst offending authorities'† and there were indications that this was beginning to have some general effect on Scottish local authorities. Nevertheless, he would be 'watching developments' and pointed to the opportunity which the next Scottish Housing Bill would provide for reviewing the statutory provisions relating to the fixing of rents.

Maclay also thought it should be possible to attract more private housing in the proposed new town. Private building for sale was increasing in some of the existing new towns, and 'particularly symbolic of changing trends', Glasgow had recently agreed to advance mortgages to Glasgow residents who wished to buy houses outside the city.

Maclay was not yet in a position to determine a specific location for the new town and, in view of its importance to the Scottish economy, and particularly to the relief of unemployment in the Glasgow area and to the diversification of the industrial structure in central Scotland, he would consult the President of the Board of Trade and the Minister of Labour before reaching final conclusions about location. The indications were that an area immediately to the south-east of the British Motor Corporation's new plant at Bathgate would offer the best prospects. The BMC project—which as it developed would have to draw labour from Glasgow—would give the project an industrial support from the start, and there were other sites in the area which were potentially attractive to other industrial developers. This location ('only thirty miles from Glasgow') would

---

* This referred to the reforms brought about by the Valuation and Rating (Scotland) Act 1956—in particular the abolition of owners' rates and the valuation of houses on the basis of rents. (See footnote on p. 131.)

† This was a reference to Glasgow, Dumbarton and Dundee: see *Report by Mr C J D Shaw, QC, on the Local Inquiry in the Matter of a Review of Rents of Corporation Houses in Glasgow*, HMSO, 1958; *Report by Mr G C Emslie, OBE, QC, on the Local Inquiry in the Matter of a Review of Rents of Council Houses in Dumbarton*, HMSO, 1961; and *Report by Mr Manuel Kissen, QC, on the Local Inquiry in the Matter of a Review of Rents of Corporation Houses in Dundee*, HMSO, 1963.

secure a self-contained development with only a very small proportion of commuters, but well linked in communications with both Glasgow and Edinburgh and with the south. Further inquiries, however, were necessary to establish whether the site selected was suitable for development on the most economic lines.

Ministers gave their approval, and Livingston new town was designated on 16 April 1962.

*Population Growth and Regional Development**

At the same time as policy was being reviewed on new towns for overspill from the conurbations, major changes in thinking were taking place on broader issues of the distribution of population and employment. These resulted from the prospect of a sharp increase in population for which housing and employment would have to be found; the continued pressures on the south-east and the midlands; and the continued problem of decline in the older industrial areas.

A landmark in the development of new thinking came, not from Government, but from the Scottish Council (Development and Industry) which in 1961 published a report on the Scottish economy, prepared by a committee under the chairmanship of Sir John Toothill. At this period, regional development policy was aimed at concentrating government assistance on areas of high local unemployment. The Toothill Committee argued the case for a more positive 'growth area' policy. Instead of the heavy emphasis on areas of unemployment, priority should be given to encouraging the growth of industrial centres and complexes:

> 'We do not think that the immediate provision of employment should be the only factor in giving assistance; nor do we want dying industries propped up or assistance directed to areas of high unemployment to the exclusion of potential growth areas. If new industry is guided to wherever local pockets of unemployment exist without adequate regard to the possibility of building up promising industrial centres or complexes, the full benefits to be had from attracting it may be dissipated. The build up of industrial complexes and centres which offer prospects of becoming zones of growth cannot be the only aim, but it should be one of the principal aims of policy.'

On 15 December 1961, the Secretary of State for Scotland (Maclay) circulated a paper to the Economic Policy Committee referring to the Toothill report. Its recommendations for fostering economic growth and selecting growing points could not be considered in a Scottish context alone, but involved consideration of the over-concentration of population and the economic congestion in the chronic labour shortage areas of London and Birmingham. He therefore proposed that a committee of officials should examine the issues and focus them for ministers. This was agreed, and a group of

---

* EA(61)33rd Meeting, 20 December 1961 and PE(62)1.

officials was drawn from the Ministry of Labour, Ministry of Transport, Board of Trade, Scottish departments, and Ministry of Housing and Local Government, under Treasury chairmanship. In anticipation of their report, a Cabinet Committee on Population and Employment was set up in July 1962 'to consider major questions in relation to the pattern of employment and population in Great Britain'. The chairman was Henry Brooke.

Though the initial concern of the group of officials was with the specific problem of the location of industry in Scotland,* they found it necessary to consider much wider issues. Indeed, the first and major part of their report dealt with long term problems of population growth, employment trends and the 'south-eastward trend'. This was followed by medium term proposals relating to industrial location in Scotland.

The Population and Employment Report†

The first draft report to the Population and Employment Committee was presented in July 1962. The starting point was the sharp and continuing rise in the birth rate which, coupled with immigration from overseas, pointed to a large population increase over the following twenty years. By 1981 the increase was estimated at 6·3 million, of which about 4·2 million would, on current trends, be in the south-east and midlands regions. (By comparison these regions then contained about a half of the population of Britain.)

A high proportion of the increase in population in the south-east and the midlands would be natural growth. In fact, of the 2·6 million increase in the south-east, only half a million would come from other parts of Britain: a further half million would be immigrants from overseas, while 1·5 million would be natural growth.

Important population movements within certain regions would also take place because of the need to provide for overspill from the conurbations: at least a million people from London, half a million from Birmingham, and smaller numbers from Liverpool and Manchester.

Despite continued Government action to discourage the growth of industry in London and Birmingham, and to encourage it in the development districts, there was markedly greater growth in the midlands and south-east. It was expected that the pressures for growth would continue—and would be intensified by entry into the Common Market.

All this was clear: but it was a very different matter to form a judgement on whether, or to what extent, the trend was damaging to

---

* The group of officials produced their first draft report under the heading 'Steering Committee on the Toothill Report'.

† PE(62)5, PE(62)1st Meeting, 25 July 1962, C(62)157, C(62)158, CC(62)62nd Conclusions, 25 October 1962 and CC(62)63rd Conclusions, 29 October 1962.

the public interest. In economic terms, it would require 'large collective disadvantages' to offset the economic advantages that individual firms appeared to find from developing in the midlands and near to London. The social and transport investment required to cope with a continuance of the trends in the congested areas would be very large,* but it was not evident what saving would result from alternative locations for the increase in population; and although the congestion necessarily involved some economic losses from labour shortages and wages drift, transport difficulties and the like, these did not appear to offset the gain to the individual firm, and might not do so to the economy. On the other hand, there might well be large social and political disadvantages in the development of a state of affairs in which one half of the country was achieving rapid economic expansion while the other half stagnated.

More sure-footedly, the officials were all agreed that the existing procedures for checking industrial development in the midlands and south-east (by IDC control) and for encouraging it in development districts were 'unlikely to make much headway against the tide'; nor would minor changes be likely to achieve more. (The possibility of controlling office employment was a different matter on which a separate report was to be submitted to ministers.)

Officials explicitly assumed that more positive direction of industry would be impracticable, damaging to economic growth, and repugnant to both sides of industry. If ministers wished to take action 'to reverse the tide', the only remaining alternative was to seek to provide more attractive environments for industry outside the midlands and south-east 'and so set in operation "natural" economic forces in an opposite direction to the tide'.

This would imply developing centres of population and industry at places and in conditions which 'would be attractive to industry in their own right'. A 'tough' policy of refusing industrial development certificates for the congested areas would have to be maintained; but instead of trying to use this to force industry to go to development districts ('which are prima facie unattractive'), the Government would permit and indeed encourage industry to go to the new centres, 'without of course direct financial assistance to the firms concerned'. Labour would likewise be encouraged to move from the high unemployment areas to these new centres.

A policy of developing 'growing points' on these lines would be a major modification of the policy of 'taking the work to the worker', and of the 1960 Local Employment Act. The objective of government

---

* A report by the Minister of Transport suggested that, if the growth of employment in central London were not controlled, there might be 250,000 more commuters by 1971 and 500,000 more by 1981. Most of these commuters would have to travel by train, necessitating 'at a very rough guess', a 'new generation of capital works' of the order of £1,000m 'or indeed significantly more' (PE(62)4).

policy would be to develop new industrial centres rather than to try to bring new industrial enterprises to places with relatively high unemployment (though some action under the Local Employment Act would continue to be necessary).

To develop this line of thought, four questions would need examining in detail:

'(a) How big a programme of government-sponsored development would be necessary to exercise a lasting influence on the present patterns of population and employment distribution? Would a programme of this size be manageable?

(b) Where should the development take place? Outside the immediate orbit of London and the other conurbations; concentrated enough to exert a countervailing pulling power; and in places attractive enough economically to expand under their own steam once they have been got going?

(c) What kind of development? New towns, expansion of existing towns, or even the expansion of a group of closely inter-related towns?

(d) How large should the unit be? Really big developments of 250,000–500,000; something more modest (say 50,000–100,000); or even smaller schemes?'

The Government's freedom of action on these issues was circumscribed by the existing pattern of development and by the availability of natural resources. In this connection, the Ministry of Housing and Local Government were making physical studies of the possibilities. A draft study of the south-east (covering the area from the Wash to the Solent) would be available early in 1963, and studies for the midlands and south Lancashire were to follow.

Parliament had been told that this work was proceeding, and the local planning authorities affected were holding back their advance land planning in the expectation of policy statements. In some of the conurbations, the stock of housing land was down to four or five years' supply. Since it took several years to mount an expansion scheme of any size, the first instalments of the provision to be made for the 1961–81 population increase had to be put into the pipeline very quickly.

It was suggested that ministers should first consider the kind of approach that they would regard as being possible as a matter of public policy, and then give instructions for the relevant research work to be done. For example, ministers might begin by forming a view on such propositions as the following:

'(i) Is it desirable to take action as far as possible to check or even reverse the trend of population to the midlands and the south-east?

(ii) If so, is the present distribution of industry policy likely to achieve this?

(iii) If not, is it possible to sharpen the distribution of industry policy to enable it to contribute effectively?

(iv) If the present distribution of industry policy is not effective for the purpose of checking the south-eastward trend, and cannot be made so, is there a prima facie case for substituting for the present policy one of developing "growing points" designed to provide a countervailing power to the south-eastward trend?'

If it were desired to develop a policy on these lines, a great deal of research would be needed in order to appraise the experience of the last decade. This was essential as a basis for the fundamental decisions which would be required 'which would seek to affect the shape of the country's location of industry and population for a generation ahead'. It would be necessary to devote substantial resources to this research, and it was work that could not be hurried.

Having identified the broad issues which had to be considered by ministers, officials turned to the Scottish problem. Following the Toothill Report, the Scottish Office had proposed that assistance under the Local Employment Act should be available in full measure in the new towns and the areas receiving Glasgow overspill, as well as in the current development districts. In substance, the Scottish Office proposal was that, so long as Glasgow itself remained a development district, certain Glasgow overspill reception areas—the 'growing points'—should be treated as if they were in all respects development districts in their own right.

It appeared that this proposal could be effected only by an amendment of the 1960 Local Employment Act. The issue was whether the change wanted by the Scottish Office could be accomplished (if legislative time were available) by a small amendment that did not prejudice the whole basis of the Local Employment Act. It could be argued that (if it were politically practicable, and if it were possible to define 'growing points' adequately) the change could be restricted to Scotland. This course would have to face the criticism of development districts in England and Wales; for example, conditions in Durham following expected colliery closures might prove similar to those in Scotland, for here also the need would be to provide employment in selected growing points away from the mining villages immediately affected.

Moreover, the policy would be at some risk in Scotland itself, for it would have to be based on the proposition that any new industrial undertaking in one of the 'growing points' would in fact relieve unemployment in Glasgow—a proposition that would fall to the ground if unemployment in Glasgow were reduced below the point at which the city could reasonably be retained on the list of development districts. The Board of Trade, which was the responsible department, believed that the benefit which Scotland would derive from such amendment would be very small, being mainly 'diversionary'. It would arouse criticism from areas such as north Lanarkshire where unemployment had for long been high, and from which the 'diversions' might take place. The Scottish Office, on the other hand, pointed to the relative successes achieved in such overspill reception areas as East Kilbride and Irvine, where the full Local Employment Act facilities were available.

This paper was discussed by the PE Committee at its first meeting in July 1962 when attention was focused on the four questions formulated for ministers.

(i) *Was it desirable to take action as far as possible to check or even reverse the trend of population to the midlands and the south-east?* The general view of ministers was that the degree of congestion which would otherwise be created during the next twenty years or so in the south-east and midlands would be so serious that action to check or reverse the trend was highly desirable. Overspill problems were already severe, and would require a large programme of town development and possibly of further new towns. It was already an objective of policy to re-habilitate certain northern towns, and in this respect current policy 'tended sometimes to run counter to the economic forces of the attraction of the midlands and south-east'. On the other hand, it could not be expected that even changes in policy could reverse so strong a tide as the movement to London and the south-east, which would be accentuated if Britain joined the Common Market. This movement was perhaps an historical event comparable with the growth of the industrial towns in the mineral areas during the industrial revolution. But, even if the tide could not be reversed or checked, it might be effectively canalised so that it did not, for lack of planning, create such severe congestion as to defeat its own purpose of securing economic advantage. It was also necessary to consider the social implications, not only of increasing congestion, but also of a division of the country into two areas, one where there was a shortage of labour and the other where there was excessive un-employment.

(ii) *Was the present distribution of industry policy likely to check or reverse the trend to the south-east?* Ministers agreed generally that existing dis-tribution of industry policy would not check or reverse the trend to the south-east. On the other hand, it would be a mistake to criticise the policy as being 'insufficiently tough'. Industrial development certificates were firmly withheld in the event of any proposal which ran counter to the policy, unless there were overriding reasons of economic advantage in making an exception. But there were practical limitations. The first development of industry often occurred in a small way with a small firm, and the increase was not such as to make a transfer to a development district sensible. Indeed, the finances of small firms might be unable to bear the cost of a move, even over a comparatively short distance. Secondly, there was no power to prevent a small factory being opened, since there was no control over the construction of factories of less than 5,000 square feet. Despite these limitations, considerable successes had been achieved. In the years 1959 to 1961, the employment position in parts of Wales had been transformed, and a great deal had been achieved in Scotland and on Merseyside. Though this period had been one of industrial expansion, the cost of government assistance had been substantial. When industry was not expanding, however, the policy in its current form could hardly be made to work satisfactorily.

(iii) *Was it possible to sharpen the distribution of industry policy to enable it to contribute effectively?* Several suggestions were made for the modification of existing policy, for instance by imposing control of the construction of new factories of less than 5,000 square feet; by differential rating or fiscal arrangements; or by the expenditure of public funds on the sterilisation of industrial sites. But other ministers felt that the determining factors were the rate of expansion of the economy itself, and the distribution of the particular industries which were expanding or contracting.

(iv) *Was there a prima facie case for substituting for present distribution of industry policy one of developing 'growing points'?* There was wide agreement among ministers that the existing distribution of industry policy needed to be supplemented by 'growing points'. It was felt that, as had happened in certain new towns, it would be at first difficult to induce industry to go even to a 'growing point', and that expenditure, which might be substantial, would have to be incurred in the initial stages to induce industry to go, for instance by construction of advance factories. However, once a 'growing point' had become established as such, experience suggested that there would be no lack of industry wanting to go there.

Discussion ranged over many related issues. A great deal of work was in hand, for example, on regional studies for the south-east and the west midlands* and on future transport patterns. Many avenues of policy needed to be further explored. Further effort might be made to transfer civil servants to the provinces. Consideration might be given to admitting immigrants from abroad more freely to areas outside the midlands and the south-east than to those regions.

The general conclusion on the long term problem was that it was necessary 'to visualise what the country would be like twenty years hence if present trends continue unchecked', and to report to the Cabinet what changes of policy would be needed to bring about any desired changes in the developing pattern. The requisite research

---

* These were published as *The South East Study 1961–1981* (1964); *The West Midlands: A Regional Study* (1965).

should be put in hand and carried through quickly. As for the short term problem, it was necessary to establish whether such severe unemployment problems might soon arise as to require a review of existing policies on the distribution of industry.

After further meetings, the report was extensively revised and much greater stress was placed in the new version on employment trends and the adequacy of existing policies. The report concluded that there were impressive features in the existing policies. The distribution of industry policy had had success, 'when times have been favourable', in steering industry to development districts by means of the Local Employment Act. Between April 1960 and August 1962, the exchequer had committed £41m to projects to provide 30,000 new jobs in Scotland and £4m to provide 9,000 in the north-east. Of course, this was a relatively slow operation: it took time to obtain land and build factories. But the committee were impressed by the fact that, broadly speaking, it was only in a boom that industries had occasion to seek new premises and could thus be influenced by the policy. On the other hand, it was precisely because of local boom conditions, mainly in the south-east and midlands, that the Government had had on occasion to adopt national dis-inflationary measures. These measures 'hit relatively depressed areas twice over': by aggravating their own state, and by cutting off the source from which relief might have come.

It was stressed that this was not to be taken as criticism of existing policy: 'it is simply a statement of the limits within which that policy has to work'. The significant fact was that the usefulness of the Local Employment Act depended heavily upon the rate of industrial growth. Subject to this, and also to any expedients that could be devised in particular localities, there was little that could now be done by means of existing policies to alter the situation in regard to higher levels of unemployment in certain regions and pockets of high local unemployment within the next three years, even though in that period other projects might be started which would bear fruit later. In this connection the Board of Trade were working out a further programme of advance factories.

There were many questions to be answered. How was the present imbalance to be rectified? Could a policy be devised which restrained labour demand in areas of shortage while not penalising areas where it was too plentiful? Could the full use of the country's resources be secured without so interfering with industry's own preferences to such an extent as to damage the very process of growth on which the success of existing policies depended? The anticipated population increase would call for social expenditure of the order of £6,000m: the problem was whether this could be spent to better social and economic effect under existing policies or under new policies.

There were two approaches to the problems. One view was that nothing should be done which might impose additional burdens on particular businesses, lest their ability to compete in world markets be impaired. The corollary was that if this led to further industrial and commercial development in the south-east and the midlands, the consequences should be accepted. Among these consequences would be new investment in housing, transport and services in those regions. This would not necessarily be uneconomic investment, even in terms of direct revenue, nor would it necessarily be additional to that which would be required elsewhere if these developments did not take place. There might be a period of congestion to be faced while the services were built up; and there would be pressure for incursions into green belt land. Moreover, some ministers expected that this would lead to a slower rate of growth, or even a gradual decline, in other areas except in so far as existing distribution of industry policy could reverse such tendencies.

Another view was that such consequences could not be accepted or risked, and that, even at some risk in other directions, it was essential that new policies be elaborated particularly in relation to 'growing points'. Growth centres could be developed in Scotland, the north, Northern Ireland and Wales primarily to relieve regional unemployment, while in the south-east, the west midlands and the north-west they would be primarily for overspill. Some of these growth centres might be in key positions for trade with the Common Market. The aims would be to relieve unemployment more effectively, to hold population in the declining areas to a greater extent, to bring about greater mobility of industry and to provide enough industry for the overspill programmes in the various regions. The hope would be that by the intensive development of a variety of inherently attractive centres a greater degree of industrial growth and mobility would be achieved. Though a policy of this kind would certainly have its difficulties, it might well offer a constructive approach to the problems of growth, unemployment and overspill.

The committee were not yet ready to make recommendations. Further study was needed of the main kinds of industry that would be concerned; what kind of environment they would need; how readily labour of the right kinds might be found; what sites, broadly, might be suitable; what pattern of transport would be available or would need to be provided; what scale of investment would be involved; and what the net effect might be on the development districts. Research on these and other points had been put in hand, and the research teams had been asked to produce ideas 'however radical'.

The report, together with a paper on the growth of office employment and measures to control it, was examined at length by the Cabinet in October 1962. Brooke said that while there were differences between ministers, these should not be exaggerated. All agreed that there could be no question of reversing the trend towards more concentration of population in the south-east. The problem was rather to devise means by which the Government could channel such trends so as to create better conditions for economic growth and at the same time produce social advantages.

> 'An instance from the past was the development of new towns, which had been successful politically, financially, economically and socially. Existing policies for the distribution of industry were designed as it were to soak up pools of unemployment. This was satisfactory as far as it went, but somewhat negative . . . There was a case for trying positively to bring about, by taking Government action in good time, the kind of location of population and industry that would bring the greatest benefit to the lives of people generally.'

But the major part of this meeting was occupied by a lengthy exposition by the Prime Minister (Macmillan) of the broader issues of the modernisation of Britain which should form the context to the discussion on population and industry.

Macmillan first asked whether the present machinery of ministerial government and of parliamentary procedures was properly organised to cope with the pressures which were being put on it. Perhaps the Government should work out a plan to modernise these machineries 'and seize the initiative in demonstrating that changes must be made to help the country to operate successfully in modern conditions'.

Secondly, the solution of the problems of population and employment did not lie simply between *laissez faire* and *dirigisme*—the alternative was a pragmatic compromise. The Government should not attempt to reverse existing trends, but positive action was required to build up growing points, which should take account of social and political requirements. It was out of the question to allow Scotland or the north-east or any large area to be abandoned to decay. The remedy did not lie in trying to preserve each individual community which had grown up for reasons long since irrelevant to modern conditions, such as a cotton town whose location originally depended on the presence of water power to drive a water wheel. More imaginative changes were required; the Highlands of Scotland which had been the playground of the rich might be developed into the playground for the masses, but the industrial belt in Scotland must remain industrial 'in a modern constructive form'.

Thirdly, the pattern of industry should be considered. During the war, industry had been geared to war production, and after the war the sellers' market had masked the need for industrial change, which had been further masked by the extent to which the advantages of technology had tended to flow from the defence programme. If disarmament became a reality, there would be an immense problem in substituting civil development and technology for the contribution made by the defence industries. There was a tendency for problems of industrial change to be viewed in terms of declining industries such as the railways and shipbuilding, but it was important to put equal effort into the industries which should grow in their place.

On the office problem, Macmillan said that he did not altogether like the proposal that it should be tackled by restrictive measures. Generally he would like to see all matters looked at not from the standpoint of what the Government should prevent, but rather of what they should do. This should be the central principle of a coherent body of doctrine, a blueprint for the modernisation of Britain, which should guide the Government's policies for the future. The studies which the Committee on Population and Employment had put in hand would clearly be valuable in this context. As an earnest of their determination to carry through a complete plan of modernisation, the Government should aim at implementing the first elements of such a plan in the life of the current Parliament.

In the meantime, it was necessary to make progress on the specific issues which the Cabinet had been invited to decide, namely, whether to invite the Chancellor of the Exchequer to consider a tax on offices, and whether to amend the Third Schedule to the Town and Country Planning Act, 1947, so that there would no longer be any liability to pay compensation if permission were refused for the redevelopment of pre-war offices to provide more than 10 per cent additional floor space.*

The North East and Scotland†

In December 1962 ministers considered a proposal that the Government should concentrate their attack on the unemployment problem in the north-east and Scotland, and make an immediate start on a long term plan for the modernisation and rehabilitation of selected areas within them. Thus priority would be given to these regions, and within the regions priority would be given to certain 'growth points' rather than to localities where unemployment happened to be serious. It would be necessary to provide a system of road and rail communications, the right kind of port facilities and provision for air travel; the derelict areas should be cleared; and some incentives to industry to go to Scotland and the north-east must be settled.

The term 'growth point' was taken to mean an area of a radius of perhaps ten to thirty miles within which travel to work would be feasible. Within the area there would be a concentration not only of

---

* This was agreed in November 1962. For further discussion see *History Vol IV*, chapter VII.
† PE(62)20, PE(62)7th Meeting, 12 December 1962, and CC(63)3rd Conclusions, 10 January 1963.

industry, but of good shops, amenities and cultural and educational facilities, including technical colleges and a university, so that generally superior conditions would be offered. The distinctive characteristic of such a growth would be that it should generate demand and further employment in surrounding areas, including employment in services other than manufacturing industry. It did not necessarily imply the development of a new community, 'though this was not ruled out'.

To promote regional development in the north-east it was proposed that a 'government representative' should be appointed 'to act as a contact between the Government and the north-east'. There was some doubt about this and particularly on its implications for the machinery of government, but, in January 1963, in view of the rising level of unemployment in this region, Macmillan appointed Lord Hailsham as the minister to be charged with undertaking 'a comprehensive review of the local situation and to prepare plans for the redevelopment of the area as a whole'.

*Washington**

Hailsham's reports to his colleagues were in broad terms, and the details were filled in at numerous meetings of ministers and officials during the middle part of 1963. The proposals were ultimately published as *The North East—A Programme for Regional Development and Growth* (Cmnd 2206), with a corresponding paper on central Scotland (Cmnd 2188). They were essentially similar, both suggesting planned development based on 'growth places', on greater inducements to industry, and on 'articulated' public service investment programmes.

For the north-east it was assumed that a better environment could best be achieved by the provision of improved town centres, housing and municipal standards generally. The need was particularly great in the Tyneside area, and schemes under the Town Development Act were already under way at Cramlington and Longbenton on the north of the river. On the southern fringe, Washington provided an excellent site for a new town; its population could be expanded from 20,000 to 70–80,000 and would do much to relieve the projected population increase on Tyneside of 165,000 by 1981; it was convenient for travel-to-work to and from Newcastle and Sunderland; it would be attractive to industry as lying on the line of the A1 Motorway and the entrance to the Tyne Tunnel and was well located in relation to the Team Valley trading estate; and a shopping centre could serve a wide surrounding centre. The estimated cost of building a new town for 50,000 people (14,000

---

* PE(o)(63)23 and Treasury File 2AT 806/01.

houses) was put at £80m of which £45m would fall on the development corporation, £16m on local authority services and £19m on private development.

The Treasury viewed Washington as 'a good bet generally'. The only real risk was the extent to which efforts 'to rehabilitate the north-east' might fail, but, as an internal Treasury minute noted:

> 'its real merit is that although a new town is directly more costly to the exchequer than an equivalent amount of housing undertaken by local authorities plus private builders, it enables building to be directed into the right place and prevents haphazard housing, quite a bit of which might get into the non-growth areas. And secondly, to the extent that the exchequer is shouldering a greater liability this should help us to resist any claims from local authorities for additional exchequer help because of their rising commitments generally.'

The Washington proposal was agreed and, after a local inquiry, was designated as a new town on 24 July 1964.

The Hailsham reports had also called attention to the potentialities for rapid growth in the Aycliffe–Darlington area, where the new town was demonstrating its attractiveness to industry, and it was argued that its ultimate population should be increased from 20,000 to 45,000. Peterlee, the other new town in Durham, was felt to lie too far from the main road network to provide a nucleus for rapid growth and, although a small additional area was designated for industrial development, no increase in the target population was then proposed.

Irvine*

Whereas the white paper on the north-east included a specific commitment to an additional new town (Washington), the Scottish white paper merely stated that 'the Government do not rule out the designation of a fifth Scottish new town in the Irvine area'. This was much less of a commitment than SDD had wanted, but they encountered strong Treasury resistance. Though SDD argued that the Irvine proposal was parallel to that for Washington, the Treasury insisted that 'the case for the use of the New Towns Act machinery at Irvine needs to be justified on its own merits and not by reference to what may or may not happen in the case of Washington'. Certainly it was not to be expected that every regional study would establish the case for new towns 'as a matter of course'. Furthermore, the Scottish new towns were more unprofitable than new towns elsewhere and, for this reason, 'we are bound because of the Scottish rent position to look particularly carefully at any proposal for further new towns in Scotland'.

---

* Treasury File 2AT 823/01, and SDD Files NT 5 series; EP(64)100 and EP(64)33rd Meeting, 29 July 1964.

SDD did not, at this stage, press the case: the compromise form of words (which appeared in the white paper) were accepted *pro tem.* But, following the publication of the white paper and discussions with the local authorities in the Irvine area, a formal request was put to the Treasury for agreement to a new town. An internal Treasury minute noted:

> 'This brings us to the parting of the ways. We can either seek the chief secretary's agreement that we should oppose the designation of a new town in principle or we can start discussing with the Scots the details of the case they have put to us. If we pursue the latter course our eventual agreement to the designation of a new town in this area is almost inevitable, even though it should be possible to scale down the present proposals.'

The general Treasury view was that 'the chief secretary ought to be given the opportunity at this stage of opposing this on general grounds'. There were several good reasons for so doing: the scale of investment in housing and environmental services in Scotland was rapidly growing, and there was already an overload on the building industry. It was proving impossible 'to get the Scots to agree to any control over their local authority programme', and there was a clear danger that the building programme would get out of hand. Moreover, the exchequer commitment for the Scottish new towns was growing rapidly. The conclusion was that 'we can reasonably press the Scots to put off any such move until we see how the public investment situation in Scotland is developing'. The chief secretary agreed, though it was recognised that there would be an immediate ministerial appeal. The Treasury therefore wrote to SDD asking for a deferment of the Irvine proposal for some six to nine months.

The expected appeal was forthcoming: on 9 July 1964, the Secretary of State for Scotland (Noble) wrote to the Chief Secretary (Boyd-Carpenter). Agreement could not be reached and the matter was referred to the EP Committee for resolution. Noble maintained that none of the Treasury arguments took account of the 'real issue':

> 'which is the identification in the Central Scotland Study of the economic growth potential in the Irvine area. There can be no argument that this growth potential exists. The question is whether we are prepared to let it be dissipated in a partially planned development, or whether we realise it as fully as possible by appointing a development corporation to plan and carry out a properly integrated expansion. The four existing new towns are proving their worth in terms of employment growth; the increase in their investment programmes is a direct result of their success in this field. This cannot reasonably be used as an argument against the commitment of a fifth new town, in an area whose expansion is fundamental to the whole Central Scotland Plan, and where no other means exist of securing a phased expansion of the order required. For this reason, while the new town proposal has important implications for the housing programme, it cannot be looked at in terms of housing expenditure alone'.

Noble's arguments prevailed and ministerial approval in principle was given for a new town at Irvine.*

Joseph Asks for More New Towns†

In January 1963, Joseph sought authority for new towns at Redditch (for Birmingham), and at Runcorn (for Liverpool), together with a site in south-east Lancashire (for Manchester). He explained that Redditch and Runcorn had previously been considered for treatment under the Town Development Act and the reason for the change was that:

'It is clear we cannot look to town development under its present statutory arrangements for fast and large housing build-ups. The fact is that town development is making no adequate progress anywhere, except where the LCC are giving massive financial support, and themselves taking a direct part in getting the development forward . . . Elsewhere . . . progress depends on relatively small district councils who have not got the organisation or the resources to tackle major development. In particular they do not feel able to charge the really high rents which would be needed to cover the cost of the houses (even after allowing for the subsidies from the exchequer and the exporting authority) nor alternatively are they willing to contribute to the cost of houses for people coming from elsewhere.'

Joseph said that he was considering how, in the long run, better progress might be made for dealing with overspill by way of town development. Much depended upon getting a higher level of municipal rents and, associated with that, a revised subsidy structure. In the meantime, he did not despair of achieving better progress in the provinces:

'and if it is agreed that the new town machinery should be used to drive Redditch and Runcorn, I shall make it clear to Birmingham and Liverpool that I expect them to help themselves by tackling other approved developments in association with the district councils concerned'.

Redditch was close to Birmingham and there was sufficient land to allow a major expansion. Its communications were sufficiently

---

* Thereupon discussion began with the local authorities about the size and nature of the development, but it rapidly emerged that useful progress was unlikely until there was a clearer picture of what was involved, including the line of the projected bypass to Irvine, and the allocation of industrial sites in relation to housing. Accordingly the Scottish Development Department in September 1964 engaged consultants (Hugh Wilson and Lewis Womersley) to make an interim report on the major land uses they would propose for the area, together with the major communications network. This became available in May 1965 and gave substance to the lengthy negotiations which were proceeding between the SDD, the local authorities and others, and which resulted in the publication in February 1966 of a draft designation order for an area of 13,700 acres and for an expansion of population of some 55,000 in addition to the existing population in Irvine-Kilwinning of 36,000. A public inquiry was held in July 1966 at which opposition was made mainly by agricultural interests and, after exclusion of 1,200 acres to meet their objections, the order was confirmed in November 1966.

† PE(63)1, PE(63)1st Meeting, 14 January 1963, PE(63)6 and PE(63)3rd Meeting, 7 February 1963.

good not to make the development necessarily dependent, at least initially, on the provision of matching industry. People moving to Redditch could continue to work in Birmingham and other nearby places where employment existed, so that the initial development need not prejudice the policy of giving immediate industrial priority to the north-east and Scotland. Nevertheless, he believed that the town would be attractive to employers and, in time, industry tied to the west midlands could be expected to build up there.

The merits of the Runcorn site were similar to those of Redditch—good rail and road communications with Liverpool, and a site which seemed likely to be attractive to industry as and when it could be encouraged to go there. The Ministry of Agriculture had withdrawn their objection to the development of Runcorn on what was admittedly good agricultural land.

Joseph believed that his proposals were acceptable to the departments concerned. In his view, the two new towns were essential if Birmingham and Liverpool were to forge ahead with their slum clearance programmes. Indeed the proposals would be insufficient to meet long term needs, even with Dawley, Skelmersdale and 'whatever town development progress may be possible'. Some 'incursions' into the green belt would probably be necessary both in the short term before the new towns got under way and in the longer term. 'Announcement of intention to make further use of the new town machinery will make it easier to put across some incursion into the proposed green belts.'

A NEW TOWN FOR MANCHESTER

The Manchester proposal was of 'a rather different type' since, although the city had been arguing for some time that the Government should build them a new town, 'a decision to do so would represent a fresh stage in the arrangements for Manchester's overspill'.

There was no question that the Manchester conurbation had a housing problem which would need a great deal more land over the following ten years than was at present in sight. This was in spite of great efforts which Manchester (and Salford) had made 'to help themselves', including a decision by Manchester to build over 12,000 houses at Westhoughton in Lancashire.* With this and with such town development schemes as had been agreed (Macclesfield,

---

* Manchester's compulsory purchase order for land at Westhoughton was confirmed—with substantial modifications—in February 1965. 'Manchester found themselves unable to accept this as a basis for a viable town development scheme, and the minister offered to contribute to the cost of employing consultants to produce a master plan acceptable to all the authorities concerned. After prolonged discussions it became apparent that the differences of opinion between Manchester and Westhoughton were so fundamental that this would clearly be impossible. In October 1966, the minister reluctantly withdrew his support for the scheme.'

Winsford and Crewe) the two authorities 'could see their way' to building something over 5,000 houses a year for the following four years, after which completions would tail off. At best, however, this programme would fall short of the target which they had set themselves, which should result in a building rate of not less than 6,000 per annum. 'Manchester think that they are owed at least one new town; and it is very difficult to dispute this.' Their attempts to build one themselves, close to the city, had been defeated by the combined opposition of Cheshire and the agricultural interests. They had sought alternative sites with more vigour and determination than any other of the great provincial cities, which was why their immediate programme was as good as it was. Recently they had located scattered sites in Cheshire totalling 1,300 acres which they were negotiating with the county council; but some of this would be the subject of bitter opposition, and much of what could be agreed would be best suited to private enterprise.

> 'In short, Manchester say, with justice, that they have done everything they can. But looking ten years forward, as every major housing authority with a continuing programme ought to do, they see production of houses beginning to run down by 1967. They want the Government's assurance that a new town will then be coming into production. I believe the need for this is established and that, while the selection of the site will require study, I should be able to inform Manchester that their long-term needs are realised by the Government, and that subject to our being able to find a suitable site, it is our intention to build a new town to cater for the land needs of Manchester and the south-east Lancashire conurbation generally.'

This proposal had been considered by a committee of officials who agreed that, in the long term, there was a case for some form of new town for Manchester which would also meet the wider needs of south-east Lancashire and Merseyside. They considered that while there was an immediate priority to be given to Scotland and the north-east in steering industry, that should not be regarded as preventing a reasonable development of other parts of the country in the medium and long term. In this connection it was thought that there must be industrial growth in the north-west which was a major industrial centre with a population increasing faster than the average for the country. Officials considered that there should be inter-departmental consultation on the question of location, that it would be advisable to pick a location where employment could, if necessary, be found by travel to work in Manchester, and that it would be unwise to encourage any public discussion of the project until these questions had been provisionally agreed upon by ministers.

Joseph was prepared generally to agree with the views of the officials, and was proposing to arrange for the issue to be further pursued. In the meantime, some general statement of government policy in relation to Manchester was, he thought, essential. It would be politically 'most unwise to make no mention of provision for Manchester's needs when we announce our measures to meet the needs of Liverpool and Birmingham. I believe that in all three cases new towns would be justified and that the general approach, including new towns as a contribution, would be popular with our Party.'

In January and February 1963, ministers considered these proposals. Redditch and Runcorn were approved. The change to 'exchequer financing' was acceptable and would not reduce the amount of money available for north-east England and Scotland provided that it was intended to charge sufficiently high rents. It was agreed that this should be discussed by officials of the Ministry of Housing and the Treasury.

Though Joseph had pointed to the likely criticism of the nearness of the sites to the parent cities ('too close to be consistent with the concept of a new town'), this was noted to have the advantage that there would be no need for industry 'which might have been steered to the north or Scotland'. Both new towns could, if necessary, depend on commuting for their employment, though it would be preferable to provide some local employment since the cost of travelling coupled with the necessary high level of rents might make it difficult to persuade people to move.

Fears were expressed that the announcement of these two new towns would lead to questioning about the Government's future policy on town development and to renewed pressure for the use 'of the new town technique' to assist the expansion of other towns. It would therefore be an advantage to introduce the announcement in a general statement on housing policy.

The Manchester proposal proved much more troublesome, but it was agreed that it would not be wise to announce new towns for Birmingham and Liverpool without indicating some measure of government assistance to Manchester's problems. Joseph said that he now took the view that the search for a site should be limited to areas within commuting distance of Manchester. Since the purpose was slum clearance, people would be displaced regardless of their jobs, and their existing jobs would have to be filled if they were rehoused beyond daily travelling distance. In addition, it was unlikely in the foreseeable future that Manchester could generate enough employment to match an exported population and create a balanced community. This ruled out the Leyland-Chorley area, the most promising site to the north of Manchester, which was well sited to take overspill from some county boroughs lying to the north. Similarly, Crewe, the most obvious site in Cheshire, was well beyond daily travelling distance, and its development would tend to weaken the attraction to industry of Merseyside and the Lancashire overspill districts. It was likely, however, that a suitable site could be found to the west of Manchester near enough to allow travel to work. Risley was an obvious possibility, although it lay on good agricultural land, and the National Coal Board might want to work seams of coal beneath it. Lymm no longer had a rail service. Nevertheless, there might be other possible sites and a further survey of areas to the west was to be undertaken. Since it was by no means sure that a suitable site could be found, any government announcement would have to be made in general terms.

Despite the likely agricultural objections, ministers generally supported Joseph's approach. It was, however, stressed that in any public announcement it was important to make reference to 'a development on the scale of a new town' in order to avoid a financial commitment to the same extent or on the same terms as existing developments under the New Towns Act.

Redditch and Runcorn were designated in April 1964, and Risley was announced in June 1964 as the site for a Manchester new town—though, as we shall see in the next chapter, this ran into considerable difficulties.

The South East Study*

Towards the end of 1963, a pre-publication draft of *The South East Study* and a draft white paper were ready for discussion by ministers.† In presenting these, Joseph laid emphasis on the severity of the London housing problem. There were some 5,000 homeless people, and a shortage of some 150,000 houses. The rate at which new households were being formed was increasing as the standard of living rose. The study showed that very little land could be found in London to deal with the housing problem. Joseph said that he had hoped to be able to ease the problem somewhat by purchasing industrial land and allocating it to housing, but the cost was prohibitive. Moreover, land had to be found in the region not only for the needs of London but also for the growth in the population. The population increase to be accommodated over the next two decades was about 3·5 million. Once the implications of this were made clear to the local planning authorities (a main objective of the study) the greater part of the growth could be provided for by the allocation of more land for housing.

But the study suggested that 1 to 1·25 million people would have to be provided for in new 'planned expansions'—new towns or

* RD(64)1 and RD(64)1st Meeting, 22 January 1964; RD(64)6 and RD(64)2nd Meeting, 30 January 1964.

† For a discussion of earlier ministerial consideration of the problems of the south-east and the 1963 white paper *London—Employment: Housing: Land* see Vol IV of this History, chapter VII.

substantial expansions of existing towns. The need for this arose partly from London overspill and partly from the need to ensure that as much as possible of the inevitable population and employment growth took place well away from London in order to avoid exacerbating the problems of congestion and overspill. The normal land allocations of the local planning authorities would not provide for the planned expansions; and the development process would have to be both induced and controlled in order 'to bring it along as and when it is needed, and to phase it'. As soon as the study was published, the local authorities would want to know how these planned expansions were to be brought about and, in particular, how the cost was to be borne. Joseph argued that three things were needed: first, a timetable—to be kept under review—for the development of the planned expansions, phased to a programme for the implementation of the whole plan for the south-east; secondly, the advance acquisition of the necessary land; and thirdly, controls exercised by local authorities able to ensure, through their ownership of the land, that development took place, whether by private or by public enterprise, as and when needed.

The broad phasing of the whole programme of development was important, both in relation to the competition with other parts of the country and within the south-east itself. It was, however, important that the land needed for the planned expansions—the bigger schemes—should be publicly acquired, and that this should be done as early as possible. Only by means of public acquisition would it be possible to ensure that land was brought forward as required and that it was used to meet the needs of inescapable growth. Planning control alone would not ensure this. It did not follow, of course, that the land would necessarily be developed by public authorities, nor that it had to be retained in public ownership indefinitely.

The problems—and the measures required to deal with them—were 'on a massive scale'. They also raised difficult political problems of timing and presentation 'to avoid damaging the Government's declared policy of giving priority to the development of central Scotland and the north-east'. It was this which worried ministers, and it was feared that the policy proposals might appear to be giving 'too much encouragement to expansion of employment within the south-east and not enough discouragement to expansion of employment in the area, particularly in London itself'. The building of houses in the centres proposed for major new development would make it difficult to resist pressure for heavy public investment and for an accompanying growth of employment. This could aggravate the problem of immigration into the south-east. Added force was given to this point by a current inquiry into distribution of industry policy which had shown that its results and potentialities were disappointing: in the previous three years over 90 per cent of the applications for industrial development certificates for the south-east had had to be allowed, and yet it was difficult to see how the policy governing these decisions could have been made more strict. (On the other hand, there was no measure of the number of applications that would have been made if the policy had not been as strict as it was.) Moreover, by relieving the pressure of congestion in London, the proposed policy would reduce the deterrents to further immigration there at the same time as new attractions were created for immigration into other parts of the south-east.

Nevertheless, the Government could not ignore the problems of the inescapable growth of population in the south-east, and, in terms of mere numbers of people involved, these problems overshadowed the problems of loss of population from the north, difficult as that problem was in other respects. The demand for industrial employment in the proposed new centres in the south-east should not be over-estimated. Services and office employment was already absorbing over 54 per cent of the working population in the south-east, and the new centres could be expected to rely to an even greater extent upon office work moved out from London.

To improve the balance of the Government's regional policy and to reduce the risks of uneconomic congestion in the south-east (which might be gravely aggravated if the Channel Tunnel were constructed) and of 'frustration of the revival' of the north-east, it was suggested that the deterrents to further growth of office employment in London should be reinforced. The proposal for some form of levy on office space (which had been earlier rejected) should be reconsidered, and some form of development certificate control might be introduced which discriminated, for instance, between concerns which had to be in London and those which could be located elsewhere.* However, the proposal for a levy had been rejected because it would add to the costs of concerns which had to be in London as well as to those of others not so tied; and control by certificates would be very difficult, if not impracticable. It was also difficult to modify so early the Government's recently declared policy of relying mainly on persuasion to relieve the pressure for offices in London. These considerations suggested that it was the more important to provide in plans for the south-east for new centres of office employment outside London—a policy which would work in harmony with the economic pressure of rent differences between London and the provinces.

It was also suggested that it would be a serious mistake to adopt a policy for the south-east which made insufficient provision for those

---

* See *History, Vol IV*, chapter VII.

born in the area to find employment there. The object of policy for Scotland and the north-east was to mitigate this very defect in those regions. Restraints on development in the south-east must also take account of the need to avoid impairing the economic progress of the country.

A revised draft of the white paper was considered in January 1964 and again there was a lengthy discussion. It was noted that the draft would commit the Government not merely to accept the basic strategy of the study but also to accept the specific proposals that a second generation of new and expanded towns to accommodate 1 to 1·25 million people would be needed and that some of these would need to be large. How wise was it to include a passage committing the Government to this extent? On the one hand, it was suggested that to do so would give the impression that public investment would be needed on a scale which would be incompatible with the Government's policy of giving priority to central Scotland and the north-east, and would pre-empt resources which might be required to deal satisfactorily with the needs of Merseyside, Wales and other areas 'as they might be disclosed by individual studies of those regions'. The Government would find themselves under very heavy pressure to build up the infrastructure required to implement the proposals in the south-east study. They had given a pledge that if it became necessary to moderate public investment, the public investment programmes required for the plans for central Scotland and the north-east would be maintained. It was already clear that the nation was committed to heavy public investment until well into the 1970s. It might therefore turn out that sufficient public investment resources would not be available to meet the demands arising from a specific commitment in the form envisaged in the draft. Moreover, the announcement that there would be large new centres of population in the south-east would tend to accentuate migration into that region from elsewhere in the country, to intercept movement of population and employment which might otherwise have gone further afield, and to thwart the Government's distribution of industry policy. If heavy public investment had to be incurred to provide for London population to be housed and employed well away from London, then this might be better directed to destinations outside the south-east altogether. It might therefore be best merely to refer to the proposals in the study as ideas which the Government considered deserved to be published for general public discussion.

On the other hand, it was pointed out that the study contained a fully argued analysis leading to the propositions that, for lack of accommodation in London itself, 1 to 1·25 million people ('and this was probably an under-estimate') would have to be accommodated elsewhere and that means had to be found to relieve the pressure on

London of the growth of employment, particularly in offices. The Government would be exposed to serious criticism if they produced a white paper which presented these propositions without indicating what should be done about them. Successive Ministers of Housing had found themselves without the means to deal with the problems of housing Londoners, and standards were deteriorating there while they rose throughout the rest of the country. The study showed that London's problem could be solved only by finding land outside London. Moreover, it was the availability of jobs in London that attracted people to move there; and these were very largely office jobs. There was authoritative advice that it was unrealistic to expect firms to move offices away from London by more than the distance that could be covered in a day return journey by road or rail; and if enough were to be achieved by such moves to stop the growth of office employment in London, large new centres within this distance from London were essential. Moreover, earlier advice from officials had been to the effect that while the proposals in the study might tend to bring forward public investment in development in the south-east they would probably involve no more in total, and might well involve less, than any practicable alternative policy. This was due in part at least to the very heavy cost of developing transport that would be entailed in an alternative policy. It was important that the white paper should show the magnitude of the task specifically, and for this reason the reference to 1 to 1·25 million overspill from London should be retained; otherwise each local planning authority would be liable to argue that the problem could be solved without their contributing to its solution. Finally, both the study and the white paper made it clear that the proposals for the south-east assumed the success of the Government's policy of giving priority to regional development in central Scotland and the north-east.

It was generally thought that the draft contained a reasonably satisfactory presentation of the 'reconciliation' between the policies for central Scotland and the north-east in terms of the underlying statistics of migration and of the phasing of investment, but additional drafting amendments were required which would lay further stress on the priority accorded to central Scotland and the north-east, and possibly to other areas. There was, moreover, concern about the degree to which the Government should at this stage commit themselves to particular arrangements for dealing with the problem of population increase in the south-east. It was therefore decided that a further draft should be prepared which would leave open the question of the size of particular developments that would be needed: this would stress that, under their policy of regional development, the Government would be doing all that they could to attract people as well as employment to the north.

There would, nevertheless, still remain a major problem to be solved in the south-east. It would take time for particular proposals to be fully worked out and for local opinion to be consulted on them and, in the meantime, development in the regions to which the Government accorded priority would be going ahead. The scale, nature and location of development and the extent to which it would be financed publicly or privately should be referred to in terms which did not commit the Government to rely either upon large or exclusively upon small schemes; but it should be made clear that in total the measures would make a real impact on the problems of London.

*Problems of Implementation**

Though general agreement was reached on the regional policy implications of *The South East Study*, Joseph's proposals for implementation proved much more troublesome. The main issue was whether there should be a policy of advance acquisition of land by some kind of public body and, if so, what form this should take. Joseph argued:

> 'It will be important that the land required for the planned expansions should be publicly acquired . . . as only by this means can we ensure that the land is brought forward as required . . . Public ownership is essential at the outset to ensure that the land is made available when needed . . . [and] will enable the public to recoup the cost, through the enhanced values which the services create . . . Early acquisition is important because values rise as services are provided and the prospects of development get closer.'

If it were agreed that there had to be a phased programme for developments in the south-east and a policy of advance acquisition of land for the bigger schemes, it remained to consider the machinery for implementation. So far as any new towns were concerned, the machinery already existed. When the time came for starting a new town, the land was designated for the purpose, a corporation was appointed, the whole of the land was in due course purchased, and the corporation, under the general direction of the ministry, could then build or secure the building of the town in accordance with an appropriate timetable.

There was no similarly satisfactory machinery for inducing and controlling the substantial expansion of existing towns. The Town Development Act 1952 envisaged that local authorities prepared to receive overspill from a congested town would carry out the expansion themselves, aided by exchequer grants towards the cost of expanding main services, and by housing subsidies. (These were higher than normal in recognition of the fact that local people could not be expected to contribute to the rents of incomers.) Experience

---

* RD(64)5, RD(64)3rd Meeting, 10 February 1964, CP(64)44, CP(64)45, and CM(64) 15th Conclusions, 27 February 1964. For further discussion see chapter IX. The issue is also dealt with at greater length in Volume IV of this History.

had clearly shown that very few local authorities felt able to carry through major expansions under these powers. The initial expenditure on acquisition of land, provision of services and recasting of the traffic pattern and (sometimes) of the town centres was heavy; and it was necessarily some years before the development began to cover its costs and to pay its way—though in time it should. Authorities were understandably reluctant to incur any substantial rate burden for the purpose of taking people from elsewhere, even though the town would eventually benefit. Moreover, local authorities were bound to feel considerable uncertainty about the outcome since the Government was in control of the distribution of industry and of the investment programme on which the success of these ventures largely depended.

In Joseph's view, it was necessary for the Government to participate in responsibility for major expansions of existing towns. This could not be done in exactly the same way as the building of a new town. Local authorities would want and ought to have a much bigger part to play especially in handling the impact of the expansion on the existing town. The right method seemed to him to be government-appointed and financed town expansion corporations which would be empowered to buy land required for the expansion, and to control its development in partnership with the local authority.

The main function of these corporations, Joseph suggested, would be to ensure that land was brought into development as required. They would buy and service it; and they might proceed largely by way of disposal to developers who would carry out the development needed. But they should be empowered to carry out development themselves where necessary. They might also be the channel for grants to assist the local authority as necessary in enlarging their services and dealing with the impact on roads and the existing town centre.

The precise relationship between these corporations and the local authorities needed further working out. The Ministry of Housing would be having informal discussions with selected local authorities experienced in town development, in order to obtain a clearer view of the financial implications for a local authority of major expansion, and to determine how best a satisfactory partnership between a local authority and a government appointed corporation could be established. Further, commissioned studies of what would be involved in the substantial expansion of three towns (Ipswich, Peterborough, Worcester) were now available and, after examination, would be published. Pending the outcome of these discussions and the examination of the studies, Joseph was not able to formulate detailed proposals; but he did need to know whether his general approach to planned expansions was agreed by his colleagues.

It was not envisaged that there would be an independent town expansion corporation for every major expansion. It would probably be right to have one corporation responsible for several expansions in a group of neighbouring counties. The corporations would be able to phase the various expansions in accordance with the needs of the overall programme and to provide highly qualified central professional and technical services.

Joseph's proposals were exhaustively considered by ministers early in February 1964. There was a major division of opinion on the wisdom of asserting that advance acquisition of land should be the general policy, or indicating the way in which town expansion corporations, if these were formed, should operate. Some ministers urged that alternative ways of providing for the development of the south-east should be fully explored before any decisions in principle were taken on the proposal that the instruments for acquisition of land should be new town corporations and town expansion corporations. It was questioned whether major new developments of the kind envisaged in the study were necessarily the right way of providing for the expanding population of the south-east. Smaller expansions at a larger number of places might meet the need without creating the problems and expenditure which could flow from concentration on a few very large developments. The use of corporations for town expansions would be publicly regarded as implying, not merely that all the land required for the major developments would be acquired at the expense of public funds, but also that a high proportion of it would be retained in public ownership. This might be interpreted as an indication that the Government thought that the required development could be carried out only by public authorities. It was undesirable that the Government should commit themselves to such implications. Advance acquisition of land was necessary, but it should be the policy that as much as possible of the land should be sold again for development by private enterprise or local authorities in accordance with a plan for the whole development.

Other ministers, however, argued that the size and nature of the problem of London's housing were such that only large expansions could cope with them, and the Government would be severely criticised if their policy appeared not to be commensurate with the problem. Moreover, the greater part of the million or so people whom it was envisaged would be housed in the major expansions could not afford other than subsidised housing, nor could they afford to travel long distances to work. Private enterprise had, so far, shown no disposition to cater for the housing of such people, and not even housing associations were likely to be able to provide houses at rents low enough to meet the need for some years to come, though as prosperity increased and rents rose generally this position might alter. Construction of houses at commuting distances from London for owner occupation or higher levels of rent would not touch this part of the problem; the policy had to ensure that sufficient subsidised houses were provided, with matching provision of jobs in the locality. Moreover, new communities were needed on a scale which would reduce the attraction of London to migrants who would otherwise enter London for employment and maintain the pressure on London's housing. The proposed new and expanded towns were the means of providing for these requirements, but this did not imply that there would not be considerably more scope for participation by private enterprise than had been given in the existing new towns.

There was general agreement that some measure of advance acquisition of land would be necessary in the action that would follow from *The South East Study*, and that the sanction behind this policy had to be compulsory purchase powers. But the wisdom of asserting that advance acquisition would be the general policy was thought to be doubtful: it was arguable that land could be released for development at the appropriate time and on the required scale under the normal processes of planning, and that only relatively small quantities of land would need to be acquired in advance. Moreover, a policy of advance acquisition by public bodies might be taken to imply that all or most of the land so acquired would be retained in the ownership of those bodies, whereas ti might be better that it should be sold. In the proposed white paper, therefore, it would be necessary to use words describing the proposals for acquisition of land in advance which left open both the extent to which the powers would be used and the extent to which any land so acquired would remain in public ownership.

Ministers differed in their views on how far the Government should commit themselves at this stage to large developments in a few places, and therefore on the proposal that town expansion corporations should be established. Apart from this, however, opinions were divided on the role which might be played by new town corporations and town expansion corporations, if these were formed. It was common ground that a larger share of development in any further new town or large expanded town in the south-east should be entrusted to private enterprise than had been done in existing projects of this kind. However, some ministers felt that it might be practicable to deal with the required developments in the south-east under some general comprehensive plan agreed between the local authorities and the Government which would be implemented jointly by local authorities and private enterprise; the local authorities would deal particularly with provision of subsidised housing, and they would have available for use if necessary their powers of compulsory purchase of land. Other ministers pointed to experience under the Town Development Act as ground for thinking that this approach would not be effective, and they stressed that central control was necessary to bring in the required employment, to ensure the required proportions of subsidised and unsubsidised housing, and to phase the whole operation correctly in relation to regional development elsewhere. Most of them were inclined to think that new town corporations and town expansion corporations would be the appropriate instruments for this purpose. Because of these differing views, it was concluded that the white paper should be drafted in such a way that the Government would not be committed to any particular method of implementation. This was to be left open for further consideration by ministers after the local authorities concerned with the study had been consulted.

In the draft white paper submitted to the Cabinet the relevant paragraph read:

> 'In the planned expansion schemes it will be necessary to keep a close control over the provision of land for two reasons. The first is to enable the whole programme to be phased correctly. The second is to ensure that land is brought forward as it is required for development, whether by private enterprise or public agencies. Where the development takes the form of new towns broadly satisfactory machinery exists. The Government intends to work out fresh arrangements for carrying through major town expansion schemes in partnership with local authorities, and they envisage that the land needed for these schemes should be acquired well in advance of needs.'

When the draft white paper came before the Cabinet, Joseph argued that there was a big issue of policy which was concealed here —an issue 'involving our whole attitude both to land and to regional development agencies (on both of which we are under fire); and it is for consideration whether we ought not to write a good deal more into the white paper than has so far been suggested'.

The study had suggested that the only effective way of housing one-third of the expected growth in the south-east was through a few major new and expanded towns. 'The question is how such major development schemes should be organised.' Joseph's view was clear: they had to be organised on the basis of 'public ownership of the land, in the hands of public agencies empowered to see that the necessary development takes place as it is required, whether carried out by private developers, by local authorities or by the agencies themselves'.

The matter was the subject of some controversy at several meetings of ministers during February 1964* and was finally settled by two small but significant changes in the draft white paper. The revised version (as published)† read as follows (the original words are given in brackets while the changes are underlined):

---

* For further discussion see *History Vol IV*, chapter VII.

† The white paper *South East England* was published as Cmnd 2308 in March 1964.

'The Government intend to work out <u>similar</u> [fresh] arrangements for carrying through major town expansion schemes in partnership with the local authorities, and they envisage that the land needed for these schemes should be acquired <u>as necessary</u> [well] in advance of needs.'

Informal discussions later took place between the ministry and some of the local authorities concerned.* From these, it emerged that, of the schemes proposed for growth in *The South East Study*, most were either small enough to take place as part of the normal growth of the town without special machinery, or a sufficiently large expansion of a small place to be handled without difficulty as a traditional new town. Only three schemes fell between the two— Ipswich, Northampton and Peterborough—and, before the election in October 1964, it was felt within the ministry that legislation specifically to deal with them was hardly justified: the new town machinery, with designation of the whole of the existing town areas, would be suitable, notwithstanding the political and technical problems that would be involved.

---

* See chapter IX, p. 512 *et seq.*

CHAPTER V

New Towns Policy 1964–69

IN the last chapter an account was given of the marked change in policy towards new towns which took place during the years between 1960 and 1964. Three factors were of particular importance in this change: the expectation of a huge increase in population; the intractable overspill problems of the conurbations; and the growing acceptance of the concept of 'growth points' as a major element in regional development. Against this background the Conservative Government had agreed to an additional eight new towns. Six of these (Dawley, Livingston, Redditch, Runcorn, Skelmersdale and Washington) had reached the designation stage before the return of the Labour Government in October 1964. The other two encountered various difficulties which delayed designation until 1966 for Irvine* and 1968 for Warrington (Risley).

In addition to these agreed new towns there were the proposals in *The South East Study* for the expansion of several of the London new towns and for major developments at Ipswich, Northampton, Peterborough and elsewhere.

During the six years 1964–70 the Labour Government embarked on many of these proposals, decided upon the further new towns of central Lancashire and Newtown (in central Wales), the extension of Dawley (renamed Telford) and the commissioning of studies of large scale development in Humberside, Severnside and Tayside.

Each proposal involved detailed investigation by a number of government departments, followed by negotiations with local authorities and statutory undertakers, and consultation with the newly formed regional economic planning councils. Inevitably, therefore, specific proposals tended to come to maturity in an erratic fashion and this accounts for the episodic character of the narrative which follows.

Review of the South East Study†

The most urgent outstanding issue at the time of the 1964 election was that of London and the south-east where *The South East Study* had indicated that by 1981 there would be a population increase of

---

* Irvine was not discussed at Cabinet level after the Conservative Government's agreement in principle in July 1964: see chapter IV, p. 192 footnote.

† ED(64)39, ED(64)9th Meeting, 21 December 1964; and Treasury Files 2AT 636/01 and 2AT 335/02.

at least 3·5 million. An overspill of at least one million people was expected from London, of whom 400,000 would find houses within commuting range, and 600,000 would need to move further out. It was also expected that the strong growth of employment would continue and that there would be an acute land shortage around London. The study outlined three main approaches to the problems: first, to take strong measures to encourage growth outside the south-east; secondly, to ensure that no employment growth took place in the south-east which could be diverted elsewhere; and thirdly, to plan for the best possible distribution of the population growth that seemed inevitable. The study indicated that most of the region's new population could be provided for by the normal process of allocating land in development plans, but that the overspill of over one million from London would necessitate a further generation of new and expanded towns. Major new cities were suggested for the South-ampton-Portsmouth area, and for the Bletchley and Newbury areas. New towns were suggested for Ashford (Kent), and for Stansted (Essex) where a new airport was contemplated. Large expansions were also proposed at Ipswich, Northampton, Peter-borough and Swindon, with smaller expansions elsewhere.

The study had been prepared by officials, and in a white paper published in March 1964 (Cmnd 2308), the Conservative Government accepted it as a reasonable assessment of the nature and scale of the population problem in the south-east, but had not committed themselves to any of the specific proposals. The study was circulated to local planning authorities and the local authorities in the south-east as a basis for consultation and comment.

In their election manifestos, both the Conservative and Labour Parties explicitly committed themselves to a positive policy in relation to new towns. The Conservative manifesto stated:

'Our regional studies showing land needs for twenty years ahead will enable planning authorities to release ample land in the right places and without damage to the green belts . . . When major developments are in prospect—such as the many new towns or town expansions which are being started or proposed—land will be acquired well in advance* and made available to private and public enterprise as necessary.'

The Labour manifesto laid greater emphasis on public initiative and the mechanism (the Land Commission) by which land would be acquired:

'. . . control over the location of new factories and offices, inducements to firms to move where industry is declining, the establishment of new public enterprises where these prove necessary—all these measures will be required to check the present drift to the south and to build up the declining economies in other parts of our country . . . Regional planning is necessary if we are to

---

* The phrase 'well in advance' appeared in the draft version of the white paper *South East England* but, as recounted in the previous chapter, was rejected in favour of 'as necessary'.

solve the problems of slum clearance and overcrowding in our major cities; to carry out a vigorous programme for new towns and overspill development, including the proposed new town for central Wales . . . The Crown Land Commission will buy the land at a price based on its existing use value plus an amount sufficient to cover any contingent losses by the owner . . . Labour will also increase the building of new houses both for rent and for sale.'

The Labour Government took office on 16 October 1964. George Brown became First Secretary of State and Minister for Economic Affairs, and R. H. S. Crossman became Minister of Housing and Local Government. Under the new regime, the Department of Economic Affairs assumed responsibility for, *inter alia*, the broad strategy of regional development, and quickly became immersed in the problem of inducements or disincentives which should be made available to persuade or direct industry to contribute to economic growth, particularly in the development areas. In parallel with this problem was that of dealing with the expected population growth which had been highlighted by *The South East Study*.

The study had not had an entirely enthusiastic welcome, and an early decision of the new Government was that its basic assumptions on population, migration and employment should be reviewed. Nevertheless, Crossman wrote to Brown on 2 November 1964 that 'as things are, the prospects for housing Londoners are worse than anywhere'. He proposed to announce in a forthcoming debate that he intended 'to take early action to start three of the large town expansion schemes proposed in the study [not specifying which] and also one new city [not specifying which].' On this, sparring took place at the official level, where the lines of responsibility between the new Department of Economic Affairs and other departments were not yet clearly established. MHLG wanted to go ahead, but the Treasury were nervous about the effect on land prices and about the financial commitments that were involved. The Department of Economic Affairs objected to the announcement of a new city, and felt that the plan for the south-east should be considered in the context of a national plan. In the upshot, Brown circulated a note to the ministerial committee on economic development (of which he was chairman and which consisted of most ministers for the home departments). This dealt with a paper prepared by officials on London's housing problems and recommended as an immediate step 'to keep going a minimum flow of new houses over the next ten to twenty years', the expansion of the new towns of Stevenage, Harlow and Basildon, and major new schemes at Ipswich, Northampton, Peterborough and in North Buckinghamshire.

The paper by officials stressed that the review of the study could hardly reduce the estimate of overspill from London, since this was based on the expected natural increase within, and the physical capacity of, the London conurbation. The population of the conurbation had been falling as the densely populated inner areas were redeveloped. The study suggested that the policy should now be to keep the population up to its current level of about eight million. Even this would involve building at high density and thus at high cost. To attempt to do more would involve redevelopment at densities which would be unacceptable both socially and economically, and there was no practical prospect of housing the continuing natural increase estimated at one million. At least an equivalent number of Londoners would therefore have to move out as 'overspill'.

The study assumed that of those one million, 400,000 'would make their own arrangements', many of them commuting back to London to work. This assumption might need to be reviewed but, even on this basis, there was a need to provide for at least 600,000 London overspill in planned expansion schemes, which implied a twenty-year programme of around 10,000 houses a year.

Planned schemes were needed to cope with this substantial proportion of the overspill for two reasons. First, much of the housing need would be for rented dwellings: these could be provided only in planned schemes. Secondly, planned schemes gave the best control to ensure that the development effectively helped London's housing problems and did not simply attract more people into the south-east. (Experience of the first generation new towns had shown that some 80 per cent of the incomers were from London; the remainder were mainly managers and key workers, many of whom came from elsewhere in the south-east.)

These planned schemes needed to be well away from London so that they did not add to the congestion of the metropolitan area. Planned schemes based on commuting would hardly be practicable even if they were desirable, in view of the cost of commuting to the tenants and the possible heavy investment which would be involved for British Railways.

Large schemes had advantages over small ones: they gave bigger and quicker results for the same administrative and technical effort; they gave more scope for the efficient large contractor and for industrialised building; and they could offer the inhabitants a much greater range of employment. It was recommended therefore that the programme should rely heavily on large schemes.

Anticipating objection, officials raised the question as to why decisions were necessary at this stage, before the review of *The South East Study* and the preparation of a national plan. Was there not a danger that this would prejudice the outcome of these wider exercises? The main issue was one of timing. A full-scale review of the study would take at least nine months to complete, but decisions were already badly overdue on the minimum action which in any case would be necessary to deal with the London housing problem.

The output of the London new towns had already fallen from the Conservative Government's peak of over 10,000 houses in 1956 to 3,300; and there were only 20,000 houses left in the programme. To this should be added the London County Council's programme of town expansions, but the output of this had been disappointing and the scope for an immediate increase was limited.

Thus there was need for some schemes which could produce substantial results quickly. The only way of achieving this was by the expansion of existing new towns, where a highly effective machine was already in operation. An immediate decision on these could have a worthwhile effect on house completions in 1966 and a substantial one in 1967. Nevertheless, these schemes would bridge the gap only for a few years and would fall away steadily from 1971 onwards. Entirely new large schemes took five years at least to reach a substantial housing output, and thus a decision was needed immediately on these also if they were to be ready 'to take the load' in time. With these factors in mind, the departments concerned proposed an 'interim programme' (which constituted the schemes proposed by Brown in his covering note).*

By the time that land was acquired for development, the Land Commission might be in operation but, even under existing legislation, the land costs for new schemes (as distinct from extensions of existing new towns) need not be excessive. Provided that the schemes were carried out under the New Towns Acts, the special provisions of the Land Compensation Act 1961 would apply to the terms on which the land was acquired (with the effect of excluding any enhancement of value by reason of the development itself). This applied to all the land acquired, whether it was ultimately developed on public account or leased to private developers. But these special provisions did not apply to acquisitions for the extension of existing new towns. In these cases the price of acquisition would take account of the development value in the land created by the existence of the new town.

If all the land required for these extensions had to be acquired under existing legislation, the additional cost of paying for the development value might be very great. Development could begin at Basildon on land within the designated area, but some acquisition of land outside the designated areas would be necessary at Stevenage and Harlow (possibly 200 acres at each place) at prices which might range up to £10,000 an acre or more, although part at least was expected to cost no more than land in the designated area which had been fetching about £1,000 an acre.†

---

* See page 209 above.

† The provisions relating to compensation for acquisition of land for extensions of new towns were amended by the New Towns Act 1966: see appendix C.

The cost of the capital investment involved could not readily be calculated at this early stage but, broadly, it was expected to be of the order of £700m–£750m over the fifteen years from 1967. The case for this programme of large development carried out as 'new towns' rested primarily on considerations of practicability and physical planning, but it was also arguable that, in terms of physical resources, it was probably the cheapest method.

Hitherto, expansion of existing towns had been carried out under the Town Development Act, but these had been comparatively small schemes and the machinery, dependent as it was on the local authorities, was quite inadequate for carrying out schemes of the magnitude now proposed. Moreover, the towns were not willing to go ahead under those powers, and even the largest of the towns concerned (Ipswich) was, at 120,000, much too small to mount a programme of the order of 1,500 houses a year in addition to its own needs.

Although the use of large new towns was economical in physical resources, a much higher proportion of the capital finance came from the exchequer, as compared with other methods of development. This proportion was not fixed, and there was scope for considerable flexibility in the proportion of developments carried out by private enterprise. Moreover, the expansion of large towns was a new departure, and the relationship with the three large existing towns in the programme (viz Ipswich, Northampton and Peterborough) would be different from that with the very small communities existing at the beginning of the first generation new towns. For example, it was already clear that the local authorities would want a share in the equity of the profitable central areas. If this were eventually agreed, they should be expected to share in the cost of the town development as a whole. Even so, the exchequer share of total investment would be high. In any event, the specific financial arrangements to be adopted would remain to be determined in the light of detailed consultation between MHLG and the Treasury.

The proposed programme also had to be considered in relation to other new town commitments and to the housing programme. The firm commitments for England and Wales were:

	£m
Outstanding balance of first generation London new towns	200
Outstanding balance of other first generation new towns	70
Second generation new towns in the north and midlands already firmly committed	520

This total of £790m included some £560m of exchequer investment. In addition to these firm commitments, there was the likelihood that the review of *The South East Study* would establish a case for at least some further new towns. If these were on the scale proposed in the study, the total investment on them would be of the order of £1,500m. Moreover, a case for further new towns for the midlands and the north might emerge from the studies being undertaken in these regions.

It thus had to be recognised that the proposals involved decisions on a substantial programme of new towns in the south-east, and a major exchequer commitment in principle, in advance of any indication of the further new town requirements elsewhere in the country, let alone the final requirements for the south-east itself. This consideration had to be weighed along with the case for immediate decisions.

If the programme were approved in principle, the timing of its implementation and the acceptance of specific financial commitments would be matters to be determined by the normal processes of consultation between the Ministry of Housing and Local Government and the Treasury and other relevant departments. The investment would have to come within the total investment figures accepted for housing and other environmental services, while the number of houses represented by this programme would be one element in the national house building programme. It would pre-empt a relatively large allocation of exchequer capital finance, but even when these schemes reached maximum output, the annual number of houses produced would represent only one-fifth of the estimated total required to meet London's needs.

These proposals by officials were warmly supported by Brown and Crossman, but Jay (President of the Board of Trade)—while agreeing to the need for early action—had major reservations about the effect of the London new towns on the growth of the south-east and their insufficient contribution to the London housing problem. (He developed his arguments at length in a letter to Crossman.) Callaghan (Chancellor of the Exchequer) agreed in principle to the proposals for the new towns, but felt that further consideration was necessary on the methods by which developments should be financed. There were also doubts on the wisdom of announcing decisions relating to the south-east before the development of a national plan which would contain proposals for new towns and for opportunities for employment in areas where the traditional industries were contracting. Notwithstanding these hesitations, ministers approved the proposals in principle. The announcement as ultimately made by Crossman in the House of Commons on 3 February 1965 was as follows:

'In co-operation with the local authorities, I am making every effort to stimulate house building within the conurbation. But there are limits to the extent that London can be built up, and there can be no doubt that the needs of the existing population call for a new programme of building in new and expanded towns in order to end the housing shortage, replace houses lost through slum clearance and other redevelopment, and keep pace with natural increase.

A critical fact is that the output of houses in the present new towns is running down as they near completion. Immediate decisions are necessary if we are to avoid a disastrous gap in housing for Londoners.

To prevent this the Government propose, as an interim measure, to go ahead with a new town in North Buckinghamshire and with the expansion of Ipswich, Peterborough and Northampton. I will shortly be discussing with local authorities concerned the measures needed to implement these proposals including the surveys that will be needed to determine the precise siting of the development. In particular, I shall be considering with them the desirability of using the machinery of the New Towns Act for these schemes.

I am also discussing with the Greater London Council the possibility of an expansion of some of its existing overspill schemes.

There remains the question of land for people who move themselves out of London into the home counties. Some of these will move well away, but many will want and will need to live within reach of London and they must have the chance to do so. Moreover, land must be made available for the new households of the population already living in the 40-mile ring. My department will shortly be discussing with the individual local planning authorities where, in the outer metropolitan region, this additional land can best be provided, leaving aside, for the time being, the question of any provision for migration into the south-east.

These measures are urgently needed to ensure a continued housing programme for people who have to move out of London. In order to avoid prejudicing the south-east review, especially in relation to migration from other parts of the country, the Government's aim will be to secure that an even greater proportion of houses provided will go to Londoners than in the existing new towns: also, that the employment provided will be in activities that cannot be located further away from London, and not, for example, in new industrial growth that could take place elsewhere in Great Britain.'

In the course of the ministerial consultation which took place on this statement, Jay wrote a full letter on 1 January 1965 which was supported by Ross (Secretary of State for Scotland) who argued that:

'there is genuine apprehension in Scotland that new major developments in the south-east may increase the magnetic pull there, unless the build-up of population in the new and expanding towns there is very strictly controlled as Douglas Jay suggests, and pretty rigorous action is taken to make sure that they really do cater for Londoners'.

Jay's letter is of particular importance and is worth summarising at some length.

*Jay's Letter to Crossman**

Jay fully appreciated that it was necessary to provide for the housing of a large natural increase of population in London and the south-east during the following twenty years. He also agreed that some of the necessary town expansion schemes to take London overspill would have to be put in hand in advance of the completion of the review of *The South East Study*. He was anxious, however, that these interim schemes, and any additional schemes which might be agreed upon after the review, should not result in an expansion of employment in a way which would intensify the pull of the south-east 'and so serve to worsen and perpetuate rather than solve the housing shortage'. He also had in mind that any restraint of avoidable expansion would lighten the burden on the economy as a whole, ease pressure on the balance of payments, and help the Chancellor with his problems.

He felt safe in assuming that all this was generally accepted. But he saw two important practical implications. First, net immigration into the south-east should be kept to the absolute minimum. Secondly—and this was a way of achieving the first—steps should be taken to ensure that the new and expanding towns in the south-east were 'genuine vehicles for housing surplus population from London, and not engines for the attraction of population from outside the south-east'.

Jay suggested four ways in which employment growth could be checked in the south-east. In the first place, industrial development certificate (IDC) control could be stricter. Currently, the rule was that a firm had to satisfy the Board of Trade that it could not move to a development district; and if a move involved a material expansion, the likelihood of its satisfying the Board of Trade on this point was much reduced. Nevertheless, Jay proposed that in future it should normally be a specific condition that a London firm moving to a new or expanding town should not materially increase its labour force in the course of doing so; and that IDCs should be granted on this understanding. He accepted that it would not be possible to be rigid in the application of this policy, and account would need to be taken of the particular circumstances of individual firms, but at least it should be a clear objective to effect the move without significant expansion. This was not to suggest that IDC policy should operate more strictly in the new and expanding towns than elsewhere in the south-east: only that it should be applied with equal strictness, and that substantial expansion should not be permitted solely because a firm was moving to a London overspill area.

Secondly, though he did not advocate control of vacant factories

---

* Treasury File 2AT 335/02.

as such, Jay felt that, as far as possible, factories vacated by firms moving from London to the new and expanded towns should be taken out of industrial use. In particular, more sites could be acquired for housing—if necessary with direct exchequer assistance. This might be costly at the outset, but it would be 'in the nature of an investment' which would appreciate over the years. There might also be scope for the defence departments or the Ministry of Public Building and Works to take over factories for storage purposes, and this was being investigated.

Thirdly, greater efforts could be made to ensure that houses in new and expanded towns were allocated exclusively to families from London.

Fourthly, he asked whether it was not possible to insist that new town development corporations should normally retain ownership of the factories in their area, or should only sell to private firms on condition that, if the firms sold again, they could sell only to the corporation. This would prevent firms outside the south-east moving into these new towns.

Jay added that, from his own personal experience as a London MP, even where migrants to the new towns did come from London, they very seldom came from the high priority groups on the council housing lists:

'I think it is not realised in Whitehall how virtually impossible it is for the worst housed families in central London to get a house in a new town. In the hundreds of cases I have handled over fifteen years I can hardly recall a single one where the new towns were a real help to the housing problem. This is because we have paid too little attention to real housing needs and too much to the doctrine that people should have a job before they get a house (instead of allowing them to go to the new towns and get a job there subsequently, if they wish, or to commute to work in London if they prefer). It seems to me that there should be a much greater effort to get people nominated from the London local authority housing lists into homes in the new towns than has been achieved by the present industrial selection scheme. This would mean modifying the rule that people must have jobs in these towns before they can get housing. I do not myself believe that any public authority should dictate to people how far they should travel to work.'

Jay appreciated that it might be 'difficult and vexatious' to carry out some of these proposals, but he believed that they could ensure that the proposed further round of new and expanding towns would be a genuine rehousing operation. Without such measures, 'we may be inadvertently launching another uncontrollable drift into the south-east and depopulation of other areas'.

*Review of Policy for the South East**
The strategic policy issues raised by Jay fell within the scope of the

---

* ED(65)79 and ED(65)18th Meeting, 2 August 1965.

review being undertaken by officials, an interim report on which was presented to ministers in July 1965.

As a first stage in the review, a detailed analysis was made of recent trends in population and employment in the south-east and of likely developments up to 1981. The analysis revealed no reason to disagree with the total volume of population increase estimated in *The South East Study*. Newly available statistics, however, showed that the bulk of the net migration to the region up to 1981 (now estimated at 900,000) was likely to come from the Commonwealth, the Irish Republic and foreign countries. In particular, a large proportion would consist of dependants of Commonwealth immigrants. (These dependants formed such a large part of total Commonwealth immigration that recent measures taken to reduce immigration would not have a significant effect on the figures.) It was assumed that the efforts to strengthen the Scottish economy would be successful and that, as a result, net migration from Scotland would gradually diminish—and, by 1981, would cease. On current trends, employment growth would continue in the south-east outside Greater London but, in the conurbation itself, there were signs that the growth might be coming to a halt. The reasons for this were complex, but it was suggested that it was due to the cumulative effect of both 'natural' factors (congestion and the long term movement of employment outwards) and government policy (IDC control). This was one of the more important issues revealed by the review which—if confirmed—would have an important bearing on transport planning and location of employment policy.

Overspill from London was estimated in the study at one million between 1961 and 1981 but, in the light of more recent information, it was apparent that the London 'housing deficit' was greater than had been assumed. As a result, it was now estimated that there would be an overspill of one million over the shorter period 1964 to 1981. Measures to restrain employment growth in the south-east had already been strengthened (for example by the introduction of controls over office development)* and further proposals to improve the effectiveness of these and of positive inducements were being considered by ministers. On balance, officials concluded that it was unnecessary to strengthen further the disincentives to the growth of employment in the south-east since it might prejudice economic growth in the region (which, they pointed out, produced 40 per cent of total British output). The situation in Greater London was such that the time did not seem to be right to introduce severe measures until it was clearer whether the new employment trends would continue. This conclusion, however, was taken within the

---

* See *History Vol IV* chapter VIII.

limited context of the south-east and, in any case, the situation would need to be kept under review.

The Scottish Office disagreed with this conclusion. In particular, they challenged the contention that efforts to strengthen the Scottish economy were all that was necessary to reduce net migration from Scotland. They considered that this would not occur without the assistance of further disincentives—notably fiscal disincentives—operating against the south-east and other areas where there was heavy pressure on manpower resources.

When this report was considered by ministers, Jay reiterated his argument that it was wrong to base policy for the south-east on the assumption that there would be a net immigration of 900,000 people between 1961 and 1981. He was not satisfied that in practice the new Commonwealth immigrants would in fact settle in the south-east. The Government's policy of encouraging development in other regions might well lead immigrants to settle there. If, however, the conclusions of the report were taken as the basis for policy, and houses and other facilities provided for an additional 3·5 million people then, in fact, population growth on the projected scale might well take place. Further study was required before any government statement was issued.

The issue was an urgent one since Crossman needed to open discussions with local authorities in the region about their long term development plans. These discussions had been held up for eight months while officials reconsidered the figures which had previously been published. Quick decisions were required about the handling of the London overspill and the treatment of the London green belt. The figures for population growth in the report by officials were the best working assumptions which could currently be made. There could be no advantage in further delaying a statement setting out the figures.

After further discussion, ministers agreed that the best working assumption that could be made of the growth of population in the south-east between 1961 and 1981 was 3·5 million as set out in the report by officials. This working assumption was based on existing policies. It should be used as the basis for discussion between the Minister of Housing and Local Government and the local authorities. It should, however, be kept under review. Parliament would be informed that a further review of the position had resulted in these conclusions.*

Regional Policies†

The review of policies relating to the south-east was undertaken

---

* See statements by Brown, HC Debates, Vol 717, Col 347–8, 4 August 1965, and by Crossman, HC Debates, Vol 722, Col 2117, 22 December 1965.

† ED(65)75, ED(65)76 and ED(65)18th Meeting, 2 August 1965.

at the same time as a review of regional economic policies. The latter was of immediate concern not only because of government commitments to a positive policy of regional development (which necessitated an announcement of what the policies would be), but also because the existing legislation—the Local Employment Acts of 1960 and 1963—were due to expire in March 1967.

The final outcome of a series of lengthy discussions at official and ministerial levels was the white paper on Investment Incentives (Cmnd 2874) which formed the basis for the Industrial Development Act 1966. This replaced the former development *districts* with wider continuous development *areas*, and improved the financial incentives to firms established in or moving to them. In the course of the discussions, an issue arose of particular concern to this history— namely the policy to be adopted in relation to the new and expanded towns which were expected to have to provide for overspill from the big cities on a larger scale than in the past. It was agreed that decisions on overspill schemes should not be taken without a thorough examination of the possibilities for the provision of industry and of what this implied in terms of other demands on the limited supply of mobile industry. It was accepted that once a decision had been taken in favour of an overspill scheme (involving a substantial commitment of public money) it was a proper objective of policy to achieve an adequate provision of employment to ensure its viability.

There was, however, some disagreement about how this objective should be attained. The Ministry of Housing took the view that it was necessary to give overspill areas *equal* priority with the development areas when the Government wished to encourage industrial expansion and that this equality of treatment had to apply to overspill towns even in the south-east and the midlands. The Board of Trade and the Department of Economic Affairs considered that the existing policy of giving *second* priority to overspill towns not directly connected with a development area was fully adequate, arguing that this policy had provided enough industry for these towns, and sometimes 'embarrassingly more than enough'. The issue was settled by ministers at the end of 1965 when it was agreed that there should be no change in the statutory requirement on the Board of Trade to have regard to the needs of the development areas in steering industry.*

A New Town for Manchester†

In January 1965, ministers discussed the problem of the site of a new town for Manchester, the need for which was generally accepted. The previous Government had announced (in June 1964) that a site

---

* The matter arose again in 1969: see appendix A.

† ED(65)2nd Meeting, 25 January 1965; C(65)13, C(65)14, and CC(65)7th Conclusions, 5 February 1965.

at Risley (immediately east of Warrington) had been selected for a new town for 50,000 people, subject to a detailed survey. The detailed survey had in fact shown that the site was unsuitable for a new town, mainly because of projected coal workings and the existence of peat, though a limited commuter development for some 15,000 people was practicable. The alternative therefore seemed to be either to create a new commuter town at Lymm, or to create a new town with its own industries at Leyland–Chorley.

The first solution had the advantage that it would meet Manchester's need for another overspill outlet, but was open to several objections 'on grounds of regional planning'. The second solution would make a much more valuable contribution to social and economic growth in the north-west, but would be a less direct solution of Manchester's immediate problems. It also implied a belief in the ability of the north-west to achieve the necessary industrial growth at Leyland–Chorley, in addition to what was needed for the development districts and the new towns of Skelmersdale and Runcorn. It further implied an acceptance of the probable need to provide financial incentives to industry.

Underlying the question of the actual site of the new town there were two more fundamental issues: what should be the employment base of the town, and what should be its ultimate function in the region?

A new town at Lymm would be conceived primarily as a commuter settlement with travel back to work in Manchester. There was some doubt on how satisfactory daily travel would be: there were no longer any rail services, and the existing road (A56) was heavily overloaded. But by the time a new town at Lymm began to take shape in the early 1970s, the Princess Parkway motorway from the centre of Manchester would have been extended to a point about four miles to the east of Lymm village and would later be extended closer to the site so that road travel by bus or car would be much easier. Additional commuting by car, however, would put a heavy strain on Manchester's capacity to absorb traffic.

Though a commuter new town was in principle less satisfactory than a self-contained new town, MHLG held that a commuter new town had advantages when it was intended to support a massive slum clearance programme, because people could be rehoused in such a town from the central core of the conurbation without at the same time having to be provided with new jobs.

A new town at Leyland–Chorley on the other hand would have to be supported from the outset by its own industry, since people could not be expected to travel to and from Manchester for work each day. Although there was a sizeable industrial base in the immediate neighbourhood, it would not be enough to support a new town. Under existing distribution of industry policies, new industrial employment to support a Manchester new town would have to come from industry planned out or moving from Manchester itself. The amount of mobile industry available from Manchester would, on past experience, be inadequate to provide a base for a new town. It would therefore be necessary to steer industry from other parts of the country. It would probably also be necessary to provide positive financial incentives for Leyland–Chorley in view of its proximity to the Merseyside development district and the new towns of Skelmersdale and Runcorn where financial incentives were already available.

All this would require a change in legislation. In any case, distribution of industry policy had to be reviewed since the current legislation expired in 1967. The possibility of a change was a factor that might be taken into account in considering the case for Leyland–Chorley. On the other hand, it might well be undesirable to announce a decision now which would prejudge the outcome of the review, particularly since it would worsen the prospects of attracting new industry to the development districts.

The second main issue was the ultimate function of a new town in the region. A new town at Lymm would be conceived primarily as an overspill outlet of limited size. Its purpose would be to enable the Government to give rapid and substantial support to the conurbation's slum clearance programme. Leyland–Chorley would be conceived from the outset as a regional growth point. For this it would be well suited. There was room for a town of 150,000 people, and the ultimate outcome could be a new city (based on Preston, Leyland and Chorley) of about 400,000. The site was well clear of congested southern Lancashire and it would present a unique opportunity to reverse the general drift of population towards the southern part of the region and to bring life to the Preston–Blackburn area.

There were strong agricultural objections to a development at Lymm which would be on first class agricultural land—and which had twice been rejected as a development site for this reason. There would not be such strong objections to development at Leyland–Chorley.

Lancashire County Council would welcome a large development in the Leyland–Chorley area. Cheshire County Council would be likely to oppose bitterly the revival of a proposal for a new town at Lymm. Manchester, while they would no doubt accept Leyland–Chorley ('indeed they could not do otherwise'), would probably say that it had little relevance to their immediate problems. 'They had long set their hearts on Lymm.'

In short, though the interested departments were agreed that the case for a new town to help with Manchester's housing problem was very strong, there was little agreement on where it should be located. DEA considered that it should be at Leyland–Chorley, where it would be supported by its own industrial and other employment and could be an economic and social growth point for the region. MHLG agreed with the project for a big new town at Leyland–Chorley, but they considered that it should come rather later. They believed that there was an immediate need for a new town directly related to Manchester's housing problems and that the best site for this was at Lymm. The Board of Trade found neither of these proposals satisfactory and considered that, if some immediate action were necessary, a limited expansion at Bury might provide some interim relief while long term solutions were worked out. The Ministry of Agriculture greatly preferred a new town at Leyland–Chorley, supplemented, if necessary, by immediate commuter development on a smaller scale at Bury.

It was eventually decided that the balance of advantage lay in implementing the proposal for a new town at Leyland–Chorley, provided that this was presented primarily as the second stage in a plan to meet the housing needs of Manchester (of which the development in the Risley area of Warrington would be the first stage). No reference would be made yet to the possibility that the Government might seek fresh legislative authority to provide, in this and other similar areas, new financial incentives to attract industry. The industrial content of the new town should therefore be provided, so far as possible, by the transfer of industry and offices from Manchester itself.

It was later decided that the limited development at Risley should form part of a comprehensive plan for 'Greater Warrington' and that the machinery of the New Towns Act would be used for this purpose. An announcement about the Warrington and Leyland–Chorley proposals was made in a statement in the House of Commons on 24 February 1965:

'The Government have been considering as a matter of urgency how they can help Manchester to deal with its housing problems in a way that would contribute positively to the general prosperity and growth of the north-west.

Like other great conurbations, Manchester cannot hope to provide houses within its own boundaries for all those living in slums and for its total natural increase. If decent living conditions are to be achieved in its bold schemes for central redevelopment, a substantial number of those rehoused must be found homes outside the city. In addition to all its secondary efforts to find sites for dealing with overspill, therefore, Manchester needs at least the equivalent of two new towns.

The search for suitable sites took several years. Finally, last year, the choice fell on Risley—12 miles from Manchester and only two miles from Warrington. This announcement was received with a good deal of doubt and criticism. I must now inform the House that a detailed survey has revealed that serious subsidence and other geological defects rule out a large part of the area. It has been strongly urged that the whole Risley project should be abandoned. But in view of Manchester's urgent needs and the fact that about 13,000 houses can be built quickly here, I feel that, on balance, the right course is to provide these houses as soon as possible and to use the New Towns Act for this purpose.

In view of its nearness to Warrington, it seems to me essential that the new development of the Risley area should form part of a comprehensive plan for the whole Warrington area. I propose, therefore, to start consultations at once in order to see how this can best be achieved. In particular, I propose to discuss with the local authorities whether it would not be possible, in carrying out this comprehensive operation, to achieve a partnership of the kind we are now working out in Ipswich, Northampton and Peterborough.

In addition to the Warrington–Risley project, Manchester will be able to rely on its own development scheme at Westhoughton, which I have now approved, with some important modifications. This should provide for about 13,000 houses. Manchester would itself carry out this scheme in co-operation with the local authorities concerned.

But, by themselves, these short term partial solutions—for that is all they are —would still leave Manchester without the assurance of long term relief. To meet this need, the Government have decided to designate a site in the Leyland–Chorley area for a large new town. In addition to providing for the long-term overspill needs of Manchester, this new town—strategically well placed in relation to the road–rail network—should contribute to the industrial revival of the whole region, and form a new focus for urban renewal.

I will shortly be discussing with Lancashire and the other authorities the appointment of consultants to carry out a detailed survey as a preliminary to designating the site under the New Towns Act.'*

In May 1967 a draft order was published designating some 21,500 acres covering Warrington County Borough and adjacent parts of Lancashire and Cheshire for development as a new town to provide for 40,000 people from Manchester by 1981. A public inquiry was held later in the year and, in April 1968, the minister made an order designating 18,650 acres as the site of the new town. The corporation was appointed in 1969.†

Planning for the Year 2000‡

During 1966, the Ministry of Housing and Local Government were heavily engaged in the consultations and statutory procedures for the new and expanded towns which had been proposed in the previous year. But ministers collectively were more concerned with the expected population growth and its 'long term distribution', on which a substantial report was produced by a committee of officials in May 1966. This was the first matter to be discussed by the new

---

* HC Debates, Vol 707, Col 398, 24 February 1965.
† For the continuation of the Leyland/Chorley story see p. 253 below.
‡ EP(66)2 and EP(66)1st Meeting, 20 June 1966.

ministerial committee on Environmental Planning which was chaired by George Brown and included most ministers of home departments. The report had been asked for by ministers to enable a decision to be taken on whether to commission feasibility studies of very large scale new developments in selected areas.

The work of the official committee had shown that the problem of planning for the year 2000 was too complex, and the available information (particularly on economic questions) too limited for it to be possible to prepare a full report quickly.† The work completed so far, however, was sufficient to show that large scale new developments were prima facie necessary and desirable; and that, although the full extent of the necessary new developments up to 2000 could not yet be assessed, certain places were 'obvious candidates'.

On the best judgment that could be made, the population of Great Britain was likely to grow by twenty million by the end of the century—from 53·1 million in 1965 to 72·5 million in 2000. Despite the wide margins of error to which such long term forecasts were necessarily subject, it was 'inconceivable that any adjustments to the forecasts would dispose of the need for forward planning to accommodate population growth on a very considerable scale'.

Estimates of household formation were available only up to 1981 : these showed an expected increase in households of 1·8 million— from 17·0 million in 1965 to 18·8 million in 1981. This, however, was by no means the limit of the need for new housing and urban facilities: there was a much larger problem of redevelopment. No fully adequate official statistics were available of the age of the housing stock, but the committee drew upon a comprehensive survey made in March 1964 by Dr P. A. Stone for the National Institute for Economic and Social Research. Taking seventy years as the life of an ordinary dwelling ('and with the increase of wealth that will accrue by 2000 this seems a reasonable though arbitrary life to assume'), about half of the 16·8 million dwellings which were standing in 1964 would require replacement by the end of the century.

The need for redevelopment, however, was not confined to housing but, in the absence of appropriate statistics on the number, age and condition of non-residential buildings, it was impossible to make any precise estimate of the total scale of redevelopment which would be required by the year 2000. Nevertheless, 'it is reasonable to suggest that if renewal of our urban fabric proceeds in parallel with the renewal of the housing stock, some two-fifths or more will have to be replaced by that date'.

All these figures merely represented rough orders of magnitude, but they clearly conveyed an idea of the scale of the difficulties to be

---

† The 'full' report was completed in 1969 and published in 1971: see further p. 286–8 below.

analysed and faced in planning for the year 2000. Substantial growth of existing major urban areas was inevitable,* but it was clear that a number of new areas for major development would be required before the end of the century to accommodate 'at least several million people'. The broad balance between the numbers of people who could 'most suitably' be housed in new growth points and the numbers who could best be accommodated in expansions of existing settlements could not yet be foreseen: this would be a major issue to be dealt with in a later and fuller report. The problem, however, was of a national rather than a regional character. No previous attempt had been made to determine a national strategy for long term development. To date, the location of new towns had been decided mainly in the context of the problems of particular large cities. This would be quite inadequate for the future. New developments would need to be planned in terms of their total scale and 'the increasingly close-knit national context that will affect them in terms of communications, technological change, etc.' It would be necessary to plan major expansions as national growth centres which might attract population from outside the region in which they were located. 'The problem of constructing an environment for 2000 will be a national problem and solutions must be conceived in national terms.'

On this approach, a major consideration in the selection of sites was 'their prospects of being able to create and sustain economic growth for themselves' and the extent to which the general pattern of new settlement was conducive to the growth of the economy as a whole. 'Major new cities will make too important a contribution to the economic growth and well-being of the country to be located merely where developable land happens to be available which is not required for other uses. They must be positively sited and planned so that the most effective location is chosen for the economic activities of their population.' In the same context, advantage had to be taken of the planned investment in motorways and ports that would be required in any event to serve the existing pattern of population.

Several feasibility studies assessing the potential of particular areas

---

* It was thought that some large towns might be able to accommodate more people when areas of relatively low density and 'inefficient residential lay-out' were redeveloped. These areas were the suburbs built in the inter-war years 'which should be ready for redevelopment before 2000'. Though no assessment of the long-term capacity of existing areas had yet been made, it seemed most unlikely ('given the present unplanned character and pressing problems of our present major urban areas') that they could be developed in the time scale envisaged to absorb all the additional population which would have to be accommodated. In any case, the shorter term redevelopment problems would involve lower—not higher—densities. New growth points would relieve the pressures on land for development in and around existing urban centres. Reduced rates of urban growth at these centres would provide 'a breathing space' in which they could tackle urgent urban renewal and road problems. Towards the end of the century it would be possible to turn attention to the areas which might then take a larger share of future population growth. The degree to which this would be possible would require detailed study.

for population growth were already in hand or about to be commissioned. These studies would provide not only factual analyses and guidance on the potential capacity of the areas concerned, but also useful information bearing on the general problem and broader issues relating to the optimum pattern of settlement. The areas being studied for this purpose were Swindon–Newbury–Didcot, Portsmouth–Southampton, North Buckinghamshire, Leyland–Chorley, Greater Livingston, Falkirk–Grangemouth and Cardiff. Additionally, a planning study of the Teeside conurbation 'might also throw some light on its potential for expansion'.

Other studies, of a rather different character, were in hand, for example the preliminary study of the possibility of a Dee crossing. In addition to establishing the most suitable means of crossing the river, other objectives included the possibility of associating the crossing with land reclamation, the preservation of coastal amenities and possibly water conservation. While Deeside clearly had potential for major development, it would not be worthwhile selecting it for a feasibility study for this purpose until the results of the crossing study were available. Much the same considerations applied to the preliminary desk studies of the possible use of barrages for water conservation in Morecambe Bay and Solway. Following the reports of these studies, feasibility studies of barrages might follow. Solway, in particular, would be looked at again in the committee's full report, and the work in hand would help in the consideration of the area for a feasibility study for planned population expansion.

Officials recommended that, in addition to these studies (which would 'help to point the way later to areas of suitable expansion'), further feasibility studies should be commissioned so as to enable planning for the growth of population to proceed as rapidly as possible. The areas selected were Humberside, Severnside and Dundee.

Both Humberside and Severnside had large undeveloped areas suitable for population expansion. They were large estuaries with deep water facilities and had great potential as natural growth points—as was apparent in the largely unplanned industrial development already taking place there. This development could be made more effective if it were comprehensively planned and associated with the population growth for which there was the physical capacity. Both areas had good communications, existing or programmed, with the main industrial centres of the country and thus had a considerable advantage over more remote areas. Humberside in particular had natural advantages in providing an outlet for expanded trade between Europe and the main industrial areas. Finally, major developments at Humberside and Severnside would form the poles of a major axis of growth not orientated on London.

The development of this axis would reduce the dominance of the existing Lancashire–London axis, and thus represented 'the opening out of the present urban pattern'. This would be the most advantageous way of developing the industrial heart of the country. However, a number of particular points of difficulty would have to be examined. For Humberside, the consultants would have to take into account the possibility of a road–river crossing and also the existence, in parts of the area, of high quality agricultural land. In Severnside, a particular problem was the need to control (in the interests of safety) development near nuclear power stations.

Rather different considerations applied to Dundee. Its selection should be seen 'primarily in the context of Scotland'. Government policy was aimed at reducing the net flow of migration from Scotland, and new planned development was necessary to accommodate the increase in population which would come about not only from natural growth but also by a reduction in net migration. Outside the conurbations, other areas in Scotland were potential candidates for accommodating a significant share of the population growth up to the year 2000. But the Dundee area, as the 'open end' of industrial central Scotland, was the location which would probably have the largest influx of people resulting from the general growth of the Scottish population and redistribution from the overcrowded Clyde Valley. Accordingly, early study was recommended so that this population movement could be programmed with the minimum of delay. Dundee was also identified as the area in Scotland where employment growth could become relatively rapid, not only in the city itself but also in Perth and the Strathmore towns. All lay close enough for potential development as a coherent and unified labour market. By the early 1970s the area would be well served by the Scottish motorway system and the Tay Bridge. Although the region was experiencing a run-down of its old industries, new industries were developing, and had considerable potential.

Only three places had been selected for feasibility studies at this stage, since further study was necessary before firm recommendations could be made about other areas. The shortage of competent consultants was itself a limiting factor. Three further studies probably represented the most that could be undertaken by consultants, bearing in mind the work they already had in hand.

The report was presented by Crossman to the first meeting of the EP Committee in June 1966. He said that full feasibility studies put out to private consultants would take up to two years. Pressure was, however, growing at such a rate that it was desirable that development should go forward more quickly than this. It was also questionable whether full feasibility studies undertaken by private consultants were required for the purpose of the broad strategic decisions that the Government would need to take. Moreover, development was already beginning to occur in the Humberside area, and it was desirable that firm plans for the future of the area, to which development could be properly related, should be formulated without delay. He and Brown therefore proposed that a central planning unit should be set up to undertake the studies which were necessary for decisions of this kind. This would be situated in the Department of Economic Affairs, but would draw staff from all the departments concerned. The unit would take studies to the point where decisions were to be taken on the formal designation of an area. From that point on the process would revert to the normal departmental machinery. The unit would be asked to give their attention first to the development of Humberside and to report on that within a matter of months.* Severnside might well follow next, and the unit might thereafter proceed to study the proposed development at Dundee. This was agreed by ministers.

North Buckinghamshire New Town (Milton Keynes)†

Although Verney in North Buckinghamshire had been suggested in the late 1940s as a possible site for a new town,‡ no action followed until the mid-fifties when an LCC sponsored town development scheme was agreed at Bletchley. *The South East Study* envisaged a major expansion in the area but, in the meantime, Buckinghamshire County Council put forward proposals of their own. These were for the designation of some 15,000 acres of virtually open country lying between Bletchley and Wolverton, as a comprehensive development area under the Town and Country Planning Act 1962, in which an entirely new city of up to 250,000 people would be constructed by a partnership of the county council, the government and private enterprise. On this proposal the secretary of MHLG commented:

> 'In addition to our need to ensure machinery which will see the job through (to our time-table) we would plainly have to have a machine responsible to us (and not to the ratepayers of Bucks) if we are going to put up the money— as in the end we are going to have to do . . . Even if the council said they would stand in with us 50/50, it is an impossible relationship—they are answerable to the ratepayers and us to Parliament . . . But I am content that they should find this out for themselves—with our assistance.'

In spite of discouraging advice from the ministry, Buckinghamshire pressed forward and, at the end of 1964, completed an outline scheme for a central area complex, with four housing sectors and

---

* See below p. 267 *et seq.*
† MHLG Files NT 256/53/10, NT 256/53/11, NT 256/1/2 and NT 49/28; EP(66)17 and EP(66)5th Meeting, 21 December 1966 and CC(65)7th Conclusions, 5 February 1965.
‡ See chapter II, p. 113.

four main industrial areas, each sector containing an elevated public transport system of the monorail type, the whole at an estimated cost of some £435m. The financial proposals envisaged that the county council and private enterprise would undertake most of the profitable development, that the government would be responsible for much of the housing, and 'would be expected to give some kind of assurance of a political nature to the effect that the county council would be paid compensation if everything did not go according to the forecast, and if in particular the rate burden was excessive'. The ministry recognised that the scheme put emphasis on the introduction of private capital, but in practice felt there would be a 'strong risk of breakdown': through inability to raise enough money; or dependence on deals with developers; or the lack of experience of local government in handling a massive task; or the 'county council finding after a few years that the financial burden was more than their ratepayers would tolerate'. If the project broke down, 'the government would have to take it over, in whatever state it was, together with the liabilities, and get it going properly'. The prospect was not attractive to the department whose planners were in any event doubtful of the monorail layout proposed. At a meeting with the county council on 28 April 1965, it was made clear that no guarantee could be given which would make the council's scheme financially feasible. Accordingly 'the project should be developed in the ordinary way as a new town'.

While these negotiations with the county council for their own scheme had been proceeding, Crossman had announced on 3 February 1965 that the Government would go ahead with a new town in North Buckinghamshire and expansion elsewhere, and that he would be discussing with the local authorities the measures needed to implement the proposals including the surveys needed to determine the precise siting of the development, and in particular the desirability of using the machinery of the New Towns Act.*

In view of the preparatory work which the planning officer of the county council had already undertaken, it was readily agreed that he should be associated with a team of planners headed by a principal planner in the department to examine the area for the purpose of suggesting a designation area within which a town designed initially for the reception of 150,000 immigrants, with scope for further substantial growth, could be built. The team reported at the end of July 1965 recommending designation of 26,500 acres, taking in the existing towns of Bletchley and Wolverton. The department's legal advisers were doubtful whether so large an area could properly be designated but the secretary commented: 'I think we could take what risk there is.' Crossman agreed on 17 August 1965

---

* See above, p. 214.

that the next step was to consult government departments on the proposed designation area, and this was done on 25 August 1965 when a dozen departments were informed. The most significant of the comments received came from the Ministry of Agriculture and Fisheries, who felt that it was 'a lot of land to designate and is bound to cause a great deal of heart burning and consternation in the agriculture community'. In particular they pressed that there should be no 'enclosed agricultural enclaves'. They did, however, note that they were 'partially reassured' by an official statement that:

> 'it is the minister's intention to secure that the growth of the towns is planned with full regard to the need to conserve good agricultural land and to avoid the permanent creation of large enclaves within which land would tend to become sterilised for agricultural purposes'.

Having cleared the proposal with the government departments, the next step was the formal consultation required by the Act with the local authorities concerned, and a letter was addressed on 13 January 1966, to the county councils of Buckinghamshire, Bedfordshire and Northamptonshire, to three urban district councils, to six rural district councils, and to a score of parish councils. The letter stated that the proposed new town area amounted in all to about 27,000 acres, including the built-up areas of Bletchley, Wolverton and Stony Stratford. This was a larger area than had been proposed for designation in earlier new towns. There were three main reasons for this. First, the proposed new town would be much larger in population than any previous new town. It was proposed to provide for an incoming population of about 150,000 over twenty years; and this, together with the existing population with its planned increases and further growth by natural increase, was likely to result in the long run in a total population of about a quarter of a million.

Secondly, it seemed right that from the outset the town should be planned to be capable of expanding to this total population and of catering for all its needs. This meant 'taking a bolder and more forward' view of the ultimate size and shape of the town and, because of the time scale involved, adopting 'a more flexible approach to its basic planning'.

Finally, a new town of this size was bound to introduce 'new principles of structure and design'. The traditional centralised form of a town based on a radial pattern was not likely to be satisfactory for this new town which was to be designed for the rapidly changing circumstances of the late twentieth and the twenty-first centuries. A more dispersed pattern of development was almost certain to be needed, even though the areas of development in the town (such as housing areas) would be built 'at economical densities so as not to waste land'.

Apart from the parish councils, the local authorities welcomed or accepted the proposal in principle, although various suggestions were made for minor alterations in the boundaries, most of which the ministry accepted and which had the effect of reducing the area to 25,000 acres. On 14 April 1966 formal notice was advertised of the minister's intention to make the draft designation order and a public local inquiry was held in July 1966.

The North Buckinghamshire new town proposal was, at this time, the furthest advanced of the major schemes agreed in principle by ministers in December 1964 and announced by Crossman in February 1965. It was also the first to reach the stage of requiring Treasury approval. In November 1966 MHLG wrote to the Treasury outlining the proposal and saying that the cost would be between £400m and £500m. It was not possible to make any more soundly based estimate in advance of the master plan which the development corporation would propose and on which the Treasury would be consulted.

The Treasury replied that, while the new town had been approved in principle two years previously:

> 'disappointingly slow progress had been made in working towards an over-all new towns programme, and it is by no means clear that it will be possible to afford all of the new towns and major expansions which have already been suggested, or which are likely to be suggested for the various regions . . . I suggest therefore that your minister should put in a short paper to the EP Committee stating the size and cost of the project as it is now envisaged . . . It seems only right that interested ministers should be given a chance of expressing considered views upon it before it is finally started.'

As a result, Greenwood (who had succeeded Crossman in August 1966) submitted a paper to the EP Committee explaining how this first new town to be designated by the present Government 'fits into our new towns programme as a whole'. This was discussed in December 1966. Greenwood reminded the committee that, in February 1965, the Government had announced to Parliament its decision to develop four new towns, in order to accommodate about one million people, mostly Londoners. The committee had, at that time, approved proposals for expansion at Ipswich, Northampton, Peterborough and in North Buckinghamshire. Statutory procedures had now been completed in respect of the new town in North Buckinghamshire. Following the publication of the draft order, a public inquiry had been held in July. After seeing the inspector's report, which had suggested reductions in the acreage of the area to be designated following strong objections by farming interests, he had consulted the Minister of Agriculture, and they had agreed on reductions which would save about 4,000 acres of agricultural land. He was under some pressure to make an early announcement of the

Government's decision on the designated area: there had been a parliamentary question on this subject the previous day; and local farming and industrial interests had said that the continued uncertainty was harmful to them. He proposed making an announcement not later than the end of January 1967.

Greenwood explained that he had already published a draft designation order for Peterborough and proposed to do so shortly for Northampton and Ipswich (subject in the latter case to agreement being reached with the Minister of Agriculture). Proposals for expansion at Swindon (now likely to be a GLC project) and those for Southampton–Portsmouth and Ashford were at an earlier stage. All these projects dealt with the problems of the south-east and more particularly of London. The Cabinet had also approved in principle proposals to develop a new growth area in central Lancashire by building a new city in the Preston–Leyland–Chorley area, and for a new town development at Warrington to take overspill from Manchester. The former of these schemes was not likely to be ready for final decision before late 1967. He hoped to be able to make a draft order for the Warrington scheme shortly. Finally there was a proposal, arising from the west midlands regional study, to enlarge the existing new town scheme at Dawley to include the nearby towns of Wellington and Oakengates and to make additional provision for Birmingham overspill—but this had not yet been approved in principle by ministers.

At the EP Committee it was argued that it would be desirable, before further decisions on individual projects were taken, for the committee to consider the proposed programme as a whole, with particular reference to the cost, the implications for development areas, and the relative priorities of the various projects. The North Buckinghamshire new town would be the first such major scheme to be launched by the Government since taking office. It was unfortunate that the development would be taking place south of Birmingham, in an area where rapid growth could in any event be expected, rather than in an area where the Government was anxious to encourage growth. There was, moreover, some doubt about the proposal for developing a new growth point in central Lancashire in the Leyland–Chorley area. The Government might be accused of getting its priorities wrong if the Leyland–Chorley scheme were to be subjected to further delay while the North Buckinghamshire development went ahead rapidly. On the other hand, the problems of central Lancashire were rather more intractable than those elsewhere. There was no doubt about the need for a centre of growth in the region: the question was whether this particular area was the right one, and also whether the development of a new town in close proximity to the east Lancashire towns in the former 'cotton belt' should be given a higher priority than the redevelopment of the existing towns themselves. The consultants' report on the Leyland–Chorley project would shortly be available, and the regional economic planning council would also be consulted on this question. Proposals involving new development in other parts of the north were also being given a high priority. Proposals affecting Humberside and Severnside were as yet 'in an embryonic stage'.

The committee agreed that Greenwood should announce his decision on the designated area for the new town in North Buckinghamshire, but also that a comprehensive report on the new towns programme should be prepared and submitted to ministers.

The designation order was made in January 1967 and the development corporation formally established in March. The ungainly name of 'the North Buckinghamshire New Town' was replaced by that of Milton Keynes.*

The New Towns Working Group†

Following this decision of ministers, a working group of officials was set up in January 1967 'to report on the regional, financial and economic implications of the proposed new town programme over the next fifteen years, having regard to the relative priorities of the various projects and to the prospects of other major planned expansion schemes'.‡ The group was chaired by an official of the Ministry of Housing and Local Government and consisted of representatives of Agriculture, Economic Affairs, Public Building and Works, Trade, Transport, Treasury, and the Scottish and Welsh Offices.

The group had to work quickly since decisions were urgently required on a number of projects where the statutory processes for designation were being held up pending the outcome of the review. (These included Warrington, Wellington–Oakengates, Ipswich and Northampton):

> 'Since the review is confidential, the delays cannot be explained satisfactorily and they are causing mounting criticism locally, undermining the goodwill and co-operation of the local authorities concerned, without which it will be difficult to proceed effectively with the new projects.'

---

* The name was decided by Greenwood 'after long reflection'. The choice of names for new towns would make an interesting (and amusing) story in itself. For the North Buckinghamshire new town it was agreed that the name Bletchley 'would have the wrong image' and Wolverton had to be rejected since 'it would plainly offend Bletchley'. Howard was suggested as an appropriate commemorative name but it was thought likely to invite 'future carping that the town is not matching up to Howard's ideals'. Other rejected names included Chiltern ('too far from the Chilterns'); Watling (reminiscent of the Roman engineers but 'it could relate to anywhere along that highway'); and Churchill (no comment made). (MHLG File NT 256/53/24).

† EP(67)14, EP(67)15, and EP(67)6th Meeting, 19 June 1967.

‡ See also chapter VIII, p. 474 *et seq.*

The group held ten meetings during January-April 1967. Its report was submitted to the EP Committee in May 1967. This is of such importance that it is appropriate to summarise it at some length.

THE NEW TOWNS PROGRAMME

There were twenty-three new towns in Great Britain in varying stages of development—seventeen in England, five in Scotland and one in Wales. Four of them (Crawley, Hatfield, Hemel Hempstead and Welwyn Garden City) were complete, and had been handed over to the Commission for the New Towns. Since the start of the programme in 1946, the population in the new towns had increased by half a million. The existing programme had a capacity to take a further two-thirds of a million people, including their natural increase, before planned population targets were reached. This programme would be largely completed by 1981, when only Milton Keynes in the south-east, and Livingston and Irvine* in Scotland, would still be building for the current intake of population. Proposals to increase the programme were of three types: expansion of existing new towns, new proposals approved in principle, and projects under consideration.

There were proposals to expand Basildon by 34,000, Stevenage by 25,000 and Harlow by 30,000–40,000 to provide further relief to London's housing problems during the early 1970s; to double the size of the existing Dawley new town from 50,000 to 100,000 by including the Wellington–Oakengates area; and to raise the target population of Cwmbran from 55,000 to 75,000. There might also be extensions later to some existing new towns in Scotland.

In addition to Milton Keynes, ministers had approved in principle large expansions of Ipswich, Peterborough and Northampton each to take 70,000 London overspill by 1981; an expansion of Warrington to take 40,000 overspill from Manchester by 1981; a new town in the Leyland–Chorley area of central Lancashire to be a focus of economic growth and to take 150,000 overspill from Manchester and Merseyside over twenty years; and the establishment of a new town development corporation to double the size of Newtown, Montgomeryshire, from 5,500 to about 11,000 over seven years.† This group of new projects would enable the new towns programme to provide for about 325,000 additional people from the London, Manchester and Merseyside conurbations by 1981.

Several further projects were under consideration. These varied greatly in scale, purpose and the degree of progress so far made. The extent to which new town machinery would be appropriate had not yet been settled in many cases. In England, Humberside and

* On Irvine see chapter IV, pp. 190–192.
† See below p. 279 *seq*.

The New Towns at May 1967

	New Town	Designated	Purpose
ENGLAND			
South-East	Stevenage	1946	London overspill
	Crawley	1947	,, ,,
	Harlow	1947	,, ,,
	Hemel Hempstead	1947	,, ,,
	Hatfield	1948	,, ,,
	Welwyn Garden City	1948	,, ,,
	Basildon	1949	,, ,,
	Bracknell	1949	,, ,,
	Milton Keynes	1967	,, ,,
East Midlands	Corby	1950	Housing for steel workers
West Midlands	Dawley	1963 }	West midlands
	Redditch	1964 }	conurbation overspill
North-West	Skelmersdale	1961 }	Merseyside overspill
	Runcorn	1964 }	
Northern	Newton Aycliffe	1947	To serve Board of Trade trading estate
	Peterlee	1948	Houses and work for miners
	Washington	1964	Regional growth and Tyneside overspill
SCOTLAND	East Kilbride	1947 }	
	Glenrothes	1948 }	Glasgow overspill and
	Cumbernauld	1955 }	general economic growth
	Livingston	1962 }	in the region
	Irvine	1966 }	
WALES	Cwmbran	1949	'To assist in solving the problems of working people having to travel long distances'

Severnside were under study by the central planning unit of the DEA as possible areas for major urban growth. Following the recommendation in *The South East Study* that the Southampton-Portsmouth area should be considered as a centre for a city-sized development as a counter magnet to London, consultants had been appointed to study the feasibility of accommodating a planned intake of 250,000 people. Their report, *South Hampshire Study : Feasibility of Major Urban Growth*, published in 1966, demonstrated that the existing rate of unplanned migration was nearly as high as the planned intake envisaged. The report was being appraised inter-departmentally.

Consultants had also been appointed to carry out a feasibility study of a major expansion at Ashford to take 150,000 people from London; and Stansted was a possible area for a new town of perhaps 100,000, catering for the employment needs of a third London airport. If this project were approved, work on the new town would have to be phased with the employment build-up for the new airport and would need to start about 1971–72.

In Scotland, a study of Tayside was being carried out: here it was envisaged that the existing population of about 300,000 'could grow by anything from 175,000 to 300,000 by the end of the century'. The feasibility study might indicate the possibility of developing a completely new town somewhere in the region, but currently it seemed more likely that the expansion would take place through the development of existing settlements such as Dundee, Perth, Arbroath and Forfar.

The 1966 white paper on the Scottish economy (Cmnd 2864) had drawn attention to the fact that the demographic and industrial recovery of the towns in the western Borders was being seriously threatened by migration, and recommended the introduction of some 25,000 people by 1980. A study by consultants from Edinburgh University was being carried out in the area to suggest the best ways of achieving this expansion.

Also as part of the white paper strategy, four major new settlements were being considered at Lennoxtown, north of Glasgow, at Larkhall on the M74, at Erskine, and at Lochwinnoch on the Glasgow–North Ayrshire axis. Together these would accommodate about 100,000 people by 1981. These developments were expected to be undertaken jointly by local authorities, the Scottish Special Housing Association and private developers. But the possibility that one or more might be proposed to be undertaken under New Towns Act machinery could not be completely ruled out. Erskine was already approved as a development plan proposal and was regarded as a firm project by Renfrew County Council and Glasgow Corporation, to be started in 1969–70.

In Wales, in addition to the Severnside study, which embraced both sides of the Severn, Llantrisant (some twelve miles north-west of Cardiff) was being considered as a possible site for substantial urban growth by the Welsh Office. This would cater for population growth in south Wales generally and, in particular, for the continuing shift of population from the central and eastern areas to the coastal plain. So far, the possibility of a new town with a target population of the order of 100,000 had been considered, but decisions on scale, timing and organisation of growth would await the report of consultants whom it was proposed to appoint shortly.

A consultants' report, *A New Town in Mid-Wales*, published in

1966, envisaged a new town centred on Caersws, Montgomeryshire, with a target population of 70,000 to be achieved over twenty years.* The decision whether to proceed further with this project would be taken in the light of the experience gained in doubling the size of Newtown. An alternative might be to designate six towns in Mid-Wales for expansion under the New Towns Act involving a total additional population of 25,000 if the Newtown experiment proved successful.

Not all these projects would necessarily be undertaken under the New Towns Acts. The extent to which the new towns' machinery would be relevant or appropriate had yet to be determined in many cases. The Humberside, Severnside and Tayside projects were of a very different character from the others. They were conceived as national growth areas which would promote national economic policies and contribute to dispersal policies on a national rather than regional scale. Although it was not yet certain whether the new towns machinery would be appropriate for these projects, it was clear that they would have to be financed by the exchequer.

In addition to these projects, there were the existing and proposed town expansions taking place under the Town Development Act.† In general, these were on a much smaller scale than new towns, both in size of planned expansion and in the rate of build-up. (The biggest contemplated was that at Swindon where it was envisaged that provision could be made for some 75,000 Londoners by 1981.) A total of some 50,000 houses, or accommodation for about 175,000 people, had so far been provided in town development schemes. Agreed schemes had a remaining capacity for about 325,000 people.

THE NEED FOR NEW TOWNS

The main impetus for the current new towns programme was the need to provide homes in a modern environment and in self-contained communities for overspill populations from the conurbations. Fourteen out of the seventeen English new towns (including Milton Keynes) had this primary function (the exceptions being Aycliffe, Corby and Peterlee). The programme was 'an integral part in the whole approach to the major problems of urban renewal'. Urban redevelopment and population growth necessitated a large and continuing programme of planned dispersal of population to relieve the need for costly high density redevelopment within the conurbations, and the pressures on peripheral development creating lengthening daily journeys to work and adding to existing traffic and transportation problems.

There was a limit to the contribution which town expansions under

---

* For further discussion of new towns in Wales see below p. 279 *et seq.*
† See chapter IX.

the Town Development Act could make towards meeting these overspill needs. These expansions were 'slow to get off the ground and small in scale'. The new towns machinery was the only machinery available to central government for implementing quickly more positive policies of population dispersal and economic growth, through the medium of large scale expansions executed by development corporations.

The need for new towns was increased by expectations of future population growth. Between 1964 and 1981, the population of Great Britain was expected to increase by 7·3 million.* This increase was widespread and covered all regions—though with wide regional variations ranging from 8·3 per cent for Scotland to 31·4 per cent for East Anglia. The dominant element in all regions (except East Anglia) was not migration, but natural growth.

Much of the future population growth up to 1981 was bound to take place in or adjoining existing urban areas which contained four-fifths of the total population of the country. The main overspill problems arose in Greater London, the west midlands, the northwest, and the Glasgow area. In other regions, the overspill problems were less acute. Up to 1981, overspill needs in the Tyneside subregion could be met by development at Washington together with town development schemes at Cramlington and Killingworth. In Yorkshire and Humberside, Sheffield's overspill could be accommodated in peripheral areas, and Hull's overspill could be considered as part of the strategy for Humberside. In the south-west, Bristol's overspill could be dealt with in peripheral areas.

By the end of the century, there was likely to be a further population growth of about 13 million—nearly twice that projected for 1964–81. Overspill problems would continue in London ('on a massive scale'), in the north-west and in the west midlands, and might develop in the urbanised area of West Riding and in the Notts-Derby industrialised belt. In Scotland, large scale overspill would continue from Glasgow, and overspill problems on a much smaller scale might develop in the north Lanarkshire and Renfrewshire urban areas and, conceivably, in Edinburgh. The need for a planned overspill programme could be seen therefore to extend well beyond the period after 1981.

To date, the location of the new towns had been decided in the regional context of the problems of the conurbations which they served. Several of the newer projects, however, reflected a wider and evolving regional strategy. The proposed expansions at Ipswich, Northampton and Peterborough were part of the general strategy for the south-east. They were also larger in scale than the first

* The population projections were revised annually and thus different figures were quoted at different points in time.

generation of new towns, and were based on large existing communities well away from the metropolitan area. In this way they were designed to assist with policies directed at shifting the economic balance within the south-east and moderating the dominance of London.

Policies for developing new growth areas were also now being reflected in the new towns programme. The Leyland–Chorley project had a twofold objective of developing a new urban complex to regenerate the economy of the area as well as providing accommodation for 150,000 overspill population from the overcrowded conurbations in Lancashire. In Wales, the Llantrisant project had a subregional rather than population overspill objective, and in Scotland, all five new towns had come to be regarded more widely as focal points for industrial and economic growth in the development of the whole Scottish economy, as well as continuing to have an overspill function.

Finally, there was a growing recognition that a local, or even a regional, approach to the problems of population growth and dispersal was no longer sufficient to cope with the problems ahead. An interim report of the long term population distribution study group* had already stressed the importance of a national rather than a regional approach, and suggested the need for new very large planned urban areas with an ultimate size ranging from 250,000 to one million people, thus in effect creating new city regions. The *South Hampshire Study* was to some extent in this category and the Humberside and Severnside studies were specifically intended to further this policy.

Over the next few decades, therefore, it might well be that the new towns programme would change in character—the emphasis switching from localised overspill towns with a basically housing and population impetus behind them, to the use of the machinery (suitably modified) to implement national economic and population policies through the medium of major urban growth areas. The use of development corporation machinery would also be affected if the report of the royal commission on local government were to lead to a structure of larger city-region type authorities. These authorities should be strong and viable enough to carry out themselves large planned expansion schemes of existing towns involving short distance overspill, but there could still be problems of long distance overspill involving several city-region authorities.

COST OF THE NEW TOWN PROGRAMME†

There were difficulties about long-term cost projections for projects

---

* See p. 223 above.
† For further discussion see chapter VIII, p. 474 *et seq.*

particularly where no master plan had been prepared. The cost estimates given were tentative; they were also incomplete in that no estimates were yet possible for large projects such as south Hampshire, Humberside and Severnside.

Total capital expenditure (public and private sector) for the existing and proposed programmes would increase nearly threefold over the following eight years, rising from £111m in 1967–68 to £295m in 1974–75. It was wise to assume that the level of expenditure would not fall below £280–£290m annually from 1975–76 onwards. Public sector expenditure was estimated to rise from £96m in 1967–68 to £220m in 1972–73 and, within these figures, gross development corporation/exchequer expenditure from £80m in 1967–68 to £155m in 1972–73.

The scale of investment in new towns underlined the importance of encouraging the highest possible contribution from private enterprise. The estimates assumed that the private sector would contribute 30 per cent of the total expenditure—mainly in industry and commerce and increasingly in housing 'as policies to increase the level of owner occupation took effect'. Public expenditure on new towns did not constitute a separate public investment programme and, in theory, could be met from within the approved basic programmes provided sufficient priority were given to it. In practice, however, the projected programme would involve the approval of some additional expenditure.

HOUSING

In the public sector housing programme, the English new towns were in the same priority class as the conurbation housing authorities and other local authorities with large slum clearance problems. This reflected their overspill function. It meant that the new towns were on a 'capacity to build' basis, and any restraints on the size of the national public sector programme were applied in the first place to the non-priority local authority programmes. In new towns, therefore, the restraint on the scale of housebuilding arose mainly from the management and social problems of integrating newcomers into the new community at a rapid rate and the need to provide employment, shopping and other urban facilities in phase with the build-up of population.

The English new towns programme (excluding south Hampshire, Humberside, etc) would be running at a rate of 25,000–28,000 house completions annually in the mid-seventies, ie about 5 per cent of a UK annual programme of 500,000. Thus, about a million people would be housed in the English new towns over the next fifteen years.

As in the English new towns, the housing programme in the

Scottish new towns was on a 'capacity to build' basis. The number of houses completed annually in the Scottish new towns had been rising steadily—from 1,519 in 1960 to 3,870 in 1966. It was estimated that the peak year for housing output in the Scottish new towns would be 1971–72 with about 5,100 houses completed. During the period up to then, three of the new towns (Cumbernauld, Glenrothes and Livingston) would be building at more or less their full rate. The programme in East Kilbride would be beginning to fall off, but the programme in Irvine would be rising to a level which would 'fully compensate' for East Kilbride.

Beyond 1971–72 there would be a gradual reduction in the rate of housing output as Cumbernauld, Glenrothes and Livingston approached (and in the case of the first two of these, reached) their target populations. Some building would, however, continue in all five new towns throughout the period to 1981–82, either by the development corporation, by the local authority, or by private enterprise.

In Wales, Cwmbran was nearing its target. At Newtown, 1,700 houses would be built for the doubling of population over the period 1969 to 1976. At Llantrisant, if the project took the form of a new town with a target population of 100,000, some 8,500 houses would be needed between 1970 and 1980. The proposed Welsh new town programme was expected to provide 17,000 houses by 1981, excluding further expansion in central Wales if the Newtown experiment were successful.

The total British new town programme was therefore expected to provide about 365,000 houses (public and private sectors) over the next fifteen years. It was difficult to estimate the scale of the private enterprise contribution, but it seemed likely to be of the order of 120,000 to 125,000 houses.

INDUSTRIAL EMPLOYMENT

New towns in the past had tended to be dependent on manufacturing industry to a far greater degree than was usual in other areas. In the existing London new towns, for example, manufacturing industry accounted for 57·5 per cent of total employment, compared with the national average of 38 per cent. They also had a high proportion of young families which tended to raise the overall employment needs.

The Board of Trade estimated tentatively that, taking account of actual projected new town and town development schemes (but excluding national growth projects such as Humberside and Severnside), the overspill programmes throughout Great Britain would require new jobs in manufacturing industry at a rate of the order of 40,000 per annum. Of these, about 30,000 would be required in projects outside development areas—18,000 of them for new towns.

A significant increase in the mobility of industry would be needed during the period up to 1981 if the requirements of the overspill programme and the development areas were to be met. Prospects in different parts of the country differed but, given that the economy would continue to operate at a high level, the prospects were not such as to justify contemplating drastic new methods to stimulate the flow of industry or cutting back the programme.

It was suggested, however, that further consideration should be given to a number of ways in which the provision of new employment for the programme might be assisted. A higher proportion of older people in the new towns would have clear employment advantages while at the same time having social and financial benefits. More office employment would help to achieve a better balanced employment structure. The conurbation local authorities (particularly in Birmingham and Manchester) could play a more active role in facilitating the movement of industry—as London had done. It might be possible to phase development in the new towns in a sufficiently flexible way to allow some slowing down or acceleration of individual schemes according to their ability to attract industry. Finally, more attention should be paid to training schemes for workers moving to new towns.

REGIONAL IMPLICATIONS

Currently, of the 23 new towns, nine were in the south-east region (including Milton Keynes), three were in the midlands, five in the north and north-west, five in Scotland, and one in Wales.

London's overspill needs would continue, throughout the seventies, to make a major call on capital expenditure devoted to the programme, but the policy of basing expansion schemes at an increasing distance from London, like those for Ipswich, Northampton and Peterborough, would contribute to economic growth in other regions besides the south-east. During the following fifteen years, the north-west and west midlands would, on current proposals, obtain an increasing share in the programme, and later in the seventies the regional balance would begin to shift as Humberside, Severnside, Tayside and other Scottish projects 'came into the picture'.

There were marked differences in the scale of contribution to the overspill needs of conurbations. At one extreme, Manchester was the only conurbation which now did not have a new town for its overspill needs. At the other end of the scale, the new towns in the north-east, together with town development schemes at Killingworth and Cramlington, were expected to cater broadly for the overspill needs of the Tyneside subregion up to 1981.

In London, the latest position was that existing and reasonably firm proposals for new towns and town development schemes now catered for 761,000 people by 1981 to meet the Government's declared intention to provide accommodation in planned extension schemes for one million people by 1981. There was still a need for further planned expansion schemes to accommodate about 240,000 people by 1981 before the target was reached. To meet this gap, the south Hampshire and Ashford areas were under study for large scale expansion, and the Greater London Council were discussing possible overspill schemes with many authorities over a wide area. The balance between new town and town development schemes had yet to be determined but, if all the proposals currently under study either as new town or town development schemes were to materialise, the target would be fully met by 1981.

REPHASING OF THE NEW TOWNS PROGRAMME

The need to consider some rephasing of the new towns programme arose mainly from the rapid doubling in total capital expenditure foreseen over the next five years (£111m in 1967–68 to £225m in 1971–72) and a further rise to a peak figure of about £290m in the mid-seventies. If the new towns programme were to be cut back or drastically slowed down, houses would still have to be provided in other ways—by redevelopment, peripheral expansion of the conurbations, or more town development schemes. New towns, however, were heavily financed by the exchequer, and ministers had asked for a rigorous examination aimed at reducing basic public expenditure programmes. It was necessary therefore to examine the possibilities and implications of moderating the rate of expansion of the programme.

The main courses open were to abandon some projects and concentrate effort on fewer schemes building at a fast rate, or allow all projected schemes to proceed at a slower rate. On balance, the economic arguments favoured the former approach, but this had some limitations in possible inflexibility, the creation of labour difficulties, and the social problems of absorbing immigrant populations into new towns at a high rate. The scope for this approach was, in fact, limited.

A major rephasing of the existing programme would be uneconomic in terms of exchequer investment. The scope for abandoning some new projects already approved in principle was limited by the degree of government commitment which already existed for some schemes. This had been reinforced by detailed discussions with local authorities on 'partnership' arrangements with the new town development corporations. A major outcry could be expected if these schemes were abandoned.

There was no clear cut choice of methods of rephasing the

programme because of the degree of commitment. The most practical approach would be some reduction in the pace of development proposed for some of the new towns. Some of the implications had been examined of keeping the total capital expenditure on new towns to about £200m in 1971–72, and thereafter allowing it to rise to about £300m by the end of the decade instead of by 1974–75. This would mean deferring about £200m in the four years 1971–75, and a further £100m in the remainder of the decade. It would result either in an uneconomic slowing down of the whole programme or in deferring one large project, already approved in principle, for six years, together with all other projects for at least five years with a corresponding deferment of expenditure on national growth projects such as Humberside.

There were immediate short term problems over the following five years when the total expenditure on the existing programme would still be continuing to rise as Milton Keynes, Irvine and the second generation of new towns got into their stride. None of the new projects involved any additional expenditure in the financial years 1967–68, but from 1969–70 onwards total expenditure on these schemes was expected to rise from £12m to £70m in 1971–72, with exchequer expenditure rising from £8m in 1969–70 to £42m in 1971–72. The room for manoeuvre for rephasing this expenditure was limited. There were fewer new schemes involved, most of them were already approved in principle, and they would be only in the initial period of building up as regards expenditure.

The effect of reducing the build-up by, say, 50 per cent would be that all the projects approved in principle (Ipswich, Peterborough, Northampton, Warrington, Leyland–Chorley and Newtown) would proceed at somewhat reduced rates of build-up, and expenditure on most other big projects under study, like Ashford, Severnside, Wellington–Oakengates, Llantrisant, would have to be deferred until at least 1972–73. This would reduce the new town contribution to the national housing programme by 3,500 houses in 1971–72. The expansion of Basildon would not be affected since expenditure involved would not be incurred until after 1972–73. The expansion of Stevenage would need to be deferred by one year.

RECOMMENDATIONS OF THE WORKING GROUP

The working group stressed that it was important to maintain the momentum of the new towns programme if it were to continue to make a significant contribution to overspill problems and planned dispersal of population growth. Statutory processes involved in setting up a new town were lengthy: it could take up to four years from the time a project was first mooted to the construction of the first houses. There was growing unrest locally about delays in proceeding with new town designation proposals for Ipswich, Northampton and Warrington which had been announced two years previously.

Ministers were invited to take decisions on the projects approved in principle at Peterborough, Basildon and Stevenage, and Warrington, Northampton and Ipswich. For Peterborough the decision required was whether the scheme for 70,000 London overspill should be finally designated as a new town and added to the existing programme. For Basildon and Stevenage, the decision required was whether provision should be made in the programme for further growth of the two towns in the light of the inspector's reports (when received) on the revised master plans by about 34,000 and 25,000 people respectively, so that future construction could proceed on a firm basis. For Warrington, Northampton and Ipswich it was necessary to decide whether draft designation orders should be published. (Agricultural issues still had to be settled in relation to Ipswich.)

It was recommended that the Leyland–Chorley proposal should await public reaction to the proposals when the consultants' designation report was published. As regards the projects under study, decisions might be called for in the near future on Llantrisant* and Wellington–Oakengates.†

CONSIDERATION BY MINISTERS

This lengthy report by officials was in essence a forward look from a standpoint early in 1967 (when there was an expectation of a substantial population increase) at the ways in which the new and expanded towns programme might develop over the next fifteen years. Ministers were not invited to become committed to 'the picture which was emerging', but they were asked to note the report and to agree that Peterborough should be finally designated as a new town of 70,000; that provision should be made for the further growth of Basildon and Stevenage; and that draft designation orders should be published and public inquiries held for the Warrington and Northampton new towns, followed by a similar order for Ipswich when certain issues involving agriculture had been resolved.

A later note by the secretaries to the ministerial committee reported that there appeared to be general agreement to these specific recommendations, subject only to a reservation by the Treasury that any resulting additional expenditure would have to be accommodated within whatever allocations were agreed by the Public Expenditure Committee in the year. Thus no meeting to discuss the report was necessary.

---

* See p. 283 below.
† See p. 258 below.

In the following weeks expansions were authorised for Basildon (to 140,000) and for Stevenage (to 105,000). Peterborough was designated (July 1967). Public inquiries were subsequently held for Northampton and Warrington, and these were designated in February and April 1968. The more or less firm proposals which were outstanding at mid 1967 were for Ashford, South Hampshire, Central Lancashire, Dawley and Ipswich.

Jay's Paper on London Overspill*

The report by officials on the new towns programme prompted Jay to take up the theme of his earlier letter to Crossman.† In a paper to the EP Committee, he expressed his concern that the strategy for dispersing London overspill was 'in danger of aggravating the concentration on expansion of south eastern England'. He argued for greater attention to be paid to the possibilities of transferring more of the expansion envisaged to areas further west or further north.

Though some part of the London overspill problem had to be met within moderate distance of the capital, the present review provided an opportunity for reassessment of the programme as a whole. It was necessary to reconsider how it could contribute to the wider aims of correcting regional imbalance and remedying the chief weakness of *The South East Study*: 'its concentration on the area to the east of the line drawn between the Wash and Poole Harbour'. Jay was particularly concerned that close attention should be paid to the possibility of re-examining the proposed major overspill expansions at Ashford and south Hampshire and pressing vigorously the opportunities offered in the south-west.

The South East Study linked expansion in the Ashford area with the building of the Channel Tunnel and, in November 1966, the Minister of Housing and Local Government had appointed consultants to undertake a study of the area as the site of a major development. The size of the development which the consultants had been asked to consider was for a planned intake of 150,000 people over the next twenty-five years plus their natural increase and that of the existing population. They had been advised that a fast build-up before 1981, by 75,000 additional population if possible, would be an important consideration. The consultants had also been told that they could take as a working assumption for the purpose of the study the Anglo-French agreement of 28 October 1966 on a cross-channel tunnel.

Jay said that until the consultants' report had been considered, he would not wish to comment on this proposal in detail: but it did seem that there were strong grounds for objection to an expansion of

---

* EP(67)16 and EP(67)6th Meeting, 19 June 1967.
† See p. 215 above.

this order at Ashford. It was improbable that the Channel Tunnel terminus, even with its large attendant ancillary services, would provide any large proportion of the employment requirements of such an expansion. The area lacked a diverse indigenous industrial base to build on, and the rate of growth recommended would require the deliberate steering of new industrial expansion to this part of Kent. The location of an expansion of this size in Kent would be a regrettable step, since it could in no way be seen as part of a general strategy for steering industry away from the conurbation. It would also encourage the notion that development of the Channel Tunnel of necessity made industrial location in south-east England more desirable and necessary than before. This would make the work of the Board of Trade in the application of its industrial development certificate control more difficult and less defensible. While he accepted the need for some limited expansion at Ashford to match the growth of ancillary services associated with the Channel Tunnel, he seriously questioned the desirability of encouraging further major growth in this part of the south-east.

Jay also had reservations about the possibility of major expansion at Southampton-Portsmouth. Having studied the report of the consultants, he noted that instead of framing their recommendations in terms of any target figure for planned population expansion in the area, they considered the possible growth of population in the area on a range of assumptions about alternative rates of natural increase and migration, taking account of growth over recent years. Their calculations gave upper and lower population limits of 1·8 million and 1·2 million by 2001, compared with the existing 800,000 in the area. Their most significant finding was that, on past trends, unplanned migration was, by itself, quite likely to give rise to a population intake by 1981 of the size postulated in their remit over this period. Thus the population of the area seemed likely to grow substantially, even if current policies were continued.

In view of these findings, Jay argued that it seemed sensible to question the desirability of building a large 'forced' development in an area within 100 miles of London which already displayed signs of significant indigenous growth. It would seem preferable that the resources which would be required for planned intake of population at the higher levels of population growth suggested be used in other regions where the building of such developments would stimulate economic growth in subregions more in need of new investment and economic stimulus. As part of such a re-examination, more attention should be paid to the need to steer major overspill projects away from the south-east region. The GLC were involved in negotiations with a number of local authorities in the south-west and in Lincolnshire. Positive encouragement should be given to these discussions to overcome the reluctance of those authorities hesitant about accepting overspill population. In particular, consideration should be given to the view of the south-west economic planning council that any decision taken by the Government on expansion in the south Hampshire area should have due regard to the effect on the south-west as well as on the south-east.

The report of the new towns working group suggested that, even if the schemes for Ipswich, Peterborough, Northampton and Swindon all went ahead on the scale planned, there was still a need for further planned expansion schemes to accommodate about 240,000 people by 1981. If a re-examination of the Ashford and south Hampshire proposals were carried out, and if allowance were made for the possibility that a number of existing schemes might expand more slowly than originally expected, it seemed to him that there would be room and opportunity for further proposals, possibly on a major scale, for the south-west, and indeed elsewhere in the country.

When Jay's paper was considered by the EP Committee in June 1967, Greenwood recalled that the committee had agreed without discussion the proposals put forward by officials: the addition of Peterborough to the new towns programme, the provision for the further growth of Basildon and Stevenage, and the publication of draft designation orders and the holding of public inquiries for Warrington, Northampton and Ipswich—subject to the Treasury's reservation on the public expenditure programme and the reservation by the Minister of Agriculture about the need to minimise loss of good agricultural land at Ipswich. In considering the new towns programme as a whole, he asked the committee to bear in mind that, between 1946 and 1964, eight new towns had been established within thirty miles of London to house about 350,000 people. Apart from the new towns programme, provision was being made for expanding established towns to provide counter attractions for population growth. It had to be remembered, however, that the further away from London the new towns or expanded towns were developed the more difficult it became to persuade industry to move. Moreover the rate of growth in the south-east had slowed down: currently, it was only slightly above the national average, and by 1981 it would be lower than the national average.

Jay said that he had an open mind as regards the proposed expansion at Ashford; the committee would wish to consider this proposal in detail when the consultants' report was available. The south-east economic planning council attached great importance to the proposed expansion in south Hampshire, and both local authorities concerned and the GLC wished to open discussions as soon as possible. His present view was that it might not be desirable to establish a new town in the area but that there should be planned development at selected points to accommodate an inflow of about 60,000 people. It was, however, too early to consider the proposals in detail.

The proposed expansion of Stevenage had been pruned compared with earlier proposals for substantial expansion. It now provided for the development corporation to continue building until the population had reached 80,000. This would enable the provision of some 2,000 houses for about 7,000 extra immigrants during the period 1970–75. This would not require an influx of additional industry because in recent years new manufacturing employment to match planned immigration had been largely provided by expansions of firms already there.

In discussion it was suggested that the proposed expansion in south Hampshire should be encouraged, particularly as it would relieve congestion on the roads in the London area which would be severely exacerbated if there were no halt to the sporadic development on the outskirts of London. South Hampshire appeared to be a natural growth point, and it would be practicable to make provision for a considerable increase in commuter traffic. The proposed expansion at Ashford on the other hand would have to be carefully considered. It was essential not to give the impression that the building of the Channel Tunnel would justify further industrial development in that area. Further considerations of the south Hampshire and Ashford proposals should await the publication of the consultants' reports in the late summer. The south-east economic planning council were also due then to report on the strategy for developing the south-east region as a whole. When reports were available, officials should report on the progress of the London overspill programme. In further consideration of the programme for the south-east, account should be taken of the possibility of providing for more expansion in the south-west especially as this would in time reduce the financial assistance which would have to be provided for the region if no development occurred. Care would have to be taken, however, to avoid any development requiring the surrender of good agricultural land. In any event, it was too early to consider what further expansion might take place in the south-west. This would have to await the outcome of the current proposals for the London overspill programme.

Ashford*

Following the proposal in *The South East Study*, consultants had been commissioned to undertake a study of a possible major development in the Ashford area. In November 1967, Greenwood informed

---

* EP(67)40 and EP(67)13th Meeting, 13 November 1967; EP(68)11 and EP(68)3rd Meeting, 14 March 1968.

the EP Committee that the consultants' report was now complete and ready for publication. The consultants recommended the designation under the New Towns Act of an area of about 25,000 acres to accommodate a total population of 240,000 by 1991. There should be no special labour problems in the new city but it would need to attract a substantial share of the industrial employment likely to move to the south-east, and the consultants suggested that there should be further detailed study of the problems involved. The Government were committed to publishing the report and to seeking the views of the regional economic planning council, the local authorities and other interested bodies. The matter for decision was whether the Government should take a purely neutral line by saying that they remained uncommitted to the project, or should give some indication that they were not convinced of the need to proceed with the development on the scale and at the rate considered in the consultants' report. Greenwood favoured the latter course for several reasons. The south-east economic planning council wished to make an overall study of the south-east Kent area to determine the feasibility for future growth before a decision on Ashford was taken. There would be difficulty in finding sufficient jobs for a town of this size and in reconciling the Government's policy of spreading the influence of the Channel Tunnel evenly throughout the country with a simultaneous attempt to create a large new town in its immediate vicinity. The general London overspill programme was progressing well and although some expansion would have to take place at Ashford, it would not necessarily be on the scale indicated in the report. There would be strong opposition from local interests following publication of the report. Lastly, there would be undesirable land speculation in the area if the Government merely published the report and gave no indication of their future policy. In the past, publication of such reports without Government comment had been taken to mean that the Government had accepted the recommendations. Since it was reasonably certain that the original plans for Ashford would have to be scaled down, Greenwood thought that the Government should inform the regional economic planning council and the local authorities that they were not yet persuaded that it would be necessary or desirable to develop the area on the lines recommended by the consultants and wished first to seek the views of the authorities concerned. The designation of the area as a new town should be held over until a decision in principle on whether to proceed with the project and, if so, on what scale, had been taken.

These proposals were generally accepted by the committee and it was agreed that when the consultants' report was published,* the

---

* The report was published by HMSO in 1967 under the title *Ashford Study: Consultants' Proposals for Designation.*

Government's doubts about the scale and rate of the proposed development of the Ashford area should be made clear.

In March 1968, Greenwood reported that the local authorities and local organisations were unanimously opposed to development on the scale proposed by the consultants—75,000 people by 1981 and an eventual 150,000 in twenty-five years. They doubted the possibility of matching the increase in population with new employment; and they believed that a major new city would monopolise the economic resources of the east Kent area, do harm to agriculture and the countryside, and bring less benefit to the area as a whole than distributing growth over a number of smaller centres. The Thanet towns, for example, suffered from chronic unemployment; the future of the Kent coalfield was uncertain; and Dover and Folkestone faced the need for readjustment when the Tunnel was in operation. Ashford was too far away to give much relief to these areas.

The south-east economic planning council agreed that major expansion at Ashford before 1981 for overspill reasons and as a means of stimulating economic development in this part of Kent did not seem necessary or desirable. But they emphasised the need to secure good progress with other major developments to which they attached priority—south Hampshire, Milton Keynes and Ipswich. At the same time, the council felt it was too soon to take a final decision on the development of Ashford as a major city after 1981 in line with their strategic proposals for the south-east. In this context, the decision to proceed with the Channel Tunnel and the location of its terminal were of crucial importance. They were also putting in hand an economic study of east Kent to provide additional background information which should assist future discussions about Ashford's long term future. For the period before 1981, the council recommended a more modest expansion of the town to house further overspill population from London and to benefit this part of Kent. Any plan for moderate expansion in the short term should be designed so as not to preclude development into a major city in the long term.

The results of these consultations strengthened ministers' preliminary conclusion about the Ashford study. There was, however, a case for a rather faster rate of growth of Ashford than had been envisaged hitherto under the arrangements with the Greater London Council, and both the planning council and the local authorities concerned were willing to consider expansion up to an eventual population of 75–80,000—roughly half the expansion recommended in the consultants' report. It was accordingly agreed that Ashford should not be designated as a new town for major expansion but that the local authorities concerned should be invited to consider a more

modest scale of expansion under the machinery of the Town
Development Act.

*South Hampshire**

The consultants' study on south Hampshire had been published in
1966.† Discussions with Hampshire, Portsmouth and Southampton
followed, and these resulted in agreement to set up joint planning
machinery to plan the area comprehensively. The authorities
tentatively agreed with the GLC to investigate the possibility of an
overspill arrangement to take 60,000 Londoners by 1981 (which
would make a big advance towards the target of one million—for
which schemes already approved or with good prospect of approval
would provide for 670,000). In April 1968 Greenwood reported that
he did not propose to set up a new town corporation for the area.
In the first place, the administrative responsibilities would consist
mainly of controlling growth which would take place regardless of
overspill and were more suited to local authorities than to a development corporation. Secondly, the area of growth, which already had a
population of over 800,000, was far too big for designation as a new
town.

At the EP Committee meeting it was emphasised that the proposed
development in south Hampshire should not be allowed to prejudice
the interests of the development areas. There were major firms
already in the area who were being encouraged to expand in the
development areas rather than locally. Expansion in the area would
inevitably require provision of an expensive infrastructure for public
utilities, roads etc as well as houses for Londoners, and the Treasury
maintained that no commitment should be accepted till a further
report had been received on the financial implications of the overspill
proposals. On the other hand, it was argued that a firm statement
from the Government was necessary if the planning authorities were
to proceed on a realistic basis. The aim was to ensure that the process
of expansion, which would take place in any case, should do so in
the most orderly manner, and the absorption of 60,000 Londoners
should be properly planned. The GLC needed to be able to plan on
the basis of the overspill proposed and a decision on this point should
therefore be taken now. It was not possible to estimate in advance
what the public expenditure implications would be, particularly as
development would be spread over fifteen years. Experience in other
areas suggested that the cost would be small in the early years and
then grow rapidly. The committee proposed some modifications in
the announcement to make it clear that the interests of the development areas would be fully safeguarded; that consideration would be

---

* EP(68)19 and EP(68)5th Meeting, 25 April 1968.
† *South Hampshire Study: Report on the Feasibility of Major Urban Growth,* HMSO, 1966.

given to the conservation of agricultural land and to the impact of the proposed development on adjacent areas; and that the financial implications of the overspill proposals should be examined.

After departmental discussion, the announcement was made in a written answer in the House of Commons in July 1968.* The minister welcomed the decision of the three local planning authorities to establish the necessary joint machinery to plan the area comprehensively and to study the planned intake of population. This machinery would enable particular attention to be given not only to the pattern of future development, but also to the conservation of agriculture, horticulture and to the natural features, and to the enhancement of the area's recreational facilities. The growth of the area was likely to take place largely on the basis of existing industry or other industry tied to the south-east, but it was not the Government's intention that the area should be allowed to attract industry and office expansion which would otherwise be suitable for the development areas. Arrangements would be made to ensure that the planning of the area was consistent with regional and national policies.

Following the statement, the authorities established the South Hampshire Plan Advisory Committee to direct the planning work, and the minister nominated a senior officer of the department to act as chairman.

Central Lancashire New Town†

In June 1967, Greenwood informed the EP Committee that the consultants' report on the new town in central Lancashire had been published.‡ This recommended designation of 51,000 acres to provide for an incoming population of 150,000 which, with an existing population of 25,000 and natural growth, would produce a town of 500,000 by the end of the century. He now wished for a wider study to evaluate the effect on the area over time of the staged development of the proposed new town, taking particular account of industry, employment, shopping and town centre services, with projections of population changes and movement, and of travel to work. It would examine communications and the location of major urban uses. The study would be comparative in the sense that it would compare what would happen to the area if no change was made and what would happen as a result of the proposed development. The proposals were agreed, and a summary of the report was presented to the EP Committee in March 1968. Greenwood

---

* HC Debates, Vol 768, Col 109, 9 July 1968.

† EP(67)21 and EP(67)5th Meeting, 12 June 1967; EP(68)9 and EP(68)3rd Meeting, 14 March 1968; C(68)129 (originally issued as EP(68)49, but withdrawn) and CC(68) 52nd Conclusions, 17 December 1968.

‡ *Central Lancashire: Study for a City*, HMSO, 1967.

suggested that the report should be published and consultations initiated with the regional economic planning council and the local authorities. It would also need careful consideration by departments, and the committee of officials on environmental planning should undertake this and submit recommendations for action in the light of their consideration and of the views of the regional council and the other authorities concerned. This was agreed.*

The report by officials was presented to the Cabinet in December 1968. The proposal for a central Lancashire new town was strongly supported by the north-west economic planning council and by Lancashire CC, but it had aroused apprehensions in NE Lancashire. This was a typical 'grey area' of the kind whose problems were being studied by the Hunt Committee.† Consultants had made a separate study evaluating the likely effects of the new town on NE Lancashire. This suggested that the project would have both advantages and disadvantages for NE Lancashire, but these were likely to become evident only after about 1980. This allowed time for NE Lancashire to improve its comparative position.

The NE Lancashire authorities did not oppose the new town proposal as such, but asked for safeguards. Some of these were on issues which were being considered by the Hunt Committee (such as industrial incentives) and could not be determined until the Government had taken decisions in the light of the committee's report. Others related to communications, urban renewal and a plan for the future of the area. On these some progress could be made.

It was now necessary to view together central and NE Lancashire, in the light of regional needs, and to determine what action would best help to meet the needs of the area and to advance the Government's regional policies.

Central Lancashire had been a relatively stable area in recent years. It contained some substantial growth industries in Preston and Leyland. It was well placed on national and regional communications and had sites for development. NE Lancashire had a population of nearly 500,000. It had suffered from the decline of cotton and coal, on which it was heavily dependent. The population had declined, with substantial emigration. Its urban fabric was largely worn out. It was an obvious 'grey' area. It was not however in irreversible decline. Blackburn in particular, by vigorous effort, had achieved a position of relative stability. Several substantial town centre renewal schemes were under way. Housebuilding had reached a post-war peak. Schemes in the current road programme would substantially improve the southward communications.

---

* The report was published in 1968 under the title *Central Lancashire New Town Proposal: Impact on North East Lancashire.*
† See appendix A.

A recent calculation by the Ministry of Housing and Local Government, after discussion with the local planning authorities, suggested that the Manchester conurbation would have to export up to 44,000 families by 1981 to central Lancashire or elsewhere. This figure assumed that 22,000 families would by then have been housed in other overspill schemes outside the conurbation. In fact a number of these schemes were certain to fall short of their targets and the figure of 44,000 would therefore be exceeded.

The Merseyside conurbation had even larger overspill requirements for which provision had not yet been made: the deficiency was of the order of 42,000 house sites by 1981, even allowing for the new towns at Runcorn and Skelmersdale. It was right to take these needs into account and to envisage that the central Lancashire new town should make some contribution to meeting the needs of north Merseyside.

Looking beyond 1981, in the twenty years to 2001, the population of the region—already the most densely populated of the economic planning regions—was expected to grow by some 1·5 million; provision had to be made to accommodate much of this growth outside the conurbations.

The question was whether the new town was the best way of making provision for all these needs. Distribution of the immigrant population in and throughout central and NE Lancashire—even if that were practicable—would not maximise the effect on the area's economy and prosperity. The impact (and effort) would be too dispersed. Concentration as far as possible on a single suitable location would channel population growth in this part of the country in a way most likely to raise to a higher level the facilities available to the population, to generate an expanding industrial base, and to produce the best possible modern environment. The most suitable location for such a development was in central Lancashire.

No development of this kind would secure a rapid and dramatic benefit to neighbouring areas, and the consultants' judgement that the new town would have little effect on NE Lancashire in the first decade could be accepted. The longer term effects on NE Lancashire were less easy to foretell, but the assessment of the 'Impact' report, though possibly tending toward optimism, might well be broadly right. On the narrowest view, people in NE Lancashire must in the longer term benefit from having the access to wider job opportunities and to city-scale facilities which improved road communications in the area and the growth of such a new town would give them; but in fact the attractiveness of NE Lancashire as a location for modern industry could hardly fail to be, at least to some degree, improved by the proximity and example of successful large scale expansion.

The officials' report continued that the new town proposal, first announced in 1965*, was one for the location in the northern part of the country of a substantial investment. There was no comparable proposal capable of early implementation in current regional strategies for the north. To abandon this project would be to accept the implication that the outward migration from the area and from the region should continue, to make inevitable yet further congestion of the Manchester–Liverpool belt, and to forego the opportunity to create a new area of growth of benefit to the region as a whole.

Though it was not possible to meet all the demands of the NE Lancashire local authorities, several could be acted upon. The Ministry of Transport accepted the case for an improved road link between the Calder Valley and the M6. Pilot studies of area improvement could be undertaken. The need for expansion of industrial training and retraining facilities would be kept under continuous review. A subregional physical plan for NE Lancashire should be prepared in consultation with the regional economic planning council and possibly with some central government leadership.

The movement of population to the new town would have to match an increase in the number of jobs. Over the whole period of the new town's development—which would not get under way before about 1972—this would require the movement to the new town of substantial manufacturing employment. For this, the new town would draw primarily on the SE Lancashire conurbation as well as on the region generally. Lancashire as a whole had shown a capacity to generate employment for its population, as illustrated by the extent to which the consequences of the decline of the textile and mining industries had been absorbed. Moreover, the new town was well placed, with excellent road and rail links, and could offer a markedly attractive location for industry. It also had a strong existing industrial base. Officials considered that these factors gave sufficient assurance about industrial prospects at this stage to proceed with the proposal.

A decision now to proceed with the new town proposal would be given effect by a draft designation order under the New Towns Act. This would be open to objection and to public local inquiry. If an objection were maintained by a local planning authority, the final designation order would be subject to the negative resolution procedure in Parliament.† The final stage in the statutory designation procedure would, in consequence, not be reached until fairly late in 1969, by which time the Government should have received and considered the Hunt report.

Officials put forward strong arguments for a decision to publish a

---

* See above p. 223.

† On this issue of parliamentary control see appendix D.

draft designation order. First, the need for the new town arose from population pressures for which provision had to be made. If it were deferred, there would be further search for short term and second-best solutions, such as further unacceptable spread of the conurbations, to the prejudice of this strategic proposal. Secondly, there were substantial ministerial commitments in principle to the proposal, which was first announced in February 1965, and which had been widely welcomed as an unprecedented proposal for an important concentration of public and private investment in the region, and in the north generally. Thirdly, the new town proposal was a cardinal feature in the plans of the north-west region economic planning council, and was emphasised as such in their report *Strategy II* to which the Government would soon need to reply. Finally, for these reasons there was strong pressure from the county council, the regional council, the local authorities in the new town area, and from much opinion in Lancashire, for an early decision to proceed.

Officials therefore recommended that the right course was to proceed to a draft designation order, accepting that when the time came for policy decisions arising from the Hunt report, the industrial needs of the new town would to some extent at least have to be taken into account.

The designated area proposed by the consultants was considered to be too large since it was based partly on an assumption of lower densities of development than should reasonably be achieved. Officials recommended various reductions which would have the effect of reducing the area from some 51,000 acres to 41,000 acres.

When this was discussed by ministers, the need to reassure the local authorities in NE Lancashire that the new town would not prejudice necessary development in their areas was strongly emphasised. It was widely believed in NE Lancashire that a decision to go ahead with the new town would in practice mean that funds would not be available for development in neighbouring areas, which were already suffering from depopulation and slow industrial growth. It would be very damaging to the Government to announce the draft designation order without at the same time giving definite undertakings that the specific needs of NE Lancashire would be met. In particular, any public announcement about the new town should contain a firm starting date for the improvement of road communications with the M6. The announcement should also contain a reference to the decision to carry out pilot operations in area improvement in NE Lancashire; and should make it clear that consideration would be given in the context of the Hunt report on 'intermediate areas' to the possibility of making available higher grants for clearing derelict land and for urban renewal in the area.

On the other hand, it was argued that to give an unqualified commitment of the kind proposed about the improvement of communications for a single area would represent the negation of planning. The road programme had been severely cut and all road projects were decided on the basis of careful appraisal of their costs and benefits and of an objective determination of priorities. The need for an improved road link between the Calder Valley and the M6 was accepted in principle, and a feasibility study had been set in hand, but it was not possible at this stage to say when the project should start or what precise form it should take. The impact of the new town would in any case not be substantially felt until the 1980s.

Ministers decided that there should be an early announcement of their decision to proceed with the proposed new town at Leyland–Chorley and to make a draft designation order. The announcement should make it clear that the Government accepted the case for an improved road link between the Calder Valley and the M6; and it should state that they would commission the preparation of pilot schemes of area improvement in NE Lancashire and would invite the local authorities concerned to prepare a subregional plan. The announcement should also refer to the Government's intention to hold discussions with the local authorities in NE Lancashire, when the report of the Hunt Committee was published, on the best way of meeting their needs in the light of the timetable for the development of the new town.

Later in December 1968 the draft designation order was published proposing designation of 41,000 acres. A public inquiry was held in May 1969, and the final order was made in March 1970 designating an area of 35,000 acres including the whole of Preston and parts of Leyland and Chorley, and capable of accommodating a total population of about 430,000.

Dawley–Wellington–Oakengates*

In the summer of 1967, officials considered the proposal that Wellington–Oakengates should be designated as part of Dawley new town. There was general agreement that every effort should be made to ensure the success of Dawley. They accepted that fact that it could be argued that the original choice of Dawley had been a mistake, but at this stage there were compelling political objections to abandoning the project. It was, however, by no means as clear that the proposal for an additional intake of 50,000 at Wellington–Oakengates should be accepted. The firms already established at Wellington–Oakengates did not seem likely to expand in the area, nor would it be easy

---

* EP(O) (67)59 and EP(O) (67) 16th Meeting, 17 August 1967; EP(O) (67)82 and EP(O)(67) 20th Meeting, 24 October 1967; EP (67)37 and EP(67)12th Meeting, 10 November 1967; EP(68)37 and EP(68) 10th Meeting, 19 September 1968.

to attract new industry. There was a serious danger that, if the Government committed themselves to a planned intake of 100,000 immigrants into an expanded Dawley new town they would double their expenditure but fall well short of their target because the necessary jobs would not materialise. On the other hand, if the decision went against expansion at Wellington–Oakengates, there would then be pressure for another new town to take overspill from the west midlands conurbation and this might well prove expensive. If, however, the expansion of Wellington–Oakengates were to proceed, the Government should not embark on other expansion schemes elsewhere in the west midlands until it was clear that Dawley was becoming a success.

It was suggested that the right course might be for the Government to proceed with the Wellington–Oakengates proposal, but not to specify the target of an additional 50,000 overspill from the west midlands conurbation. This would avoid any public commitment to a higher intake before it was certain that Dawley would succeed in obtaining the 50,000 immigrants originally planned. Dawley–Wellington–Oakengates could then be planned as one area and developed by a single agency, but the pace of development would be determined by the success of the expanded new town in attracting overspill. If necessary, the development of Wellington–Oakengates could be phased over a long period. MHLG explained the difficulties of this approach : when a new town was designated, it was necessary at the public inquiry to justify the area to be taken having regard to the population which it was to accommodate. The strongest objections invariably came from those who argued that overall densities were too low and that, in consequence, too much land was being taken. The area provided for in the consultants' report was based on an intake of 100,000 and could be defended only on that basis.*

But the need to justify the area of land did not form a commitment about the pace or the agency of development. It could be stated at the public inquiry that the primary purpose of designation was to ensure the overall planning of the area, although the area had been chosen with a target population and a target overspill figure in view. It could also be stated that the development corporation would give priority to the Dawley area, while local authorities and private enterprise would operate in partnership with the corporation in the Wellington–Oakengates area.

There was already much private development taking place in Wellington and Oakengates, and a great deal more was held back only by the freeze on development until decisions were taken on the future of these towns. Wellington UDC had been pressing hard for

* *Dawley: Wellington: Oakengates—Consultants' Proposals for Development*, HMSO, 1966.

three years to be allowed to redevelop their town centre, a major part of which would attract private investment. Similarly there was a wish in Oakengates to follow Wellington's example. There was also scope in the area for industrial expansion by private investment.

This meant that, if the whole area were designated under the New Towns Act, private enterprise in conjunction with the local authorities could undertake a larger measure than usual of the development required, leaving the development corporation to act as overall planning co-ordinator and to concentrate their building and financing activities mainly in the southern (existing) Dawley new town.

With local authorities and private enterprise taking up the challenge, 'as they undoubtedly would', public capital committed through the development corporation would be no more over the next five years and probably only marginally more over the following ten years than it would be if only Dawley went ahead. The Government would put little more at risk than currently; and if public faith were restored and strengthened by adding Wellington–Oakengates to Dawley, there was a very good chance indeed of getting far better returns on very little more investment than was likely with Dawley standing alone.

In the discussion at official level MHLG said that the need to develop the proposed area successfully was of such importance that other developments in the region should, if necessary, be delayed. DEA, however, considered that the progress of other projects should not be held up by the development of Dawley–Wellington–Oakengates: this was particularly true of the proposed expansion of Worcester.

It was agreed that the issue would need to be referred for approval to the ministerial committee on environmental planning. When ministers considered it they should be aware that, while at present there was no suggestion of attracting industry to Dawley by any stronger means than a small number of concessionary rentals and the flexible administration of normal distribution of industry policy for firms which wished to move there, it might well become necessary in the course of time to take positive action to steer industry to Dawley. It would, however, be inadvisable to allow this view to become public knowledge, and for the moment any queries on the means by which industry was to be attracted would be met by the reply that normal policy, which gave first priority to the development areas and second to the new towns, should be sufficient for the purpose.

WELLINGTON–OAKENGATES : MINISTERIAL DISCUSSION

Greenwood brought the matter to the EP Committee in November

1967. He explained that he was under great pressure to announce the Government's decision on the proposal that the existing new town of Dawley should be extended by some 12,500 acres to include Wellington and Oakengates to accommodate 100,000 overspill population from the west midlands conurbation instead of the present target of 50,000.

The scale of growth of population in the west midlands and the resulting problems of dispersal of population presented some critical planning issues. The conurbation would give rise to a need for some 355,000 houses by 1981 and an additional 1·5 million people might have to be found homes in the region between 1981 and the end of the century. In their report *Patterns of Growth* the west midlands economic planning council had stated that if *all* the overspill schemes, agreed and projected, were completed by 1981 (which was unlikely) these would do no more than satisfy the demand. The schemes included the provision of 15,000 houses for Birmingham in the south-west sector of the conurbation and the substantial contribution of 100,000 immigrants envisaged in the Dawley–Wellington–Oakengates proposal.

Wellington and Oakengates lay side by side immediately to the north of the new town. The area recommended for expansion (12,500 acres) had an existing population of about 48,000, contained many industrial units (including three large firms with important associated companies and known potential for expansion) and had thriving commercial centres. A number of outline planning permissions existed but were held back. The area was ripe for development and this could go ahead rapidly as soon as decisions were taken.

The planning consultants appointed to study the whole area had made a number of recommendations in their first report. The most important of these were that it was feasible to take a total immigrant population of 100,000 into the Dawley–Wellington–Oakengates area; that the whole area should be planned as one physical, economic and social community; and that the plan should be implemented by one agency.

In a supplementary confidential report, the consultants stated that the cost *per capita* to develop the existing Dawley new town for 50,000 immigrants would be £2,859 whilst the cost *per capita* to develop Dawley–Wellington–Oakengates for 100,000 immigrants would be £2,777.

There was general agreement among government departments, the west midlands economic planning council and the local authorities concerned that Dawley, Wellington and Oakengates should be planned as an entity. It was also generally agreed that this could best be achieved by extending the new town to include the area recommended by the consultants (less 450 acres of good agricultural land which the Ministry of Agriculture had asked to be omitted) and by having one development corporation operative over the whole area.

The question of the speed of development had been examined and again there was general agreement among departments that it would be more realistic to aim at getting 100,000 immigrants into the extended new town by 1986 rather than by 1981. This would still be a substantial and vital contribution to overspill needs and would demonstrate clearly the Government's determination to solve the conurbation problems.

Furthermore, it was accepted by departments that the larger area would provide a stronger and more attractive economic base for large scale expansion; that there was considerable potential for private enterprise investment in industry, commerce and housing in Wellington–Oakengates which could be harnessed to the larger expansion so that comparatively little extra public investment would be required if Wellington–Oakengates were included; and that the expansion would provide a much better economic justification and impetus for the major road works between Dawley and the conurbation which were in any case essential for the existing new town (and on which the Minister of Transport had already set aside £10m in the future road programme).

The difficulties and doubts about the proposal arose because of the disappointing performance of the existing new town. It had been slow to get off the ground, and industry had been reluctant to move to Dawley. It was not an attractive site. Existing road communications with the conurbation were poor. This deterred industrialists from moving. Failure to get a proper flow of industry bred doubts about the future prospects of the existing new town and about the proposed expansion. The expansion proposals had frozen private enterprise plans, and the delay in deciding whether or not to go ahead with them created still more uncertainty and doubts amongst industrialists. It was becoming a vicious circle. Nevertheless, Greenwood maintained, there was considerable potential for harnessing private investment if the expansion proposals were agreed. There was already much private enterprise housing being built in the Wellington–Oakengates area; developers were keenly interested in financing the redevelopment of the town centres of these two towns, and the existing firms had expansion plans which were at present inhibited partly by the distribution of industry policy but largely by uncertainty about the future of the area.

Greenwood stressed that he had to be supported by certain other actions. It was essential to secure the co-operation of Birmingham and the Black Country authorities in finding people and jobs for the new city. For this reason, among others, he had it in mind to reorganise the corporation of the new town in order to base it strongly on the public and industrial interests of Birmingham and the Black Country.

At the same time, he hoped that the Board of Trade would continue to operate IDC policy in relation to the new town in a sympathetic and flexible way. In his view this, together with some concessionary rental arrangements by the development corporation in early years, was all that was necessary to ensure that sufficient industry went to the new town. He hoped too that plans for improving road communications with the conurbation could be expedited: an early announcement of some firm dates for major road schemes would greatly help to reassure industrialists.

Greenwood therefore proposed to the EP Committee that Wellington–Oakengates should be designated under the New Towns Act as proposed by the consultants, (but excluding 450 acres of good agricultural land as agreed with the Ministry of Agriculture); that a single new town development corporation should be responsible for the whole expanded area; and that the target rate of growth should be 100,000 immigrants by 1986.

There was general agreement among ministers that Dawley was far from being an ideal site for a new town and, with the benefit of hindsight, its designation had probably been a mistake. Nevertheless, most considered it was important both for the sake of the new towns policy and to help solve the midlands overspill problem to try to make it a success. The addition of Wellington–Oakengates seemed the only way to retrieve the situation since it was clear that Dawley could not develop on its own. However, in view of the uncertain prospects of the area, it would be better not to fix a definite date for reaching a population intake of 100,000. Although it would be necessary at the ensuing public inquiry to announce the maximum number of immigrants envisaged, the date by which this level was to be achieved could be indicated only in general terms. It was, however, important to avoid giving an impression of uncertainty which could destroy confidence and turn away industrialists.

Doubts were expressed about the wisdom of promoting further economic growth in the midlands which was already one of the most prosperous areas in the country. On the other hand, it was emphasised that it would be necessary in any case to provide for the natural growth of the population in the midlands area where there was a serious lack of suitable space for development. It was not merely a question of providing houses for a rising population: it was essential to provide the necessary jobs as well. Other sites in the area had been examined to assess the contribution which they could make to accommodate overspill population, but it was clear that only the

Dawley–Wellington–Oakengates area offered the prospect of taking a substantial number. Nevertheless, it was important that the development of the expanded new town should not be at the expense of the development areas. The area should not be given any special assistance under the distribution of industry policy over and above that which was already given to existing new towns. The Board of Trade should grant certificates to midlands firms to set up or expand in Dawley only if they were satisfied that it was essential for the firms to remain in the midlands area. Otherwise firms would be directed to the development areas.

A contrary argument was put forward by the Treasury: since there was no prospect of Dawley developing on its own, and no guarantee that the addition of Wellington–Oakengates would turn a present failure into a future success, it would be better, even though £5m worth of public money had already been invested in Dawley, for the Government to cut its losses rather than to throw good money after bad. Very little industry had been attracted to Dawley so far in spite of the inducements already available, and the fact that it had conspicuously failed to develop, even though situated in one of the most prosperous regions in the country, meant that a decision to expand the new town area would be a costly and unjustifiable gamble.

A decision was not easy to reach, but ministers finally agreed 'although with great reluctance', that there was no alternative but to approve the expansion of Dawley to take in Wellington–Oakengates. There was no guarantee that the expanded area would be successful, but there was a definite and urgent problem of finding accommodation for people already in the midlands, and studies showed that Dawley–Wellington–Oakengates offered the best means of meeting the overspill needs of the area. Wellington–Oakengates should therefore be designated under the New Towns Act and a single new town development corporation should be responsible for the whole area. However, because of the uncertain prospects of this area, no date should be announced for the attainment of the target of 100,000 immigrants.

INDUSTRIAL DEVELOPMENT CRISIS AT DAWLEY

In August 1968, however, Greenwood reported that urgent interim measures were needed to deal with a grave imbalance which was developing between house building and industrial development. By mid-1970, at least 2,500 houses would be completed, but only 450 new jobs were in prospect. Even if a generous allowance were made for dwellings being occupied by building workers, teachers and others employed in service trades, there would be a minimum shortfall of over 1,000 male jobs.

The result would be a large number of empty houses in the new town. (One hundred of the 600 houses already built were standing empty.) This was a situation which could not be allowed to develop on a large scale.

> 'It would expose the Government to severe criticism on many grounds. It would do what might be irreparable and permanent harm to Dawley's prospects, thus wiping out before they can be felt the beneficial effects of the previously agreed expansion of the designated area.'

Greenwood believed that the slow rate of industrial movement to Dawley derived from doubts about the likely success of the new town and also the poor road communications with Birmingham and the Black Country. Experience in other new towns suggested that once the movement of industry was successfully under way it progressively gathered its own momentum. The immediate and very urgent need was to prime the pump by securing an initial move of some sound concerns to Dawley.

Great efforts had been, and were being, made to prime the pump. Greenwood had strengthened the development corporation by appointing 'a new and very energetic chairman with wide relevant experience', and a 'sound deputy chairman from the locality'. Officials of the Board of Trade, in co-operation with officers of the corporation, had, within the constraints imposed by their policy instructions, done their best to steer industry from Birmingham and the Black Country to Dawley. The Ministry of Transport were working towards a position where a public announcement could be made about the improvement of Dawley's road communications.

In spite of all this, there were no present grounds for believing that the 1,000 male jobs required by mid 1970 would be forthcoming unless further action were put in hand at once. Greenwood proposed that as a purely temporary measure IDC controls should be relaxed and that any company in the west midlands which wished to establish in Dawley in the immediate future should be given an IDC. This could be done administratively without any public announcement of a change of policy and would not prejudice the development area policy. The number of jobs required in Dawley was comparatively small: for the west midlands as a whole in 1967–68 IDCs were issued for enterprises which would provide just over 5,000 additional jobs. The applications for IDCs which were refused in that year might have been expected to provide about 1,500 jobs. IDCs were granted in development areas in 1967–68 for 52,800 jobs. When IDCs were refused a relatively small percentage of the enterprises concerned were in fact set up in development areas. It would be helpful if in borderline cases the Board of Trade could indicate that they would grant an IDC if the enterprise were established in Dawley.

At the EP Committee meeting in September 1968 it was argued that the proposed change in IDC policy for Dawley at this time would have unacceptable repercussions in the development areas where there was serious unemployment, and particularly in Wales. Even if no public announcement were made, the change of policy would become known and there would be a storm of protest which would be more embarrassing for the Government than the criticism which would be aroused if houses in Dawley were left empty. Since August 1966 the Board of Trade had applied the IDC policy very flexibly and liberally to Dawley, and this policy was by no means the only or the most important factor inhibiting Dawley's development. Any application from a firm in the Birmingham conurbation with a case for moving to Dawley was sympathetically considered, but the Board of Trade could not agree to relax the policy further. Industrialists were more likely to be deterred from moving to Dawley by the poor road communications and the attitude of local authorities, who were often reluctant to encourage industry to leave their area. In the long term, the solution lay in improving communications and putting pressure on the Birmingham City Council and local industry. Meanwhile, the Hunt Committee on the 'grey areas' had been asked to consider the case of Dawley, and it would be wrong to take any further special action for Dawley in advance of the committee's report, which was expected in two or three months' time.

Others, however, argued that the population in the conurbation was expanding rapidly and the expansion could not be dealt with solely by steering jobs to the development areas. Development area policy did not require progress on the new towns to be stopped, and the possible repercussions of the proposed concession for Dawley on the development areas had been overstated. Dawley had an unhappy background, but the Government were now committed to going ahead with the new town and unless further positive action were taken now it might not get off the ground. There would be pressure for Birmingham to expand in the green belt, and the Government's effort to restrain the sprawl of the conurbation would be frustrated. The Government were already under heavy criticism locally.

On balance, the committee decided that there was not a sufficient case for relaxing IDC policy for Dawley as proposed by Greenwood. But it was clear that Dawley was 'in an unhappy position' and that the Board of Trade should continue to give it priority within the west midlands when considering IDCs for firms which could not go to the development areas.

After a local inquiry in May 1968 the designation order including Wellington–Oakengates was made in December 1968. The town was renamed Telford in honour of the noted engineer who had spent many years in the neighbourhood. This name also avoided invidious reference to any particular locality in the area.

The Humberside Report*

A study of the development potential of Humberside had been commissioned by ministers in June 1966.† The work was undertaken by the central unit for environmental planning and presented to the EP Committee in November 1968. The main conclusions and recommendations were that Humberside had the physical potential for a major new settlement of population, and could become a highly attractive city region, at a cost 'not inherently excessive' in relation to the benefits it offered. Nevertheless, major growth on Humberside should not be planned to take place earlier than 1980. A final decision on this was not needed before 1972, by which time the economic implications of the decision (both locally and nationally) should be capable of better assessment in the light of new information. When the final decision was taken, it should (if favourable) include provision for planned growth on a very large scale approaching a total of 750,000 extra population by the end of the century; the creation of a planning and development agency with a highly qualified staff and the necessary wide powers to plan and execute the work; and the institution of financial incentives sufficient (in the light of information available at the time) to provide the inflow of industry and maintain the growth of employment on the necessary scale.

In the meantime, the prospects of major development being needed in the 1980s should be regarded as sufficiently strong to justify certain measures to preserve the area's potential and make it ready for rapid development. Construction of a Humberside bridge should be undertaken early enough to ensure completion for service by 1976, and this implied a decision to proceed with construction in 1969.

When the report was discussed by ministers, however, the immediate question was whether it should be published and, if so, in what form and when. It was feared the publication would inevitably be taken to imply that the report was endorsed by the Government and this was bound to cause embarrassment. It seemed possible that publication would encourage land speculation in the areas likely to be affected by development; and any large windfall profits which resulted would also create embarrassment. Officials had recommended therefore that the views of the chairman of the Land Commission should be sought on the extent of the risk of

---

* EP(68)43 and EP(68)13th Meeting, 20 November 1968; EP(69)4th Meeting, 2 April 1969; SEP(69)41 and SEP(69)9th Meeting, 21 April 1969.
 † See above p. 228.

profitable speculation. They had also drawn attention to the possibility that the Land Commission could exploit their advance knowledge of the report to buy land in the areas affected at agricultural value.

In discussion, it was emphasised that a published report by civil servants, in whatever capacity they were acting, was bound to be regarded as representing the views of the Government. Although publication would create difficulties for the Government, there was in fact no alternative to it; and there could be no question of editing parts of the report before publication as this would lead to even greater embarrassment. It would help to minimise the difficulties if the report were published in as unofficial a form as possible ('not looking like either a white or a green paper') and the preface should make clear the nature of the central unit which had carried out the study, and the fact that the report did not commit the Government.

A range of differing views was expressed by ministers. It was argued that it would be absurd to reach a decision on the construction of a Humberside bridge some three years in advance of the decision (which would alone provide the justification for the bridge) on whether or not to undertake a major new urban development on Humberside. The cost of construction would be some £23m which could only be found, unless resources were diverted from other regions, by postponing the construction of roads in the Humberside area which had a higher priority than the bridge.

It was finally decided that the report should be published without amendment but that it should be made clear in the preface that the Government were in no way committed to its conclusions or recommendations.* It was also agreed that the chairman of the Land Commission should be asked whether publication of the report would be likely to provoke profitable land speculation. A copy of the report could now be sent to the Hunt Committee who could take account of it in preparing their own report. But publication should not be delayed once the question of land purchases by the Land Commission had been resolved and the views of the chairman of the Land Commission on the likelihood of speculation had been obtained.†

---

* It was published by HMSO in 1969 under the title *Humberside: A Feasibility Study*.

† At first sight this seemed to be an ideal opportunity for the Land Commission, but it quickly became apparent that it was not so (MHLG Files HLG 73/5 and PLUPI 660/30). The Government were making it clear that they were not committed to the report's proposals and thus acquisition would be risky. In any case 'there would be little, if any, advantage to the commission' from 'advance information' since it was already public knowledge that the study was in hand and that the area was being considered for planned growth. As a result, land thought to be well situated for development would already have been purchased by builders or secured by means of options. Alternatively, owners would have decided to hold on to their land for sale when there was a clear prospect of its full development value being realised. There was nothing the commission could do about this since their powers of compulsory acquisition were limited to land on which a planning decision had been taken. This, of course, was not so in this case. (*History Vol IV*, chapter XIII.)

The discussion was taken up at later meetings when there was general agreement that a major planned expansion on Humberside was not necessary in the 1970s and that a more detailed study was required before a final decision was taken on whether it should be undertaken in the 1980s. Differing views were, however, expressed on whether the Humber bridge should be built by 1976 and, if so, on how the necessary resources could be provided. It was argued that the bridge could make an important contribution to the development of the Humberside area, and that it was generally preferable to use whatever funds might be available for additional road projects in the intermediate areas for one substantial project which could have a real impact locally. Moreover, this measure was specifically recommended in the Humberside report. On the other hand, it was pointed out that if the bridge would not be justified by the date proposed on normal criteria it would be difficult to justify it as an urgent regional priority, linking as it did an area to which no priority was to be attached.

It was difficult to quantify the wider benefits, but it was felt they were likely to outweigh the opportunity cost of two or even four years deferment of other marginal road programmes. There was a strong expectation, in view of past government statements, that a decision would be taken to build the bridge at an early date.

After lengthy discussion on the public expenditure implications, it was finally agreed that in view of 'the strong economic case for the bridge', and the expectations which had been raised by earlier commitments, the bridge should be built.

Ipswich*

It had been officially announced in February 1965 that the expansion at Ipswich to take 70,000 Londoners by 1981 would go ahead.† Consultants were appointed and, in their report,‡ they recommended the designation, under the New Towns Act, of land to the west and south-west of the town. The original proposal of the consultants covered some 22,900 acres, but in subsequent work it had been found possible to reduce the acreage to 20,100.

Though there was general agreement between the authorities concerned that Ipswich should be expanded, there was considerable debate on whether the expansion scheme should take place wholly to the west and south-west of the town (as proposed by the consultants), or partly to the east in order to minimise the loss of good

---

* EP(67)11th Meeting, 23 October 1967; EP(69)7, EP(69)8 and EP(69)2nd Meeting, 24 March 1969; EP(69)14 and EP(69)5th Meeting, 1 May 1969; SEP(69)53 and SEP(69) 13th Meeting, 5 June 1969.

† See p. 214 above.

‡ *Expansion of Ipswich Designation Proposals: Consultants' Study of the Town and its Sub-Region*, HMSO, 1966.

quality agricultural land. In order to make an assessment of the possibilities of a compromise solution, the consultants were asked to examine the costs of their original proposals as against possible alternatives using land to the east of the town. They showed that the extra capital cost of the least costly alternative was £5·634m and the extra recurring costs £957,000 per annum. (Using the same data, but applying the methods of evaluation recommended by the working group on the valuation of agricultural land for planning purposes, which was submitted to ministers for approval at the same time as the Ipswich proposals,* the net extra costs in terms of resources, of the cheapest alternative over the preferred solution, would be of the order of £18·5m. This calculation took into account the value of the agricultural production that would be lost.) The Ministry of Agriculture, however, did not agree that the planning considerations outweighed the agricultural and political factors, and they did not accept the cost–benefit calculation which they considered was a spurious and prejudicial figure based on false premises.

The matter had to be decided by ministers: the agricultural arguments were rejected and it was agreed that a draft designation order should be made in respect of some 20,100 acres of land to the west and south-west of Ipswich.

After further discussions, the Ministry of Housing and the Ministry of Agriculture agreed to exclude a further 1,200 acres of high quality agricultural land from the area to be covered by the draft designation order, the area so reduced allowing for growth after the end of planned expansion only up to about 1991 (rather than up to 2001 as envisaged in the consultants' original proposals).

A public local inquiry into objections to the draft order was held in June 1968. The inspector's report showed that by far the greatest weight of objection related to the high agricultural value of the land. He reported that the farming interests were claiming that 'this was the most important example so far where some of the country's best land (however defined) could be lost for all time from agricultural use'. The NFU and Country Landowners' Association argued that the proposal should be abandoned, while the county council argued on agricultural grounds for the exclusion of part of the land. The inspector also reported that a second basic objection raised at the inquiry was that it was not right to reach a final decision on the new town before regional plans for the south-east and East Anglia had been prepared and accepted. Ipswich County Borough Council, who supported the proposal in principle, lodged a formal objection in

---

* A major issue in the Ipswich case was the method by which agricultural land should be valued. On this see appendix B.

order to be able to argue their case for financial support to prevent the new town being an undue burden on their rates.

The inspector concluded that development should take place on the west and south-west as recommended by the consultants, but that the draft designation area should be reduced by the exclusion of 1,359 acres in the north-west as requested by the county council, together with 427 acres in the south-west and two smaller areas. He recommended these exclusions on the ground that 'no more land than was required should be used'. The area remaining after the exclusions would meet overspill needs up to 1981, and it was unnecessary to plan for post-1981 growth until the planning strategy for the south-east had been determined.

POST-INQUIRY DEVELOPMENTS

Meanwhile, there had been increasing discussion of the prospective decline in GLC population and, therefore, of the need for an overspill programme on the scale originally envisaged. This had become public knowledge in various documents prepared by the GLC as part of their work towards the GLC development plan. It was now estimated that Greater London's population, which it was thought would have to be deliberately restrained to 8 million by 1981, would have fallen to 7–7·3 million by that date largely as a result of voluntary movement of people out of London.

The current programme of London's new towns and town expansions was based on the earlier hypothesis: and on the inference that in order to keep the GLC population down to 8 million, planned development for 660,000 Londoners would have to be provided in new towns and town expansion schemes. The minister's case for the new town at Ipswich was argued on this basis at the public inquiry.

The full effect of the recent changes in assumptions had not been worked out, but it would probably result in some reduction in the original target for overspill provision. To that extent one part of the case for Ipswich ('the last in the line') became rather more difficult to establish. Moreover, it might affect the rate of expansion in other new towns recently established, at least in the early years. Nevertheless, the indications were that London's housing problem would remain a major social problem. The number of unfit houses was likely to be larger than was originally envisaged. Furthermore, the emphasis on improvement of houses and rehabilitation of whole areas itself produced further housing needs because of the need to reduce overcrowding in these areas.

In reviewing the target much depended on the proportions of planned and 'unplanned' movement from the metropolis. The high proportion of 'unplanned' movement was due in part to the delay in getting the major new town schemes started and to the shortage of houses for sale in the older London new towns. It was reasonable to assume that as the large new towns got into their stride and the policy for providing 50 per cent of the houses for owner occupation 'began to bite', it should be possible to change the balance between planned and 'voluntary' movement. Moreover, substantial long distance overspill schemes would help to channel some voluntary movement away from the outer metropolitan area and help to reduce the pressures of population growth there.

The matter was brought to ministers for 'a final decision' by Robinson (Minister for Planning and Land) in March 1969. He pointed out that a decision was 'not entirely straightforward'. The land was of good agricultural quality and the inspector had clearly been impressed by the strength of agricultural objections. Overspill needs were under review, and the NFU (who had noted the recent trends in GLC thinking) might well seek to challenge a decision.

On balance, Robinson concluded that it would be right to let the scheme proceed. The agricultural arguments had been faced in advance of deciding to go ahead with the draft designation and the public inquiry. There was nothing to show that total overspill provision would finally prove to be excessive. Ipswich was a natural growth area and its expansion was regarded by the south-east and east anglian regional economic planning councils as an important contribution to their total regional policies. Moreover, Ipswich itself had suffered from four years of uncertainty, arrested development and blight since the original government announcement in 1965; and London would have a pressing housing problem for a long time to come.

In view of the strength of the agricultural objection, it would be inadvisable to reject the inspector's recommendations completely. But to accept them *in toto* would leave a most unsatisfactory planning situation. In particular, it would destroy the basic concept of two large separate new districts, one to the north and one to the south of A12, each with its own district centre. The reduced area north of A12 (with a capacity of some 20,000 people) would be too small to support a viable district centre. Moreover, its physical shape would make it very difficult to plan as a coherent district development. The consultants' basic planning proposals would have to be scrapped or very substantially revised, producing further delay before development could proceed. Reduction in the scale of the development would also be likely to produce higher costs per head in terms of both capital (eg for roads, water and sewerage) and management, though it was not possible to quantify them at this stage.

Robinson therefore proposed, as a compromise, to exclude a further 363 acres in the north-west rather than the 1,359 acres which the inspector recommended, plus the other three areas which the inspector recommended for exclusion. The area north of A12, with a capacity of 35,000 people, could then support a district centre and be satisfactorily planned and developed in balance with the larger district to the south. The total capacity of the designated area outside the county borough would be reduced by about 10,000 people. It would thus be capable of accommodating a planned intake by 1981 of up to 70,000, leaving room for growth for a further six years or more thereafter. The total area of land proposed for final designation would thus be some 17,130 acres of which some 7,400 acres were outside the county borough boundary.

There was an additional complication. From the time of the earliest discussions with Ipswich, it was recognised that expansion would throw additional financial burdens on the town in advance of the growth of rateable value, and that financial arrangements between the development corporation and the county borough council would take account of this. In accordance with a promise given at the public inquiry, there had been discussions with the county borough about the nature and scale of the financial burden. The council had made it clear that they would maintain their formal objection to designation and would not participate in the development of the new town until satisfactory financial arrangements were made. There was no prospect that negotiations would be completed to the satisfaction of the council by the time a decision was announced. It, therefore, seemed likely that the county borough council (as well as the county council) would maintain their objection and arrange for the tabling of a motion to annul the order which could lead to parliamentary proceedings. But this was not unusual and there was no reason to hold up the decision on this account. Robinson concluded that the need for a new town at Ipswich still stood.

THE TREASURY CASE AGAINST IPSWICH

Robinson's proposals were not acceptable to the Treasury who put forward three arguments for a 'reappraisal': the prospective decline in London's population; the problem of providing adequate employment at Ipswich; and the current public expenditure outlook.

Hitherto it had been the agreed aim to provide new and expanding towns in south-east England for a total of one million people by 1981 (two-thirds from London, one-third from elsewhere). Schemes so far agreed were expected to provide 590,000. If Ipswich were approved, and if allowance were made for the expanding town schemes in the pipeline, the total provision would become, at most, 750,000. There would be, therefore, in any case, a substantial shortfall on the one million target, even if the Ipswich new town went ahead. But that target was approved because it was understood to be necessary in order to contain London's population at eight million by 1981. In the event, London's population had already fallen below eight million; and the GLC's latest studies suggested a possible reduction to between 7 and 7·3 million by 1981. It was the sheer size of this reduction which called in question the earlier one million target. It pointed clearly to a need to postpone a decision on Ipswich until some more considered assessment could be made of the GLC's latest estimates and of their implications for policies of overspill and planned expansions.

A second major consideration was that while the supply of mobile industrial and office development in the years ahead would inevitably be limited, the prospective demands were already greater than ever before. The planned growth that had already been approved for new and expanding towns (not only in south-east England) was so high that there had had to be some doubt about the adequacy of the resources of mobile industry in the coming decade.

Within this overall framework, Ipswich seemed a favourable site for a new town development and, in particular, might prove a more attractive area for office dispersal than some other major new town developments in the midlands. It would, however, be competing for industry with all the existing overspill towns, and there would be formidable new competition from the new towns which were getting under way at Milton Keynes, Northampton and Peterborough.

The construction of a new town at Ipswich would require investment of the order of £220m, of which about £160m would be public expenditure. It was uncertain whether, in the long term, much of this expenditure would be additional since, if the new town did not go ahead, the growing population had to be housed and provided with basic services elsewhere. A new town, however, involved a firm advance commitment to the location of this expenditure; a much larger proportionate contribution by the Government; and, in the early years, additional expenditure on the initial acquisition of land and the advance provision of roads and sewers. The bulk of the estimated £9·5m which would be spent on Ipswich in the first three years would therefore be an additional call on public expenditure.

If the proposed new town were designated now, it would not be practicable at a later date to reconsider the decision or to reduce the proposed scale of expansion. If, therefore, it were to be discovered subsequently that too many new towns had been commissioned, this would have to be corrected by slowing down several of them: 'this would be a most uneconomic way of proceeding'.

It was recognised that a postponement or reversal of plans for Ipswich had considerable political disadvantages. The Government would be criticised for vacillating, and would appear to have decided in favour of the NFU, the landowners and the Conservative county council and against the Labour members of the council at Ipswich.

On the other hand, the background to the original decision had radically changed and the GLC had made no secret of their revised population estimates. 'If we were starting with a clean sheet the arguments against Ipswich would be overwhelming.' To approve the new town would involve a commitment at vast public expense to a project which appeared to be unnecessary, which would have to compete for industry with the development and intermediate areas and which, unless given priority over them, might encounter serious difficulties in building up.

REVIEW OF LONDON'S POPULATION TRENDS

In the face of these arguments, it was decided that officials should undertake a further quick review of the position. A report was presented to ministers in May 1969. It dealt with future population estimates for London and their implications for the overspill programme in general and for Ipswich in particular; and also the risk that there would not be enough mobile industry to meet Ipswich's needs.

On the basis of their latest estimates (prepared for the Greater London development plan), the GLC argued that policy must now be directed towards keeping London's population from falling below 7·3 million as opposed to the previous policy of keeping the population down to 8 million. The GLC were conscious of a falling work force and future labour shortages. They also feared a structural change in London's population in view of the loss of skilled workers moving to new towns and potential owner occupiers moving to the outer metropolitan area. They considered that 7·3 million was a desirable minimum population below which the economic viability of London would be threatened.

Officials noted that this last proposition would need careful examination in connection with the Greater London development plan when it was formally submitted, but at this stage the main question was whether the GLC's estimates of their future population could be accepted.

Both the demographic and the housing calculations were somewhat complex, and required careful and detailed study. The demographic projections assumed the continuance until 1981 of the high rate of net outflow of population from London experienced over the previous four years, ie 80,000 to 90,000 people a year, making some 1·5 million over the 1964–1981 period. There was some evidence that the rate of net outflow reached a peak in the mid 1960s and was now falling. Even so, total net outward migration 1964–1981 was likely to be well over one million. The population figures produced through the housing calculations involved assumptions about occupancy rates where a difference of three per cent could well result in a population error of 250,000. Officials had made a quick review of these figures and their initial conclusion was that the population forecast of 7·3 million might well prove to be on the low side, though the old forecast of 8 million was clearly much too high, particularly as by mid 1968 the population had already declined to some 7·8 million.

London's overspill need could not, of course, be measured solely in terms of size and population. It had to be related to housing demand and housing capacity in the metropolis. The housing situation in London remained a major social problem. Obsolescence was widespread in the inner London boroughs and called for large schemes of rehabilitation and redevelopment. These areas of housing stress—unfit housing, overcrowding, multi-occupation, etc—were also areas with a poor environment, cramped schools, little open space and lacking in social and welfare facilities. Their redevelopment would involve 'not only housing but the total environment' and would inevitably produce lower overall densities and a net outward movement of population.

There was an increasing shortage of land in London for all purposes. Because of this, the housebuilding effort had to be concentrated on replacing existing housing, and there was only a slow net gain of housing stock for London as a whole. For example, the GLC estimated that in the five years 1967–71, a total of some 225,000 houses would be built by local authorities and private enterprise, but the total net gain would be only 90,000. After 1971, the rate of building was expected to fall because of the shortage of land. London was thus likely to be an area of major housing stress for the foreseeable future, and the relief of this stress would necessitate a substantial house building programme for Londoners outside the GLC area.

The Government had declared their intention to house one million people in the London new and expanded towns between 1964 and 1981. About two thirds of these people were expected to come from London. This would necessitate an average planned outflow of about 40,000 a year. Currently, the 'planned outflow' of Londoners to new and expanded towns was running at about 25,000 a year. However, there had been in the last few years much larger 'voluntary outflows' (60,000 a year net) than had previously been expected, mainly to the outer metropolitan area, adding to the land pressures in that fast growing area.

The existing levels of planned movement were low because the first generation of new towns were now reaching the end of their build-up and the later new towns had not yet got fully under way. When they had, a larger planned outflow of population would be possible. It was a desirable planning objective that as much as possible of the movement out of London should be attracted to these new towns to relieve land, commuting and infrastructure pressures in the outer metropolitan area. There was therefore a strong case on the evidence available for continuing provision of housing in new towns at a high level.

Nevertheless, the declared target of one million had in fact been reduced to 750,000 (though this had not been publicly announced), and the GLC were no longer actively pursuing new overspill schemes throughout southern England. The GLC had been approached at official level about their attitude to the development of Ipswich and had said that they would co-operate in the supply of population and industry to the new town. But it was pointed out that GLC officials could hardly say less than this without appearing to sabotage government proposals. The conclusion could be drawn, as it was by the Treasury, that the GLC, especially in view of some doubts they appeared to be developing about further dispersal of industry from London, now felt no positive need for Ipswich new town.

Officials also examined the second main issue raised by ministers, namely the supply of mobile industry to match planned expansion at Ipswich. The Board of Trade took the view that Ipswich was a reasonably attractive site for new town development. It was already a centre of some size with a fairly wide variety of industry which might help to attract newcomers. Ipswich would, however, be competing for industry with all the existing overspill towns and with other schemes getting under way at Milton Keynes, Northampton and Peterborough. Given that the volume of mobile industry was limited and that Ipswich would be facing competition from other reception areas, the Board of Trade could not be certain that the required flow of industrial jobs could be secured, particularly in the early years. To the extent that it did compete successfully, some of the other new towns might suffer. On the other hand, the good rail communications between Ipswich and London might make the town an attractive centre for office development particularly as the area was now outside office control. An increase in office employment (over and above offices linked to factories) might help to meet any shortfall in industrial jobs.

Ipswich would not be making employment demands in the immediate future—the most likely period of greatest difficulty. From the mid-seventies onwards the situation might be easier. The Board of Trade felt that, because the supply of new jobs might fall short of what was required to meet the target of 1981, it would be prudent to introduce some flexibility into the time scale of the proposed development so that it could be extended beyond 1981. There was no major difficulty about this, provided that the rate of development was not slowed down to a degree that it became uneconomic.

In conclusion, the officials' report noted that the Government had announced their intention to proceed with a major expansion at Ipswich as long ago as February 1965. The lengthy statutory procedures had been complied with and it would be difficult to produce convincing reasons at this very late stage to justify abandonment. Postponing a decision, on the other hand, would continue the present planning blight.

On balance, the majority of the officials considered (with the Treasury dissenting) that the Ipswich new town project should be allowed to proceed. It was recommended, however, that no time should be lost in putting in hand a more comprehensive review of London's overspill policy based on the current study of the GLDP and the strategies for the south-east emerging from the south-east joint planning study, together with a fresh appraisal of the likely demand for and supply of mobile industry in the 1970s.

IPSWICH ABANDONED

Ministers had lengthy discussions on the officials' report, and opinions were evenly divided. On the one hand it was argued that there were strong economic as well as political arguments for proceeding with the expansion of Ipswich. The migration of people to the rest of the south-east region from London was very much larger than to the rest of England and Wales. Since this outward migration, which was proceeding more quickly than had previously been assumed, was certain to continue, 'it should preferably be planned rather than allowed to take place piecemeal in a way which added to the already serious problems of the outer metropolitan area'. There was no reason why the existing rate of planned overspill should not be accelerated. Unless people could be moved out of the inner London boroughs, progress with slum clearance and redevelopment of areas with poor environments would be hindered. If the GLC were so concerned about reductions in London's labour force, they would not have gone ahead with their overspill project at Swindon. The development of Ipswich would not, in its early stages, call for much additional public expenditure. Most of the money would probably be spent anyway since the population would have to be provided for elsewhere. There could be some competition with other overspill towns for the supply of mobile industry, but no substantial demands would be made until the mid 1970's when the supply position was likely to be easier. Ipswich would be unlikely to affect the development areas, since by that time the present economic disparity between them and the rest of the country should have been reduced. Because of the delay that had already taken place there was no prospect now of completing the development by 1981 and the build-up could always be rephased if necessary.

On the other hand, it was argued that since the project had proceeded so far on assumptions which now appeared inaccurate, the project should not go ahead at this stage. The decision must be based on the best available information without undue regard to previous commitments. While it was desirable that the population outflow from London should be planned as far as possible, there was no evidence that the existing overspill programme could not adequately cater for this migration without Ipswich. A new town was the most expensive way of housing overspill population because of the extra infrastructure required. Also it had too readily been assumed that Ipswich would not attract new employment at the expense of the development and intermediate areas. There was only a limited supply of mobile industry available and some doubt that Ipswich itself would be able to attract the share it needed. The political difficulties of abandoning the proposals for Ipswich should not be exaggerated. A decision not to proceed could be defended on the basis of the continuing need for restraint in public expenditure and of the latest population forecasts for London. Such a decision would undoubtedly be criticised, but on the other hand there would also be strong opposition to the Ipswich project if it went ahead.

With this even balance of arguments a decision was not easily reached but it was finally accepted that, in view of the substantial additional public expenditure which would be incurred, particularly in 1970–71 and 1971–72, the Ipswich project should be abandoned.

The Welsh New Towns

A NEW TOWN FOR MID-WALES*

In the Labour Party's 1964 policy statement for Wales *Signposts for the New Wales* it was stated:

> 'Labour believes that radical action is needed to revitalise the central area of Wales. A new town would act as the focal point for economic and social development throughout Mid-Wales and under a Labour Government an active search for a suitable site would be undertaken as a matter of urgency.'

This was taken up by Griffiths (Secretary of State for Wales) at the ED Committee in March 1965. Mid-Wales (Merioneth, Cardigan, Montgomeryshire, Radnorshire, and part of Breconshire) was the largest area of rural depopulation and 'economic unviability' in England and Wales. It had been losing population, especially younger people, for several generations—agriculture, mining, quarrying, and rural crafts had been on the decline since before the turn of the century. It had become increasingly difficult 'to keep society going' without extensive exchequer subsidies; four-fifths of

---

* ED(65)24 and ED(65)8th Meeting, 9 March 1965; EP(O)(67)3 and EP(O)(67)2nd Meeting, 1 February 1967.

the cost of local authority services already came from this source, and the basic industry, agriculture, was more heavily subsidised than in any other area of similar size in England and Wales.

Ministers agreed that the possibility of a new town in Mid-Wales should be examined, and that consultants should be appointed to advise on the possibility, through the machinery of the New Towns Act, 'of establishing an economically viable centre in Mid-Wales, which, by making available new opportunities for employment, and by offering suitable services and facilities, would arrest and possibly reverse the depopulation and strengthen the area's economy'.

The consultants' report was published in July 1966.* They concluded that a new town in Mid-Wales would not be economically viable in terms of Mid-Wales alone but, if considered in conjunction with the acute overspill problem of the west midlands 'the case for a major development such as a new town is strong'. A new town should be centred on Caersws (near Newtown) in Montgomeryshire, and a population of 70,000 was suggested as being a viable entity. The town should be built up to its target population over a period of twenty years and should be planned and built by a development corporation under the New Towns Act. There should be a series of parallel developments in some of the smaller towns of Mid-Wales outside the area of the new town, to be managed by a new statutory authority on the lines of the Highlands and Islands Development Board. This would require special legislation.

These conclusions had been considered by the west midlands economic planning council, the Mid-Wales industrial development association, the Development Commission, the county and local authorities most directly concerned, and various other local bodies. With the exception of the west midlands economic planning council, these bodies were generally in favour of a concentrated urban development centred on Caersws provided that action was not limited to this development but included also the expansion of existing communities and the improvement of basic services, particularly roads. Some Welsh bodies favoured the establishment of a Highland Development Board type of organisation to undertake the work. The west midlands economic planning council took the view that:

'a new town primarily dependent on large scale movement of industry from the west midlands region would be a less difficult proposition when population and industry in the west of the west midlands region have been built up, and when communications between Mid-Wales and Birmingham have been improved. Until then such a development would present considerable difficulties in so far as it is dependent mainly on industry from the west midlands for impetus and growth'.

---

* *A New Town in Mid-Wales—Consultants' Proposals*, HMSO, 1966.

Officials considered that, in the light of the consultants' report and the reactions to it, the two obvious possibilities for consideration were either to build a substantial town together with some build-up of selected existing towns; or to set up a development authority on the lines of the Highlands and Islands Development Board.

The first of these would conform to the policy statements already made, and had the backing of the consultants' report and of the majority of the Welsh bodies that had been consulted. If successful it would provide an urban centre of great value to Wales as a whole. As the consultants pointed out, the prospects of success would be greater if efforts were concentrated on building one sizeable town rather than a number of smaller projects. But it was estimated by the consultants that a new town of 70,000 people would cost £137m while the expansion of existing towns would add an extra £60m making a total sum of £200m. Although incoming industry would not be limited to west midlands firms, there was the risk that the industry needed to support a town of this size would not be forthcoming on a sufficient scale.

The alternative also had attractions, but it would 'contradict' previous statements of policy. Moreover, the setting up of a development authority would need special legislation which would take time, and an authority of this kind, if it were to be effective, would weaken the position of the local authorities and conflict with the proposals which the secretary of state was working out for strengthening them.

The nature of the Caersws development proposed by the consultants suggested a third possibility which would avoid most of the difficulties of the first. While most of the Caersws development would be centred at Caersws itself, the consultants thought that a substantial part of it should be located at the nearby centres of Trefeglwys, Llanidloes and Newtown. The latter, which had a population of 5,500, would have added to it three new residential areas with a total population of 9,900. Of all the existing towns in Mid-Wales, Newtown was the most suitable for expansion in terms of location, existing size, communications and general attractiveness to new industry, particularly now that it could offer development area incentives. There was no need to rely on the west midlands or indeed any one region as the source of incoming industry. A number of firms had expressed their interest in the town, which had already attracted new growth. An examination of the area by Welsh Office planners had confirmed the suitability of Newtown for a doubling or more of its present population. The town centre facilities already existing there would suffice for a substantially larger population. Moreover, it was necessary in any case for more money to be spent on flood prevention at Newtown, and a scheme costing £0·25m had been prepared by the river authority for this purpose. The cost of a doubling of Newtown by the construction of some 1,700 houses with some 1,000 new factory jobs and other ancillary development was estimated at £11m. The third possibility was, therefore, for the Government to commit themselves at this stage only to the expansion of Newtown. This would involve much less expenditure and risk than commitment to the Caersws project as a whole. If it proved successful, the Government of the day could then decide whether to proceed further with the Caersws project.

Alongside the expansion of Newtown, it would be necessary in any event to provide for some smaller scale industrial and housing development at other small towns in rural Wales. This was justified by the size of the area and the need for constructive policies to match the continued run-down in agriculture. Industrial development of such towns was proceeding with a good deal of success, but progress was handicapped by shortages of houses.

The most appropriate machinery for the doubling of existing small towns in Mid-Wales as well as for the possible complete construction of the Caersws project would be a development corporation set up under the provisions of the New Towns Act, which appeared to be flexible enough for the purpose. Experience had shown that the use of the Town Development Act machinery would not be satisfactory. Under the New Towns Act, a development corporation would be set up with a title such as the Mid-Wales development corporation and with a suitable geographical representation on its board. Its first task would be the doubling of Newtown over a period of seven to ten years, involving the construction of some 200 houses a year, after the normal statutory procedures of consultation, preparation of a draft order, public inquiry and designation. It would also be able to deal with other town developments provided that the statutory procedures were followed on each occasion.

Expansions such as that being studied for Rhayader, to which great importance was attached, could be carried out by the appropriate local authority with the government assistance available for housing and factory development or, alternatively, these towns would be designated as new towns and their populations doubled by the corporation.

For a project of the limited size now in mind, it would be difficult to justify a separate new town staff of adequate calibre. The Cwmbran development corporation, however, had such a staff which would become increasingly available for other activities and it should be possible for them to undertake the relatively small amount of planning and design work needed in Mid-Wales.

Officials agreed these proposals and the matter was settled by correspondence between ministers. A statement was made by the secretary of state to the Welsh Grand Committee in March 1967.* Although there was some public disappointment that the proposal for a larger town had been dropped, the statutory procedure was carried through and the designation order made without objection on 18 December 1967. The new development corporation rapidly formed a link with the Mid-Wales industrial development association and the same individual served both bodies as secretary and chief executive. Cwmbran development corporation provided assistance with planning, house and factory design, engineering, land acquisition and finance.

LLANTRISANT†

By the beginning of 1966, several planning studies had come to the conclusion that there was need for major urban development to meet the expected population growth in SE Glamorgan, and the Welsh Planning Board were recommending development in the Llantrisant area. At a meeting of Welsh ministers in Cardiff in July 1966, two main arguments were submitted against the Llantrisant proposal: first, that it would act as a powerful magnet which might denude the valleys still further; and secondly, that it would seriously restrict the growth of Cardiff. On the other hand, it would enable work to be provided near enough to the valleys to reduce the drift to the coast, thus enabling people still to live in the valleys.

It was pointed out that the local authorities in the west were becoming increasingly concerned with recent industrial expansion east of Port Talbot, and would therefore be expected to oppose the Llantrisant project on the ground that it would make it even more difficult to induce new industry to settle in their areas. It was, however, agreed to accept in principle that sustained growth should take place in the Llantrisant area, and confidential discussions took place with the county council, the City of Cardiff, local MPs and the Welsh Planning Board on the basis that the area should be developed as a new town for a population of 100,000.

This proposal was ripening at the same time as the decision drastically to curtail the Caersws project in Mid-Wales. The Treasury expressed their apprehension to the Welsh Office that, without a good deal more information and discussion, it could be an embarrassment to the Government to become committed, even in principle, to a new town at Llantrisant. Accordingly the Welsh Office proposed that consultants should be appointed to carry out a feasibility study. In so doing they set out the case for the new town at length.

---

* Welsh Grand Committee, *Rural Development*, Third Sitting, 15 March 1967, Col 6 *et seq.*
† Welsh Office File WNT 3/1; EP(O)(67)20, EP(O)(67)7th Meeting, 20 April 1967 and EP(O) (67)8th Meeting, 28 April 1967.

The biggest problem facing south Wales was the need for new job opportunities. The mining valleys already had a high level of unemployment, and colliery employment would almost certainly drop by some 20,000 in the next five years. It was essential that new jobs should be located in areas which were attractive to industrial growth. The valleys themselves were already congested, had little room for new development and were not attractive to industrialists. Although there was a need to rehabilitate the valleys, experience had shown that large scale industry would rarely go to them. Much of the housing was substandard and, in order to avoid long daily travel to work with its high cost to the community and to the individual, it was important, where circumstances were appropriate, to have both houses and factories in the same localities. This argument applied with particular force to the Rhondda and Taff Valleys. With a population of 270,000 there was virtually no further suitable land for development, and the original *raison d'être* of this concentration of population had almost disappeared with the closure of most of the local collieries. There was male unemployment in some areas of about 10 per cent with the strong probability of it rising much higher without new industry. There was a lack of land to provide open spaces, playing fields and the sites for new houses, of which some 2,000 a year were needed to cater both for natural increase and the replacement of substandard dwellings.

The problem of accommodating the growth of Cardiff also needed consideration. Continued growth of the city at the rate of some 2,000 houses a year was difficult to provide for because of the geographical nature of the area—sea on the south, hills on the north, open country to the west and the unsuitability of the land to the east for housing. Moreover, continued peripheral growth would make the city's road traffic problems more intractable.

Apart from the problems of the valleys and Cardiff, and the need for a suitable new location attractive to industry in Wales, there was the problem of outward migration. A new town would enable at least some of this to be channelled to a location within the Principality.

Llantrisant was well suited for major urban development. It was located immediately to the south of the Rhondda and Taff Valleys. It was near Cardiff. The country was generally undulating land of good quality, clear of coal fields and free from subsidence problems. The surrounding area had considerable natural beauty with long stretches of relatively unspoilt coast. The A48 trunk road ran through the area and any extension to the M4 would be nearby. The area was served by the main line railway, by the Bristol Channel ports and by Rhoose Airport. Essential services, including water, gas and electricity, were available. Llantrisant and the surrounding area had already attracted important industrial development which indicated that the area was a natural growth point attractive to industry. The local planning authority (Glamorgan County Council) strongly favoured Llantrisant as a suitable area for expansion.

A target population of about 100,000 was envisaged. Net outward migration from the valleys was estimated to be at the rate of some 3,000 annually. In addition, any large scale development could be expected to attract population from Cardiff and elsewhere. An intake of some 3,000 persons per year to a major urban development was considered entirely feasible. This would give, over twenty years, a population build-up to 60,000. Since the existing population of the area was 14,000 (and, with natural growth alone, could be expected to reach 20,000) the total build-up over twenty years would be to a population of 80,000. By allowing for natural growth after this period, a target population of 100,000 persons might be expected to be reached after about thirty years.

When the Welsh Office submission was discussed interdepartmentally, in April 1967, it was pointed out that the committee would shortly be considering a report from the new towns working group on the future scope of the new towns programme.* It might therefore be sensible to defer any decision on Llantrisant until it could be examined in the light of this report. Although a feasibility study would not constitute a commitment to proceed with a new town at Llantrisant, the announcement (especially if it were contained in a white paper) would be taken to mean that the Government were examining the proposal seriously: and it would be difficult to draw back if the results of the feasibility study were at all favourable. This was agreed; in the meantime the Welsh Office could circulate draft terms of reference for the feasibility study, 'bearing in mind that a number of departments . . . had indicated that they would more readily be able to agree if the terms of reference were couched in broad terms'.

Draft terms of reference were circulated in the following week. These were 'to advise on the desirable future scale, timing, lay-out, cost and organisation of urban growth in the Llantrisant area and its neighbourhood'. But delay then ensued about the terms of reference to be given to the consultants, particularly on a point raised by the Board of Trade that it was inappropriate to expect consultants to express a view on the amount of employment likely to be available either in the south Wales area as a whole or in Llantrisant in particular, as the amount of new industry available would depend in the last resort on government policies. Although this point was cleared, trouble then arose about the consultants to

* See above, p. 233 *et seq.*

be appointed and the terms on which they should be engaged—a matter on which the Public Accounts Committee had recently expressed concern.*

Eventually consultants were appointed and their report was published in 1969.† (This was followed by a draft designation order in 1972 but, after a public inquiry—at which strong local opposition was registered—the Secretary of State for Wales announced his decision in January 1974 not to proceed.)

Overview

During the five years 1964 to 1969 approval was given to the development of new towns at Peterborough, Northampton, Warrington, Central Lancashire, Milton Keynes and Newtown, and to the extension of Dawley (renamed Telford). As with the preceding Conservative Government, a major stimulus for these new towns was the enormous increase in population envisaged by the Registrar General's projections. Whereas the 1955 projection gave a GB population of 51·5m for 1990, by the time of the 1964 projection this had been revised to 65·1m (with 72·5m for the year 2000). Later revisions reduced these figures: the 1966 projection gave a 1990 population of 63·3m, and each subsequent projection during the sixties reduced the figure by a further million or so. But once the policy of creating additional new towns was embarked upon it was not easy to change; and, in any case, there was—throughout this period—little doubt about the need for new towns to accommodate overspill from the congested conurbations. Only at the end of the sixties did doubts begin to reach ministers that changing circumstances were such as to require a major review of policies. Ipswich, however, was the only new town proposal which was immediately affected.

Of course, in 1969 the downward trend in population forecasts could not be seen for what it became in the 'seventies (when the projection for the turn of the century became lower than envisaged by the projections of the 'fifties). The last major report dealing with new towns which was considered by the Labour Government of 1964–1970 still referred to an anticipated population increase of a quarter (from 54 million in 1969 to nearly 67 million in 2001). This report—the final report of officials on the long term distribution of

---

* The ministry spent over £1·1m on eight new and expanded town studies, all of which were commissioned on the basis of a negotiated fee. Competitive tenders were thought to be unsuitable since 'the ministry judged that only five firms of consultants were capable of carrying out such large and complex studies'. The PAC considered this to be unsatisfactory and also criticised the ministry for paying out 'large sums for the time of professional men without knowing how long they actually work on the projects and whether the charge for overheads is reasonable'. (Fifth Report from the Committee of Public Accounts, Session 1966–67.)

† *Llantrisant—Prospects for Urban Growth*, HMSO, 1969.

population—did, however, mark the end of an era. No further new towns were approved by the Labour Government or, indeed – with one exception* (up to the time of writing) – any subsequent government. In the period under discussion the revised population projections were of less importance than other factors. These were spelled out in the report from officials, and a quotation from that report forms an appropriate conclusion to this part of the history:†

'Since the war 600,000 people have been accommodated in new towns and town expansions and present plans provide a further one million to be so accommodated by 1981. This will amount to over 20 per cent of the expected increase in national population by that date. Thus most of the population increase—to which must be added those displaced by urban redevelopment and migration from remoter rural areas—will have to be accommodated in and around other urban areas.

Any major planned expansion scheme represents a very considerable use of resources. Decisions on a national strategy for population distribution should ideally be taken against a background of the relative costs and benefits not only of alternative locations but also of developing new large sites as against expanding existing major urban areas. Work on this subject is in its infancy, and because of the complexities progress is bound to be slow. We recommended more work on these fundamental questions which can be pursued in the context of the individual planning studies recommended later.

New town development corporations are financed by capital loans from the exchequer. It is the Government's policy to encourage the highest possible contribution from private enterprise in new towns and, in particular, to raise the proportion of owner occupied houses which should diminish the exchequer contribution. It is likely that the extent of the call on the exchequer will continue to be a relevant factor in future consideration of any additions to the new towns programme.

Over the period to 1981 as a whole, the flow of mobile industry, after taking account of the needs of development and intermediate areas, should be about sufficient to sustain the planned rate of new town development, though there may be problems in the shorter term. There seems little scope at present for major expansion of the programme before 1981. These are, however, complex issues which need to be frequently reviewed. The group's interim report recommended that feasibility studies for major population growth should be undertaken for Humberside, Severnside and Tayside. The Humberside study has suggested that, although there is good physical potential for expansion, it would be preferable to defer a decision on a major expansion on Humberside to the early 1970s. The Severnside and Tayside studies are not yet complete. No new feasibility studies of this kind should be undertaken at this stage; but the issue should be reconsidered when final decisions on Humberside are being taken when the conclusions of the Severnside and Tayside studies will also be available. Some of the presently planned new towns will have major potential for expansion after 1981 and consideration should be given to the exploitation of this potential.

Broad estimates of the amount of mobile industry that might be available

---

* The exception was Stonehouse which was designated in 1973. This was abandoned in 1976 following a reappraisal of the housing needs of Clydeside and the problems of the declining inner urban areas.

† A revised version of the report was published by HMSO in 1971 under the title *Long Term Population Distribution in Great Britain: A Study.*

between 1981 and the end of the century suggest it may be sufficient only to provide employment to support a population of up to 3–4 million in new planned development well away from present urban areas. These estimates assume that the present development area problems are substantially reduced by 1981 and that incentives and controls broadly similar to those now in force for the development areas are used to promote the growth of such planned expansions.

There are yet other possible limitations on planned movement. For example, it is difficult to foresee how willing people might be to move substantial distances to new planned developments when they can find employment and housing near at hand. The implications for the location and planning of new developments of such social considerations should be further investigated.

The pattern of urban living has been changing rapidly as the range of variety of people's economic and social needs have increased and as facilities for movement and communication have developed. This trend towards a looser but more extended urban structure within each individual city region is likely to continue.

It is clear that whatever the scale of new major expansions, most of the land needed to house the extra population and to meet the increasing demand for urban and recreational land will have to be found in and near existing centres. This will constitute a major challenge to planning. But with proper foresight and imagination it should be possible to plan future urban development in the relatively dispersed form of the city region in such a way as to avoid many of the disadvantages hitherto inherent in large conurbations, while retaining the main social and economic benefits of cities.'

PART TWO

CHAPTER VI

Organisational Issues

THE previous chapters of this history have proceeded chrono-
logically, from the inception of the new towns programme to
its position at the end of the 'sixties. Throughout this quarter
of a century, certain issues constantly intruded themselves whether
as a result of changing ministries (or ministers), because of changing
political and economic climates, or simply because the new towns
policy was inherently in conflict with other policies. The new towns
did not fit easily into established systems of control. They involved
huge long term commitments. Major policy decisions needed several
years (typically the lifetime of a government) before they could be
implemented. It is not surprising, therefore, that the new towns were
continually under review.

Some reflections on this are attempted at the end of this history.
In the present chapter a number of strands are brought together.
How was the new towns programme administered and subjected to
ministerial, Treasury and Cabinet control? What administrative
systems and procedures were tried out—or abandoned before they
could be tried out?

As with the earlier chronological account, the focus is on the
debates which actually took place at ministerial and departmental
level. Some of the issues might appear trivial (such as whether
members of development corporations should be paid for their very
part-time services). Others are of obviously great importance (such
as whether new towns were the best means of accommodating major
geographical shifts—or national growth—of population). But what
characterises the issues which come before ministers is not the
intrinsic importance of the questions but the political difficulty of
answering them. The history of the new towns is replete with such
issues.

Appointment of Corporation Members*

The New Towns Act of 1946 prescribed that each new town
development corporation should consist of a chairman, deputy
chairman, and not more than seven other members, to be appointed
by the minister after consultation with such local authorities as
appeared to him to be concerned with the development of the new

---

* MHLG Files NT 97/2, 91650/26/49 and 91650/260/26/1.

town. In making appointments, he was to have regard to the desirability of securing the services of one or more persons resident in, or having special knowledge of, the locality in which the town was situated.

Twelve new town corporations in England and Wales were formed between the end of 1946 and 1950. The general procedure was that immediately Cabinet approval had been given to the site, and the formal machinery for designation put in hand, a letter was sent to the local authorities informing them that a small informal advisory committee would be required and inviting them to make nominations, some if not all of whom would later be appointed members of the corporation. These letters were sent on a liberal scale to county councils, borough, urban and rural district councils (and in some cases to parish councils) in the neighbourhood of the new town and, in the case of overspill towns, to the exporting local authorities. The result was a medley of a score or more names, generally of members of the majority party on the various councils. In the case of the London towns these tended to be Conservative, while in the provinces they tended to be Labour. The department did the best it could, after such discreet inquiry as was practicable, to select four or five. These generally included one county councillor, one nominee from the exporting authority, and two or more nominees from the district councils. It was considered desirable to have at least one woman, a balance between party allegiances, and if possible nominations from the local authority of people with specialist qualifications which would be useful to the corporation. Meanwhile, the minister had been sounding industrialists, administrators and others to act as chairman and deputy chairman. These consultations took time, and generally the advisory committees when appointed could make little progress before the designation order was made. The members of the advisory committees were then formally appointed as members of the corporation, with the addition either immediately or shortly afterwards of one or two people qualified in such fields as estate management, business or finance if this type of experience was not already represented.

When the names of members of the corporation were announced, there was generally a flood of protests from the local authorities whose nominees had not been selected, and complaint from the local political parties that they were not adequately represented. These protests normally died down until consultation was resumed on re-appointment, but an undercurrent of resentment was liable to remain which tended to show itself in friction between the corporation and the local authorities, and in some jealousy of the councillors who had been selected for the paid appointments on the corporation.

The difficulties in making the initial appointments to the twelve corporations should not be underestimated. They were made in the aftermath of the war when individuals were anxious to re-establish their own lives. The nationalisation measures at the time were involving appointments to national and local boards, and to regional hospital boards and management committees, which sucked away some latent ability. The department had no ready means of judging the qualifications of the nominees of local authorities. It was not easy to find a chairman and deputy chairman willing to take on a part time job, and to lead a diverse team of people with whom they had no previous acquaintance, with the prospect of frustration from local authorities and the central government.

What is surprising in retrospect is the degree of success which each corporation did achieve in the early days, notwithstanding the difficulties and suspicions with which it was regarded not only locally, but nationally. It was the apprehension of 'jobs for the boys' that led to the practice in 1948 of all persons proposed for appointment or re-appointment to the corporations being approved by both the Lord President (Morrison) and the Prime Minister (Attlee). Morrison raised several queries and refused assent to the appointment of the wife of an MP. He also firmly discouraged the appointment of those who had lost their seats in Parliament at the 1950 election. The practice of referring the appointments to the Prime Minister lapsed in 1951 but, by 1960, his concurrence was sought to appointments of chairman and deputy chairman and, in December 1966, it was laid down that the Treasury was to be consulted about a wide range of public appointments, including those of chairman, deputy chairman, and non-local authority and non-specialist members of the development corporations and of the Commission for the New Towns.

The initial appointments were all made for a fixed term of three years. When, during that period, an additional or replacement appointment was made, it was timed to expire at the end of the three years. Thus, during 1950–53 the full membership of each corporation came up for review, and both Dalton and Macmillan made careful examination and dropped a few members including those whose attendance was unsatisfactory. Most members were offered re-appointment, but while neither minister laid down any fixed policy, it was noticeable that the number of local authority members tended to be reduced and increasing numbers of places were taken by local people having no direct party affiliations and suggested by the chairman or others as carrying general respect in the neighbourhood. There also tended to be an infusion of members with a financial or business background who might be in a position to influence the movement of industry into the town.

The appointments and re-appointments during 1950–53 were for a fixed period of two years and came up for review during 1952–55, but on this round relatively few changes were made, and those members who were willing to continue were generally reappointed.

Appointments made for a fixed term meant that, on expiry, new instruments of appointment were needed to keep the corporation in existence, and this involved consultation with the local authorities, although most if not all the members would continue. This formal consultation with the local authorities gave them renewed opportunity to press their own nominees, with consequent annoyance and embarrassment to those who were not selected. More important than what on one occasion was termed 'these tiresome formalities' were the 'timetabling difficulties' which arose. Consultations could not decently start more than three months ahead. Local authorities could take four to eight weeks to reply. Ministers wanted careful and prolonged reviews of membership, and needed time to consider and 'take soundings' on recommendations. The result on at least two occasions was a frantic telephone call from a general manager pointing out that his board would cease to exist in a few days' time and any business they purported to do after this would be invalid.

To avoid these difficulties, the terms of appointment were changed in 1955: all members were appointed for an indefinite period, thus making it possible to 'stagger' appointments. At the same time, the instrument of appointment provided that the minister could terminate an appointment at any time after one year on giving at least one month's notice in writing. Some members felt a good deal of resentment at what they considered to be a lack of security of tenure, and to meet their views a modification was made in 1957 whereby notice of termination would not normally be given for two years after the initial appointment. This meant in practice that the composition of the corporation was reviewed at intervals of two years, and if the minister wished to retain a member he wrote inviting him to continue for a further stated period; or alternatively, thanking him for his services which would now come to an end.

The effect of this arrangement for appointments for an indefinite period was that consultations with local authorities took place only on the appointment of a new member and not, as heretofore, on the composition of the whole corporation. This reduced their opportunity to press their own nominees, and while the point did not pass unnoticed by the authorities, the change was generally accepted.

In addition to revising the terms of appointment in 1955 Sandys enunciated two principles in the selection of members:

'(a) Avoid the appointment and re-appointment of persons actively engaged in politics whether local or national;
(b) Introduce new blood in small doses as the opportunity occurs.'

A few changes were made in accordance with these principles during Sandys' term of office, but a minute of January 1957 recorded that:

> 'Brooke does not wish to have quite such a firm embargo as did his predecessor on persons actively engaged in politics. He has said that although he would certainly not make any appointments to new town corporations solely for party considerations, he would be prepared to consider people of merit who would be likely to make a worthwhile contribution to a new town even if they are at present actively associated in politics of either party.'

It is not known whether Brooke had any particular individuals in mind at this time, but, by the later 1950s and as the second generation of new towns was emerging, the ministry had a clearer conception than ten years previously of the type of experience which a new town required, and of the individuals who might be able to provide it.*

No minister was able, even if he had wished, to make any dramatic change in the membership of the corporations in accordance with some general policy. The membership of each came up for review at regular intervals, but never all at the same time; few members gave any direct cause for complaint or criticism and, as continuity of work was desirable, there was a presumption in favour of re-appointment which was often reinforced by the loyalty of the members to each other; deaths and resignations caused vacancies from time to time which could be filled unobtrusively. When members were dropped, it was simply explained that their term had expired and they had not been re-appointed, although not unnaturally, it might be suggested locally that they had been dismissed. The most publicised case of dismissal was that of Mrs Monica Felton from the chairmanship of Stevenage in 1951 for failure to attend a meeting of the Public Accounts Committee and for unexplained absence from the country.

An analysis made of the composition of the corporations in September 1963 suggested that the principal background of the members was:

Local authority	23
Business and industry	17
Retired civil servants and service officers	9
Surveyors and architects	8
Accountants	6
Housewives	4
Others (doctors, lawyers, clergymen etc)	8
	75

---

* The procedure was changed again by Crossman in December 1965, when appointments were continued for an indefinite period and subject to termination on at least one

Of these, fourteen were women, and sixteen were under the age of fifty.

A memorandum in 1964 discussed, in the light of the department's experience, what an ideal corporation might be. This maintained that though there could be no set pattern, it was helpful to include:

'A surveyor or architect—	with experience in property transactions, valuation and development;
An industrialist, businessman or accountant—	with experience in finance or management;
A county councillor—	aware of the problems and methods of local government;
A social welfare worker or educationalist—	with knowledge of human problems and able to understand people's troubles;
One or two local people—	who carry general respect and know the area and its people intimately;
In the case of an overspill town—	someone who understands the problems of the people moving in.

(At least one should be a woman).'

The memorandum emphasised the importance of the chairman: he should have the ability to weld his team together; he must carry weight with the local authorities and keep on good terms with them; he must be able to negotiate with industrialists and others on important issues; he must have a flair for picking suitable people for key jobs and be willing to delegate to them the day to day work without interference, but at the same time giving guidance when needed and exercising watchful supervision; above all he should be interested in the job and able to give the necessary time to it and not let other commitments crowd it out. The deputy chairman was no less important, as he had to deputise for the chairman and, in the event of the chairman's death or retirement, was likely to take over.

The memorandum continued by discussing the position of the local authority members. The consultation with several local authorities usually resulted in protests that their nominees had not been selected. Yet when they were appointed there was often a conflict of loyalties on matters where the authority and the corporation did not see eye to eye, and there were also suggestions of leakage of information. While there had been 'some very good and competent local authority members', the general tendency had been to avoid district councillors and to secure local representation by some well known, respected and capable local residents. County council members did not present such a problem since they were more removed from the purely local atmosphere and the danger of conflict of interest was correspondingly

month's notice, though members were told that 'it is not expected that the notice of termination would generally be quite so short'; but the previous initial period of two years' security disappeared. A further change was made by Greenwood in November 1966, who decided that the normal term of appointment should in future be for two years for members and three years for the chairman.

more remote. Purely political appointments were rarely made, although the political element could not be avoided completely if local authorities were to be represented. When the political complexion of a council changed, it was left entirely to the member whether he wished to continue with the corporation.

Such was the outline of past practice available to Crossman, the new minister in the Labour Government of October 1964. He was aware of the frictions which had developed with the local authorities, and of their resentment of the New Towns Act 1959, which had put the new towns 'out of their reach'. In consequence and as opportunity offered, he began to reverse previous policy and to increase representation of local authorities—a policy he confirmed in a speech at Redditch on 20 August 1965:

> 'a new town will not develop healthily either if the members of the corporation are standoffish and secretive about their policies or if the local authorities get a chip on their shoulders and go on the defensive. Here a special responsibility rests on members of the local authority selected to serve on the corporation. I want to increase this number'.

Early in 1967, Mellish, the parliamentary secretary, conducted a full investigation into the membership of the corporations and of the Commission for the New Towns. Of the 100 members then in post, he found that 45 were also members of local authorities—a proportion which he regarded as satisfactory (compared with 23 out of 75 in September 1963). He also found that of the 100, 45 were aged over sixty, and of these 25 were aged over sixty-five. Of the thirteen chairmen and twelve deputy chairmen, those over sixty numbered eight and eleven respectively. Mellish recommended to the minister (Greenwood) that as the members came under review, younger persons should be appointed—and the point 'was borne in mind'.

The Standing Ministerial Conference*

Though Silkin had rejected the Reith Committee's proposal for a central advisory commission,† some machinery for co-ordination and exchange of ideas between the different corporations and between them and the ministry was required. This initially (at the end of 1946) took the form of a standing ministerial conference, attended by the chairmen and deputy chairmen, with Silkin in the chair. The chairmen had originally proposed that they should meet alone, but Silkin explained that he was not anxious for any formal consultation which would make the corporations 'too remote from the ministry',

---

* MHLG Files 91650/50/5, 91650/19/8 and NT 140/1–10.
† See chapter I, p. 25. (Reith continued to press for a central advisory commission after his appointment as chairman of Stevenage Development Corporation but he was 'rebuffed by the minister'. It is recorded that the ministry considered the proposal a 'muddled' one which 'would have trenched deeply into the functions of the ministry itself'. (Lord President's File 1352/4.)

that he wished to keep in close touch with them, that the relationship should be settled gradually as work progressed, and that in the meantime it was undesirable to establish too many or too formal procedures. Originally, the meetings were held at monthly intervals and tended to be concerned with questions of recruitment of staff, and the nature of the financial control to be exercised by the ministry and the Treasury, but the particular problems of individual corporations loomed large. Certain of the chairmen (particularly Reith, Mrs Felton and Beveridge) were liable to dominate the discussion and there was frequently difficulty in agreeing the minutes of the conclusions that had been reached. At the meeting in September 1948, Silkin said that with new designations the size of the meeting was growing, many of the topics were of interest to one corporation only, and generally the conference was not operating as he had originally hoped. It was therefore agreed that in future meetings should be at two monthly intervals, although Silkin offered to see the chairmen separately as often as they wished.

Regular formal meetings between the minister and the chairmen ceased when Dalton succeeded Silkin in February 1950. Meanwhile the chairmen had begun to meet privately among themselves and a loose form of chairmen's conference emerged which over the period became well-established, with the chairmanship rotating among the corporations and with formal minutes of the proceedings. In parallel, meetings were held by the general managers and by various of the professional officers. The meetings provided a useful forum for an exchange of views and experience but, as those present were from towns in different stages of development and the day to day problems with which they were faced were rarely the same, they were not anxious to see the establishment of any formal piece of machinery between them and the ministry which would deprive them of the opportunity of pressing their own case.*

The day to day contacts between the corporations and the ministry were normally conducted by correspondence or by meetings between officials. Matters of more general import were the subject of circulars of virtual instruction from the ministry, and the more important of these had generally been discussed in advance with the general managers' conference whose members would as necessary have consulted their chairmen.

While Dalton and his ministerial successors were always willing to see a chairman on a matter affecting his own town, meetings between the minister and the chairmen collectively were held erratically at intervals of one or more years. With changes of ministers and changes in the chairmen there was little continuity in the meet-

---

* This attitude extended to arrangements for research: see below p. 348 *et seq.*

ings over the period. Discussion of individual cases was avoided, but the following are some of the more significant matters on which discussion arose.

1952   Building costs and 'people's houses'
        Disposal of land to government departments and local authorities
        Rents
        Relationship of the corporations with the ministry
        Diversification of tenants
        Lack of industry
1955   Future of new towns when building complete
        Rents
        Industrial selection scheme
1956   Increase in interest rates
        Owner occupation
        Pooling of rents
1957   Private enterprise housing
        Amenities
        Rents and need for economy
1958   Proposals for a New Town Commission
1962   Rents
        Owner occupation
        New building techniques
1964   Rents and housing subsidies
1965   Rents and housing subsidies
1967   Owner occupation
1968   Private enterprise housing
        Housing cost yardsticks
        Housing revenue account and general development expenditure
        Standing machinery for consultation

So far as there was any pattern to these meetings, it would seem that the minister took the opportunity to press the need for economy, or for raising rents, or for getting more owner occupation, or for speed of building, or for increasing the intake of Londoners, or for action on some other apparently intractable problem. For their part, the chairmen outlined their difficulties arising from shortage of finance, from increasing interest rates and building costs, from reluctance or inability to raise rents, from shortage of industry, or from some other equally intractable problem. Firm decisions were rarely taken, and in 1966 it was being suggested within the ministry that the meetings might be more useful if they were held informally after a dinner.

At various times there had been proposals for some more formal machinery, but in the absence of any pressure from the chairmen,

the ministry took no action until 1968 when it was complained
that:

> 'there is no continuing machinery for collective consultation: there are the
> chairmen's conference, the general managers' conference and meetings of
> professional officers, none of which do we attend as a matter of right. In
> present circumstances this no longer seems to be satisfactory. We now have
> new issues of policy which require to be discussed. We have a new crop of
> chairmen, many of whom are likely to have pronounced opinions'.

At the minister's meeting with the chairmen in October 1968 there
was an inconclusive discussion about the establishment of some
standing machinery for consultation, but the matter was overtaken
by the report of the working party on new towns structure (which is
discussed later in this chapter).*

Ministerial Doubts on Machinery, 1948†

The salaries of the chairmen and deputy chairmen were fixed, at
an early stage, at £1,500 and £1,000 respectively. Other members
were paid £400. It was contemplated that none of the appointments
(originally made for three years) would be full time, although it
was expected that the chairman and deputy chairman would devote
more attention to corporation affairs than the other members.
Execution of policy agreed by the corporation would be in the
hands of the general manager and the principal officers.

While there was relatively little difficulty in finding the part time
members, many of whom had generally been recommended by the
local authorities in the neighbourhood and of which they were
members, it proved more difficult to find suitable persons to take the
posts of chairman and deputy chairman, for which high professional
or administrative qualities were sought. There was also difficulty in
recruiting the general managers and senior staff. At the beginning
of 1948, when new town problems reverted to the Lord President's
Committee, Morrison, whose view was that the policy of depriving
local authorities of their trading services might be going too far, was
considering the possibility that some of the larger local authorities
with their experienced members and staff, should play an active
part.

At the LP Committee in April 1948, (when approval was given to
Basildon and to a new town in Scotland, and reference made to the
possibility of new towns at Mobberley and in south Wales), most
attention was directed to the suggestion by Morrison that the
larger local authorities (such as the London County Council and

---

* See p. 372 *et seq* below.
† LP(48)6th Meeting, 23 April 1948, LP(48)7th Meeting, 30 April 1948, LP(48)82,
LP(48)86, LP(48)17th Meeting, 26 November 1948; and Lord President's Files 1352/4
and 37/03.

Manchester) should be encouraged to carry out housing developments on new town lines. Several ministers supported the suggestion, but Silkin argued that the position had been thrashed out when the New Towns Act was being drafted, and had been rejected. Local authorities were not really anxious to provide new towns of the character proposed in the Act, and their natural inclination was to develop estates close to their own areas which might eventually be incorporated in these areas. It would be difficult to justify the financing of a new town by the exchequer if control was to be entirely in the hands of the local authority. After lengthy discussion it was agreed that Silkin and the Minister of Health (Bevan) should 'explore the extent to which use could be made of the organisation of the larger and more progressive local authorities in the housing work of some of the new town corporations'.

It seems that this exploration was side-tracked by private conversations which took place during the summer of 1948 between Morrison and Silkin, at which a proposal was canvassed that, instead of local authority participation, there might be a national corporation which would have responsibility for all new towns. Silkin appears to have felt that, with the development corporations already existing and those likely to be established, it was wasteful to have them all performing the same function in different parts of the country. There were somewhat strained relations with some of the chairmen already appointed, and there was difficulty in finding chairmen for the corporations shortly to be established. A national corporation on the lines of the nationalised industries, working through regional offices, might overcome some of the difficulties, and Silkin was believed to feel that one of the existing chairmen would be a suitable chairman of the national corporation. Morrison appears to have considered favourably the introduction of the necessary legislation, but officials in the Lord President's office and in the ministry urged strongly against it on the grounds that there was not a sufficient case for upsetting the present corporations. It would be criticised as centralised bureaucratic administration, and the ultimate transfer of a new town to a local authority would be more difficult from a national corporation than from a local corporation.*

In parallel with these private conversations between Morrison and Silkin on a national corporation, Morrison became aware of the

---

* An official minute to Morrison noted that Silkin 'approaches the subject of a national corporation primarily from the point of view that he is finding it increasingly difficult to keep personal track of the activities of the various corporations. He has always wished to know in great detail what is happening in each new town, and he has not been content with the channels of information open to him through his officials and the chairmen of the corporations. The position has been accentuated by somewhat strained relations between the minister and one or two of the chairmen. Some doubt is felt whether the minister is not wishing to keep too close an eye on what the corporations do.'

view of some of the chairmen that it was unfortunate that the part-timers had ever been paid. Some of these 'were not sufficiently interested in economical administration'. Moreover, while a member of a local authority paid rates on his own property and was liable to be thrown out at the next election if he had been too extravagant, these checks did not apply to a minister's nominee. The chairmen were also troubled that they and their deputy chairmen could be outvoted, a result which was appropriate in an elected body, but of doubtful propriety on a board appointed by the minister. The chairmen had some mild hope that the part time members might be regarded as advisory only.

These various issues were discussed by the LP Committee in November 1948. Both Silkin and Woodburn (Secretary of State for Scotland) circulated papers in advance. Silkin said that he had considered whether he should propose amending legislation to alter the organisation radically and substitute either one centralised corporation or fewer corporations, each looking after two or three or more towns. He had concluded that there would be great difficulties in the way of a centralised corporation. He was clear that on every ground there had to be, for each new town, some committee on the spot to represent local interests and to give decisions on matters of local or day to day importance. A body that was merely advisory would not meet the case. To superimpose on these local bodies a central corporation would mean adding an additional filter through which matters would have to go before a decision was reached. In so far as some central authority was needed for co-ordination of questions of general policy common to all corporations, that must, Silkin suggested, be the minister, who in any event had to come in on such matters because he provided all the money and was answerable to Parliament. Over and above these arguments, there was the point that to justify such a major change in organisation within such a short time would necessitate demonstrating that the existing organisation had been proved to be radically wrong. He could not pretend that the present machine was perfect. It had not been easy, for example, to find people with the best qualifications and experience to serve on the corporations and this task was becoming harder as the number of corporations increased. But there was no sufficient case on which legislation making a root and branch change could be based.

The other possibility (*viz* one corporation looking after several towns) had the double disadvantage that it would still be necessary to have some local body for each town and that one would not have secured a single central corporation.

The alternative course was to make improvements within the existing framework and without amending legislation. In the first place, whilst he could hardly reduce the remuneration of existing members until the term of their appointment expired, he would consider before the end of 1949 whether new or renewed appointments (other than of chairmen or deputy chairmen) could be made at a lower figure. Secondly, he thought that it might be practicable to reduce the actual memberships of corporations to a maximum of six or seven members including the chairman and deputy chairman. Thirdly—though here he was more doubtful—it might be possible to arrange for the same chairman and deputy chairman to look after two corporations in close proximity, and to some limited extent this might also be practicable for those ordinary members who were not appointed as primarily local representatives. But those who gave more time than was required for one corporation would naturally expect additional remuneration.

Silkin also referred to the possibility mentioned at a previous meeting of entrusting in certain instances the development of new towns to some of the larger local authorities. This proposal, which would also need amending legislation, was one which he had examined very carefully at the time of the introduction of the New Towns Bill and rejected. Upon reconsideration, he still felt that the arguments against this proposal were overwhelming. New towns were wholly financed by the exchequer and were normally developed in rural or semi-rural areas at a distance of anything up to twenty miles or more from the large town. The county council of the area would strongly resist development by the county borough council of a virtual colony in the county. Where a larger local authority had an interest in the new town it was never the only one with the interest. Moreover, it was socially and politically undesirable that one local authority should be the sole or predominant landowner in the area of another local authority.

He added that the only local authority which had seriously suggested that it should develop a new town was Manchester and then only in connection with the proposed site at Mobberley. But as this site adjoined the existing city boundary he felt sure that to a large extent they were influenced by the possibilities of a boundary extension.

He was, however, considering whether it would not be possible in some cases to carry out the expansion of an existing town which virtually amounted to the development of a new town through the local authority of the area. The point here was that there was a local authority *in situ* which in some cases might be capable of undertaking the job, though generally administrative and financial assistance would be needed.

In conclusion, Silkin expressed the hope that his colleagues would agree that it was neither desirable nor practicable at the present time to take any formal steps to reduce the payment made to members of new towns corporations.

Woodburn's paper pointed out that, to date, only two new town development corporations had been appointed in Scotland, and in each case the chairman had agreed to serve without remuneration. The circumstances were, however, exceptional, and he thought that, generally, it would be difficult in other circumstances to get the right people to serve as chairmen and deputy chairmen if the appointments were unpaid. The salaries currently payable for these appointments seemed to him to be no more than adequate for the work involved. On the other hand, he thought that there was a case for reducing the salaries payable to other members of the corporations from £400 to, say, £200 or £250 a year, though not for reducing the number of development corporation members since they had to represent a very wide range of interests. In particular, it was necessary to give reasonable representation to the local authorities concerned to secure their co-operation in the development of the new towns and in the utilisation of their technical staff and resources. If the number of members were reduced below nine it would be difficult to make the corporations fully representative.

He agreed with Silkin that it would not be practicable to make one central corporation responsible for the development of all new towns, but it might be possible to arrange for a single corporation to look after, say, two small towns if they were both in the area of one local authority: sufficient powers were available under the New Towns Act to enable this to be done. He also agreed that the responsibility for the development of new towns could not be placed on the local authorities. In Scotland, the special problem of providing accommodation for substantial numbers of immigrant miners required to develop the expanding coalfields was national rather than local in character and, because of their heavy commitments to provide housing for their own people, the local authorities could not deal with this wider problem from their own resources. In addition they would be involved in 'irreconcilable loyalties between the claims of the new town and their own needs for priority'.

Woodburn thought that it was most important that, in all cases, the local authorities (who would be securing the benefits of additional rateable value arising from the development of the new towns) should be pressed to accept responsibility for the provision of rate-borne basic services, such as roads, water and drainage. At East Kilbride and Glenrothes, the development corporations had succeeded in persuading the local authorities to assume this responsibility although, of course, it would be necessary for the development corporations to give the authorities some financial assistance.

At the LP Committee it was agreed that there was a strong case against the idea of having a central corporation for new towns. Some local organisation was essential, and a central body would tend to become a bottleneck between the local bodies and the responsible department. But there was strong local feeling, particularly in Durham, about the payment of salaries to ordinary members of new town corporations in respect of work which was no more onerous than membership of one of the larger local authorities. The same difficulty would occur in Glamorgan and elsewhere, when further corporations were established.

The LP Committee then discussed whether a reduction of payments to ordinary members should be by the fixing of a smaller salary, as proposed by the responsible ministers, or by payments on a fee basis, or by treating members on the same basis as members of local authorities (ie refunding expenses). It was suggested that payments on a fee basis might lead to fears that unnecessary meetings of a corporation and of its committees were being held, and to even more damaging comparisons with the conditions of service on local authorities. Several ministers felt that the right course was to equate the conditions for ordinary members with those of services on a local authority. Attention was, however, drawn to the presence of 'specialised members' of new town corporations who might expect more generous treatment. The suggestion was also made that deputy chairmen should receive £500 a year instead of £1,000.

There was agreement that, where it could conveniently be arranged, a chairman or deputy chairman of a corporation might be asked to serve in a similar capacity on another corporation, but a general reduction in size was undesirable. Silkin said that, while he was prepared to envisage a reduction in the size of corporations to six or seven members (including the chairman and deputy chairman), the size depended on the conception of the functions of the corporation. If it were desired to bring in persons of wide experience in particular fields, such as estate management, it might be necessary in some cases to have a corporation of nine members.

Morrison said that he hoped that the question of employing some of the larger local authorities with their experienced members and staff on the development of new towns would not be overlooked. He thought that in such a case the local authority might reasonably be asked to bear a part of the cost.

Whiteley (chief whip) drew attention to the organisation which county councils were developing in connection with their duties under the Town and Country Planning Act. He suggested that in some cases it might be possible to have no more than a manager in a new town, who would take his instructions from the county authorities.

Silkin was not in principle opposed to a large local authority, such as a county council, undertaking responsibility for the development of a new town within its boundaries, or to special arrangements by which a county borough developed an adjacent area, but he thought that this would involve serious difficulties. The development of a new town of 60,000 inhabitants in a period of ten to fifteen years was an immense undertaking which raised major problems and involved a mass of detailed work. Existing local authority officers could not take this work in their stride, and some form of high level local organisation was required to deal with major problems as they arose.

Attention was drawn to the danger that a county council responsible for a new town might feel obliged to meet the housing needs of its own population before it provided houses in a new town intended to meet the needs of a large urban area outside its boundaries. There was also the difficulty that county councils were not always experienced in the problems of urban development and that, in England and Wales, they were not at present housing authorities. Legislation would be required to enable local authorities to develop new towns.

The discussion was inconclusive and it was decided to convene a working party of officials to take further the matter of payment of members of the corporations. That there was considerable feeling on the issue is illustrated by a note from the Prime Minister to Morrison in which he said that 'I fear that we are paying a good many people for doing practically nothing'.

The Working Party on Payment of Members*

The working part of officials reported in March 1949 setting out the arguments for and against the payment of members. In favour of the voluntary principle (which was taken to mean no remuneration but with compensation for expenses and loss of remunerative time comparable to that received by members of local authorities) the arguments were, first, that it would be 'in accordance with the long and honourable tradition of voluntary public service in this country', and it was important to maintain this principle as far as possible. Secondly, the new town corporations were more closely analogous to the local authorities than to any other public bodies, and thirdly, there had been criticism of the apparent anomaly whereby members of local authorities who did their local authority work without pay received salaries as members of a development corporation for what was supposed to be comparable work.

On the other hand, it had been argued that in modern conditions fewer people than formerly could be expected to undertake public service without payment. It was easier to get people to serve volun-

---

* LP(49)30, LP(49)32, LP(49)9th Meeting, 5 April 1949, and CM(49)34th Conclusions, 12 May 1949.

tarily on local than on national bodies, but even the local authorities were said to be experiencing increasing difficulty in finding suitable people. Moreover, the comparison between the development corporations and local authorities was superficial, and there was a closer analogy to the boards which had been set up to administer the socialised industries. There were three specific points here. First, local authorities were elective, their members chose to offer themselves for election, and they enjoyed the prestige and the authority of democratically elected representatives of their own communities. There was no true comparison between them and bodies nominated by ministers.

Secondly, while some of the work of development corporations and local authorities was similar (for instance, in relation to housing, water, sewage disposal), much of it was more closely analogous to that of a major commercial undertaking. They had the task of creating 'a highly diversified economic organism'. Thirdly, though it was true that there were notable exceptions in local government, the amount of work and the burden of responsibility of the ordinary member of a development corporation were greater than those of the majority of local councillors. In the nature of things, a development corporation could not afford to carry a proportion of 'passengers' such as might be carried by local authorities without undue harm to the public interest. The evidence received by the working party showed that the average amount of time devoted to their duties by corporation members was from one to two days a week, and there was comparatively little variation from one member to another. This was in contrast with the position on most local authorities, where their information was that the majority of councillors gave up considerably less time and there was a big difference between chairmen of committees and other leaders and the back benchers.

There were two additional points. The Act itself and both government and opposition spokesmen in the debates on the New Towns Bill envisaged payment. All the chairmen would be opposed to a change, and it would be difficult to avoid the impression that it was a reflection upon the adequacy of the existing members. Finally, it had been suggested that payment induced a greater sense of responsibility and conscientiousness in discharging the corporation's work, and tended to strengthen the sense of being the minister's instrument responsible for funds wholly derived from the exchequer.

The working party were of the opinion that there was not a complete or exact analogy with either local authorities or boards of socialised industries. It did not seem to them to be particularly profitable to argue which was the more analogous. The important question was the effect on the efficiency of the corporations if a change of policy were made.

It was 'difficult to be sure about this'. The working party had been told that some useful members of the corporations would have had to decline appointment if there had been no payment. On the other hand, it seemed likely that many of the existing members would have been prepared to serve in any event, either because they were persons of substantial means or because, as their records showed, they were accustomed to giving unpaid public service on local authorities or otherwise. The two Scottish chairmen and some members served without payment, though it was understood that in the case of the chairmen the reason was that they already received substantial income from public funds. Nevertheless, there was no doubt that payment had turned the scale in some cases, and it had been suggested that even with a business man to whom the amount of the payment was not of special account, it was of assistance to him in persuading his partners that he was not lavishing their time as well as his own upon public service which left his firm out of pocket.

They concluded that, if ministers did decide to change to a voluntary system, it would be even more difficult than it already was to find suitable people to serve on the corporations. There would also be a risk that the efficiency of the corporations would suffer because of the resentment which would be caused among the chairmen and existing members: 'this would not contribute to the best relations between the government and the corporations.'

The working party examined and rejected payment on a fee basis for attendance since they thought that it might lead members of the public to think that meetings of corporations tended to be multiplied with a view to inflating members' remuneration. This in turn might act as an unjustifiable deterrent leading some corporations at any rate to hold fewer meetings than their business really demanded. In any case it was doubtful whether if this basis were adopted it would lead (on current practice) to any substantial saving in the total cost of remuneration.

The working party also considered whether there was any ground for differentiation in payment, for example, by distinguishing between those members who had professional qualifications and those whose main qualification was their connection with a local authority. They found it impossible to draw such a dividing line. Ministers had consistently emphasised that when they had selected as members people who were already members of a local authority they were in no sense selected as representatives of that authority, and that those with professional qualifications—such as architects, surveyors, accountants and engineers—were not selected to fill a narrow functional role as specialists. In all cases they were chosen because their experience and background fitted them for a large scale enterprise of this sort. Members of a corporation thus did not in fact fall into two distinct, mutually exclusive groups, and it was not desirable that they should.

Finally, they considered the position of deputy chairmen. Experience suggested that a deputy chairman was really needed only as such when the chairman was absent. At other times, his work was more in line with that of ordinary members than with that of a chairman. While, therefore, he should be paid more than the members in recognition of his position and his contingent liability to act as chairman, the difference need only be relatively small. It was difficult to suggest what the figure should be but they felt that a payment of 50 per cent in excess of that paid to ordinary members would constitute an appropriate recognition of the extra responsibility resting on him. Such a reduction from the existing £1,000 should, in their view, take effect only on new appointments and reappointments. Thus the only specific change proposed was a reduction from £1,000 to £600 per annum of the remuneration paid to deputy chairmen.

In commending the report to the Lord President's Committee, Silkin expressed his support for the view that no change should be made in the terms of service of existing members during the currency of the existing appointments and that the pay of deputy chairmen should (at the appropriate time) be reduced from £1,000 to £600.

On the central issue of whether members should be paid at all, Silkin was of the definite opinion that, despite the comment that might be expected from such areas as Durham and south Wales, payment should continue to be made:

> 'The creation of a new town is a vast and complicated task, novel in many of the problems it presents, and urgent. It is also a considerable economic undertaking. I am not satisfied with the quality of the existing membership of corporations and I am convinced, like their chairmen, whom I consulted confidentially, that if payment ceased, a situation already not entirely satisfactory would materially deteriorate. I am satisfied that the fact of payment does turn the scale with just that group of men from the professional and business world whose disappearance would, more than any other single factor, vitally impair the efficiency of the corporations.'

At the LP Committee the various arguments were repeated and it proved impossible to reach agreement. The matter was, therefore, referred to the Cabinet who decided that the remuneration of the deputy chairman should be £750, but that no other change should be made.

Public Statements by Development Corporations*

A serious difficulty arose at the end of 1948 on the propriety of development corporations expressing public disagreement with

---

* GOC(49)5, GOC(49)1st Meeting, 2 February 1949 and MHLG File 91650/50/5.

government policy which they were required to implement. The issue related to the control of public houses in the new towns. The chairmen had previously been consulted on this and had expressed little enthusiasm for the Government's proposals for state management, but the Licensing Bill published in November 1948 provided for state management on the lines of the Carlisle scheme.* The chairmen proposed that they should make a public protest on the ground that silence on their part could lead to local misunderstanding and difficulty. They considered that, in the interests of establishing and maintaining good relations with the local inhabitants they should let it be known that they did not like some of the policy decisions of the Government which they were nevertheless required to carry out.

This raised a major issue of principle and the matter was referred to the Government Organisation Committee—a body of permanent secretaries of which Sir Edward Bridges (permanent secretary of the Treasury) was the chairman. In a paper to this committee, Bridges drew a distinction between the position of the corporations acting as such and the position of individual members. On the first, he suggested that it seemed clear that the corporations should not engage in politics, that is they should not take public part in any current political controversy concerning their functions. On the other hand, it seemed equally clear that they could not be prohibited entirely from making public statements of any kind about their duties. Indeed, they were required to make an annual report to the minister who had to lay it before Parliament. In these reports they would no doubt wish to give an account of their stewardship, and it would be difficult to deny them the right to refer to any events in the year under review which they honestly believed had affected, favourably or unfavourably, their capacity to carry out their task. Such events would include the actions of the government, and provided these were referred to objectively and without controversial comment, Bridges did not think that such references could be regarded as objectionable. The difficulty, however, lay in the application of these general ideas to particular cases, when the manner and timing of a statement might be more important than its actual substance. Bridges commented that his instinct was to avoid trying to formulate hard and fast rules, partly because it would never be possible to cover all possible circumstances and partly because such a legislative approach would be in danger of missing the main point—that, by and large, the corporations and the government must maintain a harmonious working relationship. It was the need

---

* The Bill was enacted as the Licensing Act 1949. It was repealed by the Licensed Premises in New Towns Act 1952. (See LP(48)26, LP(48)6th Meeting, 23 April 1948, C(51)33 and CC(51)14th Conclusions, 4 December 1951.)

for this, rather than any set of formal rules, which ought to be the guiding consideration.

So far as the position of individual members of the corporations was concerned, this was linked with the wider problem of the political activities of members of public boards.* The Cabinet had decided, in February 1948,† on certain rules, of which those relevant to new town corporations (whose members were part time) had been communicated to the chairmen. These were that they should not serve as officers carrying out executive duties in any political party; and that they should remain conscious of their general public responsibility and exercise a proper discretion particularly in regard to the work of the board of which they were members. On matters affecting that work they should not normally make political speeches. Subsequently, objections were raised to the application of these rules to members of new town development corporations, and ministers had decided to re-examine the matter—though not until a decision had been reached on the related question of whether appointments to these bodies should continue to be on a salaried basis.

The general issue had thus been reserved by ministers for further consideration, but Bridges thought that it would nevertheless be appropriate and useful for the Government Organisation Committee to consider the narrower question about matters falling within the sphere of activity of the body on which they served. The most important point was the relation of individual members to their colleagues on the corporations. A public statement by a member on a matter connected with the functions of the body was always liable to raise the question whether or not the body agreed with him. It might, in many cases, be embarrassing for both sides, if the corporation had to make up their mind on whether or not they agreed with a public statement by one of their members. The members should be regarded as having a collective responsibility for their duties, 'not unlike that of ministers'. Normally therefore they ought to consult their colleagues before making any public statements on matters with which they were officially concerned, unless, of course, they were contemplating resignation.

The matter was exhaustively considered in February 1949 and, in the upshot, a letter was sent to Reith (as chairman of the chairmen's conference) on 4 April 1949 as follows:

'This matter has been examined in the light of a good deal of experience of relations between the government and public bodies of different kinds. It has not, however, been found possible to arrive at any more precise formulation of the principles which should govern the public utterances of corpora-

---

* See D. N. Chester, *The Nationalisation of British Industry 1945–51*, HMSO, 1975, p. 931 *et seq*.
† CM(48)17th Conclusions, 26 February 1948.

tions than that primarily the matter is one for a corporation's sense of what is proper, having regard to the relations which should subsist between them and the minister.

On this basis there seems in general to be no reason why a corporation, in giving an account of its stewardship in its annual report, should not, if circumstances warrant such a course, include an objective and impartial statement of the effect on its activities, whether favourable or unfavourable, of some government policy or decision. There would, on the other hand, be obvious objections if a corporation were to align itself in some political controversy with the views of one or other of the political parties.

When, however, it comes in practice to deciding whether a particular statement on a particular occasion would contravene the principles suggested above, the question cannot be settled in general terms but depends entirely on the facts of the particular case. If therefore a corporation should wish in future to publish a statement referring to a government decision or proposal (other than a reference in their annual report of the kind referred to above) it is felt it would be only reasonable for them to consult the minister beforehand.'

This letter was accepted by the new towns chairmen, and the opportunity was taken in the annual reports to comment critically on ministerial policies.

The Treasury Report on Development Corporations*

The various issues discussed above illustrated the general unease about the character and role of new town development corporations in the late 'forties. This culminated, in November 1948, in a proposal from Morrison (Lord President) to Silkin that there might be an investigation by officials:

'It is always difficult to work out the relationship at the official level between outside bodies, such as the new towns development corporations, and the responsible department. So far as I have heard, there is no serious difficulty between your ministry and the new town corporations, but it is a tricky business and I should have thought that it would do no harm to ask the O and M Division of the Treasury, who I think act for you in these matters, to make an examination of the relations between the corporations and the ministry. They might pick up one or two points which would not occur to your staffs or to the staffs of the corporations, and which would contribute to the smooth working of the machine. One way of handling the matter would be to have a small committee, with members drawn from your department, O and M Division and the staffs of the new towns. As you know, I am chairman of the Machinery of Government Committee, and from what I have seen in other departments, an informal investigation of this kind often yields excellent results.'

Silkin agreed, and the proposal was put to the Government Organisation Committee. In a note by the permanent secretary of the Ministry of Town and Country Planning, it was pointed out that

---

* GOC(49)5, GOC(49) 1st Meeting, 2 February 1949, MHLG File 91650/26/31/1 and Treasury File SS 385/54/01.

though it was envisaged that corporations should have as much independence as possible and should be 'bodies of real standing and responsibility' there were some inevitable restrictions on their freedom of action. In the first place, the minister was empowered to give them directions—both general and particular. Secondly, their capital requirements (which might amount to £38m for a new town of 60,000 people) were advanced wholly from the consolidated fund and had to be repaid over such periods and on such terms as were approved by the Treasury. The ministry could make grants to them from their vote of such amount as was approved by the Treasury towards expenditure on revenue account. Thirdly, the Act required them to submit their development proposals from time to time to the minister and, before making capital advances for these, the minister and the Treasury had to be satisfied that each proposal was likely to yield a return which, in all the circumstances, was reasonable.

The minister 'had made every effort to secure smooth working arrangements'. He himself had regular conferences with the chairmen and deputy chairmen to discuss problems of common interest, and there was almost daily contact between officials of the ministry and of the corporations. Nevertheless:

'It has been inevitable that, with a new piece of machinery for which there is no exact counterpart, there should be difficulties in the initial stages. A good many of them have been overcome and on the whole the relations between the corporations and the ministry have been got on to a good footing. It is, however, probably true to say that on the part of some corporations at any rate there is still some sense of frustration and unease, because they have not got as wide liberty of action as they expected or as is possible under the Act. This has been aggravated by the slow, piecemeal progress which financial and economic restrictions have made necessary.

Procedure has been worked out in consultation with the corporations, but the root facts remain that the corporations are wholly financed by the exchequer, that they cannot in the nature of things be regarded as trading bodies which may be expected to pay their way in the commercial sense, and that in the first place the accounting officer of the ministry is answerable to the PAC for the money they spend. In the circumstances it seems impracticable to give them as free a hand as some of them desire. It may, however, be worth while to consider whether the time has come for an examination of the question whether the structure of financial control provided by the Act is sound and reasonable or whether some modification is called for.'

This was agreed by the GOC Committee and, after some delay owing to pressure of other work, the inquiry was started by the O and M division of the Treasury. The inquiry was subject to delay occasioned by the death of the Treasury official who carried out most of the preliminary work but, in April 1950 a first draft of a report was sent to the ministry. In a covering letter, it was explained that it had been found impossible to restrict the inquiry to the 'narrow field' of the relationships between the ministry and the corporations. Indeed, the conclusion was that the problems stemmed from 'weaknesses of policy rather than of organisation'.

The report listed a number of policy issues which were 'still in doubt'. First, the precise duties of the development corporations had never been defined: no attempt had yet been made 'to draw up anything in the nature of a guide to the phasing, finance and construction of a new town in sufficient detail to ensure that each corporation sets about its task with the same objectives and standards in mind'. Secondly, it was not clear whether corporations were to base their planning on the fundamental assumption that they must ultimately pay their way, including the repayment of their capital borrowing with interest. Thirdly, the financial relationships between the corporations and the local authorities were still far from clear. This issue was under discussion by a working party set up by the ministry, but no definite conclusions had yet emerged. Fourthly, no decision had yet been taken on the question of whether corporations should acquire all the land within their designated area. In the main, the corporations wished to do this, but the Treasury had taken the line that land should be acquired only as and when it was needed for development.

There were several major conclusions of the inquiry. As already indicated, the most important was that 'one of the major causes which to some extent pervades the new town corporations is the absence of any clearly defined policy on a number of major issues: indeed, until definitive rulings have been given on these issues, little or nothing can be done to improve matters by changes in organisation'. In particular, the corporations needed a clear memorandum of guidance on such matters as the performance of their task, laying down the limitations within which they must work, their relations with government departments and local authorities, and the standards to which they must conform.

It was thought that two assumptions should be made as a basis for the exercise of controls. First, the corporations were not to be regarded as specially privileged bodies (except in that they enjoyed special facilities for borrowing, and grants towards revenue deficits). It followed from this that corporations had to be subject to the same controls as any other undertakings concerned with development. There was no doubt that some of the current feeling of frustration derived from the existence of controls over development plans, investment programmes, the use of labour and scarce materials, and so forth. But the corporations were in no way peculiar in this respect. Secondly, it was assumed that the corporations must eventually pay their way: this 'must surely be made if there is to be any real hope of achieving the avowed objective of giving the corporations as free a hand as possible'. (A corporation which was to be subsidised indefinitely would have to remain subject to close government control, 'and would in effect become little more than a branch of the responsible government department'.) On this assumption the aim should be to base departmental and Treasury control on the scrutiny of programmes and the approval of standards, thus avoiding the meticulous examination of detailed projects. The main issue here was the current necessity for the *ad hoc* submission of development proposals: 'this is scarcely consistent with the idea of the maximum of autonomy for the corporations'. The report continued:

'The obligation on the ministry and the Treasury to judge whether the return on a development project is "reasonable in the circumstances" makes nonsense in relation to one small item in a major plan; for example, how can one judge the reasonableness of the return on a sewage scheme *per se*, without some knowledge of the other development proposals (housing etc) for the area which it is designed to serve?'

The 'ideal instrument for control' would be a costed master plan, but there were serious difficulties in elaborating this accurately. Moreover, development would have to continue while such a plan was being prepared. Nevertheless, it was recommended that costed master plans should be prepared as soon as possible and, in the meantime, control should rest on annual programmes, budgets and accounts, supplemented by triennial programmes.

The draft report was received by the ministry with a marked lack of enthusiasm and it was several months before departmental comments were collated. These were, in the main, critical of the Treasury recommendations, many of which were thought to be impracticable. But, of overwhelming significance was the fact that the report had been overtaken by events. Much of the sense of frustration had been due to the restrictions which applied to *all* development at the time when the inquiry was being undertaken. Moreover, some of the policy deficiencies had been made good, for example by the comprehensive range of circulars which had been issued to development corporations.

This was accepted by the Treasury who wrote, in September 1950 that:

'It is clear that the material for the report was collected so long ago that as at present drafted it really deals with a state of affairs which no longer exists.'

The question remained as to whether the report should be updated or whether it would be better 'simply to let the whole matter go to sleep in its present untidy state'. It was the latter course which was adopted, though a Treasury official expressed his apprehension that 'the Government might be deliberately setting out to create what were in effect new special areas which would require indefinitely additional subsidisation from the exchequer, additional to that from local authorities'.

The Future Ownership Issue*

In the reviews of new town policy which took place in the early 'fifties, the emphasis was on reducing what Butler termed the 'alarming commitment' to investment in fourteen new towns. The way in which Macmillan dealt with this has been outlined in chapter III. The new towns prospered, and by the mid-fifties it was becoming clear that some of them were likely to prove highly profitable. As a result, the problem of meeting a major investment burden changed to one of determining the means by which the 'profits' should be allocated. The solution eventually decided upon was to transfer the assets to a new central body, the Commission for the New Towns. This was in line with the recommendations of the Reith Committee, but quite contrary to the intentions of the Labour Government which passed the 1946 Act. Before proceeding to a discussion of the legislation which provided for the establishment of the Commission for the New Towns, it is appropriate to recall the original thinking on this matter and to summarise ministerial discussions during the 'fifties. This involves some repetition of the account given in chapter III but at the same time allows for a fuller discussion of some relevant issues.

In their second report, the Reith Committee discussed the position that would arise when a new town reached maturity, and whether the development corporation should then be dissolved and its assets and liabilities be taken over at a valuation by the local authority, or whether the corporation should continue in being, modified in constitution, as land owner and estate manager. A large majority of the committee felt that:

> 'it may prove unwise to combine the functions of land owner and local authority in a single body [but] the matter will be unlikely to need a decision for some twenty years, and the issue may be determined in the meantime by national land policy . . . When the major work of construction is completed we suggest that it would then be appropriate to include in the governing body a minority of members—possibly two—resident in the new town and elected by the inhabitants by direct vote'.

When Silkin met the associations of local authorities in March 1946† he said that he differed from the Reith Committee on the ultimate fate of the corporation. 'It is the committee's view that the

---

* EA(53)106, EA(54)27, LG(54)2nd Meeting, 26 May 1954, CM(56)47th Conclusions, 5 July 1956, HA(57)77, HA(57)78, HA(57)16th Meeting, 8 July, 1957, C(57)172, CC(57)57th Conclusions, 25 July 1957, HA(58)67, HA(58)11th Meeting, 20 June 1958, HA(58)78, HA(58)13th Meeting, 30 June 1958, HA(58)117 and HA(58) 19th Meeting, 17 October 1958; and MHLG File 95351.

† See chapter I, p. 17.

corporation should continue indefinitely, living side by side with the local authority . . . but I think that when its job is substantially done, the corporation must go, and the assets and liabilities be handed over to a local authority.'

The New Towns Act of 1946 provided that when the minister was satisfied that the purposes for which a development corporation had been set up were substantially achieved he should by order provide for the winding up and dissolution of the corporation and the transfer of its undertaking to the appropriate local authority or statutory undertakers. The order (made with the consent of the Treasury) would specify the sum due for the transfer, and in the event of objection the order would be subject to special parliamentary procedure. In welcoming a government amendment to the Bill which improved the details of the winding-up procedure, W. S. Morrison speaking for the Conservative Opposition, said '. . . it would be far better to let [the corporation] pass out of existence than to prolong its existence after the date when the place ought to be governed democratically by a local authority'.* (The Labour Party made the most of this statement when the New Towns Bill was under discussion in 1959.)

While it was the general policy of the Treasury and the department that local authorities should shoulder the full cost of the services which they should properly provide in the new towns, and to discourage the corporations from contributing towards the cost, the general gloom surrounding the finances of the corporations in the early 'fifties made it unrealistic at that time to consider any ultimate disposal. (The general view was expressed in the 1953 MHLG/Treasury report: 'there is no real ground for expecting a profit'.)†

Nevertheless, in the ministerial discussions in 1952 and 1953 about the possibility of reducing the exchequer commitment, some hope was expressed that the new towns could be handed over to the local authorities before completion. It was recognised, however, that this would involve legislation, and in any event the local authorities might not have sufficient resources 'to carry on the job'. Even if they had, it was doubtful if they would be willing to take it on since they would be apprehensive of the magnitude of the investment to carry the towns to the point where profits would begin to show. But, by March 1954, Macmillan was asking 'whether handing over to the local authorities is our policy at all' and tentatively suggested that a central corporation should be established to hold and manage the property, and exercise 'a shrewd discretion' about its disposal. On this, ministers decided that as legislation would be required, and as

---

* HC Debates, Vol 424, Col 2377, 4 July 1946.
† See chapter III, p. 121.

there was no chance of introducing a Bill in the session 1954–5, there was no need to reach a decision at this time. At ministerial level the matter lay dormant for two years.

Within the department, however, serious thinking and discussion developed. In February 1955, the secretary set out a number of emerging issues, foremost among which was the future ownership question. He had never liked the idea of giving the monopoly of purchase to a single authority, but he had not pursued the matter earlier because he thought it would be academic for so many years that it was unnecessary to worry about it.

'But things are going faster than we were entitled to hope and the time has now come when we ought to be thinking about this. There are quite a lot of objections to handing over these great undertakings to the local authority whatever it may be:

(a) If they are the only potential purchasers we shan't get a fair offer.
(b) I feel most doubtful on economic and social grounds about handing these very valuable assets over to an authority which, on any view, cannot be judged really equipped to manage undertakings of such magnitude. They will be authorities without sufficient experience or background to cope with problems of the size that will pass to them.
(c) The most peculiar consequences might follow. Thus, [the general manager of a major company in one of the new towns] thinks he sees which way the wind is blowing and has got himself elected to the local council. He is looking forward to the time it becomes a borough and when the assets created by the development corporation are handed over to that council. He then argued that the profits on the industrial and commercial properties will be so great that they will be able to make an all-round reduction of four or five shillings a week in the rents. That seems to me startling economic doctrine, and it also strikes me that the county council who, through the general county rate, have provided very expensive schools, may dislike intensely the idea of the ratepayers getting off very lightly in comparison with anybody else just because they have become the owners of highly profitable property which has nothing to do with schools.
(d) There is the major question whether it is healthy for the local authority to own all the houses in the town. It is already a serious enough problem in some areas. It becomes far more serious from the electoral point of view if all the property, especially the subsidised houses, is owned by the local authority.'

From initial soundings among the development corporations, it appeared that there was a general dislike of the idea of handing over the assets to a local authority. There were several alternatives which could be examined. The first was to sell industrial and commercial assets to financial institutions 'such as the Prudential or the Church Commissioners'. A second was to establish some form of national holding corporation. Macmillan had had some ideas on this line but had never developed them. Though this had attractions, it had to be recognised that it would be difficult for a responsible local authority to run its town when there was a powerful remote body in the background which owned all the property in the place.

There were minor problems connected with the sewerage and water supply schemes which strictly ought to pass to the local authority:

'but we are in the dilemma that if they go over on the basis of the outstanding debt, the burden on the local authority will be too great. It would make them all the more angry if they saw the corporation deriving handsome revenues from the industrial property whilst they got this burden with the heavy cost of major sewerage works carried out at the present time. On the other hand, if they were transferred at a largely written down value the local authority might overlook the burden which the development corporation was being left to carry because they would look primarily at the profits the development corporation was getting from the industrial estates'.

Another problem to be considered was the distribution of the increasing profits on revenue account which the development corporations were expecting. It was felt that corporations were probably suffering slightly 'from an excess of optimism'. So long as there was no trade recession and there was plenty of overtime being worked, it did seem that within a year or two they would be showing a very handsome profit. Some of them said that they were already out of the red and that they had slightly adjusted their accounts or had been glad to keep on the burden of sewerage so as to prevent the industrialists and the house owners from grumbling about the profits that were being made.

On the assumption that there was no recession, several corporations would undoubtedly be showing very substantial surpluses. What was to be done with them? Strictly (though local people would have to be persuaded of this) they ought to be applied in large part to writing off the accumulated deficiencies. But was it not reasonable for the corporations to argue that at least some of the profits should be applied for the benefit of the new towns, for example in better community buildings?

There was another very different important point:

'The atmosphere has changed. After many years of constant denigration new towns are now becoming popular. *The Economist* talks of them as "boom towns" and noble Lords in the House of Lords are saying they are so successful that there should be more of them. Up till now we have always held off this for a number of reasons. First we had enough on our plate with the existing bodies. Secondly the Treasury were very suspicious since there was so much money at stake and they were afraid they might lose. Moreover the Treasury don't like paying the equivalent of the rate contribution which ought to be paid by a local authority. Thirdly, almost all other ministers were hostile to the whole idea of new towns.'

The secretary himself was very doubtful 'about venturing on any more provincial new towns'. Though experience had shown that people and (more important financially) industry would readily move to the London new towns, he was by no means convinced that this could be done in the provinces. In London the problem was that expansion of existing towns under the Town Development Act was going slowly and was faced with many difficulties.

> 'Before long someone may wake up and say, "Why do you launch out on all the difficulties of expanding existing towns when you have already to your hand growing and successful development in the shape of new towns which are going admirably? Why don't you concentrate on increasing their size very much, so as to deal with London overspill at an accelerated rate?" '

There were, of course, difficulties with green belts, agricultural land and the adequacy of town centres, but nonetheless the possibilities ought to be explored quickly.

The secretary's minute started a spate of internal discussions and notes. Not all officials were convinced that the new towns would be profitable. The provision of main services and the general costs of development involved heavy burdens, and the extent to which these would be set off by profits from industrial and commercial development depended on the extent to which the corporations themselves built and let at rack rents. One minute from the accountant-general's division noted that, in some of the existing new towns, special difficulties had to be dealt with. For example, at Basildon, it might cost the corporation between £500,000 and £1m to deal with the shack development; at Harlow and Stevenage exceptional expenditure on main sewers had cost nearly £2·5m; at Hemel Hempstead the clearing away of much of the old town centre to make way for the new would absorb most, if not all, of the profits from the new town centre development. In others, Aycliffe and Cwmbran, Corby, Hatfield and Peterlee, little or no new industry was required. At Welwyn Garden City and Hatfield there was already an effective town centre when the corporation was set up. In these places profits on this sort of development would not be available to set off against the cost of main services.

It was too early to say whether one or two other new towns (eg Harlow and Stevenage) would not show a more favourable financial picture, 'but several of them would show a worse.' All told, taking the position as it was likely to be when the new towns were finished, but excluding any exchequer liability in respect of housing, it was rather too much to hope there would be a profit overall, though if the reckoning was deferred until the first leases of the profit making development fell in, the position would be more favourable. But if regard was had to the exchequer liability for the rate fund contribution on subsidised houses built by the corporations, it was doubtful whether new towns as a whole would show a profit until after the capital had been repaid in sixty years' time.

There was, however, general agreement that 'something better' than 'disposal to local authorities' was wanted. But this posed a dilemma: if assets which local authorities normally provided (water, open spaces, playing fields etc) were transferred to local authorities there would be large outstanding liabilities which would probably have to be written off, and 'the less we give the authority in the way of a nest-egg out of which they can pay, the more we shall have to write off.' Disposal to private interests could 'go like steel and road haulage': shops and factories 'would go like hot cakes, but what about the rest?'

There was also 'a political point'. If a Conservative Government encouraged the corporation to sell to the Church Commissioners and the Prudential, the Opposition would cry 'dissipating the national assets' and ask why they should be 'handed over to the profiteers and not to democratically elected custodians of the nation's social conscience'. This would not be easy to argue over the floor of the House.

Financially it would be more attractive to retain the new towns under central government control than to 'sell out' to local authorities. It would also be more profitable than 'selling off the wheat and being left with the chaff'. Even if one could be sure of selling all the assets on terms which enabled the outstanding commitments to be liquidated, it might suit the Treasury just as well, or even better, to take the profits as annual revenue rather than as capital.

There were several possible legatees. The Commissioners of Crown Lands had already been suggested, but this did not seem to be a satisfactory idea: 'the dust of Crichel Down hasn't settled; they probably wouldn't want to take over so much developed land; Crown immunity on such a large scale might be awkward from the point of view of planning, public health, etc legislation.' State-financed housing associations on the lines of the North Eastern Housing Association 'would be all right if it were thought right to sell all of the wheat, because the chaff would probably be almost all housing'. Alternatively, a new body might be formed possibly out of the existing corporations. There were several variations on this theme: eg a pyramidal organisation of central boards and area boards to run all the new towns, or individual corporations for each town while building continued and a single holding corporation to take over as each was finished.

It could be that the future of town development would be relevant: 'the 1952 Act isn't going to bring home more than a fraction of the bacon, and if we mean business we shall have to take over most of the job'. There might be something to be said for an organisation capable of dealing with finished new towns and unfinished new towns and also of doing some town development. On the other hand, the jobs were different, and probably the powers ought to be. When a new town was finished, the managing body probably ought to stop all but small scale development and ought to have no compulsory purchase powers (except perhaps for the purposes of its water and sewerage undertakings). Equally, the planning administration which was suitable for new towns was not suitable for town developments, which, being by comparison of a relatively minor character, ought to remain subject to local planning control.

Whatever happened about town development, there was a good case for a single small holding corporation to which each new town development corporation handed over 'at the right moment'. This would be a suitable body, whatever its duties might be decided to be. If the policy were to hold on to the assets on a long term basis, a small body of this kind was all that would be needed to manage the estates and collect the rents for the Treasury. If the policy were to dispose of the assets, such a body could take its time, selling off smallish bits here and there as good bargains could be made. A long term plan for selling off to a variety of buyers in fairly small lots would produce better social and financial results than a rushed plan to divide all the spoils at once between the local authorities, the Church Commissioners and the Prudential on the best terms that could be obtained at the time.

The single holding corporation would need legislation. If that were impossible, the existing corporations might be given the same job, 'but it would be stretching the terms of [the 1946 Act] pretty far'.

THE VIEWS OF THE NEW TOWN CHAIRMEN

Meanwhile, the chairmen of the new towns were expressing increasing anxiety about the future uncertainty and stressed the need for early decisions. In a private meeting between one chairman and the secretary in June 1955 the urgency was underlined. For the time being, 'by a certain amount of perfectly legitimate fiddling', the development corporation could avoid showing a large profit on their general revenue account. Within two years or so, however, the profit was bound to be very large because of the big revenues they would be getting from their industrial estates, their shops and their town centres. Tenants' associations were watching the position very closely and would undoubtedly say that if the corporation were making such profits the rents ought to be reduced. More serious was the fact that the industrialists themselves were almost bound to join in with their workmen. The fear was not so much that the industrialists would demand reduced rents for their factories (though this was a risk) as that, in their determination to keep their employees, they would join with them in demanding reduction of rents as the corporation's accounts showed an increase in profits.

The secretary pointed out that 'to begin with at any rate there was an unanswerable case for applying profits in writing off the accumulated deficiency'. The new town chairman agreed, but said this would not take as long as one might think. He fully recognised that as the State had taken the risk and put up all the money, it was entitled to the lion's share of the profits. Furthermore, he agreed that it would be wrong on general economic policy to use large profits from industrial estates in reducing house rents beyond the proper market rate. He did, however, suggest, and the secretary agreed, that there was a good case for applying some of the profits in easing the burden of such services as sewerage, water and highways.

> 'Clearly, we should be in great difficulties with the local authorities if we kept all the profitable services and handed over to them major works like sewerage schemes and water undertakings, the more so as they have been carried out at a time of very high cost. On top of this there is the argument that local authorities wouldn't be slow to take the point that under Town Development the exchequer does grant aid things like sewerage services.'

Following this meeting, the new town chairmen submitted a lengthy memorandum to the ministry. The need for an early decision was stressed. The absence of any decision was creating a general air of uncertainty and might well mean that wrong decisions were now being made. For example, assets might be disposed of which might be better kept, in the light of the conclusion finally reached as to the future of the new towns. Moreover, the general assumption that all the assets of development corporations would be made over to local authorities had influenced the financial dealings and relationships between development corporations and local authorities, and had resulted in requests from the latter for indemnities and assurances which the corporations were unable or unwilling to give. This inevitably delayed progress.

Various methods of dissolving new town corporations and of disposing of their assets were analysed: the transfer of all assets to local authorities; the sale of some assets; and the deferment of dissolution.

The prospect of local authorities owning entire towns or the major parts of towns was thought to be 'disquieting from the social and political point of view'. That practically the whole of a town's residential area should be composed of subsidised housing administered by the local authority might well give 'undue prominence to the housing tenant as a voter'. Furthermore, commercial and industrial tenants might be concerned lest their economic importance to the area was not reflected in their voting capacity if their local authority were at the same time their landlord. Certain types of property, such as public houses, might not, in any event, be suitable for local authority ownership.

Secondly, the borough or urban district council to whom the new town assets would be transferred would necessarily be a young body, or at least one which would have grown rapidly and recently. It would have experienced a sudden increase in its responsibilities, many of a kind with which it would be unfamiliar, and would be fully engrossed for the first years of its existence in grappling with the normal local government problems inherent in its enhanced status. It was doubtful whether such an inexperienced local authority would be capable of shouldering the heavy responsibilities involved in managing, as a business concern, the bulk of the properties in its area.

Thirdly, though it had originally been thought that the practical problems of transfer could be overcome if the local authority took over the staff of the development corporations (at any rate in so far as they were engaged on the management of properties transferred) this would be unlikely to happen, except in the case of some junior staff. The difficulty of amalgamating parallel departments (particularly where two chief officers were concerned), the disparities in salary ranges, and the adjustment of development corporation practices to the quite different procedures of local government, would discourage the local authority from taking over development corporation staff.

Transfer to the local authority would involve considerable financial problems. The New Towns Act left the position vague: it merely empowered the minister, with the consent of the Treasury, to prescribe the terms on which the transfer should be made, although the local authority might, in effect, appeal to Parliament against them. The Act gave no guidance as to the basis upon which any payment by the local authority was to be assessed. The obvious alternative bases of transfer of assets were either written down book value (or—what in the circumstances might be little different—the outstanding loan debt) or current valuation. The first basis should ensure that the exchequer recouped the advances made to the development corporation but only if unprofitable developments such as main sewerage works were included. The local authority might make a considerable profit out of the transaction or, conversely, if all the unremunerative development were included, a considerable loss. The local authority could not, it was suggested, be forced to take over the latter. Moreover, on taking over a development corporation's housing estates, a local authority would become liable for the rate fund contribution. The sudden need to find these contributions could result in a startling rise in rate poundage. This could be avoided only if the terms on which the dwellings were transferred discounted the capitalised value of the contributions, at a further sacrifice to the exchequer.

The second basis, ie current valuation, should prevent the local authority from making any considerable profit or loss, but would not necessarily guarantee that the exchequer recovered the outstanding balance of advances. The current evidence was, however, that in most new towns the exchequer might expect to make a reasonable profit, provided that the right moment in the development of the new town were chosen for the transfer to be made.

Having thus rejected the idea of total transfer of assets to local authorities, the chairmen turned their attention to a selective transfer, with some assets being sold. This involved dividing assets into (a) those which in other areas were normally administered by a local authority, and (b) those which elsewhere were normally provided by private enterprise, even though to some extent they might fall within the statutory powers (as distinct from obligations) of the local authorities. Thus, main sewerage, main roads, open spaces, fell into the first class, while factories and shops fell into the second. Borderline cases would cover community buildings which might be put into the first class. Development corporation housing estates might either be treated as falling within the second class or might be arbitrarily divided between the two in proportions which would reflect something like the average division between council and private housing in normal towns of the same size. Assets to be transferred to local authorities would, on the whole, be unprofitable but since they would represent only a portion of the development corporation's capital expenditure, the transfer might safely be made at valuation.

Assets to be sold ought to be dealt with in a different way. They would be remunerative and ultimately, if not immediately, should be profitable. They ought to pass into hands other than those of the local authorities, and in dealing with them it would be legitimate, as the New Towns Act implicitly recognised, to protect the taxpayer, as distinct from the ratepayer, by ensuring that as far as possible the capital which had been provided for the development of the new town should be repaid in full. Possible alternatives were that these assets should either be sold and the capital sums realised paid over to the exchequer, or continue to be held by the development corporation or some government holding and managing agency.

This idea led neatly into the chairmen's favoured solution: the deferment of the dissolution of the corporations. Section 5 of the original New Towns Act prohibited development corporations from transferring the freehold or granting of a lease for more than 99 years save with the minister's consent, which could only be given in 'exceptional circumstances'. The Town Development Act, 1952, removed this limitation upon the minister's power to consent,* so

---

* See chapter III, p. 117.

that it was now possible for all the saleable assets of a development corporation to be disposed of by sale before it came to be wound up, leaving only such things as sewers, roads and open spaces to be transferred to the local authority. It was therefore argued that it was possible to contemplate—without further legislation—that a development corporation's assets need not automatically be transferred to the local authority on the completion of the new town, but they might continue to be held by a corporation, or be sold, either before or at the time of its winding up. Fresh legislation would presumably be needed if a transfer of assets to a government agency were contemplated.

The circumstances of new towns would vary, but it seemed desirable that, as each approached completion, a careful investigation should be made to determine the optimum point in time (financially) for it to be wound up. In this inquiry, account should be taken not only of the repayment of advances, but also of the funds made available by the central government in subsidies, etc and contributions to local authorities. Development corporations should not be wound up until this optimum point had been reached. Alternatively (though it would presumably involve fresh legislation) their assets might before then be transferred to some new government holding agency, if in this way economy in administration might be found.

Beyond this, even if it should be decided as a matter of policy that development corporations had to be wound up as soon as the taxpayers' interest in their finances had been met, consideration should be given to the disposal by way of sale of many of their assets, particularly industrial and commercial assets, before the scope of the residual transfers to local authorities was settled. But it had to be emphasised that the moment of disposal of the saleable assets must be most carefully chosen, having regard to the particular circumstances of each new town.

In view of the submissions made by the new towns' chairmen it was clear to departmental officials that the rapid progress with the new towns meant that decisions would have to be taken more quickly than had been anticipated. At the end of June 1955, the secretary minuted that 'our objective ought to be to aim at legislation within the next two years or so, before the trading and other estates begin to show large profits'.

A working group of officials of the ministry and the Treasury met in September 1955 to consider the issues raised by the secretary and the chairmen. It was agreed that the water and sewerage undertakings of the corporations should be disposed of to local authorities quickly, and that it would be worth some financial loss to have them free from the larger general questions of disposal of more profitable parts. But the wider question got confused with argument about the possibility of increasing the size of the towns beyond the original targets, and so determining the point at which development was substantially completed.

POLITICAL PRESSURE FOR ACTION

This side-tracked the issue, which was not revived till Sandys, evidently under political pressure, minuted on 25 April 1956 that he was 'convinced the time has come to make some statement of our intentions in regard to the future ownership of the assets of the new towns'. In response, the department prepared a draft paper for the Home Affairs Committee asking them to agree to a Bill to provide that the assets should not be transferred to the local authorities, but that a central agency should be established to hold and manage the property, with power to dispose of the marketable assets as and when a favourable opportunity occurred. The draft sought authority to make an early announcement of intention because

'the local authorities are assuming that they will shortly inherit all the assets of the corporations; and some Labour councils are beginning to make political capital of their intentions eg by suggesting that they will devote the revenue from the profitable development to reduction of rents and provision of amenities. Also I want to have discussions with various people about the constitution of the central agency, and cannot do so till the intention is announced'.

The draft proposed that the ultimate objective in each new town should be to make them 'as much like normal towns as possible'. This implied diverse—mainly private—ownership. Marketable property should be sold off as and when the most favourable opportunity arose. In the meantime, provision was needed for holding and management. Public utility undertakings, where owned by the corporations, should be transferred to local authorities or statutory undertakers, on terms to be agreed, before the corporations were wound up. Housing presented a special problem. The corporations were already authorised to sell houses, but there had been few purchasers. The local authorities had built some houses themselves, but they owned fewer than the authorities of comparable sized towns. It might be right to transfer some of the corporation houses to the local authorities if satisfactory terms could be agreed, but Sandys thought that they should not own more than 'a normal proportion' of all the houses in the town. The remainder should be transferred to a central agency. It might prove desirable for the agency to create a housing trust for the ownership and management of housing, and this might become a permanent arrangement.

Sandys approved the draft on 13 May 1956. It passed through his parliamentary secretary (Enoch Powell), and was circulated for comment on 23 May to the Treasury and the Scottish Office. In acknowledging the draft, the Treasury commented that 'this is a quite momentous document, both for you and for us, and will need wider circulation here than most new town matters'. Later they stressed that 'it should be made clear that the agency could dispose of properties to bodies, private or public, who in the Government's estimation can be relied upon to manage them efficiently'.

The Department of Health for Scotland replied to the effect that Sandys' proposals were premature in relation to Scottish conditions, and the general policy would be difficult to justify but, apart from the Scottish difficulties, the timing and nature of the proposals were inopportune. It seemed odd to announce a decision about the future of the new towns at a time when the whole financial relationship between central and local government throughout Great Britain was under review; when the structure of local government in England and Wales was also being examined; and when important changes in valuation law affecting all Scottish local authorities were being made. It was also doubtful whether the proposal to centralise holding powers would be popular on either side of the House. Government supporters were unlikely to welcome the appearance of an organisation of this kind, and the Opposition would point to the history of the disposal of the British Transport Commission's road haulage assets. The minister's proposal for the transfer of all the assets in the new town (minus some undefined proportion of the houses) to a central agency would be interpreted as a rather dramatic expression of no confidence in local government in general, and a marked lack of confidence in particular in those local authorities who were currently responsible for the areas in which the new towns were situated. Apart from the immediately detrimental effect of such an announcement on local government opinion generally, the announcement might be particularly damaging to those new towns (and they included all the Scottish ones) which had some distance to go and which would have to rely for many years on the continued collaboration and goodwill of the local authorities in the areas in which they were established. The effect of the announcement on the prospects of local authorities co-operating in the development of any additional new towns might well be disastrous.

Apart altogether from the fact that in Scotland any announcement of policy on this matter would be premature, there were other differences which made it particularly difficult for the secretary of state to follow Sandys' main proposals. The Scottish new towns had incurred substantial deficits on their housing operations, largely due to the Scottish rating system (which was in process of amendment). These accumulated deficits on housing could only be met—if they were capable of being met at all—in the long term by the profits on other parts of the new town undertakings, such as shops, offices and factories. The local authorities in Scotland would certainly be reluctant to take over the house property in the new towns unless the accumulated deficits were wholly or partly written off. On the other hand, it would be bad business for the exchequer to write off these deficits unless they were absolutely satisfied that the appreciation of the remaining assets could be calculated so precisely as to cover the amount of the 'write-off'. In all respects, therefore, it would seem more businesslike in Scotland for the total assets to be retained, at least for a time, as a *unum quid* town by town. This economic argument for the new town undertaking to be held as a whole by some holding body was a more satisfactory and palatable argument than one based on the theory that it was wrong in principle for local authorities to own the bulk of the property, particularly house property, in their areas. This argument would not be acceptable in Scotland where it was not uncommon for a local authority to own and manage more than 50 per cent of the house property in the town; in some Scottish burghs, indeed, the local authority already owned over 80 per cent of all the houses.

Sandys was faced with a debate in the House of Commons on new towns and overspill on 9 July 1956 and, as he had been unable to put an agreed memorandum to his colleagues in the Home Affairs Committee, he took the unusual step of raising verbally in the Cabinet the question as to what he should say if he were asked about the future ownership of the new town assets. He explained that as a matter of social policy it was preferable that some of the factories should pass to private ownership, and that some at least of the houses should be privately owned or owned by a housing association. He wished to make it plain that it should not be assumed that the assets would all pass automatically to the local authority. The Cabinet authorised the statement accordingly.

The debate on 9 July 1956 was wide ranging, covering progress on the new towns, action under the Town Development Act, the housing situation generally and the office problem in London. Sandys did not refer to the future but, in the winding up of the debate, the parliamentary secretary (Enoch Powell) said:

'My right honourable friend is well aware of the importance of a clear understanding as to the manner in which these great enterprises will at that stage [ie when work is drawing to a close] be dealt with. He is in consultation with the corporations themselves on the subject, and it is his intention in due course to make a statement'.*

POLICY ISSUES
The hint of a statement gave rise to some apprehension on the

---

* HC Debates, Vol 556, Col 152, 9 July 1956.

part of the Whitley Council for new town staff about possible redundancies, but in a departmental minute of 7 December 1956, it was stressed that detailed discussions with all concerned could not proceed until the broad lines of policy had been decided. A revised draft paper for the Home Affairs Committee was submitted to the minister. This had previously been agreed in general outline with the Treasury. A covering minute from the secretary noted that:

'Scotland, as always, are difficult. Their new towns are not as far on as some of ours; they think that an announcement about the future would be premature and might prejudice co-operation with local authorities; that they would prefer to let the new town corporation run on; and generally that if an announcement is made as proposed Scotland would want to be disassociated.'

But Scotland could not be 'disassociated from the general principles'. Apart from this problem, there were others—particularly in relation to housing—but it was not possible to elaborate detailed proposals until there had been discussions 'with people who know a great deal more than we do about the problems of large scale land ownership, and of housing trusts; and we cannot have those discussions until broad policy is announced'.

There were at least five questions which had to be resolved. First, what form of organisation would be most appropriate? Should there be one parent corporation, with managers in the different towns, or should there be a separate organisation for each town or for groups of towns? The secretary commented: 'I am inclined to think one parent organisation'. This might consist of a board with a 'chairman and deputy chairman (financial types) giving most of their time, with part time members, and a full time highly paid general manager'.

Secondly, what directives were to be given to the board? Were they simply to manage the property in the interest of the minister? Were they to be free to spend some money on improving the amenities of the towns?

'I think the second is necessary; but how do we give effect to that? I am inclined to think that for a start we stick to the pattern of the New Towns Act (substituting the function of holding, managing and disposing of the property for that of developing the town). The Act empowers the minister to give 'directions' to corporations; and it also provides, in effect, that any proposals for capital expenditure must receive the prior consent of the minister, and that we have to get the concurrence of the Treasury. This is a tiresome business; but I think we may have to start off this way until we get more experience.

Generally, in this connection, I hope that we will try to establish a form of organisation which would not necessarily be upset in the event of a change of government. The Opposition are bound to declare in favour of ultimate municipal ownership; but I think that they might concede that the State must retain control until it has got as much as possible of its money back. A corporation which is not bound by statute to pursue certain policies (eg disposal of freehold) but which could be directed by the government of the day, seems to me to have a better chance of survival than one with policies closely defined by statute. To which I would add that I think in any event that we need to feel our way.'

Thirdly, what precisely were to be the functions of the board? Were they to be empowered to carry out development? Would they be allowed to spend money on the town? The answer to both questions was probably in the affirmative but 'only experience can show us the needs'. However, it would be wise 'to get the views of the most sensible people at present on new town boards before coming to conclusions'.

Fourthly, what was to be the relationship of the board to the department and the Treasury? What was to be its accountability? What was to happen if and when the board started to make an overall profit on any one town, or on all the towns?

'I think that on the first two questions again we should follow the precedent of the New Towns Act; but new town experts will have some advice to give. The third question I would hope to leave till it arises; but we need to examine when that is likely to be in relation to any one town. For the whole lot is a long way off.'

Fifthly, how did one establish a housing trust? Should it be a subsidiary of the main body, or independent? What would be its financial basis?

'These are questions I cannot begin to answer until I have talked to people with experience of such trusts as well as to some of the new town experts.

My idea would be, after you have made the announcement, to collect a party consisting of such people as the best of the new town experts, leading surveyors with experience of large scale building management, one or two people from the housing trust world, one or two good people from local government (not in a representative capacity), perhaps someone from building societies. I would hope to agree with the Treasury the questions on which we want answers; and also to start working with them on the questions which are mainly their affair—financial basis, accountability etc. But I cannot start on this until the broad announcement is made.'

No immediate action was taken on the draft paper for the Home Affairs Committee, but it was submitted in broadly the same form to Brooke after he had succeeded Sandys as Minister of Housing and Local Government in January 1957. Brooke approved it without amendment.

Meanwhile the minister and the secretary had met the chairmen's conference who expressed the hope that the winding up of the corporations could be dealt with on the basis of agreement between the political parties. In a minute of 26 February 1957 to the minister, the secretary said:

'It is obviously most undesirable that the Opposition should pledge themselves to undo whatever the Government do if they are returned . . . Their
ultimate object might be municipal ownership; whereas the ultimate object
of the Government is disposal of the assets to private interests, possibly
retaining the houses in a trust. But they need to contemplate an interim
management agency (while the exchequer gets its money back) as much as
the Government. The main difference would be, I imagine, that they would
not allow the agency to sell.'

Brooke thought an agreement with the Opposition was probably
impossible, but suggested the right tactics might be to prepare a
white paper reviewing the position of the new towns and the progress
made, as the background to an announcement about future policy,
and which might do something to avoid a snap declaration of
disagreement by the Opposition. Meanwhile he agreed that steps
should be taken to find out the line the Scots were taking and to
settle outstanding points with the Treasury.

The Department of Health for Scotland repeated their reservations, though they agreed that 'in the end of the day it would be
awkward and difficult to contemplate some basically different
arrangement in Scotland from that adopted in England and Wales'.

'Our view is that we should first examine more closely whether we cannot
get all we want by invoking the safeguard in Section 15(1) of the Act as it
stands, whereby disposal of a new town can—indeed must—be deferred if the
minister and Treasury are satisfied that the circumstances render this
course expedient. If the conclusion is reached that something more radical is
needed, then we suggest—as I believe the Treasury do also—that we should
have in our minds fairly definite ideas about the form that any new holding
agency or agencies might take, before making any announcements or entering into any discussions with local authorities or other bodies. Only then do
we think the time would be ripe for an announcement, which might initially
be confined to a simple statement that the Government were proposing to
enter into consultation with the local authorities and other interests concerned so as to evolve some method of preserving the interests of the taxpayers
in assets created by government expenditure, while at the same time maintaining the local interest, identity, and character of each of the new towns.'

On 9 April 1957 Brooke wrote to Butler (chairman of the Future
Legislation Committee) seeking authority to combine a New Towns
(Money) Bill—to increase the exchequer advances—with a New
Towns (Ownership and Management) Bill for introduction in the
1957–58 session: 'members concerned with the new towns are most
anxious to get this over quickly; they have particularly approached
me about this, and I think they will be greatly disturbed if the Bill
does not come next session.' The Future Legislation Committee
agreed provisionally that the combined Bill should be placed in the
list for the next session and noted that the minister would submit
proposals to the Cabinet.

On 10 May 1957 the secretary minuted 'I am finding this very difficult': all (except Scotland) were agreed that an announcement should be made of the Government's intention not to hand over the towns to the local authorities, and to provide a new agency whose main function would be estate management and disposal; but there were some difficult questions to answer in 'this uncharted field'. What was to be the ultimate aim? The new agency would act as trustees for the public, but was this to be the general public or the inhabitants of the new towns? What form of local organisation was desirable and should it have any executive responsibility? So far as the houses were concerned, the great majority would remain as rented. The secretary believed that a housing association – or rather several housing associations – was the right solution, and that it should be a subsidiary of the main body. But its financing presented difficulties. It was becoming clear that the statutory annual subsidy of £32 per house would not be normally sufficient to keep the housing accounts in balance: in other words the rents could not be raised sufficiently to meet the balance.

There were other problems:

'It looks as though the corporations will still be left with some sewerage and water undertakings when they wind up. The Treasury believe we shall get a better bargain by delaying disposal of these undertakings: and even if we could reach agreement with them we can't *make* any local authority take these over if they don't want to do so on any terms we think reasonable. So we shall have to provide for continuing to operate these.

There will still be some development to be carried out after each new town is "substantially completed". In particular, more houses will be needed (for the growing population, and possibly to meet unlooked for industrial expansion). Should the commissioners have any powers to build? I would be inclined to think not (certainly not to build houses) though they could sell or lease for development by others. But whether such a complete break would be practicable I do not know.

I would like to think that the commissioners could be given as much freedom as the Commissioners of Crown Lands—who are simply required to comply with instructions given to them, but who do not have to submit their daily operations for comment—as new town corporations do. Crown Lands have their own accounting officer, and operate really as an independent department subject only to the general ministerial responsibility of (now) the Lord Privy Seal. But whether we could possibly get that far on the new towns I do not know. Perhaps it is too much to hope.'

The secretary hoped that a working party or a departmental committee could be set up to consider questions once a broad announcement had been made. This would provide the opportunity to consult publicly the new town experts, surveyors and others knowledgeable in estate management, the housing association experts, and the local authorities. But this would take time and it would not be possible to introduce a Bill in the 1957–58 session if it were to be combined with a New Towns Money Bill which had to be passed before Easter 1958. In order to meet the minister's need for legislation in the 1957–58 session, she therefore suggested a short Bill to enable the corporations to carry on for the purposes of estate management after their original job was substantially completed, while the committee or working party was set up to advise on the ultimate form of organisation.

At a meeting with officials on 15 May 1957 the minister said that 'the Conservative Party would not stomach the handing over of new towns to local authorities, and would expect legislation to be passed before the end of this Parliament to ensure that this did not happen'. ('This Parliament' would end its five year term in May 1960, with the possibility of a general election during 1959.) The secretary explained that adequate legislation could not be worked out in time for introduction in 1957–58, and it was agreed that the best course was to aim at making a statement before the end of July 1957 to say that the Government did not intend the new towns to be handed over to local authorities, that the 1946 Act would be amended to make alternative provision, and that a small committee would be set up to start work in September 1957 with a view to reporting in time for the introduction of a Bill in the 1958–59 session. The Treasury and the Scottish Office were to be consulted with a view to putting a paper to the Home Affairs Committee by the end of June.

CABINET DISCUSSION

At a meeting with officials of the Treasury and the Department of Health for Scotland on 19 June 1957, the terms of the paper for the HA Committee were settled. This was circulated at the beginning of July and proposed 'that for England and Wales there should be established a new body or bodies to take over the property and to own, manage and dispose of it as appropriate, their duty being to secure the maximum return for the exchequer, proper regard being paid to the interests of the inhabitants of the towns; that a committee should be appointed to advise on the organisation best suited for the purpose; and that an announcement to this effect should be made towards the end of July'. The Scots were still unhappy at the trend in events, and the secretary of state submitted a paper in which he said that, since none of the three Scottish new towns was nearing completion, the problem of future management had no practical urgency. While he agreed that the transfer of new town assets en bloc to the local authorities could not be contemplated, it would not be appropriate to ask the proposed expert committee to deal with the Scottish problem, as 'insofar as it was not looked on as a purely academic exercise it would merely stir up controversy'.

The HA Committee considered both papers on 8 July, and the proposals and the draft announcement were agreed, subject to the

Prime Minister's approval. The Prime Minister, however, minuted:
'I do not see what is to be gained by making these statements. You
merely open a flank without the chance of dealing a blow at the
enemy. Why not wait for legislation to be ready?'

Brooke replied on 15 July:

'The Conservative members for the new town constituencies are pressing me
strongly to get a government statement made without delay. They say it is
imperative. Industrialists with factories in the new towns are most apprehensive
at the possibility of entire ownership passing to the local authorities. There is
a widespread belief that this government cannot really mean to let that
happen, but as the months go by and nothing is said anxiety increases . . .
The decision to have a committee to advise us on the appropriate organisation
makes it imperative to announce the policy. We must legislate before the
election, which means in the 1958–59 session. For that I must appoint the
committee this summer and ask them to report by June next year. Even if we
did not have a committee I should still need to announce the policy in order
that we could openly consult those whose advice we need.'

On 15 July the Prime Minister minuted that he was not convinced:
'no statement should be made until the matter has been discussed
and approved by Cabinet'.

Brooke raised the matter with the Cabinet, referring to the pressure
from Conservative members, and saying that he needed outside
advice before he could put forward detailed proposals. 'If we are to
do the job properly and carry the public with us, it is desirable not
merely to consult outside opinion, but to do it in such a way as to
reassure the inhabitants of the towns, and to avoid creating any
impression that the Government is settling their future without
giving everyone concerned a reasonable chance of being heard.' He
therefore asked for authority to make an announcement of the
Government's intention to introduce legislation in the 1958–59
session for the transfer of the assets of the new towns in due course to
commissioners who would be responsible for managing and disposing
of them in such manner as to secure the maximum return to the
exchequer, while paying due regard to the interests of the inhabitants; and for the appointment of a committee to advise on the
arrangements to give effect to the Government's intentions.

The Cabinet were in general agreement with the proposals, but
doubted whether an independent committee, 'whose report might
have to be published' was appropriate. Alternative methods of
securing the necessary advice should be examined. It was agreed
that Brooke should make a general statement in the House during
the course of a forthcoming debate on local government. The
statement, as made on 29 July 1957, was as follows:

'One matter about which people have asked me is the relationship of the new
towns to all this. That raises the question whether the ownership of all the

land and buildings in the new towns when the development corporations disappear is really a suitable function for local government to discharge and, if so, for what sort of authorities. Several of the corporations, established in England and Wales under the New Towns Act will have substantially completed their tasks in the next few years. The Government have been independently examining this matter and have reached the conclusion that it would not be the best plan to transfer wholesale to local authorities the ownership of the properties which are now in the hands of corporations.

We propose, instead, to establish a new agency to take over the property and liabilities of the corporations in England and Wales as they are wound up. This will, of course, all require legislation. Meanwhile, the Government are examining a number of questions relating to the organisations and functions of the proposed agency. There will be consultations on these questions with local authority representatives and with other expert opinion. The local authorities of the new town areas are, and will continue to be, responsible for all normal local government services just as similar authorities are elsewhere.

The only exceptions to this have been in a few cases water supply and, I think in a majority of cases, main sewerage. Now that that phase of early development is over, the aim of the Government will be to ensure that in new town areas responsibility for those services passes to the normal local authorities as soon as suitable arrangements can be made.'*

The public reaction to the statement was mild, except in the new towns themselves, and the department received a number of hostile letters from local councils and residents' associations. In the course of a speech at Horsham on 10 October 1957, Brooke explained that the new agency would have power to sell some properties or to grant leases if they thought fit, but they would be required always to consider the interests of those living in the towns.

Towards the end of 1957 and early in 1958, the department were considering the form which legislation might take, and a confidential memorandum of proposals was discussed with a group of experts in large scale property management. As a result of these meetings, it was envisaged that there should be a central commission, appointed by the minister, who would establish local organisations as the towns were taken over. The local organisation would be headed by a member of the commission and otherwise consist of local personalities appointed by the commission after consultation with the appropriate district council, and with the approval of the minister. The local organisation should have responsibility for the management of rented houses, and for such other dealing with day to day matters as the commission might delegate. This conception was not subsequently challenged by ministers, and remained a cardinal feature of the Bill.

The ministry's proposals were also discussed with the Treasury, who in a letter of 25 April raised two points: first, that the legislation

---

* HC Debates, Vol 574, Cols 924–5, 29 July 1957.

should clearly lay on the commission the function of *disposing* of the properties as and when appropriate; and secondly, that the commission should not be an instrument of social improvement and betterment, and therefore there should be no power to contribute to local authorities and others on the provision of amenities.

There was a meeting between ministry and Treasury officials on 29 April 1958. On disposal, the secretary said that while the minister had previously laid emphasis on the need to promote diverse ownership, he was now reluctant to press this aspect for three reasons; first, disposal of the freehold was unlikely to be a commercial proposition for a good many years; secondly, it was by no means certain that disposal would be a sound policy; and thirdly it would be disastrous to provoke the Labour Party to come out in favour of municipalisation. If disposal policy were left in the background there was some hope of avoiding major political controversy. On amenities the secretary said that it was proposed to do no more than what great landlords had always done, and there should be no prohibition on making the sort of local contribution to certain local projects (to be agreed with the department) that any good landlord might be expected to make. 'It would be a mouse in terms of money but a lion in terms of public relations.'

Detailed proposals for the legislation were being worked out, and an outline of them was discussed with the chairmen of the new town corporations in June. Among other points, they emphasised the variety of local problems which would require close local knowledge and local handling, and the need to watch localised economic movements to which a central authority could not be sensitive; but they were concerned at the prospect of local authority representation on local bodies, who could not be entirely trusted to pursue a realistic rent policy. The chairmen also expressed the belief that the commission should not need powers of compulsory acquisition by the time the towns were taken over.

In the meantime, the Treasury had 'done a great deal of rethinking' about the matter. On the general financial arrangements, the exchequer would have dealings with the commission (a) as creditor in respect of capital advances and (b) as shareholder to whom profits, if any, should go. Disposal of property:

'is the most difficult point . . . we remain convinced that the best interests of the exchequer lie in the disposal of property so as to secure the rapid repayment of the exchequer advances, provided that the property is not disposed of before it has reached a full value . . . We see the force of your "political" arguments and are disposed to concede a great deal to them. We are content that the duty to dispose should not be in the forefront of the terms of reference, but we think it must be there (as indeed it is in your version) and should not be drowned in phrases about the best interests of the towns . . . It seems to us that on this key point the commission cannot have a free hand, but must be under the effective directions of the government of the day.'

On amenities, the Treasury continued:

'You suggested that all that was involved was the sort of thing that any good landlord does, and that the expenditure was not necessarily pure charity, since it might enhance the value of the estate. We agree there is something in this, but would not like the argument pressed too far. There is a danger in allowing these towns to have special treatment from the exchequer by a side door.'

In June 1958, Brooke submitted to the HA Committee detailed proposals for legislation. He said that the Cabinet had approved in principle the setting up of a new agency to take over the new towns as the work of the development corporations came to an end, and that he had been authorised to announce this. The decision had had two purposes—to prevent the transfer of the new towns to local authorities, and to ensure their gradual transformation into 'natural towns' by disposing of the property to diversified ownership. While the second of these remained the ultimate objective, it had become clear, since the Cabinet's decision in the previous year, that the time was not yet ripe for large scale disposals of new town property. What the new towns needed was a period of settled management, which would, from the exchequer point of view, also give time for the appreciation of property values. It would not, however, be expedient to announce now that the Government's intention was the ultimate disposal of the property to private ownership: that would only goad the Opposition into declaring that they would as soon as possible disband the new commission and transfer the towns to the local authorities, which 'would injure the towns only less than a decision actually to transfer them'. The question for immediate decision was whether the proposed Bill should empower the commission generally to dispose of property when directed by the minister at the appropriate time to do so, or whether their power should be limited by the Bill to disposals incidental to estate management. Brooke himself was inclined to favour the latter.

Discussion showed that there was general agreement that, as a matter of policy, there should be no large scale disposals of new town property in the near future. On the question of the commission's powers, there was considerable support for the view that these should be limited in the Bill to disposals for the purposes of estate management. It would be unwise to reach a decision, and to legislate now, on a problem which would not in practice arise for perhaps ten years. Moreover, the issue was of such importance that, when the time came for large scale disposals, they ought not to be effected without parliamentary control in the form of further legislation. Limitation of the commission's powers in this sense would simplify the passage of the present Bill through Parliament and would avoid raising the whole issue of leasehold enfranchisement.

On the other hand, the accumulation of property in public ownership was open to objection, particularly among government supporters, on general grounds and as much as possible of the new town property should be disposed of as soon as its value had reasonably appreciated. But by that time great pressure would have developed for giving the new towns themselves, rather than the exchequer, the benefit of the appreciated values, and it might be very difficult to secure legislation for the disposal of the property and the transfer of the profits to the exchequer. The difficulty would be avoided if a general power to dispose of the property subject to the direction of the minister were written into the Bill and, at the same time, the Government declared that their policy was not to allow large scale disposals in the near future.

On balance the committee were generally in favour of inserting in the Bill a further legislative bar to large scale disposals of new town property but it was felt that no decision should be taken until the views of government supporters were established: they might, indeed, not welcome the proposal to set up a new centralised agency to take over the towns.

A week later Brooke reported that he had discussed his proposals with 'nearly all the Conservative members representing new towns, together with the officers of the Party's housing committee'. They welcomed the proposals but stressed that, to prevent the towns passing into municipal ownership, it was imperative that there should be legislation in the current Parliament. Brooke continued that the officers of the housing committee were emphatic that the Bill should not take priority over or squeeze out of next session's programme a Bill to improve the compensation payable on compulsory acquisition.* They also stressed the great importance of:

'presenting it as a sensible alternative to the unwise Socialist plan of municipalisation, lest Conservative supporters in the country gained the idea that we were arbitrarily creating a new nationalised board. They asked whether I had considered and rejected the possibility of doing without a central body and entrusting ownership to the local bodies.'

At the Home Affairs Committee, discussion was mainly concerned with the extent to which the Bill should empower the new commission to dispose of property. Brooke proposed that the commission's powers in this respect should be similar to those at present enjoyed by the development corporations, who could sell or lease properties subject

---

* ie the Town and Country Planning Act 1959 which provided for compensation at market values: see *History Vol IV*, chapter VI.

to the minister's consent to the disposal of freeholds and the granting of leases for more than 99 years. In the debates on the Bill he would make it clear that there was to be no policy of general disposal of new town property and that the powers, like those of a development corporation, would be used only for the purposes of estate management. There might be some danger that unless the disposal powers were more closely circumscribed in the Bill itself, a future government might be able to dispose of the new towns to the local authorities without further parliamentary control, but it ought to be possible so to draft the Bill—perhaps on the lines of the Iron and Steel (Denationalisation) Bill—as to require the commission to obtain a proper price for any assets disposed of. Brooke undertook to circulate to the committee a draft of the Bill (or at least of the clause on disposal powers) before final decisions were taken on the precise content of the Bill and the form of any statement which might be made on the Government's intentions. Instructions were sent to parliamentary counsel early in July 1958.

Brooke submitted the draft Bill to the HA Committee in October. He reminded his colleagues that on 30 June they had wished to be satisfied that Bill would not enable the minister of the day either to turn the proposed commission into a general realisation agency, or to direct the commission to hand over all the assets to the local authorities. The provisions of the Bill in this respect (which was later enacted virtually unchanged as section 2 of the New Towns Act 1959):

> 'will equally preclude a Conservative minister from allowing or compelling the commission to bring about wholesale disposal of the new town properties to private enterprise, and a Socialist minister from allowing or compelling the commission to hand them over to the local authorities'.

The HA Committee 'agreed that the clause could be regarded as satisfactory' and, on 17 October 1958 Brooke reported to the Prime Minister that there was entire agreement between ministers that:

> 'what the new towns will now need is a period of some years of good management, husbanding and enhancing the value of the assets. After a further period of years it will then no doubt be desirable to decide whether a policy of general disposal should be followed; but that will need further legislation when the time comes. For the time being the commission would have the same power of disposals as corporations; no more and no less. There would be deep perturbation among our members representing new towns and among industrialists with factories in them, and indeed among development corporations themselves, if the law were not changed before the end of this Parliament'.

The Prime Minister minuted that 'this seems all right'.

The Commission for the New Towns*

THE BILL IN PARLIAMENT

The Bill, introduced in the House of Commons on 17 November 1958, applied only to England and Wales. It provided for the establishment of the Commission for the New Towns, consisting of a chairman, deputy chairman and not more than thirteen other members (who would be paid) to which the minister, after consultation with the local authorities, would transfer the property of the development corporations when he was satisfied that their purpose had been substantially achieved. The commission's role would be to manage the property transferred to them from development corporations and to maintain and increase the value of the estate while at the same time paying proper regard to the purposes for which the town had been developed and 'to the convenience and welfare of persons residing, working or carrying on business there'. The minister's power of control over the commission would be linked to this role; the disposal of property could not be pursued as an end in itself, and without general or specific authority from the minister the commission were debarred from transferring the freehold or granting a lease for more than 99 years. With the approval of the minister and consent of the Treasury, the commission might make contributions towards the cost of amenities. Any financial surplus after providing for reserves and future requirements would be surrendered to the exchequer and accrue to the taxpayers, 'who had provided the means for building the new towns'.

The Bill made provision for the commission's local organisation. The intention was that housing management would be handled locally by a committee appointed by the commission after consultation with the appropriate district council and with the approval of the minister, but in other respects the commission would have a free hand to make their own arrangements.

On second reading on 1 December 1958, ministers justified the Bill on the ground that the immediate practical effect of transferring the new towns to the local authorities would be that the latter would own at least 75 per cent of the properties in their areas. Property ownership on this scale was quite outside the normal functions of local government. Moreover, while the towns were continuing to grow, it would be unwise to make a financial settlement for transfer: the taxpayers' investment should be allowed to mature. It was pointed out that there were three stages in the evolution of a town: development, consolidation and ultimate ownership. The Bill dealt with consolidation, 'and no one could forsee how long that period

---

* MHLG Files NT 11/1, NT 11/2, NT 50/1, NT 50/4, NT 50/7 and NT 50/8; Treasury Files 2AT 830/201/01 and 2AT 649/01.

would be'. The Bill 'was not a swindle' to cheat the local authorities of something which they were intended to have. The commission would have the duty of maintaining and enhancing the value of their estate and, in doing so, to 'have regard to the general interests of the town and the convenience and welfare of the people'. They would not be 'a disposals board' and certainly 'would not go on a general spending spree'.

The Opposition moved 'not to proceed with a Bill the principal object of which is to provide for the transfer of new towns in England and Wales to a central nominated body instead of to appropriate local authorities'. Dalton (who had been Minister of Local Government and Planning in 1950–51) referred to the commission as a 'bureaucratic bumbledom in Whitehall' and as 'a group of people set up by the minister who have no living touch or contact with the new towns and who are wholly without knowledge of the special requirements of the new towns except what they may get from the local committees [which] are a very sketchy fifth wheel to the coach'.*

The Bill was in standing committee on fourteen days between 17 March and 14 May 1959. The principal government amendment was to enable the commission to sell houses for owner occupation without specific approval of the minister. The Opposition moved a large number of amendments, which were not accepted, whose objects were *inter alia*—to ensure that the properties would in due course be transferred to local authorities; to place a complete embargo on disposals; to widen the scope of 'amenities' by including education and improvements to the town; to deprive the exchequer of surpluses; to secure more extensive consultation with local authorities; and to require that the local committees would be composed of the nominees of the local authorities.

THE ORGANISATION OF THE COMMISSION

In general, the commission's functions were those of a large estate company although with certain differences. The most important difference (in the words of an internal MHLG minute) was that, 'among all landlords of a comparable size, it will have to be, and be seen to be, the most enlightened of all'. This was implicit not only in the statement of its functions given in the Act, but also in 'the many exchanges during the passage of the Bill when Opposition members sought and received assurances on such topics as the commission's responsibility for amenities, and the fear that the commission would operate solely as a profit making enterprise, without regard to the needs of the towns or to the necessity to cater for further growth and

---

* HC Debates, Vol 596, Col 883, 1 December 1958.

new employment'. It was this difference which created the largest single problem in settling the form of the commission and its 'local offshoots', and deciding how their duties should be divided and their respective lines of responsibility fixed.

Because of the commission's responsibility to government, and bearing in mind the nature of the primary task—to manage an estate—it must (subject to ministerial direction) 'be the sole source of policy decisions on all subjects falling within its province; and centralise so far as possible all the accounting and administrative arrangements for which it is responsible'. The first of these propositions was self evident: 'the second only a little less so, for probably all the present new town chief officers would agree that eventually considerable economies could result from abolishing most, if not all, of the chief officer posts and transferring their duties to headquarters'.

There was a 'basic organisational conflict which is to centralise or decentralise the new towns affairs under the commission'. The decentralisation theme had found favour with Opposition members during the passage of the Bill, when they painted 'a lurid picture' of the new towns being 'remotely controlled by a soulless, profit-making body in London, packed with city financiers'. Though it was thought there was 'some merit' in this argument, 'the real fact remains—that the main job is one of holding and consolidating, and in the process we shall be faced with opportunities to rationalise and economise which it would be folly to disregard'.

After much internal discussion, it was proposed that in addition to the chairman and deputy chairman, there should not at the outset be more than three or four members (the Act authorised thirteen in total). They would all be part-time—and paid. It was part of the MHLG conception that each chairman of a local committee would be a member of the commission. The commission would need a central staff, 'though at the outset quite a small one'. Day to day management would continue to be carried out locally, the staff in the towns transferring to the commission's service.

The commission was established on 1 October 1961 with Sir Duncan Anderson as chairman. The other initial members were the chairmen of Crawley and Hemel Hempstead, a Hertfordshire county councillor, and a financial expert. Later appointments included industrialists and local authority members. Sir Henry Wells became chairman in 1964.

Crawley and Hemel Hempstead were the first of the new towns to be transferred to the commission (in April 1962). Originally it was proposed that Crawley should be taken over in 1961 'but the change to 1962 was made so that the commission could . . . have one profitable one (Hemel Hempstead) to offset the more doubtful financial

343

asset of Crawley'. Hatfield and Welwyn followed in April 1966.

THE ROLE OF THE COMMISSION

It was hoped to give the commission considerable freedom in the management of their estate, subject only to a broad direction of policy by the minister—though financial questions still had to be settled with the Treasury. However, 'they should not have to carry out much development—but there may be some which must be done and only they can get done'. Both the ministry and the Treasury assumed that, once new towns were transferred to the commission, exchequer commitments would come to an end 'except for a few tidying-up operations'. But this quickly proved not to be the case, particularly in relation to house building. The ministry noted that it was difficult to decide who was to provide such further rented housing as was needed:

'We dare not allow a great deal of building for owner occupation because of the risk that such houses would be taken by commuters. In Crawley about 200 of the houses each year may be privately built. Hemel being further behind on owner occupation could probably stand more. The county councils as the planning authorities are strongly opposed to much building for owner occupation, fearing that it will mean an increase of population well beyond target. But we want to keep local authority house building to a minimum; these towns have more than enough subsidised housing. We have encouraged the corporations to start on schemes for housing to let at economic rents, believing that it should be possible to attract into such houses the better off tenants in the subsidised houses and so free more of these for the younger newly marrieds. The commission will carry this on through the local committees. New town subsidy will be cut off soon after the hand-over, but rents of new houses can still be pooled with those of the older ones.'

This proved to be a difficult issue and it became entangled with that of the provision of 'better class housing' (which is discussed more fully in chapter VII). In essence the question was that of the function of the commission and its relationship to local authorities. Until that was settled satisfactory decisions could not be taken on a number of issues which had led to friction between the commission and the local authorities concerned—particularly on the responsibility for providing subsidised housing for meeting the future needs of industry, 'and coping with second generation families'.

In the development stage of a new town, the local authority was 'generally relatively small and weak', and was overshadowed by the development corporation which was the dominant authority in the town and took all the decisions of significance: 'the local authority is almost a shadow'. It was the original intention that, when the commission was appointed, it should act predominantly as the landlord holding the government's assets and that it should no longer be the dominant authority in the town. This was reflected in the powers given to the commission and indeed in the organisational structure established. When Hemel Hempstead and Crawley were transferred, there was still a considerable amount of work to be done in providing housing for immigrants and in enlarging the town centres and industrial areas. In practice, therefore, the commission (which had carried over the staff of the development corporations) continued to operate 'in much the same way' as the development corporations. The ministry thought that:

'We have not discouraged this enough. If we think of Crawley we tend to think of the commission first and not of the UDC, and outside bodies do the same. The commission believe that they bear responsibility for the future welfare of the town, that they must answer to local industrialists on questions about provision of houses and future growth and that they alone are capable of providing houses on a reasonable scale.

It is essential that we should state very clearly to the commission the limitations on their functions and also make very clear to the local authorities the extent of their responsibilities and that they cannot now hide behind the commission but must stand on their own feet. It is for the local authorities to take all the decisions on the future of these towns, and the commission as the largest landowner should co-operate with them. The commission have an important function in managing their property but this must be subject to the responsibility of the local authority for managing their town.'

In April 1964, MHLG wrote to the commission stressing that Crawley and Hemel Hempstead 'should become more normal' and should no longer be treated as 'new towns'. The local authorities of the two towns should be made to accept their proper responsibilities and the commission should withdraw into the background leaving the local authorities to take the initiative in local affairs. The commission's function was to act as the landlord of a large part of the property in the town and 'although they are expected to act as enlightened landlords, they must be extremely careful not to usurp in any way, or to appear to usurp, the responsibility of the local authorities'. MHLG would not pay subsidy on any further houses in Crawley 'unless, exceptionally, there is a strong case for limited building for old people coming from London'. At Hemel Hempstead, building of subsidised houses by the commission should be run down.

The commission could build for disposal by sale or for leasing at economic rents. If there were need for further subsidised houses for new workers or for second generation families, it would in the future be for the local authority to make its case for them on the same basis as other local authorities. In practice, in view of the very large number of existing subsidised houses, it would be difficult for the local authorities to show need for many more in addition to those that were available for reletting out of the large existing stock.

In May 1964, it was noted that the commission 'had apparently accepted' most of these points, but they were now arguing on only one point of substance—the role of the commission in the context of *The South East Study*. This had suggested that there was some scope for further expansion at Crawley and Hemel Hempstead, and the commission wanted to be responsible for undertaking the additional growth necessary. MHLG thought this was 'largely academic': the scale of further growth envisaged was likely to be achieved without any positive steps to encourage development. It would probably be enough for the local planning authority to allocate land and 'let private enterprise carry on'.

But if positive development were required, so long as there was a development corporation operating in a new town the local authority was inevitably pushed into the background: the development corporation held the initiative in all substantial matters. When the development corporation was wound up, the local authority would begin 'to come into its own'. If the commission were to undertake the development as they proposed, they would be acting as a development corporation (without, incidentally, having the compulsory powers that were necessary) and would inevitably incur the strongest opposition from the local authorities.

In any case, it was felt that the commission were not 'an ideal body' to carry out this operation. The staff of the pre-existing development corporations had been run down; the headquarters of the commission was organised for estate management and not for development, and they would certainly have to recruit further staff, particularly planning and architectural staff, if they were to undertake a major development role.

In June 1964, the secretary met the commission, and noted that they were 'of course bored and frustrated that expansion of their work seemed to be indefinitely postponed'. They were told that Welwyn and Hatfield would be transferred to them in April 1965 'unless political difficulties prevented this'. But 'they had to face the fact that nothing else was in sight'. The commission were upset by the phrases in the MHLG letter that they 'should withdraw into the background' and that they 'do not have primary responsibility for living conditions in the two towns'. As landlord of the greater part of the property in the towns they did not think they can or should 'withdraw into the background' and they felt that they must carry a major responsibility for living conditions.

It was conceded that from their point of view these phrases 'were not entirely happy', but it was important 'to get the local authorities to feel the responsibility normal to authorities of their size'. This they would never do (particularly in the case of Crawley UDC) unless it was emphasised to them that this was expected of them. As regards housing, the secretary was 'firm that we could not agree to their doing any more subsidised housing for general purposes (subject to what remains to be done in Hemel)'. Indeed she was doubtful whether the local authorities 'ought to do any either':

> 'There must be more than enough subsidised houses in both towns, even accepting that they are very much "working class" towns. I thought that they should concentrate effort on houses for owner occupation—or go out for a housing association, perhaps to build for co-operative ownership.'

She did, however, agree that MHLG might consider whether they should not be allowed to carry on with some old people's housing (subsidised) where they had the land for it—if the local authorities agreed that they would like them to do so. 'Certainly if they can bring old people out of London, possibly also if they can clear family houses by rehousing, in smaller units, people whose children have grown up, this seemed a proper completion of what the corporations had left undone.' But there could be difficulty on subsidy. The matter would be explored with the Treasury.

Finally, on their suggestion that they should have some role in implementing *The South East Study*, the secretary said that this was impracticable. 'We couldn't put them in to build a new town or carry out a major expansion.' The commission suggested that they might undertake a series of minor expansions (for which MHLG envisaged no special machinery). On this the secretary minuted:

> 'I was fairly discouraging: but said that anyway machinery was still not settled and that we would of course keep them in mind. (I didn't want to be too flat-footed; but of course I don't see a role for them in development work. Whether they might have a role in acquisition is another question.)'

THE FUTURE OF THE COMMISSION

After the change of government in 1964, Welwyn and Hatfield were transferred to the commission but, in answer to questions in the Commons, the minister stated that he was opposed to the continuation of this type of ownership:

> 'The present commission is from our point of view a temporary form of government which we do not approve of and which we want to replace by a more democratic form in which the local authorities would play a far more direct and important role.'*

However, statements concerning transfer of houses to local authorities were restricted to the transfer of management. The parliamentary secretary said in October 1966:

> 'What is already abundantly clear is that local authorities who are, after all, the statutory housing authorities, should eventually become responsible for managing all publicly owned housing. When a new town has been fully developed, there should be only one housing list and one housing policy.'†

---

* HC Debates, Vol 720, Col 910, 16 November 1965.
† HC Debates, Vol 734, Col 1585, 28 October 1966.

It was solely in relation to the new wave of new towns, the 'partnership' towns, that the minister promised that *ownership* (as distinct from mere management) of assets should be transferred:

> 'When the job is finished and the corporation bows out, I envisage the acquisition by the town council of the land and assets created on terms to be agreed between them and the corporation. But the timing of this must depend on the government securing a fair return for its investment.'

In 1966 the Labour Party Manifesto *Time for Decision* again promised 'real democratic self-government' and 'the abolition of the New Towns Commission' but gave no more positive indication of what form of ownership would replace the commission. This gave rise to complaints by the commission of the uncertainty and the effect on their staff. They felt that the charges that the commission was undemocratic took 'no account of the arrangements made for delegating certain functions to the local committees and for decentralising the day-to-day work in the towns'.

Crossman was dissatisfied with the situation, but felt that further investigation was needed before a decision was taken about the ultimate ownership. In a speech at Redditch (20 August 1965) he elaborated this theme:

> 'I am particularly anxious that in this respect we should learn from the mistakes of the last twenty years and I want to ensure that in future we take as much trouble about the social and administrative problems of the new towns as we have about the planning and architectural problems.
>
> Should housing ownership and management—at present almost a corporation monopoly in most new town corporations—be turned into a municipal monopoly? Or should we try to evolve new forms of decentralised housing ownership and management to fit our new communities? These are questions which have been far too little considered either by the planners or by the politicians.'

It was to help fill this need that a study was commissioned:

> 'to examine the present pattern of ownership of housing in new towns and of all those factors, physical, economic, social, administrative and legal which may be relevant to, or may condition, ownership and management in the future'.*

The report of this study was published in 1968,† but no action was taken before the change of government in 1970.

Research Organisation 1947–50‡

> 'It is, we think, clear that, with a number of independent agencies, even if all of precisely the same constitutional type autonomous within the wide limits

---

* On this see chapter VII, p. 438 *et seq.*
† *The Ownership and Management of Housing in the New Towns*, HMSO, 1968.
‡ MHLG Files in the 91650/68 series.

of their constitutions and subject to ministerial direction in matters of major policy only, some instrument for harmonising policy and practice and also for pooling information and experience will be not only desirable but essential.'*

So stated the Reith Committee. Such an 'instrument' could not, in their view, be provided either by government departments or by a standing conference of the chairmen of the new town development corporations. What was needed was a central advisory commission.

No action was taken on this recommendation but, as soon as the first development corporations were established, a standing ministerial conference was set up.† Among its first actions was the appointment of a subcommittee 'to consider and evaluate, for the purpose of new towns, the factors that go to make up a balanced community for work and living, and to recommend how such a balance should be achieved'. Mrs Felton‡ was appointed chairman.

Mrs Felton, however, very soon urged that the issue demanded 'the expert study of a full time detailed sociological inquiry'. The subcommittee were inclined to agree, but asked her to prepare 'a statement of the problems requiring examination', if necessary with the assistance of 'someone else to be chosen after consultation with the ministry'. It was recognised that 'it would probably be appropriate to pay a fee to such a person for the work involved in preparing the initial statement'. Mrs Felton contacted the London School of Economics and, in May 1947, a meeting took place with officers of MTCP, Mrs Felton and Professor T. H. Marshall.

The first question was 'who was to pay?' MTCP readily accepted that this was 'essentially a research job for which this ministry should take responsibility and pay'. But immediately a further issue arose which was to become a familiar one throughout the period covered by this history: the inquiry was concerned with matters which were not limited 'to the interests of the four new towns: it was a general problem which applied as nearly as much to the expansion of existing towns'. This was agreed, but it was not so easy to determine how the research should be tackled. The secretary admitted: 'frankly, I don't quite know how to get this matter started'. He asked whether MTCP should:

'go to one body like the LSE and ask them to take general charge or whether we ought to collect the steering committee from representatives of a number of universities or schools. Where do we look for the whole time director and what sort of man should he be? Do we aim at an arrangement under which by virtue of our putting up the money we have a large say in the lines of

---

* *Final Report of the New Towns Committee*, Cmd 6876, paragraph 283.
† See above p. 297.
‡ Mrs Monica Felton had been a member of the Reith Committee and, in 1948, was appointed chairman of Peterlee Development Corporation; she later became chairman of Stevenage Development Corporation.

inquiry but subject to that leave those undertaking it a pretty free hand and also the right to publish their results? Or do we ask for an inquiry which is in effect a report to us which we can either publish or keep for our own use?'

In June 1947 the secretary reported that Mrs Felton and he had discussed with Professor Marshall the machinery which would be appropriate for an investigation of the type required. It was contemplated that such an investigation should include extensions of existing towns as well as new towns and should accordingly be undertaken and paid for by the ministry. It should be controlled by a steering committee which might include both academic members and representatives of interested government departments and of the new town corporations. A full time research worker would be responsible to the steering committee, and would have a number of field investigators to assist him. Though the full investigation might take as much as two years, some preliminary guidance should be available after about six months.

It was decided to adopt this suggestion in principle, and to discuss more considered proposals at a later date. It was agreed that, in the circumstances and in view of the wider inquiry now contemplated, there was no useful purpose in establishing the committee originally proposed and that the corporations should be so informed, but that some machinery should be devised for keeping corporations fully and constantly informed of the progress of the inquiry. In addition, the scope of the proposed report should come before the standing ministerial conference before a start was made with the work.

Another issue which proved to be one of long standing was raised in a subsequent minute to the secretary: in discussion with the chairman of the general managers' committee it was agreed that, where the planning division, the research division or, indeed, any other division of MTCP undertook a substantial piece of research or the preparation of any general memorandum which was likely to be relevant to the work of the corporations and helpful to them in formulating their policy, 'we should first secure that the corporations are informed that such research is being undertaken, or such a memorandum prepared and, secondly, let them have the fruits of our labours once they are gathered'. It was also agreed that this should be 'a two way traffic'.

At this time the pace was set by Crawley development corporation and, in February 1948, they sent a paper to MTCP and the other three new towns. This raised a host of questions:

Population and Household Structure : what policy should be followed for land use as regards the ratio between area and population, and how could the principles on which policy should be based best be ascertained?

Employment and Industrial Structure : what economic structure would give the

350

fullest employment with scope for individual choice and opportunity? What was the distribution of the different age and sex groups in the various types of employment?

Social Facilities and Organisation : what social services should be provided and how should they be grouped in relation to each other? These would be such services as schools, hospitals, clinics, welfare centres, churches, halls, meeting places, libraries, public houses, restaurants, theatres, cinemas, playing fields and parks.

Economic Services : what economic services should be included, such as banks, insurance companies, hotels, laundries and shops; and what criteria should be established for assessing the extent to which provision should be made for these organisations?

It was quickly appreciated that there were two aspects to questions of this nature. First, there were general matters on which wide-ranging research was needed; but, equally important, there was the need 'to work out the application' of general research findings to the particular circumstances of individual new towns. It was less easy to establish appropriate machinery for this purpose. Within the ministry, it was suggested that 'a special research section' should be set up 'to collect and disseminate answers to the sort of questions' set out in the Crawley paper. On the other hand, Crawley argued that they 'must themselves appoint a small staff to tackle these questions as a matter of urgency'.

At a meeting of the standing ministerial conference in April 1948, Silkin argued that the necessary research into subjects of a general character should be undertaken on behalf of all corporations and that the most appropriate agency to do this would be the ministry. This arrangement would avoid duplication of work at a time when research workers with the necessary qualifications were very scarce. The ministry would work in close co-operation with the corporations, so as to avoid any overlapping in research activities. It was urgent that the problem should be tackled in the immediate future, and that some agreement should be reached on the nature of the task and the dividing line between general problems and those which were particular to each individual town. He thought that a committee should be established for directing the necessary research.

Despite some reservations (for example from Crawley who maintained that they needed to undertake some field work immediately) Silkin's proposals were agreed. A research worker was appointed and, in May 1948, the conference agreed to set up an 'exploratory committee' which would 'survey the subject and make recommendations for future work before any further steps were taken'.

Internally, MTCP officials foresaw problems: one minute noted that 'the possibilities of trouble are fairly considerable'. An 'exploratory committee' would help, since its report would have to be accepted by the standing ministerial conference 'before anything can be put into operation, but even there we want to avoid friction and delays that would result from the submission of an unacceptable report. If we are to guide the exploratory committee away from lines of thought that would be likely to result in trouble (or, if need be, to smother trouble after it has started) we must have a representative who is (a) tough, (b) fairly senior'. The official suggested for this role protested 'I am not tough', and the upshot was that the writer of the minute became the representative.

In a draft report, the committee outlined a programme of research and suggested that the first stage should be the preparation of preliminary bibliographies and papers. They also commented that:

> 'A great deal of the information which corporations need is already available or is continually becoming available. The ministry has an admirable library, which either has much of this material among its own stocks or can obtain it from other allied sources. We understand that the library is available to the staffs of corporations and that, in addition, arrangements have been made for one member of each corporation to borrow publications from the library. We are, however, impressed with the need for some automatic machinery for disseminating this information, or at least the knowledge that it exists to corporations, who might otherwise work in ignorance of it.'

At the same time, the information which corporations needed was often somewhat scattered and, 'in the interests of completeness, it was necessary on occasions to seek it out'. If this were to be done, some machinery would have to be created, or some existing body charged with this task. It was accordingly recommended that a permanent committee should be set up consisting of representatives of corporations. Corporations should make a return of all research work on which they embarked, stating in the return the subject matter of the work and a brief description of its scope. These returns would be deposited with the ministry, who would inform all corporations periodically of all the returns made. The ministry library should thereafter be prepared on request to lend or issue to corporations, according to the circumstances, any of the papers prepared as a result of such work. The permanent committee would review research projects proposed by corporations and co-ordinate them.

Following the circulation of this draft, the chairman (J. E. MacColl) wrote a paper in which he suggested that there were a number of 'general questions of principle affecting the organisation of research' which the committee would need to consider before finalising their report:

> 'There are difficulties in the way of a government department carrying out research of its own. In the first place, most subjects for research are the concern of more than one department. In our field obvious examples are the design of housing which is of interest to both the Ministry of Town and Country Planning and the Ministry of Health, and the location of industry

which concerns both the Ministry of Town and Country Planning and the Board of Trade. There is a danger of reduplication of work and it may not always be easy for one department to get access to material possessed by another. In the second place, it is important in a field as ill-defined and as controversial as that of the social sciences, that the inferences and conclusions drawn should be accepted as objective. Departmental work is liable to be regarded with some suspicion, both because it may be thought to be influenced by policy considerations and because other departments may feel they are the proper experts in a particular subject.

There is therefore much to be said for avoiding a very elaborate research organisation in the ministry and for getting as much as possible done by independent bodies like the universities.

This committee is made up of representatives of the new towns corporations and its attention has, therefore, most properly been directed to the special needs of new towns. But much of the work which is to be done will be of wider interest to other departments and also, within the department, to those responsible for other types of development. Though it is perhaps not for this committee to say so, the research unit should not become obsessed with new towns to the neglect of other development, and its work should be presented in such a way that it can be used by all.

The function of the department's research unit must influence the kind of supervisory committee established. There are, it seems to me, two pre-eminent requirements this body should fulfil. It should be in very close touch with the day to day difficulties facing new development if the right problems are to be identified and the right priorities settled. It should not be, or, as importantly, be suspected of being a co-ordinating authority whose endorsement of research papers could be construed into a declaration of policy. These considerations make me doubt whether a committee representative of the boards of corporations is the most appropriate body to act as the kind of working party that is needed.'

At a more earthly level, a MTCP official minuted that 'it was never intended to make the library available for the use of all the staffs of all the corporations'. Moreover, the bibliographies referred to in the committee's draft report related to 'papers now in the hands of various government departments'. Since these papers were not to be published, the issue of a bibliography to new town corporations 'would not help members to get any information'. If, on the other hand, 'we keep only to non-confidential documents, a bibliography would be exceedingly meagre'.

A comment was also made on MacColl's paper who, it was suggested, was labouring under a misapprehension:

'The very fact that the information is in the possession of government departments means that only another government department can have access to it and that a university or similar body cannot. That is the reason why some of this research is being undertaken within the department. A second misapprehension arises from the very nature of the work suggested. We are concerned with collecting available facts, not with enunciating policy. We are not even contemplating doing detailed research work in the proper sense, ie original collection of information.

Within these limits I am quite confident that we can do our job without

353

overlap and in a much more direct and workmanlike manner than if it were farmed out to several universities. I hope we shall persuade Mr MacColl accordingly.'

Further notes on the draft report and the chairman's note were prepared by the research officer who stressed that the term 'research' was misleading since much of the work would consist chiefly of the collation and analysis of existing material. Though relevant material was scanty in some fields, in others the problem was that it was not readily accessible. As a result, there had been few attempts at synthesis.

'As most of the available material exists within the ministry or in other government departments, a small group within the ministry appears to be the most appropriate agency for the work of collation. Though, to quote the chairman, "it may not always be easy for one department to get access to material possessed by another", it is certainly easier for a government department to obtain such information than for an outside agency. As far as can be seen, the ministry already has access to the necessary information and is aware of the work being done in other government departments.

Original research, however, as distinct from collation, could be more suitably carried out by outside agencies. Therefore, the possibility of obtaining the co-operation of universities and other independent agencies is now being explored.'

The setting up of an elaborate research organisation within the ministry had not been contemplated. Only a small group was required to carry out the current programme. If, however, the new towns required the investigation of additional subjects from time to time, the staff position would have to be reviewed again. It would be the object of this work to provide the new towns with information on their specific problems. But this could be done only with reference to the general context of planning, and such work would be applicable to other aspects of reconstruction as well. This was yet another reason for suggesting that a good deal of this work should be carried out within the ministry, so that the experience and work of all the different sections could be fully utilised. Papers containing such objective information would not represent policy, nor could they fulfil their function if their preparation were influenced by policy.

Following discussion of these and other papers, the exploratory committee redrafted their report. Their recommendations included: that the collation and analysis of existing material—and some original research—should be undertaken by the research staff of MTCP (but that other work 'would be most advantageously done by independent bodies'); that the ministry's research staff should be increased; that 'a clearing house of information' should be established 'of which the ministry's library would be the pivotal point'; and that a permanent committee should be set up 'to co-ordinate research work relating to new towns'.

Appended to the report of the exploratory committee was a paper by the department's research officer outlining a programme of research to be undertaken centrally either by or on behalf of the ministry. This underlined the fact that much relevant information on some issues was already available either in published form or, more commonly, in departmental reports, files and statistics. The starting point of the research programme should be the analysis of this material interpreted with particular reference to the problems of new towns. A skilled research staff was necessary for this purpose: it was far more than a bibliographical exercise.

Some important issues, however, required original research—such as population and household structure, and the neighbourhood pattern. These might best be dealt with by universities, though the ministry would have to co-ordinate the work and ensure that it fitted into the general research programme.

It was shrewdly pointed out that research could not provide authoritative statements: 'the more the problems are analysed, the more evident it becomes that new town planning has to be based on a series of conjectures, all of which have to be fitted together in a highly complex jig-saw puzzle'. This made it all the more necessary that information was collected efficiently and competently, that 'theories should be distinguished from ascertained facts', and assumptions should be clearly stated. 'A vast programme of original research might reduce the conjectural elements of the planning process', but this was impracticable and attention had to be focused on indispensable and readily available information, though gaps in knowledge (and hence the need for specific items of original research) should be identified.

All the different (but inter-related) aspects of a new town—its population and household composition, its employment structure, and its neighbourhood pattern—were dependent upon the assumptions made about its ultimate size and rate of development. This raised major questions about the determinants of urban growth in the past and their relevance to new towns. It also raised a question (which must have appeared much more academic in 1948 than it did twenty years later): 'is it likely that once the population target for each new town has been reached, the population will remain stationary, that there will be no further substantial growth through natural increase or immigration?'

The research implied by these questions included an analysis of the relationship between the size of existing towns and their functions, their employment structure, and their potentiality for growth. The population growth of the new towns would depend on a range of factors which needed investigation, such as household structure, the types of dwellings provided, and densities. Again these factors were inter-related. Household composition would affect the need for dwellings of different types and sizes, and these in turn would affect densities. At the same time, the population structure would affect the need for services and social facilities. But a basic factor would be the employment and industrial structure of the new towns: what types of industries would move to new towns, and what would be the need for service industries?

A further area of research was 'the neighbourhood pattern'. There was a considerable literature on this, but it consisted 'almost entirely of theories'. In practice, it appeared that there were few 'natural' neighbourhoods 'because people's movements in urban areas tend to be dispersed rather than concentrated in a given district'. This was inevitable as long as services were 'located haphazardly rather than sited deliberately in relation to each other'. There were many unanswered questions here—relating, for example, to 'social mix', social relationships, and the spatial distribution of services and facilities. Studies were required 'to show which tendencies exist already and which would have to be created'. At the same time, the economics of different forms of design needed investigation. Such work would help in developing detailed and realistic designs. 'The new towns cannot hope to be perfect, but they should soon become concrete examples of progress within an imperfect world.'

The report of the exploratory committee was considered by the standing ministerial conference in January 1949. Silkin pointed out that very little of the work now contemplated could influence the form of master plans shortly to be submitted for his approval, but he thought that this was 'not likely to prove fatal'. A great deal of the work was of a long term nature, and much of it would be extremely valuable in connection with general planning standards and problems and not merely in connection with new towns.

Lord Reith said that he could not endorse the recommendation to establish a permanent committee. He agreed that some co-ordinating machinery was required, but he thought that the general managers' committee was the right body to assume this function. Lord Beveridge also doubted whether a permanent committee was necessary and suggested that each corporation should individually make its own representations to the department when necessary. Silkin said that the question was mainly one of how to arrange for the work to be shared among the corporations and the department. This could be undertaken either by the department (by a committee such as was suggested in the report) or by the general managers' committee in consultation with the department. He himself was not attracted by the suggestion in the report, but he was prepared to examine the matter further.

At a later meeting, Silkin said that the method of co-ordinating future work which appeared to have most support was that the responsibility should lie in the first instance with a subcommittee of the general managers' committee.

Sir Thomas Bennett, who was supported by Mrs Felton, said that his corporation was of the opinion that during the initial period of about a year, so many matters of principle would require to be settled that it was important that members of corporations should be closely associated with the work. His corporation would have preferred a committee consisting only of members, but in order to take advantage of the knowledge and experience of certain officers who were particularly qualified to speak on such matters, they were prepared to take part in the establishment of a mixed committee.

Lord Reith mentioned that, since Sir Thomas Bennett had originally expressed a preference for research matters to be handled by members of corporations, a chairmen's conference had been constituted, and he imagined that if the main responsibility for co-ordinating research was placed upon the general managers' committee they would report to the chairmen's conference. Sir Thomas Bennett, on the other hand, though agreeing that the establishment of a chairmen's conference was a substantial if not a material factor, thought that it did not quite meet the case since there were no officers in its membership, and he thought such subjects required study 'by the best team available'. Lord Reith suggested that the chairmen's conference could, where suitable, appoint an *ad hoc* committee, and Sir Thomas Bennett agreed that this might well solve the problem.

Silkin noted that questions such as that of the neighbourhood unit would affect all town planning and not merely new towns; though he would welcome a fresh examination of many such questions, he would not want any decisions on policy to be made which might embarrass him in dealing with problems outside new towns. Lord Reith said he did not envisage that the chairmen's conference or any *ad hoc* committee appointed by them would wish to make any decisions on policy, but merely that they would settle the agenda for the study of research problems by the general managers' committee. He agreed with Silkin that when the general managers had considered any given subject, the department would have an opportunity of relating their findings to town planning in general.

It was accordingly agreed to ask the general managers' committee to establish a research subcommittee consisting of social development and other suitable officers of corporations, it being understood that the chairmen's conference would give special consideration to research matters of policy importance. Subject to this, the report was accepted as a general basis for future research. The research subcommittee was set up in April 1949.

While these organisational issues were being discussed, research proposals were being drafted and, in December 1948, the research officer produced a rough outline of a method of recording the history of new towns. A standardised record and registry system was proposed. Details should be kept of the designation of the site, membership and staffing of the corporations, internal organisation and procedures, the new town plan and any amendments, the programme of development, the movement of industry to the town and their characteristics, employment, community structure, social facilities, schools, selection of people for the new town, occupational and income structure, household characteristics, turnover, natural growth, and so forth.

A further note was prepared on 'possible variations in stages and periods of growth and their impact on the ultimate picture of a new town'. The ultimate characteristics of a new town would be influenced by the stages and the length of the building-up period and, therefore, its population, social and economic characteristics had to be discussed with reference to the actual process of growth.

If development were slow, there would be a scarcity of services and amenities in the early stages. Since these stages might be prolonged, the first groups of immigrants might not find the new town a very satisfactory place in which to live. Their environment would be similar to that of an interwar housing estate, and thus their reactions, too, might be similar to those of the early tenants on such an estate. Would they be willing to stay? And if they did so, would their attitude to the new town be affected for a long time by their early difficulties and disappointments. On the other hand, such difficulties might also have a positive effect on the growth of the 'community'. They might help to draw people together and to promote a spirit of pioneering, a sense of a joint responsibility for the building of the new town. But even this attitude might wane if visible signs of success were long delayed.

Reliable answers to questions of this type could not be found, even through detailed studies of the social history and the relationships in existing communities—garden cities and housing estates—which had recently grown up. Nevertheless, studies of this type would help to give a clearer picture of all the intricate problems associated with the social development of new towns. They would illustrate both the advantages and disadvantages of slow or rapid growth. Some of these could already be observed through the experience of the new towns to date. It was evident that if their growth were rapid, it would be far easier not only to formulate, but also to adhere to, definite planning principles than if their growth were slow. Some of the specific and cumulative practical difficulties of a long building-up period would be avoided. But, of course, the responsibility of the planners and administrators were far greater if the town was built quickly, for then they could not count on being able to learn from, and to correct, mistakes.

At a meeting (in December 1949) of social development officers, the research work of the various new towns was discussed. Crawley reported on progress with a report on the size, age and sex structure of the population of the designated area (and referred to a report on communal laundries which was not yet ready for circulation). Hemel Hempstead referred to a forthcoming paper on 'small meeting places'; Harlow to a report on house sizes and types.

The ministry's research officer introduced a paper reviewing the work of the new towns research section. This stressed that, owing to considerable turnover of staff, the section had scarcely ever possessed its full complement of officers. Currently, the staff comprised two assistant research officers, a senior technical assistant, three research assistants and one clerical officer. In addition to the work carried out by the new town research section for the new towns, other sections of the ministry also had to be supplied with information.

The exploratory committee had envisaged a clear division between the work of the new towns research section, which would concentrate on general issues, and the work of new towns' research officers, who would deal with local matters and the application of general research. Experience during the past year had shown that this division of work could not be rigidly maintained; corporations from time to time needed to explore general issues whilst, on the other hand, the new towns research section needed local information in order to assess the problems being faced by the new towns. The subcommittee decided to report to the general managers' committee that 'without ignoring the need for some long term research', priority should be given to a limited number of subjects 'which experience has shown to be of immediate practical importance'. These were:

(a) The sociological aspects of density problems and standards.
(b) A study of the economic factors relating to the number of shops of different types and sizes to be provided at neighbourhood centres and the town centre.
(c) A study of the problems of population growth and the concurrent requirements of industry (both service and manufacturing), education etc.

The general managers, however, expressed grave doubts about the value of the work:

'It has become apparent that practically all the subjects of immediate practical interest to corporations in their social development programmes carry with them policy implications of fundamental importance which it is unfair to expect social development officers to interpret in their relationship with the new towns research section. The timing of the disclosure of policy decisions may also be important.'

The functions of the subcommittee were therefore curtailed and its name changed to that of the 'social research co-ordination sub-committee'. At the same time corporations were allowed to nominate 'those officers whom they consider best qualified to deal with the subjects under discussion'.

The ministry were none too happy about this though they had to accept that the matter was one for corporations to decide. There was 'some history behind all this' and clearly there were tensions between the various corporations which could not be resolved at the level of social development officers. Moreover, not all the corporations had social development officers. One MTCP official commented that he did not think 'that the new arrangement will be a good one . . . [it] may result in merely another advisory committee advising somebody to advise somebody else and so on'. The final result would probably be that the MTCP research workers would 'have to supply the information'. However, there was nothing MTCP could do about the matter and it was felt that they should 'let it run and see how it works'.

A review of research on new towns, written by MTCP in August 1950, outlined 'the principal defects of the present situation'. First, a great deal of work produced 'was not research in any real sense', but purely a synopsis of existing accessible works on particular subjects. Such of this work as was necessary and of use was usually best done centrally. Secondly, there was too much work of a general kind undertaken by new towns which was properly the concern of a central department. The resultant work was often of such a standard that it was of little real use. At the same time much vital local work seemed to be disregarded. Thirdly, there was too little information on what occurred to work once it had been initiated. 108 items had been notified as having started, many of them more than one year ago, but only 65 had been completed. Of these 65 papers only 28 had been circulated. Fourthly, there was too little co-operation between new towns and the department and between new towns themselves. This was reflected in the number of subjects simultaneously studied by new towns at any time, or sometimes following each other. The resultant papers were of little value and were remarkably similar. Much time and effort was thereby wasted. Finally, too many subjects were being studied which were either inappropriate or were being studied out of their proper time, while simultaneously much local and vital work remained undone.

A detailed analysis of subjects chosen showed that there was 'a tendency among some new towns to spend a great deal of their time on items which are either of little value or upon subjects which are

hardly relevant at this time as, for example, is seen in the preoccupation with the subject of old people or in the detailed examination of a subject such as burial facilities'.

The social research co-ordination committee of the general
managers' committee began to function in September 1950. It had
much the same terms of reference as the previous social development
officers' subcommittee. An internal MTCP minute noted:

> 'It must, however, be regarded as a low powered body, few of the members
> having any qualifications for research. Apparently, it does little in the way of
> real co-ordination. Corporations undertake such pieces of research as they
> feel required for their own needs, and the committee does little more than to
> make itself aware of what is being done and exchange information on
> technique. It seems that no substantial work of general value is being carried
> out. Corporation research consists of local fact finding jobs and the local
> application of the general results embodied in ministerial research papers.'

An official of MTCP attended the monthly meetings 'by tacit
rather than express invitation'. There was clearly a lack of co-
operation. The committee were fully informed of what the ministry
was doing, 'but apart from what he picks up in the meetings, he is not
made aware of what the committee or corporations are doing'. The
assistance of the ministry was not sought, and they did not even
receive copies of the minutes of the proceedings of the committee.

Within this climate of opinion, the future of new towns research
became increasingly problematic, and the subcommittee itself faded
out of existence during 1951. The ministry's new town research
section 'ceased to function' towards the end of 1950.

During its short existence, the research section had embarked on
an ambitious programme, involving investigation of size and growth
of towns; populations, households and dwellings; employment and
industrial structure; and the neighbourhood pattern. A number of
memoranda on particular aspects were produced and circulated but,
partly owing to personal and staff difficulties, and partly to the day
to day demands for information about individual towns, progress
was slow and erratic. The section was unable to secure the confidence
of the general managers who resented a tendency for questions to be
put to their staffs without their knowledge, and who in their anxiety
to make progress felt unable to wait for the results of research into
aspects where concrete experience was then lacking, or where
available might be long delayed. In the prevailing atmosphere of
suspicion, and after some incidents where it was felt that reports had
been misleading, the section was wound up at the end of 1950 'as a
means of economy', and certain of the outstanding work transferred
to the ministry's social and economic research section, which had a
wider remit.

With hindsight this was most unfortunate—as was widely

appreciated in the early sixties when a second generation of new towns was conceived, and when the ministry were criticised for 'the lack of a consolidated body of research experience'. But there was justification for the department's coyness which is well illustrated by the *cause celebre* of the Welwyn research saga. It is worth discussing this at length.

The Welwyn Research Saga*

The report prepared by a ministry research officer on Welwyn Garden City was not of any special intrinsic importance, but it has a significant position in the history of new town research. It became a focal point for opposition to ministry research. Moreover, in the folk-lore of the department, it became the 'reason' for the virtual abandonment of research at the beginning of the 'fifties. Certainly, it figured largely in many discussions on the development of new town research. It reinforced doubts about (or at least provided what was considered a sufficient reason for objecting to) the role of the central department in research. At the same time, it made the central department extremely cautious about developing a research capability. It also aroused fierce passions and resulted in exchanges between ministry and new town officials of a very unusual character. The conventions of administrative dialogue were abandoned in favour of an acrimonious duel which, though laced with humour, was deadly serious. It was many years before this was forgotten.

The initial intention was sensible, simple and apparently innocuous. A large scale programme of government-sponsored new towns was to be implemented: surely it was appropriate to investigate what lessons could be learned from the practical example of Ebenezer Howard's philosophy? Perhaps: but the first paragraph of the report sounded a note of caution:

> 'For all those concerned with planning, the history of Welwyn Garden City has not only intrinsic interest, but also appears to be specially relevant to the planning of new towns. However, although the development of the second Garden City illustrates many of the problems which especially the London new towns have to face, it does not provide a ready made recipe for their solution. The social and economic conditions, the ideas and the forms of organisation of a particular period are reflected in Welwyn's growth, and these cannot be entirely disentangled from any of the general features which might be present in the planning of new communities.'

Welwyn had a number of special features: its history reflected the changing economic fortunes of the nineteen-thirties and of the war and postwar years. It was developed, not by a statutory body but by private enterprise, and 'thus resources were limited'. As a result of

* MTCP Files 91650/68/6 and 91650/68/1.

these 'two distinguishing features', it developed slowly. When the company was formed in 1920, it was the intention to create a garden city of 40,000 to 50,000 people, but by 1948 Welwyn had a population of only about 18,000. Although this was 'a warning to those now responsible for the London new towns', it had to be remembered that Welwyn had to contend with the many unfavourable conditions of the interwar years. In particular, the great depression of the early thirties broke just as the town's industrial development was getting under way.

When Welwyn was started, the term 'self-contained and balanced community' had an even less definite meaning than it had in 1950. The objective was 'to plan a town with industries, a commercial centre, and houses for all classes of the community'. Thus Welwyn was intended to be self-contained in the sense that it had an economic and social life of its own, and balanced in the sense of having a varied social structure.

It was soon realised, however, that 'the only practicable way to start the town' was to build houses first. 'To wait for manufacturers to build factories on an empty site, and then to erect cottages and houses for the employees of the factories, would have meant waiting in vain.' The report commented that this policy itself need not have prevented 'an eventual co-ordination, and a variety of industry and population'; but two facts made this impossible. First, a large proportion of houses were built for middle class people, and secondly, the industries which settled in the town were chiefly dependent upon manual labour, 'and apparently upon a high proportion of semi-skilled and unskilled labour'. Moreover, at various stages, the company changed its policy of timing housing and factory construction. In the early period, its chief concern was the provision of utilities and homes, 'and no definite effort of co-ordinating population and employment growth appears to have been made'. Until about 1930, housing was in advance of industrial development, but in the next decade the opposite was the case: by 1939 there were more jobs than resident workers in the town—even counting those who worked elsewhere.

'But the surplus of jobs was less serious than the fact that there were not the right kinds of jobs for the people living in the town. At all stages, a high proportion of the houses were far too costly—either in terms of rent or purchase price—for wage-earners and were taken by—and indeed intended for—people working elsewhere, usually London. Only just over a third of all Welwyn's houses in 1948 were rented from the local authority, two fifths were rented from the company and most of these were too expensive for working class people. The same was true of all the remaining houses which were privately owned. Because the general shortage of local labour in the later stages was accentuated by the special shortage of local manual labour, there was not only a considerable volume of daily journeys to work, but also a curious pattern of daily criss-cross travel: an efflux of the better off, and an influx of the poorer workers.'

Thus a lack of balance was caused by two factors: 'the structure of population and that of employment were not matched, nor was the timing of housing and factory construction co-ordinated'. It followed that 'definite lessons for programmes of development' could not be deduced from the Welwyn experience. There was, for instance, no evidence that population and employment could not ultimately be brought together if in the early stages housing preceded industrial building.

The report discussed issues such as this at length but finally concluded that there was little that could be learned from the Welwyn experience:

'A good deal has been written about Welwyn Garden City, but all of it, including the present paper, is bound to be inadequate because essential information is lacking. Although Welwyn was intended to be a vital social experiment which should influence policy, its experience was not systematically observed and recorded, and thus its purpose of providing principles for future planning was not fulfilled. Indeed the intention not to repeat this failure is the only definite lesson which the contemporary new towns can now derive from its history.'

The copy of this report on the ministry's file has a handwritten addition: 'RIP'. But it was not to be so. Captain R. L. Reiss (formerly of Welwyn Garden City and now deputy chairman of the development corporation) expostulated in no uncertain terms. After a detailed (though by no means relevant) critique of the report, he concluded that it was inaccurate and misleading. At this clinical level matters might have rested had he not gone on to state categorically:

'To be of value, a research such as this must be conducted by people who:
(a) Are competent to perform the job.
(b) Go to the right sources for information, checking the one with the other.
(c) Are accurate in their figures and in their use of them.
(d) Form the correct deductions from the facts they ascertain, checking these with responsible people.

In all these respects, those responsible for this research have failed, as a result of which government money has been wasted and the preparation of these comments rendered necessary.'

Reiss was not alone in his attack. Eccles (the former manager of the Welwyn Garden City Company) wrote to the ministry:

'I think this report one of the most laughably silly and painfully misguided documents it has ever been my doubtful privilege to read.

I cannot possibly embark on a reasoned criticism of the presentation of the facts, and of the opinions of the writer—life is too short—but if this is the kind of waste of money going on in the Ministry of Town and Country

Planning, involving the employment of ignorant people who appear to be hopelessly misguided in their approach (this coming on top of another queer and even absurd document from the ministry about the town plan) it makes me wonder, with, I think, some justification, what on earth goes on in the ministry.'

He concluded that 'perhaps the best thing is to laugh heartily and forget about it'.

A frenzied correspondence ensued. MTCP tried to keep the temperature down to a moderate level:

'The writing of your letter has evidently given you a lot of fun and I hope it has eased your mind! I have searched through it and also the copy of your letter to Reiss but I can find nothing in your destructive comments to give me a clue to what it is you particularly object to in the report.

I can well understand that you have no particular love for the ministry, but if you can really find some points in the report which you feel are misconceived or inaccurate, why not come in and have lunch with Rutland and myself, and discuss them? You will be very welcome. You will find me in a perfectly amiable frame of mind, but you really can't write silly letters of this sort and then expect to "laugh heartily and to forget about it".'

The matter became even more significant when Reiss circulated his critical notes, not only to MTCP, but also to the other new towns. The ministry commented:

'Mr Reiss makes unfounded accusations against the research staff of the ministry, suggesting that they are incompetent, have got their information from wrong sources, are inaccurate, and have made wrong deductions. I entirely reject these allegations which are not borne out by the comments which Mr Reiss has made. Unfortunately, he has seen fit to give them wide circulation and some counter-action ought to be taken to correct the bad impression which is created by the inaccuracies of his allegations.

Mr Reiss starts his comments by saying that they are his own, and not those of the corporation, which is all the more surprising that, as an individual, he should circulate to all the new town corporations, presumably without the authority of his corporation. He goes on to say that although he was an original director of the Garden City Company, no one asked him for any information. The technical officers behaved in a perfectly proper manner and sought their information from the company's offices, through Mr Eccles, who was the general manager. At first, Mr Eccles was reluctant to produce any information, but I wrote to him a personal letter, after which he did co-operate with us. Mr Page of his office was, at all times, most helpful. If his officers did not inform Mr Reiss, that is nothing to do with the ministry. The fact is that he knew perfectly well that these inquiries were being made, and had he been so minded, could have produced or refused information which his officers gave us. By implication, he suggests that he has sources of information which the company could not apparently give us: if so, we should be glad to know what they are.'

A detailed commentary followed on the specific points raised by Reiss, and the matter was passed up to the secretary. By this time (December 1950) the research section had 'ceased to function', but the secretary commented that 'the point . . . that does strike me forcibly is that, in my opinion, it was extraordinarily bone-headed to have carried out this detailed investigation in the town without ever going near Captain Reiss. After all, he had been intimately connected with Welwyn Garden City for many years and it seems to me quite immaterial that he is now on the corporation. I am not surprised that he is offended'.

A senior MTCP official remonstrated:

'The point is that Welwyn New Town Corporation asked us to prepare a paper on the economic history of Welwyn Garden City, which we did. Mr Reiss is now making unjust accusations against your staff, and unfortunately, instead of following what I should have thought was the normal course of coming to you, or even to me, he has seen fit to broadcast his comments on the paper to the parliamentary secretary, all the other development corporations, and to the chairmen's conference. I feel bound to ask you to defend the staff from this sort of thing.'

There the matter seemed to end (at least to judge from the documents preserved in the files). But the repercussions were felt for over a decade. Research had clearly been shown to be a dangerous matter which was more likely to give rise to embarrassment and indeed acrimony than to produce useful guidelines for policy.*

The Resumption of Research on New Towns†

It was not until the early sixties, when the second generation of new towns was emerging, that the question of a new towns research programme was raised again. In response to a suggestion that research might provide the new corporations with some of 'the distilled wisdom' of fifteen years' experience of the building of new towns, internal minutes referred to the earlier history. It was noted that the department's research unit had completed part of its programme early in 1950, but had clearly failed to get the support or confidence of the corporations. This might have been 'partly due to

---

* In February 1951 another issue arose which, at first sight, seemed parallel to the Welwyn drama. The chairman of the general managers' committee wrote to the department about a journey-to-work survey in Basildon being undertaken by the social and economic research section (which had taken over the work of the new towns research section). It appeared (to the general managers) that this task was being undertaken without the knowledge of the Basildon corporation or its general manager.

Within the ministry it was noted that the research in question had been undertaken in agreement with the architectural staff at Basildon. There was no need to refer to 'the acrimonious correspondence about the piece of Welwyn research', but there was a similarity in that there was 'much ado about nothing'. The corporation should have known about this research—had they had adequate internal communications. Any reference to the Welwyn case should be deprecated. The matter was settled peaceably—but with a final comment from Basildon that:

'This of course emphasises the need for proper co-ordination between the ministry and the various corporations and in particular the fact that it would be advisable where any research work is contemplated that the general managers, through the general managers' committee, be consulted.'

† MHLG File NT 49/1.

personalities', but even after changes of personnel, the corporations' suspicions of the research unit remained, and 'my impression from the file is that new towns division were, at best, lukewarm about their activities'. By December 1950, the research outfit had been disbanded, and it was laid down that future research projects must be sponsored by the administrative division. 'As if to put the seal on all this', there was the acrimonious correspondence about the Welwyn report. Very few research projects had been sponsored by the ministry since then. It was 'a pity' that the research team was disbanded, and 'an even greater pity' that the records which might have been kept 'are simply not there'.

As to future programmes, it would obviously 'be prudent to try to sell them in advance either at the chairmen's conference or at the general managers' committee:

> 'No doubt the right thing to do would be to write to the general managers, telling them what we are after, referring if necessary to the past history and assuring them of our co-operation, etc etc. But research there must surely be. It seems incredible that after fifteen years there should be so many basic questions about which we are still speculating—very largely in the dark.'

A draft research programme had already been discussed internally and ten issues had been identified:

1. How big should new towns be?
2. How far from their parent cities should they be sited?
3. How much land should they occupy?
4. How valid is the neighbourhood concept?
5. What sort of town centres are called for?
6. Could the existing industrial layouts be improved?
7. What had been learned about communications and traffic?
8. What kind of housing layouts do people prefer?
9. What social provision should be made, and when?
10. Are new towns really profitable as investments?

There was a great deal of discussion on this list and it was generally felt that the questions were far too broad and, in any case, constituted a very ambitious programme. Moreover, it was quickly established that few of the development corporations had maintained adequate or consistent records; and 'some were none too anxious to give the ministry access to such information as they have'. Ministry policy on natural increase had had to be based 'mainly on Crawley statistics'. The Hook plan was also based on Crawley experience, 'for want of anything else'. 'Harlow says it doesn't apply to them: whether they are right or wrong we have no means of telling.'

Recent attempts to formulate policies on three subjects—youth employment, social provision, and the development functions of the Commission for the New Towns—had had to be done hurriedly, on the basis of inadequate statistics or hurriedly collected data. It was an unsatisfactory basis for advising either ministers or corporations. For the new corporations currently being set up, MHLG ought to insist that they obtained and maintained full demographic records, 'and MHLG must be ready to advise them on this'. Some more systematic research was desirable: indeed it was essential now that more new towns were being started. It was accepted that the main object of research should be the provision of information needed for the purpose of taking policy decisions in the ministry or advising corporations. The research team would need, however, the co-operation of the development corporations and, at some stage, a paper ought to be circulated on research proposals to the general managers' committee (and possibly the chairmen's conference) inviting both their comments and their help. 'Somehow we must avoid a repetition of the rows of earlier years and step a little more carefully.'

It was agreed that research into the new towns ought to be resuscitated and that it should be widened to cover expanded towns. New towns corporations ought to be told what MHLG were doing— 'before there is any approach to them by any of the research people':

> 'Reading the old papers, it looks as if the general managers felt, with I think some reason, that the then research sections were going around asking questions of general managers without the general managers themselves knowing what was going on. We must make sure that this kind of thing does not happen again. Indeed, it might be helpful to discuss the research pro-gramme with them, for I think they might have some ideas to contribute.'

Internal discussions continued and, in July 1962, a letter was written to the general managers' committee. This itself took some time to produce since it was felt that the issue was a delicate one. One official commented that the development corporations of 1962 might possibly be less thin-skinned than Welwyn was twelve years previously, though 'it would be unwise to rely on this': 'if there are any left among them who happen to have long memories, the mere word "research" will be like "Glencoe" to a Scotsman'. Reopening this subject called for 'the touch of velvet'.

The general managers agreed to co-operate, though in somewhat guarded terms. They were willing to co-operate with the ministry's research team in making factual information available, and would authorise their staff to discuss matters freely. However, it was thought that it might take years to collect and publish the informa-tion under the various headings; the scope of the research was probably too ambitious, and it might be necessary to consider reducing the scope to those questions on which the ministry most urgently required information.

Despite fears for the extent of the research, it was suggested that the team might also care to investigate 'how to stop new towns growing', together with problems of population structure and natural expansion. It was also considered that the time might be opportune to review the New Towns Acts, particularly in regard to the relationship between development corporations and MHLG and local authorities. Finally, the hope was expressed that the information collected would be made available to all existing new towns as well as to any new ones.

In October 1962 the issue went up to deputy secretary and secretary level, and it was agreed that the time was appropriate to respond to the increasing pressure for assessing the experience of the first generation of new towns. 'The present seems not a bad moment to look at this since the first batch of towns has reached a stage of development at which it should be possible to assess the results without too much labour or crystal gazing.'

In the following month, decisions on priorities were taken. Questions relating to the cost and profitability of new towns were the first priority,* followed by those dealing with housing layouts and the neighbourhood concept. The questions of housing layouts and the neighbourhood concept had implications that went much wider than new towns, and some aspects were already under consideration in other technical branches. Close touch should be kept with other technical branches concerned. The priorities for the remaining questions should be settled at a later stage in the light of progress and needs. Every effort should be made to draw on the researches being made in other spheres—eg the universities, the various professional or social organisations, the new town corporations themselves—and to advise on suitable areas and methods of research on new towns which such bodies might wish to undertake in the future.

The story now became complicated and—for the historian—difficult to unravel. There was further correspondence with the general managers, who agreed to consult the ministry before instituting any surveys, but commented that they felt sure that they would similarly be consulted 'before the ministry start knocking at doors in new towns'. Three 'expansion studies' (of Ipswich, Peterborough and Worcester) had been set up. At the opposite extreme, detailed studies of the validity of the neighbourhood concept and of social reactions to different housing layouts were being explored. These overlapped with the consideration being given by the housing side of the ministry to family life in high density local authority schemes. At the same time, the Central Housing Advisory Committee had set in motion a review of community facilities in expanding towns.†

---

* See chapter VIII, p. 457.
† MHLG, *The First Hundred Families: A Guide to the Community Services and Facilities which should be available for the first hundred families arriving in an Expanding Town*, HMSO, 1965.

Further inquiries revealed a wide range of studies in progress or under consideration by other parts of the ministry, by the Ministry of Transport, by the War Office, by the Building Research Station, and by universities. At the same time, internal reorganisation of MHLG included the establishment of a directorate of urban development in May 1965, and a strengthening of the statistical machinery. There was also the formation of a study group with the Treasury to establish general economic criteria for assessing the merits of proposals for new town and town development schemes,* and a further enquiry by the Central Housing Advisory Committee.† Additionally, there were renewed efforts to establish a proper system of statistical records of new town populations, and a resuscitation of the proposal to establish some central organisation for the pooling of information on new towns.

New Towns Information Bureau‡

The proposal to set up a new towns information bureau was floated by Henry Wells (chairman of the Commission for the New Towns) towards the end of 1964, and a firm proposal was put to the chairmen's conference in early 1965. It was stressed that there was a 'considerable and valuable body of information and experience' which development corporations and the commission acquired in carrying out their respective functions. It would be to their mutual advantage—and particularly for the newly established corporations —if this information and experience could be made available to all corporations and the commission. This could be achieved without undue burden if, by voluntary action, they established an 'information bureau'.

The chairmen and officers of corporations and the commission attended the chairmen's conference and the meetings of its various committees, and the commission were willing to make their secretarial staff available to service these meetings and provide and accommodate all necessary secretarial and other staff to co-ordinate the activities of the bureau. Officers in towns with special knowledge could be nominated for consultation and the secretarial staff would maintain close contact with them. Such a bureau could collect, collate and disseminate information of value without the wasteful duplication of effort entailed in separate inquiries. The conference and committee could indicate, from time to time, particular topics to which the bureau should give their attention.

Initially, the bureau might be mainly concerned to assemble and analyse information of particular value to newly established develop-

---

* See chapter VIII, p. 462 *et seq.*
† *The Needs of New Communities*, HMSO, 1967.
‡ MHLG Files NT 49/1 and NT 49/18.

ment corporations. These corporations would undoubtedly welcome collated information on a number of practical problems they would meet in their early days, such as staff structure, staff rules, standing orders, tendering and contracting procedure and housing management. All corporations and the commission would no doubt benefit from information comprising the pooled experience of various development, management, industrial and commercial questions.

The proposal was debated by the chairmen and, in May 1965, they decided that a bureau should be established 'under their general direction'. The ministry, however, took exception. In the first place, certain changes in administrative machinery were likely to be introduced in some of the latest generation of new towns. 'Already large towns' such as Northampton, Ipswich, and Peterborough were to be doubled:

> 'Naturally enough, in such towns, some of which are county boroughs, there are powerful councils and well qualified professional staff. The arrangements for developing these towns are, therefore, aimed at creating a partnership between council and development corporation, at using jointly the professional skills possessed by one party or the other rather than duplicating those skills, and at creating a greater existing town rather than a new town.'

This meant that development corporations would be 'less prominent' than in the older new towns, and that the local councils might have to be considered equally with the development corporations when it came to collecting and disseminating information. In so far as local councils were concerned, therefore, activities by the commission might be slightly 'off side'.

Secondly, the department were reorganising some of their research activities. Though the proposals for a new towns information bureau specifically excluded research, research could not be undertaken without the collection of information, and the results of research could not be disseminated without the distribution of information. A much greater impetus than hitherto was to be given to research and, therefore, 'correspondingly, a much greater need than most of us have seen or admitted in the past for the collection of factual information'. Time was required to assess the outcome. Related to this was a third point. It was intended that the new towns information bureau should not handle any information already collected and collated by the department.

> 'Here again we are busy revising what we should collect and we hope soon to consult corporations on this. This operation could and should be aligned with the activities of a new towns information bureau, but perhaps there would be some advantage in completing or nearly completing our work first.'

Finally, the department intended 'to go as far as we possibly can to make known to development corporations and other interested parties, the information which we gather in the course of our normal administration'. The qualification 'as far as we possibly can' was necessary because:

> 'it has been our custom (and it is a good custom) to seek the agreement of all those who have supplied information before we publish it. The response has generally been good and I feel confident that in these enlightened days the response in the future will be even better.'

In the light of this, the general managers decided for the time being not to pursue the idea of an information bureau. The matter was, however, resuscitated by the secretary in August 1965. She thought that there were limitations on the ministry's role of disseminating information, and that the chairmen's conference and its committees would function more effectively if it had its own machinery for pooling information. She added:

> 'I think it was the GMs who killed the idea; whether because they don't think they need any information bureau or because they don't want the Commission in it. If the idea is to run at all it will have to be supported by the GMs—and they will have to say what sort of information might usefully be pooled.'

Steps were therefore taken 'to see what the temperature is', but it appeared that 'the basic difficulties remain'. It was difficult to distinguish 'information' from 'research', and the majority of chairmen had 'no enthusiasm at all for this . . . and the majority are against it'.

There the matter rested until 1968, though it is apparent that it continued to be discussed both within and outside the department. In June 1968 it was noted that 'the question of a secretariat is still a live one, with the possibility in mind of combining with it some functions on information'. It became more alive when the working party on new towns structure was established in this month. The story at this point thus merges with other wider issues to which we now turn.

The Working Party on New Towns Structure 1968–69*

At various points in the foregoing discussion reference has been made to ministerial doubts on the organisation of new towns. These included the payment of salaries to members of the development corporations, the greater use of local authorities for projects of new town character, and the idea of a single central corporation. There was also intermittent discussion of a central research unit and the future ownership of new town assets. Finally, there were the numerous investigations undertaken or prompted by the Treasury: these emanated from Treasury concern at the huge commitment

---

* MHLG File NT 49/51.

arising from the new town programme and the difficulty of controlling it. These different strands came together in 1968 when a wide ranging review of the statutory and administrative machinery was undertaken by a working party of officials from MHLG, SDD, the Treasury, the development corporations and the Commission for the New Towns.

This 'working party on new towns structure' reported in May 1969, and in this section a summary is given of those parts of the report which relate to issues raised elsewhere in this history.

The report began by pointing out that the statutory and administrative arrangements for the development of new towns were conceived in circumstances very different from those now existing. The need foreseen in the 1940s (when it was envisaged that the national population would remain relatively steady) was for the development of towns of finite size with total populations of 50,000 to 60,000. Generally, they were conceived as satellites to major cities whose congestion they would help to relieve. Such towns would cover an area of five or six thousand acres, mainly on green fields, in places where the local authorities were not considered to be able to undertake such development. The first generation of new towns were essentially of this nature—although some of them were directed to purposes other than overspill, and it had proved possible to develop a number of them substantially beyond the populations originally contemplated.

The essential characteristics of the new town machinery were that the development was undertaken by a separate government agency for each development (the development corporation) and that the agency operated within a limited and precisely defined physical area. The area was determined by the minister and served to settle the field of operation of the corporation and the general scale of the development. The corporation was appointed by and dealt directly with the minister; had the exchequer as its sole source of capital; and was outside the ordinary system of planning control. It had the functions of making the plan for the development of the area; of carrying out a substantial part of the development and of securing that the remaining development conformed with its plan and programme; and of ensuring that the provision of new jobs matched the provision of new housing. And above all it had the less easily definable task of building a new community.

The advantages of this system had been demonstrated by experience. It had provided the government with a direct initiative in large scale development which could be used effectively to promote regional and national policies. Within the framework of government policy and planning and financial controls, it had provided agencies with a single overall purpose, undistracted by wider or different objectives, responsible for the success of each enterprise and with scope for local initiative. The agencies had been so operated as to avoid many of the impediments to action inherent in local government undertakings. The existence of a separate agency for each development had meant a substantial measure of local identification, and the support of exchequer capital had made it possible to undertake large scale development on a long term view of the viability of the undertaking as a whole.

The working party thought that the achievements had been 'strikingly successful'. A new population of some 600,000 had been accommodated in prosperous new towns. The housing developments had been in the forefront of advance in standards and design. The commercial centres and the industrial estates presented a prosperous picture. The planning concepts applied had had wide influence. The new towns had achieved a world wide esteem, and were undoubtedly the outstanding British contribution to the postwar development of land use and social planning.

Despite these achievements, new towns suffered from a number of real difficulties—the detailed nature of central controls, the recruitment of staff for the limited life of the development corporations, the division of responsibility for local services between development corporations and local authorities, and the lack of research and collated information on the experience of new town development. The first and last of these warrant some discussion in the context of this history.

The problem which presented itself most immediately to all development corporations and to the government departments was that of departmental control over the activities of the corporations. This was currently exercised mainly by the examination and approval of individual projects. Such a system of control was laborious to all parties. With the best intentions, it could lead to one set of professional officers going over in detail the work of another. Moreover, the volume of work could become a significant bar to action and policy examination. In the working party's view, it was necessary to devise broader and more expeditious forms of control.

There were two forms of control involved : financial and planning. As regards financial control, the aim should be to move from control on individual projects to a broader control through annual budgets and longer forward estimates.* This, however, had to be matched by the development of broadly uniform systems of management accounting within the development corporations in order that their financial performance (at least in relation to their remunerative

---

* See chapter VIII, p. 477 *et seq.*

activities) could be judged on a comparable basis in terms of rate of return on capital. Such a movement away from the existing project-oriented and detailed central controls over corporation expenditure on individual developments would not imply any slackening of the government's responsibility to regulate public expenditure. It would still be necessary for the government to control the totals of corporation expenditure in any given period, and the establishment of capital investment programmes would still be required for this purpose. For the same reasons the government would still be concerned with laying down general standards and unit costs, since these affected what could be achieved with the investment available. As in other fields, large capital projects would no doubt continue to require separate approval, because of their significance both for investment programmes and for returns.

The working party considered that the procedures for designating and planning new towns had not been wholly satisfactory. Problems arose at the very start of the designation process. This process was the responsibility of the minister: it fell to him to put forward a proposal for designating the site of a new town; to subject this proposal to objections and public inquiry; and then to reach a final decision in the light of the report of the inquiry. All this necessarily engaged the minister in detailed examination and justification of the site and its boundaries far beyond what was required to satisfy the broad government responsibility of determining the general location and objectives of the town. It had recently been the practice to engage consultants to make an examination and bring forward specific designation proposals; but by the time the inquiry was reached these had been replaced by the minister's proposals which might in some respects differ. The difficulty did not end there. It was important that the area for designation should reflect a con-sidered view about the structure of the town. There was, therefore, in making the designation proposal, the need to examine in sufficient depth the structure which the town should have. Moreover, if the designation order were finally made, the development corporation needed as soon as possible a basic plan for the town before they could embark on substantial development. With these two considerations in mind, the practice had been adopted of engaging the same consultants to go forward immediately after their designation report to prepare a draft master plan, but this had proved less successful than originally hoped. The employment of the consultants to draft a master plan before the designation was decided laid the minister open to criticism that he was committed to the proposal to the prejudice of his consideration of objections. To limit this criticism, it had been necessary to restrict severely the consultants' outside discussions immediately a draft designation order had been made;

and between the publication of a draft order and the minister's decision, the department were for procedural reasons precluded from contacts with the consultants. The draft master plan was often substantially completed before the decision was reached, and an awkward hiatus intervened. Changes in the final designation area might require extensive modification of the draft plan, while the development corporation came on the scene too late to have any say or part in the preparation of the draft plan which was presented to them.

The working party thought that what was ideally needed was an arrangement by which the minister should propose the designation of a new town in a certain locality: that the precise proposals for designation accompanied by the necessary master plan should be prepared by another body (preferably a body likely to be concerned with the execution of the proposals) and submitted for the minister's decision after public inquiry; and that the final master plan and initial development proposals should be approved as quickly as possible thereafter.

The existence of an increasing number of development corporations, much of whose work was similar if not identical in content, necessarily raised the question whether the management of the new town undertaking as a whole was not divided up into too many independent parts. This question recalled the recommendation of the Reith Committee, which was not adopted, for the establishment of a central advisory commission:

'It is, we think, clear that, with a number of independent agencies, even if all of precisely the same constitutional type autonomous within the wide limits of their constitutions and subject to ministerial directions in matters of major policy only, some instrument for harmonising policy and practice and also for pooling information and experience will be not only desirable but essential. We do not think this would be seriously disputed. We considered whether these ends could be served either by the ministries concerned or by a standing conference of the chairmen of the several corporations, or by a combination of both. We concluded that they could not.'

The fact that these aims had not been achieved was a matter of frequent criticism. Though it was plainly desirable that corporations should have the widest opportunities to devise solutions well tailored to the problems of individual towns, nevertheless, the experience of the first new towns was not codified and published for the benefit of later new towns, and the arrangements for achieving the necessary 'harmonisation of policy and practice' and for avoiding the waste of skilled resources when each corporation tackled afresh problems already faced and solved elsewhere were inadequate.

Certain 'piecemeal arrangements' existed, such as the department's *Handbook for New Town Corporations* and various statistical returns. The new towns themselves had standing arrangements for discussing problems of common interest through the medium of the chairmen's conference, the general managers' committee and various professional subcommittees. There was, however, no permanent secretariat to provide continuity and liaison; or to undertake any research into problems affecting all new towns.

The report continued that the recent generation of new towns suffered from the lack of co-ordinated research and information, but they also faced problems of a different order of sophistication and complexity. Central Lancashire, for instance, (as currently proposed) covered 40,000 acres and included a large county borough, two other substantial urban areas and a number of other districts. Here inter-authority relationships would be 'of an unprecedented order of complication'. The 'partnership' towns of Peterborough, North-ampton and Warrington likewise would give rise to inter-authority problems. In these towns the designated area covered both the old town and the expansion area. A single master plan for the whole area was to be drawn up in agreement between the local authorities and the development corporations but, broadly speaking, the local authorities were to be responsible for development for their own needs and within the old town areas, while the development corporations would be responsible for development of the expansion areas—though the corporations could, with the authorities' agree-ment, also develop in the old towns. All this clearly involved a much closer association of local authorities and development corporations, a role for the corporations which fell well short of responsibility for the total planning and development of the designated area, and a melange of powers, jurisdiction and management responsibility, the resolution of which had to be worked out in the particular circum-stances of each case.

When the first new towns were designated there was a desperate housing shortage throughout the country. The eight first generation towns serving London were intended to help meet pressing housing needs. Over most of the country the absolute shortage of houses was now in the process of being met, though a continuing housing problem would remain for many years in the major conurbations. But other changes required a large continuing building programme. In the 1940s, the forecasts at the time indicated that the size of population was likely to remain relatively stable. The eight first generation towns serving London were seen as part of the solution to a finite problem of reducing congestion in the metropolis. The situation in 1968 was very different: the population forecasts had for some time indicated a rapid population growth to the end of the century. In addition, in all towns a major process of urban renewal would go on, partly to restructure urban road networks in response to rising traffic pressures and partly to deal with the obsolescent housing and environment of the twilight areas surrounding the centre.

It was unlikely that future new development would normally take the form of a 'self-contained' town on a green field site—if only because sites suitable and acceptable for such development were now much harder to find. In this sense, Milton Keynes was possibly 'the last of the line stemming from the first generation towns'. It was more likely that the major expansion of existing towns under partnership arrangements would become the norm, and that such developments would increasingly become a major feature in regional and sub-regional plans.

It was also likely that the development corporations' task of matching up the recruitment of people and of employment would become progressively harder. Where a new town drew both people and employment from a single conurbation and where an acute housing shortage increased people's readiness to move from the conurbation, the task was relatively straightforward though not easy. Now, however, new towns in areas enjoying development area status attracted employment from distant parts of the country and still drew their population primarily from nearby conurbations. (In the Scottish new towns only a small proportion of incoming industry came from areas in Scotland, the great bulk coming from England or overseas.) Conversely in Peterborough and Northampton, a significant proportion of the employment was expected to be provided by growth of local industry while the population had to be drawn from London over a substantially greater distance than in the case of the first generation towns. In such a situation matching people and employment was inherently more complex and difficult, particularly since the easing of the housing situation might make city dwellers more reluctant to move.

The future location, scale and programming of major new development would be broadly channelled and directed by the regional planning process in which the government would play a major role. The degree to which the government would have to intervene to promote particular developments would to some measure depend on the future structure of local government. If the boundaries of local authorities were considerably extended, it might be possible to accommodate urban overspill within the boundaries of a new larger authority without such intervention becoming necessary. But government intervention, and the establishment of development corporations, would be required where substantial movement of population to a place outside the new larger authority's boundaries was needed.

A reform of the structure of local government would be likely to alter in a number of ways the relationships between local authorities and development corporations. The problems of co-ordinating the provision of different local government services by different authorities might be eased. The 'partnership' basis of proceedings might become more common and, if successful, might ease the financial and programming problems arising from conflicts of priorities, particularly if the individual units of local government were financially stronger. The question of direct appointment of corporation members by the local authority might arise in a new form (as it already had to a limited extent in the special circumstances in the 'partnership' towns). The role of the local authority in carrying out part of the development might be increased; and the question might in any case arise whether the building organisations of the conurbation authorities should help in the building of houses in new towns.

In the future it was to be expected that proposals for new towns would emerge from regional planning studies in which there would for a long time be a large government component. Proposals for new town development would at that stage be publicly canvassed and open to public discussion. They might then come forward as specific proposals within the structure plans which local planning authorities would prepare under the new planning legislation.* In this way the proposal for the location of a new town could go forward from the local planning authority, to be open to objection and public inquiry and ministerial decision, without obligation on the minister to carry the burden of making and defending the proposal. An 'urban structure plan' would then be needed, in which the sites for the first phases of development might be distinguished as action areas, and further areas added as development progressed. In this way the concept of 'a finite development and a final boundary' might be avoided.

Against this background of new trends (and others such as the increased role of private enterprise) it seemed likely that the nature and implementation of new town building might be profoundly modified. As the trends developed, it might be that the formula of a separate and sovereign corporation (subject to ministerial control) for each new town area on traditional lines would be inadequate. A more flexible arrangement might be needed, within which agencies of different types could be devised for particular tasks.

As a starting point, the working party considered what functions must necessarily continue to be performed by central government on the one hand and by local agencies on the other: possible forms of new organisation would fall in the middle ground between the two.

---

* ie the Town and Country Planning Act of 1968 and its Scottish equivalent of 1969.

It was felt that the central government must have final responsibility for decisions about the location of new towns as an important instrument of national policies and about the pace and scale of their development; must control public sector capital investment; and must ensure that exchequer funds were well spent.

Other responsibilities had to remain with a local agency such as a development corporation. The local agency had to assemble land required for development and either be directly responsible for the provision of basic services, the carrying out of development and the attraction of industry and population, 'or co-ordinate for those purposes the activities of other bodies on the basis of an agreed physical plan and an agreed programme of development'.

The working party then examined possible arrangements for dealing with the 'middle ground' between the central government and the local agency, and discussed the possibility of a national corporation. They suggested that, if the current scale of the new town programme had been envisaged in the mid-forties, the case for a single national corporation would have been a strong one. It would have had 'a continuing nature' which would have been able to provide a central body of experience (and staff) which could have been applied to each new development.

It would have avoided many of the difficulties of the current arrangements. As matters stood, government initiative was confined to projects which could be described as 'a new town'. This had been given very wide interpretations and a diversity of tasks had been undertaken; but for each the same apparatus of a single designated area and a development corporation on a single pattern was required. Already the major expansions of existing towns which were being undertaken in the 'partnership towns' were straining these concepts. The working party pointed to the advantages of a more flexible approach, in which the role of a local executive agency could be tailored to the particular task. It was thought that this might be more easily achieved by a national corporation operating in different ways in different localities than by trying to devise different agencies for different purposes, each dealing with the departments.

However, the working party recommended against the establishment of a single national corporation. Development corporations had recently been set up under the existing arrangements with the responsibility of building a number of important new towns. The main task for the 1970s was the vigorous development of these towns and the completion of the earlier new towns. To set up a new national body at this juncture would be untimely, and would undoubtedly check the impetus of development.

Having concluded that they should not recommend any radical change in the nature of the bodies responsible for new town building the working party proceeded to consider what improvement of the existing arrangements was indicated by their consideration of the experience of the past and the tasks of the future. They were particularly concerned with the middle ground between the responsibilities of the government departments on the one hand and those of the individual development corporations on the other. This was the area of management policy, where corporations shared common needs and would benefit from common action.

The main objective set for all new town corporations was to achieve a certain pace of building. The newer new towns were being expected to achieve a pace of development substantially greater than anything so far sought. Yet there was no well documented body of experience to show the measures necessary to achieve rapid development or the constraints which operated. The corporations undoubtedly needed a full and continuing exchange of information and appraisal, covering the methods adopted to achieve the pace of development sought, the obstacles that were encountered, the physical and social consequences of quick building, and the opportunities and advantages of accelerating or slowing down. This process would at the same time bring up for monitoring and review other concepts in new town building such as the extent to which they should seek to be 'self-contained and balanced communities' and the extent to which they should draw their population from particular areas or particular classes.

The report continued with a lengthy list of issues on which a full exchange of information and experience was needed: on social development; on promoting owner occupation; on organisation, management and financial controls and techniques; on negotiating private finance; on attracting population; on the management of industrial and commercial property; on housing estate management. There was also need for joint collection and dissemination of management statistics and for a joint approach to research. Here it was important to draw a distinction between short term 'research and development' and long term fundamental research. On the former there was 'the need to secure that day to day tasks undertaken by individual corporations have their results evaluated and made generally available; the potential for groups in individual new towns to undertake the development of specific solutions to common problems; and the need to keep in touch with research and development work undertaken elsewhere in government departments or research stations'.

The needs of new towns in relation to fundamental long term research were not in principle special, since research of relevance to them would be equally relevant to planning elsewhere. Moreover, the co-ordination and steering of long term research in the planning and social fields was the responsibility of the Centre for Environmental Studies and the Social Science Research Council. New towns were, however, something of a special case. They might provide a special opportunity for the collection of the data necessary as a research basis and it was, 'if anything, more important in the rapid development of large new communities than in the relatively slower pace of change elsewhere to secure that the lessons of research are directly relevant, quickly available, and promptly applied; for otherwise the mistakes will be greater and more expensive to remedy'. There was accordingly a need to establish the data which should be collected for research purposes; and to formulate the user's requirement for research in a way that would usefully contribute to the formulation of research programmes by the Centre for Environmental Studies and the Social Science Research Council.

In the light of this formidable catalogue, the working party concluded that the new towns needed more than a common forum where such matters could be ventilated at the suggestion of individual corporations. The need was for a regular process to bring out, evaluate, and either disseminate to corporations or put forward for consideration and decision the problems as they arose and the possible ways of tackling them. At the same time, this process would establish an accumulating body of experience on which any corporation could draw.

The working party felt that the existing *ad hoc* arrangements for such purposes should be replaced by more systematic ones within the jurisdiction and under the control of the new towns themselves through the chairmen's conference. All the matters were within the province of development corporations rather than of government departments and it was within the new town organisation that they should be tackled. Diplomatically, the working party noted that this was not an encroachment on the individual responsibility of the separate corporations nor in any way an impediment to direct dealings between corporations and the government departments. On the contrary, 'if these matters were effectively tackled within the existing collective framework of the new towns, the corporations collectively would be strengthened and reinforced'.

The working party were, of course, aware that in the past the department had taken the view that these functions should be carried out by the department, and that this view had found favour at least with some corporations. It was, however, necessary to recognise that the department had not in fact satisfied the need, though they had in recent years 'done a good deal to give more comprehensive advice in a readily available form'. There were important reasons why the department could not and should not fill this role. It was not only that the department had to deploy their staffs to meet a very wide range of tasks and to determine their manpower priorities by considerations in which the needs of the new town corporations were only one element. More fundamentally, the department did not in the ordinary course of their dealings with corporations need to consider many of the problems, and they could not in the nature of things satisfactorily undertake to be the source of advice on matters which were more the responsibility of the corporations than of the department.

It was accordingly recommended that a small permanent common services organisation should be established and controlled by the new towns themselves. The role of this organisation would be to collect, evaluate and disseminate information and in so doing to identify and appraise emerging problems and accumulate a central pool of experience. It would provide a central service to all corporations and to their joint consultative activities 'and would so support and supplement their individual efforts'. Its prime function would be to collect and analyse material including statistical material from corporations, thus ensuring that significant developments or difficult problems encountered by one which might be of relevance to others 'were brought promptly to the attention of those concerned'.

The organisation should also 'look outwards' to the work of various other bodies which had a bearing on the tasks of development corporations. It should keep in touch with research relevant to corporations' work, particularly in the planning, housing and sociological fields, as well as with development of management techniques and studies which did not fall neatly into any technical or professional compartment. It would maintain a constant liaison with, for example, the Centre for Environmental Studies, the National Building Agency, the Building Research Station and the Management Services Liaison Committee of the Ministry of Public Building and Works. It would thus not only be able to keep corporations in touch with work in these various fields; it would also be able to formulate the particular requirements of corporations so that these could influence the direction of work programmes of other bodies. In all these ways the organisation would act as a catalyst, supplementing the work of the corporations, enabling them to keep abreast of all relevant development and research on the one hand and providing information in an up to date and coherent form to outside bodies on the other.

Finally, the organisation could provide standing secretarial services for the chairmen's conference and the general managers' committee and its subcommittees, together with a central information and publicity office for all the new towns. Control of the organisation might be exercised through a management committee established under the chairmen's conference.

The New Towns Association*

The working party report was considered at a meeting between the minister (Anthony Greenwood) and new town chairmen in October 1969, when discussion concentrated on the common needs of corporations. There was broad agreement that there were needs which were not currently being met, though there were differing views on what these were. Those requiring examination included the definition of new town research needs; a 'secretariat' support for the chairmen's conference; and the assembly in 'useful and relevant form' of the experience of individual corporations.

It was noted that the departments already attempted some work in this field, but it would be difficult and unsatisfactory for them to extend this. The role could be only a subsidiary one 'in the many calls on the staff of the departments'. Practically all the departments' information on new towns was necessarily secondhand, and it did not seem sensible for departments to extend into an area which was essentially the responsibility of the corporations.

The chairmen doubted whether there was, at any rate at present, a sufficient case for a new organisation 'so substantially or possibly so potentially powerful' as that suggested by the working party. It was important to preserve the scope for individual initiative by corporations, and their direct access to the departments. Care was needed to avoid establishing a body which might come to be regarded as an intermediary between the corporations and the departments, and which might in the process generate a lot of work in collecting information which would not be used. The chairmen accordingly favoured more limited measures as the first step. This might take the form of some further development of the arrangements of the chairmen's conference and the general managers' committee, and the supporting structure.

It was agreed that the chairmen's conference would consider these matters further in the light of the discussion with a view to formulating proposals which could at a fairly early date be further discussed with ministers.

Tantalisingly, the story now extends beyond the period to which this history relates. But, after consideration, the chairmen agreed to the establishment of a standing committee of the chairmen's conference together with a small secretariat. Advertisements for the head of secretariat appeared in the national press in May 1970. The functions of the secretariat were 'to service the various bodies through which they [the new towns] deal with matters of common concern and to act as an information centre for the thirty new towns'. The name of the organisation was changed in 1971 to the New Towns Association.

* MHLG Files NT 140/16 and 49/51.

CHAPTER VII

Housing Issues

Housing Rents and Subsidies*

UNDER the New Towns Act 1946, no advances of money to development corporations could be made until the minister (with the concurrence of the Treasury) was satisfied that the return on the development for which an advance was required would be reasonable. Silkin decided that for standard housing, the return should cover all costs including overheads after account had been taken of the normal housing subsidies and additional grants paid in lieu of the statutory rate fund contribution made by local housing authorities.† This meant that each housing scheme had to be individually self-supporting. This was in line with the policy of the Ministry of Health (the department responsible for housing until 1951). An early Ministry of Health minute noted that if local authority standards were not exceeded, rents would be comparable with those charged by local authorities. There were, however, three factors which had to be 'borne in mind'. First, since development corporations were subject to the Rent Restriction Acts, rents could not be increased above the level initially fixed ('though it will be possible to reduce rents if costs fall later on'). Secondly, because of rent restriction and also because new towns had no prewar houses, development corporations would not be able to balance their

---

* MHLG Files NT 36/9, NT 43/1, NT 62/5, NT 62/6, PRP 6/301/3, 91650/19/8 and 910650/38/24; and Treasury Files 2AT 335/605/1 and 2AT 664/335/01.

† Public authority housing was financed over sixty years with annual subsidies from the exchequer. Until 1956 local authorities were required to make a 'rate fund contribution' equal to one third of the exchequer subsidy. Since development corporations had no rate fund an additional exchequer grant was made in lieu of the rate fund contribution.

The rates of subsidy changed periodically, but the 1946 subsidy was calculated on the following basis (for a house costing £1,070):

	£	s
Loan charges based on 3⅛% half yearly annuity for 60 years on a capital cost of £1,070	39	12
Repairs, maintenance and management	8	8
Total annual outgoings	48	0
Estimated rent at 10% of average wages	26	0
Deficiency	22	0
The deficiency was met by:		
Exchequer subsidy	16	10
Local authority rate fund contribution	5	10

accounts by increasing the rents of low cost prewar houses. In this, development corporations were in a very different position from local authorities. Thirdly, the corporations would be 'likely to find that over a period of time they will be driven to charge the same rents for the same types of house, whatever the difference in building costs'.

The solution to this conundrum appeared to be to fix rents at a level somewhat higher than those of the areas from which the tenants had moved. This was thought to be justifiable 'because of the saving in travelling expenses that the tenants may be expected to make'. Nevertheless, the Ministry of Health thought that it:

> 'would be wrong to put up rents substantially in order to provide a financial justification either for accepting higher tenders than we allow a local authority to accept for comparable work, or to embark on more expensive types of building. Higher rents will not be maintainable over a long period if tenants are able to show that they are not comparable with comparable houses in comparable districts. A public corporation and the government will be specially susceptible to pressure to reduce rents.'

Careful cost control would therefore be essential. Without this, the corporations and MTCP would 'stand to be shot at' because of the high cost to public funds of providing new town housing. Moreover, a large deficit on housing would hamper transfer to local authorities. This point was considered, in these early days, to be highly relevant to the rent issue:

> 'There are questions of policy and of timing to be considered in connection with the future transfer from the corporation to the local authority for the new town. The attractiveness to the local authority of managing their own towns will be countered by the attractiveness to the inhabitants as rate-payers of prolonging as long as possible life in a district where their housing rate is paid by the exchequer. The necessity of having in the background some power of compulsory transfer in the last resort or some power of levying a contribution from the rates which would have the same effect has no doubt not been overlooked.'

When houses were transferred to the local authority there would inevitably be a high housing rate since the majority of the houses would be subsidised and the local authority would have to pay the normal statutory rate contribution. On the other hand:

> 'the fact that the town will consist almost entirely of new houses and new scientifically planned industry should save it from much expenditure which has to be borne by towns with a large proportion of old houses, both current expenditure on sanitary services and liabilities for new houses to be built in replacement of old ones which, in the course of the next generation, may well mean the rebuilding of half the houses in some towns.'

Silkin raised the question of rent policies with the chairmen of the development corporations at a meeting of the standing ministerial conference in May 1949, and they reluctantly accepted the policy that each housing scheme would be self supporting. This remained the policy until 1955 when, following the abolition of rent restriction over development corporation housing, rent pooling was introduced. This effectively led development corporations to prepare a housing account, though this was significantly different from the housing revenue account which local housing authorities were statutorily required to maintain. In the first place, the New Towns Act did not refer specifically to a housing account, but required development corporations to prepare 'annual accounts in such form as the minister may with the approval of the Treasury direct'. The form of the accounts was established in 1951 when it was decided that the development of a new town was 'indivisible', and that all the development (housing, industry, town centres, amenities etc) were part of 'an integral estates business'. Separate accounting for individual services therefore had no special value and, indeed, would raise substantial difficulties about the allocation of 'general development expenditure'.

A new town housing account was therefore non-statutory and, moreover, no rules were laid down on the items which were to be included in it. The only guidance given by the ministry was that rents, together with subsidies, should cover costs. This policy (loosely termed 'housing must pay for itself') was part of a wider policy that corporations should pay their way, ie that their un-remunerative expenditure should be recouped from their revenue earning assets. They were accordingly expected to allocate a proportion of 'general development expenditure' (GDE) to housing. All this involved the ministry in detailed discussions with development corporations—and with the Treasury. Throughout there was a conflict of interest: the tenants did not wish or were unable to pay more; the corporations were reluctant to increase rents; the ministry tried to achieve a balance on the housing account; while the Treasury 'never accepted that housing rents should be limited to what was necessary to balance the account', and continuously urged a tough rent policy.

Moreover, policy in relation to new town rents and subsidies had to be determined in the context of both current and changing practice in relation to local housing authorities. As early as 1951 an official of the new towns division minuted the secretary on the difficulties of drawing up a comprehensive statement on new towns rent policy:

'In the earlier stages of our draft memorandum, the general intention was to issue to corporations a circular containing a comprehensive statement including policy and explaining what we were prepared to do if and when a self-supporting rent on the present basis of calcutation could no longer be

obtained. That course would have enabled corporations to adopt a uniform
basis of costing . . . and themselves to suggest which of the costing items in
certain cases be adjusted in the rent calculation. Discussions on the financial
side, however, suggested that such a course might well seriously embarrass
our colleagues on the housing side, who have to cope with the local authority
housing problems, and prejudice the ministry's stand on the housing subsidy
rates.'

One of the major difficulties facing development corporations (even
after they were allowed to pool rents) was that their houses were all
built at postwar costs. Only at Welwyn were there any prewar
houses over which current costs could be spread. As building costs
and interest rates rose in the fifties, the rent problem grew in
intensity, and the development corporations submitted to MHLG
that they could not continue raising rents. These were already
higher than those charged by local authorities. The corporations
also objected in principle to differential rent schemes or even rent
rebate schemes. On this there was some sympathy within MHLG.
A ministerial brief prepared for a meeting with new town chairmen
in December 1955 noted that there was comparatively little scope in
new towns for rents which varied according to income since the
tenants formed a relatively homogeneous group. (Local authorities,
on the other hand, housed 'a wide variety of people: from the
comfortably off to the very poor'.) Secondly, differential rents
would probably be unpopular, not only with the highly skilled
workers who would suffer most, 'but also with their employers, who
might face the prospect of losing them'. Moreover, 'neither would
have the remedy of changing the management, as corporations are
not elected'. Finally, differential rents would make it difficult for the
department to comply with the statutory duty to ensure that
housing schemes secured a reasonable return.

However, the minister (Sandys) made it clear in June 1956 that
he did not feel that the limit had been reached on rent increases.
Though it was not his policy to press differential rent schemes on
unwilling corporations, 'as long as these schemes were not used, it
was possible that rent income might be produced by one'.

As costs and interest rates continued to rise, it became increasingly
difficult to prevent the new towns from going into deficit on housing,
and MHLG (themselves under pressure from the development
corporations) pressed the Treasury to allow deficits to occur. The
Treasury, however, could not accept that the limit to rent
increases had been reached: 'we cannot let this £250m project be
run by Mr Micawber'. There was a lengthy period of negotiation on
this.

In September 1957, MHLG sent the Treasury a detailed memorandum on new town rents. In an accompanying letter it was

underlined that their general view ('which if necessary we must press upon ministers') was that 'we cannot be hide-bound about any rule that the houses taken by themselves shall not make a loss'. This rule had long been abandoned for the Scottish new towns: 'so let no one talk about sacred principles'.

The memorandum dealt with the breach in established policy threatened by housing deficits. The minister's view (now Brooke) was that, unfortunate as such a breach would be, 'the alternatives are so much worse that the best course is to put up with it'. These alternatives were to reduce expenditure substantially, or to increase rents to the extent necessary to maintain a balance.

The minister was satisfied that housing standards could not be reduced and that the proportion of 'people's houses'* could not be increased. A mere limitation in numbers of houses was no answer. The only way of achieving a substantial reduction would therefore be to stop housebuilding altogether. To do this would mean the abandonment for the time being of the government's decentralisation policy and would invite a major political attack. It would be treated as a confession that credit restrictions could succeed only at the expense of desirable social projects to which the government was itself committed. It would also be an inept course to take because it could not produce any early improvement in the accounts of corporations—who had entered into contracts for houses which would not be completed for some time but must be paid for—and because the ultimate success of the towns financially depended on maintaining the confidence of industrialists and trading interests, 'which would be rudely shattered by a decision to cut the towns off before the job had been completed'.

Several general considerations needed to be kept in mind. First, when increases affected most of the houses in a town, it was 'peculiarly easy for agitators to whip up the kind of strike which stopped Crawley industry at the end of 1955'. Secondly, 'the fact must be accepted that it is not only a question of what the tenants *ought* to be able to pay, having regard to their incomes, but also a question of what they regard as a reasonable amount'. What was a reasonable rent 'had been for years disguised by artificial rent restrictions'. Though it might be argued that a tenant could expect to devote a given proportion of his income to rent, 'and rent should be a prior charge to cars and TV, this will not be accepted overnight'. Arguments on these lines were unconvincing to tenants who were 'well aware that they were already paying more than it cost the corporation to build their houses—because they live in houses

---

* The 'people's house' was a lower standard house introduced in the early fifties at the time of the major expansion of house building. See MHLG *Houses 1952*, and *Houses 1953*.

built with cheap money and the corporation introduced rent pooling'. They also knew that similar houses belonging to local authorities were being let at considerably lower rents.

The ministry were not arguing against any further rent increases. On the contrary they proposed to urge increases whenever practicable. But this could have the effect only of keeping deficits as low as possible.

At a meeting with the Treasury, MHLG officials stressed that the main difficulty facing the corporations had been the instability of the interest rate, which had necessitated successive reviews of rents in order to preserve the principle of avoiding deficit. The rents of new town houses were now considerably higher than those of comparable local authority houses and private controlled houses. There were serious political difficulties in another immediate increase sufficient to keep abreast of the latest increase in the interest rate.

It was finally agreed, in early 1958, that corporations should be informed that the directive to avoid running into deficit on their housing accounts still stood and they would be asked to make proposals for increasing rents over a period of time to the extent necessary to work off any such deficit, current and accumulated, assuming the existing interest rate. MHLG would examine these proposals with a view to ensuring that the corporations were charging the highest rents that could be reasonably expected over the period, and fix a period of time within which each of the corporations would be required to eliminate deficits on their housing accounts.

During the next few years the position of the first generation new towns improved—largely because of inflation which enabled them to offset increased costs by raising the rents of their pool of cheaper housing built in the early 'fifties. The position in the second generation towns (of which Skelmersdale was the first) was, however, much more difficult: and similar difficulties were anticipated with Dawley, Redditch and other proposed new towns. Their problem was, of course, essentially the same as that experienced earlier by the first new towns, but it was exacerbated by the higher costs, interest rates and standards now prevailing.

These issues fell to be reviewed within the wider context of the 'complete overhaul of housing subsidies' announced in the 1963 white paper on housing (Cmnd 2050). A working party of officials and local authority officers was set up and presented a confidential report in September 1964. No special consideration was initially given to new town housing: it was agreed within the ministry that rent policy in new towns could be reviewed only when the broad lines of policy had been settled for local authority housing. In the meantime, the Treasury had agreed that the newest new towns would have to incur a deficit on their housing accounts, but the situation would be reviewed as soon as general subsidy policy was settled.

Nevertheless, internal minutes within the new towns division of the ministry and between them and the housing division dealt with a number of related issues. It was pointed out that the political reasons for not intervening in local authority rent policies applied almost to the same degree to new towns but, since development corporations were 'the minister's children . . . the minister must inevitably be vulnerable if he allows development corporations to pursue rental policies which do not represent the forefront of his own thinking'. One issue on which this was of particular importance was rent rebate schemes. Only two development corporations (Stevenage and Peterlee) had such schemes. Yet the ministry considered that rent rebates were essential if lower income households were to be shielded from the rent increases which would be necessary to offset the high costs of current building. The housing division suggested that a more positive line on the part of the new towns division was required: 'if the minister believes in rent rebates, there seems to be no reason why he should not insist that acceptable schemes are put forward for his approval and put into operation for those towns which are under the minister's control and which are his responsibility'.

No progress was made on matters such as these, first because of the ongoing review of local authority housing finance and then because of the change in government in October 1964—only a month after the review had been completed. Moreover, there were some problems of liaison between the housing and new towns divisions and, in January 1965, the new towns division minuted that they 'must lodge a mild protest' at the difficulty which they had experienced in getting a copy of the report on the review of housing finance:

> 'There has always been a strange reluctance on the part of housing division to let us know, on the new towns side, what is happening on subsidy policy and legislation. Subsidy levels are of critical importance to the new towns nowadays and if—as has been generally accepted—we are to keep in general line with the subsidy structure for local authorities it is particularly important that we should know what is in mind and have an opportunity to comment.'

At the same time, concern was mounting about the cost implications of 'Buchanan road systems in the new towns'.* Though the high costs of main roads was not a direct charge to housing, it affected housing through the apportionment of general development expenditure (GDE). The theory was that something in respect of GDE had to be added to the capital costs of every 'earning project'

---

* Ministry of Transport, *Traffic in Towns*, HMSO, 1963.

so that all GDE would eventually be met in this way. It had been left to corporations to decide what these additions should be, and they usually varied as between housing, commercial and industrial projects, partly on the basis of 'what the traffic will bear'. Some were 'well up in laying off their GDE'; others were falling behind.

Current rent policy was that housing, with the aid of the housing subsidies, should pay its way. It was therefore necessary to know the cost of housing. Main road costs were a major element in GDE. It followed, therefore, that unless alternative arrangements were made, the costs of providing 'Buchanan style road networks and all that went with them' would, through GDE allocations, fall largely on housing. This raised wider questions, and new towns division commented that 'a review of the whole GDE arrangements would be a good thing'.*

The report of a working party on local authority housing finance had suggested a possible new approach to housing subsidies based on the difference between the actual expenditure on the housing account and the notional income, taking gross values for rating (or some proportion of them) as the minimum. 'If something on these lines were adopted we would clearly have to specify what ranked as "expenditure", and the whole GDE element in the account—past and future—might have to be looked at in some detail.'

The ministry had it in mind 'to give an interest rate subsidy to hold down to four per cent the interest element in borrowing' for new houses 'but in view of the possible effect on overseas opinion this is not to be mentioned in negotiation'. This new subsidy scheme was an element in the revision of housing policy: its repercussions on the current overspill and new town housing subsidies were a matter for internal discussion. The new town arrangements were being altered already 'in effect by allowing deficits on the housing accounts of the newest towns'. It would not be possible to have one system applicable in all new towns since their housing costs varied. One possibility was to provide for a housing subsidy on a deficit basis: in this way each new town would receive the subsidy it needed. But this meant that assumptions would have to be made about the total rent income which corporations should be able to get, 'and that is difficult'.

After further discussion, it was decided that the basic 'interest rate subsidy' should be paid to new towns in the same way as to local authorities. Supplementary grants would still be needed and, in determining these, it was thought that there should be four basic assumptions:

---

* See chapter VIII, p. 480 *et seq.*

(i) that after taking into account the new interest rate subsidy, a newly built house would show a loss of £25 per year;

(ii) that it would be reasonable to increase the rents of existing houses by an average of £3 10s per house per year. It would therefore take the rent increases of seven existing houses to pay off the deficit on one new house;

(iii) that, therefore, if the number of houses built by a corporation in one year was no more than one seventh of its existing stock, the losses on the new housing could be offset by rent increases on the older stock, and no supplementary grant for the new houses would be needed;

(iv) that £25 per annum would be payable in respect of each house built in excess of one seventh of the existing stock.

The secretary initially thought that this 'one seventh formula' was too complicated but later accepted it as being workable. She did, however, express doubts about the basic assumptions that rents could continue to rise indefinitely: surely at some point it would become cheaper to buy than to rent? This was shown not to be so. The major subsidy to the tenant came from the rent pool of older and more cheaply built houses. The purchaser would always have the added cost of current market value for a single unsubsidised property. An owner occupier with an old mortgage might be better off than a new tenant, but if both started from the same base date, even under the proposed system, 'it must remain cheaper to rent than to buy'.

Agreement was reached internally—despite some reservations on the complexity of the proposals—and, in February 1966, an approach was made to the Treasury.

Within the Treasury, doubts were expressed as to whether there was 'a rational argument for making any kind of subsidy towards new town housing'. The Ministry of Housing seemed to think that it was sufficient to aim for rents which, together with subsidies, would cover loan repayments on the historic cost plus maintenance. It was hoped that 'we shall move away from this attitude with the introduction of viability programmes for each new town which will set targets not only for reduced deficits, where appropriate, but also for increased surpluses'. Practically all of the new towns which were currently in surplus achieved this position only as a result of the existing subsidy arrangements. 'There is certainly room all round for increased rentals, especially on some of the earlier estates.' The proposal 'to give more to the newest new towns and to take money away from the older ones' was applauded, but the Treasury were 'less happy' about the actual figures proposed. Continuing inflation itself gave a subsidy in real terms to new town tenants. Money incomes were rising every year, but the extra cost through inflation of each house added to the new town stock was felt only once, and thereafter the burden of meeting the loan charges on it lightened year by year with continued inflation. It was on this line of reasoning that the Treasury thought the MHLG proposals were 'too generous'.

In May 1966 the minister (now Crossman) was consulted on the housing subsidy proposals and also on the issue of housing revenue accounts. He reacted very strongly and wrote on the file:

> '*I can accept neither of these policies*. We had better hurry up and have a conference on both. Points:
>
> (1) We are *now* arranging for publication of new town housing revenue [accounts] in line with other local authorities.
> (2) Subsidy proposals: this is so palpably unjust that I cannot tolerate it. We must inform the Treasury that there will be *no* change. But we had better confirm this in our talk.'

At a meeting with officials, he stressed that he would prefer to maintain grants at their current level for all new towns, and seek additional assistance for the 'new' new towns which needed it most, rather than accept the proposed system whereby the grant to the older new towns would have to be reduced. He was strenuously opposed to taking away grant from the older new towns. A decision on the grants should be deferred until there had been a thorough examination of the possibilities of bridging the gap between rents in the new towns and their neighbouring district councils and of re-casting new town accounts so that they were closely comparable with the housing revenue accounts of local authorities.

At a later meeting, in July 1966, Crossman stressed that the question of finance for new towns had to be seen as a *housing* problem, with two closely related strands, namely the bringing together of new town and neighbouring local authority rents, and the co-ordination of new town accounts with the housing revenue accounts maintained by local authorities. New town housing accounts should not be the instruments for determining rents. It was true that new towns had to balance their accounts, but so had local authorities; the difference was that local authorities had an extra factor (the rate fund contribution) which made it possible for them to do so without throwing the whole burden on rents. As part of the process of drawing the two together, it should be considered how the new towns could obtain this flexibility, and what grant system would achieve this for them. At the same time, rent rebate schemes might further the integration of new town and local authority rents, and the corporations should be told of the minister's view on rent rebates and asked to consider introducing schemes.

Crossman rejected the 'one seventh formula' and favoured a flat rate £24 for ten years (to be payable to both new and expanded towns). Moreover, new towns should no longer be allowed to build to standards higher than Parker Morris. If new towns were to be pacemakers, they should be so 'in cost consciousness'. With regard to the items borne by new town housing accounts, the department should examine them with a view to standardising them with housing revenue accounts, and to investigating whether the housing accounts could be relieved of burdens which were not borne by housing revenue accounts.

Further progress on this broad field was made in August 1966 when it was decided to propose to the Treasury a 'tapering' grant in place of the one seventh formula which Crossman had rejected. Furthermore, since it was accepted that one major objective of policy was the transfer of housing to the local authorities, it was necessary to work towards a common rent structure for all publicly owned housing in any one new town. Accordingly housing accounts should no longer bear GDE. In order to 'assimilate' new town and local authority rents, contributions might be necessary from the new town to the local authority (or perhaps even in the opposite direction).

A formal approach was made by MHLG to the Treasury in the same month. MHLG outlined their broad policy objectives within the context of which the new proposals had to be considered. The intention was to work towards the handing over of rented housing to local authorities. In the case of any one town this meant that, at the time of handover, the separate housing revenue accounts of the development corporation and of the local authority would have to be merged, and the separate rent structure of the development corporation and of the local authority would have to be integrated.

The gap between chargeable rent plus subsidy for a currently built house in a new town and the repayment (economic) rent was of the order of £35 a year. In a second generation new town there were no stocks and therefore 'pooling' could not take place in the early years. As had been accepted in the case of town development schemes, reasonable stocks were built up in ten years, and the grant should be cut after that period. With the first generation new towns, there was some case for cutting existing grants (although not so drastically as by the one seventh formula) and it appeared sensible to propose that those grants should be terminated after each had run for some years. This had been and was the rule for town development schemes. Pursuing the parallel of town development, this suggested a grant for new houses of £24 for ten years.

In short, there was good reason for treating new towns and town development authorities in the same way as far as grant was concerned. Both received overspill, both had special financial problems brought about by rapid growth and both (later in one case and immediately in the other) had to integrate the rent structures of new houses with those of old without causing unjustifiable rises in rates or in the rents of local council house tenants.

It was thought right to require recovery from the exporting authority of £12 for every overspill family housed in a new town. This again accorded with the town development arrangements, and it was proposed to include the necessary provisions in the Housing Subsidies Bill.

The Treasury replied that they were not agreed on 'the policy background'. The objective of working towards the transfer of rented housing to the local authorities 'is not an objective to which our ministers would subscribe, or at least not without a good deal of qualification'. The Treasury view was that future arrangements for new towns should ensure that the profits of developed towns would be available to be ploughed back for the benefit of the new towns programme generally, and must not be such as arbitrarily to enrich local authorities in whose areas new towns happened to be situated. It might be that this aim was not inconsistent with the transfer of rented housing to local authorities, but clearly detailed discussions between MHLG and the Treasury were necessary before consideration could be given to proposals based on the assumption that transfer was 'settled policy'.

The specific proposals were discussed between Treasury and MHLG officials. Treasury officials reiterated the view that they would have preferred the retention of the 'one seventh formula'. Although they would not oppose the £24 per annum per house, their feeling was that new towns were of sufficient importance to warrant special arrangements which were not necessarily the same as town development schemes. However, if pressed for parity with town development schemes, the Treasury felt that there should be 'strict parity'—ie grants should be paid only on those houses which were fulfilling the purpose of the new towns, eg in the case of the London new towns, for houses tenanted by families moving from London. In addition, the Treasury wanted consideration of some variation in the arrangements for the payment of existing grants to those older new towns which had large housing stocks.

Other MHLG proposals were agreed, and the only issue which remained outstanding was the detailed arrangements for the paying of the £24 grant and the 'cut off' of existing grants.

MHLG wrote to the Treasury that their proposals on contributions to and from the housing revenue accounts of local authorities in new towns were not dependent on any particular assumption about the eventual disposal of new town assets. It was understood that the Treasury conclusion in the light of all this was that there would be no objection to MHLG taking the proposed powers provided that in justifying them they did not either commit themselves in advance of a *joint* ministerial decision, to the eventual transfer of all new town housing to the local authorities; or commit themselves to the proposition that rents of local authority and corporation houses must necessarily be brought to parity in all new towns and at all times.

MHLG accepted that their proposals could be thought to take insufficient account of the relatively more favourable financial position in the more mature new towns which were cushioned by a large housing stock. They therefore suggested that, 'if it would help' the Treasury to accept that all future development corporation houses which attracted subsidy should attract also an additional exchequer grant of £24 for ten years, they would be willing to recommend to the minister a modification of the proposals for the cutting off of grants already being paid on existing subsidised housing.

A further meeting was held with the Treasury in November 1966, and it was agreed that it was desirable 'to get all grant payments (old and new) on to a common decennial basis in the course of the next five years'. There was a lengthy discussion on the ways in which new towns and town development schemes resembled and differed from one another and the implications of these considerations for the grant system. The relative needs, in terms of grant, of different towns in different stages of development were also considered in detail. The Treasury could not accept that it was reasonable to give the same grant for a new house in a new town 'just beginning to build' (at one extreme) and for a new house in a town with a corporation housing stock of perhaps 12,000 or 13,000 houses (at the other extreme).

Tentative consideration was given to a possible scheme which would 'in a rough and ready way' relate the amount to be paid in grant to the stage reached in the town's growth—'with an eye particularly to the size of the housing stock available to cushion the impact on rents of any initial deficits on newly provided houses'. A MHLG official noted, however, that

> 'You will realise that this approach is getting me well beyond the limits of my present instructions and that even if we can agree between ourselves on a scheme of this kind I cannot promise to do more than to submit it in the department for consideration by ministers.'

The scheme agreed by officials provided for the existing grant to be cut off after a period of fifteen years in 1967–68 reducing to ten years in 1972–73. New grant would be payable at:

£30 per annum per dwelling for houses completed in the first four years

£24 per annum per dwelling for houses completed in the second four years

£18 per annum per dwelling for houses completed in the third four
years

£12 per annum per dwelling for houses completed thereafter.

All new grants would run for a period of ten years.

An internal MHLG minute noted the position reached in negotiation with the Treasury, and commented that 'the division are to be
congratulated on having achieved this result with the Treasury at
this time'. The proposed scheme represented a very substantial help
to the newer new towns; while at the other end of the scale the 'old'
new towns would continue with grants at existing levels, save only
that the £12 was to be paid for ten years instead of the fifteen years
for which MHLG had asked. It was only in commission towns that
the new proposal would result in a net fall in exchequer aid.
Negotiations were continuing with the Treasury on relief in whole
or part for the housing account from general development
expenditure.

Ministers approved the proposals, though they felt certain that
there was likely to be protest from the 'older' new towns and also
from town development authorities. Legislative effect to the
proposals was given by the Housing Subsidies Act of 1967.

While all these negotiations were proceeding, Crossman was
tackling housing rents and standards on the broader local authority
front. At a press conference in Bradford on 8 July 1966, he emphasised 'the need to ensure that the Government's new generous
housing subsidies are not frittered away but will go to those who
need them'. He criticised those local authorities who did not operate
rent rebate schemes (about three fifths of all authorities). Moreover,
existing rebate schemes did not provide sufficient assistance to lower
paid workers. He also referred to the need for cost consciousness in
building and stressed the importance of combining higher housing
standards 'with a cutting out of expensive frills'.

So far as new towns were concerned, this was followed by a
circular stating that, in accordance with this policy, the minister
had decided that 'henceforth the standard of houses built for rent
and which will receive government subsidy shall not be in excess of
Parker Morris minimum'. Attention was also drawn to the minister's
criticism of local authorities who did not have 'lively rent rebate
schemes'. There were still some corporations who had not introduced
such schemes and some others who had schemes which might not be
regarded as 'lively' in this context. 'The minister wishes all development corporations to have appropriate rent rebate schemes and to
operate them so that they effectively reduce the burden of rent upon
those in the lower income groups.'

Selection of Tenants*

'It is a fundamental aim of policy that the new and expanded towns should be developed as balanced self-contained communities in which the inhabitants will find work as well as houses.'

So stated the first MTCP circular on 'movement of population to new and expanded towns' (issued in 1949). At this time policy was conceived as embracing expanded towns as well as new towns, and much effort was expended on elaborating appropriate financial and administrative procedures.

During 1948 and 1949, MTCP were in discussion with other government departments about a number of matters of inter-departmental concern. One of these—which grew in significance in the 'fifties—was the financial arrangement between 'exporting' and 'importing' local authorities. In 1948 MTCP approached the Ministry of Health (the department then responsible for housing and local government) on the financial problems of expanded towns, referring specifically to the burden which would be placed on the importing authority of the rate fund contribution in respect of 'a disproportionate number of subsidy houses provided in their area'. MTCP suggested that:

'the difficulty to some extent would be overcome if the exporting local authorities were *required* to pay for a fixed number of years the rate fund contribution on the number of houses allocated for the population from their own areas. A power *enabling* the exporting authorities to pay the contribution might not always be sufficient . . . Whether or not authorities are required to make a contribution towards the cost of families from their areas rehoused by another authority, there will probably be a good deal of housing which will be occupied by families from outside the receiving authority's area which cannot be identified with an exporting authority and it is for consideration whether a special exchequer subsidy (equivalent to the rate fund contribution) should be provided for the number of houses built . . . under arrangements with exporting authorities'.

The Ministry of Health replied that they were currently divided in opinion on whether it was reasonable 'to expect an exporting authority to make a contribution in respect of persons from their areas who are accommodated in the expanding towns'. If such arrangements were made they would have to be matters of agreement. The point was not followed up, particularly since the Ministry of Health 'failed to get into the Housing Act 1949 the provision for the payment by the exporting authority to the receiving authority of the rate contribution'. Indeed, the Ministry of Health (for this reason) objected to any reference by MTCP to expanded towns in their wider discussions on 'the simultaneous transfer of population to overspill reception areas'. The Ministry of Town and Country

---

* MHLG Files 91650/26/13/1, 91650/73/1/1 and 91650/73/1/2.

Planning retorted that they could not limit their proposals to new towns since

'this would defeat the main purpose, which is to show the exporting authorities where they will stand under the proposed linkage scheme, and no such scheme is possible without including the expanded towns. The new towns will in the longer run make a much smaller contribution to a solution of the decentralisation problem. All the exporting authorities have been clamouring to know where they should look to for the eventual accommodation of their surplus populations . . . We are under no delusion about the weakness of our position so long as we have no financial inducements to offer to the authorities of expanded towns, and they will no doubt raise awkward questions as soon as they begin to think about the problem. We do not rule out however, the possibility that the county councils will be prepared to help.'

'More progress' was possible with the new towns. As thinking on these developed during 1946 to 1948, there was an assumption that a few selected local authorities with the more acute housing problems would be 'linked' with a particular new town (eg Tottenham and Wood Green with Stevenage; Acton, Harrow, Hendon, Wembley and Willesden with Hemel Hempstead; East Ham and West Ham with Basildon). There was also some expectation that the new town development corporations would from time to time allocate to those authorities blocks of houses for which those authorities would nominate the tenants 'and so relieve their housing difficulties'. In accordance with this expectation the minister, in making appointments to the development corporations, generally included at least one representative of the authorities with which the linkage might be made.

After designation, the immediate need of the corporations was for building and construction workers, and although some were obtained by nomination from the linked authorities, the shortage was such that the corporations were generally glad to attract workers from anywhere, and to house them in temporary labour camps, or acquiesce in daily travel over long distances.

This, however, was viewed as a temporary expedient. The longer term aim of policy was to apply a scheme of industrial selection on a geographical basis. It was believed that this would be 'particularly useful administratively in avoiding undesirable competition for accommodation in the reception towns'. It would also take into account the fact that 'people from the congested areas who are willing to move will look naturally to those reception areas which lie outwards from their present homes along the radial lines of communication'. The Greater London area (including the reception towns) was therefore divided into five sectors.* Each sector was so

---

* The County of London was not included in these five sectors because 'broadly speaking, movement out from the central areas may take place as easily in one direction

devised as to provide for a broad approximation between export need and reception capacity, 'so as to secure as far as possible equality of treatment all round'. At the same time the boundaries were drawn 'sufficiently widely so that each sector may be expected to contain a representative cross section of London industry and labour, and therefore be likely to provide an adequate field of selection for firms and workers willing to move to the new and expanded towns in that sector'.

Only firms from the London area were to be considered for accommodation in the reception towns. The firms were to be encouraged to move to the 'linked' reception towns except in cases where, in order to obtain a balance of employment, it was desirable that this working rule should be broken. It was expected that each firm would take some workers with it: these were to be provided with houses whether or not they came from the appropriate sector. The balance of the labour force was to be recruited through an industrial selection scheme. Local authorities were to prepare lists of applicants for rehousing in the new towns. These lists were to contain not only information relating to family structure but also 'particulars of the nature of the employment of the applicant and other working members of his household, and of his preference (if any) for a particular town'. A copy of each local authority list was to be sent to a specified employment exchange which was to act as a clearing house for the particular sector. This proposal was quickly abandoned as being too cumbersome. Instead, local authorities were to keep the lists and supply details of 'apparently suitable persons' to the specified exchange on request. Firms requiring labour would notify the local employment exchange of their requirements which would then be passed on to the specified exchange in the appropriate sector. This exchange was to send details of 'apparently suitable persons' in the sector to the firm. Arrangements for applicants to be interviewed by representatives of the firm and the reception authority could be made by the exchange. Finally, the exchange and the exporting authority would be notified of applicants selected for employment and for housing accommodation.

On average only about half of the working population in a normal town were employed in manufacturing industry. The remainder were employed in local distributive services, offices, public utilities, etc. It was expected that a proportion of such workers would be recruited from the families of workers in manufacturing industries. Others would be recruited through a selection procedure similar to that outlined above, again on a sector basis.

---

as another'. But, since the Thames formed a definite and realistic division of the county into two areas, the northern half was linked with the three northern sectors, and the southern half with the two southern sectors.

Although the sectors had been drawn widely, it was anticipated that there might be cases in which labour for manufacturing or service industries could not be obtained from the appropriate sectors. In such cases recruitment would have to be extended to other sectors. To facilitate this, the London regional office of the Ministry of Labour was to make available the names of suitably qualified workers on local authorities' lists in other sectors.

In essence this scheme was a regionalisation of the earlier linkage proposals. Since there was no previous experience to draw on, the scheme was necessarily experimental and was to 'be kept subject to review in the light of changing circumstances'. It was designed essentially to cover the early stages of building in the new and expanded towns and would 'probably require modification' once a substantial nucleus of industrial and housing development had taken place. Nevertheless, the proposals as a whole were thought to be soundly conceived and would 'certainly form a useful basis of discussion' with the different interests concerned. Local authorities were invited to consider the proposals and to inform the ministry of their observations within the next two months.

It should be noted that at this time local authorities made no financial contribution to the new or expanded towns. Under the then Housing Acts, local authorities received exchequer subsidies on houses provided by them and were also required to pay a contribution from the rate fund—the 'statutory rate fund contribution'. In order to give the new town development corporations the same financial aid, the ministry undertook to pay not only the normal subsidy but also an amount equal to the statutory rate fund contribution. Since no 'expanded towns' had yet been commenced no similar arrangement was devised for them at this time.

The proposed scheme was received by the London authorities with deep misgivings. The simultaneous movement of industry and population was agreed to be sound in principle, but its likely practical effects, particularly on the housing lists were viewed with scepticism. The dispersal of industry was to be on a completely voluntary basis and there was no guarantee that it would move from the most congested areas. Further, the scheme proposed would allow any migrant firm to obtain houses for all its employees wishing to move. Whilst it was agreed that firms should be guaranteed accommodation for their key workers, it was thought to be unfair that all their employees should be eligible for transfer irrespective of their housing need or the relative size of the housing problem in the area in which they lived. It was felt that a superior scheme would allow a specific number of houses to be allocated to each authority to enable them to meet their problems. The population so transferred could then obtain employment with the firms who had moved to the new towns with only their key workers. Arrangements would admittedly have to be made to ensure that the populations of the new towns were 'sufficiently balanced' in character, but this should not present unsurmountable difficulties. Further, since a certain proportion of houses erected would ultimately be needed for accommodating workers in service industries, houses could be used 'on a dormitory basis' by tenants nominated by local authorities during the interim period. In making these nominations preference could be given to any particular trade so as to ensure a balance in the new community. The allocation of such temporary 'dormitory' accommodation to local authorities should be in proportion to the urgency of their housing need.

This alternative, on which many variations were suggested, was, of course, in conflict with the policy of developing new towns as self-contained communities in which families could both live and work. Nevertheless, the local authorities considered that some compromise was essential if they were to cope with their problems of over-crowding, slum clearance and redevelopment. It was pointed out that the policy of restraining industrial expansion in London had had to be relaxed in view of the country's economic need to develop dollar-earning and dollar-saving industries. Although this was in principle 'academically' undesirable, it was a necessary step which had to be taken. Planning policies could not be operated without regard to the economic facts of life. Similarly, with housing in the new towns, a policy of industrial selection was desirable, but if these towns were to give relief to London authorities it could not be operated rigidly. Further, it was felt that no scheme would give maximum relief unless local councils were given 'adequate' powers of control over vacated properties to prevent families moving in from other areas.

These arguments were not accepted by the Ministry of Town and Country Planning, and an attempt was made to implement the scheme. However, it soon became apparent that it was impracticable for the Ministry of Labour to meet the labour demands of firms moving to the new towns by drawing on the housing lists of a limited number of local authorities within a particular sector. Apart from building workers, the needs of the industries in the new towns were predominantly for skilled workers whereas the registered applicants were predominantly unskilled. Further, even 'eligible' applicants became hesitant to move when they realised that they would have to pay comparatively high rents and receive provincial wage rates. As a result, selection of tenants became almost entirely on the basis of industrial suitability without regard for sector boundaries or any interim schemes of preferential treatment for 'linked' authorities previously regarded as having special claims on particular new towns.

Some local authorities did make informal arrangements with the 'specified' employment exchanges, and the development corporations attempted to give preference to their 'linked' authorities. But this was in practice often impossible. Unfortunately, as the new towns programme proceeded, other difficulties arose. In 1951 and 1952 general economic controls tended to work to the disadvantage of the linked authorities. For example, the restrictions on factory building (necessitated by the steel shortage and the concentration of building resources on the new Conservative Government's expanded housing programme) were such that one corporation at least (Bracknell) 'had to make their choice from firms anywhere in the London and Greater London area who had been able to get industrial development certificates and building licences, rather than from linked areas alone'. In Crawley it was found that migrant firms were bringing 80 per cent to 90 per cent of their London employees with them.

The London local authorities complained bitterly about this situation. Though the new towns were obviously providing some relief to the problems of the London area as a whole, the direct benefits to any particular authority seemed negligible. Firms were not necessarily moving from the most congested areas, and families selected for employment were not necessarily 'in housing need'. The only 'really tangible benefit' accrued in cases where building trade workers were nominated from local authority housing lists. This was the only trade required by the new towns which was significantly represented on their lists.

*The Town Development Act 1952**

It was partly because of this situation that legislation was introduced (in the form of the Town Development Bill) to facilitate other overspill schemes. It had always been contemplated that the post-war policy of dispersal would need to be carried out by means of both new and expanded towns. The need for expanded towns had long been established, but the obvious inadequacy of the new towns programme, and the need to restrict further development in the green belt, brought matters to a head. In one respect the Act of 1952 is of particular relevance to this chapter: it empowered exporting authorities to make financial contributions to receiving authorities. It was made clear that exchequer contributions towards the cost of town development would be made only in cases where exporting authorities were prepared to make 'appropriate contributions'. Thus

---

* See also chapter IX.

the principle was established that local authorities which exported overspill population to expanded towns ought to pay some contribution for the benefit received. Though the suggestion was not made at the time, it was clearly possible to argue that, if this principle were accepted, then exporting authorities ought similarly to make contributions to new town development corporations. Unfortunately, this was not appreciated when the 1952 Bill was before Parliament, and hence the matter was not discussed. But as will become apparent below, it soon became a matter of much argument.

Following the passing of the Town Development Act, the Ministry of Housing and Local Government produced a memorandum which summarised the provisions of the Act and outlined suggested arrangements between authorities participating in town development schemes. This pointed out that the methods used for selecting tenants would 'naturally have a close bearing on the question of contributions from the exporting authorities to the housing expenditure of the receiving authorities'. Two methods of selection 'which authorities might consider making' were suggested:

'(i) *Direct nomination* by the exporting authority who in return for the right to nominate tenants of a stipulated number of houses for an agreed period, would undertake to make a contribution in respect of those houses over the same period.

(ii) *Selection through the offer of employment* where it is essential because of distance that the tenant should work in, or at any rate near to, the new area. The exporting authority would undertake to make a contribution year by year for an agreed period according to the number of tenancies it secures for the relief of its housing problem.'

In the debates on the Bill, the minister (Macmillan) stressed that 'the purpose of the Bill is that large cities wishing to provide for their surplus populations shall do so by orderly and friendly arrangements with neighbouring authorities; . . . all these arrangements should be reached by friendly negotiation and not imposed by arbitrary power'.* Nevertheless, the situation in London was so complex—with eighty-seven housing authorities in the built-up area—that it was more important that arrangements should be orderly than that they should be friendly. This was particularly so in relation to the new towns. But the London authorities saw in the memorandum the answer to their problems: why should they not be allowed to enter into direct nomination agreements with the new towns? Indeed, some of them argued that in no other way would it be possible for them to carry out their statutory duty to rehouse families in acute housing need. The ministry, of course, were unable to accept this argument: to allow local authorities to select tenants would have meant the abandonment of the fundamental conception

---

* HC Debates, Vol 496, Col 727, 25 February 1952.

underlying the new towns and would have led to an aggravation of the very problems of urban congestion, journey to work and dormitory development that the new towns were intended to relieve.

The Revised Selection Procedure*

A scheme was therefore drawn up by the ministry for the whole of the Greater London area. It was circulated in draft form to the local authority associations in December 1952 and published in its final form (MHLG circular 29/53) in May 1953. Under the 1949 scheme limited arrangements for the transfer of population to new towns had been operated between the development corporations and groups of London authorities. With the expansion of the housing programmes in the new towns and the anticipated commencement of Town Development Act schemes it was necessary to make wider arrangements. The simple multiplication of directly negotiated agreements was thought to be quite inadequate for solving the overspill problem of the London area, for two reasons.

First, the overriding principle of new and expanded town development was that there should be a minimum of 'dormitory' accommodation. If direct arrangements were made between the new areas and groups of exporting authorities, there was a real danger that housing needs would predominate over industrial needs. It was therefore felt that the problem of linking the recruitment needs of the receiving areas with the housing needs of families in the exporting areas could be met satisfactorily only by a regional scheme.

Secondly, in view of the marked expansion of the total number of houses to be built in the country, the number of exporting authorities was increased and it was necessary to ensure, as far as practicable, that 'all the authorities whose areas are seriously overcrowded have an opportunity to get some of the houses in the expanded as well as the new towns for some of their people; the minister could not view with equanimity arrangements over the whole expanded town field which would restrict the opportunities they offer to a few only of the exporting authorities, and those perhaps not the most severely congested'.

Under the new industrial selection scheme exporting authorities were required to keep a register of families in urgent need of rehousing† who wished to move to new and expanded towns. The register was to include details of recent employment experience, qualifications, and the type of work required by these families.

---

* MHLG File 91650/73/1/2.

† Council tenants, of course, could be included in the register since their vacated accommodation could be used to relieve urgent housing need.

Firms requiring workers, whether they were firms already established in the receiving area or about to go there, were to notify their requirements in the usual way to the Ministry of Labour, who would then approach local authorities for names from their register. Anyone thus selected for employment would be nominated by the employer for the tenancy of one of the houses in the receiving area.

Direct arrangements between exporting and receiving authorities under the Town Development Act were to be subject to the approval of the Minister of Housing and Local Government. This would not normally be withheld if the minister were satisfied that people transferring under such arrangements had work to go to. Direct arrangements with new town corporations would be considered by the corporations only in special cases, eg for people who already worked in or near the new town area, and retired or self-employed people. The 'linkage' of exporting authorities with reception areas proposed in the 1949 scheme was retained only as 'a framework for orderly working, based on the main line of communication, but not as rigid divisions'.

The extended scope of the new scheme necessitated a change in the financial arrangements. The minister 'would prefer to leave exporting and receiving authorities to settle between themselves how the annual rate fund contribution is to be met, but that would hardly be feasible where tenants are going out to the new houses by means of the industrial selection scheme'. Further, some conformity throughout the region was desirable (if for no other reason than to avoid 'competition' between exporting authorities). Accordingly, the minister 'suggested' that 'all exporting authorities shall pay the annual Housing Act rate fund contribution for a period of ten years in respect of every family put forward by them which is provided with a house in an expanded town if they continue in occupation for that period. The position should be reviewed between the authorities at the end of ten years, in the light of their financial circumstances'.

Exporting authorities were not compelled to make this contribution, but 'receiving authorities will be entitled to assume that any exporting authority who put forward names under the industrial selection scheme accept this arrangement'. The same basic arrangement was to apply to nominees of local authorities who obtained houses in the new towns.*

The main objection of the London authorities to the new scheme

---

* There was one difference: in the case of an expanded town, if agreement concerning the rate fund contribution after the ten year period could not be reached, the case could by mutual consent be referred to the minister. In the case of a new town such arbitration would be difficult if the development corporation were still in existence (since the corporation was a government sponsored body); responsibility for the rate fund contribution, therefore, was to be automatically assumed by the corporation.

was the payment of contributions to new town development corporations, although several were also opposed to the wider linkage arrangements.* The purpose of these was appreciated, but it was thought that the new scheme ought not to prejudice the linkages already made between individual exporting authorities and the new towns. The linkage proposed in the 1949 scheme had not worked and the practice had been for individual authorities to make specific arrangements. Relationships (eg between East Ham and Basildon) had been built up over a period of time and were now 'most cordial'. Though the actual benefits received had been disappointing, they were tangible; under the new scheme authorities who had made these arrangements were likely to suffer. Further, councils who had made individual arrangements with expanding towns were likely to be penalized if the system of industrial selection was operated. The amount of 'dormitory' provision would decline. This, of course, was the ministry's intention, but to those authorities who, after spending much time and effort on negotiations, had managed to implement such schemes, it seemed unnecessary and 'quite contrary to the wishes of the families on their waiting lists'. In East Ham, for example, a very large number of housing applicants had refused to give up their existing employment to secure residence in the new towns; on the other hand, the number of families wishing to move to Brentwood (where some 600 houses were being built) was nearly three times greater than the number of houses available. Thus East Ham's experience was that the majority of families on their list wished to retain their existing employment, but to move to 'out-borough' estates. If the new towns were to make accommodation available on a similar basis it would be possible to meet the wishes of families in the borough and at the same time to provide relief to the authority's housing problem.

Not all councils shared these views: in fact the majority had not been able to obtain 'out-borough' sites. But nearly all were agreed that the payment of rate fund contributions for houses in the new towns on the same basis as for houses in expanded towns was, in principle, objectionable. The payment of a contribution in the case of expanded towns had been accepted with reluctance as what the ministry described as a 'sweetener' to encourage towns capable of expansion to accept a substantial and abnormal population movement from congested areas. In the case of new towns, however, there was no necessity for a 'sweetener'. Further, contributions had been looked upon as a price to be paid for the right to nominate

---

* The objections were, of course, registered while the scheme was in draft form. No substantial amendments were conceded by the ministry. In order to simplify the exposition, the provisions of the new scheme have been outlined before the objections are discussed. All the negotiations referred to actually took place before the issue of the circular.

tenants: if nominations were not to be allowed then no contributions should be paid.

The payment of these contributions was also thought to raise some important points of principle. First, payments of contributions in such circumstances was very often accompanied by some measure of control. Was it envisaged that new town corporations would be 'democratized', eg by the co-option of representatives from the exporting local authorities? Secondly, were contributions still to be paid even when a rehoused family moved elsewhere? It was appreciated that all houses to which families moved from an exporting area could not be 'tied' for the period of the contribution to that authority. Nevertheless, it seemed fair that the payment of the contribution should be accompanied by the right to nominate to a proportion of vacancies, or at least the right to have first option of letting, to be exercised within a short period. Thirdly, exporting authorities should be given powers of control over vacated accommodation in their areas. If this were not done, vacated houses might be occupied by families from other areas: in such cases the local authority would secure no benefit even though they were paying contributions for a family that had moved out.

Protests and deputations to the ministry secured very little alteration in the scheme. Satisfaction was reached only on the following points:

(a) Contributions were to be in respect of tenants (not houses) and would be subject to an annual check.
(b) Contributions would relate only to local authority nominees.
(c) To enable local authorities to ensure that accommodation vacated by families moving to new and expanded towns should be used to the best advantage, the development corporations had been asked 'to send to the exporting local authority as soon as they possibly can, notification of any family about to move to a new town, so that where the family is occupying a rented house or flat the local authority can try to arrange with the landlord to accept a tenant from the housing list'.

Meetings held at the ministry and attended by representatives of the local authority associations revealed widespread concern over the new scheme. The general view was that there should be no prescription to local authorities as to the extent and period of contributions. The export of families, all with one or more wage earners, would increase the prosperity of the receiving area but would have serious effects on the exporting area. The latter would be likely to 'lose a greater proportion of their younger people than older, and those who remained would still have to bear the standing charges for the various services provided by the local authority'. The amount and

terms of any contribution by the exporting authority should, therefore, be left to the free negotiation of the parties. The new scheme
made it impossible for exporting authorities to negotiate terms under
which they would pay less than the prescribed amount.

The ministry could not accept this line of argument. They thought
that if the scheme were altered in this way exporting authorities
would compete among themselves for overspill sites. This would
inevitably result in the London County Council, with their immense
financial resources, obtaining an 'unfair share'. Since it was made
quite clear that authorities who refused to make the contribution
would be most unlikely to secure any overspill housing at all, there
was little that could be done. The scheme as amended was, therefore, reluctantly accepted.

On the 10th September 1953, the ministry wrote to local
authorities in the Greater London area informing them that the
new scheme was to come into full operation on the 1st November
1953. As from that date 'no local authority lists will be used by the
Ministry of Labour in filling new town vacancies except from areas
where the authority have informed the minister that they are taking
part in the scheme'. In short, unless local authorities agreed to accept
the financial commitments involved they would not be allowed to
put forward names of families on their housing lists for inclusion in
the Ministry of Labour lists.

The administrative details of the revised selection scheme were
similar to those of 1949: the local authorities prepared lists of housing
applicants wishing to move to new and expanded towns. These lists
showed the recent employment history of the applicant, together
with his 'qualifications' and a note on the jobs he was prepared to
take. Firms requiring workers notified their requirements to their
local employment exchange which forwarded them to the regional
office in London. The requirements were then passed on to the local
authorities in the 'linked' sectors. Names of suitable applicants were
sent to the Ministry of Labour and, where necessary, preliminary
interviews were arranged at a local employment exchange when that
ministry would decide on the general suitability of the applicant for
the job. Details were then sent to the firm. Where no suitable
applicants were available in the 'linked' sector, an approach was
made to local authorities in a wider area.

The new scheme had a slow beginning, and considerable difficulties arose over classifying applicants according to their 'job
suitability'; but by the end of 1954 it was working fairly smoothly.
Employers found it useful, and in practice the procedure was less
cumbersome than it appeared. During the years 1955 and 1956
about a fifth of the houses erected in the new towns went to
Londoners who had been nominated through the scheme. Never-

theless, the amount of benefit received by the London authorities was still, in their view, disappointing. Many firms were taking a very large proportion of their labour force with them. Their predominant need was for skilled workers, but as these were in short supply they did not figure largely on the housing lists. The LCC, for example, found that the largest group on their lists consisted of transport workers, for whom there was comparatively little demand.

Criticism of the scheme continued during 1954 and several representations were made to the Ministry of Housing and Local Government. Mention of one of these was made in the second reading debates on the New Towns Bill of 1954. Mr Percy Daines, Member for East Ham North, suggested that the minister's attitude towards the new towns was 'idealistic' and that 'the type of surgical-economic operation under the industrial selection scheme will cause considerable distress to our people and will not fulfil its purpose because those who are affected will take steps to see that the purpose is not fulfilled'.* The ministry were trying to make Basildon a 'self-contained' town, yet it lay half-way between London and the dormitory town of Southend. Many families from east London had taken jobs in Basildon in order to obtain houses, but after a few weeks they had returned to their jobs in London: the higher wages obtainable in the London area made it worth their while to pay the fares involved. The development of dormitory towns was admitted to be wrong in principle but 'people will not necessarily conform' to the minister's plans. If Basildon were developed on a dormitory basis, in fifteen or twenty years time it would be a self-sufficient community: people would gradually give up travelling to London and would take jobs in the new town. Mr Daines' plea was for 'reconsideration on the question of timing'; what was needed was 'a little margin during these years of terrific pressure so that we can achieve the same object and have eventually a healthy, socially and economically balanced community'.

The parliamentary secretary (Deedes) thought it inevitable 'at this stage, when the London group of new towns is housing barely one fifth of its ultimate capacity, that some of the overcrowded London boroughs should be showing very natural restiveness' at the rate of progress, but the suggestion that new towns should be used as dormitories 'would be a major departure from policy, and, even if practicable, might imperil the new towns'. He felt that some councils had exaggerated ideas as to the contribution that the new towns could make to London's problems. Nevertheless, though he did not want to raise false hopes, he felt it safe to say that 'from now

---

* HC Debates, Vol 535, Cols 1318–1321, 10 December 1954.

on, the new towns idea will show an increasing dividend'. The preliminary works were nearing completion and the 'outward flow' was increasing in volume.

The statistics for 1954 and 1955 proved this to be right. Whereas up to the end of 1953 a total of only 14,000 houses had been provided in the new towns, in 1955 and 1956 the annual rate of completions was about 8,000. Nevertheless, the ministry were finding that the scheme was 'inadequate' in respect of families who, though not nominated by exporting authorities, were 'in housing need'. It was felt that exporting authorities should pay contributions for these families. The ministry, therefore, considered introducing a system for investigating 'the previous housing circumstances of each family transferred to see whether it could have been nominated as being in housing need'. This was rejected on administrative grounds, and ways were sought of simplifying the procedure.

The Housing Subsidies Act 1956*

An opportunity for simplification arose when housing subsidy policy was changed by the Housing Subsidies Act of 1956. Following the passing of this Act the ministry paid an annual sum of £8 (for ten years) in lieu of the rate fund contribution for each London family rehoused in the new and expanded towns. One half of this was recovered by the ministry (if necessary by compulsion) from the exporting authority from whose area the first tenant of any house came. The basis of this was simply that about half of the overspill 'represents relief of housing need'. This procedure obviated the 'frightful administrative complexity of trying to sort out with all the authorities of exporting areas the circumstances of each individual family which moved'.

In fact the new procedure did not work out as effectively as had been hoped. Although the 50 per cent basis was 'fairly accurate' over the London areas as a whole, there were considerable variations between authorities. Up to the end of 1956, the proportion of families rehoused in the new towns who had previously been on local authority housing lists ranged from 54 per cent in the case of Tottenham to 31 per cent in the case of Wood Green. Further, there was a tendency for the proportions to fall. Many of the exporting authorities complained bitterly about this situation. Not only were the new towns providing them with a grossly inadequate amount of relief, but, to add insult to injury, contributions were being 'extorted' by the ministry irrespective of the amount of relief. This was, in their view, too big a price to pay for the sake of administrative con-

---

* MHLG Files NT 15/15, NT 124/6, NT 124/11, NT 124/14, NT 124/17, NT 124/20 and NT 140/10.

venience.* Further, the apparent simplicity of the scheme was proving illusory. It was sometimes difficult to ascertain correctly where the migrant families had in fact previously lived. Cases had arisen where families had moved to a new town but had, shortly afterwards, moved elsewhere; yet the exporting authority had to pay a contribution on the houses for ten years. The ministry had 'administratively urged new town corporations to take this factor into account, and where such a family leaves the house in the receiving area after a relatively short period, to take steps as far as possible to see that a substitute family comes from the same district'. Little more could be done unless the administrative complexities were to be increased.

Various suggestions were made by the local authorities for improving the procedure. Enfield, for example, suggested that 'the minister should have regard to the following circumstances before determining that contributions are recoverable:

'(i) That the family housed in a new town should have a residential qualification within the exporting authority's area of not less than the immediate past five years.

(ii) That the family should not have owned accommodation immediately prior to being housed in a new town.

(iii) That the husband and wife who are moving to the new town should have been married for not less than two years prior to so moving.'

The ministry, however, felt that, despite some inevitable anomalies, the scheme as a whole was working fairly well. Nevertheless, there was a constant source of complaint that workers with low skills and in extreme housing need in London had little or no chance through the industrial selection scheme of obtaining accommodation in the new towns. While houses in the new towns were in short supply, employers naturally preferred to reserve the houses allocated to them for skilled workers, rather than for unskilled workers, who could often be recruited locally and who were not in need of houses. To an employer who wanted workers, it seemed senseless for a bureaucratic scheme to attempt to deny employment to those who lived in the locality; in any case it would have been futile to do so when he could engage a local worker who approached him direct and not through an employment exchange. The effect of the system was to reduce the numbers of unskilled vacancies which

* A further reason for annoyance was the fact that 'the very Housing Subsidies Act which relieved . . . local authorities of the necessity of making rate contributions in respect of families in acute housing need, at the same time put on them this new responsibility of having to make a rate contribution for many families who have no housing need at all'. (Mrs Joyce Butler, Member for Wood Green, HC Debates, Vol 569, Col 1342, 9 May 1957.)

were notified to London and on which the industrial selection
scheme could be expected to operate.

Following Jay's letter to Crossman of January 1965* in which
inter alia he complained that the migrants to the new towns seldom
came from the high priority groups on the London housing lists,
Mellish (Parliamentary Secretary, MHLG) undertook to investigate the extent to which the new towns drew their unskilled
workers from the London housing lists. He established a close
contact with members and officials of the GLC engaged in housing
matters. Much activity followed, but little basis was found for any
sound statistical judgment: the pattern of movements in and out
was complex, and was confused by the reletting of houses and
differences in the industrial qualifications of the tenants. The
ministry's figures showed that, by the end of 1964, of 82,000 houses
in the London new towns, 67,500 had been occupied by families
from Greater London and, of these, 25,000 were known to have
been on one of the London housing lists; but only 4,500 had been
placed through the industrial selection scheme. LCC figures showed
that, between 1953 and 1964, 200,000 names had been submitted
to the Ministry of Labour, as a result of which 12,100 had been
placed both in employment and housed (7,700 in expanded towns
and 4,400 in new towns). The secretary commented that:

'It is my hunch that in the new towns the employers go pretty much their
own way; they go through the motions of looking at the names from London
and then proceed to recruit by whatever means they find easiest.'

As a result of this exercise, the ministry reminded the corporations
that 'their towns should give as much relief as possible to the housing problems of the Greater London authorities'. In allocating
houses to workers recruited by new town employers the priorities
should be

'First: residents of Greater London who are tenants of or
registered on the housing waiting list of a Greater
London authority.
Second: other residents of Greater London.
Third: non-Londoners'.

The categories of persons to whom rented accommodation might
be allocated were:

'(a) Londoners already employed by a firm when it moved to a new
town.
(b) Londoners nominated by an employer already established in a
new town who are

---

* Chapter V, p. 215.

(i) tenants of or on a housing list in London and produce a certificate to that effect;

(ii) residents in Greater London or elsewhere who do not qualify under (i), but who are certified by the local employment exchange that the employer has tried and failed to obtain a worker under the ISS from a London housing list.

(c) families living in the new town who are displaced in the course of the new town development.

(d) children of first generation immigrant families who work in or near a new town.

(e) men returning to civil life after regular service in the Forces.

(f) old people who are relations of immigrants or are residents in Greater London'.

It was recognised that (b) could not be applied rigidly to employers with a number of different establishments in different parts of the country whose personnel policy involved frequent transfers from one to another; nor to public service employees such as policemen, firemen, or district nurses.

But pressure from ministers continued, and in a series of meetings with the GLC, representatives of the new towns, and the employment exchange managers, it was agreed that the new towns should accept a fixed proportion of rented housing to be made available for 'hard cases' eg unskilled workers from London with low incomes and extreme housing need. Nomination for these houses would be not by employers but by the local exchange. The exchanges would give priority to Londoners for new town jobs over local people who lived outside the new town boundaries. It was suggested that the GLC should have a publicity programme, and that employers in the new towns be urged to train unskilled workers. It was also contemplated that as there were no less than fifty bodies (housing authorities in the exporting areas, employment exchanges, expanding towns and new town corporations) involved in the operation, with no one person or authority having the duty or means of keeping watch on the working of the machine, there might be a focal point of co-ordination.

The Special Housing Allocation

The immediate result of this agreement was the issue of a circular urging corporations to introduce a 'special housing allocation' under which a fixed proportion (suggested at 15 per cent) of the rented housing becoming available (ie new houses plus relets) would be reserved for unskilled and semi-skilled workers from London who were in great housing need. The GLC would nominate 'suitable high priority workers' to be registered for this housing while the Ministry of Labour would process these registered workers, and send their particulars to the new town employment exchange ('or ask them to pay a personal visit'). The new town exchange would then try to place the worker in employment and, where successful, would nominate him to the corporation for housing within the 15 per cent quota.

The Commission for the New Towns, in respect of their four towns, quickly dissociated themselves from implementing the arrangements 'in the near future', arguing that 'as a matter of pure philosophy there should now be no scope for further immigration . . . as the margin left for further development was carefully calculated to meet second generation needs, and if the existing population was entirely stable the margin would have to be wholly reserved for that purpose'. In practice, they agreed the position was 'not quite so tight': industry was still expanding, and the demand was for skilled workers. There was the usual small turnover of civil servants, teachers and other local government officers moving from one job to another, and house vacancies could not be released for other purposes; but, 'the simple fact is that, after meeting the inescapable priorities, the balance of the houses remaining available go to second generation or elderly parents, and to take any of the un-skilled immigrants from London would mean a row with the local authorities, and a decision which made it clear that in the ministry's view housing more Londoners was more important than housing the newly weds and would-be weds who have grown up in the town'. The ministry accepted that the developed towns should not be pressed.

The other London towns were more amenable. Harlow expected to have 1,130 dwellings available for letting in 1966, and agreed to operate the 15 per cent quota when a backlog of 150 cases of un-skilled workers already engaged by two firms under the industrial selection scheme had been cleared. Basildon had no objection to adopting the 15 per cent quota which would result in 120 dwellings a year. Stevenage agreed the quota in principle, but in view of the existing backlog could not contemplate operating the scheme till April 1967. They added that the introduction of a further high proportion of low wage earners unable to meet current rents in full would put a financial strain on their housing revenue account. Bracknell were sympathetic, but as their houses were 'overcommitted' beyond 1970, proposed to adopt a quota of 5 per cent in 1967.

Such were the rather unenthusiastic replies from the new towns. The mechanics of the scheme were put into operation, but progress was slow, and the 15 per cent quota was never achieved, the main difficulty being that 'the respective employment exchange managers were not able to "sell" sufficient workers to employers'. Constant effort was made to make the scheme successful and to get unskilled Londoners into jobs and houses in the new towns, despite criticism 'that skilled men could be kept waiting for houses while less skilled men in housing need jumped the queue'. But the success of the scheme depended on job availability, and as unskilled workers could generally be recruited from those in the locality who were not in need of houses, its scope was limited. Figures for the four towns quoted in a letter from the Ministry of Labour illustrated the problem: in the two years to September 1968, the GLC had nominated 1,550 workers; 900 of those approached by the Ministry of Labour failed to reply or for various reasons were no longer interested in a move to a new town; 550 submissions had been made by the local exchanges to local employers, which had resulted in 237 placings (with a number still under consideration). There tended to be a good deal of wastage between placings and lettings for a variety of reasons, 'including unpleasant jobs, shift work, poor pay, no overtime and the waiting period for a house'.

Though the position fluctuated from time to time and between different towns, it was difficult for exchange managers, while there was a substantial pool of local unemployed, to press new town employers to engage unskilled Londoners; equally it was un-realistic for the GLC to increase their submissions of unskilled Londoners who would be unable to obtain work. In view of the situation, the special housing allocation scheme lapsed in Basildon during 1968, and at Bracknell during 1969.

Notwithstanding the rather disappointing results of the 'special allocation' scheme, it was kept in operation and, in 1970, corpora-tions were informed that in so far as the allocation was not filled by the normal procedure, the balance should be used to house Lon-doners in housing need who would continue to work outside the town. 'People moving in this way would be better placed to seek employment in or near the new town and take advantage of any job opportunities offering training and would not run in to the complication of lodging or travelling out to a new job while waiting allocation of a house'.

The London Dispersal Liaison Group

In parallel with the 'special allocation', steps were taken to form an organisation to improve the general working of the industrial selection scheme, and to match the employment needs in new and expanded towns with the housing needs of London workers prepared to move. A number of initial difficulties were encountered in view of the number of authorities with administrative powers which they could or would not relinquish, but ultimately a scheme was agreed for a standing committee of senior officials, to supervise a group of three officers drawn from the Ministry of Housing and Local Government, the Ministry of Labour and the Greater London Council. The terms of reference to the group (whose title became that of the London Dispersal Liaison Group after attempts to avoid the use of the term 'overspill') were 'to review the administrative arrangements for the removal of employees and their families from Greater London to the new and expanding towns, to pay particular attention to the problems of training and publicity, and to examine the form in which statistics of movement might best be collected'.

From the end of 1966 the group had wide ranging discussions with interested bodies, including the new towns branch of the GLC; the regional offices, local employment exchanges, and government training centres of the Department of Employment and Productivity; fourteen London boroughs; thirteen expanding towns and eight London new towns; the Engineering Industry Training Board; and the Harlow and District Industrial Employers Group. In their report, at the end of 1969, the group concluded that despite the occasional complaint about the scheme being slow moving and cumbersome, there were 'no general grounds for radical changes'.

Some administrative improvements were proposed, but the main problem was that delay in obtaining housing accommodation in a new or expanded town was perhaps the greatest disincentive to a Londoner seeking employment: 'our enquiries confirm that this is a root cause of frustration, family separation and financial difficulty for immigrants starting work in reception areas'. To encourage the flow of Londoners to the new and expanded towns, to ease the financial strain and to persuade the movement of industry generally, the group considered that each new and expanded town should keep available so far as possible a pool of empty dwellings.

The build-up of industry in new and expanded towns called particularly for skilled labour; outstanding vacancies for skilled men had on occasions out-numbered the combined total of those for unskilled and semi-skilled personnel by six or eight times. With placing of unskilled men averaging between 600 and 700 annually, only about one in eight (possibly one in ten) of unskilled Londoners registering under the industrial selection scheme was likely to be successful in securing a job and a home in a new or expanded town. Training was therefore the only hope for thousands of would-be migrants. It was emphasised that it was the unskilled Londoner who was invariably in the greatest housing need.

The evidence collected by the group suggested, however, that industrial training had had relatively little effect on migration through the industrial selection scheme and that the unskilled registrant had little inclination to accept government training to promote his prospects of finding employment in a reception area. There was insufficient demand to warrant 'off the job' group training facilities for the training of adults to semi-skilled level in new towns.

The group's inquiries suggested that many families moving to a new or expanded town suffered initial financial hardship. This sprang from the actual cost of removal, the need for some workers to run two homes until accommodation for the family was available, and the cost of furnishing a new dwelling (perhaps for the first time). These financial difficulties constituted a positive disincentive to migration and it was suggested that consideration should be given to a scheme of financial assistance in the form of a resettlement grant.

The operation of the ISS required a conscious effort on all fronts to give the best possible advice. It necessitated staff of good calibre all along the line, with adequate time to do the job properly. The group 'had gained the impression' that officials, both in employment exchanges and at county hall, were working under considerable pressure, and the question arose as to whether the ISS might in practice be the 'Cinderella' in both organisations. It was therefore recommended that the respective staffing authorities should look carefully at the volume of work associated with new and expanded town placings and ensure that sections concerned were adequately staffed and briefed at all times.

It was thought likely that the group's recommendations would have only modest effects on the successful operation of the industrial selection scheme but 'we dare to hope that our existence has had a catalytic effect, not least in the field of publicity, in creating a general awareness of and interest in the scheme and in securing the co-operation of all bodies involved'.

Better Class Housing in the New Towns*

The Reith Committee drew particular attention to the need for the new towns to be 'balanced communities' in the sense of including people of all social classes, and recommended that groups of larger houses of varying sizes should be provided for both renting and buying in all sections of the town. The major demand in the early years, however, was for 'standard housing' though, from the beginning, the development corporations were keen to provide a proportion of better class housing. In 1950, corporations were authorised to build larger houses of up to 2,000 square feet as long as these did not exceed five per cent of their housebuilding programmes. It was initially contemplated that these would be occupied by people working in the town, but in June 1957 corporations were permitted

---

* MHLG Files NT 35/1, NT 35/2 and NT 36/3.

to build better class houses for sale or lease to commuters 'who would contribute towards a balanced community'.

Brooke took a particular interest in this issue and, in December 1959 minuted the secretary that, through his wife's brother (the Dean of St Albans), he had met the vicars of three new towns—Hemel Hempstead, Hatfield and Stevenage:

'The main point they put to me was that the key to securing the future leadership which is so badly needed in the new towns is a policy of allocation of housing land for private enterprise which will ensure that there are real areas of the town for houses for people of the executive class, and that such houses will not be dribbled along in narrow bands where they will be pressed in on all sides by the houses of these men's employees. It is this fear, the clergy said to me, of not being able to live in a new town among the sort of immediate neighbours whom they would normally have elsewhere that is the principal factor inducing men of the executive type to try and live outside the new town if they can. Yet the future social life of the new town will depend so much on these men and their wives remaining within it.

I thought that this was a fruitful comment, in the light of all the thought we are giving to the provision of land for private enterprise housing in Crawley and the other new towns as they approach completion.'

Within the department it was agreed to be necessary to avoid confusing two different things—'owner occupation as such, and the need to get the really top people to live in the towns'. There was no need to 'go on banging away at the corporations' on 'lower middle class housing' for sale:

'They all know what we want: they are all doing as much as they can; and I do not think there is anything new that we can usefully say to them. Nor do I think it is really going to be useful to ask for a lot of statistical information.'

The upshot was a letter to all general managers stating that the minister was asking what success the corporations had had in attracting senior industrial executives and other people of similar social standing to live in the new towns. It was thought that all corporations shared the minister's view that 'these are the potential community leaders and that the towns will never be completely successful socially unless such people are willing to live in the towns and identify themselves fully with the towns' life'. The ministry's impression was that most of the corporations had had little success in this direction so far. The problem was seen, not simply as a question of encouraging more owner occupation by methods which had already been tried. Statistically, several towns had 'a good record of new houses made available for sale', but a high proprtion of these were not of the right kind for the purpose: the typical semidetached style which the speculative builders had generally adopted would not attract 'the type of people whom we really want to secure'. If they wanted a new house they were more likely to want something in the price range of £5,000 and upwards, 'and something which did not look obviously a mass produced article'.

Corporations were asked to provide an account of what they felt had been achieved so far and any suggestions they might have for improving the position. There were two points which were of particular interest to MHLG. First, whether, in the light of experience, the areas reserved in the master plan for really good quality houses were large enough, 'bearing in mind that the clients we are seeking do not like to feel hemmed in, either by their own neighbours or by standard housing close by'. Secondly, whether the corporations 'could usefully themselves build more of the right type of house, either for sale or for letting'.

This letter was sent out in January 1960, and a summary of the replies was prepared in March. The general conclusion was that there had been little success in attracting senior industrial executives and other people of similar social standing to live in the towns. Seven factors which made it difficult to get senior industrial executives to live in new towns were listed :

'(i) it was a present day fashion for people who could afford to do so to live outside the town in which they worked ;

(ii) many senior people in industry would not live in the same town or area where the majority of their working people lived ; they found that to live on top of the job meant that they did not 'get away from it' because they are always running across their own people ; this difficulty was possibly accentuated in new towns where industry and housing were compact ;

(iii) people in the higher salary range did not willingly accept the inconveniences inherent in the pioneering of a new community ;

(iv) expense of travel was no deterrent ; they were content to live some distance away from their places of work, in an old established community with all the amenities they needed on their doorsteps ; this attitude was influenced by the wishes of their wives and families ;

(v) it was difficult to find sites in the new towns which satisfied the requirements of the type of person in question ;

(vi) some senior people who were living in the southern home counties had preferred to retain their original houses because it was easier to travel southwards to Crawley than it was northwards to London ;

(vii) in the case of Aycliffe, Corby and Cwmbran, industry was already established before the new towns were designated ; the senior executives had already found residential accommodation, usually at some distance from the works'.

Three main requirements for 'higher class' people were identified. First, they wanted houses which were grouped on (appropriately enough) 'first class secluded sites'. Secondly, sites should be well separated from standard housing and should not have to be 'approached through standard housing'. Finally, sites should be adjacent to open space and in 'an area topographically pleasing with a mature landscape'. Most corporations agreed that 'some of the people concerned might prefer to rent rather than buy'. The provincial new town corporations in particular pointed out that senior executives were now required 'to move about the country to a much greater extent than formerly and often at short notice'. Crawley doubted, however, whether the more expensive houses would let readily because there came a point where, taking into account income tax allowances, there was very little point in paying a substantial rent where a house could be bought on mortgage for almost the same outgoings.

There was a fairly firm demand in the London new towns from persons of the 'next lower level'. Houses for sale at prices up to £4,000 or £4,500 were being built and were selling readily. In Welwyn and Hatfield (where there had been 'some success in this direction'), they had never attempted to get absolute maximum prices, but had been 'content to get a shade of profit' and at the same time offer something which was capable of being resold without the purchaser showing a loss. The indications were that when a house changed hands, the seller made a profit.

Some general managers did not accept the view that senior industrial executives were the potential community leaders. It was suggested that 'generally speaking these leaders come from a rather lower level and only exceptionally from the really senior executives'. In Hemel Hempstead, only a small proportion of top executives took an active interest in the life of the town, or could be described as potential community leaders. Stevenage, on the other hand, were convinced that the new town would begin to develop as a normal town only when they had attracted this type of person.

This summary gave rise to a series of internal minutes. One suggested that there were in fact two classes of people and two types of house in question—although there was no hard and fast boundary between either the classes or types. The two classes of people were (a) directors, senior managerial staff and their equivalents; and (b) senior executives, senior technical staff and the majority of professional people. The corresponding types of house were probably those costing (a) over £5,000; and (b) £3,000–£5,000.

So far as attracting the really 'top people' was concerned, it was clear that the corporations had had little or no success so far. This was not surprising. 'There are not very many of these people. They are not tied by economic considerations to living near their work; and social considerations may dictate that they do not live near it.' It was doubtful whether there was much a corporation could do to attract them beyond setting aside, for private development, carefully selected sites, which had 'clearly and unmistakably no connection with the ordinary housing areas of the town'. Corporations should not build speculatively themselves: the risks were too great, except perhaps in Welwyn which was 'established and fashionable'—'thanks to the corporation's continuance of the Garden City Company's prewar policy'. It was doubted whether any of the other towns would ever be so.

The new towns tended to be overshadowed by fashionable neighbours—Hemel Hempstead by Berkhamstead, Bracknell by Ascot, Windlesham, etc and Hatfield by Welwyn. Basildon might never completely escape the 'shack' stigma, although there was one site (Langdon Hills) which was potentially a very good area for expensive houses, 'with fine views and well wooded'. Perhaps Harlow and Stevenage would successfully establish their 'snob' areas, although the latter was very near Welwyn.

> 'Perhaps it does not matter very much if they do not . . . It is nice to have the top people in the town to lend their names, and to dig into their pockets, but I think the town councillors, the youth club leaders, the church and social workers, and the officers of the multifarious specialist clubs can be found elsewhere, and usually are.'

With the supply of building land in the home counties constantly diminishing, both because sites were being developed and because green belts were being extended, middle class houses in the new towns would probably become more attractive, even though they might largely be occupied by commuters. In another respect too, time was on the corporations' side: 'they are moving away from the pioneering or "gumboot" stage as it has been called'.

Both the ministry and the Treasury were agreed that better class housing should not attract housing subsidies, but a protracted argument developed on the means by which it could be provided. The Treasury argued the case for owner occupation; the new towns already had a very high proportion of rented housing, and a big rise in owner occupation seemed 'the natural development to be expected and welcomed in new towns', and one which private enterprise building would obviously meet.

MHLG, however, saw a fatal objection to an increase in owner occupation: it would be achieved by sales to commuters.* The

---

* The Treasury, on the other hand, saw 'every reason why some commuters, who can pay their way, should be welcomed to new towns if they choose to live there; it would be a different matter if there were a real danger (but is there?) that the new towns might be swamped by these commuters'. It was accepted that a balance should be held, 'but we

available land would be used up and 'what do we then do for the second generation coming along in enormous numbers. We should have to let the town burst its bounds'. It was essential to ensure a steady supply of houses to rent which would be let and relet to people who worked in the town. Though MHLG would 'go for as much owner occupation as we dare' it was essential that, for some time after the corporations had been wound up, there should be a continuing supply of houses to let.

This argument led the ministry to the conclusion that the Commission for the New Towns should provide better class rented houses. Exchequer advances would be necessary, but the commission would 'aim at economic rents . . . or as near as we can get'.

This method had substantial advantages over owner occupation:

'by building to let, we can control the tenancies; and also incidentally produce houses at less cost to the occupier since they will be financed over sixty years. This should enable us to attract some of the existing subsidised tenants who don't feel able to afford owner occupation at the moment. But as the years go on and the towns stabilise the houses might well be sold.'

The Treasury, however, were not prepared to consider this proposal separately from the general policy on housing. The provision of exchequer money for the building of better class houses for renting was an entirely new policy to which they feared that they would be committed nationally if they conceded it for the new towns. They were concerned at the wide divergence between MHLG and Treasury policy in connection with the new towns, and wished to see the new towns treated as normal towns at the earliest possible date. They therefore wanted 'no truck' with anything that looked like 'a continued differentiation from the normal'.

This particular difficulty was removed when it was agreed as a matter of national housing policy that exchequer funds should be provided to enable housing associations to build better class rented housing.* Henceforth development corporations would be allowed to build better class houses for rent (aiming at economic rents) without subsidy but with some benefit from the general housing account, 'provided this could be done without carrying these housing accounts into deficit'.

Much more difficult to settle was the question of the role of the commission as a provider of housing. The Treasury had always

---

ask you not to overdo it with public money'. (In New York State, 'the commuters—extremely well-heeled, and called exurbanites—bring a great deal of money into the local communities, of which their wives and families are part-and-parcel and to which they retire from the rat race'.)

* See white paper, *Housing in England and Wales*, Cmnd 1290, in which it was announced that exchequer loans, up to a total of £25m, were to be made available to approved housing associations.

envisaged that, when the corporations were wound up, exchequer commitments ('except for a few tidying-up operations') would come to an end:

> 'we are a bit afraid that if you are to advance money to the commission for further development on house building . . . it could prove to be the thin end of the wedge, and the Treasury would be driven into saying that they should carry on . . . receiving money to support the further natural growth of the new towns. We do not want to see this.'

Within MHLG it was noted that the real problem was that in 1958–59 both they and the Treasury were attempting 'a view of the shape of things to come that has not been borne out by events'. At that time, all were inclined to think that little or no new housing would need to be provided by the commission. It was now clear that that view was 'completely wrong'; but the Treasury seemed to have moved only to the point where they could contemplate further commission expenditure 'only on houses for sale or to let at wholly self-supporting rentals'. The real need in both of the commission towns (Crawley and Hemel Hempstead) was for a considerable further number of ordinary houses supported by subsidy in the ordinary way to meet the demand from new immigrants, and from new married couples from within the town. 'In other words, our clientele is much the same now as it was before. The mere act of takeover by the commission has made no difference to that, and Treasury can hardly have believed that it would.' The first task therefore, was to persuade the Treasury to accept that *some* additional subsidised housing was needed. The main justification for this was that immigrants were still being housed, and even though there would be a rising proportion of new families created within the town, the new town had a responsibility for them also. In any case, if the commission did not provide for them, private enterprise would not, and local authority building would not reduce the amount of subsidy payable.

It was eventually decided that the commission should provide subsidised housing only for old people, though they could also build for sale or for leasing at economic rents. Ordinary subsidised housing, as in 'normal' towns, would be the responsibility of the local authority.

So far as development corporations were concerned, however, lengthy—and frequently tortuous—discussions continued within the ministry, and between the ministry and the Treasury, on what constituted 'better class' housing and the extent to which it should be subsidised. This became further complicated by wider issues of housing finance, the role of housing associations, and housing standards.

In January 1964, the secretary noted that the most difficult issue was whether Parker Morris standards should be the minimum for all the houses in a new town:

> 'I think myself that it is too lush—even remembering that the houses must last for at least sixty years, and that the Parker Morris house of today may be thought pretty modest twenty to thirty years on.'

The new towns division commented that 'Parker Morris costs money. So does high density if it is to provide tolerable living conditions. We urge corporations to aim at both, particularly in the older towns which have an undue proportion of "standard" houses—as a result, mainly, of Treasury insistence some years ago'. They had consistently tried to stop the cutting of standards (which had resulted, in some towns, 'in a number of almost unlettable houses') and had urged 'the building of the best that the people in the town can afford to pay for'.

> 'Provided—
> (a) the planners assure us that the layout etc is reasonably good;
> (b) the architects assure us that it is value for money and passes subsidy tests;
> (c) the rent (with subsidy and normal aid from the pool) covers cost; and
> (d) the proportions of the various types and classes of house are in proper balance (and on this we have to depend largely on the corporation's assessment of demand and rent-paying capacity)—
> then I think schemes should be approved.'

This, indeed, had been the practice for some years: despite the arguments which had been proceeding between the ministry and the Treasury, the new towns had been providing better quality rented housing and had demonstrated that money spent on 'frills' enabled higher rents to be obtained which more than covered the additional cost. At least since the mid fifties, the development corporations—with the agreement of the ministry's new town division—had insisted that they were 'building new towns, not housing estates', and opted for standards higher than were typical in public sector housing. They 'even got away with some semi-luxury flats'.

To a certain extent, therefore, the arguments between the ministry and the Treasury had a somewhat academic air. However, in 1965 a formal agreement was reached that development corporations 'would be allowed to continue to provide Standard II houses' (ie those intended for renting to people in the higher and middle income groups') in 'reasonable' numbers. Subsidy was to be based upon the cost accepted by the department for a house 'having the same capacity in terms of people and built to Parker Morris standards on the same site as the prevailing Standard I houses in the same locality'.

In the meantime, attention had increasingly become focused on owner occupation in new towns—by way of the sale of houses originally provided for renting. Before discussing this, it is necessary to summarise the position in relation to the sale of council houses.

Owner Occupation in New Towns*

THE SALE OF COUNCIL HOUSES

The legislation relating to the sale of council houses provided for sales to be subject to the minister's consent. To avoid the necessity of giving specific consents in each case, general consents had been in operation since 1952. The consent governed such matters as sale price, resale and rent, and distinguished between houses built before and after 8 May 1945. Sale prices were a matter of judgement in the light of the circumstances of the particular authority: while it would be wrong to offer houses 'at sacrificial prices' at the expense of the ratepayers, sale at something less than market value could be justified to those needing houses for their own occupation. The circular therefore laid down bases for *minimum* prices intended to guard against actual loss, but emphasised that these were no more than minima for guidance. Where the circumstances justified it, there was nothing to prevent a local authority from charging market value.

Following the return of the Labour Government in 1964, policy on the sale of council houses came under review. The official opinion was that, in administrative terms, the general consent seemed to have worked well 'since few inquiries are received and authorities very rarely seek to depart from its terms'. Less than one per cent of the total number of council houses had been sold since the war and the number sold in any one year was small. Between January 1963 and September 1965, some 2,700 prewar houses and 4,000 postwar had been sold. But in policy terms, the two questions for consideration on the sale of houses built for letting were whether they ought to be sold at all, and, if so, at what price.

The main argument against these sales was a financial one. If an authority sold a house at a price below the cost of replacing it, the remaining tenants might have to pay higher rents. But aside from this, it was thought that there was in 'some quarters a less well articulated resistance to the general principle'. In the words of a housing division minute:

'One wonders how much this arises from a genuine desire on the part of existing tenants to keep the stock available for future entrants: when one sees the views expressed by council tenants' associations about paying more

---

* MHLG Files NT 203/1, NT 203/2, NT 203/3, NT 85/7 and NT 2/16; see also MHLG Circulars 64/52, 5/60, 32/66 and 24/67.

rent to help people who, being less fortunate than themselves, are only now being admitted to houses built at present day prices one suspects that this attitude has something in common with the instinctive defence of an entrenched right by any body of people with an interest in property.'

The sale of a council house necessarily involved transferring to the tenant 'the benefit of a prudent public investment'. On the other hand, exchequer subsidy stopped once a house was sold; there was a growing demand for owner occupation; and a sale transferred the burden of maintenance from the local authority to the purchaser. There was therefore 'much to be said for it'. Moreover, older council houses would become 'a decreasing asset as the requirements of maintenance and the need for modernisation increase'. But the most important aspect was that the sale of council houses was 'a way of correcting a wrong housing mix'.

In principle, sales were 'not objectionable in themselves': at least when they were made to existing tenants or people high on the waiting list. No special direction on this point was needed. It would be difficult to frame one that was not 'too stimulating in some areas and too repressive in others'. The guiding principle, however, ought to be that a high level of sales of existing houses could not ordinarily co-exist with a big programme of new building to let, since this assumed 'conflicting balances of demand'.

The ministry only set a price floor. For prewar houses, this was twenty years' rent (without taking account of any rebate) while for postwar houses it was the all-in cost. Authorities were encouraged to set higher prices if they thought them appropriate (though it was added that they could fix prices below the full open market level in recognition of housing need), and were given general authority to sell at these prices if they chose. MHLG commented that 'we cannot afford to feel too happy about these price levels'. At 31 March 1964 (the latest date for which MHLG had the general statistics published by the Institute of Municipal Treasurers and Accountants) the average net rents for pre-1939 three bedroom houses ranged from 9s 9d a week to 57s 3d according to the authority. Anybody buying a family house built between 1919 and 1939 for something between £500 and £3,000, depending on age, condition and area, could be expected to be getting 'a pretty cheap buy'. For postwar houses, the minimum price level of overall cost to the council could be 'even less satisfactory'—even though, unlike a price based on rent, it took no account of subsidy. Some of the houses built in the late 1940s 'were built to better standards of accommodation, if not better architectural quality', than many built in the 1950s; yet the 'floor' in the 1960 circular could well produce a sale price of £1,000 to £1,500. It was suspected that many authorities had gone well above this. 'My guess is that authorities selling council houses have in fact kept us out of trouble by charging well above the stipulated minimum price.'

It was agreed that current market value was the only viable basis on which council houses could be sold. The minister (Crossman) accepted this, and the fact that when there was a scarcity, councils should not exploit this by charging '*full* market value'. Indeed, it could be argued that where real scarcity existed, sales should not take place at all; but if houses were to be sold, it was 'difficult to get away from market value'. Selling at below that level would only result in an eventual capital gain for the person who bought and subsequently sold the house.

After a lengthy period of internal discussion and consultations with the local authority associations, a new circular was issued in March 1967. This generally discouraged sales 'in areas where there is still an unsatisfied demand for houses to let at moderate rents', but:

> 'in areas where the demand for rented housing is falling off, or where the local authority can keep pace with demand by a very modest building programme, the authority may decide that they would be justified in offering to sell a proportion of their houses in response to local demand. They should, of course, have regard to the effect on their housing revenue account of selling particular houses or types of houses according to the age and current value of the property. They should also consider carefully the management problems which can arise from piecemeal disposal of individual houses on estates or in terraces or similar groups.'

Subject to these considerations, the general consent to the sale of council houses was renewed. But the conditions governing sale prices were revised: though sales were normally to be at the market price this could be affected by any restrictions placed upon disposal. Under the normal restrictions (the most important of which reserved to the local authority the right to buy back the house at the original cost price allowing for improvement—if the purchaser offered it for sale within five years) the market value was reduced by up to 20 per cent. Consequently the general consent provided that houses could be sold at full market value assuming vacant possession and subject to no limitations on resale, or at up to 20 per cent below market value subject to the prescribed conditions.

SALE OF NEW TOWN HOUSING

In March 1967, ministry officials prepared a paper on policy for housing for sale in new towns. In this they recommended that, after consultation with the corporations and the Commission for the New Towns, a circular should be issued stating that new towns established since 1961 should plan for fifty per cent owner occupation, while older towns should make proposals to MHLG for increasing the proportion of houses to be built for sale. In general, corporations should sell rented houses only to the limited extent compatible with their other commitments, 'principally for overspill'. There were special circumstances affecting towns which had 'substantially completed their overspill task' (including commission towns). Here a special effort should be made by a controlled sales policy to reduce the over-whelming preponderance of rented houses. In building for sale, corporations should aim for at least two thirds of the houses to be built by private enterprise under arrangements whereby the corporation sold or leased land to developers and builders. The policy on house prices in new towns should be brought as closely as possible into line with that adopted by local authorities.

A draft circular on owner occupation was sent for comment to general managers in May 1967 under cover of a letter which attempted to forestall some foreseeable objections. In particular, the letter stated that it was recognised that demand for owner occupa-tion in the early years of a new town might be relatively low 'but it is important that some houses for sale should be available from the beginning to test the market'. Corporations would have in mind the importance of 'a realistic relationship' between standard (as distinct from rebated) rents and mortgage charges. (It was noted that the introduction of the option mortgage scheme in 1968 would help with this.)* Corporations might also consider inviting owner occupiers of older houses in the designated area to part-exchange their houses for new corporation houses—thus making cheaper houses available for sale to immigrants. The draft circular stressed the need for increasing participation by private enterprise in providing houses for sale in new towns. It was recognised that private house building on a large scale might add somewhat to the difficulty of co-ordinating the provision of new employment and community facilities with housing completions 'and it will be important for corporations to enlist the co-operation of private builders in overcoming this problem'.

The draft circular proposed two main aims of policy. First, an ultimate level of 50 per cent owner occupation in the second generation towns, and the same proportion of houses for owner occupation in the current programmes in the older towns; and, secondly, participation by private enterprise to the extent of building at least two thirds of the houses for owner occupation. It also proposed new rules to govern prices and disposal terms. Diplo-matically, the covering letter said that when the time came for corporations to submit their proposals under the circular, 'the minister will not be unmindful of the transitional difficulties inherent in this major change of policy. He will, however, expect to see clear

* See white paper *Help Towards Home Ownership*, Cmnd 3163, 1966.

evidence that corporations are tackling these difficulties in a constructive and imaginative way'.

The comments of the corporations revealed 'a fair consensus of opinion'. The principle of increasing owner occupation was accepted, provided that it could be achieved consistently with the purposes for which the towns were established, but opinions differed as to how far this was feasible. Skelmersdale for example, saw no possibility of achieving more than about 20 per cent owner occupation unless they made a corresponding reduction in their intake of people in housing need from Merseyside, most of whom had insufficient incomes to be potential house purchasers. Redditch, on the other hand, 'anticipated little difficulty in finding a fair proportion of prospective owner occupiers among their housing-need immigrants from Birmingham'. A number of corporations argued that private enterprise would be reluctant to invest in new towns on a large scale unless they were given a free hand in selecting purchasers. Limitations of sales to people working in the new town was said to depress selling prices and restrict demand and, in any case, was difficult to enforce. The London new towns in particular feared an influx of commuters. The example of Crawley was cited: over 70 per cent of the privately owned houses had been built by private developers and sold, allegedly, in the main to London commuters, with the result that a new crash building programme had had to be approved to house local workers.

The ministry thought that there was little real evidence either to support or throw doubt on these fears. Evidence about the real demand for home ownership (and capacity to pay) in the new towns would be forthcoming in due course from a study currently being undertaken.* And both the option mortgage scheme and the progressive introduction of realistic rent levels, coupled with rebate schemes, would tend to make existing tenants look more favourably on home ownership, 'with the possible result of making older houses available for overspill'. Similarly, it was not known how far private enterprise would be deterred by restrictions on purchasers, or even insistence on pre-emption rights, from increasing their output in new towns. 'No one has yet tested them to see.'

The ministry were disposed 'to resist pressure to water down' the draft circular. Instead, it was thought that a paragraph might be added insisting that corporations 'put their fears to the test as a matter of urgency' by approaching suitable private developers with positive offers of attractive sites for building for sale subject to the *minimum* conditions necessary to ensure that a proper proportion of the houses were sold (at least initially) to people already living and

---

* See below p. 438.

working in the new town or moving their jobs and homes from an exporting area.

An internal minute of July 1967 noted that the current pressure to reduce public sector investment in housing reinforced the need to obtain a maximum contribution of private sector finance. The problem, however, was to maintain a proper balance between the need for new towns to make the maximum direct contribution to housing pressures in the conurbations justifying 'the vast amount of exchequer expenditure being poured into the new towns programme', and obtaining the maximum amount of private sector housing investment compatible with this. It should be possible 'to step up the private enterprise contribution in new towns', despite the fears expressed by corporations that private enterprise would be reluctant to invest on a large scale unless they were given a free hand in selecting the purchasers.

Earlier in the year there had been discussions with representatives of the National Federation of Building Trade Employers who stated that experience showed that there was no demand for private enterprise housing at the early stages of the development of a new town. They did, however, suggest that some of the incentives needed would be:

(a) areas set aside for private enterprise—segregated and not amongst corporation housing—with more 'freedom' from corporations' architectural controls over specific house designs;
(b) an embargo on new town corporations building houses for sale in competition with private enterprise;
(c) arrangements for deferring payments for land until the houses had been sold—a point of importance for small builders with small capital resources; and
(d) disposal of land at something less than market value as a *quid pro quo* for building to Parker Morris standards which the NFBTE thought were too expensive.

They were also floating the idea of some form of underwriting arrangements whereby the development corporation would buy back unsold houses—'in short insulating them completely from market risks'.

It was thought that private enterprise should not be 'featherbedded' to the extent advocated by the NFBTE, but the ministry could certainly press corporations to ensure that suitable areas for private housing were made available in the development of the town, that niggling architectural controls were abolished, and consideration might be given to amending the draft circular to limit the building of houses for sale by the corporations 'and go instead for virtually a 100 per cent private enterprise contribution'.

The draft circular was sent to the Treasury in July 1967. They commented that they were basically concerned to ensure that houses were sold 'for as much as they could fetch', and that progress towards the 50 per cent target should be as rapid as possible. They were 'somewhat bothered' by some aspects of the proposed circular. In particular, it did not seem really consistent with this aim to tell corporations as a general principle that, while they were still catering for overspill, they should sell houses only to a limited extent. 'We would have thought that "real efforts" were called for at all times, qualified only by having regard to overspill needs where these cannot be met in other ways'. They also considered that it would be necessary to keep under review the effect on selling prices of the proposed pre-emption clause on houses with vacant possession. Moreover, they were unhappy about some of the proposals in relation to price: what, for instance was meant by current market value in the case of sitting tenants (current market value with vacant possession?) Though they were 'sorry to pose all these questions', it did seem to them that the draft proposals 'set up quite formidable barriers in the way of implementing our policy on owner occupation as well as eroding some of the financial benefits we expect to get from it'.

Within the ministry it was thought that there was 'not much in any of the points raised', though it had probably been a mistake not to clear the draft circular with the Treasury before it was sent to general managers.

In August 1967 the circular was issued. In new towns established since 1961, and those about to be established, it was to be the objective of development corporations to achieve 50 per cent owner occupation by the end of the planned intake period—or sooner if possible—and they should plan accordingly. It was recognised that the scope for building for sale in the early years was likely to be limited if national investment in the town was to serve the purposes for which the town was set up. Nevertheless, corporations should ensure that some houses were available for purchase from the beginning in order to test the market.

In the older new towns, though it was probably too late to achieve an overall 50 per cent (except by large scale disposals of existing rented housing), development corporations should move 'steadily towards an equal division between houses for sale and for rent' in their house building programmes.

One obvious way of increasing owner occupation was by the sale of existing rented houses to sitting or other tenants. The minister took the view that very different considerations applied in the case of first generation new towns (where the great majority of the housing stock was rented), from those applying to local authority housing, (which was provided to meet the continuing demand for houses to let at moderate rents and where tenants who wished to become owner occupiers had ample opportunity to buy privately). Where corporations were still catering for overspill, it was clear that policy on such sales must have regard to the need to maintain a sufficient stock of rented houses to meet overspill needs. On the other hand, in towns which had completed, or almost completed, their planned build-up and were now catering mainly for natural increase, there were special considerations. In these towns the proportion of public rented housing was abnormally high, and the minister thought that, as soon as the demands of immigration slackened, real efforts should be made to alter the balance between renting and owner occupation by offering substantial numbers of rented houses for sale to existing tenants.

As a general rule, current market value should be charged for all houses sold by development corporations whether originally built for rent, built specifically for sale, or acquired, and whether sold with vacant possession or to a sitting tenant.

In new towns having an overspill function it might be necessary for development corporations to ensure, when selling a house, that if the purchaser decided to sell the house it would again become available to the corporation to accommodate overspill—and this was normally done by including a pre-emption clause. If owner occupation in the new towns was to be encouraged, potential owner occupiers must not be deprived of the prospect of a capital appreciation of their investment. Accordingly, pre-emption clauses should be so worded that if the development corporation eventually exercised the right to pre-empt they would re-purchase at the then current market value. The minister was advised that the reservation of the development corporation's right to pre-empt at *current market value* ought not to have any significant effect on selling prices since it was unlikely to result in any significant financial disadvantage to the purchaser on subsequent resale. The duration of the pre-emption clause should be related to the expected duration of the town's overspill function. If the sale was made at the beginning of a planned build-up period of fifteen years or more, a pre-emption clause of a similar duration would not be inappropriate. On the other hand, where the planned build-up was nearing completion a pre-emption clause of shorter duration might be thought sufficient.

The issuing of the circular was immediately followed by a letter from the secretary of MHLG to new town chairmen:

'It will have been clear to you from the minister's remarks at the last chairmen's conference that he attaches great importance to the redirection of housing policy in new towns called for in the circular. He recognises that some corporations doubt whether the targets set up in the circular are attainable; but he is confident that all corporations accept the need to move as quickly as possible towards them and will take a vigorous action to that end.

We in the department shall, of course, do everything we can to help you in overcoming the difficulties. I have already had some discussion with the Building Societies Association—who are anxious to assist. I shall soon be inviting you and your colleagues to attend a meeting with representatives of the Association to discuss what practical steps can be taken to extend the activities of building societies in new towns as a contribution to the increase in owner occupation for which we shall now all be working.'

It would be tedious to summarise all the replies received from the new towns, but some illustrative examples can be given. Redditch was optimistic provided that they could attract 'the right industries and occupations'. Washington stressed that they had a particularly difficult task in a region where the proportion of owner occupation was low:

'Our obligations to take overspill from Tyneside and Wearside are unlikely to be fulfilled by making houses available for sale for some time to come. We have a peculiar and possibly unique problem in this area where the demand for houses for owner occupation does not continually outstrip the supply in that there is severe competition between speculative builders for the limited market and they tend to build down to a price rather than up to a standard. We shall be severely handicapped in fixing a competitive selling price for our houses built at economic costs to Parker Morris minimum standards, by the necessity to add GDE—which are inevitably higher at this stage of the town's development than those of a speculative builder.'

Harlow emphasised the problem of sales to commuters. Skelmersdale could not see how the ministry's proposals could be implemented within the terms of the present brief for the new town which was to contribute to the overspill problems of north Merseyside. The industrial selection scheme gave priority to local authority tenants or applicants: these 'are not among those whom one would expect to find large numbers of owner occupiers'. In addition to 'these social factors', demand was likely to be limited by the necessary requirement within the new town that building for sale by private interests or the corporation should be to Parker Morris standards, (while in the surrounding areas many builders were constructing new houses at lower standards).

Peterlee stressed the 'traditional indifference to owner occupation' in the area. It was 'patently clear' that this new town had to rely heavily, almost totally, on large scale disposals of rented housing to make any appreciable progress towards a 50 per cent target. This would, inevitably, 'dictate a slow and rather laborious progression' but it had to be accepted as being a realistic appraisal of the situation.

In October 1967 a meeting was held between ministry officials, the new town chairmen and the Building Societies Association to discuss the practical steps which could be taken to extend the activities of building societies in new towns as a contribution to the increase in owner occupation which MHLG wanted to see achieved. The purpose of the meeting was to explore methods by which the minister's stated policy of increasing owner occupation could be implemented. It was undesirable that new towns should develop 'in a different way from the rest of the community by becoming enclaves of rented housing'; there was a danger of settling into such a pattern and this could prejudice their capacity for growth. The department had been fortunate in obtaining all the finance it wished for new towns but, if some building society funds also could be directed to new towns, they would be able to develop even faster than currently. The option mortgage scheme would come into effect on 1 April 1968, and negotiations were in progress with the Building Societies Association and the insurance companies about the introduction of the 100 per cent mortgage scheme. This could come into operation at the same time. One would not anticipate a large increase in owner occupation as a result of these schemes, but new towns contained many people in the very income bracket which would benefit most from them. It was known that building societies had been less active in new towns than elsewhere, but the historical reasons for this were becoming 'less compelling'.

The Building Societies Association said that they had given this question much thought and were enthusiastic about the policy. The amount of money likely to be involved was not large and was quite within their capacity. They would also be willing to help builders with finance. Each new town would need to be treated individually. In towns where there were currently no building society offices, development corporations should contact the Association. In some towns, one or two societies would probably open branches; elsewhere an energetic agent might be the answer; in others, consortia could be arranged; in short, they would aim to establish an organisation commensurate with the funds likely to be lent.

An internal minute said that it was clear that there were three main impediments. First, the difficulty of reconciling an ultimate limit of 50 per cent owner occupation in the second generation towns with the requirement that as high a proportion as possible of the immigrants should be people in housing need from the conurbations. The likely maximum ultimate percentage in these towns ranged between 20 per cent and 40 per cent. Secondly, in the London towns, it was similarly difficult to switch half of the current building programme towards owner occupation without prejudicing provision of rented houses for immigrants. In some cases this could be met to a certain extent simply by increasing the overall programme, but land availability was a limiting factor at places like Stevenage.

Thirdly, trouble was likely to arise over standards. Most corporations insisted on private enterprise building to Parker Morris, but could standards be relaxed as an aid to increased sales?

In January 1968, a further internal minute took up this point about Parker Morris standards. In Dawley, for instance, one large developer was building houses in neighbouring areas for sale at about £2,500, and so were the urban district council themselves. How could the corporation hope to compete? The only possibility was some lively advertising to create a demand for houses of a high standard:

> 'Perhaps the corporation should advertise *Happy Family Homes* with a pertinent story, showing first an ordinary housewife scalding herself in the cramped kitchen—husband falling over the child in the confined sitting-room—recrimination, and marriage on the verge of breakdown—wise bank manager advocating a Happy Family Home—husband buying such a house —the couple now reunited and agreeing that the new house is roomy enough for more children.'

Yet, even with such advertisement, there were two 'probably fatal impediments'. The first was that building societies would not lend a man more than three times his gross earnings. The second was the existence of 'many social commonplaces, ie possessions that are so commonly owned that the lack of them is apt to make a householder feel small. Who is there among workers in new towns who is going to boast or even confess, that he does not possess a television set because he has bought a house with fifteen power points, or that he does not own an automobile because he has spent his money on a house with two wc's?'

In areas like Dawley the position might be even more grave than expected. There was concern about the sale of houses, 'but they might also run into difficulty in letting houses'. The rent for one of their £5,000 houses was about £250 a year, ie over £20 a month. 'The tenant for his rent gets external repairs done, which as an owner occupier he would have to pay for himself. If we subtract for repairs, the rent is about £18 a month. For £18 3s. 8d. a month, however, a man can buy a £3,000 house with the 100 per cent guaranteed 25-year loan on option terms. So granted that, as they say, the cost of renting a £5,000 house is within the capacity of tenants in the £1,250–£1,500 range of wages, it is worth while using the same sum to buy a cheaper house, and it is no wonder that some Dawley tenants have been buying a house in Oakengates.'

In early 1968, officials of MHLG re-examined prospects for increasing owner occupation in the new towns. It was appreciated that there was 'an inherent contradiction' between the increased pressure they had put on the London new towns to raise the proportion of Londoners housed and the necessarily looser arrangements which had to be accepted for private enterprise housing. This dilemma could become acute in some of the first generation towns which had 'only a limited life'—and limited land available. Nevertheless, it was agreed that increased pressure should be put on the new towns. An opportunity to do this was provided by the completion of the final draft of the Cullingworth Report on the future ownership and management of housing in the new towns.

THE REPORT ON OWNERSHIP AND MANAGEMENT OF HOUSING IN THE NEW TOWNS*

In April 1968, a minute to the secretary dealt with the final draft of the Cullingworth report on ownership and management of housing in the new towns, which had now been received.† This showed that the immediate and over-riding need was greatly to increase the opportunities for owner occupation in the new towns and to attract private enterprise on an increasing scale. On average, about half of all new town tenants wanted to buy a house in a new town, but relatively few could afford to do so. This was not because incomes were unusually low (on the contrary) but because new town houses were unusually expensive (5 to 10 per cent higher than in the country as a whole). The minute commented that 'costs must be reduced—if necessary by reducing standards'. There was also need and scope for the development of a range of housing associations in new towns. Further diversity of tenure could be obtained through co-ownership societies.

The department 'fully endorsed' Cullingworth's conclusion that the overriding need was for a substantial increase in owner occupation. The report underlined and strongly supported the Government's current stated policy that the second generation and later towns should plan from the outset for an ultimate level of 50 per cent owner occupation; that the older towns should move towards an equal division between houses for sale and to rent in their future building programme (although it was recognised that in these towns 50 per cent owner occupation could not be achieved without substantial sales of existing rented houses); and two thirds of all new houses for sale should be built by private enterprise.

An underlying theme of the corporations' evidence to Cullingworth and of their representations to the department was the difficulty of reconciling a policy of increasing owner occupation with their responsibility to cater for overspill. But a major contribution of the report was to bring out the extent of the suppressed demand for owner occupation that already existed in the new towns, and the

---

* MHLG Files NT 49/25 and NT 85/7.
† See also chapter VI, p. 348.

way in which that demand was held back largely by the absence of low cost houses for sale.

The report examined various methods of making owner occupation easier in new towns. The first, a wider use of public sector mortgages, was dismissed as incompatible with the aim of reducing public investment in new towns. This accorded with the department's view. The alternative suggestion was increased subsidies for owner occupiers. 'We are clear, however, that there can be no question of introducing any special measures that would not be available for purchasers generally'; and there was demonstrably no need for additional subsidies to stimulate owner occupation in the country at large.

MHLG suggested that they should now concentrate on two issues: first, a vigorous sales drive on the part of the corporations, particularly of the older towns, 'who could do much to create a more favourable climate for owner occupation'; and, secondly, loosening restrictions on private enterprise. The latter point raised difficult issues. It meant allowing private developers to lower standards in order to build at prices which prospective purchasers could afford. It might also mean allowing developers a freer hand in selecting their own purchasers, 'subject to clearly defined priorities', instead of requiring all purchasers to be approved by the corporation and at the same time imposing pre-emption clauses 'to an unnecessary degree'. Both would be unwelcome to some corporations. However, given cheaper houses, there seemed no reason why private developers should have any difficulty in selling almost entirely to corporation tenants, or even to people from the exporting areas. The important thing was to give them the opportunity to meet the demand that undoubtedly existed and not to price them out of the market as frequently happened at present. This would require some detailed discussion with corporations.

On 'assets', the major point to emerge was the strong support for a vigorous policy of offering commission houses for sale to tenants, to help meet the demand for owner occupation. The Government had said that local authorities should eventually be responsible for *managing* all publicly owned housing. The evidence in the report did not introduce any substantial new arguments on this (except for the suggestion of co-ownership societies as possible organisations to take over some of the houses already built). It remained the case that the 'normal' situation achieved by this transfer would—with the local authority as landlord of all rented housing—be itself abnormal, though not unprecedented. The report did not consider whether any special arrangements for local authority management were desirable in these circumstances. The numbers of houses to be transferred would be somewhat reduced by a vigorous policy of sales to tenants. That policy might well need to be continued after a transfer, and the transfer arrangements would need to provide for this and for the disposal of the proceeds.

Another official commented, 'after a hurried reading of the report', that it was clear that it raised so many issues that detailed comment would have to await a decision on the issues which needed to be pursued actively. At many points throughout the report Cullingworth had stressed that the issues raised (particularly on the future management of the rented stock and on rent policy generally) often went far wider than the particular problems of new town housing. 'One can heartily endorse his suggestion' that the guiding principles in future policy decisions should be that:

> 'the most desirable pattern of tenure is one which provides the widest range of choice to the consumer, meets the needs of all groups in the community, involves the least charge on public funds which is consistent with giving assistance to those who cannot afford housing of the standard determined politically as being acceptable, and presents the fewest obstacles to mobility.'

But, as he repeatedly pointed out, these objectives were very inadequately served by the present financial and organisational structure of housing. MHLG were thus faced with the dilemma that, while the present arrangements in the new towns were abnormal, and while the general aim was apparently to achieve 'normality', there might be little to be gained by this, since the present 'normality' was by no means satisfactory. Yet, as Cullingworth observed, there was a limit to which reform of housing finance (or any other aspect of housing) could go at one step and, in the context of the new towns issue, the object should be rationality within the confines of this issue.

On the sale of houses, Cullingworth had succeeded in expressing in a phrase 'what we have spent months trying to establish'—ie 'the only reason why it "pays" to sell council houses (even at below market prices) is that the rent rate of return is so much below market rates'.

All that one could conclude from the survey material in the report was that there was a substantial demand in the new towns for owner occupation, but that effective demand was much more limited. Nevertheless, it seemed clear that the corporations had made little attempt so far to meet even this effective demand, and if sales were actively promoted the demand might well grow surprisingly quickly. 'At the least, therefore, the corporations should be required to pursue an active sales policy, and one of the first steps (as Cullingworth suggests) would be to try to get the building societies to take a more active interest in this market.' So far as building for sale was concerned, 'Cullingworth was surely right in suggesting that cheaper houses would have to be provided for this purpose, and the first step would be to ascertain whether private enterprise are capable of meeting that demand'.

There was no justification for giving special subsidies to new towns tenants to enable them to become owner occupiers, but there were other means of widening the scope of house purchase which might be considered: longer period mortgages; 'escalator' mortgages with no capital repayments in the early years; leasehold disposals at nominal rents, related to the historic cost of the land; discounts to sitting tenants, with restrictions on resale price; 100 per cent guarantee with option mortgage; and nominal transfer charges.

The aim of achieving 'normality' in the new towns should not itself go unquestioned. The new towns were unusual places and there were great advantages as well as disadvantages in living in them. If one of the aims of housing policy was to widen the area of consumer choice, then there might be much to be said for retaining the new towns as a distinct form of housing provision, rather than attempting to suppress their special characteristics and merge them in the conventional pattern of local authority landlordism on the one hand and owner occupation on the other. Variety of choice should not necessarily mean that everyone should have the same choice in every area. Apart from the desire for owner occupation (which might not be attainable within the new towns) the report did not suggest any marked demand for any change in the current system of management, and it might well be practicable to retain it under more permanent sponsorship and with a greater degree of tenant participation.

The main issues raised by the report were the need to develop a more significant role for housing associations in new towns; the transfer of housing to local authorities in the completed new towns; and the need to increase opportunities for owner occupation. The first two issues required 'further work' within the department, but on owner occupation 'we can move forward'. The problem was one of finding ways of encouraging private enterprise to build houses at a price which people would pay. 'We suspect that development corporations are being unduly pernickety about layouts, standards and general architectural control and are not giving private enterprise a real chance to test the market.'

It was therefore proposed that action should be concentrated on two aspects of increasing owner occupation. First, a vigorous sales drive on the part of the corporations, particularly in the older towns; and, secondly, a loosening of the restrictions on private enterprise housing so that house prices could be brought more within the range of potential demand.

POLICIES TO INCREASE OWNER OCCUPATION

The first step was the preparation of a new circular. The initial draft of this was admitted to be 'a very controversial document' which was 'bound to provoke strong reactions from the development corporations that we are sacrificing housing standards in new towns and encouraging private house-builders to make profits from cheap and nasty housing'. It referred to 'complaints' that some development corporations were seeking 'excessively high prices' for land and exercising 'over-meticulous control over the detailed design of residential layouts . . . insistence on full Radburn layouts' . . . and 'an undue insistence on full Parker Morris standards'. It was stressed that private developers should be given 'reasonable latitude', and that the requirements of the National House Builders Registration Council should ensure that houses could be built of a standard similar to that of Parker Morris recommendations 'except perhaps on the number of persons designated to occupy them'.

This draft created a flurry among technical staff of the ministry. Considerable objection was registered to expressions such as 'over-rigorous insistence on planning and architectural conditions', 'unnecessary restrictions', and such like. One minute exclaimed that:

'The plain fact is that private enterprise housing in this country has had in the past, and to a very large extent has still, an extremely poor reputation. If evocative terms are in order, I would remind you that "jerry building", "by-pass variegated", and "stockbrokers' tudor" are some of the epithets which have passed into the language and which apply exclusively to the private enterprise field. There are of course some honourable exceptions to this, but by and large the private builder still remains, for all planners and architects who care about quality in design, the number one nigger in the woodpile.

The new town corporations are, rightly in my view, anxious to maintain their own high standards and very nervous about opening their doors to those who would seek to provide lower ones. Moreover, they are guardians of public funds. "Why", they may well say, "should all these enormous sums be laid out in acquiring land and providing roads, services, schools, hospitals, playing fields and goodness knows what else all at the taxpayers' expense, only to have two thirds of the housing ruined by speculative builders who care nothing but lining their own pockets?"

I really do not think I am exaggerating the dangers. In fact if I add the proposition that the policy of supplying new town immigrants from agreed catchment areas should also be weakened in order to please the private builders, I begin to wonder whether the whole purpose of the new towns movement as it was originally conceived is not about to be seriously undermined.'

The conclusion of this minute was not that the draft circular should be amended, but that it should be postponed until the 'evidence' had been more carefully assessed. But while others agreed, senior administrators saw the opportunity provided by the Cullingworth report 'to intensify the campaign' for more owner occupation.

Moreover, the fact that this implied 'accepting more modest standards' raised serious doubts about the existing policy 'of insisting on a much higher standard in all houses built to let, paying large subsidies to enable them to be let at prices people will pay and even then making large losses on them. Does it not raise the question whether at least some houses of the more modest standards necessary to achieve an increase in owner occupation should not be built for letting to those who still prefer to rent than to buy?'

At the same time as these internal discussions were proceeding, tentative approaches were made to the Treasury, whose immediate reaction was one of hoping that the ministry's efforts would 'lead to results'.

The circular was held in abeyance for a while, but a paper was prepared for discussion at a minister's meeting with new town chairmen. This included four contentious issues. First, on standards, though Parker Morris standards were not mentioned, the requirements of the National House Builders' Registration Council were recommended: this implied 'a realistic readiness to accept something less than Parker Morris'. Secondly, there was great emphasis on private cheap houses. Thirdly, plot costs implied 'less elaborate layouts'—for example in the way of full pedestrian segregation—than were usual in new towns. Fourth, on land costs, MHLG envisaged that land might have to be sold to private developers at costs which did not include a full allocation of general development expenditure. This was done with the consent of the Treasury.

The new town chairmen were alarmed, and pressed for a postponement of the issue of any circular until there had been further consideration. The ministry, however, argued that no postponement could be entertained now that the Cullingworth report had been published.* Accordingly a circular was issued in December 1968. This was very different from the original draft which had created so much discussion within the ministry. Emphasis was laid on a clear 'developer's brief' which would be 'flexible and realistic and . . . designed to obtain the highest possible standards of layout and house type *consistent with the price level aimed at*'. To this end, in addition to providing the information about the site which developers needed in order to be able to formulate proposals for development, it should define clearly the market for which the corporation wished the developer to build and the range of prices at which the houses were to be sold. It should also specify minimum planning and design requirements but, within those limits, developers should be given the maximum freedom to adapt the product to their assessment of the market. Thus, a typical brief might 'specify density but not the

---

* It was published by HMSO in 1968 under the title *The Ownership and Management of Housing in the New Towns*.

proportion of houses of different sizes, and the proportion of car spaces—but not of garages—to be provided'. It could give guidance on pedestrian safety, but not prescribe any particular solution. It could leave plan types free, and give as much freedom as possible on elevational treatment. The developer should be able to go ahead in the confidence that corporations would not subsequently seek to enforce design requirements which were not set out in the developer's brief—otherwise he would be likely to lower his bid to cover that risk.

If private developers could be shown a strong potential market for houses within a given price range, they could be expected to compete to provide the best possible commodity within it. It was believed that once the objective was clearly defined there would be found to be considerable scope for new and productive thinking along these lines. Corporations should not be afraid, if necessary, to leave it to the purchaser to bring his house up to a higher standard by the addition at a later stage of central heating, a garage or an extra room. There was overwhelming evidence that people preferred this to being unable to satisfy their ambition to become owner occupiers. All houses for sale must conform to the National House Builders' Registration Council's requirements. Corporations would also 'have in mind' the design standards recommended in the Parker Morris report. However, it had to be remembered that some of the Parker Morris recommendations, in particular the space standards, were related to the number of people who would occupy a house, and these could not be applied if the number of people was not known when the house was being built. More generally, the extent to which Parker Morris standards (apart from those which were NHBRC requirements) were met, must depend to some extent upon market considerations since a purchaser should not be put in a position where he was no longer free to decide for himself what amount of accommodation and what standard of equipment he could initially afford.

Stress was also laid on offering 'clearly defined and attractive sites for private enterprise housing', and various methods were outlined for achieving 'effective competition between developers' while, at the same time, ensuring that 'only developers likely to be able to produce satisfactory results' were allowed to compete.

Four methods were suggested. First: competitive tendering on the basis of a detailed brief and specification, the tenderer who offered the highest price for the land being selected. This had the advantage of ensuring that a competitive price was obtained for the land, though it was open to the objection that it deprived the developer of flexibility, and the corporation of much of the benefit of the developer's expertise. Secondly, a design competition on the basis of a flexible developer's brief and a fixed price for the land, the tenderer who submitted the scheme with the highest overall standards being selected: this procedure sacrificed price competition and was, moreover, wasteful of technical resources (since each bidder had to prepare a scheme but only one would be used). Thirdly, two stage tendering: selected developers would be invited to submit tenders including a sketch layout (but not detailed plans) which conformed with such a flexible developer's brief, it being clearly understood that, if agreement could not be reached between the selected developer and the corporation on a detailed scheme, he would be free to withdraw his tender. After excluding tenders which did not conform to the developer's brief, the corporation would ask the tenderer offering the highest price for the land to prepare a detailed scheme. If the corporation and the tenderer could agree on this (or some modification of it) a binding contract could be entered into. If not, the developer might withdraw his tender and the corporation could turn to the next highest tenderer. In this way the corporation could ensure a good standard of development, whilst contractors would be encouraged to put in favourable bids in the knowledge that if they were subsequently subjected to unacceptable planning or design requirements they could withdraw their tender. It was, of course, important that corporations should not unreasonably introduce new requirements at the detailed design stage. Finally, negotiation with a developer selected by means of a preliminary competition: corporations might invite selected developers to submit proposals, including a formula for arriving at the price to be paid for the land, on the basis of such a flexible developer's brief. From these submissions, after discussion with the developers, the corporation would select the one who seemed most likely to meet their requirements in terms both of financial return and standard of provision within a prescribed range of selling prices. Negotiations would then proceed with him on the detailed financial terms and on the layout, design and programming of the development. Though the importance of giving opportunity to small local developers was underlined, it was suggested that it might be desirable for corporations to make special arrangements with selected large developers. Moreover, land sales might not be possible at prices which covered the cost of servicing and an appropriate allocation of GDE—but the price should not be below the district valuer's estimate of current market value taking into account the conditions imposed by the corporation.

CONCESSIONS TO SITTING TENANTS*

Peterlee and Aycliffe corporations pressed the ministry to allow

---

* MHLG File NT 203/3.

for a reduction in the valuation of houses to sitting tenants. This was thought to be particularly necessary in their area where there was a 'deep resistance to house purchase'. An internal minute noted that the draft circular on owner occupation sent to the corporations for comment would have allowed them to give sitting tenants a 20 per cent discount subject to pre-emption clauses. When the circular was finally issued the concession was withdrawn; the rule was that all sales were to be at current market value. In commenting on the draft circular, many corporations had expressed a dislike of the proposed concession. Few had ever been prepared to grant such concessions themselves. The Treasury also objected to the proposal— purely on grounds of 'diminution of the return'.

Peterlee and Aycliffe were very unhappy that the concession was not in the event offered. They made two points. First, morally, if not technically, it was not possible to charge a sitting tenant vacant possession value. Secondly 'the deep resistance to house purchase' in the area justified the use of special incentives.

The issue was discussed within the ministry, and the conclusion was that 'there is nothing in it'. The concept of 'sitting tenant value' only had validity in the private sector where a house was sold *with* a sitting tenant, ie the purchaser acquired 'not the house as such but the rental income'. But any sale *to* a sitting tenant was, by definition, a sale with vacant possession since that was what the tenant obtained. What caused confusion was that, in the private sector, a landlord's only alternative to a sale to the sitting tenant was a sale with a sitting tenant (at a greatly reduced value), and so he often gave the tenant a discount from vacant possession value—in other words 'they split the difference'. In new towns, however, (and local authorities) the situation was quite different, partly because the tenant had no statutory security of tenure, and partly because in any event no corporation would sell a house which was occupied by a sitting tenant. Consequently there was no reason at all why corporations should not charge a sitting tenant vacant possession value. If they wanted to give a concession to recognise the tenant's marginal nuisance value, this should be accepted as a straight discount from current market value.

As for the other point, if MHLG were disposed to make special arrangements for Peterlee and Aycliffe, they would have to obtain the Treasury's concurrence. An informal word with the Treasury made it clear that 'the prospect of obtaining their agreement would be pretty bleak'. The Treasury saw the objective of selling houses as being essentially that of obtaining the maximum return. 'If you are not going to obtain the maximum return you might as well keep the houses.' MHLG could not, of course, 'go all the way with this'. There were social and political advantages in increasing owner occupation as well as the financial ones. It might be that allowing the discount would permit at least some sales to take place which would otherwise fall through 'and to that extent we should have gained something'. In some cases too, where houses were being subsidised from the rent pool on top of exchequer subsidy, a sale at a discount might still show a net return. But in view of the Treasury's attitude, and the ministry's very valid reasons for not allowing concessions to sitting tenants, 'I am still inclined to say no'.

Despite further correspondence, this decision was held. Nevertheless, this position was difficult to reconcile with the policy in relation to the sale of local authority houses. Local authorities had the option to sell at up to 20 per cent below market value, provided that they reserved the right to buy back the house at the original cost price (subject to any improvements) if the purchaser offered it for sale within five years. MHLG officials felt that there was a certain oddity about a situation in which the minister made no difficulty about concessionary prices for sitting tenants being offered by local authorities—whom he was certainly *not* encouraging to sell rented houses; yet in new towns, where such sales were a positive objective of policy, he refused to consider a similar concession. This, however, remained the policy until the return of a Conservative Government in 1970.

CHAPTER VIII

Financial Issues

*The Financial Framework**

THE new town development corporations were a novel concept hurriedly devised in 1946. They were not local authorities composed of elected members disbursing rate fund monies levied locally; nor were they nationalised industry boards taking over a going concern with accumulated assets. The corporations were agencies nominated by government; they inherited no organisation and no assets; and they could give no security for borrowing the funds required for the development they would undertake. Inevitably therefore finance had initially to be provided by government, and section 2(2) of the 1946 Act prohibited borrowing from other sources. Since a nominated corporation using public money might be expected to have less incentive to economy than an elected council responsible to the ratepayers, a degree of central financial and technical control had to be imposed. Departmental approval was required for the master plans when they had been prepared by the corporations; projects for development had to be individually submitted to the department for approval as likely to secure a reasonable return (which might be nil) and these were examined by the Treasury if more than £200,000 was involved; financial agreements with local authorities and statutory undertakers were submitted; in the early stages, all proposals for land acquisitions were referred, and the department expected to be consulted about any unusual property transactions. The corporations were required annually to submit a rolling programme of works for several years ahead, a detailed budget of capital and revenue requirements, and a forecast of their cash requirements, which were liable to be severely examined before approval was given in whole or in part. The central control extended not only to the appointment of the chairman and members of the corporations and to approval of the salaries of the principal officers, but indirectly to junior staffs whose costs were included and scrutinised in the revenue budgets. Each corporation was required to keep proper accounts in such form as the minister, with the approval of the Treasury, directed, to be audited by an auditor appointed by the

---

* MHLG Files NT 62/6 and NT 4/2; and Treasury Files SS 385/54/01 and SS 385/02.

minister. These accounts, together with a report by the corporation dealing generally with their operations were presented annually to Parliament. In addition, corporations were liable to be called on to produce regular *ad hoc* financial or statistical returns on particular aspects of their activities.

The 1946 Act provided the framework for the provision of government funds to the corporations either by way of grants towards revenue expenditure from monies voted by Parliament, or by advances from the consolidated fund (now the national loans fund) towards the cost of capital expenditure, including working capital. Advances to the corporations were made with the approval of the Treasury for working capital and for development proposals 'likely to secure for the corporation a return which is reasonable, having regard to all the circumstances, when compared with the cost of carrying out those proposals'.

At the outset, the Treasury laid down that all advances should be on terms providing for repayment over sixty years by equal instalments of principal and interest combined, at the rate of interest prevailing at the date the advance was made. Until 1952 the rate on all advances was 3 per cent; subsequently it moved up erratically to $9\frac{5}{8}$ per cent in 1970—the average rate in that year on all advances varying from 5·54 per cent for Harlow to 9·05 per cent for Peterborough.

The rise in interest rates in the later 1950s (in 1958 the rate was 6 per cent) caused much concern to the corporations and they argued that they should be given discretion 'to follow normal commercial practice and borrow for short periods when rates are unfavourable'. The issue was constantly raised at minister-chairman level, but the ministry adhered to the Treasury line that the corporations had the advantage of borrowing long term at fixed rates, that much early borrowing had been at 3 per cent, and that they must be prepared to take the rough with the smooth. To the claim that corporations might go to the market and borrow short, the secretary commented that it would be 'a revolutionary new concept—a power privately to mortgage government assets'.

This was one of the numerous financial issues with which the ministry and the Treasury were involved. Others included the provision of amenities, the form in which the accounts of development corporations should be kept and published, and the sharing of the financial burden between development corporations and local authorities of the provision of main sewerage and roads. There was also the problem of determining the division of responsibility for financial control between the Treasury and the ministry.

The primary interest of the Treasury throughout was to ensure that the new town programme was kept within reasonable bounds and did not 'go beyond what the country could afford'. In 1949, Treasury officials were 'expressing apprehension that the Government were deliberately setting out to create what were in effect new special areas which would require indefinitely additional sub-sidisation from the exchequer, additional to that from local authorities'. In writing to the ministry in 1951, they expressed the wish 'to find the best way of enabling the Treasury to maintain the broad supervision of finance which is incumbent on us, while giving you in your turn reasonable freedom of administration, and which will permit you in your turn to give the corporation whatever measure of financial autonomy is desirable'. An internal Treasury minute of 21 March 1952 stated:

> 'From the investment point of view the twelve new towns are an alarming commitment. The homes will of course have to be built somewhere, but if they are built in a new town it is necessary to spend far more on the provision of services, such as water and sewerage and gas and electricity, and also to provide shops, offices, hospitals, entertainment buildings, public houses and so on, which are the types of building which are rigidly limited elsewhere. But in addition, because it is intended that the new towns should not be dormitories, it is necessary to build factories for the future occupants to work in.'

Treasury officials were generally resistant to the establishment of any new town, but when ministers had approved, the decision was accepted that there would be a continuing call on public finance, although the rate at which expenditure was incurred generally or on individual projects was subject to a control which the ministry and the corporations were liable at times to find irksome or irrational.

Policy and Finance

Individual towns were designated for political and social reasons, and at the time of designation there was only the sketchiest financial estimate of the ultimate cost. The general argument was that all the houses would have to be built somewhere, and the extra cost of building them in a new town with a good environment was only marginally higher.

After designation they fell into the financial framework briefly described above. Apart from argument on architectural and technical matters, endless argument arose between the corporations, MHLG and the Treasury on estimates and approvals of individual projects. This resulted, in some cases, in abandonment, but more generally in modification of the original proposal or delay in starting. The corporations were subject to continuous pressure to increase their revenues and reduce their borrowings, and all this gave rise to a good deal of irritation.

But looming behind these specific arguments was a much broader concern with the cost of the new towns policy. Apprehensions were expressed—at different times, by different people, and in different contexts—about the economics and finance of new towns and their relative advantages and disadvantages compared to expanded towns or other forms of development. Various strands of this have already been discussed.* In this chapter an account is given of some of the *ad hoc* attempts which were made to wrestle with the broad financial and economic issues. It is noticeable that each of these attempts was made *after* a political decision had been taken, and when officials (particularly those in the Treasury) were wondering where policy was leading: for example, the 1955 investigation after the Town Development Act; that of 1963–65 after the second generation of new towns had been agreed; and that of 1967 after Milton Keynes had been approved and proposals for further new towns were maturing.

Much of this work was inconclusive and stillborn. Studies were undertaken at lengthy intervals of time, and typically none of the officials in the Treasury or the departments had taken part in a previous exercise. (Indeed there is little indication that they had any close knowledge of them.) In any event, circumstances and the political climate were constantly changing. But some discussion of the investigations is useful as an indication of the thinking in official circles which would have been reflected if not necessarily accepted in ministerial decisions.

The Cost of a New Town†

The Reith Committee estimated that the total cost of a new town of 50,000 people would be between £27m and £36m. The greater part of this would be borne by local authorities, statutory undertakers and private enterprise. Apart from housing (which would cost between £12m and £15m) the expenditure necessarily to be borne by a development corporation would be at least £6m to £7m. Silkin's original estimate of the cost falling on public funds was £19m, while Westwood's corresponding estimate for East Kilbride was £23·7m.‡ Neither of these estimates covered private development. Such were the financial considerations on which the first generation of new towns were approved.

In the later part of 1946 and early in 1947, Treasury officials were becoming apprehensive about the new town proposals and suggested that they were a very expensive way—in money, labour and materials—of relieving the housing shortage. They were also doubtful of the capacity of the Ministry of Town and Country Planning to

---

* See, eg, chapter V, p. 233 *et seq.*, and chapter VI, p. 372 *et seq.*
† Treasury File SS 385/02; HA(45)21, LP(46)85, LP(49)91, LP(49)21st Meeting, 9 December 1949; and Reith Committee Final Report, Cmd 6876.
‡ See chapter II, p. 45 *et seq.*

handle the large programme; and it was their view that the programme should be slowed down. It was no doubt a reflection of these views that led Dalton (Chancellor of the Exchequer and chairman of the ministerial committee on the distribution of industry) to resist the priority which Silkin was giving to the London towns. However, it was not until July 1949, when Silkin sought authority for the designation of Corby, that serious apprehension was expressed about the financial liabilities which were being incurred in respect of existing and prospective new towns. The Chancellor of the Exchequer (now Cripps) and Silkin were invited to submit a memorandum on the financial and running costs.*

Cripps submitted a note to the LP Committee in 1949 covering a lengthy memorandum by Silkin in which, subject to many qualifications and assumptions, he gave a broad estimate of the capital expenditure on a new town for 50,000 at £45·8m, of which £36·21m would be borne by public funds and £9·59m by private enterprise. In addition, there would be a deficit on revenue account, to be met out of grant or advances, which was estimated at £1·5m over twenty years, and payments of grant in lieu of rates contribution in respect of housing (additional to exchequer housing subsidies) which would amount to £0·6m. This gave a total of about £48m.

Silkin claimed that, of the total capital cost, 47 per cent was in respect of houses which would have to be built in any case either in a new town or elsewhere, and that much of the other expenditure would also have to be incurred whether in a new town or on the fringes of an existing town. The additional expenditure due to the establishment of a new town rather than an expansion he estimated to be at most £2·3m or five per cent of the total.

Cripps commented that the Treasury had been consulted in the preparation of the paper; on the assumptions made, and bearing in mind the question of timing (which was more rigid for new town development than it would be for the extension of existing towns), he considered that the estimates were as reliable as any estimates of this kind could be. However, he stressed three points. First, the calculations made no allowance for special difficulties arising from the choice of site. In fact special difficulties of this kind had figured prominently in new town development, and it was thought unlikely that there would be greater success in finding 'perfect' sites in the future. This might add considerably to the capital cost of particular new towns, and though sometimes it would be expenditure which would have had to be incurred in any case, whether there had been a new town or not, this might not always be so (eg the works to counteract mining subsidence at Peterlee would never have become

---

* See chapter II, pp. 109–110.

necessary if it had not been decided to build a new town there). Secondly, new towns were being established in a period of high prices. Corporations, unlike local authorities, could not make a profit on older revenue-producing property built when costs were lower, because they had none; and their revenue from property would tend to fall as prices fell (as they were expected to). Thirdly, the final transfer to the appropriate local authorities might well present difficulties: local authorities might be much more reluctant to take over responsibility than they would have been to build up the same services gradually, in their own way and choosing their own time. Cripps did not, therefore, feel optimistic about the possibility of handing over the new towns without an appreciable continuing burden on the exchequer. Moreover, new town development differed from local authority development in that it did not take place under the close and careful scrutiny of the ratepayers and of a local authority finance committee. It was of the utmost importance, therefore, that the Government should secure for the new towns 'a thoroughly competent administration and a sound financial control'.

There was a full discussion of this paper at the Lord President's Committee in December 1949. It was pointed out that, though the paper had been prepared in consultation with the Treasury, the Chancellor doubted whether it was possible to forecast future expenditure with the degree of precision attempted. Difficulties were foreseen when the new towns were handed over to the local authorities, as there was a risk that those which took them over would accept the greater amenities they afforded but decline to pay for them. This would create two classes of local authorities, one of which would enjoy exchequer assistance over and above the normal assistance to local authority services.

It was suggested, however, that the new towns policy should not be judged by financial tests alone: 'it was an essential part of the Government's programme of social reconstruction'. On the other hand, 'people who were not so fortunate as to live in a new town with its special advantages would not take kindly to the idea of subsidising the new towns out of general taxation . . . The new towns competed with other claimants for a share of the country's capital investment and there was a danger that more important projects would suffer. There was a danger of drifting into the piecemeal adoption of schemes which in the aggregate were beyond the country's capacity and might have at a later stage to be abandoned or curtailed'. The committee concluded that further investigation of the financial and economic question involved was necessary, but no immediate action followed in view of the imminence of the forthcoming election.

By 1950 four estimates of the capital cost had been made for an English new town of 50,000:

July 1945:   'Of the order of £10m, plus £2·3m on building by private enterprise'.
April 1946:   £19m, plus expenditure by private developers.
July 1946:   £27–36m, including expenditure by local authorities and private enterprise.
December 1949: £45·8m, including expenditure by local authorities and private enterprise.

It is clear that none of these estimates was more than an inspired guess. Each was compiled on a different basis, and different assumptions were made about expenditure which might be met by local authorities, statutory undertakers and by private enterprise. In effect, when each new town was authorised, the ministry and the Treasury were accepting a virtually unknown commitment for its completion, with the prospect of a continuing deficit on revenue account.

The return of the Conservative Government in 1951 quickly led to exchequer pressures for 'economies in the new towns', as well as the passage of legislation to facilitate the alternative of town expansions by local authorities. But, as has been recounted in chapter III, Macmillan safeguarded the existing new towns programme, despite the verdict of a report from officials that, financially, 'there is much more probability of a loss than a profit'. Sandys, who took over from Macmillan as Minister of Housing in 1954, pressed for an expansion of the new towns programme to assist in meeting the overspill needs. It was in this connection that, in 1955, his department undertook a study of the comparative costs of new and expanded towns.

Comparative Costs of New and Expanded Towns*

Sandys was concerned to establish the relative costs to the exchequer of housing the same number of people in a new town and in an expanded town. The study carried out within his department concluded that new towns were considerably more expensive to the exchequer than expanded towns. The position was illustrated by reference to Bracknell. The capital cost to the exchequer of providing houses 'and everything else required for the 20,000 people proposed to go to Bracknell' had been estimated in 1954 at some £18·5m. The average cost per person on this basis would be about £925. If Bracknell had been developed under the Town Development Act, the exchequer might have been expected to pay, say, 50 per cent

---

* MHLG Files 91650/15/8, NT 62/6 and NT 91/9.

of the capital cost of providing water and sewerage. This would amount to £840,000, or £42 per head. This comparison in gross capital cost—£925 per person as against £42—was regarded as being 'plainly unhelpful', but it did underline the major point, namely that 'new town machinery inevitably involves the exchequer in large scale expenditure at the outset'. The expanded towns could make a start with very much less exchequer money. On the other hand (as the Treasury would probably acknowledge) there was a reasonable expectation 'not only of getting their money back from new towns but also of securing a profit in the long run', while, in the case of expanded towns, they could not reckon 'to get anything back'. In current circumstances, however, the Treasury were heavily preoccupied with the scale of capital investment required for a new town 'and I can see no means of persuading them that they ought to overlook the importance of this short term consideration'. A more helpful basis of comparison would be between the net cost to the exchequer of using new town machinery over a long period and the cost of grants under the Town Development Act. This, however, was 'excessively difficult' for two reasons. First, it was impossible to forecast with any accuracy the outcome for the new towns until some progress had been made with disposing of the statutory under-takings. Secondly, it was not yet possible to establish whether the exchequer would be called upon to pay to the expanded towns 'something in the nature of a rate fund contribution' after the initial ten years. In some expanded towns, redevelopment of central areas might impose an additional charge on the exchequer. In other words, 'we cannot get at net costs without indulging in mere crystal gazing'.

Another MHLG minute commented that the idea of using development corporations for the job 'by the expectation that they would command greater skill, expertise, singleness of purpose and sustained attention than a comparatively small local authority subject to political influence' was 'sound in principle so far as it goes'. However, there could be an element of special pleading since the corporations had a desire to perpetuate their existence, and their staffs were worried about their future. There was also the serious constitutional failing of the corporation that it was 'neither competitive nor answerable to electors', and was therefore likely to spend more. To favour development corporations on the grounds that the exchequer 'gets its money back may not be true at all', but the prospects of this proving true were poorer in the case of expanded towns than in 'wholly new' towns, for a number of reasons. First, the bulk of the expenditure on the expansion would be on housing—'a normal activity of local authorities, and not a very remunerative one'. Secondly, expansion of a town might require expansion of the shopping centre or the construction of a new centre: this was 'a most expensive business'. Thirdly, to the extent that existing industry expanded on its existing sites, recoupment of unremunerative expenditure would not be forthcoming in the shape of revenue from industrial estates. Fourthly, the amount of expenditure which would be required on basic services would depend on local conditions and the extent of the expansion, but if a development corporation was employed they would have to carry the whole of the capital expenditure. The local authority would be relieved of this burden (or as much of it as was left after Town Development Act grant) although it would obtain the rate revenue from the housing. The corporation's prospects of recovering their expenditure eventually from the local authority would depend 'on the bargain which would be struck when the corporation was wound up—in conditions of monopsony, and subject to the hazards of politics'.

If it were argued that the risks might be reduced by ensuring that the local authority had a stake in the activities of the corporation, then it was difficult to see what advantage there was in not making the local authority carry the main burden of responsibility itself. 'It ought at least to be seen how local authorities get on with the job under the Town Development Act before suggesting that development corporations might do it better'. To multiply agencies on the basis that they were individually more efficient seemed questionable: there might be an increase in efficiency, but there might also be an increase in overheads and also some further loss of opportunities for local authorities to exercise really responsible functions. The conclusion was that 'the suggestion that development corporations should expand towns has little to commend it at present, either on financial grounds or on grounds of good government'.

The theme was picked up again in the early 'sixties in relation to studies of the expansion of Stevenage and Harlow. These were examined 'to see what light they shed on the financial effects of large scale expansion'. The conclusion was that 'they don't throw any clear light on this at all'. And, so far as the wider examination of comparative costs of new towns and town expansions was concerned, they contributed little except to confirm the impression that 'one can draw some pretty broad general conclusions on commonsense lines but that, for the rest, however detailed an examination of a defined expansion of a particular town may be, it will prove nothing but what that particular expansion would cost. It is possible to proceed from the general to the particular, but not from the particular to the general'. Large scale development would enjoy a financial advantage wherever there was unused capacity in main services such as roads, water, sewers and sewage disposal. The most advantageous would be that which used the spare capacity to the full. If, however, there was no unused capacity in existing services, or no services at all, financial advantage depended on the circumstances. The most advantageous circumstances might be where there was an up to date basic capacity which could be expanded. This was the position in Harlow and Stevenage. The least advantageous circumstances might be where existing services were old and incapable of expansion. The problem then was that of providing new facilities for both existing and new development, and for closing down and writing off the existing useful though out of date capacity. 'In between' came the making of new provision from scratch: 'more expensive than the first but possibly less so than the second'. In every case financial comparisons between different developments were greatly affected by the physical characteristics of the alternatives and the availability of main services.

The actual cost of building was 'very much the same everywhere subject to physical characteristics'. Comparison between one town and another or between town expansion and new towns would be misleading unless it was 'like with like in physical circumstances'. The conclusion was that 'in the end, big expansions will be new town jobs because town expansion doesn't deliver the goods; and the locations will mostly be determined by considerations other than costs because, within broad limits, cost is not a dominating factor in choosing between one place and another'.

The New Towns Research Group 1963*

The change in policy of the Conservative Government in the early 'sixties led not only to the designation of the 'second generation' of new towns but also to the reawakening of interest in research on the new towns. As a result the ministry established a new towns research group which took as its primary task a study of the cost and profitability of new towns.† This showed that the average all-in cost per 'dwelling unit' was £2,661, but with a range for individual towns from £2,194 to £3,176. The conclusion was that 'there is no standard, or near standard, unit cost for a new town. So much depends on the town's purpose, local conditions and circumstances; and even the policy of the development corporation'. At Crawley, it had been the consistent aim of the (erstwhile) development corporation to seek, by land lease, the highest possible private capital investment in industrial buildings. At Stevenage, the development corporation were delayed in their start through legal and other difficulties, thus running into higher prices for initial development. Basildon had major site development difficulties: the local soil was clay containing a sulphur constituent, requiring the use of a special

---

* MHLG File NT 49/3.

† See chapter VI, p. 366 *et seq.*

sulphur-resistant cement for foundations. Special piling was also required, even for house building, against clay shrinkage. These two requirements led inevitably to increased building costs. Despite this and other problems, the Basildon overall unit cost (£2,721) 'stood comparison with other towns'.

Overall unit costs changed as development proceeded. They might well fall towards the end of development, when heavy initial expenditure (roads, sewers, etc) could be more economically absorbed. (This was a 'factor doubtless considered' by both Harlow and Stevenage 'who, in effect, said in their expansion surveys that expansion beyond their present "targets" would benefit finances'.)

Recoupment of heavy new town expenditure on basic services and special development had to be sought from the profit on industrial and commercial development. Currently, no real profit could be expected on housing development for renting: constant review of rents was necessary to keep income 'at least level with outgoings'. New town assets (houses, factories and commercial buildings) were not revenue-producing for substantial periods after the provision of basic services and the beginning of building. In those periods, interest charges had to be borne on revenue account 'without contra rent credit: a constant drag on profitability during the period of build-up of a new town'. In comparison with the limited, personal aims of the private developer, development corporations had 'the greater, social task of producing a new, balanced community'. After the provision of adequate basic services, this demanded fine assessment of priorities for, and the marrying-up of, housing, industrial and commercial development. This was a continuous process, and one which demanded 'running judgment as the town develops, calling on all the skills of management'. Priorities, or the reversal of current priorities, for the main classes of development could not at any time 'be laid down from outside'. This was essentially a task of management, 'on the spot and aware of all changes and fluctuations in local conditions and circumstances'. No inspired formula could be given to any group of people charged with the task of building a new town: 'it would be foolish, perhaps dangerous, to attempt'. But this was not to say that valuable advice could not from time to time be offered: there was now some fifteen years' accumulated experience of new town building.

Difficulties (running from the earliest days up to the 1950s) in persuading industrialists to establish enterprises in the new towns (particularly in the London new towns and Peterlee) resulted periodically in a surplus of new town houses. There 'could be no hope of a profitable showing' until industrial development was 'brought into reasonable balance'. It was this type of difficulty which gave rise 'in some quarters' to pessimistic predictions about the outcome of new towns. It took time ('and battles with the Board of Trade') to restore the balance: 'time that has not altogether expired for Peterlee'.

This problem 'could easily recur' in any future new town development; but it was hoped that the fifteen years' experience gained would aid the formulation of advance measures to meet it. Profits should accrue on industrial and commercial development so soon as the asset was revenue producing. Indeed, there could be a revenue account surplus at a fairly early stage in the build-up of a new town; but this by itself was largely illusory, since as soon as the work in progress mounted ('with corresponding interest charge') the surplus disappeared. It was inevitably a long haul before all revenue deficiencies could be overtaken. How soon that point could be reached depended on the speed of build-up of the town and the attraction of industry and commerce. The degree of profitability at any point depended much on external factors: 'notably the market, and what it can be induced to pay'. It was therefore clear that there would always be difficulty in predicting in any one case when 'balance' would be reached.

It did not follow that it was necessary to wait till a new town was substantially completed before any assessment of probable financial outcome could be made. Financial results might be analysed annually and considered over reasonable periods. Nine towns had a general revenue account surplus in 1961–62, while three had a deficiency. Both Crawley and Hemel Hempstead had disposed of their sewerage undertakings. Crawley had cleared the sewerage revenue deficit by capitalisation and writing-off over ten years. Hemel Hempstead had written-off their sewerage revenue deficit to general revenue, covering it by re-crediting to general revenue account excess depreciation from previous years, and (irregularly) making no provision for repairs and maintenance for 1961–62 (ie immediately prior to transfer to the Commission for the New Towns). For the first time, there was an overall surplus in 1961–62 (taking account of general revenue and sewerage revenue accounts together): 'this after some fifteen years'. The new towns, as a comprehensive investment were now therefore paying their way 'on a cash footing'. But this was with the aid in 1961–62 of housing subsidies totalling £2·7m: 'all are still net borrowers'.

Much depended on the stage of build-up of the towns, and local conditions. Both Crawley and Hemel Hempstead had had to buy existing town centre areas, thereby diminishing the return. Population would largely determine when the larger, multiple stores could be attracted. Land leasing rather than building produced a higher return on a small capital expenditure: this was the main explanation for the 'good showing' at Basildon and Harlow. The return on capital was not currently such that 'take-over bidders' were attracted. It was smaller than a commercial developer would expect; but taking into account the wider, social task of the development corporations, the return could not be regarded as bad. Inflation had doubtless distorted the return on capital. A current valuation of new town assets would reveal a capital gain running into millions of pounds: return calculated on that revaluation would immediately suffer severe reduction.

In the post war inflation, new town development corporations had had two advantages: the terms of (exchequer) borrowing and the ability to increase rents at short intervals. The biggest component of the expenditure side of the revenue account was the debt interest, payable for a long period (sixty years) at a fixed rate. It was paid in a depreciated currency. While housing subsidies were paid to corporations in the same depreciated currency, general inflation had enabled the corporations to seek fairly regular house-rent increases to offset rising costs. Industrial and commercial rent increases were necessarily slower in operation, dependent as they were on the lease terms originally agreed, 'some being more sagacious than others perhaps'. Precise assessment of 'how new towns would have fared without inflation' was not feasible:

> 'A stable currency has been unknown for a century or more; market and economy conditions in such unknown circumstances could be a matter for many and varied opinions. The most that perhaps could be said was that for the last forty years at least, ordinary housing for renting had not been capable of provision without subsidy; and whether, without inflation, new town development corporations could have made sufficient profit on industrial and commercial development to offset the deadweight of housing would probably depend much on the location and purpose of the town. A town like Crawley in the south-east of England might have stood a better chance, than, say, Peterlee, in the north-east.'

Objections to 'Piecemeal' Decisions*

Such was the thinking within the Ministry of Housing and Local Government but, in the Treasury, an internal minute of December 1963 expressed anxiety about likely 'pressure for piecemeal decisions' on new towns. The Treasury wanted a forward programme for new towns, but MHLG maintained that they were in no position to provide this. Instead, they suggested that any such programme would have to await the completion of regional studies in the south-east, north-west and midlands. It was precisely this 'piecemeal' approach which the Treasury wished to replace by a forward programme.† They were particularly worried about the argument

---

* MHLG File PRP6 382/1, Treasury Files 2EAS 420/01 and 2AT 636/372/01.
† See also below, p. 477 *et seq.*

(favoured by MHLG) that new towns constituted the most economical means of providing for housing and industrial needs which had to be met 'in some way or another'. The Treasury considered that the statistical evidence for this was 'by no means clear'. In any case, the proposition was open to doubt since 'almost by definition, everything in a new town was planned to be "of the best".' Though this might, in the long term, give better value for money than the cheaper or more makeshift provisions of private enterprise or ordinary local authorities, 'it certainly costs more initially; and there must be limits to the extent to which we can afford to set our standards high for the future at greater present cost'.

In financial terms, a new town was also different from ordinary housing expenditure in that it involved in each case the *commitment* of between £50m and £100m of exchequer money over a long period. Starting slowly, the implementation built up over the years to annual expenditure which, in total, was formidable. Though the rate could be varied within limits, the ultimate commitment was inescapable—unless the new town were to be left half finished. Moreover, the exchequer received little return on this investment in the early years. It was wholly at risk, and, even for new towns which were 'successful', the return currently envisaged was only of the order of five per cent on historic cost, *less* housing subsidies at higher than normal rates. For towns which proved to be 'unsuccessful', a revenue deficit might have to be met in perpetuity. It seemed to be 'simple common sense' that there should be a programme of future commitments, whether in terms of the number of new towns to be started or in terms of a financial ceiling to annual expenditure. This inevitably involved consideration of the question of whether new towns were the 'best' method of dealing with specific problems. In turn, this raised issues concerning the current criteria of 'economic profitability'. Furthermore, even if new towns were 'not unduly expensive in investment per head', there still remained the issue of the relative shares of public and private investment and, within the public sector, the relative shares of exchequer and local authority investment.

The Treasury felt that MHLG, 'in their present frame of mind' looked upon economic criteria as a 'Treasury gimmick—that the figures are meaningless and the exercise worthless'. Experience with nuclear energy and the Channel Tunnel suggested that:

'unless the other side concerned can be got to see that the exercise is worth undertaking, we shall not get very far. After all, the other side in this case will have to do a good deal of work, and as they are rather short staffed anyhow, they need some fairly powerful arguments to make them undertake their part of the job.'

In December 1963, the Treasury informed MHLG that they had been giving a certain amount of thought to the possibility of finding economic criteria for use in assessing the merits of proposals for new towns or town development schemes. The subject was one which had been discussed from time to time previously, but never with any very conclusive results; 'and indeed, it is not an easy one with which to get to grips'. Nevertheless:

'both from your standpoint and ours there would be advantage in tackling it in a systematic manner. There are bound to be continuing discussions about new towns and town development over the following few years, when we come to work out the implications of regional plans; and we could get on with these more quickly and effectively if we had established the nature of the data needed and the criteria to be applied.'

An attempt therefore had to be made to establish the most economic method of accommodating population growth in defined circumstances and in particular types of area:

(a) 'Green field' new towns;
(b) New towns of the Redditch type;
(c) Development on Town Development Act lines;
(d) Normal 'fringe' development on town and city outskirts;
(e) Redevelopment within cities and conurbations.

It was suggested that a working group should be established to attempt a comprehensive assessment of the comparative economic costs of these alternatives—'and perhaps also an estimate of the distribution of cost between the public and private sectors, and the public part between the exchequer and local authorities, in each case'.

A meeting was held to discuss this in January 1964. MHLG did not oppose the proposed study, but stressed that economic costs were neither the only nor necessarily the most important factors in determining the location of particular developments. There were many others such as general strategic ones, the existence of local self-generating growth, communications, the speed at which projects could be executed, timing, local attitudes and so on. In practice, the ministry's field for manoeuvre was restricted and their problem was not so much a matter of selecting the cheapest form of development, but the most efficient. Nevertheless, it was agreed that a joint Treasury and ministry group (at under-secretary and assistant secretary level, with assistance from the economic section) should be established to examine the problem, including the distribution of costs between the public and the private sectors, and within the public sector between the exchequer and local authorities.

*The Study Group on Economic Criteria 1964–65**
The first meeting of the study group was held in February 1964. As

* MHLG Files PD 2/282/1 and PRP 382/1.

a start, copies of the consultants' reports on expansion studies of
Ipswich, Worcester and Peterborough were circulated. The ministry
pointed out, however, that the reports were not comparable in
detail because the three consultants had differed to some extent
in their interpretations of the instructions. Perhaps more importantly, however, they had differed considerably in the extent to
which they had proposed to deal with the redevelopment and traffic
problems of central areas. Only the Peterborough report had dealt
with these in any comprehensive manner, and even there it seemed
certain that the proposals fell short of what would in fact be required
'in Buchanan terms'. Simultaneously, an analysis was being made of
the costs of developing the new towns, but it was quite clear that an
analysis of historic costs was of little value. It would be almost
impossible to correct historic costs to make them comparable with
the current costs used by the consultants and, in any case, it was
difficult to make comparisons between the costs of a green field new
town and the expansion of an existing town.

The examination of these reports showed that many elements of
cost were common to all methods of development. Thus a house
would cost virtually the same whether it was built as part of a new
town or on the periphery of an existing town. There was no evidence
from the consultants' reports of any significant spare capacity in
services and, as long as one was comparing the cost of building a
substantial number of houses, the costs of providing water and
sewerage and, for example, schools, would not differ—or at least, in
so far as they did differ, variations caused by differences in the
geographical circumstances would be more significant than variations attributable to the method of development. In any case, the
costs of some of these services were very small compared with the
capital cost of the houses. The cost of a house was roughly £1,000
per head of population against which the cost of providing water was
about £20 per head and for providing for main sewerage and sewage
disposal about £44.

The preliminary examination of the consultants' reports had,
however, disclosed that three aspects of development displayed
significant financial differences from scheme to scheme. These were
the cost of buying land, the cost of providing roads, and the cost of
providing 'town centre' facilities. Peripheral expansion accompanied
by town centre redevelopment and major road improvements was
'the most expensive way of dealing with the problem'. Redevelopment was 'vastly more expensive than development on clear sites'. The
ministry had therefore set up a group, under the chairmanship of a
principal planner, to examine a number of other methods of providing for expansion of an existing town, to study the traffic implications,
to cost them, and to try to discover how far it was possible to provide

additional population in close association with an existing town but as cheaply as constructing 'a green field new town'. Among other things, this group should be examining 'the constituent elements of town centres' to determine how far they needed to be sited in close proximity and what the possibilities were of simplifying traffic problems by dispersing them.

There was general discussion about the subjects that the group should pursue. The Treasury drew attention to the need to have regard not only to the amount of expenditure but to its timing (because of the importance of interest). Reference was made to the need, not only to assess costs, but also to try to assess, in qualitative terms, the benefits derived. Moreover, there was a need for analysis of the comparative costs of building at different densities since there was clearly a relationship between the cost of roads and the density at which houses were built. The lower the density, the greater the time and cost involved in travel. Finally, it was necessary to consider, not only costs, but the division between the private and public sectors (and, less importantly, the distinction between exchequer expenditure and local government expenditure).

While the first meeting had been concerned primarily with an explanation of work which was already under way in the Ministry of Housing, at the second meeting the group considered further some of the points that had arisen during the earlier discussion and debated what should be the pattern of further work of the study group. Two illustrative examples can be given: densities and 'comparative costs'.

MHLG explained that increases in density beyond a certain point had little, if any, advantage because construction costs rose rapidly with height, but only small further savings in land were made because the uses which had to remain at ground level (such as garages, open space and schools) accounted for the majority of the land needed. Increases in density would not therefore necessarily materially reduce travelling distances. A 1962 planning bulletin (*Residential Areas: Higher Densities*) had recommended net densities within the range of twelve to twenty houses per acre, but there was a need to re-examine the whole basis of residential areas in the context of the Buchanan report* and to determine the optimum size and the principles governing the design of residential environmental units. This task was being undertaken by the new towns research group and would also involve a review of open space standards.

On comparative costs, it was accepted that, although density was relevant to assessing the absolute cost of development and the economics of the design of a particular project, it was not relevant to

---

* Ministry of Transport, *Traffic in Towns*, HMSO, 1963.

comparisons between the types of project with which the group was concerned. This was true also of many of the other aspects of development. It appeared, however, that for some items of capital investment, geographical location might be significant. Thus the cost of water supply would clearly vary with locality, but this was a relatively insignificant element in cost. It was probable that 'capital investment less than the cost of a single power station' might solve the problem of water supply in the whole of the south-east for a long time. The cost of provision of public utilities, notably gas and electricity, however, might well be more significant.

After a further meeting, the chairman produced a paper in which he tried to set a framework for further study. So far, the group had tried to establish economic criteria for comparing five different types of town expansion and, from the discussions, it appeared that the significance of small changes in geographical location should also be considered. It was possible to isolate the elements in cost development, which were affected by one or other of these variables and to show their significance in relation to total cost. Direct expenditure, however, was not a sufficient measure of 'relative economic advantages'. There were other factors which had to be taken into account, such as the waste of resources by traffic congestion (lost time of workers, inefficient use of vehicles, etc) or the increase in efficiency of industrial production arising from change in environment, or the effect of taking different types of agricultural land out of production. Additionally there were social factors of environment or convenience which it might be impossible to put into monetary terms: for example, availability of facilities, convenience for work and for leisure, amenities and 'the social significance of traffic congestion'. It might be that some aspects of social and economic benefit would not be significant for comparison of types of development or of detailed locations but would relate to the absolute size of a town or community—thus adding a third variable.

Various papers on such subjects were prepared for the group. As an illustration a summary can be given of a MHLG paper on 'social criteria'.

SOCIAL CRITERIA

It was suggested that, in assessing social benefit, there was a need to define some criteria which could be used to give, in measurable terms, a means of judging the differences resulting from alternative methods of town expansion. From a social point of view, these differences would relate to the scale, timing and distribution of various amenities, services and facilities. If it were possible to rate these in some way so that an ideal pattern of geographical distribution could be devised, the town development schemes could be judged against this 'urban amenity' standard.

A possible criterion was that of 'convenience'. This was a useful form of measurement because it varied in relation not only to distance but also to the amenity itself. In other words, people would tend to regard a journey of twenty minutes or one mile to the local shops as 'inconvenient', but this time and distance would be 'convenient' for the major shopping centre. Nor was convenience a fixed factor in terms of physical distance; for example, people walking would regard half a mile taking ten to fifteen minutes as a 'convenient' distance, 'but the same amount of time by car would mean that the distance regarded as "convenient" would be very much greater'. By accepting the criterion of time rather than distance, a flexible standard was achieved varying for changes in transport facilities, amount of congestion and so on. However, the use of this criterion could perhaps be criticised because it would tend to favour the most densely built areas or those with rapid and good transport. One of the problems was that a rating scale of social benefits depended on the priorities people gave to certain amenities and the extent to which they saw the advantages outweighing the dis-advantages. For example, those who liked a spacious type of housing layout said they rated these amenities more highly than the incon-venience of a long journey to work. In these circumstances, priorities would vary between social classes, age groups, those with and without families, and so on. They were also closely related to the present, rather than future, distribution of facilities. However, it might be possible 'to measure the point at which people considered that the disadvantages outweighed the advantages and made a change in their priorities'.

Finally, at each stage of a town's growth, a certain range of facilities was possible. The maximum ideal standards could probably be drawn up from a study of catchment areas required for different services, the use made of them under optimum conditions, and so on. The different methods of town expansion could then be compared, at each stage of their growth, against these standards.

This paper on 'social criteria' was circulated to the study group under cover of a note by the chairman. In his view, there was not likely to be any single set of criteria which could be used for such measurements. It might, however, in theory be possible to split the population of a town (or the population for which a town was being planned) into several groups each of which would have its own criteria of social advantage or disadvantage. Thus, one could envisage a group that was very conscious of its surroundings and wanted low density with plenty of trees and was little concerned about distances for travel. Another group, on the other hand, might be quite unconcerned about environment but very much concerned with distances either from work or from shops and entertainment facilities. In theory, it might be possible to weight the importance given to various social criteria by each of the groups, to take account of the numerical size of each of the groups, and then to arrive at some composite figure to represent the degree to which a particular scheme for development satisfied the total population.

'I stress that this might in theory be possible. I have considerable doubts about the practicability of such an analysis in quantitative terms. I am very sure, however, that any attempt to measure social benefit by taking only a single factor such as closeness to work or closeness to shops would be quite misleading.'

FIRST DRAFT REPORT

After discussing various papers of this nature, the study group prepared a first draft report. This stressed that the five methods of accommodating population growth were not comparable since 'they confuse physical form of development with agency for development'. The study group were concerned primarily with 'population growth on a considerable scale'. Redevelopment alone could not deal with this, and the impact of peripheral development on a conurbation was not easy to assess. They therefore concentrated initially on comparing a green field new town with the expansion of an existing town. Since the inquiry was concerned with large scale development, such matters as internal design, density of development and standards were not relevant—they applied equally to a new or an expanded town. In terms of total direct expenditure, the main distinctions between a new town and an expanded town would be in the cost of road construction, the cost of land and the cost of necessary redevelopment (ie the cost of buying buildings and demolishing them 'in order to get at land for development'). Thus, the costs in a new town and the costs in an expanded town of providing houses, schools, industry and shops, were broadly the same, and the differences were certainly unlikely to be more than the differences between two separate new towns due to the differing geographical locations. There would, however, be some difference in phasing.

The cost of roads in an expanded town could be expected to be substantially higher 'in order to provide a similar standard of communication' because improvement of the old town would almost certainly be required as well as the provision of a new road framework for the expansion areas. Some credit should obviously be taken for the improvement of facilities for the old town and, indeed, it could be argued that this expenditure would have to be incurred for the old town in any case, although without expansion this might not be for some years ahead. The price that had to be paid for land ripe for development on the fringe of an existing town would obviously be very much more than the price payable for unripe land in entirely rural surroundings. The cost of land for the expansion of a town would, therefore, be more than the cost for a green field new town. But, in practice, if the expansion proposed was very substantial, only part of the land to be bought for a town expansion would be ripe for development and therefore very high priced, and also it was unlikely that a new town would be sited on an entirely virgin site 'and therefore avoid paying some development value'. Thus the cost of land for new development for a major town expansion was likely to be somewhat more than the cost for a new town 'but not excessively so'.

In the course of expanding a town, some of the new development would almost inevitably have to be placed within the old town and thus necessitate not only the acquisition of land in areas where high values were well established but, more importantly, the acquisition of existing buildings for demolition and the payment of disturbance for displacing the occupants. It was not yet possible to generalise about the scale of this other than to say that 'in town expansion redevelopment should be kept to a minimum'.

Social and aesthetic factors were clearly relevant to any cost benefit analysis. They could not, however, readily be quantified, and generalisations were difficult because any rating scale of social benefits depended on the priorities people gave to certain amenities 'and the extent to which to them the advantages outweighed the disadvantages'. The priorities varied between social classes, age groups, those with and without families and so on. Many of these social factors, however, were determined within the neighbourhood. They depended upon the detailed design of housing layouts, the availability of local shopping and schools, and other social facilities. For comparison purposes, therefore, the more significant social factors were likely to be those related to the size of a town and its regional setting, eg the range of social and cultural activities available, the range of choice available in shops, and the range of jobs available for children.

It could be deduced from the arguments used in comparing a new and an expanded town that most items of capital expenditure would be broadly the same for both. The need for expenditure on industrial and commercial development might be rather less in an expanded town because of the possibilities of spare capacity. It would be well-nigh impossible to estimate the costs of road works. Substantial additional population on the fringe of a conurbation, however, would have effects on the conurbation itself. They would create congestion within the conurbation which could be taken into account as an indirect economic cost, 'or it could lead to road improvements within the conurbation which would have to be charged as direct expenditure'. Additions to the rail service in a conurbation might also be necessary.

It was difficult to quantify the significance of the various factors but, 'we do not think that anyone would disagree with the view that the London green belt should broadly be maintained—that the conurbation within the green belt is already too large'. It could be argued that the population of London could still be allowed to grow by increased commuting in areas beyond the green belt. This, however, had many disadvantages in cost and inconvenience of travel and, although such commuting did take place already, it was only certain social groups that could afford it and were prepared to put up with the inconvenience of travel for the sake of more rural living conditions. Peripheral growth was not therefore a possible solution for the London conurbation. More examination would be necessary to determine how far it was worth considering in the main conurbations elsewhere in the country.

Whatever the form of new development, it could be carried out by central government, by local authorities or by private enterprise. Whatever the agency, the total amount of capital expenditure would be the same and the total return on capital should be the same. It was the distribution of costs and profits that was at issue. If everything possible were left to private enterprise, planning control could in theory prevent development taking place where it was not wanted, but by negative control it was impossible to ensure that it took place where and when it was wanted and, in practice, the available negative control was 'not sufficient to prevent entirely development where it was not wanted'.

Private enterprise development for the expansion of an existing town was certainly possible: 'indeed this is happening all the time'. But if it took place very rapidly it created a need for the provision of social facilities and public services which could place a heavy burden on local authorities. Private enterprise undertook the profitable part of the operation and left the unprofitable part to the public body. Growth might be haphazard and could not be phased 'to form part of coherent social policy'. Positive public intervention in the expansion of a town or the creation of a new town was justified by the need to try to achieve a change in the pattern of population movement. Such intervention called for a public body to be in control of the development and with powers to carry out any of it. However, it did not follow that all the development would in fact be directly financed by the public purse. The extent to which a public body undertook development directly depended upon' the balance of the disadvantage of increasing expenditure within the public sector and the advantage of securing for the public sector the immediate and long term profit from such expenditure to offset the unprofitable elements which had to be done by the public authority'. The justification for public intervention in the growth of towns depended primarily upon how far this was necessary in order to implement a social policy of population movement. Very much more information was needed about the factors that influenced migration in order to decide less crudely the degree of public intervention and the phasing of public expenditure. A decision on whether a public scheme for growth should be run by a local authority or by a government agency should be determined on practical grounds. There was generally a preference for a government agency because this should be capable of doing the job more efficiently, because of its freedom from 'local parish pump politics', and also because, owing to this freedom, there was 'a greater assurance that the job would in fact be done and government policy secured'.

PROGRESS OF THE STUDY GROUP

The work of the group now began to spread over a wide range of issues. Within MHLG there was discussion as to whether the report did not underestimate the role which redevelopment could play in providing for growth, particularly where it was large scale and comprehensive. Within the Treasury, there was concern lest the market value of land should be too readily accepted as a good indicator of the real cost to the community of alternative uses. A paper on 'the economics of land' was produced for discussion. Another Treasury paper dealt with 'agencies for development'. This pointed out that, despite the planning advantages of public agency development 'there must be a general presumption in favour of keeping public sector investment as low as possible in any particular type of case and of favouring those types of development which in general tend to minimise the need for public intervention to secure advantages of timing and so on'. One general reason was that, in any circumstances which could be envisaged, public sector investment in catering for planned expansions of population would necessarily be very considerable and, given the scale of planned expansions which was anticipated over the next twenty years, would inevitably add appreciably to the burden of financing the public expenditure at a time when many different pressures were operating to increase it. Another reason for favouring minimal public sector intervention was that a public agency was inevitably subject to political influences which hampered its ability to concentrate on obtaining as good a return as a commercial organisation set up for the same purpose. These influences would tend to direct the public authority towards 'the attainment of objectives—possibly worthy social and aesthetic ones—but which nevertheless conflicted with viability'. Some of these objectives might be worth while pursuing because of the advantages that would be gained elsewhere, but there was reason to believe that often the advantages would be illusory and the cost greater than if private enterprise were left to get on with the job.

The argument that private enterprise undertook the profitable part of an operation and left the unprofitable part to the public body was possibly better considered 'as a criticism of the existing system of taxation and of the techniques of the development corporations as regards land purchase than as an argument for increasing public intervention'. However, whatever national policies might or might not be pursued as regards the taxation of betterment in the future, it seemed that the development corporations of new towns and, from the nature of operations envisaged, 'the authorities of future town expansions', should be able within existing powers to recoup betterment (for the benefit of the exchequer and not particular residents) to a greater extent than had been possible in the past.

The general conclusions were that developments where public investment could be kept to the minimum were to be preferred and that, where there was freedom of choice between public and private investment, the latter was to be favoured unless there was a positive net demonstrable advantage in the work being carried out by a public authority. If this were accepted, 'then it must lead to a re-thinking of the functions and of the criteria which should be used by the development corporations in deciding in what fields to operate'. The essential change that seemed necessary was 'to stop thinking in terms of the total profitability of a particular corporation or the relative profitability of different corporations but to compare the return on particular investments, where the corporation was free to obtain the maximum return, with the return that a similar firm in the private sector could be expected to obtain, whether it be property development company, industrial or commercial concern'. The current arrangement and climate of thinking tended to encourage the corporations to maximise investment in all directions, 'which was not likely to be in the national interest'.

It was generally agreed that there were good reasons for 'limiting the spread of public investment'. The presumption should be that development ought to be undertaken by private enterprise unless sound arguments could be produced against this. To justify public investment it had to be shown, for example, that the public authority could do the operation more efficiently or that there was a social requirement which could not otherwise be met. It was agreed that to make the accounts of a development corporation balance or show a profit was in itself not a sufficiently good reason for incurring expenditure. Further points were raised on the valuation of agricultural land and the effect of new town design on reducing road costs relative to expanded towns; but the main point of agreement seemed to be that the emerging report was inadequate. By mid 1965 the difficulties of the issues being tackled and changes in both Treasury and ministry representations resulted in a hiatus.

An internal Treasury minute expressed disappointment at the progress made by the study group. Discussions had been 'interesting but inconclusive' and, despite five drafts of a report, the outcome was —in the view of the Treasury—'still far too thin'. The inherent difficulties had been exacerbated by numerous changes in the membership of the study group. The basic difficulty was perhaps that, while a significant amount of work could be done on the relative costs of various types of development, it was much more difficult to see where the greater benefits lay. The main tentative conclusions which emerged from the studies were, first, that there was no one type of development which was superior to all others in all circumstances. Secondly, town expansions seemed to have considerable advantages over green field new towns, particularly if the centre of the existing town had to be renewed in any case. These advantages stemmed mainly from the existence of spare capacity, 'and employment of opportunities , so that less advance investment was necessary'. Thirdly, really large scale expansion seemed to be somewhat cheaper than smaller scale expansion.

Throughout the discussions, it had been clear that this was a field in which more study was necessary. Unfortunately, the past accounts of the new town corporations did not provide as good a guide to costs as had been hoped, because of the difficulties of discounting and the extent to which the pace of development of new towns had been affected by political decisions from time to time. The establishment of sound economic criteria, which would lead to an economic use of resources, could still leave a wide range of choice in the planning of urban environments to take account of various social factors. On the other hand, sloppy thinking about density and land use, particularly in relation to agricultural land, could well lead to the unnecessary use of resources.

Nothing more seems to have then happened until November 1965 when the official committee on regional economic planning raised the issues anew in connection with a MHLG paper on *Next Steps in the South East*. A MHLG minute noted that at this committee, the Treasury had again raised the question:

'whether we could not do more work on the costing of different forms of development . . . They dropped a broad hint that they would expect to see something attempted on this before we came along with our next batch of planned expansions for approval. We and other departments pointed out all the obvious difficulties; the Treasury nevertheless thought we ought to have another go to demonstrate what could and what could not be done.'

An internal MHLG minute suggested that 'it would be preferable not to resuscitate the working party, but to go to NIESR* and ask the unit there to work on the problems for us'. This proposal was put to the Treasury who were 'quite enthusiastic', and in February 1966 agreed it in principle.† In April, an internal Treasury minute noted that:

'We are interested in the general area in which this project falls, I take it, because we would like to know, given the increase in population of twenty million expected by the end of the century: (a) what pattern of settlement would make the best use of resources, in the sense of maximising the rate of growth of GNP while taking account of the social costs and benefits not included in GNP; (b) what implications the answer to (a) would have for the exchequer.'

The study was finally approved in May 1966.

The NIESR Report on Town Structure, Size and Cost‡

The NIESR report by Dr P. A. Stone became available at the end of 1967. An initial reaction within the ministry was:

'the broad conclusion is that green field developments are cheaper than town expansions, and that the cheapest form of town expansion is to keep the existing town quite separate from the new development . . . The conclusions emerge at the top of a pyramid of assumptions built into the synthetic town models which he has developed for population sizes of 50,000, 100,000 and 500,000. These assumptions are all set out in the report, and then analysed in great detail to their ultimate logical conclusions. If any of these are significantly wrong then much of what follows is invalidated.'

Further study led to the conclusion that 'the report is so highly theoretical that it might only have limited usefulness in shaping future planning policies for new towns and town expansions'. A major appraisal of the report was undertaken by a team of officials from different divisions of MHLG and from the Ministry of Transport. They recommended that Stone's conclusion that town expansion was relatively expensive should be used and publicised, that a register should be started of the costs of items of town building, that some further studies should be undertaken particularly of the relative advantages and disadvantages of expanding towns, as

---

* The National Institute of Economic and Social Research.
† Treasury File 2AT 636/372/01.
‡ MHLG File NT 211/50/1–5 and Treasury File 2AT 335/217/01. The report was submitted to the ministry at the end of 1967 as the first part of a wider study which was later financed by the Centre for Environmental Studies. The ministry agreed that the substance of the study should be published by Stone as part of his wider investigation. This was published in 1973: P. A. Stone, *The Structure, Size and Costs of Urban Settlements,* National Institute of Economic and Social Research, Economic and Social Studies XXVIII, Cambridge University Press.

against building separate new towns, and that there should be a steering committee for further studies of this kind.

In the meantime, Stone's analysis was being overtaken by decisions on new towns and by attempts to improve accounting and financial techniques.

The New Towns Working Group 1967*

In December 1964, ministers had approved in principle new town expansions at Ipswich, Northampton, Peterborough and North Buckinghamshire; and during 1965 and 1966 the Ministry of Housing and Local Government was making progress with public inquiries and consultants' reports. Milton Keynes was the first to come to the stage of obtaining Treasury approval and, in November 1966, the ministry wrote that the minister (Greenwood) 'envisages that the town would take 150,000 immigrants by about 1991, and that these with their natural increase would represent a population approaching 200,000 by the end of the century. The cost in resources for providing for this population would be between four and five hundred million pounds. It is not possible to make any more soundly based estimate in advance of the master plan which the development corporation would propose and on which you would be consulted'. The Treasury replied that while Milton Keynes had been approved in principle two years previously:

'disappointingly slow progress had been made in working towards an over-all new towns programme and it is by no means clear that it will be possible to afford all of the new towns and major expansions which have already been suggested, or which are likely to be suggested for the various regions . . . I suggest therefore that your minister should put in a short paper to the EP Committee stating the size and cost of the project as it is now envisaged . . . It seems only right that interested ministers should be given a chance of expressing considered views upon it before it is finally started.'

Greenwood did this in December 1966 and Milton Keynes was approved, but 'before further decisions on individual projects were taken, officials should give a comprehensive report on the new towns programme, with particular reference to cost, the implications for development areas and the relative priorities of individual projects'. Meanwhile, the DEA had suggested a working party on new town problems. A MHLG minute of 30 November 1966 commented 'I want to ensure that this working party does not drag us into fruitless discussions about priorities, economic criteria etc, duplicating the work we have already commissioned Stone to do in NIESR. If we must have a working party I think we ought to make

* MHLG Files NT 256/53/11, NT 49/28 and NT 49/31; EP(66)17 and EP(66)5th Meeting, 22 December 1966; EP(O)(67) 1st Meeting, 4 January 1967; and EP(67)14. See also chapter V, p. 233 *et seq.*

a bid for the chairmanship so that we can keep it properly under control. After all, new towns are very much a MHLG matter.'

Following a decision of the EP Official Committee, the working group was set up on 16 January 1967 with terms of reference:

'to report on the regional, financial and economic implications of the proposed new town programme over the next fifteen years, having regard to the relative priorities of the various projects and to the prospects of other major planned expansions.'

The chair was taken by MHLG, and there were representatives of the Ministry of Agriculture, DEA, Labour, Public Building and Works, Board of Trade, Transport, Treasury, Scottish Office and Welsh Office. At the first meeting on 20 January 1967, the chairman explained that the work was urgent since if it were not completed quickly there was a danger that the momentum of the English new towns would be lost. MHLG were ready to publish draft designation orders for Ipswich, Northampton, Warrington and Wellington–Oakengates but could not do this till ministers had reviewed the programme as a whole: he therefore hoped to submit a report by the end of February.

The group held ten meetings during January–April 1967, and their report was issued in May. A number of papers were circulated within the group whose contents were not directly reflected in the report, and special mention may perhaps be made of one of these which reflected the concern of the Treasury on the public expenditure implications of new towns. They pointed out that the creation of new towns meant:

'(a) Additional public expenditure in the early years through the advance provision of infrastructure, and the need to provide nearly all the houses.
(b) Probably some further addition because the quality of the social investment (including housing) is higher than it would be if undertaken elsewhere.
(c) More public expenditure because of the financing of commercial and industrial development.
(d) More financing from the exchequer which meets all the capital needs of the new town development corporations'.

Against this background the Treasury felt that any sharp rise in expenditure on new towns was bound to provoke questions about the degree of urgency or desirability of various individual projects. They understood that all the proposals for the new towns in Great Britain would in the aggregate involve expenditure in excess of £250m in 1971–72, and doubted whether it really made sense 'to become committed to more than a bare minimum of new projects until more was known of the economics and comparative costs of new town developments'. The Treasury continued that 'the case for going ahead with all the proposed new towns would be stronger if it were known with some precision how much of the population growth in the 1970s had got to be provided for in the new towns. But the estimates of need for additional new towns and expansions are inevitably carried out as residual figures from estimates of population growth and estimates of the extent to which these will be matched by the unplanned growth of existing towns. Inevitably therefore most of the estimates of requirements for new towns are subject to wide margins of error . . . It cannot therefore be assumed that approval will be forthcoming for all the proposals for new towns. The presumption must be that additions to existing programmes will have to be much more modest'.

The report of the new towns working group was a lengthy document, which was 'a first attempt to review the new town programme on a comprehensive basis' and to reflect general interdepartmental agreement. The programme currently envisaged—expansions of existing new towns plus projects at Milton Keynes, Ipswich, Northampton, Peterborough, Ashford, Standsted, Warrington, Mid Lancashire, Newtown and Llantrisant (but excluding South Hampshire, Humberside, Severnside, etc)—would provide 365,000 houses (public or private sectors) over the next fifteen years. The prospects of providing industry and other employment were not such as to justify cutting back the programme. The availability of resources within the construction industry did not constitute a major limitation. The main concern was cost: capital expenditure (public and private) for the existing and proposed programmes would increase from £111m in 1967–68 to £295m in 1974–75, and 'not likely to fall much below during the 1970s'.

> 'It must be emphasised that if approval was not given to these new towns, additional investment of broadly this order would be needed elsewhere, for the people who are to live in them will have to be accommodated one way or another. But new towns involve some extra public expenditure (and appreciably more exchequer finance) which has to be taken into account in the various public expenditure programmes (housing, roads etc).'

The report posed the questions involved in rephasing the programme, but suggested as an immediate step approval of the schemes to which there was a high degree of government commitment: designation of Peterborough; expansion of Basildon and Stevenage; and draft designation orders and public inquiries for Warrington, Northampton and Ipswich.*

The report was an agreed one, and action was taken on its specific recommendations as set out in chapter V. In view of the consensus on these, the report itself was not discussed by ministers collectively.

---

* See further chapter V, p. 233 *et seq.*

The more general issue of the control of new town expenditure thus fell to the Treasury and the Ministry of Housing. In discussing this and completing our account up to the end of the 'sixties it is necessary to go back to the beginning of the decade when the Public Expenditure Survey Committee (PESC) machinery was introduced.

Treasury Apprehensions and Management Accounts*

The 1961 Plowden Report on *The Control of Public Expenditure* (Cmnd 1432) had recommended that regular projections be made of public expenditure as a whole over a period of years and in relation to prospective resources, and that decisions involving substantial public expenditure in future should be taken in the light of those surveys. These recommendations were accepted, and the PESC machinery was established in the Treasury. Annual forecasts were made of expenditure by local and central government and by public boards several years ahead under a dozen functional headings. The results were examined by ministers in the light of the resources available, and their decisions were published in an annual white paper on public expenditure. They became an established and increasingly sophisticated part of the governmental machinery for the control of expenditure.

Expenditure on new towns was divided among three principal PESC functional blocks: housing, roads, and environmental services. In each case, the new town element was subordinate to the main issues which ministers had to consider in determining the expenditure to be allocated to that block. On housing, attention was concentrated on the total number and standards of public sector housing—of which that in new towns formed a small proportion. On roads, discussion centred on motorways and major roads elsewhere, and the new town item received no great prominence. On environmental services, new town expenditure tended to be overlooked in a total programme of several hundred million pounds which was otherwise concerned with local authority expenditure on water, sewerage, town halls, parks and so forth. In short, there was nothing in the PESC review which enabled ministers to see clearly what proposals for more new towns really involved.

In 1964, when proposals were under consideration for a substantial programme of new towns in the south-east and elsewhere, involving a major exchequer commitment in principle, it was stressed that the investment would have to come within the total investment figures for housing and other environmental services. In a lengthy minute of 29 October 1965, a senior Treasury official said he was 'much exercised about the whole business of financing

---

* Treasury File 2AT 335/24/01 and MHLG Files NT 8/9, NT 36/24, NT 49/28, NT 118/6 and NT 140/10.

the new towns and the rapidly growing demand on resources' which they represented. The time span presented great difficulty: the period covered by the public expenditure survey was too short for control, as half a dozen new towns could be designated at the start of the five year period with very little effect on spending during that period, 'but with a colossal long term commitment'. At this point he felt 'a serious philosophical difficulty' about the control of resources for new towns—namely the argument, which had 'some force', that new town investment was not additional investment, but 'investment that would have to take place any way', but which was diverted to a new, and perhaps cheaper, channel. Without new towns, the local authorities would have to invest in town expansions, overspill schemes or otherwise, to cope with the population growth. (This was the justification in the PESC exercise for bracketing new town and local authority expenditure together.) But the result was that 'it is never possible to argue seriously about whether a proposal to establish another new town will add significantly to the demand on resources, or make it compete with other proposals: new towns go virtually on the nod'. If there was any PESC resource control at all, it was only on and through housing; he felt that there was 'no real financial control either' since advances to the corporations were made virtually on demand, and the new towns, individually or as a whole, had no financial target. He continued that it was difficult to see how the slow burgeoning new town programme could effectively be brought into competition with other programmes having regard to the argument about diverting resources, 'rather than taking wholly new resources'. It would of course be possible to say that the growth rate of the new town programme was too large to be supported, unless accompanied by a sharp restraint on local authority expenditure, 'but this would merely get back to the local authority programme, and would not assist on the new town problem'.

He therefore proposed that there should be a presumption that the average new town would 'reach break even' on revenue account within a specified period (say fifteen years), and if there were special features likely to modify this (eg water and sewerage problems) 'this should be brought out at the start'. Moreover, each new town should have a target for viability; and the aggregation of targets would provide a target for the new town system as a whole. Finally, new towns 'in surplus' (including those of the commission) should contribute to financing the system, 'the exchequer providing in theory a net volume of advances'. It was these net advances which should provide the basis for discussion on forward programmes.

These proposals were put to the ministry by the Treasury in February 1966 and formed a part of the pressure the Treasury was bringing to bear to contain the size and cost of the programmes.

Other aspects were the pressure to increase private investment in housing and more particularly the instigation of the proposal to the EP Committee at its meeting in December 1966 to call for a comprehensive report on the new towns programme and a study of the basis on which agricultural land should be valued for planning purposes.* In agreeing to the proposals for the designation of Peterborough, and for public inquiries for Warrington, Northampton and Ipswich, MacDermott (financial secretary, Treasury) wrote to Greenwood on 11 May 1967:

> 'I would like it to be clearly understood between us that this is entirely without prejudice to the important decisions which we shall be called upon to take on public expenditure over the next few years. The practical effect of this is that if the Public Expenditure Review does not result in additional sums being made available to meet the expansion of the new towns programme, the necessary finance will have to be found by cutting back elsewhere in the housing block.'

On the Treasury proposals for long term estimates and targets for viability, the ministry agreed that they were not unreasonable in principle, 'but we think we must be realistic about what can be done by way of binding us in the way suggested'. In fact, MHLG had for some time been making attempts to obtain a better guide to the 'profitability' of the new towns. Development corporations had been required to submit an annual statistical analysis of their capital expenditure and income—usually referred to as a 'profitability return'. This was designed to provide an assessment of the return being obtained on investment to date. Initially, it was felt that the returns would be of greater use to the corporations themselves than to the department. In 1965 it was suggested that the returns might be summarised and circulated to all new towns. Though it was appreciated that 'this could cause a flutter', there was good reason for regarding the new towns as 'subsidiary companies of a holding company, all doing the same operation'—even if in areas of varying physical and social characteristics. On this line of argument, the development corporations should not object to, 'and ought to be stimulated by' a fair and objective comparison of results. But they did, and the accountant general's department (AGD) of the ministry minuted (some two years later) that 'I am afraid we never got it under way'.

Increased Treasury pressure forced MHLG to review their procedures, and the secretary issued several long minutes on the subject. In view of the scale of the new town operations and of exchequer financing, he thought it rather surprising that Parliament had so far shown such a limited interest, but it would be unwise

---

* See chapter V, p. 233 *et seq* and appendix B.

to count on the continuance 'of so passive an attitude'.* Quite apart from answerability to Parliament, MHLG had a duty to ensure that new towns were developed economically, 'and that we get the best possible value for money'. Leaving housing on one side (which was heavily subsidised anyway and was not run for profit) he thought that it was necessary to look critically at the return on capital invested in factories, and more especially in commercial premises. He entirely accepted that conditions might so often be variable that meaningful comparison could not be made, 'but this must not prevent us from making comparisons where these are worthwhile'. The gross return on commercial properties in the six major new towns around London (all of which were substantially completed) ranged from 6·32 per cent in Hemel Hempstead to 11·48 per cent in Harlow:

> 'Why should there be these substantial differences? Are we satisfied with the explanation offered? Is there anything to suggest faults of property or general management?'

He suggested that detailed tables should be prepared each year, and that MHLG should critically examine the rates of return on industrial and commercial premises making use, as necessary, of the knowledge of the department's estates officers. Corporations should be 'grilled' on differences that were disclosed by the analysis. Further consideration should be given to circulating (eg to general managers) a 'league table' of performance 'so as to stir some emulation among them'. Finally, a short report should be made to ministers on these activities and their assistance should be sought if the examinations disclosed any defects that ought to be remedied, 'and where the corporation is not fully co-operative'.

AGD minuted that the first step was probably to consider the action taken on receipt of the profitability assessments. The returns were examined in the AGD Branch for any obvious peculiarities or differences from the previous year's state of affairs that might seem to require explanation. In particular, a noticeable fall in the rate of income or the rate of return from investment might require explanation. Because of the effect of averaging, even a small change in the cumulative percentage figures could indicate a far bigger change in the last year.

One subject that 'would repay particular study' was the position on general development expenditure (GDE). The theory was that the total GDE incurred in building the new town should be spread over the total remunerative investment. This was usually done by a percentage addition to direct costs, and corporations had always been free to fix the percentages. To some extent they did this on the

---

* For further discussion of parliamentary control see appendix D.

basis of 'what the traffic would bear', and the tendency was to treat housing as favourably as possible. It required accurate forecasting and periodic review of the percentage allocations during the early years of a corporation's development. It was apparent from the returns that some corporations were not making sufficient provision for GDE and were therefore overstating the rate of return on their investment. The real touchstone of viability was examination of development proposals submitted by development corporations to the department for approval: 'if approval is given to a project of doubtful value it is too late to grumble at the corporation when the chicken comes home to roost'.

In July 1967, MHLG sent to the general managers a summary comparative analysis of capital expenditure. This included a statement of the extent to which GDE had been incurred and recouped to date by allocation to revenue producing land and buildings. Of course, much of GDE had to be incurred in advance of remunerative development and the rate of recoupment necessarily lagged behind the expenditure. The figures in the return, however, suggested that in some cases the allocations to date were 'on the low side' having regard to the stage of development the corporations had reached.

> 'Inadequate allocations may result in inadequate rents if these are determined as a percentage of the cost of land and buildings; where the rent is a market rent and not directly dependent on cost, an inadequate allocation of GDE produces a higher rate of return than is really being earned. The inclusion in the summary of the figure of net viability, ie the amount of the annual rate of income after providing for all annual outgoings including interest and depreciation as a percentage of the total advances, offers a corrective to such over optimistic reckoning.'

It was proposed to issue a similar summary every year as soon as possible after the analyses had been received. The issue of these summaries was not itself intended to be an occasion for comment by corporations or the commission. The department would take up directly with them any point that seemed to require elucidation or comment when the returns were examined. The corporations and the commission were invited, when they submitted the returns, 'to draw attention to any particular features'. If, however, any corporation or the commission wished to comment on the proposed arrangements MHLG would consider any points they wished to make.

In February 1968, AGD minuted that the profitability assessment amounted to an aggregation of the results of the approvals of all the individual projects that had been completed to date. The limitations of the profitability exercise had to be recognised: 'it lumps together a lot of things broadly of a kind but with some individual variation and enables a year by year comparison to be made on a broad basis'. The return would include the results of, for example, rent reviews and renewals of leases, which did not individually have to be submitted to the department. General as it was, it might nevertheless draw attention to points worth examining in depth. It did enable one to see the amount of the addition to the fructified capital expenditure in the year and what changes in outgoings and rent income had taken place in the year. The details of income and expenditure might point to items of heavy expenditure where probing might be worth while. An increase in rent income might be attributable to changes in rents of older property as well as the new rents from additional fructified expenditure, 'but only inquiry of the corporation would reveal this sort of detail'. The point for consideration was whether MHLG should ask for more detail to be supplied as a regular annual return, or whether they should be content with present information and returns and to pursue more detailed inquiries where these returns suggested that probing might be fruitful.

> 'The philosophy at one time was that the corporations were set up and had qualified professional staff to do their job and that the department should not, in these circumstances, try to take over the job itself. Unless it is prepared to push the corporation aside and deal itself with the customer or the contractor it really cannot do so. If the department thinks the corporation is falling down on the job its only sanction is to refuse to approve projects about which it is not satisfied and, in the ultimate, to dismiss the board. The department's *modus operandi* is to take a view of the corporations' results with the benefit of its own professional advice and if it does not think they are satisfactory it must show the corporation why and where they have gone wrong, and it must make sure that in its further operations the corporation does pay heed to the department's guidance.'

In all this 'it was necessary to recognise that corporations were in a difficult position'. They were charged with the task of building a new town and were subject 'to enormous pressures to do all sorts of things for social reasons which inevitably means that it cannot operate single mindedly to secure the maximum financial return from its investment'. For example, corporations were anxious to provide shopping and other facilities on social grounds 'where for maximum financial benefit it might wait until there is a stronger head of steam'. There was pressure on the architects 'to make a show which may be expensive but does not produce the maximum return'. And MHLG knew of corporations which had been short of industrial employment and had been 'ready to go to almost any lengths to get industry into the town'.

Though it might be possible to refine the profitability assessments by tightening up the instructions on the way in which they were to be compiled, 'it must be appreciated that inflexible rules that cannot be adapted to unusual circumstances are as likely to produce misleading results as relying on the corporations' common-sense in carrying out a more flexible instruction'. For example, only the corporations could say when expenditure had become fructified: this was fundamental 'and far from easy to cover by rules'. AGD concluded that there was not much that could be done apart from probing the submissions and profitability figures and making use of the results in considering approval of new projects.

Another minute took a different line. The profitability return only gave a snapshot picture of fructified return and, if strict comparisons were to be made between corporations, adjustments also needed to be made to reflect the present value of future increases in return. Efficient management, in the development corporations and the ministry, was hampered by the financial statement method of presentation of accounts and by the practice of using historic or notional land costs.

On examining the annual profitability returns, it had been suggested that 'some of the laggards will show up better in future years when commercial rents have been raised under the rising rent provisions of leases'. An increase of a current 8 per cent return to produce a 10 per cent return by a 25 per cent rise in rents (a typical rise provided for at the fourteenth year in many development corporation shop leases) would generally be regarded with satisfaction. Yet in order to keep pace with inflation alone over such a period, a 50 per cent rise in rent would be required. The financial statement therefore gave a picture of a rising rent return on original investment when the true situation was a fall in the value of the return. Furthermore, no account was taken of the fact that shops would rise in real value due to the development of trade in the town.

This example indicated the need for periodic revaluation of assets in order that management was fully aware of the true value which should be recouped rather than the original book cost. This awareness would undoubtedly influence policy and lead to insistence on more frequent fixed rent increases or rent reviews and perhaps a move towards introducing percentage rents in the peculiar circumstances of new towns where future values were difficult to assess accurately because of the rapidly changing situation arising from town growth.

There was nothing that could be done to improve past economic performance, but it would be useful to study the commercial and industrial developments of a few towns in some depth to see if the factors which had contributed to good profitability performances could be identified and whether even these performances might not have been bettered. Sharper management techniques might be suggested by such a study which could be of value to the third generation new towns.

Discussion continued between the Treasury and MHLG on the one hand, and between MHLG and the development corporations on the other. Some proposals were put to the chairmen at their meeting on 10 October 1968, who agreed that a return of viability would be a valuable instrument, but 'fair comparisons could only be made between towns in similar circumstances . . . Nor could profitability be the only way of judging the success of a town'. It was agreed that representatives of the corporations and the department should jointly consider how the return might be improved.

Lengthy discussions followed between the ministry and the chairmen and finance officers of the corporations. Trial runs were made by several corporations of methods of assessing financial performance and preparing forward estimates of expenditure and revenue as a basis for moving away from the project by project control towards a broader appraisal of each town's development programme. But it was apparent that expert advice was needed to make further progress, and in 1970 a firm of accountants (Peat, Marwick, Mitchell and Co) were appointed to advise on a suitable system of management accounting for use by the corporations and the ministry in controlling the operations and activities of the corporations. They recommended a management information system combining long term forecasts of physical development, capital investment and financial performance with a monitoring and reporting system. The system was gradually brought into use after 1971, but certain elements had been partially adopted earlier, notably the stricter enforcement of the housing cost yardstick of 1967 which involved a lessening of control on schemes which fell within it.

The Philosopher's Stone

This chapter has given a selective account of the attempts made by governments up to the end of the 'sixties to come to grips with a range of financial and economic aspects of new town development. The original estimates of costs were inevitably inspired guesswork, but fears of the 'alarming commitment' were expressed by the Treasury from the very beginning of the programme. Planning ministers made much of the point that, if new towns were not built, development would have to take place elsewhere: though new towns might be slightly more expensive, they represented good value for money and, with rising land values accruing to the public purse, would eventually be profitable. But this argument was a 'theoretical' one which could not be proved—or disproved—by the numerous investigations that were made. In 1952 officials felt that the 'extremely hazardous undertaking' of building a new town was, 'from a strictly financial point of view' much more likely to result in a loss than a profit. Opinions changed later, but there was no doubt that new towns involved a much higher degree of exchequer aid than other forms of development. It was against this background that emphasis was placed throughout the 'fifties on town expansion. The existing new towns programme was continued, but essentially for reasons of planning and housing policy, together with the political adroitness of Macmillan in parrying the Treasury arguments of 1952–54.

The conversion of the Conservative Government to a 'second generation' of new towns at the beginning of the 'sixties, coupled with attempts to improve the machinery for the control of public expenditure gave rise to a host of new inquiries. Most proved abortive. The path to conclusions was beset by numerous diversions: on densities, the valuation of agricultural land, and 'social criteria', for example. Moreover, while studies of particular sites might demonstrate the relative benefits and costs of alternative proposals for those sites, they provided no basis for generalisations. The only generalisations were 'common sense' ones such as the advantages of developing in an area where there was spare capacity in public services, and the disadvantages of embarking upon an expansion scheme which involved major town centre renewal. The more detailed an investigation became, the more questions did it raise. And theoretical exercises had to make heroic assumptions which did not obtain in the real world of decision making.

Further difficulties resulted from confusion between types of development (new towns and expanded towns) and agencies of development (development corporations and local authorities) and from the problems of discounting inflation in assessing the profitability of earlier developments.

An enormous amount of time was put into this area of study, but with little effect. Many of the questions were unanswerable in the form in which they were posed, and much of the effort was of the nature of a seeking for the philosopher's stone.

Meanwhile decisions had to be taken and, since 'rational' and 'objective' criteria proved elusive, they were based on political judgements. The problem of public expenditure control remained, however: indeed, the enlarged new town programme greatly increased it. Here some progress was made by the introduction of management accounts and, on a wider front, by the PESC machinery; but this takes us both beyond the scope and the time scale of this history.*

---

* That the issues discussed in this chapter are still very much alive needs no emphasis; see, for example, 13th Report of the Expenditure Committee, *New Towns*, HC 616 (1974–75).

CHAPTER IX

Expanded Towns Policy

Early Thinking on Expanded Towns*

THE Barlow and the Abercrombie reports had both contemplated extensions to small towns 'to secure a better distribution of population and of industry', and the initial proposals of the Pepler group in 1944† were framed on the assumption that:

> 'movement of population will generally take the form of additions to small towns or large villages rather than that of the creation of entirely new towns on virgin sites.'

To this end, the Pepler group contemplated agreements for the housing of overspill between the exporting and the receiving authorities, and accordingly some provision was made in the Town and Country Planning Act 1944 enabling a promoting local authority to acquire land in the area of another authority for the relocation of population and industry. This, however, afforded little in the way of effective machinery. Moreover, the receiving authorities were unlikely to have the resources to undertake development; the county councils were not housing authorities, and therefore were ineligible for the housing subsidies which would be essential for any progress; and there was no provision for exchequer assistance.

In the discussion at the Distribution of Industry Committee in May 1946 on the location of the new towns, Bevan (Minister of Health) and Tomlinson (Minister of Works) while not opposing the proposals, had urged that the needs of existing communities should not be overlooked and that 'means should be found for strengthening them'. But in the following months the policy of establishing new towns in virtually undeveloped areas gathered momentum, and in the prevailing shortage of labour and materials (which meant concentration on repairs and housing in the worst damaged areas) it was thought unrealistic to contemplate additionally the development and expansion of small towns on any extensive scale. Nevertheless, MTCP were concerned that the Abercrombie proposals for dispersal of one million people from central London involved twice as many people as the new towns would accommodate, and by the middle of

---

* MHLG Files 91650/12, 91650/27/5/1 and NT 42/16; Treasury File SS 48/186/01; Lord President's File 1352.
† See chapter I, p. 6 *et seq* and appendix E; also *History Vol I*, pp. 135-137.

1947 were considering the administrative and financial problems that could arise. The general philosophy was that the Government had decided on decentralisation, and this involved development in 'unnatural' areas. The 'natural' thing was for a town to expand outwards, but since there was general agreement that some towns were 'getting too big for comfortable or civilised living', planning powers were being used 'to draw a fairly tight ring around the great urban masses', and to protect this by a green belt policy.

The ministry saw the problem as being one of stimulating development in places where local authorities could be induced to provide subsidised housing for 'foreigners' and to service land for industrial development. In short, the need was 'to prime the pump'. In a departmental minute of May 1947, it was commented:

> 'A council setting to work on a major town expansion, which is little if any short of a construction of a new town, can get no financial help except grant towards acquisition and clearing of the land although the initial expenditure on water, sewerage and drainage may be very heavy. I cannot help thinking that this defect in our set-up will frustrate many expansion proposals. I do not understand why in framing the New Towns Act we did not accept the recommendation that local authorities should be allowed to initiate the creation of new towns, particularly in the case where a county council or a district council with sufficient strength wishes to promote a major extension of a small town within its own area. It seems to me a major misfortune that we did not take power to assist county or district councils financially on new town lines where they were undertaking this sort of operation.'

A series of inconclusive studies followed in an attempt to establish whether there was a general case for more financial help being made available to local authorities faced with considerable expansion problems, but this seemed 'doomed to failure in the absence of any specific proposals where the figures could be analysed'. But while MTCP were concerned with decentralisation and redistribution of the population, and were responsible for the new towns, the problems of expanding existing towns, including water, sewerage, housing and local government finance were within the scope of the Ministry of Health, who felt that it was:

> 'unfortunate that the new towns were not administered by the Minister of Health since the development of new towns was hopelessly mixed up with housing policy . . . they were not enamoured with development by local authorities of large estates outside their own areas . . . as regards new towns outside the London area, they had long felt that the policy was being developed too quickly.'

Nevertheless, in September 1948, the two departments put to the Treasury a proposal for enabling them to stimulate town expansion for overspill with grants at the rate of eighty per cent of the annual costs of land acquisition and provision of main services for a period of ten years, subject to review in the light of the burden on the local rates. It was argued that the decentralisation of population and industry necessitated, not only the creation of new towns, but also the large scale expansion of some existing towns. The London plans budgeted for the dispersal of 1·25 million population, and the eight new towns so far projected would provide for not more than 250,000 to 300,000. Some additional new towns might ultimately be needed, but it was intended that most of the remaining million would be provided for by expansions, both large and small, of existing towns. The same type of problem would arise on the dispersals from Manchester, Merseyside and other overcrowded provincial centres.

Wherever a planned expansion was within the capacity of the district council, it was obviously preferable to make them responsible for it. A major expansion would require substantial strengthening of their staff but, assuming this to be possible, local authorities should be able 'to undertake a doubling of or even a trebling of their towns'. This would require assistance with the initial expenditure entailed in preparation of the detailed plan and advance provision of essential services, but 'this would be substantially less expensive than the alternative of setting up a development corporation to do the job'.

The matter had been discussed with a number of local authorities and, while they were naturally anxious for the work to be left with them and not entrusted to a development corporation, they were apprehensive that the initial cost would be beyond their resources. The big financial problem arose in the early years, before the rateable value had significantly increased, when they had to incur heavy administrative expenditure on survey and preparation of plans, on the acquisition of land in advance of development and on the cost of services. Sewers and water supply had to be provided not only in advance of construction work, but probably also on a scale sufficient for the whole of the additional planned population, although it would take the town upwards of fifteen to twenty years to achieve the target. MTCP had considered the matter with the Ministry of Health, and the conclusion was that additional grants from the exchequer would have to be made available towards the cost of these services if the local authorities were to undertake the work. The proposal, in brief, was that a decision on assistance to a district council in order to 'force' expansion would be made by MTCP, in agreement with the Ministry of Health, the two departments satisfying themselves that the necessary expenditure in the early years attributable to the reception of overspill would be more than the local authority could reasonably be expected to bear. It was not proposed, of course, that any assistance should be given towards the cost of any natural expansion which might be necessary to meet the needs of the existing community.

The cost of assisting the district council was 'certain to be less than the cost of setting up a development corporation' since there was an existing organisation, and it was not proposed to relieve the authority of all expenditure due to expansion. It was accordingly to the advantage of the exchequer that the local authorities should be entrusted with the expansion where this arrangement could be made. It was therefore proposed that the assistance from the exchequer should be not less than 80 per cent of the approved annual expenditure, including loan charges, attributable to the plan for the reception of overspill and falling to be met by the expanding local authority during the first ten years, but subject to review at the end of five years. It would be necessary to be able to extend the period up to, say, fifteen years in exceptional circumstances, for example where progress with revenue earning development fell short of the programme for reasons outside the local authority's control.

An internal Treasury minute noted that MTCP were proposing a new exchequer grant in respect of towns, other than county boroughs, carrying out large and rapid expansion of population, and that 'the minister wants to legislate in the 1948–49 session'. There had been no approach to the Treasury until now, and no notice of the proposal to legislate in 1948–49 had been given to the Future Legislation Committee.

> 'One cannot say that the new towns corporations at present promise to be a very brilliant success, and I certainly think we should welcome the idea that, wherever possible, the local authorities should carry out their own expansions. But this grant proposal raises many difficult points both of principle and detail.'

All local planning authorities were supposed to be producing development plans by 1 July 1951, 'preceded by elaborate surveys', and subject to local objections, and public inquiries. These plans would indicate how towns were to grow and what land would be needed for the purpose. 'Is it right to short-circuit this in a few selected cases?' If it were, 'then surely other towns will be unwilling to propose expansions on their own. They would rather wait to be "forced" and thus qualify for grant'. The decision whether or not to 'force' would determine whether a town would get 80 per cent or nil—'a spectacular difference'. If the principle were conceded, the Ministries of Education and Transport 'will be holding their plates out too, and I think we should have to discuss fairly closely with all departments concerned before we could put the matter before the Chancellor'.

There seemed no chance of being able to agree with MTCP 'of getting on to the 1948–49 band wagon':

> 'I doubt if the Chancellor would be willing, at this short notice, to authorise us to commit him in any way. The chance of getting a place for this in the 1948–49 programme must surely now be poor, even if the ideas were fully

baked. And it seems to me altogether premature to legislate now on the presumption that specially intensive work—apart from paper work—on expanded towns can be undertaken in the immediate future. Blitz schemes and new towns, which must surely have a prior claim, are themselves held back. I feel therefore that even if something on the lines of these proposals is acceptable in principle—which I doubt—legislation should be postponed till the 1949–50 session and not bounced through in a hurry now.'

It was also suggested that the proposal was, in essence, 'for a grant towards expenditure on work for which the Ministry of Health are the central authority and it ought, I suggest, to be administered by them and not by the Ministry of Town and Country Planning'. But another Treasury official minuted that this 'proved too much':

'So far as I know there is no essential difference between the purposes for which they propose to grant aid LAs and those for which they finance the development corporations. Nor can we argue that because we are working here through the LA, the Ministry of Health ought to provide the grant, because other departments beside the Ministry of Health, including the Ministry of Town and Country Planning, grant aid local authorities. In particular, Ministry of Town and Country Planning grant aid acquisition of land by local authorities for comprehensive *re*development, which is what, in essence, the "forced" towns are to do . . . If you pursue the argument you soon prove that the Ministry of Town and Country Planning oughtn't to exist at all as a separate department from the Ministry of Health. I don't think it ought, but we can't say it! Moreover, is it good tactics, when you are arguing that something ought not to be done, to argue also that someone else ought to do it?'

In September 1948 there was a meeting between officials of MTCP, the Ministry of Health and the Treasury. The Treasury note on the meeting records that they put forward two reasons why it was necessary 'to go slowly on this issue'. First, it was unrealistic in current conditions to consider increasing the volume of social service investment: and, without an increase, 'the Paul of expanding towns could only be provided for by robbing a more immediately fruitful Peter'. Secondly, the right time to consider town expansions was after, and not before, the problem could be considered in the light of development plans submitted under the 1947 Act.

On the first point, MTCP said that there was no question of expanding social service investment. The current position was that, in the absence of any further plans for providing for overspill from the London area, the LCC could not be restrained much longer from undertaking, in the green belt, housing developments that the minister wished to avoid. The question at issue was whether the overspill for which the projected new towns did not provide was to be catered for by LCC housing in the green belt, or by town expansions at such places as Ashford, Basingstoke and St Albans. Whichever alternative was chosen, the pace of development could be regulated to meet the economic situation.

On the second point, the reply was that the overall plan for Greater London was already settled and that this involved the expansion of certain towns to provide for London overspill. The problem now was how to bring that about. Without the establishment of further new towns, 'which would be wrong and very extravagant', no progress was possible unless some financial help could be offered to the county districts proposed to be expanded. ('This would really have been the right way to deal with Hemel Hempstead if it had been available.')

Passing from these points, the Treasury foresaw great difficulty in limiting the claimants for assistance if there was to be 'no half-way house between no grant and 80 per cent grant'. Most towns would wait to be 'forced' in order to qualify for grant. The next question was what exactly would be grant aided. On the costs of land acquisition, the Treasury put forward, 'and I think got accepted', the proposition that land acquired and developed for expansion should, after roads have been made and services installed, be appropriated out to the various services for which it would be used at cost. This account could then be wound up when this stage of development had been accomplished. Grant would take the form of a proportion of the loan charges payable from the initial development account. In this way it might be possible to avoid having an arbitrary period after which grant would cease, an arrangement somewhat vulnerable to pressure. The Treasury objected to meeting part of the cost of surveys and plans, 'but the reply was that progress would be impossible unless we did so'. They then suggested that the problem might be met by charging these costs as capital.

The Treasury note recorded 'several conclusions'. First, to double the size of such places as Ashford, Basingstoke and St Albans was probably slower and more expensive than building by the LCC in the green belt. This did not mean that to adopt it need raise the volume of social service investment in any particular year, but it did mean that it would be 'less immediately productive of new houses'. Secondly, it was not practicable to use town expansion 'to stop the LCC from doing what the planners think wrong', unless there was an earlier prospect of such expansion than there would be if the selected towns were to be left to their own financial resources. Thirdly, 'we ought, if possible, to avoid creating more new towns'.

If, therefore, town expansions were to go ahead, there was a case for legislation during the current Parliament. The Treasury accepted that 'we cannot refuse to entertain the idea of legislating', but the Chancellor's authority was needed before detailed discussions continued. If he agreed, MTCP would have to be warned that they were not being offered a place in the 1948–49 legislative programme: 'they must fight their own battle on that'.

In view of the unlikelihood of legislation, of the latent friction between MTCP and the Ministry of Health, and particularly of the absence of any specific proposals for town expansion from the authorities likely to be concerned, the matter drifted until the housing and local government functions of the Ministry of Health were amalgamated with town planning functions in the Ministry of Local Government and Planning early in 1951. The matter was then again raised with the Treasury on the basis that there should be additional exchequer assistance for housing and the cost of main services; and that county councils should be enabled where necessary to provide services and housing for people coming into the county from a county borough or from another county. Legislation was needed quickly.

'We gave the Treasury notice that something like this would become necessary rather over two years ago, but your people were not then much disposed to look at it until it became urgent. This it has now done.'

At the same time, MLGP wanted to include in the legislation two other proposals 'designed to assist us carry through decentralisation'. The first was that the use of existing factory premises in London (and possibly also in other badly congested areas) should be subject to the same distribution of industry control by the Board of Trade as was the erection of new factory building. Secondly, that in the same areas, the grant available under Section 94 of the 1947 Act should be increased from 50 to 80 per cent where non-conforming industry was being extinguished. The reason for these proposals was that decentralisation would be defeated if industry could not be induced to move out, and new industry prevented from taking over vacated premises. 'Our minister is extremely anxious that the powers of government to reduce industry in the London area particularly should be strengthened, and these two methods seem to us to be most practicable.'

On finance it was proposed that where a 'scheme' was approved by MLGP, the exchequer should be empowered to contribute the amount of the statutory rate fund contribution for all or some of the houses provided under the scheme. The period of contribution would depend on the circumstances of each case, though it might be expected that assistance would be needed over a period of ten to twenty years, with provision for review from time to time as revenue from the new development increased. Experience in the new towns had demonstrated that the burden of large scale development was high in the beginning and only decreased as commercial, industrial and other development reached substantial proportions. In the new towns, it had been estimated that the overall profitable stage would not be reached until towards the end of the work of the development corporations, and there was no reason to expect that expanded towns would enjoy any better experience. Indeed, some of the more remunerative developments (such as shops) were likely to be more delayed than in new towns, since the expanded towns 'would already be comparatively well equipped in this respect from the beginning'.

Exporting authorities had made it clear that they were unwilling to provide the finance for houses for which they would get no rent or rates and whose tenancies they would not control. They would rather have either peripheral expansion or 'out-county' estates (where they could have ownership control) even though this would mean 'some sacrifice on the green belt'. Alternatively, by refusing to co-operate in the 'expansion' schemes, they would try to force MLGP to agree to development in green belts—or drive them into proposing more new towns which would immediately be much more expensive to the exchequer. On the other hand, town expansion as envisaged would be of financial benefit to exporting authorities in that it would relieve them of the cost of the development that they would otherwise have had to undertake themselves. There was a strong case for expecting them to recognise this. Indeed, one or two of them had already indicated their willingness to contribute, and, providing a satisfactory scheme was drawn up for ensuring that houses were reserved for persons on their waiting lists, others might be expected to do likewise.

It was also proposed that legislation should provide power to make an exchequer contribution to the cost of acquiring land pending appropriation to its ultimate use, and to the cost of providing main services in advance of the increase of rateable values. Section 11 of the New Towns Act provided that a new town development corporation could contribute towards expenditure incurred by any local authority or statutory undertakers in performance of any of their statutory functions, and the powers applying to expanded towns would need to be as wide. 'It would be impossible to defend to local authorities applying to "expanded" towns a narrower power than to "new" towns, since some of the former will involve as major an operation as the latter.' If the power were narrowed, 'it will only mean that operations which might have been carried through as expanded towns will have to be carried through as new towns, at much greater cost to the exchequer'.

An internal Treasury minute noted that the new proposals differed quite substantially from the 1948 proposals. 'I do not know that we have much hope of choking this off altogether': it seemed that the houses had to be provided in one way or another 'and we certainly do not want any more new towns'. Whereas the 1948 proposals were virtually confined to London, the new proposals were not. This re-opened the objection 'which our predecessors saw to short-circuiting development plans which local authorities are due to prepare under the Town and Country Planning Act'. The 80 per cent grant which had been earlier proposed had now been replaced by proposals relating to rate subsidy, plus a proposed power to make an exchequer contribution to land acquisition and main services, on the analogy of Section 11 of the New Towns Act.

'This latter is a pretty vague proposal and obviously needs a lot of thought. Section 11 has not by any means worked smoothly so far: Town and Country Planning organised a working party to draw up principles of financial assistance by new town corporations to local authorities, but its conclusions were rejected both by the new towns corporations and by the local authority associations, and at the moment things are happening in a very piecemeal and *ad hoc* fashion. While we do not want a flat percentage grant for expanding towns, I should have thought we do want something more precise than Section 11.'

No contribution to county council services was proposed, but it had been recorded in 1948 that 'the Ministry of Transport and the Ministry of Education would have something to say about that.'

As regards industrial decentralisation, 'the ministry's proposals on this seem to me the sort of thing that will have to be shelved in present circumstances; in particular I do not at all like the idea of increasing grants under Section 94 of the 1947 Act, which were agreed with the local authority associations quite recently after exhaustive discussion'. Another Treasury minute commented:

'I am afraid that the departments have a case, if policy on some related questions is to be regarded as sacrosanct. One way of looking at the proposal would be to say that it represents yet another attempt to evade the problems created by the Rent Restriction Acts, high housing standards, and rising building costs. Wherever they are built, expensive local authority houses which have to be let at uneconomic rents, mean an additional burden to local rates. In the case of these "overspill" houses, the economics of the situation are so unpleasant that the local authorities have already dug their heels in. I do not think they are to be blamed, for, beyond a certain point, it is only possible to subsidise people living in new houses at the expense of those living in old ones, by starving environmental services enjoyed by all inhabitants. The only effective way of breaking out of the vicious circle—raising rents—is not likely to commend itself to ministers, and we are left to look at this proposal on its merits.'

The effect of the proposal was likely to be that, beyond a given point (related to the amount of land at their disposal), a local authority would have their population rehoused by another local authority in houses all of which would attract subsidy at £22 a year. The idea was that the higher subsidy would be paid only for a few years, 'but I am not convinced that it will be at all easy to turn off the tap: so long as costs continue to rise and rents do not rise, the local authorities will have a case for retaining the extra subsidy on the grounds that these factors are "outside their control", and they will make the most of it.' The other form of assistance would be contributions to services. Though MLGP hoped to limit contributions to county services to exceptional cases, 'we shall no doubt find before long that most cases are "exceptional" '.

Another Treasury official asked whether the accelerated defence programme was not 'a ground for suspending action altogether'. The Prime Minister's defence statement of 29 January 1951* had said that the ministers in charge of civil departments would 'consider to what extent they can discontinue or retard peacetime activities of their departments in order to free staff for defence work. It may also be necessary for local authorities to make a similar diversion of effort to defence planning'. The Prime Minister's directive, of 1 February,† required all ministers in charge of departments to consider the extent to which they could discontinue or retard their peace-time activities accordingly, and to report to the Treasury by 28 February showing what balance of staff they could consequently make available for transfer to defence work in other departments. Similarly, the Minister of Local Government and Planning was to consider what guidance could be given to local authorities regarding the transfer of local authorities' staff to defence work. 'This looked like a good candidate for relieving both MLGP and the local authorities of civil work. If Mr Dalton does not offer himself, might we not suggest that he should?'

A further possible 'solution—or at least a partial solution—to this problem of overspill' was looked for in Dalton's 'apparent willingness to re-examine present housing standards to see if they cannot be reduced without sacrificing any essential amenities'. But this was not to be so:

> 'It is true that Mr Dalton started off by being keen to reduce standards, and he let it be known to the local authorities that his mind was not closed to the idea—as his predecessor's had been. On examination, however, he has found that it is going to be more difficult than he had at first thought, without resorting to such expedients as reducing the amount of square feet by having the staircase in the living room.'

By April 1951, Treasury attitudes appeared to be hardening: though MLGP had 'a good logical case' which sounded 'very plausible and is certainly attractive to the Treasury if the alternative is more new towns', there were strong reasons for not accepting the proposals. In the first place, legislation providing for more housing subsidies looked 'out of keeping' with the general line of the Chancellor's budget speech. 'We may not be able to (and indeed may not want) to cut

---

* HC Debates, Vol 483, Col 579, 29 January 1951.
† CP(51)36.

down the social service provisions we have, but let us not start new ones.' Secondly, legislation would be very likely 'to bring about more pressure for more housing'. Though, in theory, it would involve only a 'transference' of building within a pre-determined total programme, 'the minister would be less than human if he did not start it off with something of a flourish so that it would lead to increased demand against the restricted programme and therefore increased difficulty in maintaining the latter'. More generally:

> 'the problem really arises out of two matters which have got to be tackled sometime, the failure to tackle which so far has brought the redistribution of population by way of housing into a condition of stalemate viz the increasing gulf between building costs and the level of rents, and the need to readjust local government areas and boundaries. I do not like removing difficulties from these causes by the simple expedient of putting in more exchequer aid to the rates. It must diminish local incentives to economy of provision and management and it must increase the degree of central supervision, so leading to increases of staff. Departments have been told to say what normal activities they can cut down to help the rearmament programme. So far, the Ministry of Local Government and Planning has made only an exiguous offer, if I remember right. This sort of scheme will mean that they will be asking for more staff.'

At this stage, Dalton wrote to Gaitskell (Chancellor of the Exchequer) expressing the hope that he would 'find no difficulty in agreeing' to the proposals which had been discussed at official level. Gaitskell replied:

> 'I can see a logical case for dealing with these expansions by some form of assistance between housing subsidy on ordinary lines at the one end and the creation of new towns at the other. But these intermediate schemes have their difficulties and it seems to me that there are a number of matters which ought to be further explored departmentally before the subject is broached with local authorities. For example, the new houses will presumably have to be provided without increasing the total housing programme, which means I think, that the small towns in question will have to be given a bigger allocation than they would otherwise get on condition that they allot houses to immigrants. But if they get this, will not the usual and natural willingness, or indeed anxiety, of authorities to increase their towns lead them to be willing to do a good deal, in fact possibly as much as circumstances will permit to be done, without special assistance? And, if they have increases of programme on any substantial scale, where is the labour to come from?
>
> Secondly, I feel that there are special difficulties in starting grants in connection with housing schemes for the extra cost of the general services of local government. Such grants may take us a long way with an entirely new form of general assistance.
>
> In short, I feel that the scheme needs further examination before we commit ourselves to it even to the extent of putting it forward for discussion with local authorities. I suggest that our departments should explore the subject on these lines. We were, in fact, about to suggest this to the ministry when your letter arrived.'

Further discussions at official level continued, and the Treasury admitted (internally) that 'it is an awkward business', but it seemed that the MLGP arguments were convincing. The 'need for extreme caution' had been impressed upon MLGP and they were indeed 'already alive to that need'. Moreover, the Treasury felt that they had 'diminished the risk of their weakening when they come to discussion with representatives of local authorities'. There were, however, two difficulties as seen by the Treasury. First, the danger of the concept of giving special financial treatment to any one local activity which was labelled as being of national interest was that the concept 'might spread until local authorities would seek to find reasons for labelling part of everything they did as being "national" '. Secondly, there was the danger that the proposals would lead to pressure to increase house building 'since those concerned would try to get it as an addition to the housing programme'.

MLGP stressed that the matter was urgent because the housing programme in certain areas could not be maintained unless powers of this kind were taken—'unless one took the more expensive alternative of creating another new town'. Greater London, Manchester, Liverpool and Wolverhampton were all running out of land. 'If Treasury refused to help', they would build on the edges of their own boundaries and then expand. This met the second point: there was to be no addition to the housing programme 'but rather the prevention of a drop'. On the first point, the Treasury were reassured that MLGP thought that it should be possible 'to limit the concept very closely to cases where the programme is of considerable size and also has to be carried out much faster than is normal'.

On the basis of these understandings, Treasury officials took the matter up to the Chancellor again and, in May 1951, Gaitskell wrote to Dalton:

'Our officials have discussed the matter further and have dealt with the questions which I raised in my letter to you. I see the strength of your case, but equally you, I am sure, will realise my difficulties. We shall want to proceed with great caution and to make sure that the scheme is set out in such a way that we can resist any extension of the principle of assistance to local authorities in respect of activities which they are to label in some way or another as not being of direct local importance.

In the light of the explanations which I have had, I agree that you should start discussions with the local authorities and see if you can work out something satisfactory, bearing in mind (as I understand you are ready to do) the points which I have made.'

The Town Development Bill*

Discussions with local authority associations followed and, in July

---

* LP(51)44 and LP(51)17th Meeting, 20 July 1951; HA(51)3 and HA(51)1st Meeting, 23 November 1951; LC(52)2nd Meeting, 22 January 1952 and LC(52)3rd Meeting, 29 January 1952; and Secretary's Bill Papers 271.

1951, Dalton sought the authority of his colleagues to introduce a Bill to give financial help to local authorities to carry out major town expansions in their own areas to relieve overcrowding in the areas of other authorities. He explained that some of the population of the big towns had to be rehoused in expanded towns in other local authority areas, and that the problem was urgent as some local housing programmes would soon run down, and continuity of building should be assured. The new towns were meeting part of the problem, but 'the right people' to carry out the expansion of existing towns were the local councils, who in view of the burden of expenditure on water and sewerage and site preparation for factories, and payment of rate contribution, could not expect any early and worthwhile increase in rate income. He therefore proposed that exchequer help should be given towards the statutory rate contribution for houses contributing to the relief of overcrowded areas, and, where necessary, towards the provision of main services and towards the acquisition and opening up of land for development—the amount of assistance to depend on the circumstances of each case. He proposed that the county councils, as local planning authorities, should be responsible for planning the expansions, and for actually carrying them out where the borough or district council could not or would not tackle it. He said he had agreed his proposals with all the local authority associations other than the Association of Municipal Corporations who, although not disputing that the job must be done, disliked the proposal that county councils should come to the help of the borough and district councils.

Dalton's proposals were agreed on 20 July 1951 but, as the Government fell shortly afterwards, no action was taken on them. However, in November 1951 Macmillan sought authority for preparation of a Bill in very similar terms. He urged the scheme on the basis that he would be able to secure that town developments were begun at the time and on the scale required, that no increase in the total housing programme was involved, and that the purpose was to secure that the houses which were to be built were built in the right places.

Macmillan's proposals were approved, though the Board of Trade warned that experience with new towns suggested that it would be difficult to induce industrialists to establish factories in new areas. Those who had done so with reluctance in the new towns might now find themselves faced with increasing competition from these new developments. It was important that there should be consultation with the Board of Trade to ensure that any proposals were consistent with plans for the proper distribution of industry.

The Bill came before the Legislation Committee in January 1952. A point was raised as to whether assistance under the Bill should be given to the cost of providing schools but, following interdepartmental discussions, it was reported that it had been agreed that such assistance should not be given, as the Bill itself did not create the movement of population, and the poorer counties were already assisted by the exchequer equalisation grant. The committee agreed with this view but it was pointed out that the transfer of population put an increasing burden on county councils and that this was a general problem which might at some future date have to be considered further.

After discussion, the committee authorised the introduction of the Bill, in which town development was defined as 'development in a county district which will have the effect, and is undertaken primarily for the purpose, of providing accommodation for residential purposes (with or without accommodation for carrying on of industrial or other activities, and with all appropriate public services, facilities for public worship, recreation and amenity, and other requirements) the provision whereof will relieve congestion or over-population elsewhere'. The Bill provided a framework for agreements to be made between county boroughs (as exporting authorities) and county districts and county councils (as receiving authorities) which, if approved by the minister, gave him discretionary power to make grants towards the expenditure of the receiving authorities in respect of the annual rate fund contribution for housing; the acquisition of land for development; site preparation; the provision, extension or improvement of main water supplies and sewerage services; contributions to water undertakers to obtain supplies; and contributions to river boards or drainage authorities in respect of work necessitated by the town development.

The Bill had an unopposed second reading on 25 February 1952, but during the committee stage a large number of minor points were raised on behalf of local authorities and statutory undertakers. The most significant was an objection to the original proposal that the financial provisions of the Bill should not apply in the case of movement of population from one district council to another in the same county. Macmillan justified the distinction on the ground that the population were already within the county and it was the responsibility of the county to look after its proper redistribution. The matter was of some importance in the case of the boroughs in south west Essex which were part of the London conurbation and any relief to them would contribute to the general London problem. Macmillan was hard pressed and the Government had a narrow majority, whereupon he wrote to Butler:

'I developed the argument against the proposal with considerable intellectual skill and some fervour. But in the atmosphere of non-partisanship which surrounds this Bill I was left with scarcely a supporter. Give me a good Party Bill, the closure and the guillotine, and I can guarantee to drive it through. But a non-controversial Bill is Hell.'

With Butler's agreement an amendment was later made which removed the restriction on 'in-county moves'. The Bill received the Royal Assent on 1 August 1952.

*The Early Operation of the Town Development Act**

The Conservative Government had pinned their hope on the machinery of the Town Development Act 1952 in place of the New Towns Act, and in their view it was important that 'quick action should be taken in getting houses built in the right places on the scale required'. But the Act was regarded with some suspicion. The potential exporting authorities, whose housing needs were urgent, felt that they should have had the right of initiating schemes. Potential receiving authorities in rural surroundings had an instinctive dislike of a 'mass invasion of town dwellers with their industry and of the modernisation of their local amenities'. Few had a staff or facilities able to plan for extensive development, and there was a natural preference to let matters remain as they were. Both the receiving and exporting authorities were uncertain of the financial assistance they could expect from the government, and consequently of the residual burden they would ultimately have to assume; and both were unaccustomed to think in terms of the rate of interest then prevailing (about 5 per cent) which, after the era of cheap money, was regarded as high.

However, the London County Council were active in exploring possibilities and, by the end of 1954, were reaching agreements with Bletchley and Swindon for the provision of houses for Londoners with government contributions calculated on the basis of estimated cost and the probable burden on the rates of the district. Elsewhere progress was slow and, in a letter to the Treasury of 23 February 1955, it was stated:

'The minister is convinced that we must find a way of showing that the Government mean business . . . The great defect of the present system of adjusting the rate of grant to individual cases is the long period of uncertainty . . . It is not until the scheme has been worked out in considerable detail, and the negotiations between the authorities pretty well completed, that we can give an indication of the rate of grant. This inevitably means heavy delay . . . The Town Development Act is in evident danger of being labelled unworkable; we rather think it is on the approach we have so far adopted, but the obvious thing is to alter the approach rather than abandon the Act. If we can talk in terms of 50 per cent for any approved scheme, we shall undermine much of the rising clamour.'

The Treasury agreed and, on 26 April 1955, the Minister of Housing

---

* MHLG Files 95300/5/1 and 95300/8/1.

(now Sandys) announced that, to remove uncertainty, grant would be payable at the uniform rate of 50 per cent for extension of water and sewerage services attributable to town development.

While the ministry were negotiating with the Treasury on a uniform rate of grant, they were also pressing the Board of Trade and the Ministry of Labour to agree to some industrial development in small country towns where there was possibility of expansion under the Town Development Act. In May 1954, ministers had agreed that the expanded towns programme should be limited to ten towns.* By April 1955, negotiations were in various stages of progress in respect of a number approaching ten, and although it was expected that some would fall through, the ministry proposed that they should work up to a maximum of twenty schemes, most of which would be modest expansions of 5,000 people (or 1,300 houses) or less. The Board of Trade 'with some reluctance' agreed that in the case of small schemes they would expect to give industrial development certificates for any industry being moved out of a congested area or for some reason tied to the area being expanded, but reserved the right to try in any particular case to persuade the company to go to a development area. This relaxation enabled the London County Council to proceed with their negotiations for expanded towns in East Anglia.

The Housing Subsidies Act 1956†

The election on 26 May 1955 caused a pause but, in September 1955, the secretary minuted that satisfactory arrangements had been made with the Treasury for financial assistance. Arrangements were in hand with the Board of Trade about a range of places where they would be prepared to contemplate industrial expansion by way of decentralisation from overcrowded areas. Satisfactory progress had been made with exporting towns and it was hoped to get 'the confused business of their financial contribution' settled in the forthcoming Housing Subsidies Bill.

This Bill, which became the Housing Subsidies Act 1956, revised the basis on which housing subsidies were based. The statutory rate fund contribution (previously in the proportion of one to three of the exchequer contribution) was abolished, and local authorities were left free to decide for themselves how to finance their house building, and in particular to determine the extent to which the cost should be met out of rates and rents. A special subsidy of £24 (compared with a standard subsidy of £22.1s.) was provided for houses for overspill, but when the overspill agreement allowed the exporting authority to nominate all or a high proportion of the occupants of the new

---

* See chapter III, p. 147.
† MHLG Files EST 4669/3 and 92038/1/394/2.

dwellings, the exporting authority would pay an additional contribution of not less than £8 direct to the receiving authority. Where the overspill scheme was based on a substantial transfer of industry from the exporting area, the minister would pay the additional grant of £8 for ten years direct to the receiving authority, and recover half from the exporting authority of the area from which the first tenant came.

This complicated arrangement was based on the premise that in new and expanded towns it was not fair to expect that the existing residents should have to carry the rate burden of the immigration of population who were the proper responsibility of another local authority. Conversely the exporting authority, with responsibility for providing accommodation for people in their area with housing need, should contribute when accommodation was vacated by migrants from that area to new or expanded towns.

The justification for recovery of half the additional grant by the minister was that about 50 per cent of overspill 'represents relief of housing need'.* The industrial selection scheme, designed to ensure that migrants with suitable skills came from congested areas, was the foundation for the arrangement, but it caused strong feeling among exporting authorities who felt the recovery provisions were inequitable, partly owing to the difficulty of determining the area in which the migrant had had a bona fide residence, and partly owing to the complexities arising when dwellings were relet. The arrangement was adjusted from time to time in an attempt to reduce anomalies in respect of persons who had little more than accommodation addresses, but for the ministry, for housing managers, and for local authorities it was expensive and troublesome to operate in keeping track of tenants and tenancies. Nevertheless, to maintain the principle that exporting authorities had responsibilities for their migrants, the Treasury and the ministry adhered to the point that the additional grant should not be paid unless recovery could be obtained from the exporting authority.

Disappointing Progress†

Despite all this legislation and interdepartmental activity, progress under the Town Development Act continued to be disappointing. In September 1955 the secretary suggested that 'what we want is an imposing person to encourage hesitating receivers, to answer their questions about how to start, and to preside on occasions over meetings between exporters and receivers to bring agreements to conclusion'. In the result, General Sir Humphrey Gale (the chairman of the Basildon New Town Development Corporation) was appointed

---

* See further chapter VII, p. 412.
† MHLG Files Est 4669/3 and 95300/8/1.

to 'advise and assist the minister in securing the speedier progress in the promotion of schemes under the Town Development Act for relieving congestion of population in the larger cities'.

Gale visited some fifty county and district councils before his appointment terminated in 1958. By this time sixteen schemes had been approved. But they made little impact on the overspill problem of the major conurbations. There had been regular opposition from potential receiving authorities who did not wish to be swamped by large numbers of people from their big neighbours, and who were apprehensive that any change in the Government's financial or industrial policies could put the development in jeopardy. Potential exporting authorities who were liable to lose population, industry and rateable value were looking for more financial assistance than the Treasury were able to contemplate. In the attempt to make the Act work, the ministry were continually pressing the Treasury during 1957 for an increase in the rates of grant or of housing subsidies, but the Treasury maintained that the ultimate responsibility for dealing with overspill lay upon the local authorities, that the exporting authorities had no more need of subsidy than if they had built the houses within their own boundaries, and that the 50 per cent grant to receiving authorities for water and sewerage was generous. The argument, which became acrimonious, had an air of unreality since the ministry had no specific proposals for large town expansion schemes to put to the Treasury, while the Treasury claimed that they could hardly give *ad hoc* approvals in the absence of knowing how many schemes there would be, what the commitment would cost, and what was an order of priority among the exporting authorities. The argument in its general form had a further air of unreality in view of the limitation on capital expenditure and the increase in interest rates which made many of the provincial towns reluctant to proceed.

Little progress was made during 1958 and 1959 and, in any event, the ministry were heavily engaged in the problem of the future of the existing new towns, and in drafting the New Towns Bill which provided for their transfer to the Commission for the New Towns. But pressure continued and came to a head early in 1960 with the minister's rejection of Birmingham's proposal to develop 2,400 acres at Wythall on the ground that it would involve a serious incursion into the green belt. In the course of a debate on 2 May 1960* when he was urged to agree to a government sponsored new town, Brooke said:

'Birmingham seems to be approaching all their housing difficulties less robustly than other cities. Manchester was anxious to go forward at its own

---

* HC Debates, Vol 622, Col 851, 2 May 1960.

expense with development on a new town scale at Lymm. The LCC came to the Government and asked for approval in principle for its looking for a new site which it might develop as a new town and the Government said "Yes, in principle we agree". Liverpool has been entering successfully into arrangements with Lancashire and Cheshire. Among the big cities it seems that only Birmingham shies at the idea of finding a solution to its own problems . . . I do not at present see any clear site anywhere where a wholly new town could suitably be built. I may be wrong, but it seems to me that we are more likely to find a solution by way of expansion of a number of existing towns.'

Shortly before, on 23 February 1960,* he said in answer to a parliamentary question, 'there is still room for many thousands more new houses in several of the new towns around London; and meanwhile other towns are expanding under the Town Development Act. I should like to see still better progress made with these town expansions. I have no proposals for starting further new towns for Greater London, but I understand that the LCC may be putting forward a proposal to build a new town itself'.

Such was the publicly stated policy of the Government early in 1960 but, as was shown in chapter IV, commitment to this policy was, by this time, being undermined. Town expansion schemes were developing at a painfully slow rate and were clearly unable to meet the housing problem of the conurbations.

Review of Machinery for Town Expansion†

By the early sixties there was widespread disillusionment on town development schemes. Though subsidies were increased (by the Housing Act 1961) it was clear that the schemes could make relatively little contribution to the solution of the overspill problem. At the same time, the expectation of a massive growth in population made it necessary to build more new towns and to secure the large expansion of a substantial number of existing towns.‡ An internal MHLG minute of March 1963 noted that there were two pieces of machinery available—new towns and town development schemes: 'the first works, the second is totally inadequate'. Until recently, the ministry had hesitated to use the new town machinery for the expansion of a town which already had a 'fair sized' population, but it had now been decided that Redditch (with a population of over 35,000) should be a new town. Macclesfield (where the population was approaching 40,000) might be similarly treated. The scope for using the new town machinery was thus becoming greater. However, many of the envisaged expansions would be of towns larger than 50,000, and it seemed probable that local authorities of this size

---

* HC Debates, Vol 618, Col 33, 23 February 1960.
† MHLG File NT 42/16.
‡ See chapter IV.

would wish to take a larger part in the development than was normal in 'an orthodox new town'.

Experience had shown that small authorities could not tackle town expansion:

> 'We have the sad examples of Bletchley and Winsford who have tried, and of other places like Ashford and Bury St Edmunds who have promised but never tried. The only successful independent scheme has been at Swindon and there the town had an initial population of nearly 70,000, and even so expansion was only by some 20,000.'

Schemes had been carried out with success only where the LCC and the local county council had undertaken the major part of the financing and the bulk of the work of organisation. It was doubtful whether the London County Council (or their successors, the Greater London Council) and the county councils could be relied upon to tackle the schemes now necessary. Many more schemes were needed, each being very much larger than anything which had previously been tackled (with the exception of Basingstoke), and it was unlikely that even the Greater London Council would have the resources in staff and money to cope with a job of the magnitude envisaged. Moreover, there was nothing comparable to the Greater London Council in the provinces. There was, however, a more decisive objection. Town expansions in the south-east would in future 'be directed as much to stopping people getting to London as dealing with people coming from London'. In these circumstances the Greater London Council's interest would clearly be small. They could scarcely be expected to spend time and money in providing for people who had never been and never would be Londoners.

In the provinces, some county councils were hostile to any development in their counties, and it was obviously impossible to count on all of them co-operating in future. Though 'the more intelligent councils—for example Buckinghamshire, Hampshire, West Suffolk and Northumberland'—had been willing to initiate and support development for the benefit of the neighbouring cities, it seemed highly improbable that the counties could be relied upon to bear the bulk of the burden. Many of the towns to be expanded would grow to a size which would 'on current rules' enable them to claim county borough status. 'Clearly we cannot rely upon the counties willingly putting up money for development which will be snatched away from them.'

There was a further problem which had been raised by many counties. Development of a particular part of the county meant that county investment in schools, roads and so forth had to be concentrated on the town being expanded. However justifiable this might be in the national interest, it caused jealousy in the county, and since the representatives of the other parts of the county were in a majority, there could be 'no certainty that a county would steadily plough ahead with a policy which favoured particular places at what appeared to be the expense of the rest of its area'. Finally, it was doubtful whether any county could willingly face the expenditure which would be involved in schemes of the magnitude now contemplated. The counties which were most willing to co-operate had made it clear in informal discussion that if they were to tackle the job themselves they would expect special government guarantees about finance and grant aid which were likely to be totally unacceptable to the Treasury and which, if given, would turn the counties into nothing more than agents for the central government.

The weakness of the machine and the magnitude of the financial operations made it desirable that the central government should take an active part and bear a substantial proportion of the cost of big town expansion schemes. Using the model of the Basingstoke scheme (which was a joint scheme between the London County Council and Basingstoke) a proposal was outlined for a standing corporation (or series of corporations) to cope with the bigger town expansions to be expected, and which could be ready to swing into action anywhere at any time. It would operate, not by 'taking over' from the local authorities as the new town corporations did ('which would anyway be inappropriate in the case of sizeable local authorities') but by working in association with the local authorities on a joint committee which would be responsible for the whole development.

In April 1963, the secretary minuted that 'before we can settle machinery we must be clear about the means by which implementation of the results of the regional studies is to be achieved'. The assumption seemed to be that the problem was 'to make town development—in the sense that we have always known it—work'. But town development had always been concerned (as had new towns) to promote overspill housing.

'It seems to me both that our conception how to do that may need radical reconsideration, and that anyway we are looking primarily at a different problem; which is to make land available for development. Given the growth of population for which we are planning, I would not have thought our problem was how to induce development, but only how to make it possible in the places where we want it. To my mind, the key to this lies first, of course, in getting the land planned for development; and then in public acquisition of the land and development of the main services. The building is a separate, subsequent question; it may well be that it could and should be carried out largely by private enterprise, use and phasing being controlled through the public ownership. I doubt whether exchequer "grants" are the right approach at all. Should not the development, in the long run, pay for itself? If so, whoever buys the land should finance the bringing of it into development; the problem is how to carry the cost until the revenue is sufficient to recoup it. But if we can envisage that the cost will be recouped, then we surely have to think in terms of loans rather than grants.'

She continued that the assumption ought to be that 'housing will look after itself', and in so far as it had to be subsidised ('which I would hope that the greater part would not') the subsidies would be sufficient. For making the land available, she agreed that a corporation was needed.

> 'But I think that the power of acquisition, coupled with the power (whether by bribery or direct action) to secure expansion of the services should be vested clearly in one authority: either the corporation, or the county council or the district council as may fit the particular case. The authority that buys must be in control (subject to the minister) and should, it seems to me, carry whatever cost has to be met in expanding the main services and opening up the land (subject to arrangements enabling them to bridge the gap till disposal and development begins to pay).'

A joint committee was inappropriate and, in any case, would be 'a horrifying piece of machinery to get committed to'.

The heart of the problem 'as always' was a financial one. Where the corporation was the body buying land it would be financed by the exchequer, though the problem remained of enabling the sewerage (and possibly the water) authorities to expand in advance of rateable value. This might be dealt with by way of grant (as in the new towns) or by interest free loans. Similarly, where a local authority was undertaking responsibility for bringing the land into development, interest free loans or deferment of repayment and capitalisation of interest charges could be considered. All these possibilities could be explored.

It was assumed that acquisition of the land and expansion of the services could be made to pay for itself by the subsequent disposals, 'though I wouldn't rule out industrial and commercial development by the managing authority'. It was necessary to obtain some idea of the order of initial cost and the prospects and timing of recoupment, 'looked at as an exercise for bringing land into development'. Moreover, would there not also be a major problem of phasing? If land were to be brought into development over a twenty year period by acquisition, expansion of services and disposal, regional plans would be required for this purpose. This could be a function of a corporation ('armed with powers and money').

Much more thorough study of the financial implications was needed. But first it was necessary to establish whether this general approach was accepted—ie public acquisition of land, development of services, disposal (whether to public authorities or private interests) and ultimate recoupment (no exchequer grants, but arrangements to bridge the long, non-remunerative period). However, whatever approach was agreed, there was the major policy question of the acquisition powers; 'but it seems to me possible that the Government will be willing to agree (subject to consideration of cost) to very large scale advance acquisition'. A relatively simple procedure would have to be worked out: 'we surely do not want to get involved in the process of designation if we can help it.'

The matter was held up for some three months 'pending results of the first look at possible future developments in planning machinery in general, since if that review had suggested that regional bodies for both planning and development were a strong possibility, machinery for town expansion would have had to have been fitted into that context'. By the end of June 1963, it seemed that the balance of argument was against such bodies, and it could be assumed that although the arrangements for implementing regional plans would be improved, development would require separate machinery. In a very long note, a senior official pointed first to the substantial regional differences both in the nature of the forces which required the forced expansion of some towns and in the scale of the problem ('and in many parts of the country there isn't a problem at all'). But, whatever their origin, the problems were all on a much greater scale than those which had been tackled in the past. Indeed, it was simply the size of the job which necessitated the re-examination of the machinery and prompted doubts about the adequacy of the existing powers.

In the north-west, the core of the problem was the building of homes for families displaced from the slums of Liverpool and Manchester. Growth was so small that it did not create difficulties. Any solution necessarily required large scale house building by public authorities. The draft regional study suggested that the task could be carried out 'by building three new towns (Skelmersdale, Runcorn and a town for Manchester), the two cities building on their periphery, and some comparatively small town development schemes'. The powers and grants, with minor improvements, currently available were thought to be adequate for this job. The study of the midlands was not so advanced, but roughly only a third of the problem stemmed from slum clearance; the remainder arose from growth and immigration. Orthodox new towns could help, as could town development at places such as Daventry. These were not sufficient, though it was not clear what further would be needed and whether this would require new powers and machinery.

The real difficulties arose in the south-east where the numbers to be accommodated were so much larger than elsewhere and the problems of development so much more complex.* The *minimum* population growth in the south-east would be 3·5 million by 1981. This growth would not be evenly distributed but would fall most heavily on the counties close to London; for example the population

---

* See further chapter IV, p. 196 *et seq.*

of Essex might increase by nearly 70 per cent, and Berkshire, Hampshire and Hertfordshire by over 60 per cent. Roughly two thirds of the growth—2·25 million people—would be catered for by 'normal economic forces': most of the housing would be provided by private builders, as would much of the capital for related shopping, commercial and industrial development. Local authorities would have to extend their services to meet this growth, and should be able to do so 'though they would have to make a big effort without special help from the government'.

For the other third, which consisted partly of people moving out of London under planned programmes and rather more of people migrating into the south-east (or moving within the region) special arrangements would be needed to settle them in a comparatively small number of selected localities. This would be 'a very big job: about four times as much as has been done in present new towns and town expansions in a comparable period of time'.

The location of the places planned for expansion was also different. The main burden in the past had been borne by the new towns: 'and they have been successful instruments'. *The South East Study* suggested that there should only be four additional new towns, and of these two depended upon other events—a channel tunnel and a third airport for London—which were far from certain. In short, there might be only two more new towns. The study also showed that the expansion of small towns was a dubious operation and one which, in any case, could not meet the needs shown to exist, in particular the need to provide alternative places to London for office employment. The places chosen for major rapid growth were therefore established towns with populations of 50,000 and upwards.

In the towns chosen for 'forced expansion', growth over and above their 'natural growth' might be of the order of 50,000 to 75,000 people before 1981, in some cases continuing beyond that date. The total investment might be about £2,000m. This would be a very large programme both in total and for each centre of growth— 'substantially larger, and more complex, than the investment which local authorities are accustomed to handle'. It would have to be undertaken at the same time as they would have to make investment for natural growth. This was about twice as large in total but, because it was not concentrated, it was easier to control: 'no particular job is likely to be larger in size or complexity than local authorities are used to tackling'.

New Town Machinery for Town Expansion?

The more the arrangements for tackling 'forced expansion' could be diversified, the better would be the chances of finding the scarce managerial and technical skills and tapping every source of capital.

The possible agencies were, first, 'private capital supplied by property developers and builders'. There were some signs that private developers might be interested in large scale town expansion, but no proposal had reached a stage at which it was possible to make any kind of assessment of their terms for participation, and it seemed that public authorities might have to take a substantial part in development of the towns selected for growth. The second—town development—looked 'unpromising', but the third—the machinery of the New Towns Act—could be used to expand any town; indeed some new towns had been or were to be built where there was a substantial population before designation—20,000 at Hemel Hempstead and Basildon, 26,000 at Runcorn, 35,000 at Redditch. The machinery was adequate for dealing with larger towns; the problem was that of relationships with the local authority. The larger the authority, the more they might resent the intrusion of a powerful development corporation. The use of new town machinery for the expansion of a large town was a problem in tactics and politics—the machinery was adequate, the wisdom of using it dubious. A new town corporation was only a piece of administrative machinery; the extent to which it was used could vary. In a large town, more could be left to the local authority and less done by the corporation.

There were two difficulties if new town machinery were used for town expansion: 'one practical, the other psychological'. In a new town, planning was in effect taken from the local authority and transferred to the corporation. A large authority might (though it depended upon how much delegated authority it had) resent this change. Psychologically the authority might want formal recognition of its status and not be content with such informal machinery for co-operation with the corporation as could be established under existing arrangements. The proposals made earlier for a formal joint committee were intended to meet this objection. Their merit depended upon an assessment of the balance of advantage—a joint committee could be a most troublesome device and was not necessarily better than the friction which could (and had arisen) between a local authority and a new town corporation.

Financing new town corporations was straightforward. Finance for local authorities was more complicated. If an expansion were successful it should in the long run more than cover its costs and there was in logic no case for grant to a local authority taking part. However, local authority financial structures were not designed to cover this situation, and short term losses fell on the rates.

Local authorities had shown (at Swindon, Basingstoke and Andover) that they could tackle the job, but local government was not geared to undertaking large scale development, and it was 'an accident when favourable circumstances combined to produce the

right team'. Even then, progress was always at the mercy of elections
(Ashford had alternated in enthusiasm with changes in the council;
Andover turned on the results of a council election). While, therefore,
it was clear that local authorities could do part of the job, they could
not be relied upon 'for anything approaching the whole'.

Unless private capital were forthcoming on a totally unprecedented scale (and although this was possible there were no signs
which would justify planning on this assumption) the bulk of the
effort would have to come from government agencies. This could be
by the use of the New Towns Act, though there were political
arguments for using a modified and differently named government
agency. However, whatever its name, it would be handicapped if its
powers were less than those of a new town corporation. The experience of the Commission for the New Towns (which were still carrying
out development) showed how absence of planning and compulsory
purchase powers limited their capabilities.

Time was also a difficulty. While most of the planned expansion
would be needed in the 1970s, some should start in the late sixties. It
would be hard to do this if new legislation was needed since it was
impossible to envisage any legislation before the 1964–65 session.
The shorter the time in which the development was concentrated the
more essential it was that the instruments were 'strong and swift'.

To be certain that 'forced growth' towns grew 'at the date and the
rate needed' to secure the success of the south-east plan, and to
assist in other parts of the country, a government agency would be
needed in addition to local authorities and private enterprise. Any
such agency should have full powers to build factories, shops, etc as
well as houses, and have power to buy land compulsorily 'well in
advance of need'.

In August 1963, the secretary minuted that 'we shall need the
development corporation method to provide for most, if not all, of
the 1·25 million'. But, at the same time, local authorities should be
given the power to carry through the development themselves—
'with exchequer grants towards the initial costs where we are
satisfied that they are competent to do it and will do it well and at
the pace required'.

It was probable that subregional corporations would be required,
but this posed a difficult organisation problem.

> 'It is arguable that each new town must have its own corporation during the
> development stage—and if so maybe each major expansion being undertaken
> by the development corporation method should have its own body too. That
> leads one to the idea (as with the New Towns Commission) that there should
> be a parent body with branches in each town—which could mean ad-
> ministrative economies and high powered staff. But it also means channelling
> the exchequer money through the parent body, and a three tier structure
> (ministry, parents, child). However, that could be right.'

There was also the question of whether such an organisation should not absorb the commission, 'completed new towns falling into the subregional corporations'. However, it was not yet appropriate to spend much time on the detail of the organisation. It was first necessary 'to get the principle settled of tackling the job via the development corporation method'.

The other principle that had to be settled was that of advance acquisition:

> 'This is the basic method by which we should get the development phased, controlled and carried through; this and the power to promote and, as necessary, finance the provision of the services which will make the land ripe for development. The "development engine"—corporation, local authorities, private enterprise, the mixture varying according to needs and government policy—can be settled as and when, provided there is power to do it however seems best at the time. But the principle of public (and normally government) ownership of the land, with the right of compulsory acquisition (as in new towns) flowing from the decision to expand, is crucial.'

An important argument for public acquisition of the land was that it was the only practical way 'to grapple with the betterment problem and to recoup, in time, the initial expenditure on the services'. Equally important, it was the best way to promote development in accordance with the plan and a phased programme.

A Regional Development Agency?*

By November 1963, sufficient study had been completed to 'enable us to see more clearly the sort of machinery we need for this job'. The towns for expansion fell into three groups: *Group 1:* Southampton–Portsmouth, Bletchley, Newbury, Stansted, Ashford, Basildon, Harlow and Stevenage; *Group 2:* the Medway towns, Norwich, Poole, Reading and Southend; *Group 3:* Ipswich, Northampton, Peterborough, Swindon, Aylesbury, Banbury, Bedford, Chelmsford, Colchester and Hastings.

In Group 1, growth was so large relatively—and so rapid—that it would need a separate organisation for each town. The best investment for these was the present new town machinery ('perhaps improved in detail').

On the other hand, the towns in Group 2 were large, and the growth envisaged was less than 50 per cent of the existing population. 'Towns of this size and competence ought to be able to tackle growth of this scale on their own. It is not so far out of step with the kind of growth they would have to tackle over the next twenty years—20 to 25 per cent—come what may.'

The towns in Group 3 (which were to take about a third of the

---

* MHLG File 42/16.

expansion) were a problem. While one or two might accept orthodox new town arrangements, it was very doubtful whether the larger and more ambitious authorities would be content to do so. Nor could MHLG force them to do so. 'Yet we cannot rely on the ordinary local authority organisation in these towns to carry out a job of the cost and complexity of an expansion which at least increases their population by half and in some cases doubles it.' The cost of doubling Ipswich and Peterborough would be £218m and £198m respectively. Apart from the problems of finance and quality this raised, 'we can never be sure that a council would carry on with the expansion if it proved unpopular locally'. New machinery was needed for expanding these towns *in partnership* with the local town councils. 'Partnership is important because recalcitrant authorities of this size could effectively frustrate growth.' Planning powers were at the heart of the matter. When a new town was set up, local authorities kept all their existing powers except planning. This change was sufficient to enable growth to be effectively controlled by the minister and the development corporation.

'Partnership will therefore mean that the towns concerned will want a say in planning. They have to be given this and, *at the same time, strengthened by a partner with ample technical and financial resources.* We think that this partner should be a *regional development agency.*'

The agency would have a board consisting of a full time chairman, up to four part time members, and general managers responsible for running the local organisations in the towns in which it was working. The agency would handle central establishments and accounting, and have available specialist technical staff to provide assistance of a type and scale not required for the day to day running of the schemes in the towns concerned. It could act primarily as an estate developer, opening up and servicing the 'growth' areas for a variety of other building agencies; *or* it could itself build along new town lines. Almost certainly both these methods would be needed in the bigger schemes.

Before taking these tentative proposals further, it was suggested that they should be discussed informally with 'some of the better clerks with experience in this field'. This was agreed by the secretary in November 1963. She added that the main functions of the regional development agencies should be to acquire land, provide services (or ensure their provision) and promote development by others, rather than carrying it out themselves. In particular, she was very doubtful whether they should be regarded as a housebuilding agency (though they would have to have reserve powers). Since the plans were for 'inescapable' growth, housebuilding in theory should respond to the demand once the land was made available and employment growth assured. To the extent that the housing had to be subsidised it would be preferable for it to be provided by the normal agencies for that purpose. To what extent housing subsidies would be needed could not be determined 'till we know where we get to on rents and how the housing association movement prospers (and of course the attitude to housing of the government of the day)'.

The Treasury suggested that the other main function of the regional development agencies would be to phase the overall build-up in their sectors to the best economic advantage:

> 'Can we envisage that each agency should have an annual budget for several years ahead, which it would be up to them to get the best out of—a budget in terms both of public investment and of their own expenditure?'

In January 1964, the secretary put to the minister (Joseph) a paper incorporating the latest version of proposals by officials. Joseph replied:

> 'I like the town expansion corporations very much: perhaps you will tell me when we meet what alternatives you rejected in coming to this view. Surely we should also include the argument that such corporations will give continuity to design teams who might not in sufficient quality be mobilised for individual smaller ventures. There would also be more chance of using labour saving building methods. Town expansion corporations would build up considerable expertise in the fields of planning, town transport, housing design where skills are not all that abundant.'

An account of Joseph's submission to the Cabinet of proposals for the public acquisition of land for planned expansions—and the Cabinet's rejection of these—is given in chapter IV.* Nevertheless, the debate continued within the ministry and the secretary minuted (in April 1964):

> 'The minister is wondering whether he should make another attempt, in two or three months time, to persuade his colleagues to agree to our proposal for exchequer financed agencies. He would very much like to be able to announce intention to establish machinery which would make it plain that the Government would drive the expansions through. I have told him that I would be nervous about this, for fear we got an even dustier answer which might make it more difficult for us to make headway.'

In the meantime, discussions with officers of the local authorities principally concerned would continue.

Informal discussions took place with several town clerks from which it seemed unlikely that the proposed 'partnership' arrangements could be made to work. It would be almost impossible to divide the operation between the two parties 'without inviting acrimony' because one body rather than the other 'was undertaking the profitable part of the exercise'. The development of the new areas

---

* See chapter IV, p. 201 *et seq* and *History, Vol. IV,* chapter VII.

and the redevelopment of the old were so closely interlinked that they could not be achieved successfully without extremely close co-operation and this could not necessarily be assured.

It seemed that the solution might be to divide the projects into those which should be left to the local authority to achieve but with new machinery for town development, and those which could be 'forced into the new towns machine'. Thus Northampton, Ipswich and Swindon of the major expansions, together with Norwich, Southend, Poole and possibly Hastings, 'could do their own expansion' (Reading might well be omitted), whereas Peterborough would be taken over as a new town together with Banbury and probably Maidstone. Aylesbury might be dropped, although, if it proceeded, it could be a new town; an expansion at Chelmsford and Colchester might possibly be achieved by the construction of a new town somewhere between the two; Bedford might be dropped. It might be necessary to consider some further new towns 'of the larger nucleus type'.

For the local authority expansions, it would be necessary first to take power to enable the authority to borrow for all the activities involved in the expansion from the Public Works Loan Board over sixty years, and to borrow to meet deficit on the same basis as a new town. If a local authority embarked on a town expansion scheme financed in this way, the need to earn long term profit in order ultimately to repay the deficit would provide a strong incentive to continue with the scheme. Once launched, it would be practically impossible for a local authority to contract out.

By September 1964, however, thinking within MHLG was turning more to the use of New Towns Act machinery. The substantial expansion of a large town depended on three main factors: 'bridging finance on a substantial scale for most of the period of rapid growth; sufficient well qualified professional staff; and the will to proceed despite difficulties and to spend enough to ensure quality'. Financial problems could be solved by appropriate legislation, but it was felt to be most unlikely that a local authority would engage staff of the required calibre ('new blood at chief officer level'), and it was thought that 'it would not be safe to rely upon the will of the local authority to continue to pursue a scheme with sufficient enthusiasm and expenditure, and there are obvious difficulties in committing substantial exchequer bridging finance in the hope that the local authority will complete the scheme'. All these difficulties, however, could be overcome by the use of an area development corporation— which could be established under the existing new towns legislation. Each town would need 'staff of the corporation roughly equivalent to that in a new town of the existing type' and would have a general manager. It was proposed, however, that one corporation should be responsible for up to four projects. Such a corporation would have much greater status and, for this reason, 'and because it would appear less like a duplicate of the local authority', co-operation with it would be easier for a local authority. It would also have the advantage that it would justify some better quality professional staff and could lead to economies in use of staff. Some functions such as accounting could well be centralised, staff could be switched from one project to another as the load of work required, and specialist teams could be set up available for use in any of the projects as the need arose.

The existing new towns would be brought into the scope of the area development corporations as would new expansions. Indeed, since the New Towns Act required a designation area before a development corporation could be appointed, considerable time could be saved by creating the first area development corporations out of existing new town development corporations. It would be essential, however, to make it very clear that the 'area development corporation' was a new body, and to avoid any impression that an existing development corporation was taking on the new projects.

It was envisaged that, initially, Stevenage Development Corporation might provide the basis for an area development corporation covering Stevenage, Peterborough and Northampton, with the possibility of a fourth project being added later. Another area development corporation might cover Harlow, Basildon, Stansted and Ipswich. A third grouping might be Bracknell, Banbury and Swindon. If Ashford and Maidstone both proceeded, a new corporation would have to be established to cover these two.

Further discussion within the ministry led to the abandonment of the idea of 'linked' new towns, and agreement was reached on the steps to be taken in relation to Ipswich, Northampton and Peterborough, all of which would have independent corporations on conventional lines. Consultants would be appointed early in 1965 by the ministry to advise on the areas to be designated and would then continue with the preparation of master plans until such time as the corporations were established and took over.

The new town corporations would work in partnership with the town councils. The main proposal was that the development corporations would be directly responsible for the expansion areas but that in the existing central areas they would be used by the local authority 'just as though they were a private developer working in financial partnership with them'. An arrangement on these lines seemed to commend itself to the clerks who accepted that this job could not be done by the authority itself. This was, admittedly, not an ideal arrangement, but it was 'the only way we can see of getting the job done properly'.

'Partnership' New Towns

Following the general election of October 1964, a fresh approach was made to the Treasury outlining a 'partnership' procedure under the New Towns Act. MHLG said that it was likely that there would be general agreement that the expansion of Ipswich, Peterborough and Northampton should be started soon and that the job could be satisfactorily done only under the New Towns Acts. Some adaptation of the normal machinery would be needed 'because we shall now be dealing with large local authorities'. MHLG proposed that there should be 'more of a partnership with the local authority'. Details would vary between the towns but, broadly, MHLG expected 'a development corporation at one of these places to do less and the local authority to do more than in orthodox new towns'.

Studies showed that the significant difference between expanding a big town and a 'green field' new town lay in the cost of the redevelopment of the town centre and the road network. Town centre renewal was necessary and, indeed, was being thought about in all towns of the size of those which were now being considered. Equally they would soon have to make serious proposals for improving their roads. But forced expansion would bring the need for this forward in time. Against this MHLG believed that it should be possible, to some extent, to disperse employment centres ('the big traffic generators') and to carry out both town centre renewal and improvement of the road network at a lower unit cost than would be possible if there were no expansion. 'But we cannot be sure about this until we are well on the way to a master plan for the particular towns.' Whether or not these hopes were justified, the same machinery would be needed to integrate planning and implementation of these jobs, 'whatever may be the final plan'.

From preliminary discussions, it was clear that these local authorities would not be willing to surrender control of the future of their town centres. Equally, they knew that they could not tackle the job themselves (indeed, in most town centre schemes all the local authority did was to plan and to acquire land, leaving development to a property company). This was 'a very real dilemma for them and us'. MHLG therefore proposed, for any necessary redevelopment of the town centres, that the new town corporation should be able to act in relation to the local authority as a 'development company'. For example, the local authority would acquire the town centre land and hold the freehold, giving a long lease to the development corporation and sharing, after the payment of the appropriate ground rent by the corporation, the equity profits.

Town centre work was expensive, but equally it should in these towns produce an earlier return and be profitable: more so than in ordinary town centre schemes because the increase in population would result in 'rapidly increasing shopping values'.

At a meeting with the Treasury on 4 January 1965, Treasury officials stressed that current ideas on new towns and town expansions increased the need to draw up a programme embracing the various individual schemes. MHLG said that the main factors which prevented the completion of such a programme currently were that the balance of priorities in the south-east had yet to be determined; a report had yet to be received from the west midlands study group; and it would be some time before the study group on the north-west reached any firm conclusion. It was agreed, however, that MHLG would provide the Treasury, on the basis of currently available information, with a summary of new town and major town expansion projects in England together with at least provisional figures of their cost and a table showing the phasing of total expenditure in this field.* This would help the Treasury to see the trend in this expenditure and how it would fit into investment on housing and environmental services generally.

The 1965 Review of Town Development†

So far as town development was concerned, a further review was put in hand at Crossman's request. In an internal minute, a senior official commented that the minister clearly envisaged (after recent discussions in Cheshire) 'a big future for town development and a big role for the counties'. This pointed to the need to clarify 'the extent to which the financial provisions are inadequate; or whether it is simply the machinery that is wrong'.

A report was produced at the end of January 1966. Town development schemes had been approved covering some 120,000 houses, about a half of which were for London overspill. The schemes varied widely in size, organisation and financial arrangements. Progress was judged to be 'very limited' outside the south-east, mainly because of lack of enthusiasm on the part of both exporting and receiving authorities. Three issues, however, were of importance: machinery, industry, and finance.

On machinery, the problem did not lie in the absence of legal powers. The 1952 Act provided for a highly flexible list of arrangements under which development could be planned and executed by the receiving authority, the exporting authority, the county council or by any combination of them. It was difficult to believe that sufficient powers could not be found in the Act to permit any method of co-operation which local authorities were likely to desire.

---

* So far as new towns were concerned, this remit was eventually fully discharged by the report of the new towns working group: see chapter V, p. 233 *et seq.*
† MHLG File NT 91/13.

One obvious difficulty facing a small authority was the need of skilled professional staff for the planning and supervision of large scale development. Where a scheme could amount to the doubling of the size of a town it was likely to be beyond the resources of the average receiving authority. The GLC, who had the largest resources in this respect, had overcome the problem by taking over many of their schemes and executing the work as agents for the receiving authority. Outside the south-east, such help could come either from the exporting county borough or from the receiving authority's county council. County boroughs were likely to be heavily engaged on their own domestic problems of redevelopment, but tripartite arrangements, which had already been devised in some areas, seemed to offer the most promising line for further schemes. These would bring the exporting and importing councils and the county councils into partnership 'with their respective roles tailored to fit the particular scheme but each playing a part'.

The success of many town development schemes and hence the extent to which they encouraged further projects depended on their ability to attract industry. This had not been a very serious problem so far in the south-east where there had been a sufficient number of firms seeking new locations. Despite the reluctance of the Board of Trade to issue an IDC in any case where there was a chance of a firm going to a development district, expansion schemes in the south-east had generally had sufficient new industry to meet their employment needs. In other regions there had been difficulties. This was partly due to the comparative lack of mobile industry there and partly to the priority given to development districts. This was a problem on which the exporting authority and the Board of Trade might both be called upon to help—the former by encouraging industry to move and the latter by sympathetic handling of IDC applications.

It was finance, however, which was the crux of the problem. If the town development programme 'limped' at first, it was due to the doubts of receiving authorities about the ultimate extent of their liability. And the progress made in the south-east was substantially associated with 'the willingness of the GLC to foot a large part of the bill'. Under town development agreements, the GLC normally bound themselves, not only to carry out the physical work as agents for the receiving authority but also, *inter alia*, to raise the money and bear the loan charges on housing development until the houses were actually occupied, as well as to contribute towards any loss on the housing revenue account. In the case of Andover and Basingstoke they had also agreed to add a further contribution to that which the county council was making towards the expenses of the district council.

The financial fears of receiving authorities had led to pressure for increased exchequer assistance, but, though this might be possible to a limited extent, it would probably fall short, both in flexibility and in generosity with the scale of assistance given by the GLC. Moreover, it was open to question whether the exchequer should contemplate taking over a substantially higher share of town development costs. Town development arrangements were 'essentially in the hands of local authorities and while the exchequer can help, the final liability should be borne by the authorities who are likely, in the long run, to have created a very profitable piece of investment'.

The conclusions were, in brief, that:

'Conditions are not likely to favour town development unless all three authorities have a positive inducement to join in. The inducement may be the fear of a less attractive alternative, e.g. a county may prefer a town development scheme to the peripheral expansion of a county borough. But the important thing is that all three authorities should positively want the scheme to succeed.

Fresh legislation to amend the Act will not create the conditions under which it can operate successfully. Nor is it likely that they can be created by a tinkering with government grants (though we might still look at some of the points mentioned in this memorandum). Where small overspill schemes are needed—especially from the Birmingham, Manchester and Liverpool conurbations—it would be preferable to try individual approaches to the local authorities to encourage co-operation. But in the long run it would probably be best to look for large scale expansions which can be carried out under the new towns mechanism.'

This judgement was accepted and, though housing subsidies were increased in 1967 and an amenity grant was introduced in 1968, no other changes were made.

In the eighteen years following the passing of the 1952 Act, some sixty town expansion schemes were promoted in England. (There were none in Wales.) These were to provide some 160,000 houses, of which around 60,000 had been completed by 1970. A half of the schemes (and two-thirds of the completed houses) were for London.

There was constant concern within the ministry at the 'disappointing' progress with the expanded towns, but the completion of some 60,000 houses was no mean contribution to the overspill problems of the big cities. (By contrast the new towns in England had built 120,000 houses.) It was, however, clear both to officials and ministers that the anticipated population explosion demanded developments on a scale which was inconceivable within the framework of the Town Development Act. The major emphasis in the late 'sixties was therefore placed on the 'partnership new towns'.

*Scottish Expanded Towns**

Moves towards a Scottish Town Development Bill began in 1953

---

* SDD Files P/ACT/55/2 and P/NT/HOU/2; and Treasury File SS 48/186/015.

when Glasgow Corporation 'finally admitted' that their housing problem could be solved only by overspill. The Secretary of State for Scotland, James Stuart, asked the Clyde Valley Planning Advisory Committee to study the Glasgow overspill problem, to put forward recommendations for its solution (particularly the selection of sites for development), and to consider the type of legislative and administrative machinery which was needed to enable local authorities to work in partnership with each other and with Glasgow. This was in line with the current view that expansion of existing settlements was likely to be a cheaper method of providing for overspill population than the building of new towns.

To meet the existing situation (in which Glasgow would run out of housing sites within the city boundaries by 1958, and at least 300,000 people would eventually have to be housed elsewhere), the committee recommended the immediate designation of a new town at Cumbernauld as the only means of supplying a sufficiently large number of houses and proposed another new town at Houston. Scottish ministers, however, made it clear that the Government 'were not at this stage disposed to consider the approval of any new town other than Cumbernauld until the possibility of meeting overspill needs by the expansion of existing townships and villages had been closely examined'. They were of the opinion that 'a considerable proportion' of the overspill requirement should be met by the expansion of such towns and villages.

For the last part of their remit, the Clyde Valley Committee's natural focus was on the 1952 Town Development Act for England and Wales, but they thought that any Scottish legislation should be more positive and explicit, especially regarding grant provision. In addition to the expansion of existing communities, they wanted the establishment of new ones of a size smaller than that contemplated under the New Towns Act (though the government view was that town expansion was the sounder economic proposition). They thought that the exporting authority's contribution should be specified by the government, and that exchequer assistance was necessary to induce industry to move to expanding areas.

Ministers agreed during 1956 that town development legislation for Scotland, broadly corresponding to the English Town Development Act should be introduced, and that the necessary provisions should be incorporated in the forthcoming Scottish Housing Bill. The aim was to enable all local authorities whose areas were congested or overpopulated, and who had no sites for further building in their own areas, to make arrangements with local authorities for other areas to provide the necessary accommodation for residential purposes (and other associated facilities and services). The arrangements would include 'participatory payments' by the congested (or exporting) authority to the other authority (receiving authority) in respect of such accommodation as might be provided, and for exchequer grant to the receiving authorities towards their expenditure on basic services and other matters involved in the provision of the necessary accommodation.

The instructions to the parliamentary draughtsmen reveal some of the thinking behind the Bill. Exporting and receiving authorities were to be defined in wide terms because, although the main overspill problem was in Glasgow, it affected other burghs to a lesser degree, and the problem might be accentuated there in the future. Therefore, any county, large burgh or small burgh as receiving authority should be enabled to provide housing and other accommodation which would relieve congestion and overpopulation in the areas of exporting authorities. This would involve a substantial departure from the 1947 Planning Act where the small burghs had, for all practical purposes, no planning powers, and, in particular, no powers of land acquisition or disposal for planning purposes. They should now have these powers, subject to the approval of the county council, or the secretary of state.

It was generally agreed that in the case of overspill schemes, the receiving authority would receive the exchequer subsidy of £42 a house for sixty years, plus a contribution of £14 a year from the exporting authority for at least ten years. This, however, would not cover the costs which a receiving authority was likely to incur in the acquisition and clearance of land, and in the provision of water supply and sewerage services. The department therefore proposed that an exchequer grant should be available on lines similar to those in the English Act. The Clyde Valley Committee on the other hand, desired a definite obligation on the minister to pay grant (at least 75 per cent) to receiving authorities in respect of *all* expenditure incurred by them including a deficit on their housing account and an extension of grant aid to include education and highways. Considerable argument took place over the items to be covered by grant, the department maintaining their objection that to pay a percentage grant to cover a deficit on the housing account would involve the government inextricably in decisions on rents, and that any extension to education and highways would upset their grant codes.

The department, however, were receptive of the committee's argument that the grant should be payable on an annual basis so that help was given most effectively when it was most needed, ie when heavy expenditure was being incurred before new revenue had accrued. The Treasury were generally in accord; they recognised that the subsidy structure for Scotland was very different from that in England, and this would excuse differing provision for other overspill arrangements, but as each country was looking to the other's arrangement in search of some advantage, those arrangements should, like the housing subsidies, be entirely different. An internal Treasury minute noted that:

'the local authority associations in Scotland have learned from the English Act that an enabling measure is not good enough. It lines every one up at the starting post, and there is no one to fire the gun. So they want a measure that defines in advance the exchequer stake; and they also want provision on a scale which will produce houses and they regard the English 50 per cent of capital cost of water and sewerage as inadequate for this purpose.'

A series of hypothetical calculations suggested that a 75 per cent grant to a receiving authority in Scotland of the revenue deficit on the provision of water and sewerage and acquisition and preliminary development of land, might in the long run be no more expensive than a 50 per cent capital grant to water and sewerage in England. As the department were satisfied that they could cope with the formidable accountancy problems in settling the deficit, and as they preferred that the grant arrangements should be incorporated in regulations, the Treasury raised no objections to the proposals.

The scheme for dealing with overspill was included in Part II of the Housing and Town Development (Scotland) Act 1957. Three clear cut means of providing houses in a receiving area were contemplated:

(a) a straight overspill agreement whereby the exporting authority would pay £14 per house for ten years to the receiving authority, who would receive the exchequer subsidy of £42 for sixty years.
(b) by an arrangement with the Scottish Special Housing Association, normally involving an overspill agreement whereby the receiving authority would provide an equivalent number of houses.
(c) by the exporting authority itself in the area of the receiving authority, with the exchequer subsidy of £42 for sixty years.

But the Act recognised that overspill development would rarely consist of houses alone; community services and industrial employment would generally have to be provided, and the houses in the receiving area would have to be accompanied by development which without assistance might impose an unreasonable financial burden on the receiving authority. Accordingly the receiving authority was empowered to promote a 'town development scheme' containing their proposals for industrial or other development or other social requirements, and the provision of basic services. When a town development scheme had been approved by the secretary of state, an exchequer grant of 75 per cent would be payable to the receiving authority of the additional net annual charge arising from expenditure on the acquisition, clearance and preliminary development of land and on the provision of water supply, sewerage and sewage disposal services.

While the Act applied to housing authorities throughout Scotland, it was contemplated that initially the overspill provisions would be limited to those authorities which were in a position to assist with the Glasgow housing problem. In accordance with these provisions, sixty local authorities made arrangements with Glasgow to build a total of 23,000 houses. By 1970 some 9,000 had been completed.

EPILOGUE

CHAPTER X

New Towns and Government

HISTORY is never 'complete', but some histories aspire to be more complete than others. The present volume has no such aspiration: certainly in no sense can it be said to provide a full story of British new towns policy. This is not an apology for shortcomings: it is a warning statement. Its objective was primarily to chronicle those issues of policy in relation to new towns which came before the Cabinet and its committees. This, however, proved to be too restrictive and the resulting 'story' was (to the author) surprisingly episodic. An attempt was made to broaden the canvas by extending the account to those issues which came to individual departmental ministers for decision. But this gave rise to two major difficulties. First it was necessary to delve into huge collections of departmental files to identify issues which did come before ministers while, at the same time, collating sufficient background material to enable a comprehensible account to be given of the nature and source of the issues. More important, it proved quite impossible to define satisfactorily what was meant by 'ministerial decision'.

This last point was the most troublesome. True, some issues were clear—such as Silkin's deep personal involvement in establishing the first new towns, Macmillan's adroit manœuvres to safeguard them, and Joseph's increasingly pragmatic commitment to them as effective instruments for implementing regional policy. Yet most issues were not like this. For the majority of the new town issues, ministers were spokesmen for their departments: though nominally responsible for policy, ministers, on taking up office, were faced with a situation in which the 'facts' had already been defined and in which the scope for imposing new policies was restricted. The evidence of the official records shows that senior civil servants were punctilious in bringing to the attention of their ministers the issues which needed political or major decision. Yet 'decisions' are typically made by increment: commitments are gradually built up until a position is reached when it is difficult to do other than follow a clearly indicated path. It took a remarkable combination of circumstances to effect reversals in policy. Ipswich was the exception which proves the rule.*

---

* See chapter V, p. 269 *et seq.*

No doubt the point can be better appreciated (and perhaps qualified) by histories of policies in other fields but, in relation to new towns, it is of particular importance—as the Treasury were quick to appreciate. Decisions to designate new towns could be made with ease: but they assumed 'an alarming commitment' for future governments. Indeed, it was Treasury anxiety which gave rise on occasion to the necessity for formal reference to the Cabinet.

This provides another warning of the inadequacy of a history which focuses on matters which came before the Cabinet or to the attention of ministers. Such matters are frequently those on which there is interdepartmental disagreement. Had it not been for the widely held feeling on the necessity of 'safeguarding' agricultural land, some of the new towns might never have been brought to the Cabinet: with more certainty it can be asserted that the policy in relation to new towns for Merseyside, Manchester and the West Midlands would have been different. Apart from the initial designation, issues of new towns policy which were the subject of formal Cabinet decision were isolated eruptions precipitated by interdepartmental disagreements, or by attempts of the Treasury to reassert central control over expenditure, or—more rarely—by vain attempts to forge more rational and comprehensive policies in relation, for example, to the distribution of population. For the most part, Cabinet and ministerial decisions were made only when one or more of these factors emerged from the constant round of departmental and interdepartmental discussions.

It was for these reasons that it was decided to make considerable use of departmental files for this history. The difficulties to which this gave rise have been summarised in the Introduction where it was pointed out that the problems of the historian are shadows of those facing politicians. Both are easily overwhelmed by the sheer volume and complexity of material. There is an important lesson in this: what is revealed is not just the limitations and inadequacies of the historian but also an indication of the real problems of government. In a world where events move rapidly, where everything is related to everything else, and where it is impossible to take all relevant factors into account, it becomes imperative that the true nature of the difficulties of government should be appreciated.

Neatly—and hopefully not unconvincingly—this provides a rationale for the current history. It is illustrative of the problems of government. As work progressed, this increasingly became the author's bench-mark. Though the original intention had been simply to provide an 'official' history of the new towns, the emphasis shifted into an attempt to outline some of the problems of government by illustration from the field of new towns. This explains why some particular issues are included; and sufficient has been said to explain why many others are excluded. The final outcome is as much a contribution to the understanding of the problems of modern government as it is a chronicle of policy in relation to new towns.

It is not appropriate for an author of an official chronicle to enter into an extended commentary on the 'lessons' to be learned from his survey of policy formulation over a period which extends to a point which could well be embarrassingly close to the contemporary scene. Much must be left implicit—and capable of differing interpretations. Nevertheless, some issues can be highlighted, and others can be brought together to illustrate what 'the art of the possible' involves. Above all, the story of the new towns provides a particularly revealing insight into the problems of co-ordinating policy which perpetually bother and baffle all governments. Many of the policy areas with which government is concerned are circumscribed: problems of battling for more resources, of reconciling conflicts and of achieving the ideal of a harmony between the objectives of different policies (and the ministers and departments responsible for them) are inevitably settled (or, to be more precise, accommodated) either by the Cabinet or by concordats between individual ministers or departmental officials. It is clear from the account given in the main body of this volume that this was frequently the case in relation to new towns. But the new towns policy, by its very nature, raised interdepartmental conflicts in a particularly acute and clear form since it cut across a wide range of departmental functions, objectives and programmes. New towns could not be abstracted from planning, industrial location, education, agriculture, health, housing, transport and other fields which, being matters of national policy and resource allocation, were constantly in the forefront of the minds of departmental and Treasury ministers; nor could the problems of new towns be isolated from those of local government.

Much of the anxiety about new towns expressed by the Chancellor of the Exchequer and the President of the Board of Trade stemmed from the fact that, once a commitment was made to a new town, issues of overall policy control were compromised. A new town could not be made subject to the same effective controls as could be applied to other building programmes. It had its own momentum (for which a specific development agency had been established); and it was not affected by local politico-financial constraints (as was an expanded town). While a local authority housing scheme could be retarded (or accelerated) in accordance with national policies, a new town had to be considered not only within this broader framework; it also had to be judged in terms of its own viability and profitability. A new element was thereby introduced into departmental, ministerial, Treasury and Cabinet thinking. If new towns were to achieve 'profitability', they had to be allowed to continue—and possibly to

Their strongest ally (apart of course from their own Treasury ministers) was the President of the Board of Trade who was generally responsible for regional development (though towards the end of the period the responsibility was uneasily shared with the Secretary of State for Economic Affairs). The role of Jay is here of particular significance, partly by the accident of the positions which he held but also because he constantly raised pertinent questions (to which no fully satisfactory answers were forthcoming).*

One cannot but be struck by the difficulties which faced government in controlling the forces which they had unleashed in establishing the new towns programme. A motley of factors conspired to maintain the momentum of the new towns which Silkin so skilfully initiated despite the doubts of his colleagues—and which Macmillan, for pragmatic reasons, fostered. In a curious way, the new towns policy has been almost apolitical. Once launched, new towns attracted support from successive planning ministers which ensured their continuation. In Macmillan's time they were a significant contribution to the housing and overspill programmes which he sponsored. Later they were seen (first by Joseph and later by Crossman and his successors) as highly effective instruments for regionalism and for coping with 'the population explosion' which ministers were advised could be confidently expected. In the mid-fifties only a modest population growth was envisaged—of less than two million. Each succeeding annual revision raised the projected figures until, by the mid-sixties, an increase of over 19 million was anticipated. The result was a major change in attitude towards new towns—and their function and scale. A large new programme of new towns (and 'new cities') was put in hand. But—such are the shifting sands upon which policies are formulated—this had hardly got under way when the demographic scene was transformed. Falling births after 1964 led to revisions in population projections: by the end of the decade the projected increase had fallen to 10 million— and the indications were that it might fall further (as, indeed, proved to be the case).†

At the same time, the 1966 census (the first—and only—one to be undertaken five years after its predecessor‡) provided new evidence

---

* See chapter II, p. 40 and chapter V, p. 215.

† Year in which projection made	Base population in previous year	Total Population Projections (Great Britain)		
		1980	1990	2000
1955	49·8	51·7	51·5	
1960	51·1	56·1	58·9	62·0
1965	53·1	59·6	64·9	72·5
1970	54·3	56·9	60·2	64·0
(1975	54·5	54·6	56·4	58·0)

‡ Except for the war-time year of 1941, the British census has been undertaken decennially. The 1966 census was carried out on a ten per cent sample basis.

on crucially relevant issues. First, it revealed that the conurbations were losing population through 'unplanned' outward migration on a large and unappreciated scale. Secondly, the 1966 census workplace data showed that the received wisdom about a continuing increase in total employment in London was quite wrong. As a result, some fundamental rethinking on planning policies for the south-east began to emerge.

But commitments to the new new towns programme were by now firm, and only one scheme (Ipswich) was still at a stage at which it could be abandoned.

NEW TOWNS AND URBAN PROBLEMS

A major purpose of the new towns policy (and initially its predominant purpose) was to assist in the solution of urban problems. In the quarter-century covered by this history these problems have changed. In the mid nineteen-forties, the perceived priority problem was that of redistributing population and employment from overcrowded cities. London constituted the most difficult problem by virtue of its size (though the Scots rightly stressed the more intense problems of Glasgow and its urban neighbours). So far as the 'overspill new towns' are concerned their *raison d'etre* was to cater for the needs of the urban areas with which they were associated: and the criteria for their success was the extent to which they did precisely this.

This was particularly so in the case of the London new towns. It followed that strong control had to be operated to ensure that the London new towns did not have the effect of increasing 'the drift to the south' and thereby frustrate the policy they were designed to implement: hence the industrial selection scheme and the attempt to apply stringent rules to the movement of industry. The difficulties which all this set for the new town development corporations should not be underestimated. It would have been very much easier for them had their task been simply to develop new towns (attracting population and employment from anywhere). It would also have been easier had their function been simply to house people from London, leaving aside the issue of employment. But these new towns were conceived as 'balanced communities' in which the population would both live *and* work. These ideals were difficult to attain, but the difficulties were greatly compounded by the pressure upon them to concentrate on the housing of Londoners who were 'in housing need'. Local authorities were highly sceptical of any concept of 'filtering': it was insufficient that the new towns should give *general* assistance to the London housing problem by providing accommodation for anybody from London. The local authorities might have agreed that—in theory—this would give some relief in that the houses which were vacated by those moving to a new town would become available for others. But this was very remote from their thinking—as their early proposals for the control of vacated accommodation illustrates. They wanted tangible and direct assistance with their housing problems (and they pressed their case even more strongly when they were compelled to make financial contributions in respect of families moving to the new towns).

There were constant complaints that the new towns were doing insufficient to this end: the heartfelt plea of Jay echoed their strong feelings. As the new towns developed, the development corporations came under increasing criticism for failing to house the most needy. Crossman and Mellish tried to meet this by introducing the 'special housing allocation' system under which families in housing need but lacking the skills needed by new town firms could move without first obtaining a job. This, however, was limited in its possibilities (to be unemployed in a relatively restricted new town labour market was even less attractive than to be unemployed in London) but, in any case, the increasing success of the new towns in attracting modern industry meant that there was a perpetual shortage of skilled workers: and it was these for whom the houses were needed.

This specific issue of alleged failure 'to house the most needy' became more generalised in the 'sixties when new towns were criticised for 'creaming off' the more skilled, the more able and the more venturesome Londoners. (At the same time they were equally criticised for failing to attract 'the higher social classes'.) This is not the place to attempt an independent assessment of these allegations: the immediately relevant point is that these were the types of criticism levelled at new towns. They affected the thinking of ministers and officials, and underlaid some of the controls which the development corporations found so irksome. And they led to serious questioning about the function of new towns. Towards the end of the 'sixties, a new twist to these arguments began to emerge: were not new towns being instrumental in *creating* 'the inner city problem'? Though, in fact, the new towns housed only a small proportion of those who moved from the cities (the majority moved 'privately'—as analysis of the 1966 Census clearly showed) they began to become the whipping boy for a wide range of problems whose causes lay much deeper—of public sector housing, of urban redevelopment, of urban decay, of social polarisation and of urban deprivation.

In journalistic terms, the new towns had a poor press. They were under criticism for alleged failures not only in achieving the objectives for which they were established, but also for a multiplicity of other social and planning problems. Despite the constant stream of foreign visitors to new towns and the widespread acclaim

533

abroad for the British new towns,* the domestic reaction was remarkably lukewarm. Pseudo-sociological criticism (epitomised by phrases such as 'new town blues' and 'social indigestion') and architectural criticism ('prairie planning') added to the troubles of ministers who sought to defend them against their Cabinet colleagues.

Part of the reason for the growth during the later 1960s of this predominantly critical attitude may be explained by the fact that (though each new town devoted great effort to public relations) no one did so for the new towns collectively—apart from the Town and Country Planning Association.† Indeed, for most of our period, the only publication which collated statistics for all the new towns was the journal of this Association. The ministry's records were limited and its research meagre. Things might have been otherwise had not early attempts to accommodate a research section within the ministry given rise to acute discomfort: but, in the event, a promising development was killed off to the relief of both the ministry and the development corporations.‡

Be this as it may, the new towns had no protagonist to compare with their first minister. Though, as is now abundantly apparent, Silkin laid a very firm foundation, what followed was pragmatism rather than conviction. Thus, the nine ministers§ who had succeeded him by the end of the 'sixties protected and promoted new towns for a range of practical reasons: they saw the new towns as a convenient instrument at hand for implementing a variety of policies. At central government level, therefore, there was little positive projection of the new towns policy and surprisingly little 'defence' against the changing character of the criticism which it attracted. Ministers had more important things on their minds, and the real political battles were conducted privately, not in the country at large. Frustratingly to the historian whose period ends before the 'seventies, wider debates on the function, achievements and failures of the new towns assumed significant proportions later—when the problems of 'the inner city' began to emerge as an urgent but ill-defined issue of political concern. It is ironic that a policy originally conceived as part of a comprehensive strategy for dealing with urban problems should, thirty years later, be subject to attack on

---

* There is a story (the authenticity of which proved incapable of proof) that a Japanese delegation asked to visit Hook New Town. When told that it was never built they expressed incredulity and remonstrated that they had already built two 'Hooks'.

† The official New Towns Association was not established until 1970 and its role was somewhat restricted (see chapter VI, p. 384).

‡ See chapter VI, p. 348 *et seq.*

§ ie Dalton, Macmillan, Sandys, Brooke, Hill, Joseph, Crossman, Greenwood and Mellish.

For Scotland, Westwood was followed by Woodburn, McNeil, Stuart, Maclay, Noble and Ross.

the grounds that it had been instrumental in exacerbating these very problems.

This particular debate, however, was only beginning to get into its stride by the end of the 'sixties. More significant to ministers were the relative claims of new and existing towns for resources. The issue of amenities in the new towns was a case in point, but it went much wider. The new town development corporations, being directly responsible to the minister could—and did—continually press upon him the claims of the new towns. As the new towns grew and obtained political representation in Parliament, their MPs supported the case. Ministers (and their departments) were sympathetic, and added argument was provided by reports such as those produced by the National Council of Social Service* and the Central Housing Advisory Committee.†

The claims of the new towns were made in articulate and persuasive terms, and it is at the least arguable that they did receive favourable treatment compared with existing towns. Whether favourable treatment was justified or not is a question which others must answer: the point which is here relevant is that any hint of generosity towards new towns immediately brought a response from the Treasury, questioning the basis on which resources should be channelled to new towns when 'a great many other places will have as good, or better claims'.‡ This was indeed the issue. To generalise from a stream of Treasury letters and minutes (spanning the whole period of this history, and relating to a wide variety of proposals— from community centres to sophisticated transport systems): 'why should new towns, which are expensive and heavily subsidised, receive preferential treatment over old towns whose needs are typically greater?; and if we give way to the new towns, how can we resist the stronger, much more numerous (and therefore much more costly) claims of all the old towns?'

This is the very stuff of politics and was accordingly settled by argument and political decision. It thereby added to the web of controversy within which ministers were involved.

AGRICULTURAL LAND

The issue of agricultural land was different. Though new towns as a policy had little general electoral appeal, the opposite was the case with agricultural land. For reasons on which we cannot speculate here, 'safeguarding' agricultural land (like green belts) brought about an apparently clear and positive political response, and new

---

* J. H. Nicholson, *New Communities in Britain*, National Council of Social Service, 1961.
† Central Housing Advisory Committee, *The First Hundred Families*, HMSO, 1965, and *The Needs of New Communities*, HMSO, 1967.
‡ Treasury File 2EAS 420/01.

towns again became the whipping boy. The fact that new towns were economical in the use of land is important for an independent assessment: but such facts can be irrelevant to the perceived situation—and the consequent political arguments. A major additional point in this case was that, since new town proposals came before ministers collectively more frequently than did the much more significant urban development proposals for 'normal' housing (and for expanded towns), they constituted a focal point for interdepartmental conflict.

The Treasury (and its later ally—the Department of Economic Affairs) tried to take some heat out of the argument and to put matters on what they considered to be a more rational basis by pressing for more objective methods of valuing agricultural land. They failed: and the arguments assumed an untypically acrimonious character. The normal interdepartmental procedures for resolving difficulties proved inadequate in the face of the insistence of the Ministry of Agriculture that the issue was a quite abnormal one. Agricultural land could not be treated in the same way as other departmental issues. Certainly it could not be resolved 'in principle' or by recourse to 'spurious formulae'. The ministry insisted that each case should be treated on its merits by standard procedures —in which they were closely involved at various stages. Their views prevailed.

It is unlikely that the story stops there and, as is commented in appendix B the chronicle of a future historian will need to be set against the changing attitudes to the safeguarding of natural resources which emerged in the 'seventies.

HOUSING POLICIES

At the inception of the new towns programme, new towns were the responsibility of the Ministry of Town and Country Planning, while housing was the (very longstanding*) responsibility of the Ministry of Health. The relationships between these two departments on housing policy showed signs of strain as the new towns began to get under way (though the signs need interpretation by the student of departmental repartee). The inherent difficulty was that the Ministry of Health were concerned with national housing policies and programmes (as well as with other local government services) while the Ministry of Town and Country Planning were not responsible for any 'service' apart from new towns. But, before real difficulties arose, there was a major redistribution of functions, and those of the Ministry of Town and Country Planning were

---

* The Ministry of Health had been responsible for housing since the department was established in 1919, but its history goes back even further since it took over from the Local Government Board.

amalgamated with all the local government responsibilities of the Ministry of Health (except local health and welfare services) in 1951 in a new Ministry of Local Government and Planning (which changed in name, but not in function, to the Ministry of Housing and Local Government following the return of a Conservative Government later in the same year).

This did not, of course, abolish by sleight of hand possible conflict between new town and housing policies. It merely translated them from the interdepartmental to the intradepartmental arena. Conflict is perhaps too strong a word: the basic problem arose from the fact that housing policies in the new towns could not be forged without reference to national housing policies. Moreover, the latter have been in a perpetual state of change (there were fifteen Housing Acts between 1945 and 1970*). Typically, the new towns had to wait for decisions on national policy before changes could be introduced which met their particular requirements (at least in so far as these were seen by the ministry). Even with rent control, to which development corporations housing was originally subject, despite common agreement between the corporations, the ministry and the Treasury on the necessity for abolition, this had to await national policy decisions—and a place in the legislative programme.

The difficulties to which this subservient position of the new towns gave rise is illustrated by the abortive attempt on the part of the ministry to promote 'better class' rented housing in new towns in advance of decisions on national policy. Even more difficult was the real clash between national and new town policy issues in relation to owner occupation.

As the review of the future ownership of new town housing demonstrated:

'The main issues at debate on the future ownership and management of housing in the new towns highlight major problems of policy of far wider import. These major problems—of housing finance, standards and costs, local government organisation, central-local government relationships, and so forth—cannot be solved within the narrow context of the new towns. If the new towns are to become "normal" they must be treated as such. At the same time, the general problems which they pose, often in an acute form, demand attention.'†

The subsidy issue created constant difficulties, but here settlement could be reached (though not necessarily to everybody's satisfaction) by the device of providing special rates of subsidy and additional grants for new town housing. This never completely met the argument of the development corporations that their task was rendered more difficult by the fact that their rents were typically

---

* Ignoring purely Scottish legislation.
† *The Ownership and Management of Housing in the New Towns*, HMSO, 1968, p. 162.

higher than those of normal public sector housing. But this problem was incapable of adequate solution until the basic system of housing finance was changed—and this did not happen in the period covered by this history.

CENTRAL CONTROL

The Reith Committee had no hesitation in stressing the need of new town development corporations for a high degree of independence from central control:

> 'We assume that such a corporation will be invested with sufficient powers to enable it to carry out its task free from the administrative control and consequent interference which are necessarily associated with full and direct government responsibility. The appropriate Minister (the Minister of Town and Country Planning or the Secretary of State for Scotland) should have the power to give such directions as he may from time to time consider necessary in the public interest in any matter of major policy. Subject to that, the corporation must have freedom of action comparable with that of a commercial undertaking.'

But it was not to be; and, since such very large sums of public money were involved, it was inconceivable that Reith's concept would be accepted. Though it was of obvious relevance to the type of organisation of which Reith had had long experience (such as the British Broadcasting Company and Imperial Airways), it was quite inappropriate to a series of corporations which, on the basis of consolidated fund advances, were charged, as agents of central government, with developing new towns.

This was quite a new piece of administrative apparatus, and its uniqueness gave rise to apprehensions on the part of the Treasury (and on the part of others such as the local authorities involved in new town areas). Initially the key note was one of caution, except on the part of the young Ministry of Town and Country Planning— which itself was watched with a critical eye. As noted earlier, new towns formed the only 'service' for which the ministry was responsible: its major 'planning' function was a co-ordinative one, and it was quite unclear in the early days what this really involved.

There was, moreover, a basic difference of outlook on 'planning' between professional planners in the ministry (together with their counterparts in the development corporations) and the administrators in the other interested departments and the Treasury (and later between the professionals and the administrators in the Ministry of Housing and Local Government). The professional planners saw their role as being a *professional* one: they were the people who knew what 'planning' meant, and who could make technical judgements on the merits of planning proposals. The administrators, on the other hand, viewed 'planning' much more as a political process in which questions of values, and even taste and fashion were paramount.

In the 'sixties (and even more in the 'seventies) 'professional' attitudes changed, as did so much of the framework within which government operated; but, over the major part of the period covered by this history, this basic difference in outlook was of major significance. Above all, it meant that while planners viewed many of the controls to which they were subjected as being irksome and unnecessary, administrators considered it to be essential that the planners should be controlled both because of the essentially political nature of their work and because they were involved in decisions which might—and often did—imply large financial commitments.

This somewhat overstates the case. In particular, it ignores the natural inclination of administrators (in the departments, but not in the Treasury) to ally themselves with the needs and even the thinking of their opposite numbers at the local level. It also ignores the fact that, in the development corporations themselves—even though all was not sweet and harmonious—there was a clearly defined objective: to develop a new town.

The Treasury, of course, were well aware of this, and it increased their concern to ensure that new town plans and proposals were soundly conceived, economical, and made as little demand on the exchequer as possible. This concern was made all the greater not only because they feared oversympathetic treatment by the department to their creation, but also because there was no 'built-in' constraint to new town expenditure similar to that which operated in local government: hence the Treasury's initial preference for town expansion (where, additionally, development could be retarded or accelerated much more easily).

But a new element entered the debate when it became apparent that some at least of the new towns would be financially profitable. The Treasury then found themselves in the position of defending the continuation of the existing new towns programme and their retention by some organisation which would ensure that the 'profits' accrued to the exchequer. Nevertheless, even if the new towns were proving to be (in the words of Wells, the chairman of the Commission for the New Towns) 'gold mines of the future',* the future was still a long way off, and additional new towns merely pushed it further away.

Yet—as the Ministry of Housing and Local Government constantly stressed—financial issues were not the only ones; and they

---

* H. Wells, 'Gold-mines of the Future', *Town and Country Planning*, January–February 1968, p. 42.

were not necessarily the most important. When an overall assessment of the achievements of the new towns comes to be made many other issues will have to be taken into account. This history suggests that the selection of appropriate criteria for measuring the achievements will be as contentious as any conclusions.

APPENDICES

APPENDIX A

Distribution of Industry Policy

National Policy

The effects of the depression in the early 1930s coupled with major changes in the economic structure of some of the old established industrial areas led to the first legislative measure affecting the distribution of industry—the Special Areas (Development and Improvement) Act, 1934. This designated the north-east coast of England, Cumberland, south Wales and the Clyde as areas where special government assistance would be available for their social and economic rehabilitation. A few trading estates were established, but the apparently intractable nature of the problem was among the factors leading to the appointment in 1938 of the Barlow Commission which reported in 1940 (Cmd 6153), with recommendations for a central authority 'to promote a balanced distribution of industry'.

The demands during the war for munitions and for ship building stimulated the heavy industries in the special areas. Moreover, some lighter industries were diverted to these areas both for strategic reasons and to take advantage of the existing labour force. As a result a measure of temporary prosperity was restored to them. But the long term problem was not overlooked and, in July 1943 the permanent secretaries of the Treasury, Board of Trade, and Ministry of Labour, and the head of the Economic Section of the Cabinet Office were appointed as a steering committee on postwar employment and reported to the Reconstruction Committee in January 1944.* Their report dealt with control of investment and of consumption, wages and prices, mobility of labour, industrial efficiency and industrial location.† On the last point, they concluded that there was a grave danger of long term unemployment in the special areas and in certain other localities. To counter this, they recommended that there should be positive measures 'to develop the attractiveness of areas suffering from unemployment', combined with a system of inducements and aids together with 'the zoning and planned layout of great towns and contiguous areas'. They suggested that firms planning developments calculated to employ 200 workers

---

* See *History Vol I*, p. 27 *et seq.*
† R(44)6.

or more should contact the Board of Trade before plans reached an advanced stage, 'as the speed with which they could proceed would depend on the priority which could be afforded to them in the allocation of resources which would still be scarce and subject to government control'.

The report was the subject of exhaustive examination by ministers in the Reconstruction Committee and in the War Cabinet. After a number of revisions and amendments, it was issued as a white paper on *Employment Policy* in May 1944 (Cmd 6527). On the distribution of industry it was stated that it would be an object of government policy to secure a balanced industrial development in areas which had been specially vulnerable to unemployment by encouraging the establishment of new enterprises in those areas, and a number of measures were outlined. For example: the government would exercise a substantial influence over the location of new industrial development; munition factories would be released for civilian production as early as possible; priority in the granting of building licences would be given to new and extended factories in the development areas; advance factories for smaller firms would be erected by the government in development areas for lease or sale.

There had been considerable discussion,* while the white paper was being drafted, on the machinery which might be established to carry out government policy on location and, in 1944, Woolton had recommended that 'the responsibility should rest with the President of the Board of Trade. This is a policy for securing a balanced distribution of industry; it is not a policy for relieving unemployment in depressed areas'.

W. S. Morrison (Minister of Town and Country Planning) retorted that the Board of Trade's primary concern was with raising the efficiency of industry and 'their natural function may frequently be the negative one of watching that restrictions on choice of location are not imposed'. At a meeting of the Reconstruction Committee in April 1944, he argued that, in view of the extent to which town planning was involved in the application of a policy of location, his department should be given a more prominent place.

Bevin (Minister of Labour and National Service) felt that, if the general responsibility were entrusted to the Board of Trade, the impression would be given that insufficient account would be taken of the interests of unemployed workers. For this reason he thought that the special responsibility of his department 'should be more clearly defined'. Anderson (Chancellor of the Exchequer) settled the dispute by saying that the Board of Trade should have the primary responsibility, and that if there were a conflict of interest with other

---

* R(44)58, R(44)72 and R(44)30th Meeting, 12 April 1944.

departments it would have to be settled 'in accordance with normal constitutional practice by the Cabinet'.

The white paper stated that responsibilities would rest with the Board of Trade, the Ministry of Labour and National Service, the Ministry of Town and Country Planning and the Scottish Office. Standing ministerial and interdepartmental arrangements would be made for supervising and controlling the development and execution of the policy, but as 'it would not be satisfactory if the public were left to deal with a number of different departments on different aspects of the same problem', the Board of Trade would be the channel for expression of government policy.

The resulting machinery was a standing ministerial committee, with the Minister of Labour (Bevin) as chairman and a nucleus of ministers consisting of the President of the Board of Trade, the Minister of Production, the Minister of Town and Country Planning and the Secretary of State for Scotland, with power to co-opt other ministers as necessary. Subordinate to it was a committee of officials working in three panels: *Panel A* to deal with general questions of industrial distribution and projects for new industrial development; *Panel B* to deal with the allocation and disposal of government factories; and *Panel C* to deal with facilities for the expansion of civil production. The chairman and secretaries of each Panel were provided by the Board of Trade, and the Board was separately represented on each Panel. In addition to the Board of Trade, the nucleus of each Panel consisted of representatives of the Ministry of Production, the Ministry of Labour, the Ministry of Supply, and (for Panels A and B) the Ministry of Town and Country Planning and the Scottish Office. Representatives from other departments were co-opted as necessary.

Thus, at the end of 1944, a powerful piece of machinery had been established which, at the official level, resulted in the confirmation of the Board of Trade as the dominant department in the industrial location policy. Within that machinery, Panel A quickly emerged as the most influential part. (It was later absorbed wholly within the ambit of the Board of Trade.)

Panel A advised the ministerial committee on the implementation of the location policy which had been set out in the white paper, and which was enacted in the Distribution of Industry Act 1945. The Bill, as introduced by the President of the Board of Trade (Dalton), had originally contained a clause giving the Board power to prohibit the erection or extension of industrial buildings in certain areas to be later defined. Dalton faced much opposition on this clause on the ground that it would create great uncertainty. The issue was under discussion when the Coalition Government gave way to the Caretaker Government. Dalton was replaced as President of the Board of

Trade by Lyttelton who then became in charge of the Bill. Fearing that the whole Bill might be lost, Dalton (now in opposition) moved the deletion of the controversial clause on the assurance of Lyttelton that the Government would secure the passage of the remainder of the Bill during the current session. Dalton made it clear, however, that dropping the clause at that time was without prejudice to its being brought forward again by whatever government was in power after the election.

In its final form, the 1945 Distribution of Industry Act prescribed a statutory schedule of development areas (north-east coast of England, West Cumberland, South Wales and the Clyde industrial belt; to these were later added Wrexham and South Lancashire in 1946, Merseyside and part of the Highlands in 1949, and NE Lancashire in 1953). In these areas the powers of the Act could be exercised. The principal powers were that the Board of Trade could acquire land and build factories for lease or sale, and make loans to trading or industrial estate companies; the Treasury could make loans or grants to industrial undertakings approved by the Board on the advice of an independent advisory committee if the project had good prospects of success and the capital could not be obtained elsewhere; and the Board of Trade had to be notified of any proposed industrial building of more than 10,000 square feet.

With the collapse of the Coalition Government in May 1945, the ministerial committee of which Bevin had been chairman lapsed, but Panels A and B were taking what steps were practical in the circumstances of the time to steer footloose industry to the development areas. To deal with the many difficult cases which were arising, the Attlee Government reformed the ministerial committee in May 1946. Bevin, the former chairman, became Foreign Secretary, and the chairmanship of the new committee fell to Dalton (Chancellor of the Exchequer, but previously President of the Board of Trade, who had sponsored the Bill in the previous Parliament).* At the end of 1947 the committee was reconstituted at a junior level with Douglas Jay as chairman (at that time Financial Secretary to the Treasury and who, previously as a civil servant, had been a member of Panel A, where he had taken an active part in the formulation of the Bill of 1945).

The Board of Trade machinery, with the support of the ministerial committee, had a fair measure of success in steering industry to the development areas in the immediate postwar years. Firms wished to get into production quickly, and wartime factories and labour were available. Moreover, building licences were readily available for firms wishing to build or expand in these areas.

---

* It was this committee which settled the sites of the first new towns in spite of Dalton's hesitations and his anxieties to get them established in the provinces; see chapter II.

Initially, the main instrument of negative control was the need to obtain building licences from the Ministry of Works. While these were freely available for new factories and expansions in the development areas, they were strictly controlled through the machinery of Panel A for works elsewhere, and were only considered on the recommendation of a sponsoring department (primarily the Ministry of Supply and the Board of Trade for defence and civilian production respectively) within quotas allotted to them. The quotas were heavily reduced at the time of the Korean War 1950–51, and limited to projects essential to defence or which made a direct contribution to dollar saving. But during 1952 the shortage of steel and building materials eased, and the building licence control was abandoned in the spring of 1953.

Meanwhile, early in 1947, the long awaited Town and Country Planning Bill had been introduced, and included a provision that an application to a local authority for planning consent to erect an industrial building was to be accompanied by a certificate from the Board of Trade to the effect that 'the development could be carried out consistently with the proper distribution of industry'. This provision, which had been in Dalton's original Bill of 1945, attracted little attention in Parliament, although a government amendment was introduced in the Lords which limited the certificate to buildings in excess of 5,000 square feet. It was S14(4) of the Town and Country Planning Act 1947 which formed the legislative basis for the Board of Trade's continuing powers in respect of industrial development certificates (IDCs), and which gave the Board negative powers to restrict industrial development.

After the tight control through building licences and IDCs in the early 1950s, there was a gradual improvement in the economic climate and, as the threat of general unemployment in the development areas appeared to be receding, IDC control was relaxed, and considerable industrial expansion took place in the midlands and south-east (including the new towns). Towards the end of the 1950s, it was becoming apparent that parts of the scheduled development areas were no longer places where there was high unemployment or any special danger of it. As a result, the inducements to industrialists, in the shape of loans or factories to rent, were no longer being exercised, though they were not formally removed. On the other hand, a number of (mainly small) areas had become prominent in which there was a relatively high level of unemployment, but which were not adjacent or analogous to the development areas. The Distribution of Industry (Industrial Finance) Act 1958 accordingly empowered the Treasury to give assistance by way of grant or loan to undertakings outside the development areas if the Board of Trade were satisfied that the purpose for which the assistance was required was one 'likely to reduce unemployment in any locality in which in the opinion of the Board, a high rate of unemployment existed and was likely to persist'.

In 1959 a committee of officials reported that the arrangements for giving assistance, which had been built up over the years to meet changing circumstances, had become unnecessarily complex, and that the varying availability of inducements in differing and sometimes overlapping places was giving rise to confusion. In referring the report to the Cabinet, the President of the Board of Trade (Eccles) proposed that 'the Bill I have in mind would get rid of the outmoded concept of development areas and provide that we could use the powers we take wherever in Great Britain they are needed'.* The Local Employment Act 1960 followed. This repealed the Distribution of Industry Acts and replaced them by a single comprehensive statute giving the Board of Trade powers which they might exercise

'with due regard to the proper diversification of industry for the purpose of providing for the benefit of any development district employment appropriate to the needs of the district,'

which was defined as

'any locality [where] . . . a high rate of unemployment exists or is to be expected within such a period that it is expedient to exercise the said powers and (in either case) is likely to persist.'

The financial inducements of the previous legislation were improved to enable the Board, after consultation with an advisory committee and the consent of the Treasury, to make building grants to firms providing premises in development districts. These were at a rate of 85 per cent of the excess of the cost of provision over the market value on completion. On the negative side, the Act provided that, in considering industrial development certificates, the Board of Trade should 'have particular regard to the need for providing appropriate employment in development districts'. In practice the Board came to interpret this to mean that an IDC should not be granted outside a development district unless the Board were satisfied that the project could not be reasonably undertaken in a development district.

The Act of 1960 was designed to pinpoint those *districts*—as distinct from the *areas* under previous legislation—where high unemployment existed and was likely to persist, and to concentrate remedial action and financial assistance on them. The corollary was that as employment prospects improved, the districts would be 'declassified', but in practice the Board adopted the administrative

* C(59)129.

device of 'stop listing', which meant that projects in the pipeline could be completed, but that assistance for new projects was suspended until the employment prospects for the district became more certain.

The first list of development districts covered 12·6 per cent of total employees in Great Britain (compared with 18 per cent in the old development areas); in March 1962 as a result of changes in the districts (by additions and stop listing) the coverage was 7·3 per cent and in March 1963 was 12·4 per cent. The frequent changes in the list were criticised partly on the ground that industrialists were deterred from starting new projects for which they might have no further assistance for subsequent expansion, and partly that districts were removed before their problems were solved.

Meanwhile, in the Population and Employment Committee, ministers were expressing apprehensions about the markedly greater growth of industry in the midlands and the south-east than in the development districts, a regional outlook was emerging, and ideas focused on 'growing points'. In January 1963, Hailsham was appointed to make a comprehensive review of the local situation in the north-east and to prepare plans for the redevelopment of the area as a whole. Hailsham's proposals were quickly followed by the Local Employment Act 1963, which established a standard building grant of 25 per cent in place of the previous complex formula, and a standard grant of 10 per cent of the cost of plant and machinery; and by the Finance Act 1963 which allowed qualifying investment in development districts to be written off for tax purposes at whatever rate a company chose. Both measures substantially increased the financial inducements to industrial movement and development (though the grants to plant and machinery tended to be more attractive to capital rather than labour intensive industry), and were balanced by a toughening of the IDC control. The white papers on Scotland and the North-East, published in November 1963 (Cmnd 2188 and 2206), committed the Government to an improvement of the infrastructure (eg communications, water supply, housing) and to maintenance of the financial incentives to industry so long as the local economies required. Heath's appointment in October 1963 as Secretary of State for Trade and Regional Development, in addition to that of President of the Board of Trade, was designed to provide additional stimulus.

During this period there was a change of emphasis in distribution of industry policy. It had become evident that consideration had to be given not only to unemployment but also to the level of activity rates: in consequence the policy came to be justified less by the narrow social criteria of the relief of unemployment and more by the wider advantages of balanced growth and development throughout the country. The return of the Labour Government in 1964 saw further development of policy along these lines. Among the first measures of the new Government was the Control of Office and Industrial Development Act of 1965. This required office development permits for offices in London and in such other districts as the Board of Trade might designate. (The initial exemption limit was 3,000 sq ft, but the Board were given power to vary this.) Birmingham was brought under permit control in 1965, and in 1966 control was extended over a wide area of the south-east and midlands.

This was followed by the Industrial Development Act of 1966 which replaced development *districts* with wider continuous development *areas* where special measures were considered necessary to encourage the growth and proper distribution of industry. The Act required that in the selection of these areas consideration be given to all the circumstances, actual and expected, including the state of employment and unemployment, population changes, migration and the objectives of regional policies. These new development areas covered most of Scotland, most of Wales, the northern region, the Furness peninsula, Merseyside, most of Cornwall and north Devon. Towns taking overspill from development areas, although not so designated, were treated as if they were development areas provided their population intake from a development area was high enough. (Skelmersdale new town and Winsford urban district were so treated in relation to the Merseyside development area.)

Administratively in November 1967 certain colliery closure districts were designated as 'special development areas', in which additional incentives were made available over and above those already provided in the rest of the development areas.

In 1967 the Government appointed a committee under the chairmanship of Sir Joseph Hunt 'to examine, in relation to the economic welfare of the country as a whole and the needs of the development areas, the situation in other areas where the rate of economic growth gives cause (or may give cause) for concern'. The committee's report, *The Intermediate Areas* (Cmnd 3998), found that the Yorkshire and Humberside region was economically vulnerable as it was too dependent on industries which were shedding manpower, growth was slow, earnings low and there was lack of alternative employment, particularly in view of the considerable unemployment expected to arise from the run-down in mining in the Yorkshire coalfield area; moreover, much of the region had a poor environment as a result of dereliction from coal-mining. The report considered that in the case of the north-west region it was of paramount importance to evolve a coherent and balanced policy for the area as a whole by introducing policies to unify and stimulate the whole region: here too were the problems of declining traditional industries, slow growth and industrial dereliction, as well as poor amenities and much substandard housing. The Hunt Report recommended the extension of regional assistance to both these regions. The Government, however, decided that, in view of the limited resources then available, assistance must be concentrated in more narrowly defined localities within those regions, where the need was judged to be greatest.

Industry and the New Towns

THE NINETEEN-FORTIES*

When W. S. Morrison wrote to Woolton in May 1945 proposing that Stevenage should be the site of the first new town, he referred to the fact that it was well served by road and rail to both London and the midlands, and that it had proved attractive to a number of small industries which were already established there. Later in 1945, when Silkin was meeting with resistance from his colleagues to his proposals for satellite towns, he circulated an optimistic report by the interdepartmental committee on the Greater London Plan. This expressed the view that, while it was important that industry should move concurrently with population, this should be 'attained with a strong government drive and a carefully controlled programme'. The Board of Trade had a list of firms anxious to rebuild, whose decentralisation was desirable, but who satisfied the Board that they should continue to be located within the Greater London area: 'there will therefore be no clash with development area policy—and no danger of depriving existing industrial areas of industries needed for the maintenance of full employment'.

The Reith Committee, in their first interim report, stated that it was 'vital that the national policy for the location of industry should keep in step with the national policy for the development of [the new] towns'. In spite of the hesitations of ministers, Silkin had by 1950 secured the designation of twelve new towns in England and Wales (and two in Scotland); master plans were being prepared, and an extensive housebuilding programme was getting under way, the houses initially being mainly occupied by building trade workers, school teachers, and those engaged in the various forms of local government. But by the end of 1948, the chairmen of those corporations which had then been formed were expressing apprehensions in general terms about the difficulties they were expecting in attracting industry to their towns. A departmental minute of 3 May 1949 commented:

---

* MHLG File 91650/37/2.

'This ministry has real misgivings lest the policy underlying the Board of Trade's distribution of industry scheme is now out of date or deficient so far as new towns are concerned. The fact is that it was settled before the establishment of new towns became government policy, and it has never been revised so as to take account of their needs and treat them where necessary exceptionally.'

The new towns research section were invited to investigate the position, and reported in July 1949 that, in the preceding three years, 300 firms had made inquiries about the possibility of development in the London new towns. Of these only fifty, mostly small or medium size, were still interested, and of these only twelve had definitely applied for an IDC. Firms appeared to be worried whether their workers could afford the rents likely to be charged, and accordingly the corporations tended to favour those firms which paid high wages. Rents for industrial premises were thought to be 'on the high side, and to discourage some firms which otherwise would be suitable'. But it was suggested that the main difficulty was one of timing: firms that were in a position to go to a new town immediately were not willing to wait for a distant date when factories and houses would be built. On the other hand, those firms whose problems were not so immediate did not wish to commit themselves to future dates, especially as the corporations could not on their side give definite assurances for such dates. Moreover the speed of 'build-up' in the new towns was important as some firms had indicated that they were doubtful whether their workers, used to an urban life, would be happy in the present very small towns with few urban amenities. Industrialists tended to feel that the LCC quasi-satellite towns gave a better base for operations, as a potential labour force was already established, and housing and amenities already existed. In short, the report concluded that the factors discouraging firms from going to London new towns were 'not so much obstruction from government departments, as the slow tempo of growth and lack of a sufficiently definite programme of construction'.

No direct reference to this somewhat discouraging report appears to have been made at a meeting which was held, at Silkin's request, in July 1949 with the President of the Board of Trade (Wilson) and the Financial Secretary to the Treasury (Jay). Silkin expressed concern at the prospect of houses becoming available in the London new towns before sufficient industry had been established, 'so that the new inhabitants of these towns would be compelled to travel back to London to work', and he suggested that undue pressure was being put on firms to go to the development areas. If housing were to go ahead in the new towns the requisite amount of industry had to be allowed. Wilson said that 'firms capable of operating in the development areas must not be allowed to set up in the new towns'. Jay commented 'it was important to press on with steering industry to the development areas in order to bring idle resources into use; we could not afford unemployment in those areas'. It was agreed that a working party of officials from the two departments should examine the housing programme for the new towns over the next three to five years, assess the volume of industry which would be required, and consider the long term implications of the development of the new and expanded towns 'from the industrial standpoint'.

A MTCP minute commented:

'I am quite sure that the Board of Trade are apprehensive that the new towns will be an embarrassingly strong magnet to industry. That is the heart of our trouble. BOT conceive that their main function in relation to new towns is to prevent them from getting too much instead of to help them to get what they need. Since the development corporations can presumably be relied on to prevent the new towns getting too much industry the BOT might just as well occupy themselves with seeing that they get the right kind quickly.'

The working party met on 16 August 1949, but its deliberations were overtaken later in 1949 by a small but distinct improvement in the prospects of industrial development in the London towns, other than Harlow. (At Harlow the position was that an IDC had been granted to only one firm, expected to employ twenty persons; twenty houses had been completed, eighty were nearing completion, and 1,400 should be completed in 1952, 'which would then give an employment potential for some 1,500 workers, including 500 women'.) Meanwhile, a suggestion was canvassed that factories might be built in new towns 'in advance of the selection of tenants for them', but the Board of Trade rejected this unless 'suitable tenants whose production is of sufficient importance to secure the support of their sponsoring department, are found before the factories are built. To build factories "on spec" would be contrary to the Government's investment policy and the resulting strict control over industrial building'.

THE NINETEEN-FIFTIES*

In the first part of 1950, the industrial position in the new towns was showing some improvement, but the ministry continued to express concern about the imbalance between the housing programme and industrial development. An appreciable amount of employment would be required in 1952 and increasingly in the following years, and 'this means that the necessary factories must be started very soon, and we have not got anything like enough in sight yet'.

---

* MHLG Files 91650/37/2, 91650/37/25 and NT 62/6; IPC(51)30; HA(51)1st Meeting, 23 November 1951; EA(52)72, EA(52)76, EA(53)111, EA(53)16th Meeting, 13 May 1953; and LG(54)2nd Meeting, 26 May 1954.

Towards the end of 1950, the strain on sterling and the re-armanent programme consequent on the Korean War involved a much tighter control over economic development and in particular over industrial building, for which licences within quotas laid down by the Production Committee were limited to projects essential to defence, or which made a direct contribution to dollar saving. Few of the firms which were willing to move from London to the new towns fulfilled the criteria, and accordingly building licences were not forthcoming. To meet the position the ministry proposed two solutions: first, a central clearing house to deal with all applications for industrial development in the new towns, and secondly a special allocation for building licences. The proposal for a clearing house was based on the fact that unless a firm could be assured of a building licence from the sponsoring production department, and an IDC from the Board of Trade, a good deal of time could be wasted by negotiations between the firm and a development corporation. The position was complicated in that the regional areas of the various departments did not in all cases coincide, the new towns were in different regions, and when particular cases were referred to head-quarters, confusion and delay could result. The Board of Trade's reaction was that 'however attractive it may appear superficially to envisage an arrangement by which all applications for industrial expansion in the Greater London area are dealt with by a single organisation, we are not at all convinced that we should not lose rather than gain as a result'.

The question of a special allocation for industrial building licences for new towns had been discussed at the official level early in 1951, and was mentioned at a meeting between Dalton (then Minister of Local Government and Planning) and Shawcross (the new President of the Board of Trade) on 30 May 1951 when the latter agreed that, subject to the approval of the Chancellor, there should be an allocation for new towns that would be additional to the Board of Trade allocation. Dalton noted:

> 'If this could not be arranged he [Shawcross] would be very glad to consider cases where I felt BT were being unreasonable. He agreed to tell [a named official] that I had complained to him of the unhelpful attitude of BT and my desire that they should be more responsible.'

On 7 June 1951, Gaitskell (Chancellor) agreed that £1m of the 1952 investment programme for manufacturing industry should be earmarked for new towns in addition to whatever work was already authorised. On 3 December 1951 it was reported that the additional allocation was working satisfactorily, and that over half had already been committed. Nevertheless, industrial development in the new towns was slow, and in November 1951, the President of the Board of Trade in the new Conservative Government (Thorneycroft), warned his colleagues that experience with the new towns suggested that it would be difficult to induce industrialists to establish factories in them.

During the early part of 1952 the Treasury were discouraging all expenditure in new towns, and to Macmillan's request for a further allocation of £3·5m for industrial development, Butler replied

'to licence on this scale projects not of the first importance, when we are having to restrict building for manufacturing more severely than ever, will . . . create difficulties for the Ministry of Supply and the Board of Trade who will find it hard, to say the least, to justify refusing valuable projects at a time when less essential work is being done, and being seen to be done, in the new towns.'

In May 1952 Macmillan staked a claim with his colleagues for the siting of a new factory for GEC at the new town of Stevenage, which would give employment to 1,380. At the same time he renewed his request for an additional allocation of £3·5m for industrial development in new towns and proposed that, of this, £1·5m should be allocated to the building of advance factories. Thorneycroft suggested that any additional allocation for industry should come from the allocation for houses. He objected strongly to the proposal for advance factories as, owing to the shortage of steel, he had found it necessary to stop building them in development areas.

Macmillan's request for an additional allocation was deferred, but meanwhile a ministerial battle developed on the siting of the GEC factory. The main alternative to Stevenage was Portsmouth, which was favoured by Monckton (Labour) and by Thorneycroft on grounds of unemployment in that area. Stevenage was favoured by the Admiralty and by Sandys (Supply) as the factory would otherwise compete with the dockyards for skilled labour. Moreover, if it were sited at Stevenage it would be less vulnerable to attack. The EA Committee discussed the matter on four occasions during June and July 1952, and, after examining possibilities in Lancashire, ministers decided that the factory should be located at Portsmouth.

While ministerial argument over the siting of the GEC factory was raging, the edge had been taken off the Treasury attack on the new towns on financial grounds by the agreement to call for a joint MHLG/Treasury report,* but, on 4 September 1952, Macmillan wrote to Thorneycroft on the question of keeping industry in step with housing:

'If we fall down on this it will redound not only to my discredit (which does not matter) but to the discredit of the Government (which does) . . . Whatever we may think of new towns as an idea (and I do not think it was a very good idea in the immediate postwar conditions) we have inherited them

---

* See chapter III, page 120.

and we must make them work—You are the master of factory building and if you will take the lead you could direct enough of the industry you are anyway going to start to keep at least some sense in new town development . . . What I would like is to have an interdepartmental organisation of officials with your chap in the chair.'

Thorneycroft agreed that officials should discuss the matter and, under the chairmanship of Dame Alix Kilroy of the Board of Trade, a working group of representatives from the Ministries of Housing, Supply and Labour met intermittently at the end of 1952 and during 1953. This made little progress, as the representatives of the Board of Trade made it clear from the outset that they could not alter government policy on the priority accorded to the development areas. Some inconclusive estimates were made of housing in relation to jobs; suggestions were made and rebutted that the industrial rents proposed by the development corporations were high and discouraged applicants at the outset; and arrangements were made for regular meetings between the ministry, the corporations, and the regional controllers of the Board of Trade concerned with the London new towns to discuss all matters relating to the provision of industry in those towns.

In a draft report for the working party prepared by the Board of Trade on 12 October 1953, it was explained that it was current government policy to encourage industrial expansion in development and unemployment areas, and to restrain the growth of industry in congested areas, particularly in Greater London. Accordingly when an industrialist proposed to move to a new town, the Board of Trade normally insisted that the concern must be moving production from inner London, that the project must not be mainly an expansion, and that the industrialist must have sound reasons for not moving out of London altogether to an unemployment or development area.

To meet the position in the new towns, the draft proposed some easement of that policy:

'1. Production might be moved from Greater London (and not only inner London).
2. Expansion should be regarded as suitable for a new town if the alternative was expansion in another part of Greater London or not at all.
3. Concerns already established in a new town should be allowed to expand there.
4. Harlow, Hatfield, Stevenage and Basildon should be allowed to construct a small block of unit (advance) factories.'

In submitting the BOT draft, officials in the Ministry of Housing commented that the proposals 'amount to very little more than an open acknowledgement by the Board of Trade of the flexible interpretation which they have applied to the otherwise strict policy in numerous cases in the past'.

The Kilroy working party of officials was virtually ineffective in view of the entrenched position which ministers in the Conservative Government had taken from the end of 1951 to the middle of 1954. Briefly, the positions were that the Chancellor of the Exchequer was calling for a reduction in public expenditure in the new towns; Macmillan was committed to a policy of decentralisation, which involved the movement of jobs; Thorneycroft was committed to giving preference to the development and unemployment areas for new industry, and was supported by Monckton (Ministry of Labour); and the Ministers for Health and for Education were doubtful of their ability to finance hospitals and schools in the new towns.

At meetings of ministers in 1953 and 1954 the argument tended to be confused by discussion of the prospects of 'getting rid of the new towns to the local authorities', but apart from the general Treasury point on costs, the main burden of the argument rested between Macmillan and Thorneycroft. Macmillan had told his colleagues that 'if it was decided to change the existing policy for new towns, this would have to be clearly stated in Parliament'. Thorneycroft warned that any departure from the existing policy of preference for the development areas would be such a marked change that it would have to be the subject of a formal announcement which the Government would have to be prepared to defend. 'Our political opponents would undoubtedly be only too glad to seize on such an announcement as an indication of our desertion of the development and unemployment areas'. With ministerial commitments of this character on a contentious matter of policy, it was not to be expected that officials in the Kilroy working party could reach any dramatic solution, and their draft report was effectively ignored.

Ministers resolved their differences about the new town policy in May 1954.* In relation to industry it was agreed that firms which were capable of going to the development areas and which could be induced to do so, should go there; the London new towns should be expected to draw their industry wholly from Greater London; and there should be an annual review between the Treasury, the Ministry of Housing and other departments concerned to fix the rate of house building and other development in the new towns for two clear years ahead, and that the housing programme in each new town should not be allowed to run ahead of the industrial development there.

With the easing of the supplies of steel and other materials the

---

* See chapter III, pp. 145–147.

building licence control had been abolished in March 1953, the economic climate was improving, the Board of Trade were being more flexible, the rate of housebuilding was increasing, employers' apprehensions about the availability of labour were lessening, and the corporations were finding a demand for small as well as large factories.

In the second half of the decade, industry in the London new towns grew apace; the Board of Trade adopted a tough policy on IDCs for industrial building and expansions in the congested parts of the Greater London area and, while there was still encouragement to a firm to transfer to a development area, IDCs were not normally refused for a move (or an expansion) to a new town. The annual reviews with the Treasury kept the housing programmes in reasonable balance with industrial development, although the position fluctuated from time to time and from place to place when housebuilding outran industry or vice versa. Generally, it was a case of industry outstripping houses, and in February 1956 it was reported that apart from Crawley, Harlow and Basildon, none of the towns would welcome additional industry if this necessitated more houses before 1958. In the circumstances the Board of Trade was inquiring about the possibility of speeding up housebuilding in the new towns or expanding their size beyond that currently envisaged.

THE NINETEEN-SIXTIES*

By 1960 the London new towns were well established and thriving, and the Board of Trade approached MHLG about the extent to which they should continue to encourage manufacturing firms, which were tied to the London area, to set up in the London new towns, particularly if they expected to start production before 1963. The factors in the situation were that in almost all the new towns there was then a long waiting list for houses, partly due to a failure to meet the housing targets; the number of unfilled vacancies was steadily rising; most corporations had enough factory space under construction to take up all the labour likely to become available in the next two or three years; and in some cases there were signs that industrial land was being used up rapidly, with the risk that insufficient might be available if new enterprises had to be introduced in five to ten years time. On the other hand, there was the school leaver problem, likely to become significant in the mid 1960s, and careful timing would be necessary to ensure that sufficient jobs in factories and offices would be available. This, however, was some time ahead and, in the circumstances of 1960, it was agreed that the Board of Trade would not normally issue IDCs for projects in the

---

* ED(65)123, ED(65)133 and ED(65)18th Meeting, 2 August 1965; EP(69)30 and EP(69)10th Meeting, 10 December 1969; and Treasury File 2AT 634/01.

London new towns unless the firm was already established there, or the proposal was for several years ahead, or was 'one making relatively little demand on housing and labour and helping to diversify the industrial pattern of the town'. This was the counterpart of the policy in the Local Employment Act 1960, which had required the Board of Trade in considering IDCs to 'have particular regard to the need for providing appropriate employment in development districts'. In the result, the Board of Trade adopted a tougher line in their location policy, and while the first generation of new towns continued to flourish, their industrial development was at a slower tempo.

Meanwhile the second generation of new towns was emerging. Skelmersdale, Runcorn, Washington and Livingston were in, or adjacent to, areas where the special inducements to industry were available; Redditch and Dawley were to serve the west midlands conurbation, and at Redditch there was already an industrial base. But overall the employment position remained sluggish and was regarded as a major problem by the new Labour Government which took office in October 1964.

The letter from Jay (President of the Board of Trade in the new Labour Government) to Crossman (Minister of Housing and Local Government) of 1 January 1965 has already been quoted.* This was followed by a meeting between the two on 5 January 1965 when Jay suggested that firms moving from London to new towns in the south-east had been allowed to expand more than was advisable, and had led to an excessive expansion in the population of the south-east as a whole. Crossman replied that a distinction should be drawn between independent new towns such as he hoped Bletchley† would be, and those which were in an advanced state of development; in the former expansion should be welcomed, whereas a different policy might be appropriate for the others. But as natural increase alone would give rise to an overspill demand of one million by 1981, and as it was out of the question to hope that many of these people could be encouraged to leave the south-east altogether, homes would have to be provided for them in the new towns. Experience had shown that it was impossible to build up employment in the new towns unless firms were allowed to expand their labour force.

To this Jay replied that the experience of the first generation of new towns was not necessarily applicable to the early stages of the second generation; 'the general background of the first round has been a comparatively weak IDC policy; the policy was now much tougher and he intended to make it tougher still'. Jay continued that

---

* See chapter V, p. 215 *et seq.*   † i.e. Milton Keynes.

firms taking factories in the new towns had been allowed to draw more of their labour force from outside London than was desirable, and that greater effort should be made to ensure that workers came from the London housing lists. A job should not always be a prerequisite of accommodation in a new town, and commuting should be allowed on a temporary basis. Crossman felt that commuting would be generally unpopular and beyond the means of the average unskilled worker. It was left that officials would examine the difficulties of attracting industry to the new towns, and Mellish (Parliamentary Secretary, MHLG) was invited to investigate the extent to which the new towns drew their unskilled workers from the London housing lists.*

The examination by officials was swept up in the general review taking place during 1965 into regional economic policies as a whole, and the revival of the conception of development areas as opposed to development districts. The overspill aspect was peripheral to the main issue, but the Ministry of Housing argued that it was necessary to give overspill areas equal priority with the less prosperous regions. In submitting the draft of the white paper on *Investment Incentives* (later published as Cmnd 2874, and forming the basis of the Industrial Development Act 1966) a majority of officials held that the general policy of giving second priority to overspill towns had so far resulted in providing sufficient industry for their needs. They therefore recommended that no change be made.

At the ED Committee, Jay said that he was sure that he could not explain in Parliament why the Government should remove the provision that the Board of Trade should have particular regard to the need for providing appropriate employment in the development areas. Now that the development areas were being widened it would be more than ever necessary to put pressure on firms to move there if they could. It would look inconsistent if at the same time as widening those areas, the Government appeared to be reducing their efforts to send industry to them. He was satisfied that the existence of the provision would not prevent the needs of the overspill schemes being met, and it was far easier to meet the industrial needs of the overspill schemes in the south-east and the midlands than those of the development areas.

Crossman agreed with most of Jay's points, but thought that 'we must leave ourselves free to adjust our position to industrial steering'. The changes now being considered would make a big difference in the balance between the development districts and the rest of the country; their size was to be extended, and they were to be given a more effective range of inducements and priority in public invest-

---

* See chapter VII, p. 414.

ment. If the measures were effective, they would inevitably make it much more difficult to get the industry needed for the growth points in the rest of the country and in particular for the new towns and expansions essential to meet the housing needs of the big cities. The Government could not be put in a position where these schemes were stopped or crippled because they were starved of industry. He was therefore strongly opposed to the retention of a statutory provision which would prevent adoption of a more flexible steering policy.

In discussion it was pointed out that 'the repeal of the provision requiring the Board of Trade to have regard to the needs of the development districts, so as to provide a formal flexibility of policy for giving appropriate priority to the needs of the overspill towns would appear to be a major change of policy and would be badly received in the development areas. Whatever the logical arguments it would be psychologically a mistake. If the present statutory requirements were maintained, it would be possible within this framework to operate the arrangements in practice so as to give sufficient priority to the needs of the overspill schemes'. It was decided that, on balance, it would be desirable to retain the policy of requiring the Board of Trade 'to have regard to the needs of the development areas in steering industry'.

This was the firm decision of ministers at the end of 1965: the new and expanded towns outside the development areas were to have second priority in the steering of industry. Nevertheless, most of the established towns were generating their own growth, both with industrial expansions and with commercial and office development. Government pressure continued on the development areas, as evidenced in April 1967 by the Prime Minister's personal minute to the President of the Board of Trade referring to 'the great importance of reducing unemployment in the development areas and improving their relative importance compared with the midlands and the south . . . I should like you to consider whether the time has now come for a further drive in persuading firms to go not only to those areas but to get them into the pockets of high unemployment by emphasising all the inducements we can now offer and by maintaining a tight grip on our IDC control'.

However, the preferential treatment accorded to development areas led to increasing difficulties in adjoining 'grey areas' and, as a result, the Hunt Committee were appointed to study the problem. So far as new and expanded towns were concerned, they commented that 'to date there has been little real difficulty in securing an adequate supply of industry', and most were growing rapidly. Nevertheless, they recommended that the minimum for IDC control should be raised to 10,000 sq ft. Following the publication of the

Hunt Committee's report,* the Secretary of State for Economic Affairs (Shore) made a statement in the House of Commons which, *inter alia*, referred to the Government's policy in relation to new and expanding towns:†

> 'We do not accept the Hunt Committee's proposals that the general exemption limit should be increased from the present levels to 10,000 square feet or that all control should be removed from moves to overspill towns. But we do see the need for a more flexible policy for such moves where planned development may be held up if the flow of industry to overspill towns from an exporting area is impeded. It certainly is our intention that all approved schemes for new and expanding towns should be properly supported by employment opportunities.'

The statement was followed by discussions between the Distribution of Industry Division of the Board of Trade (now transferred to the Ministry of Technology) and the Ministry of Housing and Local Government. A broad measure of agreement was reached on the ways in which the secretary of state's statement was to be implemented.

First if, in any new or expanded town, housing and industry were seriously out of balance, any firm wishing to move to that town from the conurbation which it served would normally get an IDC. The Board of Trade reserved the right to press a firm to move to a development area instead if they thought the firm was particularly suitable for such an area. This had been accepted with the proviso that there should be consultation in advance on any case where the Board wanted to take this line.

Secondly, where imbalance had not yet developed but seemed likely to develop, the Ministry of Housing would give the Board of Trade as early a warning as possible. It would be necessary to satisfy the Board that the risk of future difficulty was real and significant. They would then be prepared to act in accordance with the first point of agreement.

Thirdly, the Ministry of Housing might want to press the case for admitting a firm from outside the strict limits of the exporting conurbation to help a town which was in difficulties. The Board of Trade would be prepared to consider any such case on its merits. More generally it was agreed by both departments that suitable firms in the outer metropolitan area would be allowed IDCs for new and expanded towns serving Greater London if they were prepared to recruit much of their labour from London.

Fourthly, a firm already in a new or expanded town would usually get an IDC if it wanted to expand there. There might be cases where the Board of Trade would want to press a firm to expand

---

* *The Intermediate Areas*, Cmnd 3998, 1969.
† HC Debates, Vol 782, Col 671, 24 April 1969.

receive priority in the allocation of resources—at a level which was different from that which could be considered appropriate for the old towns. The more quickly the new towns attained financial viability, the better—for all concerned.

There was thus a basic community of interest between the new town development corporations, their sponsoring departments, and the Treasury which did not apply in the traditional field of local government services. The development corporations made the most of this (it was their job to do so); and the responsible departments were inevitably in sympathy with their creations. The Treasury were faced with a real dilemma: initially anxious (or, to use the word which frequently appeared in their internal minutes, 'alarmed') about the long term commitment which the new towns represented, they were increasingly concerned with ensuring their 'success'. Yet this did not fit easily into normal patterns of Treasury thinking; and in any case, they were unsure about how success could be measured; hence their concern with establishing objective criteria for performance.

This was also an expression of the Treasury concern to elaborate an effective machinery of control over what they often saw as 'the higher flights of fancy of planners'. The Treasury files are replete with acid comments on particular proposals.*

The Treasury search for objective criteria proved in vain— neither the efforts of civil servants nor those of academics proved able to provide what was intuitively hoped for. Moreover, studies of this nature inevitably took a long time: and (even when they reached a 'conclusion') the context changed before the final report emerged. All the effort to establish a 'scientific' approach ran into the sands, and the Treasury were forced back into their well established role of attempting to subject departmental submissions to sharp questioning, objections and delay. Letters which flowed from the Treasury to the departments were frequently of an intellectual rigour which would do honour to a postgraduate seminar. But—as the Treasury feared in the early days of the new towns programme—they were in a weak position. Though they continually raised shrewd questions of import, which might modify or delay a project, they rarely had sufficient information or experience to keep an argument going on a proposal which was seriously pressed, and were liable to be swept along by the dictates of the situation, by the adroitness of ministers such as Macmillan, or the persistence of successive Scottish ministers.

---

* New thinking on transport systems was a particular target for criticisms. For example, the proposal in the Runcorn draft master plan for a rapid transit system involving the construction of a road network for the sole use of buses was described as 'one of the occasions when the architect-planner has taken a short journey into Cloud Cuckoo Land'. (Treasury File 2 EAS 420/01.)

in a development area instead: eg, where it had had a particularly long run of successive IDCs for expansion in its present location. They accepted that this reservation would be used only very exceptionally.

Finally, both departments agreed that currently only Telford and Daventry were in serious difficulties, though one or two other towns had difficulties which hopefully were less serious and which could be remedied more quickly. Milton Keynes was agreed to be a special case. The Board of Trade accepted that it needed some 'pump primers' and that, in order to get them, they should be prepared to follow the policy set out in the first point of agreement.

This agreement (which was reached at official level and among the ministers most intimately concerned) was accepted by other ministers in December 1969 on the ground that it constituted a temporary expedient to help overspill towns which were in serious difficulty. But it was stressed that 'a reversion to normal policy should follow the establishment of a satisfactory balance between housing and employment'.

APPENDIX B

Agricultural Land

Throughout the period covered by this history, agricultural land considerations have had significant effects on major development proposals. This has been equally true of new towns, expanded towns and peripheral housing developments. Some proposals have been rejected for agricultural reasons, while others have been considerably affected by agricultural objections. Every major urban area has its own history of the conflicts between the need for land for urban development and the need to safeguard agricultural interests.

So great has the conflict been that a number of cases had to be referred to a Cabinet Committee or to the full Cabinet for resolution. There have even been cases where, though the planning and agricultural ministers have agreed that urban development on agricultural land was unavoidable, the matter has been referred to a Cabinet Committee to forewarn other ministers of the likely outcry following announcement of the decision. An early example is illustrative: the development of the 900 acres site at Clifton for the City of Nottingham. In January 1950, Silkin presented a paper to the Lord President's Committee on this.* The land had been purchased by the city in 1947 'without reference to any government department'. The site was one of good agricultural land, and the Minister of Agriculture strongly objected to its development for housing. There had been equally strong representations from the city for this development. The full history is a lengthy one (and includes two local public inquiries), but eventually the lack of alternatives and the urgency of Nottingham's need forced a reluctant capitulation by the Ministry of Agriculture.

Silkin referred the matter to the Lord President's Committee, not because of the disagreement between departments, but because 'there is going to be vociferous criticism from agricultural interests when the decision is known'. He also laid down a number of conditions of which three are of particular relevance to this account. First, no further loss of good agricultural land south of the Trent would be entertained. Secondly, Nottingham would have to build to higher densities at Clifton (and on any other sites) than they had typically adopted in the past. Thirdly, development on other sites should be

* LP(50)5.

564

started as quickly as possible, 'so that although the whole of Clifton will ultimately have to go for housing, as much as possible of the agricultural land will be retained in agricultural use for some time to come'.

All new town proposals inevitably involved the loss of some agricultural land, and the area finally designated for most towns represented some compromise with agricultural interests. The compromise generally left MHLG and the Treasury with an uneasy feeling that too much weight had been given to agricultural considerations. This feeling was expressed in the abortive discussions of the working party on economic criteria for town development (during 1964 and 1965)* where it was argued that because subsidies were paid for agricultural products and agricultural land was derated, it was fallacious to allow agricultural objections to the most economical plans of development. The matter came to a head in connection with the designated area for Milton Keynes when it was argued that while the value of agricultural land should always be an important consideration, it should not necessarily be regarded as of over-riding importance in determining the area to be designated. It was at this point in time (1966) that ministers asked for a thorough study of the basis on which agricultural land should be valued for this purpose.

The outcome was a lengthy report by an interdepartmental group of officials.† It is this report which is the subject of this appendix.

The group were asked to consider and recommend the principles and techniques which should be used in calculating the value of agricultural land for planning purposes; to examine the principles and methods used in practice; and, in the light of the recommended principles and actual practice, to prepare guidance for planners on ways in which agricultural land was to be valued in the selection and preparation of planning schemes and long term population distribution plans.

The report reviewed the existing guidance given to officials of various departments, discussed the problem of quantification and, finally, recommended (subject to strong reservations by the Ministry of Agriculture) a method of valuing agricultural land as an aid to establishing the merits of alternative planning schemes.

Departmental Policies

(i) THE MINISTRY OF AGRICULTURE

The Ministry of Agriculture's policy regarding the use of agricultural land for development 'was related to the role assigned to

---

* See chapter VIII, p. 462 *et seq.*   † EP(67)28.

agriculture in the national economy'. Home agriculture produced about a half of the United Kingdom's total food consumption and two thirds of the total consumption of those commodities which could readily be grown in temperate climates. Current agricultural policy aimed at meeting a major part of the additional demand for food by 1970.

Land as a resource was an essential element in agricultural production. Setting aside differences in the degree of capitalisation and management skills as between one farm and another, the higher the inherent quality of land (as measured in terms of soil type, elevation, contour, climate, etc) the higher was the economic yield from it. The range of potential yield was considerable: the output from first class arable or horticultural land, for example in the Fens, had a value many times that of the output from the rough grazing or poor quality grassland characteristic of the upland areas of the north and parts of the south-west.

Accordingly, the contribution which the agricultural industry in the UK was able to make in the long term to the national economy depended, *inter alia*, not only on the amount of land in agricultural use but also upon its quality. Agricultural land was currently being taken out of production for non-agricultural uses at a rate approaching 50,000 acres net annually. It had been estimated by the working group on the long term distribution of population that, if the projected needs for all forms of non-agricultural use in Great Britain to the end of the century were to be met, the total amount of land taken out of agricultural production would be some two million acres.

There was comparatively little that could be done to contain or reduce the quantitative demand for agricultural land. The most that was possible was to ensure that land for non-agricultural uses was not taken out of agricultural use either prematurely or in excess of requirements. It was therefore an important part of the ministry's land use policy to urge the greatest economy in the use of land consistent with the acceptable layout of development at reasonable cost and, in the case of housing and associated development, with reasonable living conditions and amenities.

The greater scope for minimising the loss to agricultural production, however, lay in the retention for agriculture of better quality land where alternatives of lower quality were reasonably suitable for development. The application of this principle, and its reconciliation with the requirements of developers, was the main aim of the ministry's land use policy. The task was made more difficult by the fact that the greatest economic pressures and economic justification for development often occurred in precisely those regions where land quality was highest.

Nevertheless, land quality was not homogeneous; variations in quality could occur over quite narrow areas, and relatively small changes in siting could result in appreciable differences in the quality of land taken. There was, therefore, substantial scope for the exercise of judgement in considering the siting of development from the point of view of its effects upon agricultural productivity. To aid in this, the ministry's Agricultural Land Service had recently devised, and was in course of applying throughout England and Wales, a national system of land quality classification, under which land was placed into one of five grades according to the degree to which its physical characteristics imposed long term limitations on agricultural use. The productivity of most classes of land could, of course, be improved by appropriate treatment (drainage, irrigation, fertilisation, etc) and, where this would be likely to be economic under current methods, the classification normally took it into account. As techniques of land improvement developed, new possibilities for the upgrading of poor land might emerge, and to this extent land quality was not immutable. It was, nevertheless, true that under the current system the highest grades of land were those which showed the greatest promise of productivity gains from advances in farming techniques.

The ministry's instructions to regional and divisional offices on the use of land for non-agricultural development were based on these considerations. The working group examined these instructions and found that there was no requirement to undertake a quantitative assessment of the economic value of agricultural land proposed for development, or of the economics of developing an alternative site. Thus the discussion and resolution of issues involving a choice of agricultural sites depended (like the majority of decisions in other sectors) upon qualitative assessment.

(ii) THE MINISTRY OF HOUSING AND LOCAL GOVERNMENT

The Ministry of Housing were responsible for ensuring that the housing needs of the community were met, and that planning for this and other purposes took proper account of the need for economy of resources and the provision of a good environment.

There was no statutory requirement that a local planning authority should consult the Ministry of Agriculture or any other body on the allocation of agricultural land for development in the development plan. However, a 1948 circular (40/1948) recommended that planning authorities should consult the regional land commissioner of the Ministry of Agriculture 'who will advise on the agricultural quality of the land and will indicate areas where development could take place on land of the least agricultural importance and with the minimum of damage to economic farm units'. A later circular (99/1950) emphasised that the minister would require to be satisfied, when development plans were submitted, that full weight had been given to the information obtained from the provincial land commissioner. The circular also stressed the need to settle differences by local agreement at the formative stages of the plan.

At the stage of formal submission of development plans, the Ministry of Agriculture were consulted by MHLG. On all town maps the Ministry of Agriculture thus had, at this stage (as did other departments) a further opportunity to pursue with MHLG any arguments which they had failed to carry with the local planning authority during the preparation of the plan. After the public inquiry, the Ministry of Agriculture were again consulted where it was proposed to act contrary to advice which they had tendered or where any modification proposed by MHLG affected agricultural interests. Local authorities were advised that 'land, even though its cost be low, is one of the nation's most valuable assets', and they were warned against extravagant use of land in 'unnecessarily spacious' layouts. Moreover, housing densities might be rather higher than housing authorities and private developers were accustomed to propose. 'The point of this suggestion was not to reduce standards but, by skilled planning, to secure worthwhile economies.'

A 1958 circular (43/58), though modifying the arrangements for consultations about applications for planning permission, endorsed the policy for safeguarding agricultural land.

The general point which emerged from these instructions was that the case for preserving agricultural land was taken very seriously as a factor in making planning decisions. There was a clear underlying principle that good agricultural land ought to be preserved unless a very cogent case could be advanced for its development. This approach was inherent in the concept of 'safeguarding' illustrated in MHLG circulars. There were a number of other points. First, although the circulars pointed out that avoidance of development on good agricultural land could give rise to increased building costs, no guidance was given on the way in which a quantitative assessment could be made to determine whether this might be worthwhile or not. Secondly, it was not made clear that the avoidance of good agricultural land might involve not only additional capital expenditure but also additional recurring costs. Thirdly, much of the 'bargaining' process involved in making planning decisions without the benefit of 'quantitative guidance' was conducted necessarily at local or regional level.

(iii) THE MINISTRY OF TRANSPORT

In planning new motorways or trunk roads the Ministry of Transport endeavoured to find a route (or routes) which, as far as possible, would meet transport, local planning and amenity considerations, was consistent with the essential engineering standards required, and had due regard to costs. Without a detailed survey and analysis of each possible route, the Ministry of Transport could not, at this stage, make a full quantitative comparison of the costs of alternative routes except insofar as there were clearly foreseeable difficulties on one route, such as extensive bridgeworks or poor soil conditions, or where one route was much longer than the others. Thus, the Ministry of Transport usually finished with a number of routes, all of which were more or less acceptable from the purely transport point of view, and between which the variation in cost would normally be small.

Divisional road engineers or agents of the Ministry of Transport (whether consulting engineers or local authorities) had been instructed to seek the regional land commissioner's views on the general agricultural implications of the possible alternative routes as early as possible, and certainly before the detailed survey of any particular route was undertaken. The commissioners gave a broad appraisal of the agricultural implications of the various possible alternative routes and of the extent to which each might be expected to affect general, but not private, agricultural interests. After taking this advice into account in selecting a particular route or routes for detailed survey, the Ministry of Transport informed the regional land commissioner of the proposed selection. If the regional land commissioner were satisfied that there would be no serious harm to the general agricultural interest he informed the Ministry of Transport by letter that he had no comment on the proposal. The letter of 'no comment' committed the Ministry of Agriculture to acceptance of the broad line of the route proposed. On completion of the detailed survey (and before any draft scheme or order was published), the regional land commissioner was supplied with 'six inch maps' of the proposed route and, as a general rule, with ownership plans and holdings along the route. This afforded the regional land commissioner an opportunity of suggesting minor changes in route to avoid, for example, particular difficulties of farm severance which the detailed maps might reveal.

If agreement could not be reached between the regional land commissioner and the Ministry of Transport, the matter could be referred for settlement at headquarters level. This happened only infrequently.

When consultation was completed, the Ministry of Transport prepared a draft scheme or order setting out the proposed line of route. An advance copy was sent before publication to the headquarters of the Ministry of Agriculture who referred it to the regional land commissioner for confirmation that the proposals were agreed.

(iv) THE TREASURY

The Treasury, of course, had a general responsibility for sanctioning expenditure on planning schemes and for ensuring 'proper economy'. They had not, however, issued any general guidance to departments which might assist in resolving planning matters where the interests of departments often differed. There was thus no agreed quantitative advice, nor even any 'neutral qualitative guidance' which might indicate the lines of a co-ordinated approach to the problem.

The Effects of Current Policies

It was seldom possible to demonstrate precisely the extent to which agricultural factors had influenced past planning decisions because, in many cases, these factors were linked with other planning factors as the reason for the decision. Moreover, there had not necessarily been any record kept of the exact degree to which agriculture entered into the final evaluation. Only the important cases came to the attention of central government, and it was not possible to assess how far, in a climate favourable to the preservation of farmland, the use of good agricultural land for other purposes might have been ruled out from the start.

In the 1960s the increase in the demand for land for development arising from growing population had forced departments to make a more critical examination of the arguments for retaining agricultural land than was evident in the early 1950s. Nevertheless, it seemed that the amount of weight given to agricultural considerations in the past had probably led to additional costs being incurred in some cases. A case in point was the provision for Manchester overspill. Development to cater for this in the Cheshire plain at Lymm was rejected largely for agricultural reasons and, as a result, the housing of Manchester overspill had been seriously delayed. Building had had to take place elsewhere—in the view of MHLG probably at higher costs.

Part of the difficulties arising in connection with the siting of new towns stemmed from the fact that consultants' reports rarely, if ever, supplied any quantitative evidence about the merits of different sites or designation areas. Indeed, in most cases, consultants were asked simply to report on a particular broad area and were not given the opportunity to indicate whether alternative sites much further removed in distance might be more suitable, or less costly, to develop. Dawley, for example, was chosen as the area to be examined by consultants because other suitable sites within reach of Birmingham had been rejected, at least partly, for agricultural reasons. Dawley did not suffer from agricultural objections to the same degree as the alternative sites since it contained large tracts of land which were derelict or subject to mining subsidence. However, this land was relatively expensive to build upon and, moreover, the area suffered the disadvantage of poor communications. On the other hand, the decision to site a new town there was partly due to the fact that it was regarded as an area which could benefit from the rehabilitation which a new town should bring.

MHLG had fully realised, when Dawley was chosen as a new town site, that some extra costs were involved, and the Treasury had similarly been aware of this fact in sanctioning the proposals. These extra costs were probably of the order of £3m to £4m: this represented approximately 3 per cent of the total development costs. These additional costs would be incurred mainly in the early stages of development, and this fact 'accentuated their importance from an economic point of view and especially in relation to existing strains on resources'. On the other hand, offsetting these extra costs was the social value of rehabilitating a depressed area (which was difficult to quantify) and the economic value of the net agricultural advantage gained through building at Dawley rather than elsewhere.

In general, the feasibility studies of consultants did not show consistency of approach to the problem of selecting sites for urban development. Though this was probably due in part to the fact that their terms of reference were too loosely framed, a much more important factor was probably the lack of generally accepted techniques to enable the total comparative costs of urban development at different sites, and in different urban forms, to be broadly calculated.

The Problem of Quantification

The problem of measuring the comparative costs, in the broadest sense, of alternative planning solutions, was not merely one of quantifying the net benefit lost from using an area of good agricultural land. If the equation was to be fully meaningful, all major comparative costs (both capital and recurrent) for, eg the acquisition of land for housing, transport, industry, and common services of alternative sites also required evaluation. Many of these costs were broadly ascertainable in the current state of knowledge. For example, it was usually possible to calculate the extra costs of high rise housing, of building on land affected by mining subsidence, and the probable cost of diverting or building extra lengths of road. It was more difficult to quantify such costs as those of obtaining industry for relatively unattractive sites, of transporting goods extra distances and of the additional travel to work times imposed on employees. It was not always easy to determine what were 'additional' costs since some expenditure might have to take place in a given area whether or not a particular planning scheme was adopted. It was emphasised that, in the absence of precision, a considerable area remained where judgement would have to be exercised. It was desirable, however, to continue to attempt a more sophisticated quantification of planning alternatives in order that decisions could be taken with as much regard to the ascertainable cost factors as was practicable.

Two alternative techniques of valuation were suggested. The first —the discounted cash flow method—involved measuring the net output of the land under optimum conditions and discounting at an appropriate rate the annual value so obtained. The second was to take the current market value and to apply to it 'an assumed factor' reflecting the value of the land to the community.

With the net stream of output method, no attempt was made to arrive at a unique value for agricultural land. What was sought was a technique for making the evaluation; the value arrived at in any particular case would depend on the characteristics of the land, the prices of the output which it produced, and so forth. The method involved making assumptions about four main factors:

(a) whether agricultural output would tend to rise in the future;
(b) whether output should be valued inclusive or exclusive of subsidies;
(c) whether an allowance should be made in the calculations for a future rise, relative to the general price level, of agricultural prices;
(d) the rate of interest to be used in capitalising the stream of outputs.

It was not too difficult to determine appropriate figures for the first two of these assumptions. On (a) it could reasonably be assumed that agricultural output per acre would increase annually by one per cent over the next 25 years. On (b) it was also agreed that net agricultural output should be valued inclusive of subsidies so long as there were subsidies. The case for this was that the subsidies reflected the government's assessment that the value to the community of agricultural output was greater than its market value, especially for balance of payments reasons. If, at some time in the future, either the amount of agricultural support or the method of applying it were substantially altered, agricultural prices (and therefore the valuation of agricultural net output) would reflect the new arrangements and the new value of agricultural output to the community.

The prospective movement of agricultural prices relative to the general level of prices was very difficult to forecast. It depended, among other things, on the rate of rise of productivity in agriculture compared with other sections of the economy, the growth of population, and the income elasticity of demand for food. Apart from the effects of the two world wars, the long term trend appeared to have been for the prices of agricultural products to fall relative to the general level of prices. There was now, however, a new factor in the situation expected for the future—the greatly accelerated growth of population. While the effect this would have on the level of agricultural prices could not be measured, it was provident to assume some rise in the price of agricultural products relative to the general level of prices, even though stability or even a further fall could not be ruled out. The group recommended that a two per cent a year increase in the price of agricultural products relative to the general level of prices should be assumed when an explicit view on the subject was required for the valuation of agricultural land for planning purposes.

The rate of interest used to discount the future benefits from keeping good agricultural land in agricultural use was of key importance. The fundamental point was that if, in order to build on poor land instead of good, extra outlays were incurred, resources were being used to preserve agricultural output instead of being put to other productive uses. Whether it was worthwhile to use the resources to preserve agricultural output therefore depended on what return the resources could have produced in other uses. Current estimates, on which government investment policy was based, suggested a return of eight per cent net of depreciation on new investment in low risk (but not risk free) projects. On the other hand, it had been argued that, since agricultural land gave a yield in perpetuity, an interest rate should be adopted which would be very low, approaching zero. This was the view of the Ministry of Agriculture. To do this, however, would be to put a value on agricultural land, *per se*, much higher than for competing urban uses. Since the decision to incur extra costs by building on poor agricultural land was a decision on the allocation of capital investment, the group (other than the Ministry of Agriculture) recommended the use of the current rate of interest for low risk public investment (currently eight per cent) for discounting the future costs and benefits of incurring additional expenditure to preserve good agricultural land.

An alternative method of evaluation was to take the market price of the land with vacant possession, but with its use restricted to agriculture. This method had the virtue of simplicity. The economic case for this approach was that the market value was a price negotiated between willing buyers and sellers. The buyers could be presumed to be well informed about the value of the output that could be obtained from the land in question by applying to it the other inputs needed (which had alternative uses). Administratively, the market value approach had the important virtue that it was relatively readily ascertainable and, in contrast to the net stream of outputs method, would be familiar to officials and others concerned with planning processes. However, market value was not a sufficiently accurate measure of the economic value of agricultural land to the community. In some aspects it over-valued economic value, while in others it under-valued it.

There were three factors which tended to make market value higher than economic value. First, there were always purchasers who would buy agricultural land to satisfy 'social aspirations' as well as for agricultural purposes. Secondly, many buyers of farmland put an amenity value on the land in addition to its agricultural value. Thirdly, there were concessions in the valuation of agricultural land for estate duty purposes in that only 55 per cent of the normal duty was paid. On the other hand, the price a buyer was willing to pay would depend, in part, on the state in which the previous occupier had maintained the land, 'which might not be up to its inherent quality'. Inherent fertility, however, tended to be recognised to some extent in market prices. Another problematic issue was that, if the terms of trade of agricultural produce were to move against the United Kingdom as a result of a world food shortage or loss of overseas food sources, the economic value of agricultural land would rise. Whether this would, in fact, happen was as yet uncertain. Finally, short term economic fluctuations led to relatively large fluctuations in land prices, whereas the long term economic value of land was relatively stable. However, it would be possible to make an allowance for these short term fluctuations and thus arrive at a figure which would represent the average market price over a complete economic cycle.

Though these factors might limit the usefulness of market value as a measure of economic value, the balance of the arguments inclined towards the view that market value overstated the economic value of agricultural land 'considered exclusively as a productive resource for agriculture'. For example the concession on agricultural land for estate duty purposes added to the market value something which should not be included in the economic value. Nevertheless, 'for practical purposes, it could be assumed that all the factors cancelled each other out'. Indeed, the theory of market value implied that this was the case, and calculations based on capitalising the net stream of outputs suggested that market value remained a very useful guide to economic value to the community within broad limits.

However, it was desirable to recognise imponderable factors such as the future of world food supplies, the limited amount of agricultural land, and the high cost of reclaiming it from non-agricultural use. There was no wholly scientific way of allowing for these factors but, for practical purposes, this could be done by 'uplifting' market price by an appropriate percentage. In deciding on the amount of 'uplift', it was considered reasonable to have regard to the assumption used in discussing the net stream of output method of a rise of two per cent per annum in the relative prices of agricultural products. This implied an uplift of about 25 per cent. The group decided that the broad advantages lay in using market price plus 25 per cent rather than the more complex method of capitalising the net stream of outputs to calculate the value of agricultural land for planning purposes. If, however, it was eventually decided to adopt the net stream of outputs method, then the imponderable factors would be allowed for to a similar extent by adopting the assumption of a rise of two per cent per annum in agricultural prices relative to other prices.

The conclusions of the group were that current instructions to officials did not contain any quantitative guidance on the assessment of the value of agricultural land for planning purposes; that there was much freedom to bargain on this matter at local and regional levels; and that it was therefore desirable to devise a method of quantifying the economic value of agricultural land in order to assist in a more objective costing of alternatives when choosing sites for new development.

In relation to major new urban developments, particularly new towns or large planned expansion schemes, an examination of the reports made by independent consultants had not shown consistency in their treatment of the importance of agriculture and had indicated that, without any quantification of the factors involved, some areas of land had been excluded from consideration of whether urban development was desirable. The group considered that this deficiency should be remedied by an appropriate wording in the terms of reference of consultants. Moreover, the costs of development at alternative sites should be quantified and compared in all cases of major urban expansion where the preferred or most economic site gave rise to objections on agricultural grounds.

So far as roads were concerned, the group considered that although no detailed knowledge of costs of different routes was known when the regional land commissioner's advice was first sought, an attempt should be made to quantify the cost of following the commissioner's advice, if the line favoured by him differed materially from that proposed by the Ministry of Transport. The route which was shown by this method of evaluation to be the most economic should normally be adopted. Farm underpasses or bridges should not usually be provided unless they could be justified on purely compensation grounds. Finally, consideration should be given to the possibility of rearranging farms into economic units, if necessary by the use of compulsory powers.

The market value method of evaluating the economic value of

agricultural land had the attraction of simplicity, was readily ascertainable, was well known to those engaged in planning, and appeared to be a reasonable approximation to economic value. It should, therefore, be adopted; but the special circumstances of agriculture in the economy and in particular the risk of a rise in agricultural prices relative to other prices, should be recognised by uplifting the market price by 25 per cent.

It was considered that this premium recognised, to some degree, the lack of fine precision which was inevitable at this stage of quantitative planning and which was also found in other important aspects of planning for urban growth. The group therefore recommended that until further experience had been obtained, a check on the market value should be made in cases of major importance, such as the selection of designation areas for new towns, by using the net stream of output method. When this was done; the assumption should be that output per acre would increase annually by one per cent over 25 years; that net output should be valued inclusive of subsidies; that an annual rise in prices of two per cent should be assumed; and that the discount rate should be eight per cent.

It was stressed that planning decisions should not always and completely be taken in favour of the lower cost alternative. Major decisions of this kind involved questions of policy, and subjective judgement would always remain an important element. Nevertheless, decisions of policy should rest on a sound factual basis including quantitative analysis.

The Views of the Ministry of Agriculture*

While the Ministry of Agriculture did not disagree with the view that there was a case for attempting to evaluate more scientifically all the costs and benefits involved in the selection of sites for development, they stressed that agricultural land was merely one among a large number of factors to be considered in this context. In their view, the report did not make out a convincing case for concentrating on the evaluation of this one factor, since it did not present any clear evidence that the agricultural land factor received undue weight under existing arrangements. In a paper to the Environmental Planning Committee, the Minister of Agriculture argued:

'When the Labour Government introduced comprehensive town and country planning for the first time in 1947, we did so because we believed that the economy of the market place did not necessarily produce the best result in the long term interests of the nation. We thought, in my view rightly, that current market values should not be allowed to decide such

* EP(67)29.

matters as whether it was better that urban sprawl should continue or that new towns should be built; whether historical monuments should be preserved; or whether scarce and irreplaceable good quality agricultural land should be lost for ever. We considered that such values could not and should not be measured in current monetary terms, which merely record immediate individual values, but must be decided by subjective judgements in the long term interests of the nation.

Yet in this paper it is now suggested that a formula, based on current market values, should be used for guidance where planning decisions involve agricultural land. Even those officials advocating this approach seem to have seen the inconsistency of taking current market values, and have suggested that an arbitrary 25 per cent should be added to these so as to cover the unquantifiable long term benefit to the nation of this scarce natural asset. Nothing could illustrate more clearly the futility of this approach to measure the immeasurable. Why 25 per cent instead of 5 per cent or 500 per cent? There is no way of placing even an approximate monetary value on the need to conserve a scarce productive resource such as agricultural land against all the uncertainties of our food needs for the rest of the century and beyond. In the last resort such factors must be a matter for subjective judgment, and judgment is liable to be confused rather than helped by the provision of spurious figures.

This does not mean that I do not accept the necessity for a substantial annual loss of agricultural land, and for measuring the costs which would be involved in developing different sites. But it is vital to keep this loss to a minimum, and to ensure that development is steered away from good agricultural land whenever a reasonable alternative can be found. I am quite sure that this result cannot be achieved by the application of a formula.'

It was noted that the report stated that 'it seems that the amount of weight given to agricultural considerations in the past has *probably* led to additional costs being incurred in *some* cases' (Ministry of Agriculture emphasis). But the number of such cases was not stated and since, over the previous twenty years, some one million acres of agricultural land had been converted to non-agricultural use—involving several thousands of individual decisions—it was evident that such cases had been 'quite exceptional to the general run'.

Secondly, the Ministry of Agriculture stressed the limitations of the use of purely quantitative techniques. Beyond recommending that every effort should be made to arrive at a reasonable assessment of these factors, the group had not faced up to this difficulty, and was indeed compelled to admit that 'in the absence of precision there must still remain a considerable area where judgement will have to be exercised'.

Thirdly, each of the techniques for the valuation of agricultural land was open to criticism. Under the net stream of outputs method, it could not be regarded as reasonable to discount the future output from agricultural land at the rate of eight per cent currently used in relation to some (though not all) public investment projects. While eight per cent or an even higher rate might be an appropriate test for capital assets subject to a short economic life, it could not be appropriate to use a similar rate for discounting the benefit of agricultural production in perpetuity. As regards market value, it was surely fallacious to equate the expectations of individual buyers and sellers over their own limited time horizon with the considerations that should govern the community in its assessment of future needs and benefits; and the gap between the two was in no way bridged by adding to market value an arbitrary percentage.

The difficulties, however, went deeper than questions of methodology. The Ministry of Agriculture held that no basis for the valuation of agricultural land could be considered as satisfactory unless it took fully into account not only the permanence of agricultural land as a source of production—together with the fact that its amount was limited, and that a decision to convert it to other uses was to all intents and purposes irreversible—but also the whole range of unpredictable factors which might govern the future food needs of the community, including the possibility of unforeseen emergencies, natural or man made, which might call for a sudden and unprecedented expansion of domestic output.

The Ministry of Agriculture were therefore unable to accept the group's conclusions and recommendations, and were 'strongly opposed to any suggestion that they should be promulgated to officials and others concerned with planning'.

*Impasse**

Ministers discussed the report in October 1967. There was complete agreement with the principle that, wherever possible, good agricultural land should not be taken for development, 'but it was necessary to make the best possible assessment of land values if sensible planning decisions were to be taken'. The majority of ministers agreed that the evaluation techniques set out in the report should be regarded as useful tools in considering planning problems. Subject to reservations by the Minister of Agriculture, it was agreed that officials should prepare guidelines on the lines proposed in the report.

Progress on the issue of guidance was slow, and had no impact on new town development; but on the same day that the EP Committee discussed the matter, they agreed the designation of 20,000 acres of land to the west and south-west of Ipswich against the recommendation of the Minister of Agriculture who favoured development to the east to minimise the loss of good quality land.†

---

* EP(67)11th Meeting, 23 October 1967; Treasury Files 2AT 39/78/02 and 2AT 56/39/03; and Cabinet Office File C 46/A/5.
† The Ipswich scheme was later abandoned, though not for agricultural reasons; see chapter V, p. 269 *et seq.*

Nevertheless, the Minister of Agriculture maintained his strong objection to the whole exercise and there were lengthy inter-departmental and interministerial discussions and correspondence.

Eventually, an interdepartmental committee of officials (under Treasury chairmanship) was established to determine the instructions which should be drawn up to give guidance to departments on assessing the economic value of agricultural land. This committee ran into heavy weather mainly because of the opposition of the Ministry of Agriculture who, for their part, considered that the exercise was of little practical value. A basic disagreement on the question of the bodies to whom these instructions were to be issued could not be resolved by officials, and had to be referred to ministers. They decided that the 'trial' should be limited to government departments.

One year later (in November 1969) departments were requested by the Treasury to submit reports on their experience in implementing the new technique, but most departments had had no cases in which the technique could be used. (It was to be applied to any major area of agricultural land considered for development—taken to be 50 acres or more—for which an alternative site was possible.) The Ministry of Transport noted that in no case did the 'enhancement by 25 per cent of the value of any agricultural land' make a significant difference:

> 'This is not surprising since the cost of land in schemes of largely rural character is in the range 2 per cent to 12 per cent (with an average about 5 per cent) of the total scheme cost. Thus even if all the land on one line, and none on the most favourable alternative, is agricultural—a most improbable situation—the addition of 25 per cent to the value of agricultural land will only alter the cost difference between the two lines by 1·5 per cent. The effect on an economic rate of return of, say, 20 per cent would be a mere 0·3 per cent. These amounts are much too small to influence a decision on a line.'

Even the Ministry of Agriculture had 'very little' to report, referring only to three cases of which they were aware where 'some attempt' had been made at a cost-benefit calculation—Ipswich new town, the Morecambe Bay Barrage, and the third London Airport.

As a result, the committee decided that they had to report to ministers that 'the information obtained seemed too sparse to enable any definite recommendations to be made'. This was in March 1970: a date beyond that at which this history must terminate. It has to be sufficient to record that although a further working group of economists was set up to examine the issue further (to provide the basis of a submission to ministers) the Ministry of Agriculture 'considered that the importance of agricultural land made it in some ways priceless, and could see no reliable scientific techniques for valuing it'. Nevertheless, they were prepared to consider the results of the assessment to be made by the working group of economists.

Starting from such widely divergent premises it is not surprising that this issue was one on which neither officials nor ministers could possibly reach agreement. But the basic conflict remains, and the continuation of the story (which obviously must be a matter for a future historian) will need to be set against the changing attitudes to the safeguarding of natural resources which emerged in the 'seventies.

APPENDIX C

Land Acquisition

'It is the clear intention, when an area is designated, to acquire all the land in the area. The only doubt is when the land will be bought.' So said Silkin in the debates on the New Towns Bill.* This intention was confirmed by the right of an owner whose land had not been acquired within seven years to require the corporation to purchase it.

Development corporations, with the consent of the minister, were able to obtain land by agreement, or by means of a compulsory purchase order confirmed by the minister. The procedures for compulsory acquisition, and for determination of compensation, are embodied in a mass of complex legislation, which has been modified from time to time—and sometimes drastically. A detailed discussion of the successive Acts is given in volume IV of this history; but, briefly, the Act of 1947 established a comprehensive system of planning control under which land could not be developed without planning permission; development rights were nationalised; and owners had to buy back the right to develop by paying a development charge. Owners were to be compensated for the loss of development values from a £300m fund, and it was assumed that in these circumstances land would be bought and sold at existing use value. As a logical corollary, compensation for compulsory acquisition was limited to existing use value. In 1953, development charges were abolished and owners whose land was compulsorily acquired received their established claims in addition to the existing use value. This resulted in a two price system—one for private sales, the other for public or compulsory purchases, which in some cases, and particularly on the fringes of growing towns, fell far short of market value. Mounting disquiet on this led, in 1959, to the return to market value compensation. The 1959 Act established the principle that the owner of land compulsorily acquired should receive the value he could expect in a private sale in the open market. This applied generally to acquisition by public authorities, but special provision was made for new towns, where any increase (or loss) of value due to the development or prospects of development was excluded. In other

---

* HC Debates, Vol 424, Col 2559, 5 July 1946.

words, the acquiring authority was protected from paying for the value created by the very scheme for which they were buying the land.*

In 1947 the development corporations were thinking in terms of the immediate acquisition by agreement of all property which came on the market, to be followed as soon as practical by a compulsory purchase order for the whole of the designated area. In commending this conception to the Treasury, the ministry explained that it was necessary because 'landlord control is a finer and more effective instrument than planning control can ever be'; and that 'the creation of a new town will give rise to great betterment of the existing built up area . . . which should enure to the benefit of the corporation'.†
The ministry therefore proposed that development corporations should proceed by way of comprehensive purchase, and then lease the properties back to the existing or new occupiers until they were required for the development of the town, and at a premium which would reduce the capital outlay. The reaction of the Treasury was that the premature purchase of land was inflationary in giving the owner liquid resources in place of land values which were not normally easily or quickly realisable; that possession of land was a temptation to press on with physical development which in existing circumstances had to be drastically restricted; that any such scheme would place a heavy burden on technical manpower; and that they could not agree that shop property likely to appreciate in value and all property coming on the market should immediately be bought up. In their view land should normally be purchased only when needed for immediate development or redevelopment.‡

---

* When the Cabinet considered the proposals to return to market values for compulsory acquisition, the original decision was to make an exception for the new towns, where many of the corporations still had to buy a good deal of land within the designated area, and where the value had become very high as a result of the development already carried out—at market value the cost might be £5,000 per acre as against £100–£200 under existing use plus claim. As these values had been created wholly by public expenditure, it was considered that there was justification for retaining the current basis of compensation for land within areas already designated. (C(58)151 of 16 July 1958 and CC(58)63rd Conclusions, 22 July 1958.)
  In subsequent discussion with the local authority associations, it became clear that they would object strongly to any arrangement which relieved the acquiring authority from the cost of going over to market value only when exchequer money was involved. It was therefore proposed that 'the benefit of exemption from the market value principle should not be secured for the exchequer alone, and that in assessing compensation both in the new towns and in other areas of comprehensive development, the principle should be adopted of ignoring the effect on land values of the scheme for which the land was being bought. This would make rather more expensive the acquisition of land in new towns, but the cost would still be much less than market value.' It was this principle which was embodied in the 1959 Act. (HA(58)18th Meeting on 30 September 1958.)
  † MHLG File 91650/56/2/1.
  ‡ The background to the Treasury view included the fact that they were about to issue £2000m of government guaranteed fixed interest stocks for the nationalisation of coal, transport, gas and electricity, and were apprehensive of the purchasing power the sale of these stocks might release. It was at this time that the ceiling of '300 building workers' was imposed on London towns—see chapter II, p. 78 *et seq.*

Initially the development corporations tended to be restive that they could not get authority for comprehensive advance purchases but, by 1951, the position had become established that authority would normally be given for the purchase of land required for operations during the following two or three years.* Corporations were thus able to establish a steady programme of purchase geared to their programme of development, enabling them to be sure of obtaining possession somewhat ahead of need. Moreover, it rapidly became clear that there were cases where it was unnecessary to purchase particular parcels of land, for example land permanently occupied by local authorities or statutory undertakers. Additionally, there was land which it was unnecessary to acquire (unless the owner wished to sell)—particularly areas of relatively recent development. In December 1962 corporations were authorised to buy land without the limitation of requirement during the next two or three years, and in July 1963 a general consent was given to acquisition by agreement of any land within the designated area.

Compensation in New Town Extensions†
Following *The South East Study* increasing concern was expressed (particularly by the Treasury) at the cost of compulsorily acquiring land for new town extensions. Though the 1959 Act had provided that the designated areas of new towns should be subject to special provisions (ie that the value of the scheme should be ignored) this did not apply to later extensions of the designated area.

The 1959 Act (Section 6 of the consolidating Land Compensation Act 1961) extended the long established principle that, when land was bought compulsorily 'for the purposes of a scheme', value attributable to the carrying out of development under the scheme (or to the prospect of such development) was excluded from the assessment of compensation. Under this Act, the definition of a 'scheme' was widened to include a number of other cases (eg comprehensive development areas, designated new towns, and areas of town development). In the case of an extension of the designated area of a new town, however, the only value which could be excluded was that which was attributable to development (or the prospect of development) on other land within the boundaries of the compulsory purchase order under which the land was being acquired.

At the time when the 1959 Act was passed it had not been envisaged that new town extensions would be significant. In fact major extensions were made to the designated area of Bracknell in

---

* MHLG File 91650/56/2/4.
† H(66)54 and H(66)15th Meeting, 1 July 1966; and Secretary's Bill Papers 424.

1961 and 1962 and to Corby in 1963. There were also firm proposals for Aycliffe as well as for Harlow and Stevenage.

In spite of the higher prices involved in the acquisition of land in these extended areas, the ministry were reluctant to accede to Treasury pressure for amending legislation. They were particularly concerned at the opposition which would develop against extensions (which had already been 'strong enough' in Stevenage). Moreover, if amending legislation were to be passed, 'it would sterilise the land on the outskirts of every new town designated area for fear of further extensions in the future'. In their view it was wiser to await the Land Commission Bill which would 'take away much of the need' for additional 'safeguards' and would avoid the political embarrassment of a separate Bill. In any case, the costs of land acquisition were not sufficiently substantial in relation to the total costs of new town development 'to make it worthwhile arousing more opposition'.

Following exploratory discussions with the Treasury, the Ministry of Housing proposed that they should discuss with the Ministry of Land the possibility of an appropriate provision being included in the Land Commission Bill. The Ministry of Land, however, were strongly opposed to this. The Land Commission Bill would in no way affect the basis of valuation and they were 'emphatic that it should be kept this way'. The proposal would greatly complicate the work of parliamentary counsel (who was already having difficulty in coping with the Bill in 'the extremely tight timetable'), and would considerably widen the scope of the Bill—and thus the opportunity for debate and amendment.

The Treasury, however, were insistent that amending legislation was necessary, and eventually the Ministry of Housing accepted, though 'without enthusiasm'. Since it was agreed that it would be undesirable to widen the scope of the Land Commission Bill, some other vehicle had to be found for the appropriate single clause provision. It was finally proposed that this should be the new towns money Bill of 1966.

The matter was taken to the Home Affairs Committee in July 1966 when it was explained that the original exclusion 'seemed right and sufficient at the time bearing in mind the small extensions to which we were then accustomed, in relation to which public or private losses would have been minimal'. The position now was very different:

'New town areas are now being extended by incomparably larger areas than was contemplated in 1958. Possible losses can no longer reasonably be ignored. It is therefore proposed to amend the law so that where, after the Act comes into operation, an order extends a new town designated area, the price paid on public purchase of land in the extension area, while still taking full account of values attributable to the new town as already designated (those values would have been established before the area was extended), would exclude all increase or diminution attributable to the extension.

Amendment of the law in this way is likely to save large sums of public money. It should cause no actual loss to owners and will be more fair than the present law to the small number of owners whose property has diminished in value as a result of new town extension.'

This was agreed by the Home Affairs Committee, though some concern was expressed at 'the increasing tendency to add additional points to straightforward and non-contentious essential Bills'.

In deciding not to make these provisions for extension areas in 1959, the Conservative Government had had it in mind that land adjacent to a new town would change hands between initial designation and extension at prices which would reflect changes in value caused by the new town. It followed that an owner might receive less in compensation than he had paid for the land. The same point worried ministers in 1966 and this was dealt with by making the extension area 'self-contained' for the purposes of assessing compensation. In other words, the price to be paid by a public authority in an extension area would still include any development value reflected on to that land by the existing new town. It would exclude only the enhancement arising from development (other than the land in question) in the extension area itself. (The same applied to any diminution in value.)

There was a curious corollary of this: prices in the original designated area would be similarly calculated without taking into account any effect on values of the extension. This was justified on the ground that, without it, a new anomaly would be created which would be closely akin to that which the proposed Bill sought to remove. Whereas the owner in an extension area would receive at least half (and 'probably much more') of 'the total new town values allowed to him', the owner in the initial designated area would get none. Thus a new two price system would be introduced.

The issue was one of particular concern to Dawley new town where an 'extension area' of huge proportions (more than double the original area) was under consideration. Had it been possible to 'amalgamate' the original designated area and the extension a very large saving in land acquisition costs could have been secured. A ministry official commented:

'I would not deny that the solution we are adopting is not a theoretically perfect solution but I do believe that it goes just as far as we possibly can in a practical world bearing in mind the general climate regarding compensation, the fact that we are unwilling to impinge in the slightest upon compensation which would become due to any landowner surrounded by normal development processes (as distinct from major new town developments) and remembering also that the alternative to the present proposals would be to designate an extension as a separate new town. If in fact we resorted to this device (as we might be forced to if the legislation does not go through), then the situation would be precisely the same as if the legislation did go through. Such a situation would be no different from that which has existed for many years between Hatfield and Welwyn Garden City.'

In fact, of course, no 'theoretically perfect solution' could be attempted while ever the two price system remained.

APPENDIX D

Parliamentary Control

The Act of 1946 gave the minister general powers to initiate a programme of new towns. The Act of 1959 provided for the establishment of the Commission for the New Towns and enabled the minister to transfer the property of the development corporations (in England and Wales) to the Commission when he was satisfied that their purpose had been substantially achieved. In neither case was the minister required by the Acts to obtain the specific approval of Parliament to the creation of a new town or to its transfer to the commission.* Nevertheless in accordance with the general principle of ministerial responsibility, the minister was answerable in Parliament for the generality of the action—or inaction—he had taken; and in practice this extended to questions in Parliament relating to a wide range of matters such as designation, appointment of members, approval of master plans, the making of grants and advances, and the tempo at which work proceeded.

The Act of 1946 provided for an annual report, with accounts audited by professional auditors, to be submitted by each corporation to the minister, which he was required to lay before Parliament. In addition, the minister was required to transmit to the Comptroller and Auditor General an account of the sums advanced by him from the consolidated fund together with the accounts of the corporations, and the Comptroller and Auditor General was required to examine and certify these and to lay copies with his report before each House of Parliament. But this financial control only became exercisable *after* a new town had been designated and the corporation had been appointed.

In the early years the reports of the Comptroller and Auditor General were considered by the Public Accounts Committee, who took the opportunity to examine in a friendly spirit several of the chairmen about the progress they were making and the difficulties they were encountering.† But the main control which Parliament had over the new town programme was the limitation placed on the

---

* A Treasury view (which was not sustained) is given in chapter I, p. 24.

† On 27 February 1958, the Public Accounts Committee examined the permanent secretary on the financial arrangements with the corporations. In the course of her evidence she said 'there is an extremely close control by the ministry and the Treasury on all spending by the corporations. I would myself venture the opinion, too close a control . . . a harrowing control'. The committee made no report on her evidence.

amount of advances which could be made from the consolidated fund for capital purposes. The Act of 1946 limited the amount for new towns in England, Wales and Scotland to £50m. By 1950 the advances were about £20m, but the Public Accounts Committee pointed out:

> 'If Parliament is not asked to increase the present limit on advances until commitments approaching this amount have been approved, its right of determining what sums it will make available to the executive will to some extent be prejudiced, since part at least of the expenditure already incurred would be wasted unless further advances were then authorised.'*

Accordingly, the practice developed of introducing the Bills which were required to increase the limit of advances at dates when approvals were significantly below the limit previously authorised. Thus a margin was provided for completion of work should Parliament decide on restriction. The limits were set as follows:†

New Towns Act of:	Limit of Advances	Advances Approved at Date of Introduction
	£m	£m
1946	50	
1952	100	42
1953	150	89
1955	250	141
1958	300	225
1959	400	253
1964	550	335
1966	800	535
1969	1,100	720

The Acts of 1952, 1953, 1955, 1964 and 1969 were single section measures simply increasing the limit. In addition, the Act of 1958 removed a duplication in the printing and presentation to Parliament of the annual accounts of the corporations which previously had appeared both in the annual reports of the corporations and in the report of the Comptroller and Auditor General. The Act of 1959 established the Commission for the New Towns (applicable to England and Wales), while the Act of 1966 extended the provisions of the Land Compensation Act 1961 to extensions of an existing new town.‡ The short Bills extending the limit of advances were generally unopposed, but the occasion was taken for ministers (including Scottish and Welsh ministers) to report to Parliament on

---

* Fourth Report of the Public Accounts Committee, 1950, paragraph 106.

† At the time of writing the limit (set by the New Towns Act 1975) is £1,750m and, subject to an affirmative resolution of the House of Commons, can be increased to £2,250m.

‡ See appendix C.

progress and prospects, and for a wide ranging debate on the problems surrounding the new towns.

Two other Acts were consolidation measures—the New Towns Act 1965 (which applied to England and Wales), and the New Towns (Scotland) Act 1968.

Despite the very large amounts of public expenditure involved in the new towns, there had been little pressure for a greater degree of parliamentary control. The issue was raised by the Public Accounts Committee in 1950 when Reith (then chairman of Hemel Hempstead Development Corporation) suggested a royal commission to examine the relationship which ought to exist between Parliament, the minister and the various public boards which had recently been established—including but not confined to new towns. The committee did not pursue this, but suggested that:

'although the minister is not required to seek the approval of or even to inform Parliament before additional new towns are designated, it might be well to consider whether Parliament should be informed of the minister's intention before he embarks on the heavy commitments involved.'*

The Treasury minute on this suggestion was:

'My Lords have given careful consideration to the proposal but hesitate to recommend its adoption. The committee are of course aware that Parliament placed upon the minister the responsibility of designating new towns. In view of this My Lords feel that it would hardly be proper now to invite him to exercise that responsibility only under the further sanction of Parliament in each case.'†

The point was raised on 31 March 1952 during the debate on the New Towns Bill. Macmillan, who was then Minister of Housing and Local Government, argued that it was unsatisfactory that there was no parliamentary control, and that 'I have the right to designate any number of new towns I like.' He implied that in future he would inform Parliament of any additional proposals for new towns.‡ The issue arose again in 1963 when it became known that there was a possibility of expanding Stevenage beyond its target population of 80,000 to 130–140,000. A local agitation arose and, in a debate in the House of Commons on 20 January 1964, the Hertfordshire members voiced strong objection to what they regarded as 'the creation of a vast new conurbation in the county under which Stevenage would merge with Luton, Welwyn and Hatfield'. These objections led to what was apparently the first serious consideration of parliamentary control over the designation of new towns and, indeed, to legislative change. It is worth summarising this short story.

---

* Fourth Report of the Public Accounts Committee, 1950, paragraph 107.
† Included in First Report of PAC 1950/51.
‡ HC Debates, Vol 498, Col 1308, 31 March 1952.

THE MADDAN BILL*

The Hertfordshire MPs were predominantly concerned with opposing the proposals for the expansion of Stevenage, but this quickly led them to press for parliamentary approval for all new towns and new town extensions. Notice was given by Maddan (MP for Hitchin) that he proposed to introduce a Private Member's Bill under the Ten Minute Rule to give effect to this.

Within the department, the immediate reaction was one of some surprise that the issue had not arisen earlier. At ministerial level, concern began to mount over the strength of the opposition to the specific Stevenage extension proposal, and it was felt that the general case being put forward by Hertfordshire MPs for parliamentary control had some merit. These doubts probably account for the decision of the Legislation Committee that, though the Bill 'need not be opposed, it should not be allowed to make further progress'. But also of importance was the fact that a convincing case against the Bill had not at this stage been elaborated: there was merely the feeling that existing arrangements had worked satisfactorily, that Maddan's proposals could be 'the thin edge of the wedge' and could arguably be applied to a wide range of other areas (for example new motorways, airports, or universities), and—less explicitly in the records—that the Hertfordshire MPs were merely deploying general arguments to assist them on a specific case.

However, the Bill began to attract considerable support from government backbenchers and from the Opposition. Ministers— and officials—expressed increasing concern about the delays which the Bill, if enacted, would create. Moreover, the issue was politically embarrassing: 'we should help Conservative members *if* it can be done without loss of face or disruption of principle'; yet, at the same time, there was a lack of conviction at least on the part of ministers, that the case against the Bill was adequate. In the result, the Home Policy Committee compromised and agreed that, if the Hertfordshire members could not be persuaded to drop the Bill, the Government 'would not object' to applying the negative resolution procedure to orders establishing new towns, but they could not accept the use of this procedure to orders relating to the extension of existing new towns. Since it was precisely the latter which the Hertfordshire MPs wanted, they rejected this compromise—and they obtained sufficient support in standing committee to defeat the Government: Maddan and his supporters were joined by the Opposition, and the voting against the Government was ten to three.

---

* LP(64)8th Meeting, 10 March 1964, LP(64)13th Meeting, 28 April 1964, HP(64) 15th Meeting, 1 May 1964; and Secretary's Bill Papers 416.

The Government accepted the defeat, and the Bill passed all stages without further debate in the Commons on 26 June 1964. In the Lords, though Silkin mildly complained of the delays which would ensue he expressed the view that the issue was relatively unimportant. The Bill was passed without a division.

The resulting New Towns (No 2) Act 1964* provided that orders designating a new town or extending the area of an existing new town by 10 per cent or more (but with a minimum of 500 acres), *and* if objected to by a local planning authority, should be subject to annulment by either House of Parliament within forty sitting days.

This procedure was invoked on 27th November 1967, when the MP for Peterborough, supported by several members for neighbouring constituencies, moved the annulment of the Peterborough designation order. The purpose was not to object to the scheme, but to record the apprehensions of the local authorities 'as to who pays for what'. The parliamentary secretary (MacColl) in replying said that on certain matters he 'hoped to make a generous agreement with them', but the main responsibility would rest with the development corporation when they had been appointed. This satisfied the mover and the motion for annulment was withdrawn without a division.†

Though the Maddan Act is of interest it is, in fact, only of peripheral importance. It arose almost by accident and is, perhaps, of more significance to students of the political process than to those concerned with the history of the new towns. Of greater noteworthiness is the fact that, during the period covered by this history, it was the only occasion on which Parliament came near to debating the issue of parliamentary control over major decisions by the Executive on new towns. It was not until 1974 that the first major review of new towns was instigated by Parliament.‡ By this time, total expenditure on all British new towns had reached the figure of £1,500m.

---

* On consolidation this became S53(5) of the New Towns Act 1965.
† HC Debates, Vol 755, Cols 171–197, 27 November 1967.
‡ See *Thirteenth Report from the Expenditure Committee, Session 1974–75: New Towns*, HC 616, HMSO, 1975.

APPENDIX E

Report of the Interdepartmental Group on Administrative and Legislative Arrangements Needed for the Development of Satellite or New Towns (Pepler Report)
1944

In view of its historical importance, the Pepler report, of which a short summary was given in chapter I,* is reproduced in full in this appendix. The report makes reference to the Town and Country Planning Bill which was before Parliament during the later stages of the group's deliberations. This became the 1944 Act, and reference to its relevant provisions are given in an addendum to the report.

1. The group was set up to pursue in greater detail the problems already discussed at the twelfth meeting of the interdepartmental conference held on 3 January 1944, under the joint chairmanship of Sir John Wrigley and Mr Neal, and to make proposals as to the administrative and legislative arrangements needed for the development of satellite or new towns; and in particular as to the constitution, functions, and finances of the necessary developing body or bodies.

2. At the meetings held on 2 and 26 June and 20 July, the group considered existing legislative powers which might be used for the purpose. The nearest approach to the legislative provision required was found in section 35 of the Town and Country Planning Act, 1932 concerning garden city development by a local authority, a combination of local authorities, or an authorised association. Consideration was also given to 'joint bodies' authorised under an operative planning scheme to carry out the scheme (section 11(2) of the Town and Country Planning Act, 1932) and 'joint boards' constituted under section 6 of the Public Health Act, 1936. The position of housing associations generally, the Central Housing Association and of the special North Eastern Housing Association Ltd, was reviewed in relation to housing aspects of satellite development (sections 93–96 of the Housing Act, 1936).

3. The group also had regard to the provisions of the Town and

---

* Chapter I, pp. 6–8.

Country Planning Bill which has passed the second reading, in so far as it proposed to provide powers for an 'exporting local authority' compulsorily to acquire land, outside its own boundaries if necessary, for the settlement of its 'overspill' (clauses 2 and 9) and to carry out operational development on such land (clause 16).

4. Past experiments in the nature of large scale developments undertaken by big exporting authorities were considered. Amongst them are Dagenham, providing for overspill from London, and Wythenshawe from Manchester. Both have largely taken the form of extensive suburbs and dormitories, and Wythenshawe has been incorporated in the parent town. Neither was designed to provide for adequate industrial development, and neither possesses balance, or the corporate consciousness of a separate township.

5. The trading estates at Slough and Trafford Park resulted in lack of balance in the other direction, as industry outpaced housing and workpeople had to find homes elsewhere and spend much time travelling to work.

6. At Corby a new town had been built by a single industrial undertaking. It appears, however, to be undesirable for any town to be dependent upon a single industry because of the danger of paralysis in the event of a slump in that industry. The Government's employment policy is definitely against any locality having all its eggs in one basket.

7. The most successful experiments in the construction of new townships are those at Letchworth and Welwyn Garden City, both developed by special corporations which took the form of public companies registered in 1903 and 1920 respectively under the Companies Act and limited as to distribution of dividends. The process was necessarily slow, far too slow to meet the requirements of postwar development in areas 'designated' under clause 1 of the Town and Country Planning Bill. Moreover, since these experiments were initiated, local authorities have been given, and under the Bill will be given, wider powers which will enable some of them to undertake expeditiously the kind of work which the Letchworth and Welwyn companies achieved as pioneers by long negotiation, anxious trial and much ingenuity. These companies did, however, achieve the development of balanced townships, much nearer to the group's conception of what a new town should be than any of the other experiments carried out in this country. This was due no doubt to the fact that they started with the ideal of a complete self-contained township as their objective and were free from the predominating influence of a large town seeking mainly a place of residence for

people whom it wished to retain within its own sphere of influence, if not within its own administrative area.

8. The group felt that the postwar problem of the resettlement of overspill from war-damaged and over-populated cities was not likely to work out in practice merely as a simple transfer from a parent town to a new town, not far distant, to be built on virgin soil. There would be many combinations each postulating its own variant in local organisation and administration. Examples are ready to hand and already require urgent attention.

(1) London required numerous new developments, each to provide for overspill from several metropolitan boroughs and extra-metropolitan areas, and the position in the reception areas will vary according to the extent of existing development in the reception areas selected. Oxhey for example would naturally be built on to the substantial Borough of Watford while a new town erected at Chipping Ongar would itself far exceed in new population the nucleus on which it is to be grafted.

(2) Portsmouth has already purchased land, partly in Havant and Waterloo urban district and mainly in Petersfield rural district, for the settlement of a population of 30,000 where there is now no development to speak of.

(3) Plymouth contemplates on overspill of 40,000 divided into five or six developments, some based on a small borough or urban district (Saltash or Torpoint) and others in neighbouring rural districts, but all grafted on to some existing development, and, though outside the county borough boundary, within the range of the one joint planning committee area.

(4) There will be further variants concerning Manchester, Liverpool and Leeds.

9. Apart from the provision for overspill problems there are other circumstances in which the establishment of new towns must be contemplated. The following are examples:

(1) In some parts of the country (eg south-west Durham and south Wales) there are villages which have been derelict for a long time and have no hope of industrial revival. The Government have already announced its intentions to make some provision for these places without having recourse to compulsory long distance transfer. The establishment of industry in each village is quite impracticable but the development of some industrial undertakings somewhere near is feasible and probably essential. There is, however, no local authority in the neighbourhood strong enough or suitably equipped to plan and execute any scheme for establishing a new

township nearby (see paragraphs 29 and 30 of the white paper on Employment Policy—Cmd 6527). Some means must be found, probably with the help of central government initiative (see paragraphs 23, 24 and 26 below) and finance (see paragraph 18 below), to develop new towns in these areas and hand them over either to existing or to new local authorities for administration.

(2) There are instances where industrial undertakings have evacuated themselves to rural areas, or where wartime factories have been erected in country districts and where, in both types of case, they will remain for peacetime work. In some cases a new town may be required. It will have no particular parent town to relieve of its surplus population but will be open to all comers. Ashchurch in Gloucestershire, where the possibility of establishing a new town has been considered, is a case in point.

Recommendations

10. *Development by Existing Authorities*

(1) The group consider that movement of population will generally take the form of additions to established small towns or large villages rather than that of the creation of entirely new towns erected on virgin soil. Where the receiving area is a moderate sized borough or an urban district, or even a rural district having substantial nucleus development and some experience and adequate technical assistance, the receiving area itself should normally undertake responsibility for development in agreement with the exporting city or town (usually a county borough), and with the backing of the county council. It will greatly facilitate such an arrangement if the exporting and receiving authorities are members of the same joint planning committee. The agreement should provide, *inter alia*, for the exporting town or towns to pay to the receiving authority the state subsidies and rate subsidies which they would have received or paid if they had undertaken the development themselves. The receiving authority would have power under section 79 of the Housing Act, 1936, to sell or lease land for housing development, and to invoke the assistance of housing associations. In this connection it is now proposed that government subsidies may, for a limited period, be available for private enterprise in housing as well as for local authority housing schemes. When a large addition is made to a small town it will need a measure of redevelopment of the existing town to enable it to absorb the addition without putting undue strain upon the old fabric. Inasmuch as the provision for readjustment is inevitable when any expansion takes place, it is not thought that it would be reasonable to charge the cost of it to the exporting authority as a part of the new development. If the exporting

local authority is unable to agree with the receiving authority on the basis outlined above, a joint developing body should be constituted on the lines recommended in paragraph 11 below.

(2) Where the receiving area local authority (or there may be two of them affected) is a small urban district or rural district with little nucleus development or experience, the county council for the receiving area might undertake the major responsibility but with such help as can be provided by the exporting and receiving authorities respectively.

(3) Section 35 of the Town and Country Planning Act, 1932, provides that land required for this form of development, either by local authorities (including county councils) or authorised associations (see 11(2) below) shall be acquired, either by agreement or compulsorily, by the minister on their behalf. It is essential that the receiving authority, (1) above, or the county council, (2) above, should be able to acquire the necessary land either in their own right or through the minister. Clause 1(2) of the Town and Country Planning Bill only provides for purchase by the war-damaged exporting authority (see 12(2) below).

11. *Constitution of Joint Developing Body*

(1) Where, in the receiving area, there is no local authority with adequate experience or resources to undertake development on the required scale as in 10(1) above, and the county council does not accept responsibility as in 10(2) above, or where the exporting local authority is not prepared to co-operate along the lines of 10(1) or 10(2) above, the group consider that it would be advisable to create a joint developing body. This should be a joint body representing the local authorities concerned (exporting and receiving authorities and the county council of the receiving area) with the option of co-opting private individuals. The object of co-option should be to secure the services of individuals able, either by personal qualifications or representative influence, to render special services. This body should be a body corporate with power to acquire land, to undertake operative development, building, etc to lease, and, subject to Ministerial approval, to sell land and buildings. It should hold powers to carry out all functions set out in paragraph 12 below. (See paragraphs 13 and 14 below for legislative powers and paragraphs 15 to 21 on finance.)

(2) Provision should also be made to enable a private company (subject to limited dividend) such as Hampstead Garden Suburb Trust Ltd to acquire land and develop it for similar purposes. If compulsory acquisition is necessary in this case it should be exercised

by the minister for the company as at present provided in section 35 of the Town and Country Planning Act of 1932.

12. *Functions of Joint Developing Body.* If a joint developing body is appointed, it should have complete control from the commencement of the scheme with the object of producing a balanced township, whether its immediate object is to absorb the overspill of the exporting town or towns or to create a new town open to all comers. Its aim should be to secure the town's complete physical development within reasonable time, and ultimately, in the case of a completely new town, its independent political enfranchisement as a new urban district. This involves:

(1) *Planning.* It is particularly desirable that all the local authorities represented on the joint developing body should be members of the same executive joint planning committee which will undertake the planning of the satellite development.

(2) *Acquisition of necessary land.* The Town and Country Planning Bill provides for compulsory acquisition by the exporting authority, but ownership should be transferred to, or vested in, the joint developing body. Also provision should be made for acquisition by the minister on behalf of a joint developing body.

(3) *Preparation* of roads, services and sites for building of all types.

(4) *Erection and estate management* of buildings, houses (not all working class), shops, community centres, schools, etc and some industrial buildings, sufficiently to establish a nucleus and bring the town up to the stage at which private enterprise would be attracted and would progressively undertake independent development. Clause 16 of the Bill limits these powers to the exporting authority. They should be in the hands of the joint developing body. Some control of private enterprise would be essential in cases where provision is to be made for overspill from congested areas to ensure that, so far as necessary, the new town is occupied by people from the area needing to be reduced in density.

(5) As owner and sole landlord the joint developing body would receive all estate revenue, rents, leases, etc while rate revenue would go to the local authority (or authorities) for the receiving area.

(6) *Final transfer of property and of assets and liabilities* (eg outstanding loans) to the new local authority for the new town.

13. *Legislative powers required for Joint Developing Body.* As indicated in paragraph 2 above, section 35 of the Town and Country Planning Act, 1932, provides the nearest approach to the legislative provisions required for the establishment of a joint developing body. In the opinion of the group, however, the provisions of the section fall short of requirements in the following respects:

(1) Local authorities may act jointly but nothing is said as to how joint action is to be operated.

(2) Local authorities cannot join up with or be represented on an authorised association, nor can they contribute to its finances.

(3) There is much doubt as to the meaning of the words 'to develop' and 'development' as used in the section. The group took the view that the definition of 'development' in section 53 of the Act did not apply to the use of the word in section 35. The term as it stands might be interpreted as limiting a local authority to the powers of development which it possesses under other statutes (eg housing for the working classes), whereas the powers now required are to develop anything needed for a new town, such as the powers contemplated in clause 16 of the Town and Country Planning Bill.

(4) The term 'garden city' is not adequately defined and hardly covers the type of development now contemplated.

14. The group recommends, therefore, that section 35 be repealed at the earliest possible opportunity and that its re-enactment should be in wider terms to cover the constitution of a joint developing body set out in paragraph 11 above, and giving powers to fulfil all the functions defined in paragraph 12 above, and to raise money and dispose of its assets as suggested in paragraphs 15 to 21 below.

15. *Finance of Joint Developing Body.* As far as the provision of housing for the working classes is concerned, permanent financial provision is already available under sections 105–134 of the Housing Act, 1936 for local authorities responsible for slum clearance, reduction of overcrowding, etc. In addition, further state subsidies are to be made available for the immediate postwar years both to local authorities and to private enterprise. Under clause 5 of the Town and Country Planning Bill government financial assistance is provided for exporting towns which have suffered extensive war damage to cover the loan charges which the authority are required to pay for a period of two years. The extension of such assistance for a further period up to eight years and in special cases up to thirteen years (making fifteen years in all) does not apply to land outside those areas which may be purchased compulsorily for replacement purposes.

16. The group recommend that such of the resources mentioned in paragraph 15 above as are available for either the exporting or receiving authorities, should be applied to approved satellite development and be made available for a joint developing body.

17. For all other purposes, eg operative development other than working class houses, the joint developing body should be financed by loans from the Public Works Loan Board. Subsection (5) of

section 35 of the Town and Country Planning Act, 1932, already makes this provision for an authorised association and similar provision should be made for any approved developing body.

18. In the special type of development referred to in paragraph 9(1) above there will be no contribution from large exporting towns and special exchequer grants may be required on lines similar to those made during the slump period through the special areas fund to the North Eastern Housing Association for the provision of working class houses in the Tyneside and Durham special area. The group understood that the problem of satellite development was of first urgency and, therefore, have not yet given full consideration to the problems referred to in paragraph 9(1).

19. In exercising the functions outlined in paragraph 12 (see also paragraph 22), a joint developing body may have constructed roads, laid sewers, erected working class houses and public buildings and laid out open spaces etc. As regards some items it may have acted, in effect, as agent for an existing local authority, or may have provided sites for such an authority to operate upon. In the opinion of the group it is desirable that, ultimately, all works and buildings of a public character should be handed over by the joint developing body to the appropriate local authority at a cost; and that, where a new local authority is established to administer the new town, it should become possessed of all works and buildings which an authority of that status is entitled to hold and administer.

20. With regard to other property (eg cinemas, private houses, factories) it was not easy for the group to formulate agreed proposals. It was represented that the joint developing body should have power to sell both land and buildings in the open market (houses to occupying tenants and factories to industrial undertakings) and so to realise development values and pay off some of its loans to the Public Works Loan Board. On the other hand it was thought that the body should only lease property and should aim at handing over to the new urban district council all its assets and liabilities when the development operations were completed. It was agreed however that before selling, the prior consent of the minister should be obtained.

21. There was also a difference of opinion as to whether, in cases where development has taken place in a rural district, the new urban district council for the development area, when formed, should take over from the rural district council the latter's membership of, and financial interest in, the joint developing body. (In some cases it may be appropriate to give the whole of the rural district urban status.) On the one hand it was considered that the new council should be aloof from the joint developing body, as it would have financial

transactions with it on the takeover, and on the other hand that, as the new receiving authority, it should take over the responsibilities and interests of its predecessor. The general opinion was that for political reasons the new council should link up with the joint developing body for the remainder of the latter's period of operation.

22. *The administrative organisation of the joint developing body and the uses it may make of existing agencies in development operations.* On assuming responsibility for the construction of a new town the joint developing body will have many agencies available to undertake operations:

(1) In the first place the site of the new town should have been selected with due regard to the availability of statutory undertakings for essential services—railways, electricity, water, gas and sewers. The maximum use should be made of statutory undertakers.

(2) Highways would be the concern of the county council and estate roads of the joint developing body. The body would have to provide sewers for its own development, but in some cases they could be linked up with neighbouring systems.

(3) Schools and hospitals would be undertaken by the county council.

(4) Housing might be shared between the exporting authority and the receiving authority. The assistance of housing associations may be invoked.

(5) Public buildings, libraries, and community centres would be the responsibility of the joint developing body and, under powers similar to those in clause 16 of the Bill, that body could undertake a measure of industrial development (eg flatted factories), except where industry would be attracted on its own footing. Private enterprise might undertake the erection of cinemas from the commencement. If not, the joint developing body, as in the case of industrial buildings, might make a start with a cinema which would soon be taken over by private enterprise. Land could be leased for churches, banks and licensed premises, each of which would be ready to look after themselves from the commencement.

(6) Reference is made in paragraph 7 above to the experiences of the Letchworth and Welwyn Garden City companies, and it is thought that some record of these experiences might be helpful to joint developing bodies in connection with operational developments. A technical booklet might be prepared and circulated for this purpose.

23. *Central control.* Central control in some form is needed to ensure that satellite development is undertaken where necessary and in order to secure uniformity in finance. At present the initiative rests with the exporting authority, and possible areas, suitable and ripe for satellite development, wait either for a raid upon their territory in the form of extensive land purchase by the exporting town, or an

invitation by the latter to collaborate on its own terms. It is thought that the initiative should not be left entirely to local bodies, but that there should be guidance and direction from the central government. The whole question of the need for, and location of, a new town is directly affected by the government's policy on location of industry, including decisions on the postwar use of wartime factories, and by its application regionally of its employment policy.

24. The group consider that it is not within their terms of reference to devise a plan for relating these broad issues of policy to the details of local development, but throughout their discussions they were conscious of the vital connection between the successful establishment of new townships or the satellite developments grafted on to existing towns and the location of industry. They therefore submit these proposals on the functions, constitution and finances of joint developing bodies, confident that, if their proposals for the repeal of section 35 of the 1932 Act and for its re-enactment in wider terms are accepted, the minister's control thereby secured will enable him to relate local development to general policy.

25. *Initiating procedure*

A proposal to establish a satellite town will ordinarily arise in the course of the preparation of either local or joint planning schemes. The more obvious and urgent cases will come to light in providing for the overspill from war damaged and congested areas. At present in these cases the initiative rests with the exporting local authorities who have been, and are, laying their own plans with varying degrees of collaboration with the authorities of such receiving areas as they may select. Most of the important cases are already known to the Ministry of Town and Country Planning through the normal planning contacts and, as all exporting authorities affected by serious war damage will require formal approval of their plans for compulsory purchase and financial assistance under the Bill, the group recommend that, in giving his approval at that stage, the minister should determine in consultation with the Minister of Health which authority should be given charge of the satellite development and, failing agreement, on what terms, or whether the responsibility should be placed in the hands of a joint developing body on the lines indicated in this report. In this connection the group do not recommend that satellite development should rest solely with the exporting local authority.

26. In the special types of satellite development mentioned in paragraph 9 above, the group consider that it will normally rest with the Minister of Town and Country Planning to take the initiative. In so far as derelict mining villages in Durham and south Wales are already proceeding with plans for postwar housing, urgently

needed on account of the unsatisfactory nature of present accommodation, the problem has already arisen. The Ministry of Health feel unable to reject proposals for first year housing sites and, unless the whole question is to be prejudiced by the erection of new houses in villages without any prospects of industrial revival, a decision on this matter is needed at an early date.

(NOTE: The group have attempted to make the above recommendations in as specific a form as possible but they are aware that the whole matter is related to possible changes in the structure and finance of local government.)

22 August 1944

Addendum

1. After the issue of the report on 22 August, 1944, the Town and Country Planning Bill was substantially amended and the Act now passed has made certain provisions affecting some of the group's recommendations. These are summarised below (with references to the sections of the report affected).

2. *Purchase of land by importing authority.* The most important change is in the authorities that may be authorised to purchase land for 'overspill' development. (When the group report was made, the Bill provided that only the exporting authority could buy. The Act provides that either the exporting or the importing authority may buy (section 12).) Section 55 enables a local planning authority to delegate to a county council the power of securing the designation of an area under section 1, but the Act confers no power on the county council to purchase the land, except in their capacity as a local highway authority. These provisions implement to some extent the group's recommendation in paragraph 10(3) of their report.

3. *Section 35 of the Town and Country Planning Act, 1932.* Section 20(1) of the new Act enables planning authorities to carry out any development for which they have not already got statutory powers. Subsection (7) of the same section enables them (with the minister's consent) to enter into arrangements with an authorised association as defined in section 35 of the 1932 Act, under which the association can carry out the development, and to make payments or loans to the association. No amendment has been made in section 35 itself, however, so that the criticisms in paragraph 13 of the group's report remain, except that the local planning authority now has power to make arrangements with, and payments or loans to, the association.

4. *Financial assistance to local authorities in 'overspill' areas.* Paragraph 15 of the group report refers to the financial assistance to cover loan charges which the authority are required to pay for a period of two years. Section 5(1)(ii) of the new Act increases the measure of assistance to the extent of 50 per cent of the next two years' loan charges.

11 December, 1944.

APPENDIX F

New Town Statistics

Table 1 : New Towns : Date Order of Designation and Original Population

Great Britain	Date of Designation	Population at Designation
Stevenage	November 1946	7,000
Crawley	January 1947	10,000
Hemel Hempstead	February 1947	21,000
Harlow	March 1947	4,500
Aycliffe	April 1947	60
East Kilbride	May 1947	2,400
Peterlee	March 1948	200
Hatfield	May 1948	8,500
Welwyn	May 1948	18,500
Glenrothes	June 1948	1,100
Basildon	January 1949	25,000
Bracknell	June 1949	5,100
Cwmbran	November 1949	12,000
Corby	April 1950	15,700
Cumbernauld	December 1955	3,000
Skelmersdale	October 1961	10,000
Livingston	April 1962	2,000
Dawley*	January 1963	21,000
Redditch	April 1964	32,000
Runcorn	April 1964	28,500
Washington	July 1964	20,000
Irvine	November 1966	38,700
Milton Keynes	January 1967	40,000
Peterborough	May 1967	80,500
Newtown	December 1967	5,500
Northampton	February 1968	131,000
Warrington	April 1968	124,700
(Central Lancashire	March 1970	234,500)

* Extended in October 1968 to include Wellington and Oakengates; renamed Telford with a 1968 population of 70,000.

Table 2 : The New Towns Programme as at December 1969

	Year Designated	Population at Designation	Population at 31.12.69	Planned Population Capacity
Aycliffe	1947	60	22,000	45,000
Basildon	1949	25,000	79,000	140,000
Bracknell	1949	5,100	36,000	60,000
Crawley	1947	10,000	66,000	75,000
Corby	1950	15,700	50,000	83,000
Cumbernauld	1955	3,000	31,000	90,000
Cwmbran	1949	12,000	45,000	55,000
East Kilbride	1947	2,400	65,000	95,000
Glenrothes	1948	1,100	29,000	70,000
Harlow	1947	4,500	77,000	90,000
Hatfield	1948	8,500	26,000	29,000
Hemel Hempstead	1947	21,000	70,000	80,000
Irvine	1966	38,700	42,000	100,000
Livingston	1962	2,000	11,000	100,000
Milton Keynes	1967	40,000	46,000	250,000
Newtown	1967	5,500	6,000	11,000
Northampton	1968	131,000	131,000	230,000
Peterborough	1967	80,500	85,000	190,000
Peterlee	1948	200	22,000	30,000
Redditch	1964	32,000	36,000	90,000
Runcorn	1964	28,500	34,000	100,000
Skelmersdale	1961	10,000	23,000	80,000
Stevenage	1946	7,000	64,000	105,000
Telford*	1968	70,000	73,000	220,000
Warrington	1968	124,700	124,700	205,000
Washington	1964	20,000	24,000	80,000
Welwyn	1948	18,500	43,000	50,000

* Smaller area designated as Dawley in 1963 with a planned population capacity of 90,000.

Table 3 : New Towns Accounts, 31 March 1970

Development Corporation/ Commission for the New Towns	Advances by Minister/ Secretary of State outstanding	Capital Expenditure (at cost, less disposals and depreciation)	General Revenue Account Deficiency or [Surplus]	Ancillary Undertakings Revenue Accounts Deficiency
	£	£	£	£
Aycliffe	15,412,262	15,235,834	39,392	117,576
Basildon	84,437,833	79,426,530	2,778,899	2,734,912
Bracknell	41,583,102	40,784,386	1,002,275	916,424
Corby	23,110,983	23,692,351	95,212	—
Harlow	62,590,852	66,840,539	[5,152,573]	165,644
Milton Keynes	3,666,944	3,371,326	179,549	2,491
Northampton	2,188,974	2,331,471	121	—
Peterborough	2,132,756	2,965,470	1,577	—
Peterlee	23,512,070	21,171,605	1,955,685	196,268
Redditch	23,392,888	22,828,641	1,781,254	115,490
Runcorn	21,286,667	20,080,889	1,315,628	440,388
Skelmersdale	35,360,406	32,808,434	2,460,540	666,155
Stevenage	58,427,939	57,890,750	[2,268,247]	1,880,084
Telford	25,735,632	24,573,552	1,970,573	412,227
Warrington	174,996	193,860	—	—
Washington	12,946,427	12,646,882	821,279	114,588
Cumbernauld	44,399,850	40,281,655	4,706,885	—
East Kilbride	63,386,299	57,239,091	4,807,942	4,075
Glenrothes	29,164,373	25,730,803	2,741,812	13,732
Irvine	2,693,483	2,903,191	140,943	—
Livingston	28,107,543	22,212,488	2,418,564	
Cwmbran	28,020,386	27,032,953	1,235,165	172,596
Newtown	472,066	808,368	229	704
Commission for the New Towns	104,901,232	103,256,053	[649,190]	—
TOTAL £	737,105,963	706,307,122	30,453,524 [8,070,010]	7,953,354

NOTE ON NEW TOWNS ACCOUNTS

The figures relate to development corporations and the Commission for the New Towns. They therefore exclude expenditure by other public authorities and by private enterprise. The source is *Accounts Relating to Issues from the National Loans Fund 1969–70*, HC 269, 1970–71.

		£m
Capital expenditure (at cost, less disposals and depreciation)		706·3
Deficiency on general revenue accounts	30·5	
less surpluses	8·1	
	—	22·4
Deficiency on ancillary undertakings revenue accounts		8·0
Other and cash in hand		0·4
		737·1

This has been financed by:

Advances from the Consolidated and		
National Loans Funds—total	759·2	
—less repayments	22·1	
	—	737·1

The total commitments for which ministerial approval had been given at March 1970, including those for which advances had already been made, were approximately:

	£m
England	628
Scotland	175
Wales	31
	834

It was estimated, at the end of 1970, that the total liability which might eventually have to be met from the National Loans Fund in respect of all the new towns (including Central Lancashire) might be of the order of £3,000m. The actual figure would depend, of course, on changes in price levels, the degree of participation by private enterprise, and how far short of the ultimate population figure the new towns stopped their own development to leave room for natural expansion.

In addition to advances to meet capital expenditure, the new towns

received the normal housing subsidies and also grants in respect of
certain subsidised houses (analogous to those repayable in respect of
overspill and to the contributions from the rates that local authorities
could pay in respect of their own subsidised houses). In the year to
March 1970, these amounted to £1·4m.

APPENDIX G

List of Ministers

Principal Ministers Concerned with Environmental Planning 1944–70

This list contains the names of the ministers who were closely concerned with environmental planning, together with those offices which they held at the time at which reference is made to them in volumes III and IV of this history.

Amory, Heathcoat — Chancellor of the Exchequer, Jan 1958–July 1960

Anderson, John — Chancellor of the Exchequer, Sept 1943–July 1945

Attlee, Clement — Prime Minister, July 1945–Oct 1951

Bowden, Herbert — Lord President, Oct 1964–Aug 1966

Boyd-Carpenter, John — Financial Secretary, Treasury, Oct 1951–July 1954

Bevan, Aneurin — Minister of Health, Aug 1945–Jan 1951

Brooke, Henry — Financial Secretary, Treasury, July 1954–Jan 1957
Minister of Housing and Local Government, Jan 1957–Oct 1961
Paymaster General, Oct 1961–July 1962
Home Secretary, July 1962–Oct 1964

Brown, George — First Secretary of State and Secretary of State for Economic Affairs, Oct 1964–Aug 1966

Butler, R. A. — Chancellor of the Exchequer, Oct 1951–Dec 1955
Lord Privy Seal, Dec 1955–Oct 1957
Home Secretary, Jan 1957–July 1962

First Secretary of State, July 1962–Oct 1963
Foreign Secretary, Oct 1963–Oct 1964

Callaghan, James — Chancellor of the Exchequer, Oct 1964–Nov 1967

Churchill, Winston — Prime Minister to July 1945; Oct 1951–April 1955

Corfield, Frederick V. — Joint Parliamentary Secretary, Ministry of Housing and Local Government, July 1962–Oct 1964

Cripps, Stafford — President of the Board of Trade, July 1945–Sept 1947
Chancellor of the Exchequer, Nov 1947–Nov 1950

Crosland, Anthony — President of the Board of Trade, Aug 1967–Oct 1969
Secretary of State for Local Government and Regional Planning, Oct 1969–June 1970

Crossman, Richard — Minister of Housing and Local Government, Oct 1964–Aug 1966

Dalton, Hugh — President of the Board of Trade, Feb 1942–May 1945
Chancellor of the Exchequer, July 1945–Nov 1947
Minister of Local Government and Planning, Feb 1950–Oct 1951

Douglas-Home, Alec — Prime Minister, Oct 1963–Oct 1964

Eccles, David — President of the Board of Trade, Jan 1957–Oct 1959

Eden, Anthony — Prime Minister, April 1955–Jan 1957

Erroll, F. J. — President of the Board of Trade, Oct 1961–Oct 1963

Gaitskell, Hugh — Chancellor of the Exchequer, Oct 1950–Oct 1951

Gardiner, Gerald Lord Chancellor, Oct 1964–June 1970

Greenwood, Anthony Minister of Housing and Local Government, Aug 1966–June 1970

Griffiths, James Secretary of State for Wales, Oct 1964–April 1966

Heald, Lionel Attorney-General, Nov 1951–Oct 1954

Heath, Edward Lord Privy Seal, July 1960–Oct 1963
Secretary of State for Industry, Trade and Regional Development, Oct 1963–Oct 1964

Henderson, Lord Lord in Waiting, Oct 1945–June 1948

Hill, Charles Minister of Housing and Local Government, Oct 1961–July 1962

Hughes, Cledwyn Secretary of State for Wales, April 1966–April 1968
Minister of Agriculture, April 1968–June 1970

Jay, Douglas Economic and Financial Secretary, Treasury, Dec 1947–Oct 1951
President of the Board of Trade, Oct 1964–Aug 1967

Jenkins, Roy Chancellor of the Exchequer, Nov 1967–June 1970

Johnston, Tom Secretary of State for Scotland, Feb 1941–May 1945

Jones, F. Elwyn Attorney-General, Oct 1964–June 1970

Joseph, Keith Minister of Housing and Local Government, July 1962–Oct 1964

Jowitt, Lord Lord Chancellor, July 1945–Oct 1951

Lloyd, Selwyn Chancellor of the Exchequer, July 1960–July 1962

Lyttelton, Oliver   Minister of Production, March 1942–May 1945
President of the Board of Trade, May 1945–July 1945

MacColl, James   Joint Parliamentary Secretary, Ministry of Housing and Local Government, Oct 1964–Oct 1969

MacDermot, Niall   Financial Secretary, Treasury, Oct 1964–Aug 1967
Minister of State, Housing and Local Government, Aug 1967–Sept 1968

Maclay, John   Secretary of State for Scotland, Jan 1957–July 1962

Macmillan, Harold   Minister of Housing and Local Government, Oct 1951–Oct 1954
Minister of Defence, Oct 1954–April 1955
Foreign Secretary, April 1955–Dec 1955
Chancellor of the Exchequer, Dec 1955–Jan 1957
Prime Minister, Jan 1957–Oct 1963

McNeil, Hector   Secretary of State for Scotland, Feb 1950–Oct 1951

Manningham-Buller, Reginald (Lord Dilhorne)   Solicitor General, Nov 1951–Oct 1954
Attorney-General, Oct 1954–July 1962
Lord Chancellor, July 1962–Oct 1964

Mason, Roy   President of the Board of Trade, Oct 1969–June 1970

Maudling, Reginald   Economic Secretary, Treasury, Nov 1952–April 1955
President of the Board of Trade, Oct 1959–Oct 1961
Chancellor of the Exchequer, July 1962–Oct 1964

Maxwell-Fyfe, David (Lord Kilmuir)   Home Secretary, Oct 1951–Oct 1954
Lord Chancellor, Oct 1954–July 1962

Mellish, Robert   Joint Parliamentary Secretary, Ministry of Housing and Local Government, Oct 1964– Aug 1967
Minister of Housing and Local Government, May–June 1970

Mitchison, G. R.   Parliamentary Secretary, Ministry of Land and Natural Resources, Oct 1964–April 1966

Morrison, Herbert   Lord President, July 1945–March 1951

Morrison, W. S.   Minister of Town and Country Planning, Dec 1942–July 1945

Noble, Michael   Secretary of State for Scotland, July 1962– Oct 1964

Peart, Frederick   Minister of Agriculture, Oct 1964–April 1968

Powell, Enoch   Parliamentary Secretary, Ministry of Housing and Local Government, Dec 1955–Jan 1957
Financial Secretary, Treasury, Jan 1957–Jan 1958

Rippon, Geoffrey   Parliamentary Secretary, Ministry of Housing and Local Government, Oct 1961–July 1962
Minister of Works, July 1962–Oct 1964

Robinson, Kenneth   Minister for Planning and Land, Nov 1968– Oct 1969

Rosebery, Lord   Secretary of State for Scotland, May 1945– July 1945

Ross, William   Secretary of State for Scotland, Oct 1964– June 1970

Salisbury, Lord   Commonwealth Secretary, March–Nov 1952
Lord President, Nov 1952–March 1957

Sandys, Duncan   Minister of Housing and Local Government, Oct 1954–Jan 1957

Shawcross, Hartley	President of the Board of Trade, April 1951–Oct 1951
Shore, Peter	Secretary of State for Economic Affairs, Aug 1967–Oct 1969
Silkin, Lewis	Minister of Town and Country Planning, Aug 1945–Feb 1950
Simon, Jocelyn	Financial Secretary, Treasury, Jan 1958–Oct 1959 Solicitor-General, Oct 1959–Feb 1962
Skeffington, Arthur	Joint Parliamentary Secretary, Ministry of Land and Natural Resources, Oct 1964–Feb 1967 Joint Parliamentary Secretary, Ministry of Housing and Local Government, Feb 1967–June 1970
Stewart, Michael	First Secretary of State, Aug 1966–March 1968
Stuart, James	Secretary of State for Scotland, Oct 1951–Jan 1957
Thomas, George	Secretary of State for Wales, April 1968–June 1970
Thorneycroft, Peter	President of the Board of Trade, Oct 1951–Jan 1957 Chancellor of the Exchequer, Jan 1957–Jan 1958
Willey, Frederick	Minister of Land and Natural Resources, Oct 1964–Feb 1967 Minister of State, Ministry of Housing and Local Government, Feb 1967–Aug 1967
Westwood, Joseph	Secretary of State for Scotland, Aug 1945–Oct 1947
Williams, Tom	Minister of Agriculture, Aug 1945–Oct 1951

Wilson, Harold

President of the Board of Trade, Sept 1947–
April 1951
Prime Minister, Oct 1964–June 1970

Woodburn, Arthur

Secretary of State for Scotland, Oct 1947–
Feb 1950

Woolton, Lord

Lord President, May 1945–July 1945; Oct
1951–Nov 1952

Ministers Responsible for New Towns

COALITION AND CARETAKER GOVERNMENTS (TO 26 JULY 1945)

| Works and Buildings (to Feb 1942) Works and Planning | Reith | Oct 1940–Feb 1942 |
| | Portal | Feb 1942–Nov 1944 |

| Town and Country Planning | W. S. Morrison | Dec 1942–July 1945 |

| Scotland | T. Johnston | Feb 1941–May 1945 |
| | Rosebery | May–July 1945 |

LABOUR GOVERNMENT 26 JULY 1945–26 OCTOBER 1951

| Town and Country Planning (to Jan 1951) Local Government and Planning | L. Silkin | Aug 1945–Feb 1950 |
| | H. Dalton | Feb 1950–Oct 1951 |

Scotland	J. Westwood	Aug 1945–Oct 1947
	A. Woodburn	Oct 1947–Feb 1950
	H. McNeil	Feb–Oct 1951

CONSERVATIVE GOVERNMENT 26 OCTOBER 1951–16 OCTOBER 1964

Housing and Local Government	H. Macmillan	Oct 1951–Oct 1954
	D. Sandys	Oct 1954–Jan 1957
	H. Brooke	Jan 1957–Oct 1961
	C. Hill	Oct 1961–July 1962
	K. Joseph	July 1962–Oct 1964

Scotland	J. Stuart	Oct 1951–Jan 1957
	J. Maclay	Jan 1957–July 1962
	M. Noble	July 1962–Oct 1964

LABOUR GOVERNMENT 16 OCTOBER 1964–19 JUNE 1970

Housing and Local Government	R. Crossman	Oct 1964–Aug 1966
	A. Greenwood	Aug 1966–May 1970
	R. Mellish	May–June 1970

| Scotland | W. Ross | Oct 1964–June 1970 |

Wales	J. Griffiths	Oct 1964–April 1966
	C. Hughes	April 1966–April 1968
	G. Thomas	April 1968–June 1970

APPENDIX H

List of Abbreviations

AGD	Accountant General's Department (MHLG)
AMC	Association of Municipal Corporations
BH	Committee on Birmingham Housing (Cabinet)
BOT⎫ BT ⎭	Board of Trade
C ⎫ CP ⎭	Cabinet Papers
CC ⎫ CM ⎭	Cabinet Conclusions
CCA	County Councils Association
CNT	Commission for the New Towns
DEA	Department of Economic Affairs
DEP	Department of Employment and Productivity
DHS	Department of Health for Scotland
DI	Distribution of Industry Committee (Cabinet)
EA	Economic Policy Committee (Cabinet)
ED	Economic Development Committee (Cabinet)
EP	Environmental Planning Committee (Cabinet)
EP	Economic Policy Committee (Cabinet)
EP(O)	Economic Policy Committee (Official)
GDE	General Development Expenditure
GEC	General Electric Company
GLC	Greater London Council
GLDP	Greater London Development Plan
GLP	Official Committee on Greater London Plan
GOC	Government Organisation Committee (Official)
GM	General Manager (New Town)
GNP	Gross National Product
GTC	Government Training Centre
H ⎫ HA ⎭	Home Affairs Committee (Cabinet)
HC	House of Commons
HL	House of Lords
HRA	Housing Revenue Account
IDC	Industrial Development Certificate
IPC	Investment Programmes Committee (Official)
LA	Local Authority

LC	Legislation Committee (Cabinet)
LCC	London County Council
LG	Committee on Local Government Reform (Cabinet)
LP	Lord President's Committee (Cabinet)
LP(DI)	Lord President's Committee—Subcommittee on Distribution of Industry
MAF	Ministry of Agriculture and Fisheries
MGO	Machinery of Government Committee (Official)
MHLG	Ministry of Housing and Local Government
ML	Ministry of Labour
MLGP	Ministry of Local Government and Planning
MTCP	Ministry of Town and Country Planning
NCB	National Coal Board
NHBRC	National House Builders' Registration Council
NIESR	National Institute of Economic and Social Research
NT	New Towns
NTWG	New Towns Working Group (MHLG)
PAC	Public Accounts Committee (House of Commons)
PE	Committee on Population and Employment (Cabinet)
PESC	Public Expenditure Survey Committee (Treasury)
R	Reconstruction Committee (Cabinet)
RD	Committee on Regional Development (Cabinet)
RDC	Rural District Council
REP	Regional Economic Planning Committee (Cabinet)
SDD	Scottish Development Department
SEP	Steering Committee on Economic Policy (Cabinet)
SEPD	Scottish Economic Planning Department
S of S	Secretary of State
TDA	Town Development Act 1952
UDC	Urban District Council

INDEX

Abercrombie, P., 4, 5, 9, 27, 35, 38, 86, 486
Adams, W. E., 162, 163n
Agricultural land
  in Merseyside Plan, 34
  Peterlee, 75, 77, 107
  in Cheshire, 95–101, 151–5, 194
  report on loss of agricultural land in
    England and Wales, 101–2
  Corby, 109
  and housing densities, 154n
  Tadley, 160
  Allhallows private enterprise new town,
    163
  Swynnerton, 167–8, 172
  Dawley, 167–8, 261–2
  Skelmersdale, 168
  Wythall, 169–70
  Brooke's assurance on, 170
  Runcorn, 193
  North Buckinghamshire (Milton Keynes),
    230, 231
  Ipswich, 269–71, 272
  valuation of, 536, 564–80
  Nottingham, 564
Allhallows private enterprise new town,
  162–3
Amenities in new towns
  Macmillan's arguments for, 128–9, 136,
    144
  Treasury's views on, 134, 147–8, 338
  agreement on, 146, 147–8
  research on, 351, 358, 359
Amory, Heathcoat, 152–4
Anderson, Duncan, 343
Anderson, John, 544
Andover, 161, 510, 511, 519
Annual reviews of new town development,
  146, 148
Ashford
  proposed as site for new town, 113, 208,
    232
  feasibility study, 236, 243, 249–52
  linked with Channel Tunnel, 246–9
  decision not to designate as a new town,
    251–2
  town expansion scheme, 490, 505, 511, 512
Attlee, Clement, 293
Aycliffe (Newton Aycliffe)
  new town proposed, 36, 42
  agreed, 44, 60
  supported by Treasury, 78n
  attractiveness to industry, 190
  sale of houses to sitting tenants, 445–7
Aylesbury, 34, 62, 512, 515

Banbury, 512, 515, 516
Barlow Report, 3, 11, 28, 486, 543
Barnes, A., 44, 48–54
Basildon (Pitsea and Laindon)
  first mention, 70
  new town approved, 82–6
  possible expansion, 161, 209, 211
  expansion agreed, 245–6
  cost of clearing shack development, 320
  journey to work research, 366n
  links with London, 400, 408, 411
  better class housing, 423
  site difficulties and unit cost, 457–8
  advance factories, 556
Basingstoke, 34, 90, 113, 505, 506, 510, 519
Belcher, J. W., 63–4
Bennett, Thomas, 31, 357
Bevan, Aneurin
  supports Silkin on Crawley, 43
  on Bridgend, 44–5
  supports new towns, 51
  supports Basildon proposal, 82
  on Corby, 109
  use of local authorities in new town
    development, 301
  need for strengthening existing communi-
    ties, 486
Beveridge, Lord, 298, 356
Bevin, Ernest, 544
Birmingham, 35
  development at Wythall, 165, 173, 503
  need for new town, 166–75, 192–3
  overspill to Dawley, 258–66
Bishopton-Houston
  proposed as site for new town, 33, 39
  not agreed by Cabinet, 56–7
  agreed by Cabinet and later abandoned,
    89
Bletchley
  considered for expansion, 34
  start made, 134
  new city proposed, 208, 228–30
  overspill agreement with L.C.C., 500
  inability to cope with town expansion, 505
  see also Milton Keynes
Board of Trade
  responsibilities, 12, 544 et seq
  on size of Corby, 109
  Macmillan's criticism of, 120
  concern over effect of new and expanded
    towns on development areas, 139–40
  supports new town at Tadley, 160
  on Manchester, 222
  employment needs of new and expanded
    towns, 241–2
  doubt attractiveness of expanded towns
    to industry, 498
  distribution of industry policy, 543–63
Boyd-Carpenter, John, 145
Bracknell
  new town proposed, 67, 81
  approved 89–91
  expansion of new town, 160, 583–4
  industrial development, 404
  low-skilled workers from London, 415–16

Bracknell, *cont.*
    comparative analysis of cost of development as a new town and an expanded town, 454–5
    possible area development corporation embracing Banbury and Swindon, 516
Bradford, possible need for a new town, 35
Bridgend
    possible site for new town, 33, 36
    normal expansion preferred, 38
    Bevan's views, 44–5
Bridges, Edward, 310–11
Bristol overspill, 35, 238
British Drug Houses, move to Hatfield, 63, 64
British Petroleum, and Allhallows private enterprise new town, 162–3
Brooke, Henry
    Hook new town, 156–60
    changing attitude to new towns, 164
    new town for Birmingham, 167–73, 503–4
    chairman of Cabinet Committee on Population and Employment, 179
    on composition of development corporations, 295
    on future ownership of new towns, 331–40
    view on housing deficits in new towns, 389
    on better class housing in new towns, 420
Brown, George, 209, 224
Buchanan Report, 391, 464
Buckinghamshire, North, *see* Milton Keynes
Burton Constable, satellite town for Hull, 35
Butler, R. A.
    presses for economies in new towns programme, 117–25, 141–2
    on Lymm proposal, 155
    Town Development Bill, 499–500

Caersws, proposed new town, 237, 279–83
Calder Valley, road link with M6 motorway, 256
Callaghan, J., 213
Cardiff, 76, 226, 283
Carlisle, state management of public houses, 310
Central advisory commission for new towns, 15, 25, 297, 348–9, 376
Central Housing Advisory Committee, 369, 535
Central Lancashire New Town, *see* Leyland-Chorley
Centre for Environmental Studies, 382
Channel Tunnel
    would encourage congestion in S.E. England, 198
    linked with Ashford development, 246–51
    referred to in *The South East Study*, 509
Chapman, Dobson, 98
Cheshire, 34, 59, 80, 95–101, 151–5, 194, 219–23, 504
Chessington, L.C.C. development rejected, 43
Chipping Ongar
    proposed site for new town, 6, 10, 16, 32, 33, 594
    agreed, 51
    abandoned, 53
    transport difficulties, 67

Chipping Sodbury, possible new town for Bristol, 35
Chorley, *see* Leyland-Chorley
Church Commissioners, possibility of transfer of new towns to, 318, 321, 322
Church Village
    proposed site for new town, 73, 76, 92–5
    abandoned, 95, 110–12
Clarke, C. W., 73n
Clyde Valley Regional Planning Advisory Committee, 38, 521, 522
Coalfields
    in Derbyshire and Leicestershire, 36
    in South Wales, 58, 75, 93, 110–12
    in Scotland, 61–2, 86, 87
    in Durham, 77–8, 102–7, 182, 452–3
    in Yorkshire, 550
    see also National Coal Board
Commissioners of Crown Lands, possibility of transfer of new towns to, 321, 333
Commission for the New Towns
    background to, 316–40
    Bill for establishment before Parliament, 341–2
    composition and organisation, 342–4
    role of, 344–7
    future of, 347–8
    membership of working party on 'new towns structure', 373
    low-skilled workers from London, 416
    role in housebuilding, 424–5
    limited powers, 511
Common Market, effect on industrial location, 179, 183, 186
Congleton, 95–101, 118, 119
Conservative Party manifesto (1964), 208
Control of Office and Industrial Development Act (1965), 550
Co-operative Permanent Building Society, proposal for private enterprise new town, 10
Corby
    new town proposed and agreed, 108–10
    extended, 583–4
Costain Ltd, Richard, proposal for private enterprise new town, 10
Cost of new towns, *see* Finance of new towns
Coylton, proposed new town, 86
Cramlington, town expansion scheme, 189, 238, 242
Crawley
    proposed site for new town, 16, 32, 34, 38, 44, 47
    agreed, 43
    transferred to C.N.T., 343–4
    relationship between C.N.T. and L.A., 345
    development corporation's proposals on research, 350–1
    report on population structure, 359
    rent strike, 389
    owner occupation and commuting, 431
    encouragement of private investment in industrial building, 457
    sewerage undertaking, 459
Crewe, 154, 194
Cripps, Stafford, 79, 110, 452

Crossman, R. H. S.
  Minister of Housing and Local Government, 209
  supports more new towns for S.E. England, 213
  statement to Commons, 214
  and Jay's letter on London, 215–16, 414, 559–61
  proposes feasibility studies of Humberside and Severnside, 227–8
  appointments to development corporations, 295n, 297
  on future ownership of housing in new towns, 348
  views on housing subsidies, 394–5
  on rent rebates and housing standards, 398
  on sale of council houses, 429
  requests review of town development, 518
Crowhurst, proposed new town, 6, 16, 67
Cullingworth Report on future ownership of housing in new towns, 438–43
Cumbernauld
  proposed site for new town, 33, 39
  considered and agreed, 149–51
Cwmbran
  proposed site for new town, 81, 92–5
  agreed, 95
  possible abandonment or curtailment, 122, 123, 124, 125, 128, 143, 146
  nearing housing target, 241
  better class housing, 421

Daines, Percy, 411
Dalton, Hugh
  concern over cost of new towns, 21, 43–4, 50–1, 62
  discusses Welwyn-Hatfield with Silkin, 71
  letter to Silkin on new towns, 72
  resigns from Government, 79
  Town Development Bill, 116, 496–8
  reviews membership of development corporations, 293
  opposes Bill establishing C.N.T., 342
  on reduction of housing standards, 495
  Distribution of Industry Bill, 545–6
Daventry, 169, 172, 173, 508, 563
Davies, Clement, 16, 65
Dawley (Telford)
  possible site for new town, 167–8
  considered by ministerial committee, 168–73
  agreed, 173, 175
  further consideration and agreement, 173–4
  extension to Wellington and Oakengates, 258–64
  industrial crisis, 264–7
  renamed Telford, 266–7
  financial difficulties, 390
  competition from low cost private houses, 437
  agricultural land advantage, 571
Dee crossing feasibility study, 226
Deedes, W., 411
De Havilland expansion at Hatfield, 63–6
Development corporations
  early ideas on, 6–12, 14–18, 24, 592–602
  methods of appointment, 28–9, 291–7

payment of members, 92, 300–9
possibility of a national corporation, 124, 139, 301–4, 317–19, 380, 511–12
relations with ministry and financial control of, 141–2, 312–16, 374, 448–50, 460–1, 477–85
proposed for town expansions, 201–6, 455–6, 510–18
meetings of Standing Ministerial Conference, 297–300, 349, 351, 356–7, 386–7
public statements by, 309–12
Treasury report on (1949), 312–16
views on future ownership of new towns, 322–7
attitudes on research, 351, 356–7, 359–62, 368–9
information bureau, 369–72
review by official working party (1968–1969), 372–84
views on better class housing, 420–2
on sale of houses, 429–31, 434–5, 445–7
on owner occupation, 443
  see also Future ownership of new towns and Commission for the New Towns
Development Rights Bill, 20–1
Distribution of Industry Act (1945), 545–6
Distribution of Industry (Industrial Finance) Act (1958), 547–8
Dollan, Patrick, 86
Dolphin Development and Management Company, 162
Dundee, feasibility study on expansion, 226–8, 236

Easington, 68, 73–5, 77, 102; see also Peterlee
East Ham, 37, 82, 400, 408, 411
East Kilbride
  proposed new town, 33, 39
  agreed, 45
  cost, 47–8, 51–2, 55–6
  progress, 86, 131–2, 183, 241
  local authority responsibilities for main services, 304
Eccles, David, 548
Economic Affairs, Department of
  responsibilities, 209
  supports Leyland-Chorley proposal, 222
  central planning unit, 228
  on Dawley-Wellington-Oakengates, 260
  membership of New Towns Working Group (1967), 475
  on valuation of agricultural land, 536
Economic criteria, study group on (1964–65), 462–73
Economist, The, on new towns as 'boom towns', 147, 319
Education, Ministry of, 123, 146, 494, 557
Ellesmere Port, 34, 113, 166
Employment Policy, white paper, 544

Felton, Monica, 29, 31, 295, 298, 349, 357
Finance of new towns
  Dalton's concern over costs, 21, 43–4, 50–1
  initial estimates, 22–3, 44, 45–8, 69, 451–4
  borrowing limits, 23, 69, 588

Finance of New Towns, *cont.*
cost of East Kilbride, 47–8, 51–2, 55–6
Butler presses for economies, 117–25
relative costs of housing, 136–7
financial control, 141–2, 312–16, 374, 448–51, 460–1, 477–85, 538–9
annual reviews, 148
cost of Dawley, 174
land costs for new town extensions, 211
estimate for new programme (1964), 212–13
estimates of new towns working group (1967), 239–40, 243–4
financial framework, 385, 448–50
general development expenditure (G.D.E.), 387, 391–2, 395, 480–1
comparative costs of new and expanded towns, 454–7, 462–77
study of cost and profitability, 457–60
new town accounts (31 March 1970), 605–7
see also Rate fund contribution for housing *and* Housing in the new towns
Forshaw Report, 14
Future ownership of new towns
by local authorities: initial ideas, 12, 15–16, 17
Reith Committee proposals, 14, 17, 316
consideration of immediate transfer of new towns to local authorities (1953), 123–4, 128, 131, 132, 138–9, 317
doubts on ownership by local authorities, 138–9, 145, 317
detailed consideration, 316–40
provisions of New Towns Act (1946), 317
provisions of New Towns Act (1959), 341–2
and housing finance, 386, 395–7
Cullingworth Report, 438–43
financial difficulties foreseen, 453
see also Commission for the New Towns

Gaitskell, Hugh, 106, 496–7, 554
Gale, Humphrey, 502–3
Gardiner, Thomas, 31
General development expenditure (G.D.E.), *see* Finance of new towns
Gibberd, Frederick, 163
Gibson, G., 11n
Glasgow, 38–9, 88, 124, 130–3, 149–51, 175–8, 236, 520–4
Glenrothes
proposed new town (Leslie-Markinch), 57, 61
agreed, 62
progress, 86, 132, 241
local authority responsibilities for main services, 304
Government Organisation Committee, 310–313
Government training centres, 418
Greater London, *see* London
Greenock, 87–9
Greenwood, Anthony
Minister of Housing and Local Government, 231
decides name of Milton Keynes, 233n
on Ashford, 249–51
on Central Lancashire new town, 253

appointment of development corporations, 296n
on report of working party on new towns structure, 384
Griffiths, James, 279
Growth areas policy, 178, 182, 184–7, 188, 207, 225, 237, 549

Hailsham, Lord, 189, 190, 549
Hampshire, 158–61; *see also* Ashford *and* South Hampshire Study
Harlow
proposed new town, 6, 16, 32, 34
agreed, 51, 54
link with Tottenham, 84
expansion of new town, 209, 211, 456, 512, 584
cost of main sewers, 320
low-skilled workers from London, 416
profitability, 480
difficulties in attracting industry, 553, 556, 558
Hatfield
proposed new town, 34, 62–6
agreed, 66, 71
proposal for immediate transfer to local authority (1953), 123, 138
transferred to C.N.T., 344
sales of houses, 422
Health, Ministry of
responsible for housing, 8, 12
consulted on Congleton, 96, 101
views on speed of development, 146
on housing rents in new towns, 385–6
rate fund contributions for overspill, 399
view on departmental responsibility for new towns, 487, 490, 601
Heath, Edward, 549
Hemel Hempstead
proposed new town, 16, 32, 34
agreed, 51, 54
possibility of immediate transfer to local authority (1953), 123, 138
profitability, 343, 480
transferred to C.N.T., 344
subsidised housebuilding to be run down, 345
linked with London local authorities, 400
better class housing, 422
sewerage undertaking, 459
M.T.C.P. view on development by way of town expansion, 491
Hill, Charles, 174
Hinchingbrooke, Lord, 25
Holford, W. G., 8
Holiday new town, 113–14
Holmwood, proposed new town, 6, 16, 67
Hook new town proposed by L.C.C., 155–62
Housing associations, 203, 424
Housing in new towns
rents, 117, 151, 385–98
standards, 145, 389, 398, 426, 437–9, 442–4, 495
'people's house', 145, 389
owner occupation, 145, 271–2, 344, 419–447
provision by C.N.T., 344–7, 424–5
for old people, 347, 361, 415, 425

subsidies, 385–98, 412, 501, 522
housing accounts, 387, 390, 394
better class, 419–26
sale of, 427–47
costs, 457
see also Rate fund contribution *and* Selection of tenants
Housing and Local Government, Ministry of
Macmillan becomes Minister, 116
working party with Treasury on new towns (1952), 120–1
proposals on new towns and industrial location policy (1954), 135
annual reviews on new town development, 148
minute on ministers' dislike of new towns (1955), 148
consideration of expansion of London new towns, 149
consideration of L.C.C. new town (Hook), 155–61
on changed ministerial attitudes to new towns (1960), 164–5
discussion on Birmingham overspill, 175
official committee on population and employment (1962), 179 *et seq*
on *The South East Study*, 209–13
on industrial location and overspill (1965), 219
on Leyland-Chorley, 222
on new town in North Buckinghamshire, 228, 231
new towns working group (1967), 233 *et seq*, 474–7
on phasing of development at Wellington-Oakengates, 259, 260
agree to exclusion of agricultural land from Ipswich new town designated area, 270
membership of development corporations, 296
future ownership of new towns, 318–22, 327, 330–4, 337
Commission for the New Towns, 342–7
research on new towns, 366–70
proposed new towns information bureau, 370–2
working party on new towns structure (1968–69), 372 *et seq*
housing rents in new towns, 387 *et seq*
memorandum on Town Development Act (1952), 405
selection of tenants for new and expanded towns, 406 *et seq*
London Dispersal Liaison Group, 417–19
better class housing in new towns, 420–6
sale of council houses, 427–9
sale of new town housing, 429–41
owner occupation in new towns, 442–7
relationships with development corporations, 448–51
on development corporations for town expansion, 454–7
new towns research group (1963), 457–60
and Treasury demand for forward programming, 460–2
study group on economic criteria, 462–73

N.I.E.S.R. Report on town structure, size and cost, 473–4
new towns working group (1967), 474–7
profitability of new towns, 479–84
review of machinery for town expansion, 504–12
considers regional development agencies (1963), 512–16
'partnership' new towns, 517–18
review of town development (1965), 518–520
on industrial location policy, 556–8
see also Local Government and Planning, Ministry of *and* Town and Country Planning, Ministry of
Housing Repairs and Rents Act (1954), 117
Housing Subsidies Act (1956), 412, 501–2
Housing Subsidies Act (1967), 398
Housing and Town Development (Scotland) Act (1957), 520–4
Houston, *see* Bishopton-Houston
Howard, Ebenezer, 3
Hull, 35, 238; *see also* Humberside
Humber bridge, 267–9
Humberside, feasibility study of major expansion, 226–8, 239, 267–9
Hunt Committee (*The Intermediate Areas*), 254, 257, 266, 550–1, 561–2

Industrial Development Act (1966), 219, 550, 560
Industrial location control
Jay on, 40–2, 215–16, 246–9, 552–3
Macmillan on, 127, 134–8, 142–3
Thorneycroft on, 129–30, 139–40
control over vacated factories proposed, 137–8, 492
Stuart on, 140–1
population and employment report (1962), 179–88
review of trends in S.E. England (1965), 217
review of regional economic policies (1965), 218–19
and new towns (1967), 241–2
and Dawley (1968), 264–6
and Ipswich, 274, 277
history, 543–63
see also Board of Trade, Growth areas policy *and* Office development controls
Industrial selection scheme, 399–419, 435, 532
Inglis Report, 49
Investment Incentives, white paper, 219, 560
Ipswich
proposed expansion, 207, 208, 209, 212
approved, 213
announced, 214
draft designation order under consideration, 245, 246, 269
consultants' report, 269
public inquiry, 270–1
post inquiry developments, 271–3
opposed by Treasury, 273–5
review of need for, 275–8
abandoned, 278–9, 527
machinery for development, 512–18
cost of expansion, 513

Irvine, proposed and agreed, 190–2
Isaacs, G. A., 65

Jay, Douglas
  questions new towns policy (1946), 40–2
  opposes development at Hatfield, 64
  becomes chairman of DI Committee, 79
  reservations on London new towns (1964), 213
  letter to Crossman on London, 215–16, 414, 559–61
  paper on London overspill (1967), 246–9
  chairman of advisory committee on development areas (1947), 546
  meets Silkin on industrial location policy (1949), 552–3
Jenkinson, Charles, 31
Joseph Keith
  seeks approval for more new towns, 192–6
  The South East Study, 196–8
  proposals for advance acquisition of land, 197, 201–6, 514

Key, C. W., 65
Killingworth, 238, 242
Kilroy, Alix, 556

Labour (and National Service), Ministry of, 12, 101, 475, 545
  and industrial selection scheme, 399 *et seq*
Labour Party, manifesto (1945), 13; (1964), 208–9, 279; (1966), 348
Laindon, *see* Basildon
Lancashire, 34, 165, 166, 192–6, 221, 504; *see also* Leyland-Chorley
Land acquisition
  initial ideas on acquisition of all land in new towns, 75, 314, 581–2
  proposals by Joseph for planned developments in S.E. England, 197, 201–6, 514
  proposals by secretary of M.H.L.G. for implementation of regional plans, 506–8, 512
  for new towns, 581–6
Land Commission, 208, 267–8, 268n, 584
Land Compensation Act (1961), 211, 583, 588
Latham, Lord, 16
Leeds, 22, 35, 594
Letchworth, 34, 41, 84, 593, 600
Leyland-Chorley (Central Lancashire New Town)
  first mention, 76, 113
  considered 'unrealistic' (1956), 154
  industrial base inadequate for a new town (1965), 220–1
  differing opinions on, 221–2
  balance of advantage in favour of, 221
  announcement, 223
  under study, 226, 232–3
  objectives, 239
  consultants' report, 245, 253
  impact on N.E. Lancashire, 253–8
  designated, 258
Linwood, 88, 176
Littlehampton, possible holiday new town, 113

Liverpool
  Merseyside Plan, 34
  overspill to be assessed, 81
  lack of decentralisation, 165
  Skelmersdale new town, 166–8
  Runcorn new town, 192–6
Livingston
  proposed new town, 175–78
  agreed, 178
Llantrisant
  development proposed (1948), 76, 81
  under study (1967), 236, 241, 245, 283–5
  rejected, 286
Local authorities
  development of new towns by, 7–9, 11–12, 14, 17, 24, 25, 79–80, 85, 300–1, 592–602
  consulted on initial ideas for new towns, 15–18
  representation on development corporations, 291–7
  relationship to C.N.T., 344–5
  'partnership' new towns, 377–80, 513–20
  see also Future ownership of new towns, Rate fund contribution *and* Selection of tenants for new towns
Local Employment Act (1960), 180–3, 219, 548, 559
Local Employment Act (1963), 219, 549
Local Government and Planning, Ministry of
  Town Development Bill, 495–8
  establishment, 536–7
  see also Housing and Local Government, Ministry of *and* Town and Country Planning, Ministry of
Local government reorganisation, 141–2, 239, 378–9
Lochgelly, 57, 86
London
  early postwar plans, 3–6, 9, 11, 19, 23
  interdepartmental committee on Greater London Plan, 9, 19, 27, 66, 82, 551
  reaction to Silkin's proposals for legislation on new towns, 16, 18
  new towns programme for, 33–4, 37–8
  Jay on control of employment growth, 40–2, 64
  nearness of new towns to, 43, 65, 70–1
  Barnes on transport improvements, 48–54
  review of new towns for (1947), 67
  Dalton on unchecked growth of, 72
  housing programmes of London local authorities, 83–4
  selection of tenants for new and expanded towns, 84, 399 *et seq*, 532–3
  need for Bracknell new town, 89–91
  effectiveness of decentralisation (1954), 125–9, 137–8, 140
  L.C.C. new town (Hook), 155–62
  population and employment growth (1962), 179–88
  The South East Study, 196–201, 207–14
  Jay's letter to Crossman on (1965), 213, 215–16, 414, 559–61
  review of policy for the S.E. (1965), 216–218
  future population growth (1967), 238

overspill needs, 242–3, 246–9
and Ashford, 249–52
and South Hampshire, 252–3
prospective decline in population and
   revision of overspill needs (1969), 271–9
L.C.C. success with town expansion
   schemes, 500, 505, 519
London airport, 49, 89–90, 236
London Dispersal Liaison Group, 417–19
Lymm
   overspill development for Manchester,
   151–5
   rejected, 155
   reconsidered, 220–2
Lyttelton, Oliver, 546

Macclesfield, town expansion, 193, 504
MacColl, J. E., 352–4, 591
MacDermott, Niall, 479
MacDonald, Alistair, 10, 11n
Maclay, John, 176–7, 178
Macleod, Ian, 124
Macmillan, Harold
   at M.H.L.G., 116–25
   policy reviews, 125–9, 133–9, 142–7
   industrial development in new towns
      127–8, 134–8
   transfer of new towns to local authorities,
      127–8, 138–9, 145, 317–18
   argues for amenities in new towns, 128–9,
      136, 144
   defends standards, 145
   succeeded by Sandys, 148
   on 'modernisation of Britain', 187–8
   reviews membership of development
      corporations, 293–4
   on Town Development Bill, 405, 498–500
   skill in safeguarding new towns pro-
      gramme, 485, 531
   on parliamentary control, 589
McNeil, Hector, 89
Manchester
   need for new town (1946), 34
   and Mobberley, 59–60, 80–1, 85, 95 *et seq*,
      303
   and Congleton, 96 *et seq*
   and Westhoughton, 98, 165, 193
   and Lymm, 151–5
   new town for (1963), 193–6
   and Risley (Warrington), 196
   new town for (1965), 219–23
   Warrington agreed, 223
   see also Leyland-Chorley
Margaretting, proposed new town, 6, 16, 67
Marshall, T. H., 349–50
Mellish, Robert, 297, 414, 533
Meopham, proposed new town, 6, 16, 34, 67
Merseyside, 34, 255, 431, 546, 550
Mid-Wales Industrial Development Association, 280–3
Milton Keynes (North Buckinghamshire
   New Town)
   Verney, 113, 228
   new town approved, 213
   new town announced, 214
   proposals by Buckinghamshire, 228–9
   history, 229–33
   designation order, 233

last 'self-contained' new town, 378
Treasury discussion, 474
'special case' for industrial development,
   563
see aslo Bletchley
Mitchell, Miles, 18
Mobberley, proposed new town, 59–60,
   80–1, 85, 95–9, 303
Morrison, Herbert
   chairman of L.P. Committee, 32, 79
   payment to members of development
      corporations, 92
   appointments to development corpora-
      tions, 293
   local authorities and new town develop-
      ment, 300–1
   possibility of a national corporation for
      new towns, 301
   relationship between development corpo-
      rations and M.T.C.P., 312
Morrison, W. S.
   on Stevenage, 9, 551
   presses for legislation on new towns, 11–12
   supports New Towns Bill, 25
   future ownership by local authorities, 317
   argues for prominent role of M.T.C.P. in
      industrial location policy, 544

National Coal Board, 75, 78, 87, 93, 102–7,
   110–11, 196; *see also* Coalfields
National Farmers' Union, 99, 160, 270, 274
National Institute of Economic and Social
   Research, 224, 473
Neal, L., 592
Newbury, 34, 90, 113, 159, 208, 226, 512
Newton Aycliffe, *see* Aycliffe
Newtown (Wales), 237, 241, 279–83
New Towns Acts
   (1946), 23–6, 69, 117, 317, 449, 587–8
   (1952), 119, 588
   (1953), 122, 588
   (1959), 341–2, 583
   (1966), 584–5, 588
   (Others), 588–91
New Towns Association, 384
New towns information bureau, 370–2
Noble, Michael, 191–2
Northampton
   expansion proposed, 207, 208, 212
   approved, 213
   announced, 214
   a 'partnership' new town, 377
North Buckinghamshire New Town, *see*
   Milton Keynes
North Eastern Housing Association, 321,
   592, 599
Nottingham, 35, 564–5

Oakengates, *see* Dawley
Office development controls, 180, 188, 198,
   217
Ongar, *see* Chipping Ongar
Operation Round-up, 142–5
Osborn, F. J., 14
Owner occupation, *see* Housing in new towns

Parker Morris, *see* Housing in new towns:
   standards

Parliamentary control of new towns, 24, 587–91
Partnership new towns, 377–80, 513–20
'People's house', 145, 389
Pepler, G. L., 4, 6, 10
Pepler Report, 6–8, 486, 592–602
Peterborough
 proposed expansion, 207–9
 agreed, 213
 announced, 214
 move to annul designation order, 591
Peterlee
 proposed new town, 73–5, 77
 approved, 77–8
 supported by Treasury, 78n
 difficulties between development corporations and N.C.B., 102–7
 inadequacy of development corporation members, 104
 target population not to be increased, 190
 owner occupation in, 435
 sale of houses to sitting tenants, 445–7
 difficulty in attracting industry, 458–9
Pitsea, *see* Basildon
Plowden Report, 477
Plymouth, 23, 35, 594
Pontllanfraith, 81, 92
Pontypridd, 68, 76, 92, 93
Poole, 512, 515
Portal, Lord, 3
Portsmouth, 35, 208, 226, 232, 512, 555, 594;
 see also South Hampshire Study
Powell, Enoch, 327, 329
Private enterprise
 development of new towns by, 10–11, 14, 17, 162–3, 362–4
 participation in new town development, 22, 46, 123, 128, 132, 203–6, 469–71, 510, 511, 596
 see also Housing in new towns: owner occupation
Prudential (Assurance Co), possibility of transfer of new towns to, 318, 321, 322
Public Accounts Committee, 286, 295, 587
Public Building and Works, Ministry of, 216, 383, 475
Public Expenditure Survey Committee (P.E.S.C.), 477
Public Works Loan Board, 7, 515, 598–9

Rate fund contribution for housing
 payment by exporting authorities to new and expanded towns, 16, 18, 128, 399, 402, 404, 405, 407–10, 412–13, 492–3, 501–2
 in Scotland, 133, 150–1, 176
 explained, 385n
Reading, 71, 113, 512, 515
Redbourn, proposed new town, 6, 16
Redditch
 expansion proposal, 169, 173
 Joseph proposes new town, 192–3
 agreed, 195
 designated, 196
 difficulty on housing rents, 390
 owner occupation, 431
 optimism on industrial development, 435

Regional development agencies proposed, 512 *et seq*
Reiss, R. L., 364–6
Reith Committee
 appointed, 13–14
 reports, 14–15
 rejects private enterprise new towns, 14, 17
 on future ownership of new towns, 14, 17, 316
 recommendation for central advisory commission, 15, 25, 297, 348–9, 376
 distance of new towns from London, 71
 new towns as balanced communities, 419
 estimated cost of a new town, 451
 independence of new towns from central control, 538
 industrial development in new towns, 551
Reith, Lord
 redevelopment planning for London, 3, 4
 Treasury control of new towns, 25, 538–9
 in Standing Ministerial Conference, 298
 research organisation, 356–7
 parliamentary control, 589
Rent restriction, 117, 156, 157, 385–7, 494
Research
 organisation of (1947–50), 348–62
 at Welwyn Garden City, 362–6
 resumption of research on new towns, 366–70, 457
 new towns information bureau, 370–2
 complaint on lack of research, 377
 need for research, 381–4
 new towns research group (1963), 457–60
 on economic criteria for development decisions, 460–74
 see also Central advisory commission for new towns
Risley, proposed new town for Manchester, 196, 219–23; *see also* Warrington
Roberts, Howard, 163
Robinson, Kenneth, 272
Ross, William, 214
Runcorn
 town expansion scheme, 166
 proposed new town, 192–5, 508
 agreed, 195
 designated, 207
 bus-only roads, 530n

St Albans, Dean of, 420
Sandys, Duncan
 succeeds Macmillan at M.H.L.G., 148
 presses for more new towns, 148–9, 454
 selection of members of development corporations, 294–5
 future ownership of new towns, 327
 rent increases for new town housing, 388
 siting of G.E.C. factory, 555
Scotland
 separate New Towns Bill suggested, 26
 first new town proposals, 33, 38–40, 45, 47–8, 55–7, 61–2, 86–9
 review of new towns (1953), 130–3
 transfer of new towns to local authorities, 131, 132, 304, 328–9, 332
 new town at Cumbernauld, 149–51
 fourth new town (Livingston), 175–8
 council house rents, 177

proposals for amending Local Employment Act, 182–3
Highlands as 'playground for the masses', 187
white paper (1963), 189, 190–1
new town at Irvine, 190–2
and white paper *The South East Study*, 199–200
review of *The South East Study*, 214, 218
feasibility of major growth in Dundee-Tayside area, 227–8, 236
new towns working group (1967), 233, 236, 241
expanded towns, 520–4
Scottish Special Housing Association, 236, 523
Selection of tenants for new towns, 84, 399 *et seq*, 532–3
Severnside, 207, 226–8, 239
Shawcross, Hartley, 554
Sheffield, 35, 238
Shinwell, Emmanuel, 107n
Silkin, Lewis
 proposed as chairman of private enterprise new town, 10
 appointed Minister of Town and Country Planning, 13
 establishes Reith Committee, 13–14
 discusses new towns legislation with local authorities, 15–18
 future ownership of new towns, 17, 316–317
 seeks approval of L.P. Committee to new towns legislation, 18–23
 New Towns Bill, 23–6
 Stevenage, 27–30
 paper to L.P. Committee on new towns (1946), 33–8, 43–4
 rejects L.C.C. proposal for development at Chessington, 43n
 on capital costs of new towns, 45–7, 50–2, 55, 451
 on provincial new towns, 54
 review of new towns (1946), 57–8
 new town for Manchester, 59–60, 76, 95–101
 Welwyn and Hatfield, 62–6
 faces mounting ministerial opposition to new towns, 66
 review of new town proposals (1947), 67–78
 Peterlee, 73–5, 77–8, 102–7
 review of new towns programme (1948), 80–2
 Basildon, 82–6
 Bracknell, 89–92
 new towns in South Wales, 92–5, 110–12
 loss of agricultural land, 101
 Corby, 108–10
 holiday new town, 113–14
 new town policy achievements, 114, 531
 Standing Ministerial Conference, 297–8
 possibility of national corporation for new towns, 301–2
 new town development by local authorities, 303, 305–6
 membership of development corporations, 303, 305

payment of members of development corporations, 303–4, 309
agrees to inquiry on development corporations, 312
research on new towns, 356–7
rents in new towns, 386–7
industry in new towns, 551–2
Sinclairston, proposed new town, 61
Skelmersdale
 proposed new town, 166–8
 agreed, 168
 designation, 207
 difficulty with housing rents, 390
 owner occupation, 431
 treated as part of Merseyside development area, 550
Social Science Research Council, 382
Sorn, Lord, 131
Southampton, 208, 226, 232, 235, 512; *see also* South Hampshire Study
South East Study, 196–206, 207–18, 346, 509
South Hampshire Study, 235, 239, 252–3
Special Areas (Development and Improvement) Act (1934), 543
Standing Ministerial Conference, 297–300, 349, 351, 356–7, 386–7
Stansted, proposed new town, 208, 236, 476, 512
Stapleford, proposed new town, 6, 16, 67
Stevenage
 proposed new town, 6, 9–10
 agreed, 21
 detailed account, 27–31
 investment restriction, 79
 expansion of, 209, 211, 245–6, 249, 456–7, 476, 512, 589–90
 sewerage costs, 320
 rent rebate scheme, 391
 links with Tottenham and Wood Green, 400
 low-skilled workers from London, 416
 better class housing, 422
Stewart and Lloyds, steelworks at Corby, 108, 143
Stone, P. A., 224, 473
Strauss, G. R., 66
Stuart, James, 130–3, 140–1, 521
Supply, Ministry of, 131, 545, 556
Swindon, 135, 226, 232, 237, 500, 505, 510, 512, 515
Swynnerton, 167–75

Tadley, 158, 160
Talbot Green, *see* Church Village
Tayside feasibility study on major expansion, 227–8, 236
Telford, *see* Dawley
Tenants of new towns, *see* Selection of tenants for new towns
Thorneycroft, Peter, 125, 129–30, 139–40, 555
Tomlinson, G., 64, 486
Toothill Report, 178–9
Tottenham, 9, 84, 400, 412
Town and Country Planning Act (1932), 10, 596, 602
Town and Country Planning Act (1944), 8, 23, 486, 592, 602

Town and Country Planning Act (1947 and 1962), 117, 188, 228, 547

Town and Country Planning Association, 3, 13, 534

Town and Country Planning, Ministry of
early planning for London, 3 *et seq*
early thinking on machinery for new town development, 6 *et seq*, 592–602
Stevenage, 6, 9–10, 21, 27–31
Treasury, criticism of, 44, 72, 451–2
Peterlee, 102–4
appointment of development corporations, 292–7
payment of members of development corporations, 306–9
Treasury report on development corporations, 312–16
future ownership of new towns, 318 *et seq*
Commission for the New Towns, 342–8
research organisation, 348–366
selection of tenants for new and expanded towns, 399 *et seq*
expanded towns, 486 *et seq*
see also Housing and Local Government, Ministry of *and* Local Government and Planning, Ministry of

Town Development Act (1952)
background to, 116, 404–6, 486–97
Bill, 404–5, 497–500
early operation, 500–4
review of machinery (1963–64), 504–16
Crossman's review (1965), 518–20

Training for unskilled workers, 418–19

Transfer of new towns, *see* Future ownership of new towns

Transport facilities
for London new towns, 48–54
for Dawley, 173–4, 262–3, 265
for Manchester new town, 220
monorail system for North Bucks (Milton Keynes), 229
in N.E. Lancashire, 255–7
bus-only roads in Runcorn plan, 530n

Treasury
reaction to early thinking on new towns, 10
on parliamentary approval for individual new towns, 24, 589
financial control over new towns, 25, 448–51, 538–9
criticism of planning ministry and planners, 44, 72, 133, 451–2, 530
seek to exercise restraint, 64
in support of Aycliffe and Peterlee, 78n
working party with M.H.L.G., 120–1
criticised by M.H.L.G. for delay, 133
on amenities in new towns, 134, 147–8, 338
changing attitude to new towns, 164, 539
official committee on population and employment, 179 *et seq*
on Washington, 190
on Irvine, 190–1
on North Buckinghamshire (Milton Keynes), 231
argues against Ipswich, 273–5, 278
to be consulted on appointments to development corporations, 293

report on development corporations (1949), 312–16
on disposal of water and sewerage undertakings to local authorities, 326
on future ownership of new towns, 334, 337–8
working party on 'new towns structure', 373
on housing rents, 387–90, 393–8
concern over subsidies for better class housing, 424
on sale prices of new town houses, 433, 446
objections to 'piecemeal decisions', 460–1
study group on economic criteria (1964–1965), 462–73
enthusiasm for N.I.E.S.R. study, 473
new towns and public expenditure control, 477–84
on grants for expanded towns, 489–97, 500–3
press M.H.L.G. for complete proposals for new and expanded towns, 518
vain search for objective criteria, 530
press for objective method for valuing agricultural land, 536, 565, 570
see also Finance of new towns

Treforest Trading Estate, 58, 76, 92, 110–11

Verney, 113, 228; *see also* Milton Keynes

Wales, new towns for, 33, 36, 58, 68, 75–6, 81, 92–5, 110–12, 128, 236–7, 241, 279–286

Warrington
proposed site for new town (Risley), 196, 219–23
designation order, 207, 245–6
announcement, 222–3
'partnership' new town, 377

Washington
proposed new town, 189–90
agreed, 190
owner occupation, 435

Webster Report on Peterlee, 102, 105

Wellington, *see* Dawley

Wells, Henry, 343, 370, 539

Welwyn (Garden City)
first mentions, 34, 41
development corporation proposed, 62–6, 71, 84
possibility of immediate transfer to local authority (1953), 123, 138
transferred to C.N.T., 344
research on history, 362–6
sale of houses, 422

West Ham, 82, 400

Westhoughton, 98, 165, 193

Westwood, Joseph, 22, 33, 38–40, 45, 47–8, 55–6

Whiteley, W., 305

White Waltham, proposed new town, 16, 34, 67, 90

Widnes, 166

Williams, Tom, 77, 97–101

Williams-Ellis, Clough, 29

Willis, J. R., 155

Wilmot, J., 65

Wilson, Harold, 114, 552

Wilson, Hugh, 192n
Winsford, 194, 505, 550
Womersley, Lewis, 192
Woodburn, Arthur, 86–9, 304
Woolton, Lord, 9–10, 551

Worcester, 169, 172, 369, 463
Worsley, town expansion, 134–5
Wrigley, John, 592
Wythall, housing development by Birmingham, 165, 167, 169–70, 173, 174, 503